GAY

GUIDE TO THE

USA

BY

ANDREW COLLINS

Fodor's Travel Publications, Inc.
New York • Toronto • London • Sydney • Auckland
http://www.fodors.com/

Fodor's Gay Guide to the USA

Editor: Christopher Billy

Contributing Editors: Steven Amsterdam, Karen Cure, David Low, Conrad Little Paulus, Craig Seligman

Editorial Contributors: Susan Bain, Deb Carroll, Steve Crohn, Fionn Davenport, Mitchell Davis, Audra Epstein, Ellen Mayer, Rebecca Miller, Ken Paprocki, Julius Roberge, Vicki Robinson, James Sinclair, Nevenah Smith, Russell Stockman

Map Editor: Robert P. Blake

Production Editor: Laura M. Kidder

Creative Director: Fabrizio La Rocca

Cartographer: David Lindroth; Eureka Cartography

Cover Design: Archie Ferguson

Text Design: Between the Covers

Copyright © 1996 by Andrew Collins

Special Sales

Fodor's Travel Publications are available at special discounts for bulk purchases for sales promotions or premiums. Special editions, including personalized covers, excerpts of existing guides, and corporate imprints, can be created in large quantities for special needs. For more information, contact your local bookseller or write to Special Markets, Fodor's Travel Publications, 201 East 50th Street, New York, NY 10022. Inquiries from Canada should be directed to your local Canadian bookseller or sent to Random House of Canada, Ltd., Marketing Department, 1265 Aerowood Drive, Mississauga, Ontario L4W 1B9. Inquiries from the United Kingdom should be sent to Fodor's Travel Publications, 20 Vauxhall Bridge Road, London SW1V 2SA, England.

PRINTED IN THE UNITED STATES OF AMERICA

10 9 8 7 6 5 4 3 2 1

CONTENTS

Contents

Maps

FOREWORD

A READER WRITES "My life does not begin and end with gay culture. But there is something about being in a new town—I want to know where the boys are even if I never go near the place. I can't tell you how frustrating it is to try to guess which part of town is the most like-minded. And trying to decide where to get a room ('No, we don't want to be switched to two twin beds, I want the king-size as specified on my reservation') can be rough. Luckily, I have a savvy gay travel agent. Can someone in a smaller town say the same?"

You've been there, too: Asking a B&B owner for something a little less frilly (preferably plaid). That awkward moment when room service arrives, in the room with the king-size bed, both of you in morning *déshabille*.

To help you avoid such awkward moments, this guide directs you to the hotels and restaurants where you'll be comfortable, the parts of town that are most like-minded. We hope you'll find it a wonderful traveling companion: charming, brimming with sound recommendations and solid ideas, absolutely honest, and consistently full of fascinating facts that will help you see America's cities under the brightest possible rainbow.

Karen Cure

Karen Cure
Editorial Director

AUTHOR'S NOTE

BEING GAY OR LESBIAN influences our choice of accommodations, nightlife, dining, shopping, and perhaps even sightseeing. Exactly how "gay" you want your vacation to be is entirely up to you.

Whatever you decide, this book will enable you to plan your trip confidently and with authority. On the following pages, I list and describe dozens of options, from the main gay bars and clubs to the great gay beaches; from the best shopping in New York City to the top restaurants in Chicago. You'll also find a wide range of accommodations in every destination, from exclusively gay resorts to lesbian guest houses to mainstream hotels. And you'll be shown which properties are closest to downtown businesses and which are near the gay discos. In every category, I've tried to provide ideas for every segment of our community.

Early plans for this book called for coverage of more than 50 destinations, including both the country's largest cities and some that are smaller. But the list shrank as my editors and I realized how much there was to say about each place. The options available to gay and lesbian travelers have never been richer, and if we included it all, you'd have an encyclopedia.

About Me

This is an opinionated book, and I don't hesitate to say what I think, so it might help you to know a bit about me. I'm a white gay male in my midtwenties. I grew up in Connecticut. My favorite restaurants are in New Orleans and San Francisco; my favorite bars are in Austin, Texas, and New York City's East Village; and my favorite resort communities are Provincetown and Taos. I'm prone to describe certain neighborhoods as characterless, resorts as touristy or uppity, restaurants as dumpy or over-the-top. My intention is always to relate what I've observed and what I've heard locals say. I expect that anybody reading this book will find plenty to disagree with, which is understandable.

How I Researched This Book

I spent between 5 and 15 days in most cities, and a couple of days in smaller resort towns. At every destination, I interviewed gays and lesbians—from newspaper editors to city council members to barflies to people on the street. For the most part, I traveled without announcing myself—most of the businesses in this book had no idea I was writing about them when I visited.

On the road, I often I slept in the living rooms of friends . . . or friends of friends . . . or acquaintances, who soon became new friends. Sometimes I paid for hotel rooms and in some cases hoteliers extended their hospitality on the house. At least twice I slept in my car. Without the generosity of friends and many hotels, I couldn't have written the book. But I never included a property or wrote favorably about one in exchange for a room. And I personally paid for every other expense, from airfare and car rentals to meals and club covers. I made all my own travel arrangements. In short, I attempted to experience these destinations in the same manner you will.

I've described everything as I've seen it— or as it has been reported to me. In the end, *Fodor's Gay Guide to the USA* is a service not to hotels and guest houses, or to gay bars and restaurants, or to anybody in the travel industry. It is a resource for you, the traveler.

Language and Voice
Rather than sticking to the safe PC "gay" and "lesbian", I opted for the more colorful language of my own generation; I used terms such as "faggy," "dyke," and "queer" throughout the book (even while I recognize that, for some people, these words are painful reminders of more repressive times). Much of gay and lesbian America uses these terms. And often I do personally. Please be assured that no offense or assumptions are intended.

Also, unless the context suggests otherwise, when I use the terms "gay" or "homosexual," I'm referring to gay men *and* lesbians. Where clarity was needed, I tried to specify which gender was intended.

Content

Each chapter has several distinct sections. Here's a quick rundown of what's inside each one.

The Lay of the Land

If you're looking for a quick summation of each destination's geography, its neighborhoods and major attractions, and its shopping, you'll want to read this carefully. At the end of each section are tips on getting around.

Eats

The list of restaurants in each chapter can be a bit arbitrary, but I've tried to give a range, balancing cuisine, price, and location. I've considered places named to me by gay and lesbian locals, places that advertise in gay publications, and places that were reviewed positively in local newspapers and magazines. Omission of your personal favorite does not mean that I don't recommend it, only that it's probably similar to other restaurants I did include. I ate at about 20% of the places in the guide and visited almost all the rest to study the menu, check out the decor and atmosphere, and observe the crowd.

I've tried to include choices for every budget. In most destinations, many recommendations are in or near gay-oriented neighborhoods. A handful of places are included less for the food than for the overtly festive (gay) atmosphere. A few places in each chapter are there simply because they represent some of the destination's finest or most unusual dining. Unless otherwise noted, you can assume that any restaurant in this book is at least somewhat popular with the community.

If you're looking for a great social alternative to the bar scene, you'll be happy to know that each dining section ends with a section about coffeehouses. Unless I describe the food, you can assume that each place offers only coffee and light snacks.

The following charts explain the price categories used for restaurants throughout this guide:

CHART A

Category	Cost of Dinner Entrées
$$$$	over $20
$$$	$15–$20
$$	$9–$14
$	under $9

CHART B

Category	Cost of Dinner Entrées
$$$$	over $16
$$$	$12–$16
$$	$7–$11
$	under $7

Sleeps

In large cities, I've included any gay-specific establishments that I felt confident recommending. In resort areas, I've listed a broad range of gay-specific accommodations, but in the most popular areas—including Key West and Provincetown—there wasn't space to include every possibility. I visited most of the B&Bs and small inns (usually anonymously), although I stayed in only a handful. If the establishment was straight-owned and I had no knowledge of its gay-friendliness, I checked with the owners to verify their interest in being covered in a gay publication. My descriptions of the clientele, compiled without the owners' input, are there only to give you a general sense of the place.

When I discuss larger hotels, particularly those in cities, don't assume that they are gay-friendly (or otherwise) unless the reviews specifically state so. Obviously, the degree of tolerance you encounter at a large property with many employees will depend largely on who happens to assist you. I included both mainstream properties that are in and near gay neighborhoods and those that have a strong reputation with the community.

The following charts explain the price categories used for lodging establishments throughout this guide:

CHART A

Category	Cost*
$$$$	over $180
$$$	$130–$180
$$	$90–$130
$	under $90

Cost of double-occupancy room in high season

CHART B	
Category	Cost*
$$$$	over $150
$$$	$115–$150
$$	$75–$115
$	under $75

Cost of double-occupancy room in high season

Scenes

I checked out nearly every bar reviewed in this book. If a place opened after my visit to the city, I telephoned an employee and also got a report from a knowledgeable local resource to ensure an accurate review.

Although the smallest, sleepiest, and most out-of-the-way bars aren't reviewed, I have mentioned a few of the more memorable, friendly, "neighborhood" bars—they're terrific places to meet locals, and they're usually low on attitude.

In this guide, male-oriented places outnumber those that cater mostly to women by about 10 to 1. This is not a reflection of my preferences but of America's gay bar culture—it's overwhelmingly young, white, and male. Still, don't assume that a bar described as 80% male or mostly young doesn't welcome lesbians or older guys. Descriptions of each bar's crowd and its "cruise factor" are based on my own observations and interviews and are there simply to give you a profile of what's typical.

I've tried to provide complete information on every city's entertainment scene. So, in addition to bars and discos, I've listed a few bathhouses, adult theaters, and the like. Our sexuality defines us and a sexually charged atmosphere defines many of the destinations we visit. I would be remiss if I didn't tell you what's where. What you do with the information is up to you. (I would also be remiss if I didn't encourage you to do it safely.)

The Little Black Book

This is your quick resource guide for every destination. If some establishments have closed by the time you read about them—bars and restaurants are unpredictable—

try the contacts here to get the latest scoop. Local tourist boards, as well as lesbigay bookstores, help lines, community centers, and newspapers can be helpful. Additionally, I've included a few gay-popular gyms, and the phone numbers of resources for persons who are HIV-positive or who have AIDS.

Disclaimer

This is where I'm to remind you that time brings changes, and that neither I nor the publisher can accept responsibility for errors. An incredible amount of time and effort has been spent ensuring the accuracy of this book's information, but businesses move and/or close and restaurants and bars change. Always call an establishment before you go to make sure that it will be open when you get there.

Few of the establishments in this book knew in advance that they would be appearing in *Fodor's Gay Guide to the USA*. The mention of any business, attraction, or person in this book is in no way an indication of sexual orientation or attitudes about sexual orientation. Unless specifically stated, no business in this book is implied or assumed to be gay-owned or operated.

Send Letters

Whatever your reaction to this book—delight, excitement, unbridled rage—your feedback is greatly appreciated. I'd love to hear about your experiences, both good and bad, and about establishments you'd like me to include or exclude in future editions. Send your letters to me c/o Fodor's Travel Publications, 201 East 50th Street, New York, New York 10022.

In the mean time, I hope you'll have as much fun using this guide as I had writing it.

Andrew Collins

Andrew Collins
December 6, 1995

ACKNOWLEDGEMENTS

Since I started this project, more than 300 of you have assisted me with this book by offering insights, opinions, suggestions, and advice. Some of you gave me your names, and I have thanked you personally below. Just as many of you either had no idea I was interviewing you for a book (surprise!) or drifted off before introducing yourselves—please accept my warmest gratitude.

More than a dozen members of Fodor's staff worked tirelessly on this book. Particular thanks go to Bob Blake, who coordinated all of the book's maps and continues to act as my unofficial spiritual advisor; Craig Seligman, who helped me immeasurably to get the project off the ground; Chris Billy, who spent hours editing, reworking, and coming up with new ways to improve the book; Ken Paprocki, who fact-checked the entire manuscript and wrote dozens of new reviews; and Laura Kidder, who saw the book through every single stage of production, kept me on track, edited, wrote, transferred corrections, and helped me maintain my sanity.

I'd also like to thank my agent, Daniel Bial, for not only invaluable professional advice but for constant moral support. I wish to thank dozens of great friends, on whose sofas and spare futons I've slept over the past three years. Lastly, I wish to thank my parents, Edward and Gretchen Collins, for encouraging me to pursue freelance writing, this particular project, and every other unlikely endeavor I've ever attempted.

This project is dedicated to D. Keller Beasley and Forrest H. "Woody" Bennett . . .two diamonds in the rough who, against considerable odds, taught me everything about love, a few things about patience, and never to take anything for granted.

Special thanks also go to the following:

General: Valerie Aaronoff, Stephanie Blackwood, Andrew Caldwell, Sara Cartwright, Teagan Chandler, John Frazier, Norman Hackl at the International Gay Travel Association, Thomas R. Harris, Laura McWade, Stan Metzger.

Atlanta: D. Keller Beasley; Cliff, Eddie, Kendra, Patrick, Rodney, et al; Judy C.; Cliff Edge; Debbie Fraker at Outwrite Bookstore; Dave Hayward; Les Howell; Badili Jones, Gary Kaupman, K.C. Wildmoon, and Joan Sherwood at *Southern Voice*; F. J. and R. C. McLaughlin; Jack Pelham at *Etc. Magazine*; David Verzello at Black Sheep Lager.
Austin: Craig Edwards at the *Fag Rag*, Kay Longcope at the *Texas Triangle*, John Metz.
Baltimore: Patricia Beachley, Jennie Boyd Bull and the staff at the 31st Street Bookstore Cooperative, Sally Franklin at Cafe Diana, Jack Garman at Lambda Rising, Rawley Grau at the *Baltimore Alternative*, Gwen at P. T. Max, Larry Holmes, Ed Lawrence, Tom Mayak, Stephen Ziobro.
Boston: Matthew Basile, John Caveretta, Richard DiCusati at Citywide Reservation Service, Sam Donato, Joe Haley, Eric Hess, Johanna Nackley and John Affuso, Deborah Knapp, Jon Revere, Paul A. Thurman, Jesse Wennik, Kevin Zimmerman.
Chicago: Susan Cross, Mark Kollar, Todd Savage.
Dallas: Scott Bishop, Trey Brown, Pam D., Randall Hooper, Skip Landers, Steven Lawson, John Shore, Jeff Updike.
Denver: Michelle Baker, Richard Evans, Simon Foster, Roger Hunt and Jim Tomberlin in Aspen.
Fire Island: "Casey."
Houston: Tom Fricke, Carolyn A. Larson and Tad Nelson at the *Houston Voice*, Danni Saboda at the Houston Convention and Visitors Bureau, Sandra Wilkins.
Key West: Fran, Jerry Frantz, Michael Ingram, Melissa Kendrick, Damon Leard, Michael MacIntyre, Foster Meagher, Mark Porter, Martha Robinson, Stephen Smith and the staff at the Key West Business Guild, Bob Tracy.
Las Vegas: Brad Anderson, Leigh Bucknam, Bill Haller, Wes Miller and the staff of Get Booked, Christopher Strauss, Susan L. Thompson.
Los Angeles: Patricia Archuleta, Carter Bravmann, Steven Crawford at California Riviera 800 in Laguna Beach, Robin Eckland, Jim Kepner, Rosalie Kerkochian and Dan Marroni at Atlas Travel Service,

Dona Klein, Grinnell Morris, Fred Mutter, Alex Perez, Lucky Scoles, Marsha Meyer Sculatti at the West Hollywood CVB, Mark Simon at A Different Light Bookstore, Kristoffer Tangen, Stuart Timmons, David Urquhart, Ted Zepeda.

Nashville: Paul Clere, Collette, Cindy Sanders at the Nashville Convention and Visitors Bureau, Tracey at Ralph's.

New Orleans: Will Avera; Forrest H. "Woody" Bennett III; Bill, Charles, Gloria, Jeff, Lea-Ann, Lisa, and Stacey; Russell S. Colvin; Karl D. Matherne; Kyle Scafidy at *Impact*.

New York City: Noel Ambery; Andrew Boorstyn; Michelle Bouchard; Frank Browning; Nancy Duran; Elvis, Sil, and Craig; Caroline Hickson; Jason Jercinovic; Jeffrey Kazin; Christina Knight; Matthew Lloyd; Matthew Lore; Christopher Pennington; Laura Prichard; Marcy Pritchard; Sam and Tigger; Ruth Scovill; Todd Whitley.

Philadelphia: Rita Adessa at the Lesbian and Gay Task Force; Thom Cardwell, Al Patrick, and Mark Segal at the *Philadelphia Gay News;* Jim Carpenter at the New Hope Information Center; David Covert; Ed Hernance at Giovanni's Room; Alan Krause and Shilpa Mehta at *Au Courant;* Michelle at Hepburn's; Alan Molchan at Cafe Nola; L. A. Mundy; Charles O'Donald at the Rittenhouse Hotel; Robert at the Westbury; Michael Smith; Richard Smith; R. C. Staab at the Philadelphia Convention and Visitors Bureau.

Phoenix: Daphne Budge at Out'n Arizona Tours, Bruce Carl, Maureen P. Faul, Steve Francoeur, the staff at the Heartline Cafe in Sedona, Marian at Kachina Stables in Sedona, Jeff Ofstedahl at *Echo,* JoAnn Palazzo, Graydon Williams.

Portland: Alan Jones, Robert Liberty, Dan Rooney, Susan Solari of the Portland Oregon Visitors Association.

Provincetown: Ken Esry, Esther Lastique, Arise LaVina, Alex McCune, Philip Norkelonius, Peter at the Boatslip.

Rehoboth Beach: Bob the Cabana Boy, Fred, Patty, Swan, et al.

St. Louis: Adam, Barb, and Kent; Jeff Archuleta; Tim Cusick; Michael Lance; Nancy McAdams at *LesTalk;* Nancy Milton at the St. Louis Convention and Visitors Bureau; Amy Adams Squires Strongheart; Becky Turner; Rodney Wilson.

San Diego: Albert Columbo, the staff at Jerry and David's Travel, the staff at Men on Vacation.

San Francisco: Ty Accornero, Chris Arrott at Council Travel, Jon Bain, Daniel Carrillo, Mark Chekal, Chip Conley of Joie De Vivre Hotels, the late Mark Finch, Joseph Fortier, Gary King, Jeffrey Longhenry, Don Mack, Daniel Mangin, Vicki McGrath, Jenni Olson, Paige Schaffer.

Santa Fe and Taos: Andrew Beckerman, Cathy Bugliari, John Daw, Diane Fichtelberg, Karen Ford, Beth Goldman, Carol Jensen, Steve Lewis at the Santa Fe Convention and Visitors Bureau, David McCarty, Noel Stone, Patty Taylor at the Taos Chamber of Commerce, Carole Wildman, Jess Williams.

Seattle: Steve Bennett, Rob Cunningham, Mark Hanley, Cathy Hastings, John Hickey, Peter Johnson, Nathan Kibler at Beyond the Closet, Jim Locke, Eric Rockey.

South Beach: Michael Aller, Gerry and Jeffrey at Jefferson House, Bob Guilmartin at the South Florida Hotel Network, Craig Pritchard.

Tucson: the staff at Antigone Bookstore, Carl Eynatian, Bob Griffin at the *Observer,* the owners of the Catalina Park Inn, Edie Jarolim, Bob McMahon.

Washington, DC: Garbo Afarian, Joe Rio, Erik Wolf.

The United States

PACIFIC OCEAN

0 — 400 miles
0 — 400 km

N

PACIFIC OCEAN

1 *Out in Atlanta*

ATLANTA IS THE CAPITAL OF THE SOUTH, and so it comes as no surprise that the city's lesbian and gay newsweekly is called not *Atlanta Voice* or *Georgia Voice* but the all-encompassing *Southern Voice*. Indeed, a quick survey of patrons at any of the city's more vibrant gay watering holes will reveal a broad cross section of geographic origins. The majority of today's Atlantans hail from towns east of the Mississippi River, south of the Mason-Dixon Line, and north of Florida, but there are plenty of northerners here, too.

Atlanta is the ultimate melting pot of Southern cultures, tainted—or spiced up, depending on how you look at it—by myriad Northern influences. It is not the land of Rhetts and Scarletts, nor are most of its residents mired in the Old South mentality commonly attributed to them. Atlanta is as sophisticated and tolerant as most major urban centers. It's extremely gay: There are more cars with pink triangle and rainbow decals than in any city in America (granted, there also seem to be more cars). In the last couple of years business interest in the gay dollar has risen radically; hundreds of mainstream advertisers place ads in the gay papers.

Circling Atlanta, however, is a six-lane beltway called I–285, and though much of what lies inside this ring—Atlanta proper—possesses a refreshingly enlightened outlook toward lesbians and gays, much of what lies outside it despises us.

If you were to draw a new ring around I–285 every mile out indefinitely, each band in the resultant tree-ring pattern would represent roughly a one-year step back in time. Head 30 miles outside I–285, and you'll enter pre–civil rights Georgia; here it feels as if the presence of gay symbols on your car is an invitation to have your tires slashed or your windows smashed in.

The most horrible of these Atlanta suburbs are the towns of Cobb County, which has long been a den of Ku Klux Klan activity, skinheads, and other hate groups. In August 1993, Cobb County Commission (the county's governing body) passed a resolution "denouncing the gay lifestyle." This led to a long and ultimately successful grassroots campaign by gay activists to convince the Atlanta Committee for the Olympic Games to move the volleyball competition from its scheduled Cobb County venue to a gay-friendly community. The battle to have this nasty resolution repealed is being continued; ironically, one of the leading and most outspoken voices against the resolution is the lesbian daughter (Shannon Byrne) of homophobic chairman of the Cobb County Commission, Bill Byrne.

This isn't the first oddity concerning the gay community in Georgia politics. Georgia Congressman and Speaker of the House Newt Gingrich is constantly criticized by his lesbian half sister, Candace Gingrich. The state is also home to Senator Sam Nunn, who though a major and powerful opponent of gays in the military, scored relatively high (67%) on gay and lesbian issues, according to the Human Rights Campaign Fund. Fortunately, Atlanta's own congressman, John Lewis, has worked hard for the gay community and played a major role in keeping the Olympics out of Cobb County. City politicians are aware of and generally cater to Atlanta's gay community, whose powerful voting strength is recognized by all.

On another positive note, it's worth noting that the southeast Atlanta suburb of Decatur has been a foil to Cobb County. When Cobb announced its resolution, the straight mayor of Decatur invited gays and lesbians to come live peacefully in his city. Indeed, Decatur has long been popular with lesbians and gay men who have reached the point where vegetable gardens are more important than beer gardens, and the city is also the home of the Digging Dykes of Decatur, the hottest social club in Georgia. This sapphic garden club is said to know relatively little about tulip bulbs and topsoil; on gossiping, however, they're experts.

One aspect of Atlanta's history still holds true to a certain degree. Though restaurants and clubs are slowly becoming more racially mixed, it's hard to find a core black, substantially out gay community, and that's despite the city's large black population. Blacks and whites don't mingle much, and what black presence there is in the gay community is relegated largely to entertainment venues. Politically, Atlanta's gay community remains mostly white, and African-Americans stay fairly closeted.

With its diminutive and virtually obsolete downtown, the wealthy shopping and residential neighborhood of Buckhead sprawling to north of downtown, and a few trendy areas in between, Atlanta has come to resemble the one city in America that's the virtual antithesis of a small town: Los Angeles. Like L.A., Atlanta is not a walking city. Nor is it a place that you can easily get around by public transportation. Rather, Atlanta, like L.A., is a sit-in-your-car-and-curse-traffic city.

Atlanta has always been a city of stereotypical Southern hospitality, a warm city with a friendly outlook and a genuine interest in newcomers. But these traits are changing as development booms and outsiders begin to make up a significant chunk of the population. The under-30 gay crowd is made up largely of men and women from neighboring states who have left their small, backward towns and discovered a climate where they are welcome. And so, in many of the new discos and bars you encounter equal numbers of friendly Southerners and insecure, image-conscious newcomers. It's still an inviting city, but Atlanta is not a small town anymore.

THE LAY OF THE LAND

Though Downtown, specifically Five Points, is Atlanta's official center, other symbolic centers have evolved over the past few years: The intersection of Highland and Virginia avenues, Little Five Points, Buckhead's intersection of Piedmont Avenue and Peachtree Road, Midtown's 14th and Peachtree streets. Atlanta is the land of shopping centers—there may not be a detached, single-standing shop in the entire city. And sidewalk culture is virtually nonexistent. In many places you can park your car and wander, but to travel from one neighborhood to another you need to drive. This continuous feeling of sprawl is in certain ways the bane of Atlanta existence—sitting in traffic all day can put an edge on even the most laid-back southerner—but it also contributes to the city's charm and accessibility. There is no shortage of greenery, rolling hills, attractive houses, or stunning commercial architecture.

Downtown

Although it possesses a fascinating mix of early and late-20th-century buildings, Atlanta's **Downtown** is comparatively dull, and it provides little you can't find in safer, cleaner, and greener parts of the metro area. The 1996 Olympics have spurred several massive civic rebuilding programs around Downtown, but it remains to be seen how much these new stadiums, housing units, and improved thoroughfares will enhance the area's popularity after the games have left.

Five Points, where Edgewood Avenue and Peachtree, Marietta, and Decatur streets converge, is the commercial and spiritual center of the city— as it has been since 1837, when it marked the terminus of Atlanta's railways. Now the site of Downtown's most central MARTA (Metropolitan Atlanta Rapid Transit Authority) station, Five Points is just north of a large shopping and entertainment district called **Underground Atlanta,** a relatively unsuccessful creation of the Rouse Company (known for developing Baltimore's Inner Harbor and Boston's Quincy Market). This three-level (two of them underground) network of avenues is packed with somewhat cheesy shops and restaurants. It's worth a quick visit, but in this city known for great shopping and dining, you'll find better options farther north.

A short walk south of here is the rather campy **World of Coca-Cola** (55 Martin Luther King Jr. Dr., ☎ 404/676–5151), a shameless but amusing promotional tribute to Coke history, with tastings, memorabilia, and gifts relevant to the legendary Atlanta-born soft drink.

The blocks just north of Five Points contain most of Downtown's earliest prominent buildings, including several historic churches, the neoclassical **Georgia State Capitol** (1889; 206 Washington St.), the neo-Gothic **Atlanta City Hall** (1930; 68 Mitchell St.), the Beaux-Arts **Fulton County Courthouse** (1913; 136 Pryor St.), the original **NationsBank Building** (1901; 35 Broad St.), the Art Deco **William Oliver Building** (1930; 32 Peachtree St.), the neo-Gothic **Hurt Building** (1913; 45 Edgewood Ave.), the **Flatiron Building** (1897; 84 Peachtree St.), and the ornate **Candler Building** (1906; 127 Peachtree St.). On Downtown's western edge stands the massive **CNN Center** (International Blvd. and Marietta St., ☎ 404/827–2300); 45-minute studio tours are available.

Heading up Peachtree Street, you begin to see the buildings that make up today's dramatic, modern skyline. The most striking towers are the 52-story, pyramid-crowned **Georgia-Pacific Building** (133 Peachtree St.), Philip Johnson's and John Burgee's neoclassical, 50-story **191 Peachtree Tower,** the 73-story **Westin Peachtree Plaza Hotel** (210 Peachtree St.), and the 60-story, gray-granite **One Peachtree Center** (303 Peachtree St.). This stretch of Peachtree is the liveliest bit of Downtown; there are several stores and restaurants here, most notably a dramatic old **Macy's** (180 Peachtree St.), whose grand exterior dates from 1927. Note also the Jetsonesque and somewhat silly-looking **Hyatt Regency Hotel** (265 Peachtree St.). When it opened in 1967, its glowing, blue rooftop restaurant permitted unobstructed views of Atlanta. Today, from many parts of town, you can't even see it.

Just east of Downtown is the **Sweet Auburn** historic district, a series of landmarks—most of them relating to the city's rich African-American history—stretching along Auburn Avenue from about Peachtree Street to Jackson Street. The western span of Auburn is where blacks conducted business in segregated Atlanta earlier in this century; the eastern span, beyond the I–75/85 overpass, is the **Martin Luther King Jr. National His-**

toric District, which documents the life and times of the civil rights leader who grew up and lived in this neighborhood. The **Ebenezer Baptist Church** (407 Auburn Ave., ☎ 404/688–7263), the site for many years of King's sermons and ultimately his funeral; the **Martin Luther King Jr. Center for Nonviolent Social Change** (449 Auburn Ave., ☎ 404/524–1956); and **Dr. King's Birthplace** (501 Auburn Ave., ☎ 404/331–3920) are among the many moving stops on this tour.

Midtown and Ansley Park

Midtown, where the counterculture nested three decades ago, now has Atlanta's highest concentration of gays and lesbians. Midtown's geography, like that of most Atlanta neighborhoods, is rather loosely defined. For practical purposes, it's separated from Downtown where Ponce de Leon Avenue crosses Peachtree and West Peachtree streets. Its western border is I–75/85 and the campus of Georgia Tech, its northern border is where I–85 veers off to the northeast, and its eastern border is Piedmont Avenue and Piedmont Park. Most of Midtown's popular gay bars and several of its restaurants are clustered around a grid of streets close to the intersection of 6th and Peachtree. This neighborhood also contains a few of the city's more distinct contemporary skyscrapers—most notably the South's tallest structure, the **NationsBank Plaza Tower** (600 Peachtree St.). History buffs might stop by the quirky **Atlanta Museum** (537 Peachtree St., ☎ 404/872–8233); budding Scarletts mustn't miss the **Road to Tara Museum** (659 Peachtree St., ☎ 404/897–1939), which contains enough *Gone with the Wind* memorabilia and costumes to satisfy even the most dedicated groupies; performing arts supporters should check out the esteemed **Woodruff Arts Center** (1280 Peachtree St., ☎ 404/733–4200), which is home to the Alliance Theatre and the Atlanta Symphony Orchestra; and fine-art lovers should see the adjacent **High Museum of Art** (1280 Peachtree St., ☎ 404/733–4444), whose respectable collection (19th-century European painting, American decorative arts, and a fine array of Alfred Uhry prints) is usually overshadowed by its striking, white-porcelain-paneled setting in a building designed by architect Richard Meier.

Piedmont Park, one of the loveliest urban parks in America, feels miles away from urban life, except for its views of the city skyline. Despite several construction projects, it's still common to see dykes and queens merrily blading, jogging, sunning, reading, and cruising just about everywhere. At night, the park is notoriously cruisy; avoid it then. A good number of the guys lurking around are out to beat you up or arrest you—after dark the park becomes "the land of entrapment." The park's northern edge is bordered by Atlanta's spectacular 60-acre **Botanical Garden** (1345 Piedmont Ave., ☎ 404/876–5859).

In northern Midtown you'll find the rather tony and quite gay residential neighborhood of **Ansley Park,** where many houses date from the early part of the century. Here, at the intersection of Piedmont Avenue and Monroe Drive, is a small but concentrated gay entertainment district, the focal point of which is the **Ansley Square shopping center** (1492–1510 Piedmont Ave.). Next to Seattle's Broadway Market, this is probably the gayest collection of shops, bars, and restaurants in the country—the food is fair at best. It's a drab little compound, but there are some useful stores, including **Brushstrokes** (☎ 404/876–6567), which sells gifts, cards, books, and magazines (including porn). Around the corner is **Ansley Mall** (1544 Piedmont Ave.), which is not so obviously gay-oriented but nevertheless has several shops popular with the community. The Kroger's grocery store next door to the mall is the cruisiest in town. Just down Piedmont from

Ansley Square is a great, little, gay-male fashion boutique, **Boy Next Door** (1447 Piedmont Ave., ☎ 404/873–2664).

Perhaps a mile north of Ansley Park, on the northeastern outskirts of Midtown, is a stretch of **Cheshire Bridge Road,** between Piedmont Road and the I–85 overpass, that constitutes a third small gay entertainment district. This whole stretch has a seedier feel to it than the rest of Midtown. The **Poster Hut** (2175 Cheshire Bridge Rd., ☎ 404/633–7491) sells gay gifts, cards, fetish wear, and sex stuff.

Buckhead

Posh **Buckhead** is so far removed from downtown Atlanta, that it's hard to believe it's within the city limits. Residential Buckhead encompasses a rather huge area—everything west of Peachtree Road and east of the Northwest Expressway (I–75) up to the **Perimeter** (an expanse of office buildings, restaurants, and malls), where Highway 400 runs over I–285. (Note that growth continues northward at a feverish pace, and formerly rural Roswell, Gwinnett, and Alpharetta are all quickly becoming extensions of Buckhead and the Perimeter.) A great sunny-day activity is to drive around Buckhead's winding, wooded roads gawking at the hundreds of mansions; West Paces Ferry Road and Northside Drive are two of the better routes. If you're into this sort of thing, consider stopping by the **Atlanta History Center** (130 W. Paces Ferry Rd., ☎ 404/814–4000), a 32-acre spread with several historic buildings, including the sumptuous **Swan House,** a furnished 1926 Palladian mansion.

Commercial Buckhead is where the chic go to see and be seen. Most of the nightclubs, restaurants, and shops are along Paces Ferry and Pharr roads, between Peachtree and Piedmont roads—which are also both dotted with upscale establishments. On weekend nights, this section is simply overrun with yuppies and college students. It's not a particularly gay neighborhood, although Elton John lives in a high-rise condo just south of all the action on Peachtree Road. The gays who live here tend to be older, settled, wealthy, and male. Buckhead is quite cosmopolitan, however, and the presence of both gays and lesbians gets stronger every day—as does the level of tolerance. The two most popular—and fashionable—malls in Atlanta are on Peachtree Road, north of where it somewhat confusingly intersects with Piedmont Road. **Lenox Square Mall** (3393 Peachtree Rd.) is officially the most visited site in Atlanta—it's the larger of the two, and has the most mainstream selection of shops. The snazzy **Phipps Plaza** (3500 Peachtree Rd.) has the sort of boutiques and department stores you'd find on Manhattan's 5th Avenue. Both have enough homo traffic to qualify unofficially as America's two fanciest gay community centers.

Virginia-Highlands

Monroe Drive is generally thought to be the boundary between Midtown and **Virginia-Highlands,** a funky yet gentrified residential and commercial neighborhood that's become increasingly popular with guppies. There are several good shops and restaurants where Monroe hits 10th Street from the west (by the southeast corner of Piedmont Park) and Virginia Avenue from the east. The true commercial center of the area, however, is a short drive east, at the intersection of Highland and Virginia avenues. Galleries and offbeat home-furnishings stores are abundant in these parts. Just south of Virginia-Highlands, the **Dekalb Farmer's Market** (3000 E. Ponce de Leon Ave., ☎ 404/377–6400) is the best dyke-cruising ground in the Atlanta metro area—maybe even in the whole Southeast.

Little Five Points and Inman Park

Atlanta does well when it comes to outrageousness. The city is teeming with young counterculturists, and you'll find most of them in a tiny district southeast of Virginia-Highlands. **Little Five Points** is centered, aptly, at a five-street intersection—shops and eateries stretch along Moreland Avenue between Mansfield and Euclid avenues, then on Euclid from about Moreland Avenue down to Austin. What to see? Grungers, goths, Deadheads, the tattooed and pierced, boys in ski hats in summer, girls in fishnet tights in winter, loiterers, do-nothings, poets, actors, artists, disillusioned scofflaws, slackers and rakes, ruffians and fakes, poseurs, curiosity-seekers, you name it. It's not necessarily a gay scene, but everybody is welcome (Little Five Points had a nasty skinhead problem here a few years ago, but their intolerant presence has been largely eradicated). You might pop into **Eat Your Vegetables** (438 Moreland Ave., ☎ 404/523–2671), a popular restaurant packed with punks who don't like meat. Or bumble into **Village Coffee House** (420 Seminole Ave., ☎ 404/688–3176), the coffeehouse where Atlanta's headbangers like to bang heads. There are also several experimental theaters, **Charis Books** (*see* Bookstores, *below*), and the lesbian-popular **Sevananda Natural Food Co-op** (1111 Euclid Ave., ☎ 404/681–2831). There's also a store selling Celtic trinkets and two or three Indian restaurants.

The heart of **Inman Park** is just south of here on Moreland, at about where Edgewood and DeKalb avenues intersect it. This neighborhood, Atlanta's first suburb, was eventually abandoned and worn down before a largely gay gentrification began to occur in the early '80s, with the restoration of many of its elaborate Victorian houses. It's now a wonderful place to wander.

Ormewood Park and Grant Park

As recently as five years ago, it was unheard of to live in the southeast Atlanta neighborhoods of **Ormewood Park** and **Grant Park.** But as gays and lesbians have sought bigger houses and more acreage for moderate prices, they've moved east to the extremely gay-friendly suburb of Decatur or headed to these two borderline sections. Perhaps most significant is that whites are slowly settling into a predominantly African-American area—this in a city whose racial spheres still rarely overlap. The movement first began in Grant Park, which is best known as the site of Atlanta's zoo. It has only recently begun spreading to Ormewood. In both communities, the mix of architectural styles runs from Victorian to '50s cottage; many of the houses are in dire need of repair.

GETTING AROUND

With the Olympics in town for the summer of 1996, Atlanta's extensive but often criticized mass-transit system is supposedly becoming more user-friendly for out-of-towners. Regardless, you should really not consider coming here without a car. Parking is fairly easy in Midtown but can be tough in Buckhead and Downtown. The layout is confusing, the traffic horrendous, and the roads always under construction. Nevertheless, a car is still a better weapon than a map of MARTA's bus and subway system, which is limited in coverage. People don't take a lot of taxis here, either.

EATS

Atlantans seem to believe their dining scene is far better than it really is. That there are dozens of first-rate, world-class restaurants here is not in question; the trick is separating the stars from the impostors. Eating out has become such a way of life in Atlanta that the number of dining options has quadrupled over the past decade. Especially in Buckhead and Midtown, just about every new eatery has indirect or track lighting, gobs of contemporary paintings, tables and chairs in surreal shapes and colors, pretty but often absentminded waitrons, and a menu that draws from an almost interchangeable battery of froufrou ingredients. After a while, many of these places begin to look and taste alike.

Virtually every restaurant in Atlanta has something of a gay following. Those Downtown are the least gay, and those in Buckhead (a few of which feel like extensions of sororities and fraternities) are usually packed with straight yuppies and are the trendiest. In Midtown, Virginia-Highlands, Little Five Points, and Inman Park it's gays galore. Any place where the see-and-be-seen factor is high, you're likely to have trouble parking, getting a table, and being served promptly. Be patient: You're in the South.

Southern restaurants are the minority. More usual are Southern influences on New American and contemporary Continental menus; you might see grilled swordfish, for example, with a side of hush puppies or collard greens, or you might catch a Northern Italian restaurant whimsically substituting pecans for pine nuts.

For price ranges, *see* Chart A at the front of this guide.

Midtown and Virginia-Highlands

$$$–$$$$ The Abbey. This is the place to go for special occasions. The stained-glass windows and ecumenical mood of this former church command a certain reverence—as though you should be extra careful not to dribble béarnaise sauce down your front. Food is very traditional and European, the sort of rich meals you'd expect the White House to serve to visiting French dignitaries. Check the limit on your charge card. *163 Ponce de Leon Ave.,* ☎ *404/876–8532.*

$$–$$$$ Indigo Coastal Grill. One of the major brunch spots in Virginia-Highlands, Indigo is a seafood restaurant with a Caribbean kick. Sample the faintly sweet conch fritters, the rich lobster corn chowder, or shrimp on a skewer with a tasty margarita sauce. At any meal, you're likely to see some of the gay community's movers and shakers. *1397 N. Highland Ave.,* ☎ *404/ 876–0676.*

$$–$$$$ South of France. The words RESTAURANT AND LOUNGE on the sign out front (and the location in a tacky shopping center) belie the authenticity of this fine French restaurant, which has been feeding Francophiles since 1977. Once you get past the cheesy facade, there's a refined dining room inside, where the wine overfloweth and the pâtés are plentiful. Good value, too. *2345 Cheshire Bridge Rd.,* ☎ *404/325–6963.*

$$–$$$$ Tiburon Grille. Slightly pretentious (the spelling of the name is a giveaway), with high ceilings, indirect lighting, and rather affected contemporary decor, this relatively recent addition to Highland Avenue's restaurant row churns out fresh California-inspired cuisine. You might try the hefty Caesar salad with fried oysters or the delicious rare tuna steak. There's a great wine list, too. *1190-B N. Highland Ave.,* ☎ *404/892–2393.*

$$–$$$ Cowtippers. Just about everything here but the tap water is char-grilled, making Cowtippers one of the best steak houses in town—and easily the faggiest. Set in a low ranch-style house on Piedmont Road, just up from Ansley Square, it's a rollicking place with an authentic roadhouse atmosphere. Lots of outdoor seating. *1600 Piedmont Rd.,* ☎ *404/874–3751.*

$$–$$$ R. J.'s Uptown Kitchen & Wine Bar. It's fun just to show up and guzzle— or sip, rather—wine; dozens of vintages are available, and you can get samplings of particular types of wine. But don't forget that the food at this converted service station makes a pretty great meal. It's light stuff at reasonable prices. Check out the seafood-and-artichoke dip or the pizza

8

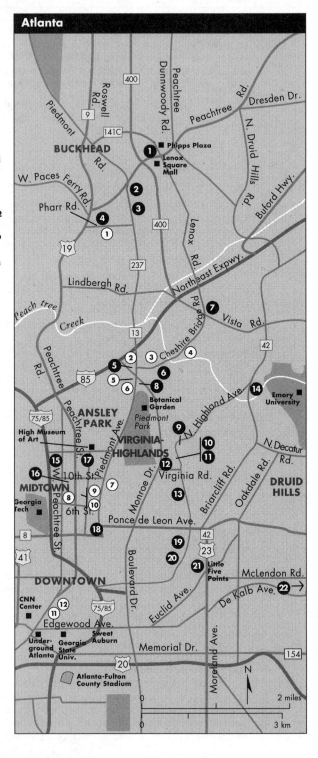

Atlanta

with goat cheese, tomatoes, and salmon. *870 N. Highland Ave.,* ☎ *404/ 875–7775.*

$$–$$$ **Veni Vidi Vici.** This northern Italian bistro is so authentic that there's even a boccie court out back—it certainly makes it easy to forget you're dining in the middle of Atlanta's Midtown. This choice spot features several rotisserie selections (including an unusually good salmon), plus a fine antipasto spread for starters. *41 14th St.,* ☎ *404/875–8424.*

$$ **Camille's.** No surprises here: just an old-fashioned, family-style Italian restaurant without too many families. You sit either in the bright dining room or out on the covered patio—both have candles and red-check tablecloths on the tables. Expect good, filling pastas, chicken, veal, and seafood—and a nice selection of wines by the glass. *1186 N. Highland Ave.,* ☎ *404/872–7203.*

$$ **Colonnade Restaurant.** Blue-haired old ladies and bleached-blond fags: two great things that go well together. Yes, the Colonnade is practically a caricature of itself; it's been serving fattening but beloved Southern fare since the late '20s. Gussied up with hunting prints and floral carpeting, it really does draw a mix of gays and old Southern Baptists (and who says you can't be both?). The chicken potpie will warm your heart and clog your arteries. *1879 Cheshire Bridge Rd.,* ☎ *404/874–5642.*

$$ **Vickery's.** This lively restaurant in the heart of Midtown is essentially Blake's (*see* Scenes, *below*) with a kitchen: very trendy, very cute staff and patrons, and a touch of attitude. It's a casual place, serving traditional American food with a few Cuban overtones. *1106 Crescent Ave.,* ☎ *404/ 881–1106.*

$–$$ **Dusty's.** You are in the South, after all, so at least once you should do as the natives do (what few of them exist in Atlanta), and hit an authentic barbecue. This one near Emory University is noted for its North Carolina–style preparation (lots of vinegar and spices, no tomatoes). *1815 Briarcliff Rd.,* ☎ *404/320–6264.*

$–$$ **Einstein's.** Set in a rambling old Southern house on Juniper Street, Einstein's is probably the gayest of Atlanta's restaurants; it's famous for its lively Sunday brunches. Getting a patio seat is tough, but worth the wait. The crowd is cruisy, loud, and vivacious. Intergalactic kitsch makes up the decor and enlivens the menu, which has several dishes with physics- and astronomy-inspired names. *1077 Juniper St.,* ☎ *404/876–7925.*

Buckhead

$$$$ **The Dining Room and Café, Ritz-Carlton, Buckhead.** Both of the Ritz-Carlton's dining rooms are usually mentioned when discussing the world's leading hotel dining venues. The Dining Room is formal, warm, and surprisingly unstuffy—maybe owing to its views of the open kitchen. The Continental prix-fixe meals are pricey but magnificent. The Café, which at just about any other first-rate hotel would qualify as the formal dining room, is off a sumptuous lobby and has lighter but no less spectacular food: The crab cakes are a specialty. *3434 Peachtree Rd.,* ☎ *404/ 237–2700.*

$$$ **Bacchanalia.** This unassuming house on Piedmont Road is home to some of Buckhead's most creative cooking, borrowing from many cultures— the south of France to Thailand. Though it's one of the city's true hot spots, it's the sort of place where you show up in jeans and a pressed shirt and enjoy a spirited, memorable evening. The menu changes weekly. Save room for homemade ice cream. *3125 Piedmont Rd.,* ☎ *404/365–0410.*

$–$$ **Buckhead Diner.** It's becoming a popular trick: You build a fancy chrome restaurant; jazz up the dining room with marble, neon, and leather; flood the menu with nouveau takes on traditional favorites; and then call it a "diner." Of course, we all know better—the diner bit is little more than a gimmick. But the food, such as tomato fondue with goat cheese and veal meat loaf, ensures that the gimmick works. *3073 Piedmont Rd.,* ☎ *404/262–3336.*

$ **Café Tu Tu Tango.** Packed most nights with beautiful people, this clever theme restaurant in Buckhead often provides a 90-minute wait as part of the dining experience. Artists and musicians actually work inside the restaurant, their oeuvres dotting the walls and filling the air. But the draw is really some 50 varieties of tapas and great pizzas, rosemary flatbread, artichoke dip, and pot stickers. The upstairs seating is quieter and has better ambience. *220 Pharr Rd.,* ☎ *404/841–6222.*

Elsewhere

$$–$$$ **Babette's Cafe.** Famous for seasonal, prix-fixe Babette's Feasts, Babette's is a modest storefront bistro that captures the essence of Southern European farmhouse cooking. Expect plenty of pâté and red wine: It keeps the French living a long time, so it should do the same for you, too. It's the best restaurant in Inman Park. *471 N. Highland Ave.,* ☎ *404/523–9121.*

$–$$ **Flying Biscuit Cafe.** Just down the road from Little Five Points, in a quiet, residential neighborhood, this offbeat café has developed an almost unheard-of cult following among every kind of person—from hip alterna-teens to dykes with tykes. Breakfast is the main draw, and it's served all day. Try the exceptionally rich orange French toast with honey and caramelized bananas. Healthniks love the scrambled tofu with ginger and garlic. *1655 McLendon Ave.,* ☎ *404/687–8888.*

$ **La Fonda Latina.** This is a busy little dive in Little Five Points—a standard Mexican restaurant and bar, extremely bare and simple inside. It was literally a stretch of sidewalk between two buildings before somebody got the clever idea of throwing a tarp over it and calling it a restaurant. Okay food, cheap beer, but a colorful crowd. *1150-B Euclid Ave.,* ☎ *404/577–8317.*

Coffeehouse Culture

Coffee culture is taking hold with caffeine-infused fervor. One of the many glitzy coffeehouses to open in Midtown in the past couple of years, **Aurora** (1572 Piedmont Ave., ☎ 404/607–9994) has quickly developed a gay following because of its location across from Ansley Mall and Ansley Square. It's a bright, contemporary place with some outdoor tables—not a lot of character but lots of handsome customers. **Cafe Diem** (640 N. Highland Ave., ☎ 404/607–7008), which is located oddly in a transient hotel, is the major lesbian and gay coffeehouse. A place to bring your dog-eared paperback and curl up with steamed milk and biscuits, or one of the good salads and sandwiches. Very intellectual crowd and quite popular late at night. With great muffins, bagels, and lots of designer coffees and espressos, amber-lighted, traditionally furnished **Gallettos Espresso** (corner of Monroe Dr., Virginia Ave., and 10th St.; ☎ 404/724–0204) is in a small shopping center near the southeast corner of Piedmont Park. Gets a fairly collegiate crowd.

SLEEPS

In the past couple of decades, as more and more corporations have moved to Atlanta, a slew of first-rate hotels has opened. The metro area now has the most impressive selection of contemporary luxury hotels of any American city. On the other hand, it lacks the characterful grandes dames you find in New Orleans, New York, and Chicago.

Only a handful of hotels are within walking distance of Midtown bars and restaurants. But since you're probably going to need a car to visit Atlanta for more than a couple of days, proximity to nightlife isn't all that important. You can drive to Midtown from the hotels in Buckhead and Downtown just as easily. Keep in mind, however, that Downtown is eerily deserted at night, and Buckhead is a traffic nightmare—especially on weekend evenings.

For price ranges, *see* Chart A at the front of this guide.

Hotels

Buckhead

The 25-story, granite **Hotel Nikko** is the most striking structure on Buckhead's skyline. The lobby overlooks a 9,000-square-foot Japanese garden and 35-foot waterfall; the dignified decor consists of soft colors and Asian designs in the esteemed Nikko tradition. *3300 Peachtree Rd.,* ☎ *404/365–8100 or 800/645–5687. 438 rooms. $$$$*

The **Ritz-Carlton, Buckhead** is the flagship property of the chain, and you won't find a better hotel. It is filled with rare art and antiques and presided over by the most efficient staff in town. The Dining Room and Café are stellar, and across the street are the Lenox and Phipps Plaza malls. *3434 Peachtree Rd.,* ☎ *404/237–2700 or 800/241–3333. 553 rooms. $$$–$$$$*

The **Wyndham Garden Hotel,** sandwiched between the Ritz-Carlton and the Hotel Nikko, is one of Buckhead's best values. Rooms are large and filled with standard mahogany hotel furniture. Guests can use the health club next door. *3340 Peachtree Rd.,* ☎ *404/231–1234 or 800/822–4200. 221 rooms. $$*

Midtown/Downtown

If you need to stay Downtown, and you have the money, choose the **Ritz-Carlton, Atlanta,** whose spacious rooms have marble writing tables, sofas, and four-poster beds. The Ritz has one of the best afternoon teas in town. *181 Peachtree St.,* ☎ *404/659–0400 or 800/241–3333. 447 rooms. $$$$*

The **Occidental Grand,** one of the more underrated hotels in the city, has the charm and elegance of a top European property. The dramatic atrium lobby centered by a sweeping staircase is lined with Spanish marble, and guest rooms are large, sleek, and contemporary. There's a great pool and health center, too. *75 14th St.,* ☎ *404/881-9898 or 800/952-0702. 244 rooms. $$$–$$$$*

Any time there's a gay event in town, the **Sheraton Colony Square** is packed with queens. It's a short walk from Backstreet and other Midtown bars, and the staff is always great to gay guests. Rooms have typical Sheraton-chain furniture; try to score one on an upper floor—the views are stupendous. *188 14th St.,* ☎ *404/892–6000 or 800/325–3535. 461 rooms. $$$*

With all the enormous convention properties in Atlanta, the attractive, redbrick **Wyndham Hotel Midtown** is refreshingly intimate and personal. It's in the center of Midtown and possesses the sort of touches that make it a hit with business travelers: coffeemakers, extra phones, and oversize rooms. *125 10th St.,* ☎ *404/873–4800 or 800/822–4200. 191 rooms. $$$*

The only historic property in town, the vaunted Georgian-style **Biltmore Suites Hotel** was built in the '20s and has hosted many presidents and, more importantly, Scarlett O'Hara's portrayer, Vivien Leigh. Sadly, it's grown a bit frumpy with age, but the price and location are right, and the suites are absolutely enormous. The duplex and triplex penthouse suites, though more costly, have fabulous Jacuzzis. *30 5th St.,* ☎ *404/874–0824 or 800/822–0824. 75 suites. $$–$$$*

🏨 The **Biltmore Peachtree Hotel,** a small, quiet property that's equally close to Downtown and Midtown, actively courts gay business. Rooms are large for such an inexpensive place, and complimentary Continental breakfasts are served each morning in the lobby. *330 Peachtree St.,* ☎ *404/577–1980 or 800/241–4288. 91 rooms. $–$$*

🏨 Within walking distance of the gay bars on Cheshire Bridge Road, the **Cheshire Motor Inn** is a good, budget option and has a certain '50s retro charm. *1865 Cheshire Bridge Rd.,* ☎ *404/872–9628 or 800/827–9628. 49 rooms. $*

Guest Houses

🏨 The **Woodruff Bed & Breakfast Inn** is a short walk from a few of the quieter bars on Ponce de Leon, but also close to Downtown and most of Midtown. This three-story Victorian mansion was once a brothel, but things have quieted down. Rooms are now done with Victorian furniture, and two suites have hot tubs. *223 Ponce de Leon Ave.,* ☎ *404/875–9449 or 800/473–9449. 12 rooms. Mostly straight. $$–$$$*

🏨 A few miles north of Midtown in quiet, unincorporated Sandy Springs, the **Hidden Creek Retreat** is technically within the city limits, but you'd never know it from its forested setting on more than 2 acres. This huge split-level ranch is big on amenities: There are VCRs and TVs in all rooms, a private gym, and a rec room with a pool table and a baby grand piano. *201 N. Mill Rd.,* ☎ *404/705–9545 or 800/605–9545. 5 rooms. Gay male. $–$$*

🏨 The **Magnolia Station B&B** is an antiques-laden private home in the up-and-coming Inman Park section, very close to Little Five Points and a short drive to Midtown. Its best feature is a pool in back. *1020 Edgewood Ave. NE,* ☎ *404/523–2005. 3 rooms. Mostly gay male.*

🏨 The **Midtown Manor** is the place to be if you're looking for cheap, friendly accommodations within walking distance of Midtown bars. It's not a fancy place, but the rooms—spread among three, linked, Victorian houses—have a smattering of antiques and a simple charm. *811 Piedmont Ave. NE,* ☎ *404/872–5846 or 800/724–4381. 63 rooms. Mixed gay/straight. $*

SCENES

Atlantans love to party. The nightlife is diverse, fairly wild, and—for a city of fewer than 400,000—quite extensive. Saturday is the big night out on the town; for some reason Fridays are relatively quiet—closer in popularity to other weeknights. But at most bars here, there's always something going on. Many clubs have opened in the last few years; the entire face of Atlanta's nightlife has changed dramatically in that time. A vast majority of the bars and clubs are in Midtown.

In Atlanta you can always find a drag show (Ru Paul got her start here). You'll find everything from serious, traditional shows put on by female impersonators to campy, outrageous productions. Big, glitzy dance clubs are also common, with Backstreet and the Armory among the biggest. The Heretic is the best leather club, but there are several other rough-edged bars that are similar in clientele, including **Bulldog's** (893 Peachtree St., ☎ 404/872–3025) and the **Eagle** (306 Ponce de Leon Ave., ☎ 404/873–2453). None of the bars has a strong suit-and-tie following, but Blake's and Burkhart's draw something of an after-work crowd.

Don't overlook the city's budding music scene. A number of popular bands hail from Atlanta and environs, including REM, Indigo Girls, Hootie and the Blowfish, the B-52s, and Arrested Development. You may not find any all-gay bands, but a ton of them have one or two gay members and substantial followings in the community. **Eddie's Attic** (515-B N. Mc-Donough St., ☎ 404/377–4976) in Decatur gets the younger crowd by frequently featuring acoustic women's groups. It's not gay per se but has a huge lesbian following.

In preparation for the 1996 Olympics, talk around City Hall has centered on shutting down strip joints, or at least those that aren't regularly frequented by local politicians. Among them, the **Coronet Club** (5275 Roswell Rd., ☎ 404/250–1534) has a mostly gay contingent on Sundays—but it's BYOB, and since you can't buy booze on Sundays, plan ahead. Also, **Guys and Dolls** (2788 E. Ponce de Leon Ave., Decatur, ☎ 404/377–2956) has a fairly strong following among both gay guys and dykey dolls. There are no sex clubs in Atlanta, although things can allegedly get frisky at the Heretic. The **Chamber** (2115 Faulkner Rd., ☎ 404/248–1612) is a fetish club where you can watch a variety of fascinating, kinky demonstrations representing every conceivable sexual taste.

Bars and Nightclubs

The Armory. The Armory is almost adjacent to Backstreet, so lots of guys wind up hitting both. If you find the guys at Backstreet too piss-elegant for words, head here where the booze is cheap and a gotta-get-laid attitude prevails. There are several bars and dance floors, one of which is country-western on weekends. Also has nightly drag shows. Fridays are most popular. *836 Juniper St., ☎ 404/881–9280. Crowd: male, all ages; similar to Backstreet's but looser and trashier; broad racial mix; very cruisy.*

Backstreet. Just about everybody winds up here at some point on a Saturday night—it's one of four Atlanta bars (but the only gay one) that never closes or stops serving alcohol on weekends. It's closed from 7 AM to 11 AM weekdays. A good number of straight folks join the dykes and fags in the upstairs lounge to catch the now legendary drag act of Charlie Brown and Lily White (and friends). There are three floors: The lower one in back is a large dance floor with a small bar; the middle one has pool tables, a sex shop, and a large rectangular cruise bar; and the upper one has a small video bar and the drag lounge. Balconies and open stairwells abound—a very smart, fun layout, overall. *845 Peachtree St., ☎ 404/873–1986. Crowd: young, white, guppie, often stuck-up, gym boys; best mix on Saturdays.*

Blake's. Of stand-and-model bars, Blake's may have the most uppity reputation in the country. But, in fact, because this is a comparatively friendly city, it's not truly all that stuck-up—it's just a bit of a scene. You enter through a front room, which is cozy, crowded, and pubby; it has a pressed-tin ceiling and walls covered with license plates and odd signs. There are some bar stools, but these guys are known to bare claws and fangs to capture them. A flight of stairs leads to a second, quieter video bar in back, off of which you'll find a rickety sunporch and off that a patio. It's nice to catch some air back here. The owners of Blake's also run **Red Square** (991 Piedmont Rd., ☎ 404/724–4915), a weird little disco that's just around the corner and opens late—apparently with the hopes of attracting guys leaving Blake's before they run over to Backstreet and the Armory. As of its first anniversary in 1995, Red Square was still pretty quiet. It is rather striking inside, with red walls, and a front lounge with love seats and other furniture to slouch on. *227 10th St., ☎ 404/892–*

5786. *Crowd: clonish and cliquey, mostly male except for a few fag hags, starched-shirt, attitudy, uniformly chiseled and beautiful.*

Burkhart's. The crown jewel of Ansley Square shopping center, Burkhart's is one of the nicest bars in town—the kind of place where you can walk up and talk to somebody, where they spin popular and current dance tunes, where a stranger is welcome to jump in and play pool with the regulars. And, contrary to popular opinion, the guys at Blake's aren't better looking, they just think they are. The whole place has a warm, taverny feel; downstairs has several small rooms and bars—no dance area per se, but there's a space in the center of the main room where you'll catch a few guys wiggling their hips. Upstairs, an open interior balcony encircles the main room down below, allowing for prime ogling, and a second room has pool tables. *Ansely Sq., 1492 Piedmont Ave., ☎ 404/872–4403. Crowd: similar to guys at Blake's but less attitude; regular guys, mostly 20s and 30s; cruisy and friendly.*

Heretic. Some leather devotees swear by the Eagle, but the Heretic has far more character and seems to exude machismo. Your first hint is a parking lot absolutely packed with monster pick-up trucks and Cadillac Eldorados. The Heretic is also along a strip of sleazy (mostly straight), girlie bars—which contributes to the forbidding atmosphere. As for the leather theme, a strict dress code is enforced on Wednesday and Sunday, and strongly suggested the rest of the time. Inside, the place lives up to expectations—that is, it's so dark and smoky you honestly can't see a thing, except the occasional bear belting down a vat of Jack Daniels. Don't say we didn't warn you. *2069 Cheshire Bridge Rd., ☎ 404/325–3061. Crowd: male; thirtysomething; dangerous-looking but warm and fuzzy underneath; leathered up.*

Hoedown's. This has traditionally been the top gay country-western dance club in Atlanta. It's in a sort of uninspiring, barn-red building, although the neon cactus outside livens things up. Inside is a huge floor that's always buzzing with dancers. At press time (fall 1995), a new country-western club, Chaps, was expected to open soon in Midtown—check the gay papers for details. *1890 Cheshire Bridge Rd., ☎ 404/874–0980. Crowd: about half-and-half cowboys and cowgirls; mixed ages; friendly, down-to-earth.*

Metro. There's something lovable about this rather tired dance club, with a mostly skeevy roster of dancers. One of the few gay-owned clubs in town, the Metro always comes through with a wild, popular event when the community needs fund-raising. Depending on the night of the week, the place can be dead or pulsing with offbeat characters. Particularly enticing is Monday's amateur strip night. *48 6th St., ☎ 404/874–9869. Crowd: male; a colorful blend of daddies, club kids, hustlers, guppies, and the occasional transsexual.*

New Order Lounge. Of the dozen-or-so dives around town, the New Order Lounge has the campiest appeal. It's hidden in back of Ansley Mall, around the corner from the Laundry Lounge Laundromat, which itself is pretty cruisy. The actual entrance is set cheerfully amid several loading docks for the mall's Woolworth's store. It's a cheap, dreary cocktail lounge with nothing especially new or orderly about it. But at 2 in the afternoon, where else is a girl to go? *Ansley Mall, 1544 Piedmont Rd., ☎ 404/874–8247. Crowd: older, male; hard drinkers; neighborhood following.*

The Otherside. More mixed and mellower than Atlanta's main lesbian bar, Revolution, the Otherside is a lively tavern with lots of space for chatting and an extremely approachable crowd. *1924 Piedmont Rd., ☎ 404/875–5238. Crowd: 70/30 f/m; fairly mixed in age and race; gals/guys next door; low attitude.*

Pearl Garden. Of Atlanta's gay African-American clubs, the Pearl Garden has the friendliest staff and the safest location. Crowd is mostly male, but lesbians are very welcome here. Good drag shows on certain nights; call ahead. *15 Simpson St., ☎ 404/522–3000. Crowd: 75/25 m/f; mostly African-American; mixed ages.*

Revolution. It's hard to understand why Buckhead has only one gay bar, and, given how few lesbians live up here, why it's mostly a women's disco, but this is a great club. Up front there's a large dance floor; in back is a smaller room that feels more like a sports bar, with video screens and pool tables. Decor is classy and contemporary—there's even valet parking out front. A good place to meet a hot, young chippie. *293 Pharr Rd., Buckhead, ☎ 404/816–5455. Crowd: 80/20 f/m; young, stylish, well-heeled and well-dressed.*

Velvet. Partly because of its Downtown location, Velvet has had some problems in the past with wild patrons and overcrowding (Sundays are especially scary), but it's still Atlanta's primary glam club. Elton John and even Madonna sightings are reported from time to time. Velvet isn't a big club: There's a small dance floor with cutting-edge music, a long bar with a standing-and-chatting area in front, and a lounge upstairs that's only open occasionally. The bad news: Velvet has the longest bathroom lines on the planet. *89 Park Pl., ☎ 404/681–9936. Crowd: mostly gay and male on Saturdays and Mondays, mixed other times; young, good-looking, lots of club kids, stylish.*

THE LITTLE BLACK BOOK

At Your Fingertips

AIDS Hotline for Women: ☎ 404/888–9991. **AIDS Info Line:** ☎ 404/876–9944 or 800/551–2728. **Atlanta Convention and Visitors Bureau:** ☎ 404/521–6600 or 404/222–6688; visitor centers at Peachtree Center Mall, 233 Peachtree St. NE, Suite 2000; Underground Atlanta, 65 Upper Alabama St.; and Lenox Square Mall, 3393 Peachtree Rd. NE. **Atlanta Department of Tourism:** 233 Peachtree St. NE, Suite 2000, 30303, no ☎. **Atlanta Gay Center:** 71 12th St., ☎ 404/876–5372; clinic at 67 B 12th St. **Atlanta Lambda Community Center:** Box 15180, 30333, ☎ 404/881–1985. **Gay Helpline:** ☎ 404/892–0661.

Gay Media

Southern Voice (☎ 404/876–1819) is Atlanta's weekly gay and lesbian newspaper; in terms of coverage and writing quality it's one of the best papers in the country. The city's other gay weekly, ***Etcetera*** (☎ 404/525–3821), is a thick, little newspaper whose emphasis is more on dining and nightlife; it also has a smattering of coverage about other parts of the South.

Creative Loafing (☎ 404/688–5623) is the city's politically alternative and very gay-friendly arts weekly.

BOOKSTORES

Outwrite Books (931 Monroe Dr., ☎ 404/607–0082) is the main lesbigay bookstore; it's relatively new but has become very popular. There's a small coffee bar inside, and in addition to its wide selection of lesbian and gay titles, Outwrite sells the gamut of gay periodicals, lube, and some greeting cards. **Charis Books** (1189 Euclid Ave., ☎ 404/524–0304) is an excellent feminist and lesbian bookstore in Little Five Points. **Brushstrokes** (1510 Piedmont Ave., ☎ 404/876–6567), the gay and lesbian variety store in Ansley Square, has a small selection of books.

Body and Fitness

Boot Camp (Ansley Mall, 1544 Piedmont Ave., ☎ 404/876–8686) is big with muscle boys and can be quite a scene. **Mid City Fitness** (2201 Faulkner Rd., ☎ 404/321–6507) has a more mainstream following and has become the most popular gym with gays and lesbians in the city. The **Fitness Factory** (Midtown Outlets, 500 N. Amsterdam Ave., off Monroe Dr., ☎ 404/815–7900) has quickly developed a gay following.

2 *Out in Austin*

AMERICA'S CITIES ARE STRIKING PORTRAITS of highs and lows, gains and losses, compromises and accommodations. We cope with New York City's crime and grime to be able to enjoy its restaurants, culture, and sophistication. L.A.'s smog and plasticity may be hard to take, but the film industry's glamour and Santa Monica's beaches keep us happy. New Orleans is an all-night party—but how much of that is too much? For almost every city a simple rule seems to hold: Opposing each of its strengths is an equally significant weakness.

The capital of Texas, however, is the exception to this rule, particularly if you're gay. Look all you like: There is simply nothing wrong with Austin, and it seems to have an unmistakably rosy future. As one gay resident commented with a hint of frustration in her voice, "Everybody is just so damned comfortable here." Even the disconcerting election in 1994 of former first son George W. Bush as governor of Texas has done little to upset people. "It's certainly not a good thing," commented another local, "but with regard to gay issues, he's really an unknown. Ann Richards appointed several lesbians and gays to high level positions—she gave us extremely high visibility in state politics. Bush claims he simply won't ask." (Former governor Ann Richards is in fact cited as often as the University of Texas as a major reason Austin is such a lovely city. And it's hard to believe Bush will be as good to this free-thinking, arts-minded, eco-concerned community as she was for so many years.)

Even if this largely conservative state now has a staunchly conservative governor, few in the gay community are overly concerned about the state of politics in Austin itself. For one thing, Austin's representative on the state legislature is none other than openly gay Glen Maxie. And Austin's mayor, Bruce Todd, is exceedingly gay-friendly and progressive.

Spend a few days in Austin and you'll even begin to wonder if it's truly in Texas. This is actually one of the most diverse cities in America, and it's thriving. While Houston slumped in the '80s, Austin had the nation's fastest growing economy. *Fortune* rated Austin's work force as the fifth most knowledgeable in America. It has the highest number of restaurants per capita in the United States, the most movie screens per capita, more than 100 live-music clubs, the sixth-highest number of artists per capita, and the highest bookstore sales per capita. It's also been cited as the nation's most computer-literate city, the fifth-best city in which to start a business (*Entrepreneur*), the most "fit city" (*Walking*), and the third-best place to live (*Money*).

The University of Texas could probably take credit for some of these startling statistics. UT attracts people to Austin, and many decide to stay. For this reason, Austin has a high number of parking attendants and burger flippers with PhDs. Only so many high-level jobs exist, and highly educated residents are often forced to take what's left. It's not surprising that the pop term "slacker" was coined here a few years back, when an amusing, low-budget documentary on the city's brightest and youngest do-nothings achieved cult status.

Yes, here in Austin, where high-tech industry thrives, slackerdom is a major force, or antiforce, to be perfectly accurate. As you stroll by the coffeehouses and restaurants along Guadalupe Street, note the remarkable number of disillusioned Gen-Xers hitting passersby up for change. In many ways a nuisance, their presence nevertheless adds a certain grungy charm to the streetscape.

Some peculiar battles relevant to the gay community have been fought here in recent years. Apple Computers nearly decided not to move to nearby Georgetown because the company's gay-friendly benefits rules clashed with the county's gay-unfriendly attitudes. Though Austin's Travis County is the most liberal in Texas, neighboring Williamson County, of which Georgetown is the county seat, is quite conservative. The county eventually relented, and Apple moved in, joining the likes of Dell Computers, IBM, and Motorola as key engineers of Austin's information highway.

Although antidiscrimination laws protecting gays have been on the books in Austin since the last decade, passing a same-sex benefits package for city employees has proven trickier. Austin actually did pass a resolution in favor of domestic-partner benefits in September 1993, but enraged Bible thumpers rose up against it, raising enough of a stink to cause a revote in May 1994. Few took the revolt seriously, but much to the amazement of many complacent Austinites, the package was repealed.

Nevertheless, residents—straight and gay—still praise Austin as one of America's best cities, and visitors keep coming back to savor a few cheap meals, catch a few bands, sun themselves along the banks of Barton Creek or Travis Lake, drive around the hill country, browse a few funky shops, and wonder why it is they live somewhere else.

THE LAY OF THE LAND

People disagree about the designations and borders of neighborhoods in Austin. Such fabled enclaves as Travis Heights, Clarksville, Red River, and Barton Springs are bandied about from time to time. The local paper, the *American-Statesman*, groups the city's restaurants in its weekly roundup into regions based on points of the compass: Northwest, Northeast, Central, Southwest, and Southeast. And real estate ads often default to listing properties in terms of their proximity to well-known landmarks (e.g., Zilker Park, the University of Texas, the MoPac Expressway). If you ask where Austin's gay neighborhoods are, most locals shrug, noting that gays and lesbians live, eat, and conduct their business all around town.

Downtown
Austin's grid-shaped downtown is defined to the west by Lamar Boulevard, to the north by Martin Luther King Jr. Boulevard, to the east by I-35, and to the south by the Colorado River (or Town Lake, as the segment that fringes downtown is called). There isn't that much in terms of sightseeing, but there's plenty to do. The area is small and walkable, and for the most part very picturesque. And what it lacks in attractions, it makes up for with shops, restaurants, and music clubs.

Sixth Street (a.k.a. Old Pecan Street) is Austin's equivalent of New Orleans's Bourbon Street. It has the liveliest array of diversions—all quite gay-friendly. Red River Street, which intersects 6th, has more of the same from about 4th through 8th streets. Most of the neighborhood below the State Capitol (11th and Congress Sts.) makes for good exploring and shopping. The outskirts of downtown are largely made up of quiet, tree-lined residential streets. If you feel you have to have a guided tour of something—anything—stop by the Renaissance Revival **State Capitol Complex** (☎ 512/463–0063), the largest in the country, a good nine feet taller than the one in Washington, D.C.

Connecting downtown to the area just south, across Town Lake, is the **Congress Avenue Bridge,** famous as the home of more than 1.5 million Mexican free-tailed bats, who hang out beneath it from March to November. Curious onlookers gather at dusk on the walkway along the river to watch the nation's largest urban bat colony emerge from its daytime slumber and take to the night skies.

South of Downtown
Here you'll discover the less prettified but still engaging **Barton Springs.** If you follow Barton Springs Road (site of many of the city's slacker-infested shops and eateries) you'll reach **Zilker Park;** an offshoot of the Colorado River, Barton Creek, snakes southwest out of the city through the park. Zilker is a popular place to tan your hide on sunny days, and a good place to meet some of the city's outgoing locals. There's also a popular swimming hole here, **Barton Springs,** whose spring-fed pool remains an invigorating 68°F year-round. Following Barton Springs Road east will bring you to South Congress Avenue and to **Travis Heights.** If Austin has an unofficial gay settlement, Travis Heights is it. It's bordered by Riverside Drive to the north, I–35 to the east, Oltorf Street to the south, and Congress Avenue to the west.

University of Texas and Environs
North of downtown is the sprawling campus of the **University of Texas,** which is bordered to the north and south by a commercially and residentially mixed neighborhood. The campus itself is bound to the west by Guadalupe Street, to the north by East 26th Street, to the east by I–35, and to the south by Martin Luther King Jr. Boulevard. The 357-acre campus (tours are available, ☎ 512/475–7348) is dotted with dozens of notable buildings, including the **Lyndon B. Johnson Presidential Library and Museum** (2313 Red River Rd., ☎ 512/482–5279) and the **Texas Memorial Museum** (2400 Trinity, ☎ 512/471–1604), which has exhibits on state history and local flora and fauna. **Guadalupe Street** (known along its border with UT as "The Drag") is another haven of Austin's slackerdom as well as *the* place to shop for locally made arts and crafts, Longhorn memorabilia, and other offbeat goods.

Lake Travis and Points West
A great way to spend a sunny afternoon is to drive out to Lake Travis. Begin by driving west on RR 2222 for several miles, then turn left onto Route 640W and take a right a short while later on Comanchee Road. This leads to the famed **Oasis** restaurant (*see* Eats, *below*), which overlooks the shores of **Lake Travis,** and, farther on, to **Hippie Hollow State Park** (populated with gay sunbathers).

To get back to Austin, return to and turn right onto Route 640W; in a few miles you'll pass a recently opened outpost of the regionally famous Mexican bar and restaurant, **Carlos'n'Charlies,** a popular party ground on weekends. Continue on Route 640W another 10 miles to the tiny city of Beehive, and turn left at the light onto Route 71. A mile farther, make another left onto RR 2244 (Bee Cave Road), and follow that 15 miles back to town. The last section of this scenic loop (particularly around Barton Creek Boulevard) will take you past some of the city's wealthiest developments.

GETTING AROUND

Austin's lively downtown is navigable on foot, and you can definitely enjoy three or four days in Austin without wheels. If you want to take advantage of greater Austin, however—the beautiful countryside west and north, many of the better restaurants, and the University of Texas—you'll need a car. Public transportation isn't really adequate, and taxis are inconvenient (and generally too expensive) for greater distances.

EATS

Even though Austin has some terrific restaurants, it's impossible to spend a lot of money on food here. Just try to find an entrée above $15—most are in the single digits! Almost every neighborhood has a few good restaurants to choose from. There are several downtown, close to major hotels and most nightclubs. Many others are farther afield, however—north and west of the city. There's a particularly funky stretch of dilapidated, queer-friendly eateries south of Town Lake on Barton Springs Road. Austinites like to dine out and often late—most places are still hopping past 10 PM, especially on weekends.

For price ranges, *see* Chart B at the front of this guide.

$$$–$$$$ **Coyote Cafe.** Mark Miller, a renowned Southwestern cook, first opened a Coyote Cafe in Santa Fe, then one in Las Vegas, and recently this one in Austin. The nouvelle Southwestern menu leans toward the grill. Popular dishes are blue-corn New Mexican enchiladas, pan-roasted salmon, Mexican green-chili sirloin fillets, and the Cowboy Steak, a 20-pound slab of black Angus rib steak. Faux adobe walls, Santa Fe shuttered windows, leather booths, handmade cowhide chairs, and earthy hues make you feel as if you're dining in a Spaghetti Western. *612 W. 6th St.,* ☎ *512/ 476–0612.*

$$–$$$ **Granite Cafe.** West of the University, the Granite Cafe with its light, airy dining room and inviting terrace is as upscale as Austin gets. The eclectic, contemporary menu changes daily (for both lunch and dinner). Recent offerings included sesame mahimahi on Asian noodles, lamb with rice pilaf and cassis-peppercorn sauce, and several varieties of wood-oven pizza. *2905 San Gabriel,* ☎ *512/472–6483.*

$$ **El Rinconcito.** The blackboard menu of this elegant little Mexican restaurant is always crammed with inventive specials like jalapeño and cheese-stuffed shrimp wrapped in bacon and simmered in a smoky chipotle sauce. The intimate dining room is suffused with warm lighting and decorated with authentic Mexican crafts. In the same shopping center as Liberty Books (*see* The Little Black Book, *below*). *1014-E N. Lamar Blvd.,* ☎ *512/476–5277.*

$$ **Mars.** An unprepossessing pale gray clapboard structure on residential San Antonio Street houses one of Austin's hottest restaurants and bars. The interior walls are fiery red and lined with glittering copper sconces, and the food is fiery hot—bistro versions of Thai and Indian standards, including wonderful naan bread pizzas with a variety of toppings. *1610 San Antonio,* ☎ *512/472–3901.*

$–$$ **Cafe Spiazzo.** Much of the interior of this chic but casual, noisy but refined restaurant is speckled with multicolor sprays of paint that would

Austin

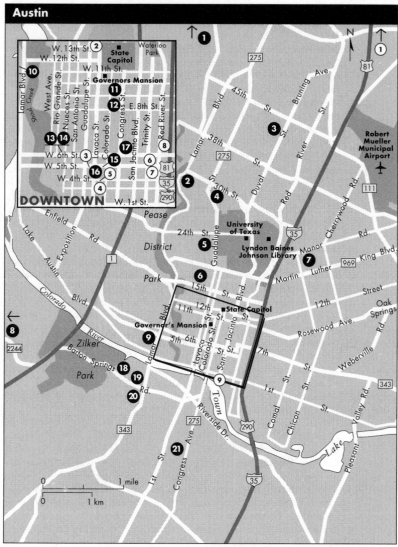

Eats ●

Cafe Spiazzo, **1**
Castle Hill Cafe, **9**
Chuy's, **18**
Common Market Cafe, **21**
Coyote Cafe, **14**
East Side Cafe, **7**

El Rinconcito, **10**
Flipnotiks, **20**
Granite Cafe, **2**
Hickory Street Bar and Grill, **12**
Hyde Park Bar and Grill, **3**
Insomnia, **5**
Katz Deli, **13**

Little City, **11**
Louie's 106, **17**
Mars, **6**
Oasis, **8**
Ruby's BBQ, **4**
Ruta Maya Coffee, **16**
Shady Grove, **19**
Thai Soon, **15**

Scenes ○

Area 52, **5**
'Bout Time, **1**
Casino El Camino, **6**
Chain Drive, **9**
Charlie's, **2**
DJ's, **8**
5th Street Station Dance Hall Saloon, **7**
Oilcan Harry's, **4**
Nexus, **3**

make Jackson Pollack proud. The designer pizzas and gourmet salads and pastas rival any in town. Very gay staff and patronage. *5416 Parkcrest Dr.,* ☎ *512/459–9960.*

$–$$ **Castle Hill Cafe.** It can be a bit difficult to get a table in this bright New American bistro in a pretty pink house west of downtown. The long menu has lots of finger food, such as the popular brie with chutney, plus a variety of grills and salads. *1101 W. 5th St.,* ☎ *512/476–0728.*

$–$$ **Hickory Street Bar and Grill.** Welcome to food-bar headquarters: Hickory has an all-you-can-eat salad bar, an ice cream bar, a bread bar, and a potato bar. This large, social hangout with red-and-white checkered tablecloths and beveled glass is the perfect place to pig out. Great New Orleans-style breakfasts, too. *800 Congress Ave.,* ☎ *512/477–8969.*

$–$$ **Hyde Park Bar and Grill.** This hoppin' college hangout well north of downtown is notable for the enormous silver fork rising from the ground in front (it must be 12 feet tall). The Grill prides itself on its diverse, healthful, and cheap menu—although the addictive Park fries (buttermilk-battered) aren't exactly good for you. Very casual. Good wine list. *4206 Duval St.,* ☎ *512/458–3168.*

$–$$ **Louie's 106.** This is one of the best restaurants in Texas (and it's still difficult to spend more than $20 on a three-course dinner). The old-fashioned city dining room, with high ceilings, marble floors, an open kitchen, and a hip, well-dressed crowd has only two drawbacks: the noise and the uneven service. A sample dish: red snapper *en croute* (in a crust) with dry vermouth, mussels, mustard, and grilled vegetables. *106 E. 6th St.,* ☎ *512/476–2010.*

$–$$ **Thai Soon.** Around the corner from Area 52 (*see* Scenes, *below*) and several of the gay bars is this cute storefront Thai restaurant with curtain valances and a perky green neon sign. The menu focuses chiefly on seafood and veggie dishes, often with a slight Texan influence (like the Thai corn fritters). The squid with vegetables is heavenly. *121 W. 5th St.,* ☎ *512/476–2356.*

$ **Chuy's.** Chuy's is one of Austin's standard cheap and cheerful, young and funky Tex-Mex restaurants—with all the standard dishes, great margaritas, and huge weekend crowds. *1728 Barton Springs Rd.,* ☎ *512/474–4452.*

$ **Common Market Café.** Has all the ingredients of a great gay deli: tasteful use of neon, contemporary art and photos on the walls, pretty floral curtain valances, and throngs of gay staff and patrons. Everything is great—from the thick sandwiches to the myriad varieties of coffee, to stay or to go. *1600 S. Congress Ave.,* ☎ *512/416–1940.*

$ **East Side Cafe.** Patronized largely by crunchy peaceniks, this café has amazingly popular brunches, sunny outdoor seating, and dishes made with the fresh produce grown in the Cafe's garden. Big lesbian and gay following. *2113 Manor Rd.,* ☎ *512/476–5858.*

$ **Katz Deli.** This upbeat, contemporary deli is busy all day and has some of the cutest staff in town. The half-pound sandwiches are more than most can eat in one sitting—especially good is the grilled three-cheese with tomatoes. Many come for cocktails after work—the martinis are killers. Has been very good to AIDS causes. *618 W. 6th St.,* ☎ *512/472–2037.*

$ **Oasis.** This huge, multidecked, hilltop compound is about 20 minutes west of the city center in the hill country and commands glorious views of Lake Travis. It's a little tacky, the food is mediocre Mexican, but the drinks (especially the margaritas) are great. Everyone—gay, straight, and in between—heads here on weekend afternoons and lingers to admire the best sunset in Texas. *6550 Comanchee Trail, near Lake Travis,* ☎ *512/266–2441.*

$ **Ruby's BBQ.** This funky spot with off-white siding and teal trim serves up real Texas barbecue. Mutton, brisket, and smoked chicken are a few of the items sold by the pound. Delicious sides of tacos, red beans and rice, and other goodies are plentiful, too. *29th and Guadalupe Sts.,* ☎ *512/477–1651.*

$ **Shady Grove.** Set in an actual shady grove south of the Town Lake and close to Zilker Park, this twentysomething slacker hangout has been around forever and is something of a landmark. The patio, gussied up with Christmas lights, odd topiaries, and plenty of kitsch, must be seen to be understood. Good, down-home Southern and Mexican standbys. *1624 Barton Springs Rd.,* ☎ *512/474–9991.*

Coffeehouse Culture

The closest thing you'll find to a coffeehouse nightclub, **Ruta Maya Coffee** (218 W. 4th St., ☎ 512/472–9637) is in an ancient brick building near several of the gay and straight clubs. The front door was once an old loading dock. It has live music and a queer, trendy, alternative following. The crowd at **Little City** (916 Congress Ave., ☎ 512/476–2489) is a little too hot for its own good, but this is a great perch from which to observe the rituals of Austin society. It's near the capitol. As the name suggests, **Insomnia** (2222 Guadalupe St., ☎ 512/474–5730) is open all night; the uncomfortable, postmodern metal furniture even seems designed to keep you alert. In the heart of Guadalupe Street's stretch of used-clothing and music stores, it attracts a collegiate, artsy bunch. It also has a big post-club following, and serves a basic munchy menu and great pies. **Flipnotiks** (1601 Barton Springs Rd., ☎ 512/322–9750) is above a terrific clothing boutique across the street from the Shady Grove restaurant. Enter through a rickety porch in back. They have great desserts, but the best feature may be the television whose tube has been replaced with a tropical fish tank.

SLEEPS

Because it's a relatively new city on the upswing, Austin has an inviting selection of sleek, relatively new hotels. Most bars, shops, and restaurants are close to downtown hotels, which range from no-frills to upscale—rates rarely go over $130, even at the Four Seasons or the Stouffer. That said, there is nothing especially showy or interesting about Austin accommodations—the lodging scene is typical of other mid-size American metropolises. There are also no gay-specific accommodations here, but a couple of the guest houses have gay followings.

For price ranges, *see* Chart B at the front of this guide.

Hotels

Downtown

🏨 In addition to being the city's most luxurious hostelry, the **Four Seasons Hotel Austin** has great views of the Congress Avenue Bridge, where Austin's legendary fleet of bats reside in the summer months. *98 San Jacinto Blvd.,* ☎ *512/478–4500 or 800/332–3442. 292 rooms. $$$–$$$$*

🏨 Austin's grande dame is the splendid, extremely gay-popular **Driskill Hotel,** an 1886 period piece that continues to witness the patronage of famed politicos and celebrities. Beyond the spectacular lobby, guest rooms, though not especially memorable, are some of the largest in town. *604 Brazos St.,* ☎ *512/474–5911 or 800/527–2008. 177 rooms. $$–$$$*

🏨 A block above 6th Avenue's bustle is the shiny glass-and-steel **Omni,** whose upper floors have great views. *700 San Jacinto Blvd.,* ☎ *512/476–3700 or 800/843–6664. 314 rooms. $$–$$$*

🏨 The most affordable centrally located options are the **Radisson Hotel** (111 E. 1st St., ☎ 512/478–9611 or 800/333–3333; 280 rooms; $–$$), which overlooks Town Lake and is just off Congress Avenue, and the surprisingly pretty **La Quinta Capital Inn** (300 E. 11th St., ☎ 512/476–1166 or 800/531–5900; 148 rooms; $), which is just a stroll from the capitol and midway between the bar district and UT.

Elsewhere

⊞ Though a 15-minute drive from downtown, the giant **Stouffer Renaissance Austin** is one of the chain's premier properties, a contemporary convention hotel attached to the ritzy Arboretum shopping center. *9721 Arboretum Rd., ☎ 512/343–2626 or 800/468–3571. 478 rooms. $$$–$$$$*

⊞ A more peaceful alternative to being downtown is staying at the intimate **Melbourne Hotel and Conference Center** over in the clean and green Barton Creek area. *4611 Bee Cave Rd., ☎ 512/328–4000. 60 rooms. $–$$*

Guest Houses and Small Hotels

⊞ The **City View Bed & Breakfast** is on a 2-acre, tree-covered hilltop overlooking downtown Austin and Town Lake. The house has characteristics reminiscent of Frank Lloyd Wright's architecture. It's furnished with '30s European Art Deco and modern classics. *1405 E. Riverside St., ☎ 512/441–2606. 8 rooms. Mixed gay/straight. $$$*

⊞ Also popular in the community is the grand **Fairview.** This Colonial Revival house was built in 1910 and is now an Austin landmark. It's surrounded by an acre of rose gardens, lawns, and trees: you feel as if you're out in the country. The rooms are decorated with period antiques and have private baths, TVs, and phones. *1304 Newning Ave., ☎ 512/444–4746 or 800/310–4746. 6 rooms. Mixed gay/straight. $$–$$$*

SCENES

Austin's gay nightlife is unusual for Texas—for all of America, in fact. Whereas many gay bars in many cities are small, off the beaten path, and hidden behind dark windows, only one of Austin's several hangouts fits this image. The bulk of them are downtown in well-decorated and often historic buildings; they have big dance floors and often live music, and they pull in equally mixed gay and straight or, at the very least, partially straight crowds.

There's only one difficulty, and that's meeting people over 30. The bar scene is young and collegiate. The most concentrated areas, Red River Street, 4th Street around Lavaca and Colorado, and 6th Street, appeal primarily to students, and typically to a somewhat alternative, nonconformist bunch. If you're looking to meet working adults, your best bets are the bars of many of the restaurants listed above, and also at **Charlie's** (for men) and **Nexus** (for women); both places get a good mix of the young and not-so-young.

Area 52. In an old downtown brick warehouse, this new establishment opened in October 1995 and replaced Club 404; it has a fantastic sound system and lighting, scaffolds, walkways, two levels, a dance floor, and a steamy, high-energy atmosphere. Nice outdoor balcony, too. Though liquor is not served after 2 AM, the club often stays open for dancing long after. *404 Colorado St., ☎ 512/474–4849. Crowd: young, mostly gay, trendy, 70/30 m/f, mix of club kids and college students.*

'Bout Time. This is Austin's only true neighborhood bar, a tavern well north of downtown just off I–35 at Rundberg Street. It has a nice big central bar, good lighting, lots of seating, and pool tables. If you're looking to strike up a conversation, come here. *9601 N. I–35, ☎ 512/832–5339. Crowd: laid-back, local, chatty; mixed genders, ages, and races.*

Casino El Camino. Punkish, grungish, stylish, freakish. Leave the loafers and khaki pants at home. This place has all the buzz of Greenwich Village—black-and-white walls, clever music ranging from punk to acid jazz to Cole Porter, and some pretty good bar food. There are three pool tables upstairs. These kids think they're pretty cool, but they are friendly. *517 E. 6th St., ☎ 512/469–9330. Crowd: mostly straight, young, goths and alternateens; gay-friendly.*

Chain Drive. This is your only choice if you're into leather. Few students come here, and it's very popular, dark, and seedy. The leather dress code is enforced weekends. Has a nice leather shop on the premises. *504 Willow St., ☎ 512/480–9017. Crowd: leather and Levi's, male, macho, bears, ages 30s and 40s.*

Charlie's. Austin's original gay bar is attractive and popular. Nowadays it looks a bit like a country-western bar, but the music is definitely of the mainstream dance variety. Since it's within the shadow of the capitol building you may be able to spot a few polymorphously perverse politicos. Several rooms, lots of video screens, pool tables. *1301 Lavaca St., ☎ 512/474–6481. Crowd: mostly male, some suits after work, mixed ages, very cruisy.*

DJ's. A disco opened by a British investor in 1995, DJ's is meant to compete with Area 52. A purple sidewalk leads you to the front door of this million-dollar-renovation dance complex, which is divided into three sections: the main bar with the dance floor and a game room, the quiet back bar, and the outside patio bar. Go-go dancers prance around seven days a week; on Sunday there's a tea dance with a cookout, and on Wednesday there's a drag show. *611 Red River Rd., ☎ 512/476–3611. Crowd: very mixed.*

5th Street Station Dance Hall Saloon. This is Austin's best gay country-western bar, and it plays *nothing* but country music. It attracts a terrific mix of people. The cow skulls and other Western trinkets hanging from the walls lend it a kitschy air. There's also a big game room with pool, air hockey, darts, and other diversions. Has great drag shows on Sundays. *505 E. 5th St., ☎ 512/478–6065. Crowd: 80/20 m/f; mixed ages but mostly young, country-western, cruisy, Nirvana-meets-Travis Tritt.*

Nexus. This is the largest women's bar in Texas, and actually one of the largest in the country. The elevated dance floor holds a sizable jumble of two-steppers and line-dancers, and there's also lots of room for comfortable mingling and chatting. Has an upscale feel, thanks to the great decorating, but all are quite comfortable here. Heavy use of neon gives the room a pink and lavender glow. Great sound system. *305 W. 5th St., ☎ 512/472–5288. Crowd: mostly women, mixed ages, butch to lipstick, country-western.*

Oilcan Harry's. Austin's only true stand-and-model bar attracts a truly hot collegiate crowd. There are a couple of bars, a nice patio in back, amber lighting, a good sound system, a tiny dance floor, and bar stools everywhere. For a guppie cruise bar, they serve some surprisingly stiff drinks. Another surprise is how relatively approachable and attitude-free the guys are. Oilcan Harry's is starched shirt, but not stuffed shirt. *211 W. 4th St., ☎ 512/320–8823. Crowd: mostly male, cruisy, young, professional, buttoned-down.*

Since Austin is one of the nation's best music cities, there are dozens of other clubs and nightspots that offer excellent entertainment ranging from country, blues, and folk to hard-driving rock, grunge, and punk (check the *Austin Chronicle* for listings). A few mostly straight clubs with gay followings include the divy **Blue Flamingo** (617 Red River St., ☎ 512/469–

0014), a little trendoid bar with pressed-tin ceilings and tortured souls—and a pool table; **Esther's Follies** (525 E. 6th St., ☎ 512/320–0553), a renowned comedy club with skits and a penchant for drag and queer-theme humor; **Ohms** (611 E. 7th St., ☎ 512/472–7136), the hub of the city's industrial, underground music scene, packed with a grim bunch of Day-Glo-haired ne'er-do-wells; **Paradox** (5th and Trinity Sts., ☎ 512/469–7615), a sprawling, warehouse-style dance club that's neither gay nor straight and plays great house music; and **Proteus** (501 E. 6th St., ☎ 512/472–8922), another warehouse-style dance club with hip decor and an extremely diverse crowd.

THE LITTLE BLACK BOOK

At Your Fingertips
AIDS Services of Austin Hotline: ☎ 512/458–2437. **Austin Convention and Visitors Bureau:** 201 E. 2nd St., 78701, ☎ 512/474–5171.

Gay Media
The biweekly **FagRag** (☎ 512/416–0100), which offers the most comprehensive coverage of gay entertainment in Austin (as well as San Antonio, Corpus Christi, and Waco) is one of the more professional and entertaining publications of its kind. Other gay periodicals include *This Week in Texas* (☎ 713/527–9111), an entertainment-oriented magazine that covers the entire state, and the *Texas Triangle* (☎ 713/871–1272), a news-oriented weekly newspaper. The gay monthly from San Antonio, the *Marquise* (☎ 210/545–3511), is also available throughout Austin. The best mainstream resource is the *Austin Chronicle* (☎ 512/454–5766), an alternative-scene arts-and-entertainment weekly.

BOOKSTORES
Liberty Books (1014-B N. Lamar Blvd., ☎ 512/495–9737), Austin's principal gay/lesbian bookstore, is small, neat, well-stocked, and evenly male- and female-oriented; it has some porn mags and some gay newspapers from other states. **Bookwoman** (918 W. 12th St., ☎ 512/472–2785) is a good feminist bookstore with plenty of lesbian titles. **LOBO** (3204-A Guadalupe St., ☎ 512/454–5406), like its Houston and Dallas branches, specializes in gay-male porn but has some other gay and lesbian titles, too.

Body and Fitness
A fairly laid-back bunch, Austinites seem to have a mild aversion to those who put brawn above brains. Nevertheless, the **Clean & Lean Fitness Center** (4225 Guadalupe St., ☎ 512/458–5326) has a strong gay and lesbian following.

3 *Out in Baltimore*

JUST AN HOUR FROM WASHINGTON by car and two hours from Philadelphia, quiet, unassuming Baltimore has experienced a rebirth in the last 15 years or so, gaining back some of the ground it lost through much of this century to other, flashier cities on the East Coast.

From the latter part of the 19th century into the first half of this one, Baltimore was a city where factory and railroad workers of many ethnicities toiled for a small elite of factory owners, merchants, bankers, lawyers, and politicians. Following the Depression and World War II, however, the white middle and upper classes began fleeing the cities en masse. With the advent of new forms of technology and transportation, many of Baltimore's blue collar jobs were eliminated. By the early '70s Baltimore's downtown was barren and boarded up, gray and undesirable.

Over the last 15 years, however, Baltimore has been transformed into a much more vibrant place to live and visit. This remarkable comeback started with the rehabilitation of Baltimore's industrial Inner Harbor. Thanks in no small part to the resulting growth in tourism, surrounding residential neighborhoods, which still contained many fine Colonial and Victorian houses, began to prosper once again. Gentrification soon brought communities like Mount Vernon, Federal Hill, and Fells Point back to respectability. A new city skyline emerged in the '80s: First came the new museums and shopping pavilions around the refurbished harbor; then came the new office towers and hotels.

It's hard to find a more genuine and down-to-earth breed of urbanites than the residents of Baltimore. Those who never fled the city retain a special affection for their hometown. It's hardly insignificant that locally bred filmmakers Barry Levinson and John Waters set so many of their works in Baltimore. This feeling of loyalty empowers Baltimore with a civic pride not found in many larger cities.

Baltimore's lesbian and gay community is not large, but it does seem to be committed to making the city as free as possible from homophobic bigotry. There aren't many firebrands here—on the right or on the left—but rare as well are egomaniacs and attention-seekers. Reasonable people are using reasonable means to turn Baltimore back into a viable destination; similar tactics are being employed by gay and gay-friendly Baltimoreans to get a gay-positive civil rights law passed, to get the mayor to set up an efficient gay and lesbian task force, and to get the police to respond effectively and sensitively to gay bashings.

The domestic partnership bill that was up for debate in the city council a couple years ago failed not so much because of right-wing opposition in Baltimore itself but because conservative watch groups from Pennsylvania came down and rallied locals against it. This turn of events points out one major weakness in Baltimore: It's a city whose residents won't usually get too excited about the passage of new laws, leaving the outcome of many controversies open to opportunistic external forces.

Don't visit Baltimore with high expectations of the gay scene. There are several lively bars, plenty of good restaurants and unusual shops and galleries, and enough tourist attractions to keep you busy for several days. But it's less in Baltimore's nature to impress you with extremes than it is to charm you with friendly hellos, moderate prices, and low-key pleasures. If you live in any of the East Coast's more intense metropolises, a spell in Baltimore may be just what you need.

THE LAY OF THE LAND

Even with its few new skyscrapers, the city retains a human scale: Residential, commercial, and tourist districts mingle together, and, for the most part, downtown Baltimore is alive with pedestrian traffic day and night. That said, sections of town that haven't yet been touched by the magic wand of gentrification remain fairly crime-ridden. Stick to populated streets and neighborhoods.

Charles Street and Mount Vernon

Charles Street is the backbone of Baltimore, running from the Inner Harbor area all the way north to Johns Hopkins University. The section that's ideal for browsing begins around Pratt Street and runs up close to Penn Station, which is where Charles crosses I–83.

Earlier in this century, the lower stretch of Charles was a fashionable shopping district. The many storefront windows that were boarded up as recently as five years ago now sport the names of art galleries, bookstores, and the sorts of shops you won't find in shopping malls. Many of the city's better restaurants are along here, too.

Be sure to check out **A People United** (516 N. Charles St., ☎ 410/727–4470), a women's clothing and arts cooperative; **Nouveau** (519 N. Charles St., ☎ 410/962–8248), which has the best selection of Art Deco and Art Nouveau furniture and collectibles in town; the **Zone** (813 N. Charles St., ☎ 410/539–2817), known for secondhand duds, grunge garb, and jewelry; and **Louie's** (*see* Eats, *below*), which is as lauded for its intelligent selection of books as for its great food and coffee.

The heart of Charles Street bisects **Mount Vernon,** which is commercially the city's gayest neighborhood. Many gay men and lesbians live here, too, although increasing numbers have begun to settle in other parts of Baltimore, most notably in Federal Hill (which is more couples-oriented) and up around Johns Hopkins University (more lesbians).

Bounded roughly by Howard Street to the west, Saratoga Street to the south, Calvert Street to the east, and Chase Street to the north, the neighborhood is anchored at Mount Vernon Square by the 178-foot **Washington Monument,** surrounded by grassy lawn, enchanting statuary, and benches. Just south of the monument is the **Walters Art Gallery** (N. Charles and Centre Sts., ☎ 410/547–9000), whose vast holdings include many Renaissance and Baroque paintings; jewelry and decorative works; and a strong collection of Byzantine, Islamic, and Oriental works. Be sure to stop by the dramatic sculpture court.

A number of streets surrounding Washington Place and Mount Vernon Place make for good exploring. Just two blocks north of the monument is **Read Street;** a hippie haven during the '60s, Read now has several vintage clothing and bric-a-brac shops. Two blocks west of Charles Street is **Howard Street,** the city's Antiques Row (most shops are between Read and Monument streets). And farther south, and then west a couple blocks on Lexington Street, is the colorful **Lexington Market,** perhaps the best of several indoor food markets; locals have been shopping for fresh produce, meats, and seafood here for more than a century. It's worth coming just to watch the vendors and shoppers dicker over blue crabs and sweet corn.

The intersection of Charles and Eager streets (two blocks north of the monument) is the center of Mount Vernon's gay bar district. All the restaurants within a block of this corner have strong gay followings.

The Inner Harbor
A compact wedge of water that cuts directly into the heart of downtown, the **Inner Harbor** was for years a thriving shipping crossroads. Six piers jut out from the northern (Pratt Street) edge of the basin. Light Street makes up the western boundary, Federal Hill is to the south, and Fells Point to the east. Only a relatively narrow passageway gives ships access from the Inner Harbor Basin to the Patapsco River and eventually to Chesapeake Bay.

The most popular attractions are the glass-enclosed **Harborplace** pavilions, which occupy the northwest corner of the harbor, at the intersections of Pratt and Light streets; here you can browse through more than 100 shops and graze your way through a serious food court. A skywalk connects Harborplace to the **Gallery Mall,** which will remind you of every other upscale suburban shopping mall in America. To the east of Harborplace, at the piers, are a few historic ships, which together make up the **Baltimore Maritime Museum** (Piers 2, 3, and 4, ☎ 410/396–3453), and the tallest pentagonal building in the world, I. M. Pei's **World Trade Center** (Pier 2, ☎ 410/837–4515), which has a 27th-floor observation deck. The mammoth **National Aquarium** (Pier 3, ☎ 410/576–3800) is terrific. South of Harborplace, along the wharf that borders Light Street, is the **Maryland Science Center** (601 Light St., ☎ 410/685–5225).

Federal Hill
South of the harbor is a regal grassy knoll that was nearly leveled in the 1850s to make a landfill out of the harbor. Fortunately, those plans were scrapped and **Federal Hill** continues to rise above the city, offering views of downtown and the Inner Harbor. It's also a nice spot to laze under the sun on warm afternoons.

The blocks around Federal Hill have become gentrified over the past decade, with many young professionals moving in and refurbishing the neighborhood's many early and mid-19th-century brick homes. A couple of blocks west of the actual hill, along Light and Charles streets, are several good ethnic restaurants and quirky shops, plus the bustling **Cross Street Market.**

Fells Point
Fells Point is one of America's best-preserved colonial waterfront settlements. Perfectly maintained Federal town houses line Thames and Fell streets and nearby blocks. This is not at all a gay neighborhood; it houses a cross section of older Italian and Eastern European immigrants (Little Italy is just north, centered on High Street) and straight yuppies. With restaurants and pubs packed nightly with J. Crew types, and a regular influx of teens and college kids from the suburbs, Fells Point is a lot like Washington's Georgetown.

Outlying Neighborhoods

Pratt Street leads west from downtown past the extremely impressive new **Oriole Park at Camden Yards** baseball stadium (☎ 410/685–9800) into a mixed-use area that includes a small garment district, the University of Maryland–Baltimore campus, and a few historic sites—including the **Edgar Allan Poe House** (203 N. Amity St., ☎ 410/396–7932), where you can tour the bare-bones studio in which the author wrote his first tale of gothic horror; **Babe Ruth's Birthplace** (216 Emory St., ☎ 410/727–1539); and the **B&O Railroad Museum** (Pratt and Poppleton Sts., ☎ 410/752–2490), which gives an excellent overview of the city's 19th-century industrial and railroad history.

About a mile west of downtown along Lombard Street is up-and-coming **SoWeBo**, an arts district, which, because of its affordable housing and proximity to a few colleges, has become a small haven of youthful bohemianism. Here also is the **H. L. Mencken House** (1524 Hollins St., ☎ 410/396–7997), the row house in which the Sage of Baltimore lived.

Just northwest of Mount Vernon is **Bolton Hill,** a lovely residential neighborhood of Victorian row houses. Continuing north of downtown, taking Charles Street, you'll reach the campuses of Johns Hopkins University, Loyola College, and the College of Notre Dame. Several residential neighborhoods up here, such as **Charles Village, Homewood,** and **Waverly,** are popular with lesbians and, to a lesser extent, gay men. This area was a hotbed of lesbian and gay activism in the '60s; Abell Avenue, which runs through Waverly, is still referred to as Lesbian Lane. Farther afield, **Laurelville** is developing a strong gay following.

The grounds of the 140-acre campus of **Johns Hopkins University** are impressive, green, and ideal for walking. Note also that Johns Hopkins's highly esteemed medical school was begun with funding from one of America's most illustrious lesbians, Mary Elizabeth Garrett. The daughter of railroad mogul John Work Garrett, Mary Elizabeth inherited a third of his fortune. When the plans to open a medical school were stalled for lack of funds, the well-educated and highly driven Garrett and her lover, M. Carey Thomas, founded the Women's Medical Fund Committee, which raised the necessary half million to open the school. More than $300,000 came from Garrett herself, with the proviso that the school admit women on the same terms that it would admit men. Garrett went on to provide the funding to help found the Bryn Mawr School for girls and Bryn Mawr College, of which Thomas later served as president.

Adjacent to Johns Hopkins is the **Baltimore Museum of Art** (N. Charles and 31st Sts., ☎ 410/396–7101), whose strengths include French Impressionist painting, 18th- and 19th-century American painting, and 20th-century sculpture.

GETTING AROUND

Most neighborhoods that are popular with visitors are within walking distance of one another and downtown hotels. Exercise caution late at night, however. In outlying neighborhoods, you'll need a car. There is an extensive bus system, and limited subway and light-rail service, but most of this transportation is geared for getting between downtown and the suburbs. Parking lots and garages are plentiful and relatively affordable downtown, and parking spaces are easy to come by elsewhere. Cabs are rarely necessary, except perhaps for traveling between Penn Station or the airport and downtown; you phone for them or catch them at hotels.

EATS

Baltimore's cooking is full of flavor—the city even has its own spice, Old Bay Seasoning, a feisty concoction of 16 seasonings used most often on shellfish but required by some locals on everything but ice cream.

Seafood—particularly oysters, clams, and Chesapeake Bay blue crabs—is a regional specialty, as is fried chicken. The trendiness factor has introduced New American, Northern Italian, and even Southwestern flavors into many of the city's up-and-coming kitchens. Most significantly, Baltimore has fostered a tremendous variety of ethnic eateries over the past couple of decades, including outstanding purveyors of Indian, Thai, and Chinese cooking.

For price ranges, *see* Chart B at the front of this guide.

Baltimore's Little Italy is quite respectable—among that neighborhood's best eateries are **Amicci's** (231 S. High St., ☎ 410/528–1096; $–$$); **Germano's** (300 S. High St., ☎ 410/752–4515; $$–$$$$); and the formal **Da Mimmo** (217 S. High St., ☎ 410/727–6876; $$$–$$$$).

$$$$ Hampton's. The city's best hotel restaurant, this Edwardian dining room allows perfect views of the Inner Harbor. Revered is a bouillabaisse that's loaded, naturally, with Maryland crab. Wild game is another specialty. *Harbor Court Hotel, 550 Light St., ☎ 410/234–0550.*

$$$–$$$$ Brass Elephant. The best place in Mount Vernon to celebrate a special occasion or to wine and dine a date, the Brass Elephant is set inside an antiques-filled town house with vast plate-glass windows. Polished parquet floors, a carved marble fireplace, brass banisters, chandeliers, and gilt-frame mirrors create an intimate, refined space. The mostly Northern Italian menu includes a filling starter of *bruschetta* and such entrées as grilled yellowfin tuna *oreganato. 924 N. Charles St., ☎ 410/547–8480.*

$$$–$$$$ Donna's Restaurant. One of the hottest Baltimore bistros, Donna's specializes in Provençal and Tuscan cooking, brick-oven designer pizzas, and salads—a great choice is the orange, fennel, and shaved pecorino on greens. Has some sidewalk seating and a more affordable café adjacent (*see* Coffeehouse Culture, *below*). *800 N. Charles St., ☎ 410/539–8051.*

$$$–$$$$ Foster's Oyster Bar, Restaurant, and Market. Though it's more than a little touristy, the crowded raw bar that serves Chincoteague, Malpeque, and Olympia oysters is worth braving. The offbeat menu has everything from your standard comfort foods to such exotic offerings as grilled antelope. Has 20 wines by the glass. *606 S. Broadway, ☎ 410/558–3600.*

$$$–$$$$ Pierpoint. Putting some innovative Mediterranean spins on traditional Maryland favorites, this popular Fells Point restaurant serves dishes that might have appeared on a city menu at the turn of the century, such as green tomatoes and braised rabbit. The emphasis is on seafood. Very chic. *1822 Aliceanna St., ☎ 410/675–2080.*

$$$–$$$$ Tio Pepe. An institution in Mount Vernon, Tio Pepe serves delicious, authentic Spanish food in a festive, cheerful dining room. It's a great place to hit with a pack of friends. The paella *à la Valencia* (chicken, sausage, shrimp, clams, and mussels with saffron rice) is delicious, and there's a great selection of tapas to start. Try one of the lusty Spanish wines. *10 E. Franklin St., ☎ 410/539–4675.*

$$–$$$ Central Station. The restaurant of the city's most popular gay bar, Central Station actually has decent, affordable, grub; it's predictable—crab cakes, veal piccata, burgers—but competently prepared. And the service is friendly. This is also one of the few restaurants along Charles Street with sidewalk seating. *1001 N. Charles St., ☎ 410/752–7133.*

32

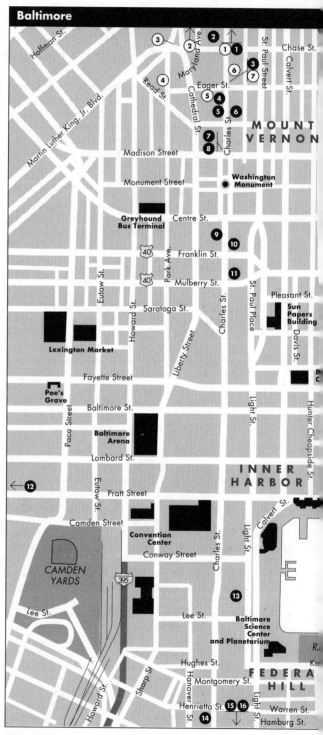

Baltimore

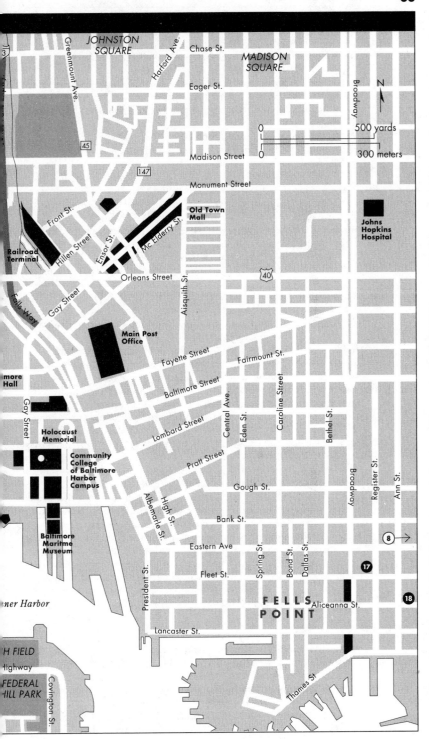

$$ Bandaloops. This is a Federal Hill favorite, where the beautiful people gather for wine and hors d'oeuvres after work. The narrow dining room has a slick pressed-tin ceiling, exposed brick, and contemporary art. Try the cheese board if you're sampling wines available by the glass. *1024 S. Charles St., ☎ 410/727-1355.*

$$ Kawasaki. A major after-work hangout, this charming little Japanese restaurant on Charles Street's Restaurant Row has the city's top sushi-and-sashimi bar, plus a wealth of tasty tempura, teriyaki, and noodle dishes. *413 N. Charles St., ☎ 410/659-7600.*

$-$$$ Mt. Vernon Stable and Saloon. A noisy, hip little pub with a small bar, red-vinyl booths, old-fashioned sconces and ceiling fans, Mount Vernon is especially popular late on weekend eves. This is a good spot to sample authentic Maryland crab soup (in a tomato-base broth with veggies, spices, and flakes of crab). They also serve salads, pizzas, and sandwiches. The actual saloon, downstairs, is not gay per se but gets a mixed crowd and carries all the gay papers. *909 N. Charles St., ☎ 410/685-7427.*

$-$$ Banjara. Perhaps because it advertises in the local gay papers, this sedate, softly lit Indian restaurant has garnered a fairly strong gay following. Among the many tandoori specialties are several vegetarian dishes. In Federal Hill, a short walk south of the Inner Harbor. *1017 S. Charles St., ☎ 410/962-1554.*

$-$$ Gampy's. The name is an acronym for Great American Melting Pot (fondue, in fact, is a specialty). True enough, Gampy's gets a great mix of real Baltimoreans—and a very large gay following. The dining room, with red and blue tubes of neon snaking along the ceiling, bright red tables, and blue napkins, is loud and lively. The food is a cut above what you'd find at a good diner: The cholesterol-laden Monte Cristo is a highlight, as is the rich chocolate malt. *904 N. Charles St., ☎ 410/837-9797.*

$-$$ Louie's. While away a Sunday afternoon here browsing through the many book racks and plucking favorites off Louie's great brunch menu. On the healthful New American menu are a soft-shell crab sandwich, orange-chicken soup, and vegetable pâté. It's also a great place for desserts and coffee. Live jazz and classical music from time to time. *518 N. Charles St., ☎ 410/962-1224.*

$-$$ Mencken's Cultured Pearl. An odd tribute to Baltimore's own famed phrasemonger, H. L. Mencken, this lively Mexican restaurant is in the heart of trendy SoWeBo. You can draw on the tablecloths with crayons or pass suggestive messages on to the cute staff. All ingredients come from a nearby organic farm. *1114 Hollins St., ☎ 410/837-1947.*

$ Henry & Jeff's. A good rendezvous point for the early evening (before heading out to Mount Vernon's bars), Henry and Jeff's has mastered the art of quick, filling food; there are more than 40 kinds of sandwiches here—11 alone with grilled chicken. You'll also find good pastas and many Mexican goodies. There's plenty of outdoor seating, too. *1218-1220 N. Charles St., ☎ 410/727-3322.*

Coffeehouse Culture

As much a popular vegetarian restaurant as a cozy coffeehouse, **One World Café** (904 S. Charles St., ☎ 410/234-0235) is Federal Hill's rainy day hangout—a warm place where you're invited to sit around talking and listening to music, read the paper, or shoot pool. Has an excellent variety of rich desserts. In a tree-lined residential neighborhood just off the Johns Hopkins University campus, **Café Diana** (3215 N. Charles St., ☎ 410/889-1319) is known mostly as a women's and lesbian's meeting space; men are welcome except on certain nights, when women's readings and music presentations are held. You'll find good sandwiches, veggie quesadillas, and ice cream. **Donna's Coffee Bar** (corner of Madison and

Charles Sts., ☏ 410/385–0180), next to Donna's well-known restaurant, has outdoor seating overlooking Washington Monument. This upscale bar has the best cappuccino in town and a fine roster of salads and soups.

SLEEPS

Most of the nation's major chains have newer facilities around the Inner Harbor, and there are some older, grander properties to the north, dotting the very gay Mount Vernon neighborhood. In most cases, downtown hotels are within walking distance of the gay bars and Charles Street's and Fells Point's restaurants. The best B&B in town, Mr. Mole, is gay-owned.

For price ranges, *see* Chart B at the front of this guide.

Hotels

🏨 A centerpiece of Baltimore's Inner Harbor project is the gracious **Harbor Court Hotel,** which is where celebrities often stay. Although the contemporary, redbrick facade reveals a relatively young hotel, the interior is appointed with sumptuous antiques meant to recall a traditional English country home. Be sure to ask for a room overlooking the harbor. *550 Light St., ☏ 410/234–0550 or 800/824–0076. 203 rooms. $$$$*

🏨 The 1924 **Clarion at Mount Vernon Square,** once an apartment building, overlooks the Washington Monument. Rooms are done with reproduction antiques, and service is first-rate. *612 Cathedral St., ☏ 410/727–7101. 104 rooms. $$$–$$$$*

🏨 Though it's a 10-minute drive north of downtown, the **Doubletree Inn at the Colonnade** is in a greener, quieter setting across the street from Johns Hopkins University, near the feminist coffeehouse Café Diana and the 31st Street Bookstore, and across from Baltimore's Museum of Art. Business travelers and academics prefer this European-style hotel. Complimentary transportation downtown. *4 W. University Pkwy., ☏ 410/235–5400. 125 rooms. $$$*

🏨 Built as an apartment house in the 1960s, the all-suite **Tremont Hotel** is one of the only properties in Baltimore with fully stocked kitchens, making it perfect for long-term stays. It's also midway between the gay district and the Inner Harbor, right off Charles Street. The staff is extremely warm and professional. *8 E. Pleasant St., ☏ 410/576–1200 or 800/638–6266. 60 suites. $$–$$$*

🏨 Around the corner from the Tremont Hotel is its sister property, the 37-floor **Tremont Plaza Suite Hotel.** Amenities are similar to those at the Tremont Hotel—including the kitchens—although a greater variety of room configurations are available. *222 St. Paul Pl., ☏ 410/727–2222 or 800/638–6266. 193 rooms. $$–$$$*

🏨 If value is a top priority, consider the **Mount Vernon Hotel,** part of a small network of properties run by the Baltimore International Culinary College. The staff is made up of students of hospitality who aim to earn high marks by pleasing guests. Be sure to check the outstanding Washington Café on the ground floor. Rooms in this historic hotel are simply furnished, although there are a few suites with Jacuzzis. *24 W. Franklin St., ☏ 410/727–2000 or 800/245–5256. 115 rooms. $–$$*

Small Hotels and Guest Houses

🏨 Formerly the Society Hill Hotel, the **Government House,** run by the Baltimore International Culinary House, comprises an 1827 Victorian mansion and several late-19th-century town houses. Rooms are decorated with period furnishings and art; many have marble, nonworking fireplaces. A couple blocks east of Charles Street's gay neighborhood. *1125 N. Calvert St., ☎ 410/539–0566. 20 rooms. Mostly straight. $$–$$$*

⌸ The only licensed, gay-operated property in town, the **Mr. Mole B&B,** in the historic, residential Bolton Hill neighborhood, is a five-minute drive from Mount Vernon. All of the enormous suites have either canopy or four-poster beds and Victorian antiques and reproductions; some have two bedrooms. Hosts Peter and Colin are extremely helpful. This is an ideal spot for couples (most single night owls tend to want to be closer to Mount Vernon bars or the Inner Harbor). *1601 Bolton St., ☎ 410/728–1179. 5 suites. Mixed gay/straight. $$–$$$*

⌸ One of the most characterful small hotels is the turn-of-the-century **Biltmore Suites**. Its luxurious, antiques-filled rooms are as popular with leisure travelers as with business types, who take advantage of the hotel's 24-hour executive business center. *205 W. Madison St., ☎ 410/728–6550 or 800/868–5064. 24 rooms. Mostly straight. $–$$*

SCENES

The gay bar scene here is straightforward, down-to-earth, neighborhoody, and casual. At least half the bars qualify as true holes-in-the-wall—local haunts seldom frequented by out-of-towners. Should you venture into any of them, you'll encounter a mostly friendly bunch, all curious to know why a total stranger has crossed their insular threshold. Though Baltimoreans complain about how segregated the bars are, there's actually a stronger racial mix in most Baltimore bars than you'll find in most American cities. The lesbian nightlife scene leaves something to be desired, however. There is one lesbian bar (**Port in a Storm**) in a working-class neighborhood in East Baltimore; it's small and not very popular beyond that territory. Of Mount Vernon bars, the Stagecoach Saloon is the top spot for women, though they're still in the minority there.

The city's most popular bars are all close to Charles Street, in either Mount Vernon or north of it, just beyond Penn Station. Exercise caution throughout this area, especially up by the train station and west of Charles, along Howard Street and Park Avenue. **Paradox** (1310 Russell St., ☎ 410/837–9110) is a straight but gay-friendly club that's big with the collegiate, pierced-navel set. There's also an after-hours club up by the Stud called **1722 Charles** (1722 N. Charles St., ☎ 410/727–7431), which is BYOB, has good dancing, and is about the only bar in Baltimore where you stand some chance of getting groped—but even that's rare. The block of Baltimore Street between South and Gay streets constitutes the city's still-lively red-light district. The neighborhood is 99% straight but **Le Salon and the Custom House Saloon** (18 Custom House Ave., ☎ 410/347–7555) has gay buddy booths and porn.

Allegro. This spot has an illustrious history dating back to the '40s and '50s when it was Baltimore's primary lesbian club—Talulah Bankhead was said to be a regular. Though women maintain a presence here and have their own night—Thursdays—it's now more of a mainstream men's fern bar. It has a tiny dance floor and some choice tropical decor. Friday is Allegro's most popular night—people come here before heading down to the Hippo. A little tough to find, it's on the small, oddly shaped block where Maryland Avenue and a closed-off span of Cathedral Street cut into Chase Street—the bar is down a flight of stairs. *1101 Cathedral St., ☎ 410/837–3906. Crowd: 75/25 m/f; the full gamut—from diesel dykes to pretty boys to older guys; easygoing.*

Central Station. Baltimore is not nearly as overrun with guppies as other Eastern Seaboard cities, but what strands of collar-shirt culture exist here thrive at Central Station. The front room is attractively decorated and well-lit; in back is a smaller room with pool tables. This is a mostly pre-dance spot; the crowd thins out after midnight. *1001 N. Charles St., ☎ 410/752–7133. Crowd: 80/20 m/f, mostly under 35, a bit clonish but very friendly for a stand-and-model bar.*

The Eagle. This is Baltimore's traditional leather bar, and it's every bit like every other Eagle you've ever been to. It has the friendliest bartenders in the city; there are no dress requirements or pretensions. *2022 Charles St., ☎ 410/823–2453. Crowd: mostly male; lots of leather and denim; similar to crowd at Studs.*

Hippo. Baltimore's main disco is smaller, quieter, and far less attitudy than Badlands in Washington, or even Woody's in Philadelphia. In fact, it's a bit dated in some respects—especially with regard to music. The dance floor is midsize, but has lots of cruising and standing room around it, and there are bars on either side. Next door is a big cruise bar with video screens and pool tables, and, on weekends, there's another smaller video bar open behind that. Most disco queens wind up here at some point. Wednesdays are more African-American; Fridays more lesbian. *1 W. Eager St., ☎ 410/547–0069. Crowd: 80/20 m/f; more white, young, male, and suburban on weekends; more diverse other nights; slightly stand-and-model.*

Leon's. One of a few clubs on the East Coast that claims to be the oldest continuously operated gay bar in America, it has been around for at least 50 years. Because it's something of a stink hole, few locals admit to coming here. At about 1:30 AM on a Friday or Saturday, Leon's is genuinely hopping with desperados from the Hippo and Allegro—they ought to rename it the Last Chance Saloon. Great jukebox. *870 Park Ave., ☎ 410/539–4993. Crowd: male, scruffy, older.*

P. T. Max. There are relatively few gay bars in America that so successfully support a predominantly African-American clientele. It is also a bar that works hard to welcome all races and types, and there are usually a few lesbians here. There are several small rooms; the main bar is particularly ambient, with dozens of small, red miners' lights, lots of pinball machines, and several tables and chairs. Though the adjacent dance floor is quite small, the music is as good as any in town. The main drawback is the bar's crummy location, a block west of Charles Street, not far from the Eagle (*see below*)—there is parking across the street, but a cab is advisable late at night. *1735 Maryland Ave., ☎ 410/539–6965. Crowd: mostly African-American and male; used to be a leather bar but little of that now; zero attitude, mixed ages but younger at night.*

Stagecoach. This is one of the few places in today's Baltimore that reminds visitors that it's still definitely, in the minds of many locals, a southern city. The Stagecoach is the best line-dancing and two-stepping club on the East Coast—and it has an excellent restaurant (burgers, steaks, Southwestern food), too. In the heart of Mount Vernon's gay bar district, the club has a great big dance floor with a railing around it allowing full views of all the dancing. The format is similar to other gay country-western dance halls, but for some reason it works unusually well here. The crowd is exceedingly friendly and open to visitors and those unfamiliar with two-stepping; lessons are given on certain weekdays. *1003 N. Charles St., ☎ 410/547–0107. Crowd: 60/40 m/f; mixed ages but mostly 30s and up; country-western.*

Unicorn. This gruff but lovable pub, the only gay bar close to Fells Point, is in a mostly Central European immigrant neighborhood on a very industrial span of the Inner Harbor. It's a great place to meet some local color (and maybe a few hustlers). *2218 Boston St., ☎ 410/342–8344. Crowd: older, mostly male, white, working-class.*

THE LITTLE BLACK BOOK

At Your Fingertips

AIDS Action of Baltimore: ☎ 410/837–2437. **Baltimore Area Convention and Visitors Association:** 100 Light St., 12th Floor, 21202, ☎ 410/659–7300. **Chase-Brexton Clinic:** ☎ 410/837–2050. **Gay and Lesbian Community Center of Baltimore:** 241 W. Chase St., ☎ 410/837–5445. **Gay and Lesbian Switchboard:** ☎ 410/837–8888. **Maryland AIDS Hotline:** ☎ 410/333–2437 or 800/638–6252.

Gay Media

The monthly *Baltimore Alternative* (☎ 410/235–3401) and the biweekly *Baltimore Gay Paper* (☎ 410/837–7748) are gay and lesbian news and entertainment rags; both are well written and comprehensive. *Woman's Express* (☎ 410/366–4507), the monthly women's forum, contains articles, resources, and some creative pieces.

The free arts-and-entertainment weekly, *City Paper* (☎ 410/523–2300), frequently has gay-oriented stories and information.

BOOKSTORES

Baltimore has both an excellent lesbigay bookstore and a renowned feminist and lesbian one. In Mount Vernon, **Lambda Rising** (241 W. Chase St., ☎ 410/234–0069) has a wide selection of lesbian and gay titles, videos, jewelry, porn and nonporn periodicals and newspapers, and out-of-print titles. It's next to the Gay and Lesbian Community Center.

Body and Fitness

The **Downtown Athletic Club** (210 E. Centre St., ☎ 410/332–0906) is gayest; very cruisy.

4   *Out in Boston*

With Ogunquit, Maine

IN 1995 THE U.S. SUPREME COURT RULED that the organizers of Boston's beloved St. Patrick's Day Parade were within their constitutional right to exclude a group of Irish homosexuals from marching that year under a gay banner. The controversy seemed typical in a city whose history has been riddled with battles involving both tradition and ancestry. Better yet, it illustrates the complex and intriguing paradox that has long characterized the city and its population: that Boston is famous simultaneously for its constant intake of outsiders, as well as for its intense derision of them.

On the one hand, a high number of Bostonians are products of the city's many prestigious universities, and are therefore knowledgeable of and sensitive to issues of diversity. On the other hand, if you lack a fine Boston education, you may be shunned—or at the very least condescended to—by anybody who possesses one. Bostonians and their suburban cousins have voted into office two openly gay U.S. congressmen, the Republican (but gay-friendly) Governor William Weld, and an entire brotherhood of Kennedys (Roman Catholic, Irish, but gay-friendly). The last few mayors have been Roman Catholic, Irish- or Italian-American, and liberal. Public opinion in Boston was largely in favor of excluding gays from the parade, but the city forbid its employees from marching in the event as a sign of support for the excluded gay marchers.

What exactly does all this mean? The blue-blooded Brahmin Bostonians have long despised the Irish, and yet when the issue of busing was bandied about during the 1970s, plenty of Brahmins and Irish joined hands either in opposition or in favor of this. Where racial issues are concerned, even the old school Irish populist is unpredictable—as is the blue-blooded Brahmin. Where gay issues are concerned, again, it's hard to tell where lines will be drawn. In Boston, when an issue of tolerance runs head-to-head with an issue of tradition, only one thing appears certain: that the city's two stubborn heads will spit fire at each other.

Still saddled with a somewhat provincial reputation, Bostonians have long been known for their appreciation of—if not obsession with—family names. Stories are still told of the eight consecutive generations of Saltonstalls or Wigglesworths that attended Harvard. Or of the city's legendary dynastic breeding: that at one time four of the seven Cabots who married, married Higginsons. When people speak of Brahmin Boston society as being closed, even incestuous, they're not necessarily exaggerating. Cleveland Amory said it best 50 years ago while explaining the gradual dilution of the city's finest families: "No longer are Proper Bostonians entirely content to choose their life partners from among the ranks of their cousins."

It was once a city where who you were meant a great deal more than what you did. But successive waves of immigration have gradually infiltrated the old Yankee guard. And being a Cabot or a Lowell means a great deal less today than it did 30 or 60 or 100 years ago. People seem genuinely less concerned about how many generations back they can trace their Brahmin or Irish or Bostonian roots.

Interestingly, gays and lesbians have been one of the first identifiable segments of Boston's population to settle across lines of heraldry and race. It is homosexuals who have gradually settled into the mostly African-American and Middle Eastern South End, into largely Hispanic Jamaica Plain, into the white working-class sections of Cambridge. And one supposes, in time, that although our "lifestyle" flies directly in the face of Catholicism, gays and lesbians will eventually be permitted to carry a banner in Boston's St. Patrick's Day Parade.

THE LAY OF THE LAND

Compact and attractive, Boston is almost the definition of a good walkers' city. Points north and east of the Common have the broadest appeal to most visitors; here you'll find most of the city's notable historic sites, museums, and shopping districts. (These sections are, incidentally, also the least settled by gay people.) Beacon Hill is a well-to-do, somewhat conservative, upper-crust residential neighborhood with a mostly Federal facade. Government Center is corporate on weekdays and always touristy. The North End, the most densely populated neighborhood in Colonial days, is today the city's Italian neighborhood. East of the Common is Boston's primary commercial and retail district.

South and west of the Common, late-Victorian Back Bay has a younger, hip spirit. The South End is more modest in scale and appearance, ethnically diverse, and extremely gay. The Fens is an eclectic blend of student, artist, and blue-collar housing interspersed with shells of pre–World War II industry and the reedy ponds and sloping meadows of the Back Bay Fens park.

The Common and Environs
The **Boston Common,** which dates from 1630, continues to be the city's hub. The sections of the park facing Boylston and Tremont streets are busier and dowdier than the stretch along stately Beacon Street, but the entire Common merits exploration. The adjacent **Boston Public Garden** (☎ 617/635–4505), the centerpiece of which is a placid pond traversed in summer by foot pedal–powered swan boats, also boasts several acres of formal gardens.

One of the nation's earliest urban residential neighborhoods, **Beacon Hill** was laid out in the early 19th century and settled by the city's wealthiest merchants. Bounded by the Common to the south, Storrow Memorial Drive to the west, Cambridge Street to the north, and Bowdoin Street to the east, Beacon Hill is a neighborhood of brick sidewalks, stately town houses, shade trees, and boutiques (the best are on Charles St.). Chestnut and Mt. Vernon streets are the most striking. At the corner of Park and Beacon streets, overlooking the Common, stands Charles Bulfinch's golden-domed neoclassical **State House** (☎ 617/727–3676).

North of Beacon Hill, just across the Charles River from the city's otherwise drab West End, is Boston's estimable **Museum of Science** (☎ 617/723–2500), which has more than 400 exhibits, the Charles Hayden Planetarium, and the Mugar Omni Theater.

Northeast of the Common is **Government Center,** a jumble of 1960s-era civic buildings and office blocks that stands on what was once Scollay Square, a patch of prostitution and burlesque shows. Just east of here is **Quincy Market,** an enormously popular complex of specialty food shops, restaurants, bars, and retail stores. The food stalls hawk everything from gelato to fried dough to Italian sausages to steamed clams.

Many of Boston's most popular sights are within a short walk of here. Highlights of the **Freedom Trail,** a mile-and-a-half self-guided historic tour marked with a painted red line along the sidewalk, include the 1713 **Old State House** (206 Washington St., ☎ 617/720–3290), **the site of the Boston Massacre** (in front of the Old State House), and several churches and burial grounds. Just east of Quincy Market, along Central Wharf, is the **New England Aquarium** (☎ 617/973–5200), home to more than 2,000 species of sea creatures and one of the city's most popular attractions.

Northwest of Government Center, across the hideous Fitzgerald Expressway, is Boston's **North End,** a network of narrow, crooked streets and 19th-century brick tenements that house one of the nation's most prominent Italian communities. In addition to a number of fine Italian restaurants, you'll also find a number of important Freedom Trail sites here, including the **Paul Revere House** (19 North Sq., ☎ 617/523–1676) and the 1723 **Old North Church** (193 Salem St., ☎ 617/523–6676).

South of Government Center and east of the Boston Common is the closest thing Boston has to a downtown, although you rarely hear Bostonians refer to it as such. High-rise office buildings now dominate this labyrinthine network of streets laid out during Colonial times, and although many prominent examples of 19th- and early-20th-century architecture still stand, this section of town is Boston's least charming. Washington Street is the main shopping avenue, where you can battle for discounted clothing in the original **Filene's Basement** (426 Washington St., ☎ 617/542–2011) or browse at nearby **Jordan Marsh** (450 Washington St., ☎ 617/357–3000). Farther south down Washington Street around Essex and Beach streets, is Boston's lively but compact Chinatown.

The South End

The **South End's** early flourish as an enclave of gentility was short-lived. Most of the neighborhood's lovely redbrick homes, many of them embellished with elaborate details, were built in the 1850s. By the turn of the century, however, the South End had fallen in stature and been cut off from the rest of Boston by rail lines. Over the next 60 years, middle-class blacks and incoming Middle Easterners, Asians, and Latin Americans began to settle here. Although the South End never experienced a period of gentrification as dramatic as that of Washington, DC's Dupont Circle and Philadelphia's South Street, the neighborhood did begin to attract students, artists, and young professionals in the '60s, and by the mid-'70s Boston's premier gay neighborhood had been born.

The rail tracks are now long gone, but the South End is still cut off from the rest of the city by the I–90 underpass, Copley Plaza, and the Prudential Center. Massachusetts Avenue forms its western boundary. Columbus Avenue and Tremont Street are where you'll find most of the gay-popular restaurants and businesses.

Back Bay and the Fens

While Beacon Hill and the South End have a distinctly British character, the relatively young **Back Bay** (a tidal flat before the 1860s), with its broad avenues of four-story town houses, its grid layout, and its bustle of sidewalk cafés and swank boutiques, recalls late-19th-century Paris. Although most of the magnificent single-family homes that attracted wealthy families from Beacon Hill have now been gutted and subdivided, it's still one of Boston's preeminent residential neighborhoods, popular with yuppies and guppies.

The only neatly defined neighborhood in Boston, Back Bay is bounded on the west by Massachusetts Avenue, on the north by Beacon Street, on the east by Arlington Street, and on the south by Boylston Street. The long east–west streets are ideal for walking: Beacon and Marlborough streets are predominantly residential and have some of the neighborhood's most impressive single-family homes. Commonwealth Avenue is divided by a gracious grassy mall. Newbury Street is lined with shops and eateries that range from high-end, up by the Public Garden, to funky and collegiate, down toward Massachusetts Avenue. Boylston is the most commercial. Both the 62-floor **John Hancock Tower** (Trinity Pl. and St. James Ave., ☎ 617/247–1977) and the 52-story **Prudential Tower** (between Boylston St. and Huntington Ave. in Back Bay, ☎ 617/859–0648) have phenomenal views for miles around Boston; the latter is surrounded by an indoor shopping mall. Just west of the Pru and southwest of Copley Square is **Copley Place,** a larger and more upscale mall anchored by the Westin and the Marriott Copley Place hotels.

West of Massachusetts Avenue is **the Fens,** the final piece in Boston's jigsaw puzzle of landfill, an amalgam of low-budget residential and shaggy industrial blocks and site of the campuses of Northeastern University and Boston University. The topographical feature that most defines the neighborhood, however, is the amorphously shaped **Back Bay Fens Park,** the only area of tidal marshlands that was never filled in with gravel as Boston expanded. Landscape architect Frederick Law Olmsted was responsible for converting this wilderness area into a manicured (subtly) park. On the south side of the park is the **Museum of Fine Arts** (465 Huntington Ave., ☎ 617/267–9300). Highlights include the Asiatic art and French Impressionists, plus works by John Singleton Copley, Winslow Homer, John Singer Sargent, and Edward Hopper. Two blocks west is the **Isabella Stewart Gardner Museum** (280 The Fenway, ☎ 617/566–1401), a stunning if idiosyncratic collection of paintings, drawings, textiles, and furniture (mostly Western European) that began as the private holdings of Mrs. Gardner, an avid, eccentric, Brahmin art collector who stipulated in her will that everything in her palazzo remain just as she left it. On the western side of the park is a small residential enclave of attractive apartment buildings and row houses that has become increasingly fashionable with young artists and students. To the north of this neighborhood is quirky **Fenway Park,** one of the smallest and oldest baseball stadiums in the major leagues. Behind the ballpark are several gay and mixed straight/gay warehouse discos.

Cambridge

Often lumped in as just another of Boston's many neighborhoods, **Cambridge** is in fact a small, independent city of nearly 100,000. It was settled in 1630 and six years later became home to the nation's first university, **Harvard** (walking tours, ☎ 617/495–1573), which remains the city's primary tourist draw. Dozens of shops and eateries line the streets around **Harvard Square** (the intersection of Massachusetts Avenue and John F. Kennedy Drive). Within steps of the Square are such impressive institutions as **Widener Library** (Harvard Yard, ☎ 617/495–2413), which has the country's second-largest book collection; the **Fogg Art Museum** (32 Quincy St., ☎ 617/495–9400), whose 80,000 holdings concentrate most on European and American painting; the **Arthur M. Sackler Museum** (485 Broadway, ☎ 617/495–9400), which emphasizes Asiatic, ancient Greek and Roman, and Egyptian, Buddhist, and Islamic art; and the mammoth **Harvard University Museums of Cultural and Natural History** (26 Oxford St., ☎ 617/495–3045).

About 1½ miles southeast of Harvard Yard is the more contemporary **Massachusetts Institute of Technology** (MIT; Information Center: Building Seven, 77 Massachusetts Ave., ☎ 617/253–4795), which fringes the Charles River and is close to Kendall Square, another strong spot for dining and shopping. Not as exhilarating to tour as Harvard, MIT's 135-acre campus does have a few small museums and some noteworthy examples of the architecture of I. M. Pei and Eero Saarinen.

Cambridge, along with Watertown to the west and Somerville to the east, has a fairly high population of both gay men and women, and in recent years the area around **Central Square**—midway between Harvard and MIT—has become especially popular with lesbians. Right off the Square are several excellent Indian and East Asian restaurants, plus a couple gay-popular hangouts and bars.

Jamaica Plain

For lesbians and gay men, **Jamaica Plain** is Boston's most desirable "streetcar suburb." The area is notable for lovely Jamaica Pond and the once-exclusive residential neighborhood surrounding it. This enclave was rediscovered over the past couple of decades by city dwellers in search of affordable housing. There's not much here of interest to the tourist, except for a handful of homo-popular restaurants and coffeehouses; **Pluto** (603 Centre St., ☎ 617/522–0054), a small shop selling gay cards and gifts; and **Crones' Harvest** (761 Centre St., ☎ 617/983–9530), which sells women-and lesbian-oriented books, crafts, jewelry, and clothing.

Ogunquit, Maine

Although it had existed as a village within the town limits of Wells since 1913, tiny Ogunquit (60 miles north of Boston) was not incorporated until 1980. Flanked by a 3-mile beach—one of the most beautiful in the state—and rich with art and theater history, Ogunquit has long been a quieter, simpler gay alternative to Provincetown. From Boston, take I–95 North into Maine; then take Exit 4 to Route 1. Head north 7 miles.

Painters first discovered the village in the early part of the century, and the Ogunquit Playhouse, one of the country's first successful summer theaters, opened in 1939. The gay presence grew in the '60s, when a beatnik contingent began summering here, and then boomed in the '70s, when the town finally opened its first gay guest house and a gay disco, Anabelle's (now The Club). There are now several more guest houses, and a second bar.

The scene is low-key and the gay and lesbian residents here are content to keep it that way. There will probably never be a gay pride parade or an attempt to pass any gay rights laws—as one local put it, "Many of us are just your average Republicans, except for the time we spend between the sheets."

The primary tourist months here are July and August, but all weekends from May though October are busy.

GETTING AROUND

Boston has an extensive bus, trolley, and subway system (referred to as "the T"). It's also extremely walkable, and, as it was laid out before the automobile, driving here is nerve-wracking. Find a parking garage the minute you've entered the city and walk or take public transportation for the rest of your stay. Only one entertainment district—the pocket of nightclubs near Fenway Park—is practical to visit by car (there are several garages near the discos). Note that taxis are difficult to hail; in a pinch, head to a hotel taxi stand.

In Ogunquit, you don't need a car; it's easy to get around town on foot (most sights and establishments are within walking distance of one another), and a trolley makes a regular loop.

EATS

The Boston dining scene is exciting and innovative—a fact that comes as some surprise to many visitors. Not that the old New England broiled scrod, steamed lobster, overcooked vegetables, baked beans, and pork chops and apple sauce have completely disappeared. There are traditional fish and steak houses all over town, many of them decades old. But younger, trendier eateries—many of them strung through the South End, the Back Bay, and Beacon Hill—borrow more from San Francisco than they do from Puritan Massachusetts.

Boston is the land of the neighborhood bistro. Here it usually takes the form of an intimate, storefront dining room with working fireplaces, exposed brick, track lighting, and menus anchored by that trinity of contemporary Italian dining: the designer pizza, the risotto, and the fish grill—each adorned with trendy ingredients: sun-dried tomatoes, artichoke hearts, smoked salmon, calamata olives, grilled shrimp, and the like.

As with any city, the most touristy areas have the crummiest food, although the food stalls at Quincy Market are consistently good spots for snacking. There are almost no late-night eateries in town; after the bars close, your best bet is Chinatown, where both the **Imperial Teahouse Restaurant** (70 Beach St., ☎ 617/426–8543) and **Ho Yuen Ting** (13A Hudson St., ☎ 617/426–2316) entertain legions of hungry disco queens.

Boston

For price ranges, *see* Chart A at the front of this guide.

$$$$ **Pignoli.** Jumbo zeppelins representing pine nuts hang from the ceiling of local impresario Lydia Shire's Italian restaurant. A casual but well-heeled crowd of gays and straights appreciates both the polished, trendy decor and the simple, hearty food. *79 Park Sq., ☎ 617/338–7500.*

$$$–$$$$ **Biba.** One of Boston's original New American restaurants, Biba is no longer *the* in place it was a few years ago, but it's still a must-do for anybody who loves eating. The foods here span the globe; a favorite is pan-fried oysters on semolina blini. It's a perfect perch from which to watch passersby on busy Boylston Street. *272 Boylston St., ☎ 617/426–7878.*

$$$ **Cornucopia on the Wharf.** This is a great alternative to the predictable fish house standbys near the aquarium and Quincy Market. The seafood entrées here are supremely inventive: Consider the Southwest lobster, which is roasted and served over a vegetable enchilada with avocado puree. Great wine list. *100 Atlantic Ave., ☎ 617/367–0300.*

$$$ **Hamersley's Bistro.** One of the first restaurants to attract serious diners to the South End, Hamersley's has both a café and a more formal dining room in an elegant but spare space inside the Boston Center for the Arts. Notable dishes include braised rabbit and duck confit with roasted shallots. The culinary influence is clearly country Continental. *553 Tremont St., ☎ 617/423–2700.*

$$$ **Icarus.** This is one of the top South End choices, meaning that even straight yuppies from Beacon Hill drop in from time to time. The clever menu, which changes seasonally, dazzles with such striking combinations as mussels with red curry broth, chili-rubbed chicken over sweet corn, or cinnamon and pecan in a heavenly meringue. *3 Appleton St., ☎ 617/ 426–1790.*

$$–$$$ Appetito's. Attractive, outgoing waiters, a festive color scheme of mustard yellow, plum, emerald, and cobalt, white napery and warm exposed brick, and well-prepared, reasonably priced food—it all adds up to a terrific restaurant. The Northern Italian fare includes such stars as polenta with gorgonzola, cream sauce, and pine nuts and a seafood risotto with marinated swordfish, scallops, shrimp, calamari, and saffron. *1 Appleton St., ☎ 617/338–6777.*

$$–$$$ Azita. Showcasing the simple, bountiful fare of Lombardy, Tuscany, and Emilia–Romagna, this stylish bistro in the small storefront basement of a tony redbrick town house is done with marble floors and shades of black, white, and lilac. The seafood stew of assorted fish and shellfish in saffron is one of the top choices. *560 Tremont St., ☎ 617/338–8070.*

$$–$$$ Claremont Café. The rustic Claremont has the feel of an old general store. On the sidewalk are several black wrought-iron chairs and tables— perfect for warm days. The menu is Mediterranean-meets-granary: tapas mix with crunchy entrées as baked polenta lasagna with goat cheese and seasonal veggies. The adjacent bakery has coffees and sweets. *535 Columbus Ave., ☎ 617/247–9001.*

$$–$$$ Club Café. Despite its slightly pretentious blend of casual and elegant furnishings and the fact that it's attached to Boston's big guppie bar, the Club Café is a great eatery: It has excellent food, a terrific wine list, and solid service. You can pick from the lighter bar menu or from the main dinner menu, which includes such New American creations as rotelle pasta with shrimp, fennel, and yellow peppers. Equally popular with lesbians and gay men, it's a good place for a date. *209 Columbus Ave., ☎ 617/536–0966.*

$$–$$$ Cottonwood Café. Both locations—there's one in Cambridge and another in the Back Bay—are major hangouts for gay Bostonians interested in eating, sucking down margaritas, and cruising in that discreet New England way. Their sleek, Southwestern decor fits nicely with offbeat dishes like Navajo flatbread with prosciutto, cherries, figs, serrano peppers, and Havarti cheese, or horseradish and cornbread–encrusted salmon glazed with Dijon red chili honey—not what you'd actually find in Santa Fe, but delicious just the same. *222 Berkeley St., ☎ 617/247–2225; in Cambridge: 1815 Massachusetts Ave., ☎ 617/661–7440.*

$$–$$$ Giacomo's. Not quite old-fashioned enough to be mistaken for a North End spaghetti house, Giacomo's is as authentic an Italian dining experience as you'll find outside of that neighborhood. In a handsome South End storefront framed with carved wooden pilasters and a forest-green door and frieze, Giacomo's emphasizes pasta, chicken, and grilled fish; the yellowfin tuna with balsamic and mint vinaigrette, grilled potatoes, and vegetables is especially good. *431 Columbus Ave., ☎ 617/536–5723.*

$$–$$$ St. Botolph's. In a romantic redbrick town house with a turret and a round peaked roof, St. Botolph's is half a formal Continental restaurant and half a lively little bistro with a good late-night menu of pastas, risottos, and salads. It's just down the block from Copley Plaza. *99 St. Botolph St., ☎ 617/266–3030.*

$$ Blue Wave Rotisserie and Grill. Though nothing about the food here stands out especially, the Blue Wave always satisfies the appetite with its long menu of comfort foods: pasta dishes, thick sandwiches, and salads. Many dishes cost less than $10. It's raucous, cheerful, and has a big guppie following. Huge floor-to-ceiling storefront windows give the sensation that you're eating in a window display. *142 Berkeley St., ☎ 617/424–6711.*

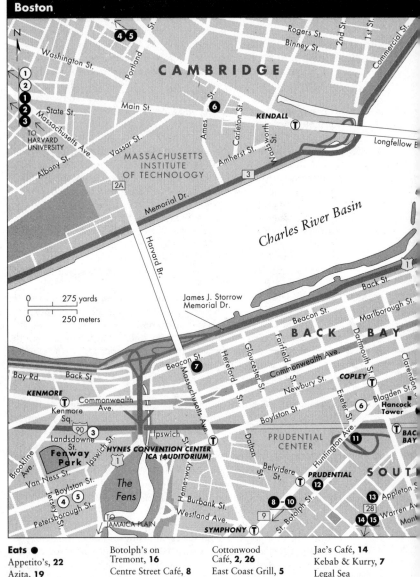

Eats ●

Appetito's, **22**

Azita, **19**

Bertucci's, **23**

Biba, **29**

Blue Diner/The Art-zone, **30**

Blue Room, **4**

Blue Wave Rotisserie and Grill, **25**

Botolph's on Tremont, **16**

Centre Street Café, **8**

Claremont Café, **15**

Club Café, **24**

Club Passim Coffee Shop, **1**

Coffee Cantata Bistro and Beans, **10**

Cornucopia on the Wharf, **31**

Cottonwood Café, **2, 26**

East Coast Grill, **5**

European, **32**

Five Seasons, **9**

Geoffrey's, **18**

Giacamos, **13**

Hamersley's Bistro, **17**

Icarus, **21**

Jae's Café, **14**

Kebab & Kurry, **7**

Legal Sea Foods, **6,11, 27**

Mildred's, **20**

Pignoli, **28**

The Rialto, **3**

St. Botolph's, **12**

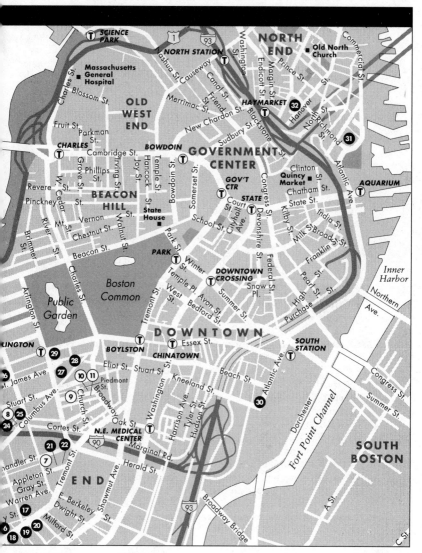

Scenes ○

Avalon/Axis, **3**

Boston Ramrod, **5**

Campus at
Man Ray, **2**

Chaps, **6**

Club Café, **8**

Fritz, **7**

Jacques, **11**

Luxor/Jox, **10**

Napoleon Club, **9**

Paradise, **1**

Quest, **4**

\$\$ **Botolph's on Tremont.** In the heart of the South End, Botolph's is where you go to model your designer duds and newly rippled abs—it's *very* popular with image queens. The pretty decor—a high-ceilinged, old-fashioned storefront with black and red chairs, black tables, and white-tile floors—provides a suitable backdrop for all this posing. The menu of designer pizzas, focaccia sandwiches, and pasta (try baked penne with wild mushrooms, gorgonzola, and tomatoes) is surprisingly affordable. *569 Tremont St.,* ☎ *617/424–8577.*

\$\$ **European.** This is one of the better of the many interchangeable Italian restaurants in the historic North End. None of these spots are especially gay popular but all serve authentic dishes. The European has been serving pizza, seafood, and 16 different spaghetti dishes since 1917. *218 Hanover St.,* ☎ *617/523–5694.*

\$–\$\$ **Geoffrey's.** Known for hearty breakfasts and lunches, Geoffrey's is one of the gayest restaurants in Boston. The bright dining room with ceiling fans, red walls, and framed prints is completely informal. Try the grilled chicken sandwich with corn and black-bean salad, or any of the filling side dishes like garlic mashed potatoes. *578 Tremont St.,* ☎ *617/266–1122.*

\$–\$\$ **Jae's Café.** This happily bizarre hole-in-the-wall has a few tables on the sidewalk, a sushi bar in the basement, and cute, flirtatious waiters wherever you look. The basement, with exposed brick, a big fish tank, and a neon clock, is the choice seating area. The Pan-Asian menu—a mix of Thai, Japanese, Korean, and Chinese—offers everything from pad Thai to buckwheat noodles to miso soup. *520 Columbus Ave.,* ☎ *617/ 421–9405.*

\$–\$\$ **Kebab & Kurry.** In a city with dozens of good Indian restaurants, this basement spot is synonymous with student eats. Has the usual curries but also some Afghan items, too. *30 Massachusetts Ave.,* ☎ *617/536–9835.*

\$ **Bertucci's.** The branch of this regional New England pizza chain just beyond the I–90 underpass in the South End has a very gay following. Pies are baked in a brick oven and come with dozens of great toppings. Portions are huge—even an order of garlic bread or a dinner salad. *3945 Stanhope St.,* ☎ *617/247–6161.*

\$ **Blue Diner/The Artzone.** Near Chinatown and the South End, this is one of only a handful of 24-hour eateries downtown. The Blue Diner dates from 1945, is gay as can be late on weekend nights, and serves the usual blue-plate specials, a great corned beef hash, a full crab cake dinner, and gooey baked macaroni and cheese. In the back room, work by local artists is displayed; exhibits change about every six weeks. *150 Kneeland St.,* ☎ *617/338–4639.*

Cambridge

\$\$\$\$ **The Rialto.** In this warm, sophisticated, yet casual, dining room with works by local artists, chef Jody Adams offers coastal French, Italian, and Spanish fare. Standouts include the halibut braised in vermouth with smoked bacon and artichokes and the spicy baby chicken cooked under a brick. Dinner only—but some of the best food in the city. *Charles Hotel, 1 Bennett St.,* ☎ *617/661–5050.*

\$\$\$ **East Coast Grill.** "Equatorial cuisine" draws crowds to this small, bright, very popular spot. Key tests of your strength: pasta from Hell (enlivened with hot sauce); North Carolina barbecue; and ethnic dishes such as grilled tuna with soy, ginger, and wasabi. It's low-key and lots of fun, though not especially gay. *1271 Cambridge St.,* ☎ *617/491–6568.*

\$\$–\$\$\$ **Blue Room.** One of the best restaurants in the area, the Blue Room is hip, funky, informal, smart, and international, with foods from Latin America, Europe, and Asia. The location is convenient to Central Square's nightclubs. The front counter seating is ideal for mingling. *1 Kendall Sq.,* ☎ *617/494–9034.*

$$–$$$ **Legal Sea Foods.** Locals sometime knock the fact that there are Legals all over metro Boston, and that eating here lacks the authentic feel of a true wharf-side seafood shanty, but you can't beat the quality and freshness. Legal is notable for its straightforward preparation of dozens of varieties of fish—broiled, baked, Cajun, or fried. The appetizers of seafood chowder and the smoked bluefish pâté are outstanding. *5 Cambridge Center in Kendall Sq.,* ☎ *617/864–3400; in Back Bay: Copley Place, 100 Huntington Ave.,* ☎ *617/266–7775; 800 Boylston St., tel 617/266–6800.*

Jamaica Plain

$$ **Centre Street Café.** Jamaica Plain's lesbo central has some great, cheap eats—like black bean burritos, smoked bluefish cakes, and bountiful veggie sandwiches—and a homey atmosphere that's good for making friends. A much-used bulletin board has tons of information on readings and meetings around town. *597 Centre St.,* ☎ *617/524–9217.*

$–$$ **Five Seasons Café.** About 80% of the dishes at this crunchy spot are vegetarian, and all use organic, natural ingredients. A good choice is the asparagus and tofu stir-fry or linguine with tofu meatballs. The bright little dining room is rife with ferns and hanging greenery. The organic wines are surprisingly smooth. *669 Centre St.,* ☎ *617/524–9016.*

Coffeehouse Culture

It took until late 1994 for gay coffeehouses to catch on in Boston, but upbeat **Mildred's** (552 Tremont St., ☎ 617/426–0008) has captured the crowds. Has great salads, pastas, and sandwiches, in addition to all the usual coffees. Watch the steady stream of gym boys. **Coffee Cantata Bistro and Beans** (605 Centre St., ☎ 617/522–2223) is a nesting ground for budding lesbian relationships. This upbeat, earthy coffeehouse in Jamaica Plain is warmed by exposed brick walls, varnished wooden tables with Windsor chairs, and a bright red ceiling. Stocked with funky cards, gifts, and jewelry, **Club Passim Coffee Shop** (47 Palmer St., Cambridge, ☎ 617/492–7679) is also a great place to stop for snacks and light lunches. It has good folk and acoustic entertainment many nights and attracts lots of cute scholars.

Ogunquit, Maine

For price ranges, *see* Chart B at the front of this guide.

$$$–$$$$ **Arrows.** This dignified farmhouse restaurant is on every critic's short list of the top restaurants in Maine (if you're planning to dine here on a summer weekend, reserve a week ahead). You may find it stuffy, but if fine food is your goal, persevere. A dinner of lobster risotto followed by grilled salmon and radicchio with marinated fennel and baked polenta is worth dressing up for. *Berwick Rd.,* ☎ *207/361–1100.*

$$–$$$$ **Hurricane.** Arguably the best, though the most touristy, seafood house in town, Hurricane has an unbeatable setting in Perkins Cove, at the end of Marginal Way and overlooking the ocean. The lobster chowder is a much celebrated starter; a typical main dish is the Cuervo and lime–glazed swordfish. *Perkins Cove,* ☎ *207/646–6348.*

$$–$$$ **Black Swan Tavern.** Just ½-mile north of downtown, the Black Swan is one of the most romantic of the town's dining options. Set in an old gray Victorian house, the French and New American menu is highlighted by a rich baked brie appetizer and chicken Yucatán (served with sweet corn, tomato, and papaya salsa). *Rte. 1 N.,* ☎ *207/646–9934.*

\$\$–\$\$\$ **Poor Richard's.** This 1788 colonial, a former stagecoach stop between Boston and Portland, is near Perkins Cove. The chef has yet to succumb to trendy, so you'll generally encounter a selection of true New England classics. It's also a nice place to stop in for a beer and chat with locals, though you should call for dinner reservations. *Shore Rd.,* ☎ *207/646–4722.*

\$–\$\$\$ **Porch Café.** The dining room of the mostly gay Front Porch bar, this cheerful little space decked out with rattan furniture serves a dependable traditional American menu of burgers, grilled chicken, artichoke dip, and a few Mexican munchies such as deep-fried jalapeños and nachos. Has live piano music most afternoons and evenings. *Ogunquit Sq. and Shore Rd.,* ☎ *207/646–3976.*

\$ **Fancy That.** Many guests staying at nearby guest houses rub shoulders here for lunch, either while they're dining at one of the simple wooden tables with bright blue chairs or while they're picking up the fixings for a picnic at the beach. You can choose from among more than a dozen creative sandwiches in addition to wines, cheeses, coffees, and sweets. You can also check out the small community bulletin board or pick up some artsy postcards or gifts. *7 Main St.,* ☎ *207/646–4118.*

\$ **Java Jive.** This tiny little coffeehouse down an alley off Main Street is painted in tropical colors, has a lovely Elvis-on-velvet among its many colorful decorations, usually has country music blaring from the stereo, and serves a pleasing selection of sweets and coffees. *Shore Rd. and Main St.,* ☎ *207/646–0969.*

SLEEPS

Boston's a great hotel city, with several historic properties, a solid range of high-end and budget hotels, and accommodations in almost every neighborhood. If being close to the gay South End is important, your best bet is a hotel around Copley Plaza, which is nearby. Cambridge has plenty of great hotels, and generally the rates are a bit lower there. The knowledgeable staff at gay-owned **Citywide Reservations Services, Inc.,** (☎ 617/267–7424) can help you find rooms in Boston, on the Cape, and throughout New England; they represent everybody from major hotels to small, gay B&Bs.

Hotels

Boston

For price ranges, *see* Chart A at the front of this guide.

🏨 Still the grande dame of Boston, the **Copley Plaza** is in the heart of the Back Bay and a short walk from the South End. Public areas are to die for, and rooms, though somewhat less impressive, are still among the nicest in town. *138 St. James Ave.,* ☎ *617/267–5300 or 800/822–4200. 373 rooms. \$\$\$\$*

🏨 The newer of the city's preeminent hotels, the **Four Seasons Hotel Boston** nevertheless retains an Old World air and specializes in luxurious personal service; the best rooms overlook the Boston Public Garden. The restaurant, Aujourd'hui, is one of the top New American eateries in town. *200 Boylston St.,* ☎ *617/338–4400 or 800/332–3442. 288 rooms. \$\$\$\$*

🏨 Also overlooking the Garden, the 1927 **Ritz-Carlton** is appropriately stuffy but professionally staffed. The public rooms here, especially the stunning rooftop bar, are the classiest—and most romantic—of any hotel in New England. *15 Arlington St.,* ☎ *617/536–5700 or 800/241–3333. 278 rooms. \$\$\$\$*

🏨 Just off Massachusetts Avenue, offering easy access to the Back Bay, the Fens, and even Cambridge, the nine-story **Eliot Suite Hotel** is all suites and ideal for longer stays. The charming guest rooms have marble baths and period furnishings. *370 Commonwealth Ave.,* ☎ *617/267–1607 or 800/443–5468. 91 rooms. $$$–$$$$*

🔟 Rising 36 stories above the shops at Copley Place, and sitting just opposite the popular bar Chaps, the sleek, contemporary **Westin** lacks the cachet of the preceding three hotels. This is clearly a convention hotel, but an attractive one, with large and bright rooms done with smart Queen Anne reproductions. *Copley Place,* ☎ *617/262–9600 or 800/228–3000. 800 rooms. $$$–$$$$*

🔟 One of Boston's oldest (1891), most dignified hotels, the restored, European-style **Copley Square Hotel** has late-19th-century ambience. Rooms are mostly quite small, although there are several exceptions; in any case, they exude character. *47 Huntington Ave.,* ☎ *617/536–9000 or 800/225–7062. 132 rooms. $$$*

🔟 A Theater District bargain, the elegant 1925 **Tremont House** has a spacious lobby with high ceilings, marble columns, a marble stairway, and lots of gold leaf. The compact guest rooms have been jazzed up with reproductions of 18th-century antiques and stately prints from the Museum of Fine Arts. *275 Tremont St.,* ☎ *617/426–1400 or 800/331–9998. 282 rooms. $$–$$$*

🔟 Owing to its remote but pretty location at the end of fashionable Charles Street, the **John Jeffries** is a little-known hotel bargain, one of the loveliest small hotels in the city. Patronized mostly by visitors to nearby Massachusetts General Hospital, the Jeffries gets its share of tourists, too—especially those planning stays of a week or more. Rooms are large and furnished with colonial reproductions and Monet-print fabrics; they all have small kitchens and spacious baths. *14 Embankment Rd.,* ☎ *617/367–1866. 46 rooms. $$*

🔟 A good budget choice close to the Fens and Boston University, the **Buckminster** feels a bit dormitorylike—with kitchen and laundry facilities on every floor—but rooms are clean, large, and have reproduction antiques. The concierge can usually give a few tips about the gay scene. *645 Beacon St.,* ☎ *617/236–7050 or 800/727–2825. 100 rooms. $–$$*

🔟 With a gay bar on the ground floor, the otherwise unmemorable **Chandler Inn** is one of the most gay-frequented city hotels in the Northeast. The small but clean guest rooms have blond wood furnishings and small writing desks; the baths are very small. You'll be treated well and the price is fair. *26 Chandler St.,* ☎ *617/482–3450 or 800/842–3450. 56 rooms. $–$$*

Cambridge

🔟 The ziggurat-shape **Hyatt Regency** is one of Cambridge's premier lodgings. Though rooms are highly ordinary, many have private balconies and views of the Boston skyline. The Hyatt is a short drive from Harvard and MIT, as well as from Boston; unfortunately, it's not within walking distance of much of anything—even the T. *575 Memorial Dr.,* ☎ *617/492–1234 or 800/233–1234. 469 rooms. $$$–$$$$*

🔟 Also overlooking Harvard Square, but possessing little charm, the clean and crisp **Sheraton Commander** is an affordable hotel popular with business travelers and the parents of students. *16 Garden St.,* ☎ *617/547–4800 or 800/325–3535. 175 rooms. $$$–$$$$*

🔟 In a favorable Harvard Square location, the relatively new **Inn at Harvard** is a refined, discreet hotel that was created to house university visitors but is open to all. Rooms have pieces lent from the Fogg Art Museum and tasteful, contemporary furnishings. *1201 Massachusetts Ave.,* ☎ *617/491–2222 or 800/222–8733. 113 rooms. $$$*

🔟 The ideal budget choice in Cambridge is the **Susse Chalet Inn,** which is a short walk from the Red Line T terminus, but a 10-minute drive from

Harvard Square. *211 Concord Tpke.,* ☎ *617/661–7800 or 800/524–2538. 78 rooms. $*

Small Hotels and Guest Houses

Boston

⊞ On a lovely tree-lined thoroughfare, **463 Beacon Street** is a charming town house; many of its rooms have bay windows that overlook, among other things, a frat house across the way. The rooms are quite large and have a mishmash of traditional furnishings; several have fireplaces. *463 Beacon St.,* ☎ *617/536–1302. 20 rooms. Mixed gay/straight. $*

⊞ Lively, rather social **Oasis Guesthouse** comprises two adjoining red-brick buildings about a 15-minute walk from both the South End and the bars near Fenway Park. Rooms are small but bright with oak furnishings and a mix of antiques and contemporary pieces. The staff is extremely friendly and helpful. There's a top deck for sunning. *22 Edgerly Rd.,* ☎ *617/267–2262. 16 rooms. Mostly gay male. $*

⊞ In the heart of the South End, two friendly women rent a room in their Victorian home with the same name: **Victorian Bed and Breakfast.** It's a large room with an Oriental rug, simple furnishings, a huge tile bath, and bay windows overlooking a pretty street. Enjoy a full breakfast in your room. *Call for the address,* ☎ *617/536–3285. 1 room. Women only. $*

Ogunquit, Maine

Ogunquit's B&Bs are not unlike Provincetown's; most are simply furnished and have small—often shared—baths. Unless otherwise noted, all are open seasonally. For price ranges, *see* Chart B at the front of this guide.

⊞ Set high on a bluff overlooking downtown and the ocean, the **Inn at Two Village Square** has one of Ogunquit's more enviable settings. Rooms in this 1886 house are small and quirkily furnished. This is not, however, a boutique B&B but rather a lively inn with chatty guests. Activities center around the pool and the sprawling wooden deck. There are informal get-togethers some nights and barbecues on Tuesdays, and the hosts reserve a block of seats at the Ogunquit Playhouse on Thursdays. *135 Rte. 1,* ☎ *207/646–5779. 18 rooms. Mostly gay male. $$–$$$*

⊞ The **Rockmere Lodge** has the best location of any guest house in town. It overlooks the ocean and the enchanting walking path, Marginal Way. This imposing gray-shingle cottage has a wraparound porch on which many guests enjoy breakfast, and is decorated throughout with antiques, Adirondack chairs, and lots of wicker. Verdant gardens and a pool. *40 Stearns Rd.,* ☎ *207/646–2985. 8 rooms. Mixed gay/straight. $$–$$$*

⊞ The grandfather of Ogunquit's gay guest houses, the **Yellow Monkey** opened in 1972 and has expanded to a compound of four houses, a fitness room, and a large sundeck and Jacuzzi. Several rooms are efficiencies, other units have two or three bedrooms; there's tremendous variety in rates, amenities, and room sizes. Owner Victor Caffese is in the antiques business and most rooms have pieces from his collection. *168 Main St.,* ☎ *207/646–9056. 40 rooms. Mostly mixed gay/lesbian. $$–$$$*

⊞ Although it's a five-minute drive north of town, the **Gazebo** is recommended for several reasons: It's open year-round; host Tony Fonts prepares an elaborate full breakfast; it's set in a stunning 1865 Greek Revival farmhouse; there's a pool and flagstone patio; and all but one room has a private bath. The decor is heavy on antiques and collectibles. *Rte. 1,* ☎ *207/646–3733. 9 rooms. Mixed gay/straight. $$*

☎ The newest place in town, the **Heritage Inn** is on a quiet residential street, a 15-minute walk from both downtown and Perkins Cove. Accommodations are in a Victorian-style house with gables and white scalloped siding; the rooms are spacious and brightened with smart fabrics and hand-stenciling (many of the touches executed by hostess Rica Shepardson). Each room is named after a famous woman, such as Lily Tomlin or Gertrude Stein. It's open year-round. *Marginal Ave., ☎ 207/646–7787. 5 rooms. Mostly lesbian. $–$$*

☎ With an inland suburban setting, the **Leisure Inn** consists of an 80-year-old main house and some cottages and apartments in back. The owner has strived for a place that would conjure up memories of visiting your grandmother's house—rooms are informally furnished with old (not antique), comfy pieces. Tends to get a more mature, professional crowd. *6 School St., ☎ 207/646–2737. 23 rooms. Mostly mixed gay/lesbian. $–$$*

☎ A schoolhouse in the late 19th century, the **Ogunquit House** is now a quiet B&B within walking distance of the beach and both clubs. Rooms have Oriental rugs, chenille bedspreads, and Victorian wallpaper. Most rooms open onto a deck. *7 Glen Ave., ☎ 207/646–2967. 6 rooms, 4 cottages. Mixed gay/straight. $–$$*

☎ Run by amiable host Bob Tosi, the **Tall Chimneys** is a simple boarding house with small, homey rooms. Continental breakfast is served on an enclosed deck, which also has a Jacuzzi. The attic bedrooms are the coziest and have air-conditioning and private baths. *94 S. Main St., ☎ 207/646–8974. 8 rooms. Mostly mixed gay/lesbian. $–$$*

SCENES

Boston's bar scene is often made fun of for being such a direct throwback to the city's Brahmin heritage—a bunch of skinny-legged, blue-blooded white guys in collared shirts chatting, without the slightest impiety, about their beloved city. In fact, though Milquetoasts are many, Boston has cultivated one of the better leather scenes on the Eastern Seaboard and one of the most popular bars (Chaps) has attained a strong following among Latinos. Gay African-Americans, however, are not a significant presence at any clubs. Lesbians—though present as a minority at many of the boys' bars—haven't had their own full-time club since the Indigo burned in 1993. As far as socializing goes, Boston crowds can seem a bit aloof. This is not to say conversation is hard to come by but only that outsiders typically have to make the first move.

Although most gay men hang out in the South End and most lesbians live and play in Cambridge and Jamaica Plain, the bar scene is spread among several neighborhoods; only in two pockets—by Fenway Park and in Bay Village near the intersection of Stuart and Church streets—are there clusters of gay bars. Bars close at 2, and Boston observes the barbaric practice of denying establishments the right to hold happy hours or offer other kinds of drink specials.

Boston

Avalon/Axis. These two adjacent warehouse discos near Fenway Park (this is as close as you'll probably ever get to playing center field for the Red Sox) join forces on Sunday for the biggest gay party in Boston. At Avalon, you can dance on a stage or on the large dance floor beneath it to a mix of house and hip hop; there are several bars, the lighting is good, and go-go boys writhe on blocks above the crowd. Accessible from Avalon via several doorways, Axis is darker, with black walls adorned with fluorescent faces and murals. The dance floor is smaller and the ceiling is lower, which gives the place a more intimate feel. Upstairs is a smaller dance floor and bar where a DJ spins disco classics. Avalon feels more like a theater, Axis like a bare-bones warehouse. *15 Landsdowne St., ☎ 617/262–2424. Crowd: gay on Sundays—75/25 m/f, mixed gay/straight rest of week; guppier and more white-bread at Avalon, more of an edge at Axis.*

Boston Ramrod. Sort of a Disneyesque vision of what a leather bar should look like—it's still seedy here, but in an intentional, self-conscious sort of way. Today's Ramrod is nothing like the rough-and-rowdy club it was 10 years ago. On some nights, the linen actually overpowers the leather. Only on weekends do things get serious, when the back room—dimly lit and filled with black-oil-barrel statuary—has a strict rubber and leather dress code. The rest of the bar is surprisingly well lit, and decorated a bit like a frat house rec room. *1254 Boylston St., ☎ 617/266–2986. Crowd: male, some hard-core leather men, more often a hodgepodge of curious guppies and overflow from the nearby discos, very mixed in age.*

Chaps. The name describes the crowd better than it does the dress code, which is to say a fairly steady flow of regular, guy-next-door types come here. It's hidden behind a series of blackened windows along Huntington Street, across from Copley Plaza. Inside are a large dark room with black walls and floors and a smaller video bar in back. The larger room has a small dance floor and several big red leatherette sofas that are nice for chatting. Tuesday's classic disco party shouldn't be missed. *27–31 Huntington Ave., ☎ 617/266–7778. Crowd: mostly men, all ages, very cruisy, more down-to-earth than the Club Café but stuffier than Luxor.*

Club Café. Despite possessing the dullest name of any gay bar in America, the Club Café is one of the smarter spots in the city. It's above the queeny Metropolitan Gym, and has a first-rate New American restaurant (*see* Eats, *above*). The front end of the bar area is a sophisticated little cocktail lounge that's popular with suits after work—this section is the most mixed gay/lesbian. In back is a larger, somewhat attitudy video space that's only open Thursdays through Sundays. *209 Columbus Ave., ☎ 617/536–0966. Crowd: 70/30 m/f, guppie, clean-cut, collegiate, generally under 35.*

Fritz. By Boston standards, Fritz gets a gregarious bunch, which means there's a slight chance somebody might actually saunter up to you and introduce himself. Often described as Boston's gay Cheers, the decor is bright and inviting, with heavy use of brass, blond woods, and old-fashioned bar fixtures. *26 Chandler St., ☎ 617/482–4428. Crowd: mostly male, local South Enders, rather cliquey, mostly ages 30s and 40s.*

Jacques. Though it's a bit sleazy, this is the place to go if you want to catch some of the city's best female impersonation shows. *79 Broadway, ☎ 617/426–8902. Crowd: older, very popular among TVs and TSs, some hustlers.*

Luxor/Jox. In the quasi-gay Bay Village neighborhood near Jacques and the Napoleon Club, this two-story compound consists of a mediocre Italian restaurant (Mario's), a downstairs sports bar (Jox), and an upstairs video bar (Luxor). Luxor is the most inviting of the three sections, with rows of seats overlooking the many video screens—which play campy movies much of the time—and a couple of small bars with lots of room to stand or sit. Great kitschy Egyptian murals on several walls. The sports bar downstairs is packed and lively whenever there's a game on—Bostonians take their sports seriously. *69 Church St., ☎ 617/423–6969. Crowd: mostly male, working-class, thirtysomething, regular Joes.*

Napoleon Club. This is thought to be the oldest continuously running gay bar in the nation, dating from 1935. They have piano entertainment most nights. *52 Piedmont St., ☎ 617/338–7547. Crowd: mostly male, older, somewhat mixed racially.*

Quest. Almost unheard of in Boston, Quest has a roof deck, and this is its strongest attribute. Its other three (long and narrow) levels aren't bad, either: The third floor is open and good for dancing; the second floor has a bar, sofas, and video screens; and the basement is a stand-and-pose bar. Friday is the most popular night, when the crowd is similar to that of Avalon's and Axis's (*see above*) on Sundays. *1270 Boylston St.,* ☎ *617/424–7747. Crowd: generally young, mixed genders, somewhat grungy; officially queer on Mondays, lesbian on Wednesdays, gay male on Fridays, and straight the rest of the week—but unofficially there's a pretty strong mix all week.*

The **Safari Club** (90 Wareham St., 2nd Floor, ☎ 617/292–0011) is the city's main sex club (with lockers, tanning tables, and workout facilities).

Cambridge

Campus at Man Ray. With several bars and a small dance area enclosed by chain-link fencing, Campus is the major alternative club in Cambridge, actually more popular with this crowd than any of the Boston clubs. Gets a big crowd on Thursdays. *21 Brookline St., Central Square, Cambridge,* ☎ *617/864–0400. Crowd: very young, lots of pierced body parts, goatees; officially gay and lesbian on Tuesday and Thursday but always very mixed.*

Paradise. Of any bar in the area, Paradise best captures the harder edge of New York's and San Francisco's cruise bars. Both floors are extremely dark and fairly cramped, sweaty, and crowded—the decorating theme is exposed air ducts and corroded hardware. Downstairs is a small dance floor, upstairs is a long room with a couple bars, on which go-go boys perform. *180 Massachusetts Ave., Cambridge,* ☎ *617/864–4130. Crowd: mostly male, on the young side, very cruisy, fairly preppy.*

Ogunquit, Maine

Front Porch Café. Known also for its casual restaurant, the Front Porch is where many people go early in the evening for cocktails before or after dinner or to get warmed up before heading across the street to the Club. The Café, downstairs, has a strong lesbian following early in the evening. Upstairs is a large, bright room with white latticework, yellow director's chairs, and bright green walls; here there's piano entertainment nightly. *Shore Rd.,* ☎ *207/646–3976. Crowd: mixed m/f; older, quieter; gets lots of straights, too.*

The Club. For more than 15 years, the Club has been the town's main gay summer disco (it's also open weekends spring and fall). On the first floor is a midsize dance floor; upstairs is a video bar. *13 Main St.,* ☎ *207/646–6655. Crowd: 80/20 m/f, younger, the disco segment of the town's resort population, but still more conservative and low-key than P'town's.*

THE LITTLE BLACK BOOK

At Your Fingertips

AIDS Action Committee: ☎ 617/536–7733. **Boston Welcome Center:** 140 Tremont St., 02111, ☎ 617/451–2227 or 800/765–4482. **Cambridge Women's Center:** 46 Pleasant St., Cambridge, ☎ 617/354–8807. **Fenway Lesbian and Gay Friends and Neighbors:** Box 928, Astor Station, 02123, ☎ 617/353–1925. **Gay and Lesbian Medical Helpline:** ☎ 617/267–9001. **Greater Boston Convention and Visitors Bureau:** Box 490, Prudential Tower, 02199, ☎ 617/536–4100. **Massachusetts AIDS Hotline:** ☎ 800/235–2331. **Ogunquit Chamber of Commerce:** Box 2289, 03907, ☎ 207/646–2939 or 207/646–5533.

The **Boston Living Center** (29 Stanhope St., ☎ 617/236–1012) is a drop-in center for all persons affected by AIDS. The **Fenway Community Health**

Center (☎ 617/267–0159) has general information for gay men and lesbians and specific programs for women, people of color, and victims of violence.

Gay Media

Bay Windows (☎ 617/266–6670) is New England's major lesbian and gay newspaper. It has extensive articles, club information, advertisements, and personals.

The best resource for women and lesbians is **Sojourner: The Women's Forum** (☎ 617/524–0415), which includes articles, resources, and fiction. Also look for **Bad Attitude** (☎ 617/395–4849), a bimonthly news and entertainment magazine for lesbians. **IN Newsweekly** (☎ 617/723–5130) is similar but more Boston-focused.

BOOKSTORES

The **Glad Day Bookstore** (673 Boylston St., ☎ 617/267–3010), directly across from the Public Library, has a great selection of lesbian and gay titles; it's especially good on women's studies and nonfiction. Toward the back is an extensive porn selection—from books to videos to magazines, new and used. Lots of postcards, too. Another great lesbigay bookstore is **We Think The World Of You** (540 Tremont St., ☎ 617/423–1965), which is in the South End and has music, cards, and a helpful staff.

Crones' Harvest (761 Centre St., Jamaica Plain, ☎ 617/983–9530) has a broad selection of feminist and lesbian books and periodicals, plus clothing, crafts, jewelry, and a bulletin board. Another excellent resource is **New Words–A Women's Bookstore** (186 Hampshire St., ☎ 617/876–5310) in Cambridge.

Body and Fitness

The major gay and lesbian gym is the **Metropolitan Health Club** (209 Columbus Ave., ☎ 617/536–3006), which is just below the Club Café restaurant and bar complex. It's a major scene.

5 *Out in Chicago*

With Saugatuck and Douglas, Michigan

IN THE 1890s, CHICAGO WAS NICKNAMED "THE WINDY City" not because the weather was so volatile but rather because its residents were thought to be a bunch of self-promotional windbags. In a bid to host the World's Columbian Exhibition, city leaders couldn't stop gabbing about how theirs was the greatest town in the world. A century later, Chicago is still one of the world's great destinations. And while certain coastal cousins have caused Chicago's "second city" status to be blown out of proportion by stealing so much of the limelight, they have also developed "windy" reputations of their own. Today, Chicago is quietly glorious—with a dramatic lakeside setting, a striking skyline, sophisticated arts and museums, bountiful shopping, and heady dining and nightlife scenes. Its gay and lesbian community is strong and visible.

Chicago's rise to preeminence was rapid. Only 150 years ago, this area was a flat, dreary tract of marshland settled by a few spirited pioneers. After the city's incorporation in 1833, developers began work on a canal to connect the Gulf of Mexico (via the Mississippi and its tributaries) with the East Coast (via the Great Lakes and the Erie Canal). Completed in 1848, the canal instantly turned Chicago into a commercial center. Between 1840 and 1850, the population grew from 28,000 to 110,000. It ballooned to 300,000 by 1860 and to better than a million during the city's grandest hour: the 1893 World's Columbian Exhibition. By then Chicago had the world's largest train station and countless grand hotels and skyscrapers.

For the exhibition, architect Daniel Hudson Burnham constructed a glimmering, electrically lighted "White City" of exhibition halls and civic buildings. His efforts not only elevated Chicago's status, but also lifted the nation's somber spirits during one of its deepest economic depressions. Although much of the White City burned in a fire the following year, some of its components still exist, including the esteemed University of Chicago, the Art Institute of Chicago, several grand libraries, and numerous city parks.

Chicago has always had a gritty, working-class personality. Many of the city's early immigrants came from central and southern Europe and quickly found work in the city's abundant stockyards, slaughterhouses, and meat-processing plants. Chicago was jokingly dubbed "Porkopolis," owing to the astounding number of hogs (as well as cattle and sheep) that were butchered here.

Chicago's scrappy, go-getter mentality has perhaps contributed to its history of labor and race problems and political corruption. Infamous are the Haymarket riot of 1886, the Pullman strike of 1894, and the race riot of 1919. Al Capone, John Dillinger, and a host of other gangsters ran the city in the '20s and '30s. A severe post–World War II housing shortage exacerbated racial strife. By 1957 the Chicago Urban League deemed this the most segregated city in America, and in the late '60s, race riots nearly tore it apart.

Although it still seems a loose collection of neighborhoods, each with its own ethnic traditions and occasional tensions, Chicago is more integrated than ever before. The South Side remains a rough, visitor-unfriendly patchwork of exclusively African-American and exclusively white districts, but North Side streets are lined with African, Latin American, eastern and southern European, East Indian, and Southeast Asian shops and restaurants. Here myriad cultures exist peacefully side by side, and this is where most of the city's gays and lesbians have settled.

Although never considered a center of gay activism, Chicago was home to one of the country's first gay rights organizations. The Society of Human Rights was formed by German-American activist Henry Gerber in the mid-'20s—long before the Mattachine Society and the Daughters of Bilitis (DOB) blossomed in California. After publishing two issues of an underground journal advocating homosexual rights, it was disbanded when a member's wife alerted police to the group's agenda. "Strange Sex Cult Exposed" was how the *Chicago Examiner* billed the episode.

Since then, Chicago's gay and lesbian community has maintained a low national profile, although Mattachine and DOB chapters were formed here in the mid-'50s. Whereas major rallies were staged in New York City, Los Angeles, and San Francisco in 1970 to commemorate the first anniversary of the Stonewall Rebellion, only a couple hundred people marched in Chicago. Attendance has increased at pride parades and rallies since then, and the city passed a gay rights nondiscrimination ordinance on February 17, 1989. Chicago is comfortable and safe for gays and lesbians, and visitors will find a full gamut of gay-friendly bars, coffeehouses, restaurants, and shops in one of the nation's more vibrant queer neighborhoods, New Town.

THE LAY OF THE LAND

Chicago hugs the southwestern shore of Lake Michigan for some 25 miles between the suburb of Evanston, Illinois, and the Indiana border; a string of suburbs skirts Chicago to the west. The city is about 5 miles deep; its streets form an easy-to-navigate grid that's traversed by only a few long diagonals.

Visitors rarely see the city's South Side, an expanse of working-class and, in many places, dangerous neighborhoods; only Hyde Park, the site of the University of Chicago, and neighboring Kenwood offer much of interest to travelers. Central Chicago—which consists of the South Loop, the Loop, and Near West Side—is the city's geographic hub and was once its commercial and cultural center. Although much of the action has inched north in recent years, the Loop is still the heart of the city in certain respects.

North of the Loop, above the Chicago River, is a slew of tony residential and shopping districts, beginning with River North and the span of Michigan Avenue known as the Magnificent Mile, moving north through Gold Coast, Old Town, and Lincoln Park. West of here are Wicker Park and Bucktown—up-and-coming pockets of bohemianism. Uptown Chicago, north of Lincoln Park, is home to the large gay and lesbian neighborhood known as New Town (which is part of Lakeview); a smaller gay community, Andersonville; and such racially, socially, and economically diverse neighborhoods as Wrigleyville, Ravenswood, Lincoln Square, and Rogers Park.

The Loop and South Loop

From the 1880s to the 1950s, people shopped, dined, partied, and worked in the **Loop** (a.k.a. downtown), a square defined by the Chicago River to the north and west, Grant Park to the east, and Congress Parkway to the south. Today, although it's still the seat of politics and commerce, most of the big-name shopping has moved north to Michigan Avenue; the nightlife and restaurant scene is now found around Rush and Division streets, in Old Town, and in several North Side neighborhoods.

State Street, which runs north–south, was once the Loop's main commercial strip. Today only a few classic pieces of the golden era remain. The leviathan department store **Marshall Field & Co.** (111 N. State St., ☎ 312/781–1000) is a midwestern monument to all that is good and for sale. Shopping and architecture are the draw at **Carson Pirie Scott** (1 S. State St., ☎ 312/641–7000), which is known for its elaborately ornamented facade. **Wabash Avenue,** a block east, provides more opportunities for window shopping, particularly between Randolph Street and Jackson Boulevard.

The streets that run from just south of the Loop to about Roosevelt Road—a section called the **South Loop** or **Downtown South**—also have a few noteworthy attractions. Perhaps the Loop's greatest attribute is its high concentration of landmark buildings. You can't miss the 110-story **Sears Tower** (Skidmore, Owings & Merrill; 1974; 233 S. Wacker Dr.), the world's tallest skyscraper, and the slightly shorter (only 300 feet) **Amoco Building** (200 E. Randolph St.), which was once clad entirely in marble (it began to fall off soon after the building's completion and has since been replaced with granite). The Loop showcases the work of many extraordinary architects and engineers; a century's worth of design milestones and styles are represented here. Dankmar Adler and Louis Sullivan's elaborate **Auditorium Theatre** (1889; 430 S. Michigan Ave.) has almost perfect acoustics and unobstructed sight lines. The **Monadnock Building** (1891–93; 53 W. Jackson Blvd.) is the tallest structure built entirely of masonry; the northern half was constructed by Burnham and John Wellborn Root, the southern half by William Holabird and Martin Roche. Mies van der Rohe's sleek, International-style **Federal Center and Plaza** (1964–1975; 219–230 S. Dearborn Sts.) is home to Alexander Calder's famed *Flamingo* stabile. The Art Deco **Chicago Board of Trade Building** (1930; 141 W. Jackson Blvd.) houses the hectic commodities trading market; take in the activity and Holabird and Root's striking interior from the observation deck (☎ 312/435–3590). The **Rookery**'s (1886; 209 S. LaSalle St.) red-stone masonry and steel-frame construction are by Burnham and Root; the marble and gold-leaf lobby, by Frank Lloyd Wright (1905). The sweeping curve of the postmodern, green-glass-clad **333 W. Wacker Drive** (Kohn Pedersen Fox, 1983) traces the turn in the Chicago River, which flows beside it. Helmut Jahn's **James Thompson Center** (1985; 100 W. Randolph St.) is provocative—people either love or hate its unusual mix of plain- and mirrored-glass cladding and its red, white, and blue color scheme. The 35-story **333 N. Michigan Avenue** (1928), an Art Deco riverfront beauty, complements the dramatic buildings just north of the river.

East of this impressive array of masonry, steel, and glass is **Grant Park,** site of the protests at the 1968 Democratic National Convention. Owing to police paranoia and misconduct (encouraged by then-Mayor Richard Daley), the situation escalated to riots involving much police brutality, all of it captured vividly on television. Today, peaceful festivals and concerts are frequently staged on the park's lush grounds, which extend several blocks south from Randolph Street to Roosevelt Road. Where Adams Street intersects the park is the dramatic **Art Institute of Chicago** (S. Michigan Ave. at Adams St., ☎ 312/443–3600), whose 300,000-piece collection spans more than 40 centuries and includes the most impressive display of Impressionist works in the United States, not to mention Grant Wood's iconic *American Gothic.* Also check out the Chagall windows and the architectural details from the old Chicago Stock Exchange.

If you stroll south of the museum through Grant Park, you'll pass the **Buckingham Fountain,** the world's largest decorative fountain when it was built in 1927. In the southern half of the park are the **John G. Shedd Aquarium** (1200 S. Lake Shore Dr., ☎ 312/939–2438 or 312/939–2426), the world's largest indoor aquarium; the **Adler Planetarium** (1300 S. Lake Shore Dr., ☎ 312/322–0304); and the humongous **Field Museum of Natural History** (Lake Shore Dr. at E. Roosevelt Rd., ☎ 312/922–9410), which contains gem rooms, a rebuilt Pawnee earth-lodge, a comprehensive ancient Egypt exhibit, and the "Life Over Time" exhibit.

Hyde Park and Kenwood

Two South Side neighborhoods worth exploring are **Hyde Park** and, just to its north, **Kenwood.** The World's Columbian Exposition of 1893 was held in Hyde Park, bounded by South 51st Street (Hyde Park Boulevard) on the north, South 60th Street (the Midway Plaisance) on the south, South Lake Shore Drive on the east, and Washington Park on the west. The **University of Chicago,** built a year before the exhibition opened, commands a large social and architectural (Gothic) presence here; it is one the most outstanding academic institutions in the country, with more than 60 Nobel laureates among its graduates. The 184-acre campus takes up the bulk of the neighborhood, long maintained, for better or for worse, by strict zoning and urban renewal projects as an island of middle-class living in a sea of poverty. Because this has involved razing bars, artists' studios, and other colorful establishments that once lined 55th Street, the neighborhood is without a vibrant nightlife or interesting shopping strip.

In the lakefront park east of the university is the exposition's Palace of Fine Arts; it now houses the **Museum of Science and Industry** (5700 S. Lake Shore Dr., ☎ 312/684–1414), one of the country's first hands-on museums. On or near the campus are several notable sites, including the **David and Alfred Smart Museum of Art** (5550 S. Greenwood Ave., ☎ 312/702–0200), whose diverse collection numbers 5,000 items; the **Oriental Institute** (1155 E. 58th St., ☎ 312/702–9520), with an outstanding collection of artifacts from the ancient Near East; and a few of Frank Lloyd Wright's most notable achievements, chief among them the **Robie House** (5757 S. Woodlawn Ave., ☎ 312/702–8374), which you may tour for free daily at noon or by special arrangement.

Near North

North of the Loop, between the Chicago River and the lakefront and below North Avenue is a collection of lively neighborhoods—some of them saddled with various combinations of old and new money and others rich with galleries and nightclubs, all of them prosperous. Closest to downtown are River North and Streeterville. North Michigan Avenue (a.k.a. the Miracle Mile) essentially divides these two neighborhoods.

Once heavily industrial, then virtually abandoned, **River North** had little going for it up until about two decades ago, when artisans began making studios of its inexpensive derelict lofts and warehouse spaces. Now you'll find a vast number of galleries, many of them concentrated around **SuHu** (where *Su*perior and *Hu*ron streets intersect with Orleans and Hudson streets). Interior designers know the area best as the home of the monolithic **Merchandise Mart** (300 N. Wells St., ☏ 312/527–7600; near where Orleans St. crosses the Chicago River). In America, only the Pentagon has more square footage. On the first two floors are retail shops open to the public; on other floors are wholesale showrooms that welcome only interior designers). Mart tours are given weekdays at noon. Fashion wholesale showrooms can be found next door in the **Apparel Center.**

Architectural landmarks along the northern waterfront include the terra-cotta–clad **Wrigley Building** (1921–24; 400 N. Michigan Ave.); the twin cylindrical towers of 60-story **Marina City** (1964–67; 300 N. State St.); the magnificent Gothic Revival **Tribune Tower** (1925; 435 N. Michigan Ave.); and the imposing limestone-and-granite **NBC Tower** (1989; 200 E. Illinois St.).

The **Magnificent Mile** and **Streeterville** are in a league with the finest American and European shopping districts. Between the Chicago River and Oak Street, Michigan Avenue is lined with retail giants: Saks Fifth Avenue (700 N.), Tiffany & Co. (715 N.), Neiman-Marcus (737 N.), F.A.O. Schwarz (840 N.), and Bloomingdale's (900 N.).

Streeterville, a landfill overrun with saloons and whorehouses at the turn of the century and now a nondescript patch of high-rise apartments, hospital buildings, and office blocks, is home to two excellent art museums: the **Museum of Contemporary Art** (237 E. Ontario St., ☏ 312/280–5161), chiefly representing post–World War II artists, and the small but impressive **Terra Museum of American Art** (666 N. Michigan Ave., ☏ 312/664–3939), with works by Whistler, Sargent, Homer, Cassatt, and the Wyeths.

East of Streeterville, along the lakefront, is the **Navy Pier,** a former commercial-shipping pier that in 1995 was transformed into 50 acres of parks, gardens, shops, and restaurants; kind of nifty and kind of touristy, it's a bit like San Francisco's Fisherman's Wharf or New York's South Street Seaport, though not as tacky—yet.

North of Streeterville, brushing the lakefront from Chicago Avenue up to about North Avenue, is that posh and precious chunk of real estate known as the **Gold Coast,** site of some of the city's grandest and most exorbitantly priced homes and apartment houses as well as impressive hotels, several good restaurants, and more high-end shopping.

Lincoln Park and Old Town

Lincoln Park, bounded by North Avenue, Belmont Avenue, the Chicago River, and Lake Michigan, is the name for both a lush expanse of green and for one of the city's oldest neighborhoods, settled in the early 1840s by German and Eastern European immigrants. The park, which began with 60 acres and now is more than 1,200 acres, includes the small but impressive **Lincoln Park Zoo** (2200 N. Cannon Dr., ☏ 312/742–2000); the **Chicago Historical Society** (1601 N. Clark St., ☏ 312/642–4600), with good displays on the Chicago Fire; and the **Lincoln Park Conservatory** (2400 N. Stockton Dr., ☏ 312/742–7736).

When the weather behaves, the lakefront from Lincoln Park north to Foster Avenue is jammed with sun worshippers; there are many gays and lesbians along the entire stretch, but the New Town section (*see* New Town, *below*) is the gayest.

The area around the park is a bit too cutesy but terrific for sidewalk strolling and people-watching and not as busy as some of the neighborhoods to the north; a good number of well-heeled, same-sex couples live around here. Still hip but increasingly monied, dapper yet daring, it might remind you of Boston's Back Bay or Washington, DC's Kalorama.

Much of the area's dining and shopping is near handsome **DePaul University;** it's centered around the intersection of Belden and Sheffield avenues. Outside the nearby **Biograph Theater** (2433 N. Lincoln Ave.), an interesting local landmark that still shows first-run movies, the notorious John Dillinger met his demise.

Lincoln Park's southeast corner, the **Old Town Triangle,** is one of its liveliest sections, with plenty of good shops, restaurants, and nightclubs along Wells Street and its intersecting one-way alleys. Here you'll find **Second City** (1616 N. Wells St., ☎ 312/337–3992), the famous improvisational comedy club where performers such as Elaine May, Mike Nichols, John Belushi, and Bill Murray first tested their comic wings.

Wicker Park and Bucktown

West of Lincoln Park are the newly vibrant neighborhoods of **Wicker Park,** which runs from Division to North avenues, and **Bucktown,** the block of streets stretching above it from North to Fullerton avenues. Originally home to immigrant Poles, Ukrainians, and other Eastern Europeans, then later to Puerto Ricans, these areas are a hodgepodge of ethnicities and lifestyles—not particularly gay, but so predominantly countercultural they're sometimes called the "new Seattle." There are several restaurants, coffeehouses, bars, and offbeat shops along North Avenue, especially near its intersection with Milwaukee and Damen avenues.

Lakeview and New Town

Lakeview is usually defined as running between the lakefront and Ashland Avenue, north of Belmont Avenue on up to Irving Park Road. Within this neighborhood is a small triangle, bound by the lakefront, Belmont Avenue, and Halsted Street, called **New Town** (a.k.a. Boys' Town). Traditionally, while most of Lakeview has been a mix of artsy types, working-class families, and young, not-yet-rolling-in-dough professionals—with a smattering of lesbians and gays—New Town has been overwhelmingly gay and mostly male. Today, New Town draws more straights and lesbians, and homosexuals form a broader presence in Lakeview as a whole; Montrose Avenue, on Lakeview's northern outskirts, is fast becoming a dyke enclave second only to Andersonville to the north.

In the heart of Lakeview is **Wrigley Field** (Clark and Addison Sts.), home of baseball's Chicago Cubs. The stadium draws thousands of fans on roughly 80 summer days and—since 1988 when lights were installed (an act still widely regarded as blasphemous)—summer nights. Lakeview is one of the most dynamic entertainment districts you'll find— with throngs of baseball fans mingling with Clark Street's already motley assortment of same-sex couples, straight kids from the burbs, yuppies, and the like.

Clark Street, which runs diagonally north–south, is Lakeview's major commercial thoroughfare, with a diverse collection of businesses—from spiffy bistros and simple fast-food joints to sports cards shops and vintage clothing boutiques. **Halsted Street,** parallel to Clark just one block east, is a strip of shops, restaurants, and bars that cater primarily to gay men. Try **Flashy Trash** (3524 N. Halsted St., ☎ 312/327–6900) for wigs, drag wear, and make-up; **We're Everywhere** (3434 N. Halsted St., ☎ 312/404–0590) for the latest gay and lesbian fashions; **Beatnix** (3436 N. Halsted St., ☎ 312/935–1188) for vintage duds; and **Cupid's Treasures** (3519 N. Halsted St., ☎ 312/348–3884) for fun toys and trinkets. East of Halsted, **North Broadway** draws a mixed bag of pedestrians with its quirky antiques shops, bookstores, and other engaging retail outlets. **Belmont Avenue,** which runs east–west and intersects Clark, Halsted, and North Broadway, has scads of cheap eateries and clothing and music shops. In the most general sense, things are gayest along Belmont the closer you are to the lake, but it's all rather diverse and busy as far west as the El. If you follow Belmont to Lake Michigan, you'll hit the main gay sun-bunny section of beach, which many people call simply the Belmont Rocks.

Uptown

The multiethnic neighborhoods extending north of Lakeview to suburban Evanston are some of Chicago's most up-and-coming. Directly north of Lakeview, from Ashland Avenue west to the Chicago River, and from Irving Park Road north to Bryn Mawr Avenue, is **Lincoln Square** (a.k.a. Ravenswood), once heavily German and now populated mainly by Southeast Asians.

From about Ashland Avenue east to the lakefront, are a few communities good for exploring. **Argyle Street,** the least touristy of the city's three Asian districts, is lined with restaurants and shops from Broadway to Sheridan Road. Most eateries are Thai, Cambodian, Vietnamese, or Chinese; many are extremely inexpensive and BYOB. **Andersonville,** an old Swedish enclave whose main commercial strip is **Clark Street** between Foster and Bryn Mawr avenues, is steadily developing into a low-key lesbian and gay residential district. It's nondescript but has some cheap eats and coffeehouses, some friendly neighborhood bars—a couple of them big with the leather crowd—and some good shops, including **Women and Children First** (*see* Bookstores, *below*); **Woman Wild** (5237 N. Clark St., ☎ 312/878–0300), an arts and crafts gallery devoted to women artists; a scattering of the neighborhood's original Swedish bakeries and eateries; and the **Swedish-American Museum Center** (5211 N. Clark St., ☎ 312/728–8111), which displays and sells a variety of crafts and decorative arts. It's possible to drive through this area without registering its true funk factor; spend a few hours poking around to really breathe in its bohemian air.

Chicago's northernmost neighborhood is **Rogers Park,** home to **Loyola University.** Rogers Park has long had a substantial Jewish population but more recently has become a true melting pot: Residents range from down-and-out to upper middle-class, from college students to retirees, from Indian and West Indian to Russian, African-American, and East Asian—all living more or less harmoniously. Since the '60s, a left-leaning, politically spirited underground of coffeehouses and folk and jazz clubs has thrived here. Although the area is not specifically gay, same-sexers usually feel comfortable here.

Evanston and Points North

If you have a car and a little extra time, consider a jaunt north of the city along picturesque **Sheridan Road,** which more or less hugs the lake shore from the city border up to the Wisconsin state line. The first town you hit, **Evanston,** has been the national headquarters of the **Women's Christian Temperance Union** for more than a century; it's also home to 104 churches. Nevertheless, because of the presence of **Northwestern University,** Evanston has some colorful galleries, shops, and eateries along

Main Street between Sherman and Davis streets—but no bars. After passing by the town's lovely old mansions and sandy beaches, you'll enter **Wilmette, Glencoe, Highland Park,** and **Lake Forest**—still other tony Chicago suburbs.

Oak Park

West of Chicago are a number of middle-class suburbs. **Oak Park,** accessible via the Eisenhower Expressway (I–290), is the biggest draw. One of the city's earliest suburbs, it's where Ernest Hemingway was born and raised and where Frank Lloyd Wright started out. Stop to visit the **Frank Lloyd Wright Home and Studio** (951 Chicago Ave., ☎ 708/848–1976) and verse yourself in the ways and means of this legendary architect. Dozens of homes designed by either Wright or his disciples are located around town; a map and self-guided tour is available from the **Chicago Architecture Foundation** (☎ 708/922–8687) and the **Oak Park Visitors Center** (158 N. Forest Ave., ☎ 708/848–1500).

Saugatuck and Douglas, Michigan

The sleepy villages of Saugatuck and Douglas comprise the only significant gay vacation spot in the central United States. A little more than two hours from Chicago and a little more than three hours from Detroit, the two towns are separated by Lake Kalamazoo, which is actually just a wide expanse of the eponymous river, which empties into nearby Lake Michigan.

Douglas, the sleepier of the two communities and the home of the area's main gay lodging and entertainment venue, successfully passed a gay and lesbian civil rights ordinance not long ago. **Saugatuck**—the larger, more commercial, and more northerly of the pair—has sunny boutiques, antiques shops, galleries, fudge shops, and eateries along a compact grid of unassuming, tree-lined streets; straight yuppies have always and probably will always be the community's bread and butter, and Saugatuck is without rainbow flags or other signs of homo-habitation, despite the fact that gay men and, increasingly, lesbians have been visiting for a few decades. Nonetheless, a straight-owned B&B allegedly refused to book one room to a male couple, sparking a relatively mild but nonetheless controversial civil rights struggle that ended in 1995 when the city council shot down a proposed antidiscrimination ordinance. Since then, there has been considerable debate in Chicago and Detroit about whether to boycott the area.

Despite these rumblings, it is unlikely that you will encounter negative vibes in either town. Both are quiet, low-key, and modestly charming. Along the sweeping, sandy Lake Michigan shoreline, **Oval Beach** is the main gay and lesbian sun spot. From downtown Douglas, take Center Street west; turn right onto Park Street; follow it north, turning left at the Holiday Hill resort and following signs to the Beach. The gay and lesbian section is at the north end of the beach; parking is $3. The setting is striking, as Lake Michigan's surf can pack a wallop, and the strong winds have formed huge shrub-covered dunes behind the parking lots. Like the area as a whole, Oval Beach has shunned overdevelopment.

The main tourist season runs from May through September, though many places stay open year-round. Fall is beautiful when the foliage is changing, and winter offers a quiet and romantic (if chilly) respite from Midwest cities.

GETTING AROUND

Public transportation in Chicago is not hard to negotiate. The excellent map published by the **Chicago Transit Authority** (CTA) is available in many hotels and at fare booths. A network of both elevated ("El") and subway lines traverse the city, and buses usually operate where there's no El. It is not impossible to get around by car, but traffic can be heavy and street parking nearly impossible, especially around the Loop and River North. On the North Side, from Lincoln Park to Rogers Park, a car can actually be handy, however; street parking is easy to come by in Lakeview and New Town, except when the Chicago Cubs have a home game or on weekend evenings when the clubs are hopping. Taxis are metered and can be hailed easily from the busier streets.

EATS

African, Chinese, German, Greek, Israeli, Italian, Mexican, Polish, Russian, Scandinavian, Thai, Ukrainian, and Vietnamese cuisines are all well-represented in Chicago. Still, though some of the nation's culinary darlings call Chicago home, it lags behind many other cities when it comes to innovative cooking.

One great thing about Chicago's restaurant scene is the amount of bang you usually get for your buck. Old World diners and cozy pubs that serve up heaps of comfort food line city streets. Pizza is a Chicago specialty—the deep-dish version was invented here—and any combination you can dream up can be found. Even a feast in one of the city's fanciest eateries can cost you less than a comparable meal in other big cities.

Gay and lesbian patrons abound just about anywhere you eat in Lakeview and New Town. Andersonville, Wicker Park, and Bucktown restaurants are also quite popular with the community. And when you dine out in other neighborhoods north of North Avenue you're likely to spy at least one or two gay couples, if not some waitrons. Things are straighter as you venture south, through Near North and the Loop; in some of the rough South Side neighborhoods, exercise discretion.

For price ranges, *see* Chart A at the front of this guide.

Lakeview and New Town Vicinity

$$$-$$$$ **Yoshi's.** Perhaps the only serious dining spot on Halsted's anything-but-serious gay entertainment strip, this intimate international eatery serves such innovative food as soft-shell crab tempura with tomato-cilantro sauce. *3257 N. Halsted St., ☎ 312/248–6160.*

$$$ **La Paella.** Gilt-frame mirrors, copper chandeliers, and leather booths give this classic Spanish restaurant an Old World elegance uncommon amid Lakeview's mostly casual chic. From the main menu, you won't go wrong with the fresh seafood or the tender rabbit braised with white wine, garlic, and olive oil. *2920 N. Clark St., ☎ 312/528–0757.*

$$-$$$ **Bella Vista.** This northern Italian restaurant with dramatic frescoed ceilings and servers as stylish as the decor is one of the most romantic spots in Lakeview. Picture-pretty salads and a long, varied wine list complement a selection of creative pizzas and pastas such as penne with grilled asparagus. *1001 W. Belmont Ave., ☎ 312/404–0111.*

$$-$$$ **Jezebel.** Pink-marble tables, sponge-painted ocher walls, and chandeliers set an elegant scene in this charming Mediterranean bistro in the shadow of Wrigley Field. Pastas and grills are elaborate and flavorful—a lemon

Lakeview and New Town

Eats ●
Angelina, **9**
Ann Sather **25**, **30**
The Bankok, **7**
Bella Vista, **23**
Blue Iris, **18**
Buddies, **20**
Cafe Voltaire, **21**
Carlucci, **32**
Chicago Diner, **10**
Chinalite, **5**
Coffee
Chicago, **22**, **27**
Cornelia's, **8**
El Jardin, **16**
Halsted Street Digital-Audio Cafe, **3**
Jerome's, **31**
Jezebel, **14**

La Paella, **29**
Le Loup, **13**
Leona's **19**
Mama Desta's, **17**
Matsuya, **15**
Melrose Diner, **24**, **26**
Mike's, **2**
Penny's Noodle Soup, **12**
Pepper Lounge, **6**
Playa Azul, **1**
Raw Bar and Grill, **4**
Star Top Café, **28**
Yoshi's, **11**

Scenes ○
Berlin, **13**
Buck's Saloon, **7**
Cell Block, **1**
Charlie's, **3**
The Closet, **11**
Gentry on Halsted, **9**
Little Jim's, **5**
Manhole, **6**
The North End, **2**
Roscoe's, **8**
Sidetrack, **10**
Spin, **12**
The Vortex, **4**

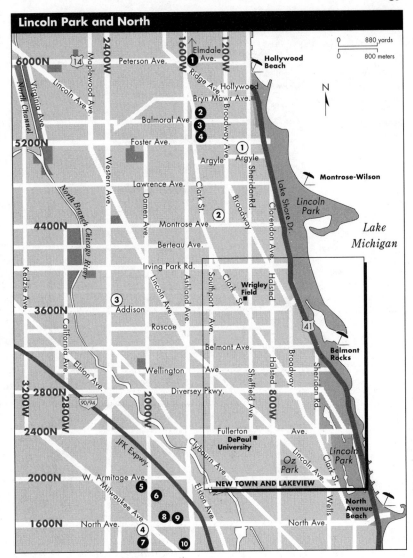

Lincoln Park and North

Eats ●
Ann Sather, **4**
Busy Bee, **7**
Heartland Cafe, **1**
Kopi Cafe, **2**
Le Bouchon, **5**
Northside Cafe, **6**
Reza, **3**
Savoy Truffle, **10**
Starfish, **9**
Urbis Orbis, **8**

Scenes ○
Big Chicks, **1**
Estelle's, **4**
The Other Side, **3**
Paris Dance, **2**

68

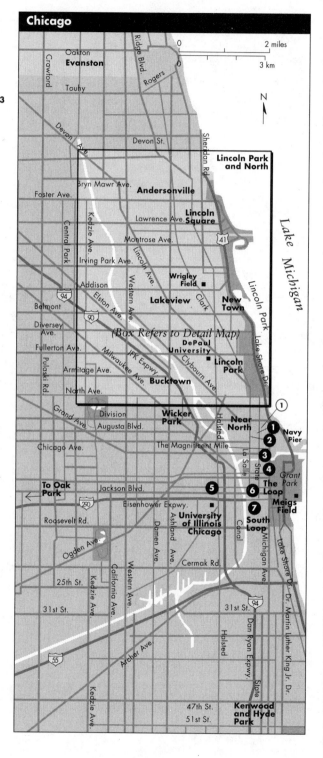

fettucini with smoked chicken, spinach, artichoke hearts, and sun-dried tomatoes is typical. *3517 N. Clark St.,* ☎ *312/929–4000.*

$$ **Blue Iris.** The white-tile floor and trim with tables the shade of blue irises will brighten your mood, and just wait until you sample the soul-influenced Southwestern cooking. Start with a basket of jalapeño garlic bread, then dig into fresh shrimp enchiladas, blackened swordfish, or pan-fried crawfish. *3216 N. Sheffield Ave.,* ☎ *312/975–8383.*

$$ **Cornelia's.** Rough-hewn wooden walls make this cozy, rustic restaurant, steps away from the Halsted bar scene, feel almost like an old farmhouse. The cuisine has a green market sensibility. A starter might be wild mushrooms broiled with seasoned bread crumbs and goat cheese, followed by shrimp with sun-dried tomatoes, tapenade, and herbs with carrot fettuccine. *750 W. Cornelia Ave.,* ☎ *312/248–8333.*

$$ **Matsuya.** This is one of the best Japanese restaurants in the area, with excellent sushi, such spicy starters as deep-fried chicken wings and whitefish with smelt roe, and many tempura, seafood, and teriyaki dishes. The dining room is spare and contemporary; a striking wooden screen separates it from the kitchen. *3469 N. Clark St.,* ☎ *312/248–2677.*

$$ **Pepper Lounge.** Behind a facade the color of port wine cheese is the hottest late-night supper club in the city (serving dinner until 1:30 AM). The entire dining room is done in red, from the rich velvet drapes to the lighting—many of the furnishings, including the elaborate chandeliers, were salvaged from an old theater. The menu is Continental with contemporary influences; a great Caesar salad comes with prosciutto, and the tasty red-pepper ravioli is filled with ricotta cheese. Has a chic, sexy crowd. *3441 N. Sheffield Ave.,* ☎ *312/665–7377.*

$$ **Playa Azul.** Nowadays it's hard to tell the real dives from the fakes. This one is authentic, from its gray linoleum floor and sickly fluorescent lighting to its plastic tablecloths. The draw? Some of the tastiest, hottest Mexican seafood on the planet. You can get fresh oysters on the half shell, several fish soups, and a variety of seafood grills in red or garlic sauces—octopus is one of the better options. *4005 N. Broadway,* ☎ *312/472–8924.*

$$ **Raw Bar and Grill.** This dark, lively tavern just north of Wrigley Field looks and feels like most of the sports bars in the neighborhood, but it used to be a lesbian bar and still retains a strong homo following. A dozen fresh fish dishes, including Maine lobster and mahi mahi, are available—plus a variety of items on the half-shell. *3720 N. Clark St.,* ☎ *312/348–7291.*

$–$$ **Angelina.** This neighborhood trattoria has two dramatic dining rooms with sweeping maroon drapes, vaulted ceilings, chandeliers, and gilt-frame mirrors. But it only looks fancy. Most of the delicious pasta dishes ring in for under $10. *3561 N. Broadway,* ☎ *312/935–5933.*

$–$$ **The Bangkok.** Thai food is a strength of Boys' Town, but if you had to pick one standout it would be this lavish dining room where museum-quality Thai bibelots set the scene for a rich, fiery cuisine. Sunday buffet brunches are as attractive as they are delicious. *3542 N. Halsted St.,* ☎ *312/327–2870.*

$–$$ **Chinalite.** A bit west of New Town, this classy Chinese spot has a sweeping wall of French windows and pressed white napery on the tables. It's nice but still affordable. *3457 N. Southport Ave.,* ☎ *312/244–0300.*

$ **Ann Sather.** You could actually survive solely on the flaky, freshly baked rolls that accompany every meal at this hallowed Swedish diner with gay-popular locations in both Lakeview and Andersonville. From the fresh, pink salmon salad sandwiches to the fluffy omelets stuffed with crab, spinach, and sour cream, every morsel is memorable. Were it possible to choose your own grandmother, you'd want her to come from the ranks of Ann Sather's doting wait staff. *929 W. Belmont Ave.,* ☎ *312/348–*

2378; 5207 N. Clark St., ☎ 312/271–6677; 2665 N. Clark St., ☎ 312/327–9522.

$ Buddies. You can't see inside from the street, but signs and decorations on the front door and windows make it clear that this is a gay establishment, more restaurant than bar. Inside, filling familiar fare perfumes the small, casual dining room: meatballs marinara, burgers, and fancier dishes like grilled yellowfin tuna are offered. *3301 N. Clark St.,* ☎ *312/477–4066.*

$ Chicago Diner. Don't expect to find meat loaf and baked ham at this diner—everything that comes out of this kitchen is vegetarian, and much of it is low-fat. Specialties include tempeh burgers, tofu hot dogs, and filling rice-and-bean platters. The storefront dining room has wooden booths and exposed brick, and the staff is friendly and laid back. *3411 N. Halsted St.,* ☎ *312/935–6696.*

$ El Jardin. This lively yuppie Mexican restaurant and bar is big with guppies and yuppies weekdays after work and on weekends. There are several noisy dining rooms, but the best seating is outside on the patio overlooking the action on Clark Street. The food is decent but predictable. *3335 N. Clark St.,* ☎ *312/528–6775.*

$ Le Loup. This "Loup" has nothing to do with Chicago's downtown or the city's elevated railway. *Loup* means "wolf" in French, and indeed, the dining room is filled with photos and decorations of the animals. This theme is diverting, if odd, for what is essentially an urbane French bistro, where big portions of veal-sausage-and-white-bean cassoulet, coq au vin, and ratatouille Niçoise are doled out for bargain prices. *3348 N. Sheffield Ave.,* ☎ *312/248–1830.*

$ Leona's. Founded in 1950, Leona's serves delicious pan, stuffed, and thin-crust pizzas as well as a mean lasagna. Everything comes in ridiculously big portions. The dining room is dimly lit and cozy, and has large windows overlooking Sheffield Avenue. Service is quick and friendly. *3215 N. Sheffield Ave.,* ☎ *312/327–8861.*

$ Mama Desta's. Because this looks like a shanty from outside, its dining room comes as a surprise: It's filled with framed art and stylish furniture. You may not know what to make of the food, either, especially if you've never sampled Ethiopian and Eritrean cooking. Vegetables and spicy, hearty stews are the feature; you scoop up everything with *injera,* a spongy bread. Delicious and affordable. *3216 N. Clark St.,* ☎ *312/935–7561.*

$ Melrose Diner. If Ann Sather's, across the street, is closed or too crowded, try this 24-hour diner that's big with club goers into the wee hours. The food is typical, although there's a bakery on premises that turns out an extraordinary cheesecake. The Broadway branch is also fag-happy. *930 W. Belmont Ave.,* ☎ *312/404–7901; 3320 N. Broadway,* ☎ *312/327–2060.*

$ Mike's. This standard greasy spoon with fabulous, striped velour seats stays open all night on weekends. Egg dishes are great, the staff's friendly, and the usual fare is well done. *3805 N. Broadway,* ☎ *312/404–2205.*

$ Penny's Noodle Shop. On those raw, windy Chicago days, there's little that warms the soul better than a bowl of piping-hot Thai noodles. The pad Thai and beef satay are both excellent. This is a small, triangular place with both table and counter seating. It's simple and quick—perfect when you're in a hurry. *3400 N. Sheffield Ave.,* ☎ *312/281–8222.*

Lincoln Park and Points West

$$$ Starfish. This hot restaurant in Bucktown/Wicker Park has been packing 'em in since it opened in 1995. It's a slick place, with exposed air ducts and brick, a handsome dark wood bar, and asterisk-shape light fixtures. The waitrons look like fashion models but are courteous and friendly. Starfish has a great menu with plenty of creative fish dishes; if you're up for a fowl evening, start with roasted quail with goat cheese and move on to the incredibly filling smoked duck and lobster tortillas with yellow tomato salsa. *1856 W. North Ave.,* ☎ *312/395–3474.*

$$–$$$ **Carlucci.** One of the most gay-popular—and urbane—restaurants in Lincoln Park, it's known for its first-rate Italian fare, wintertime fireside dining, and refreshing summer garden. A safe bet for a romantic evening. *2215 N. Halsted St.,* ☎ *312/281–1220.*

$$–$$$ **Jerome's.** This Lincoln Park favorite, a 20-minute walk south of Lakeview, has the sort of toasty dining room that'll warm you up on a nippy fall afternoon—in better weather, take a table on the vast wooden deck overlooking busy Clark Street. Expect filling, uncomplicated comfort food: Sheboygan bratwurst, strip steak, chicken with Monterey jack cheese, and zesty hummus are good bets. *2450 N. Clark St.,* ☎ *312/327–2207.*

$$–$$$ **Le Bouchon.** This Bucktown bistro is one of those off-the-beaten path spots that locals bring their friends to only after swearing them to secrecy—the charm will be lost if *everybody* finds out about it. Providing a real taste of Paris, the diminutive dining room has pressed-tin ceilings, paintings in vintage frames on the walls, and bentwood chairs; the menu offers veal kidneys with mustard sauce, garlicky escargots, and robust monkfish Provençal. *1958 N. Damen Ave.,* ☎ *312/862–6600.*

$$–$$$ **Star Top Café.** On a busy street about midway between Lakeview and De-Paul University, this place feels almost like a grunge club with its turquoise walls, its colorful but crudely hand-painted furniture, and its dour staff, who appear to have received their courtesy training at the Department of Motor Vehicles. The outlandish Asian-Caribbean-Southwestern cuisine is magnificent. Sake-marinated beef and scallops in minted chèvre sauce are good bets. *2748 N. Lincoln Ave.,* ☎ *312/281–0997.*

$$ **Savoy Truffle.** This BYOB hole in the wall is a surprising culinary oasis set amidst a row of auto repair shops and taquerias. It has only about half a dozen tables, and there can't be more than three or four people cooking and serving. The eclectic menu is extremely inventive, however, especially the veggie dishes. Try the Roquefort cheesecake to start, then the sautéed wild mushrooms or grilled eggplant on couscous. *1466 N. Ashland Ave.,* ☎ *312/772–7530.*

$–$$ **Northside Cafe.** In between Bucktown and Wicker Park, this former neighborhood hangout now attracts yuppies (mostly straight) from all over the city. The main section, a lively old tavern, has lots of brass and dark wood; adjacent is a huge greenhouse room with a peaked roof. Traditional American pub food is on tap, and there's a major brunch scene. You can play pool, too. *1635 N. Damen Ave.,* ☎ *312/384–3555.*

$ **Busy Bee.** Punks, tourists, dykes and fags, and hefty old Eastern European women feast on pierogis, beef barley soup, and blintzes in this traditional Polish diner. It's in the heart of Wicker Park, which has always had a strong immigrant population. *1546 N. Damen Ave.,* ☎ *312/772–4433.*

Greater Downtown and Near North

$$$–$$$$ **Printer's Row.** The culinary centerpiece of the revitalized Printer's Row district, this purveyor of creatively updated regional American cuisine is a popular place for sealing deals and talking futures. Seafood and game dishes are among the many notable offerings. Dressy—save it for special occasions. *550 S. Dearborn St.,* ☎ *312/461–0780.*

$$$ **Shaw's Crab House.** Fresh fish, flown in daily from all over the country, makes Shaw's the top seafood haunt in Chicago, if not the entire Midwest. Lots of dark wood, exposed brick, and the aroma of chowder and oyster stew—very good. You feel as if you're on a New England wharf. *21 E. Hubbard St.,* ☎ *312/527–2722.*

$$–$$$ **The Berghoff.** Figures are routinely destroyed by the leaden German classics churned out at this ancient beer-and-bratwürst hall in a century-old building downtown. The Berghoff brews its own beer, and has been doing so since the repeal of Prohibition. The dining room can be stuffy, loud, and touristy, but for a real taste of old Chicago, you can't go wrong here. *17 W. Adams St., ☎ 312/427–3170.*

$$–$$$ **Frontera Grill.** This sassy Mexican restaurant filled with colorful folk art has redefined Chicago's south-of-the-border dining scene. Run by the authors of *Authentic Mexican,* Rick and Deann Bayless, it offers such regional fare as duck breast in adobo pepper sauce and turkey mole; the menu changes often. In the historic Courthouse District. *445 N. Clark St., ☎ 312/661–1434.*

$–$$ **Santorini.** This is the best of the several fine Greektown favorites—a large, lively tavern with mouthwatering tzakziki with pita bread and tender charcoal-grilled octopus. Grilled lamb and seafood dishes are star entrées. *800 W. Adams St., ☎ 312/829–8820.*

$ **Heaven on Seven.** What appears to be an ordinary luncheonette on the seventh floor of a nondescript downtown office building is actually one of the city's special gems. You can always get good, plain diner food; more to the point, however, are the many authentically rendered Cajun and Creole dishes, from gumbos to filling étouffées. It's best to come in the midafternoon, when the long lunch lines have died; closes at 5 PM daily. *111 N. Wabash Ave., ☎ 312/263–6443.*

$ **Pizzeria Uno.** By now most of America knows about the deep-dish pies at this chain pizzeria. This Uno is the original and even if it looks like all other Unos, its pizza seems just a little more flavorful, the crust a hint crispier. *29 E. Ohio St., ☎ 312/321–1000.*

Elsewhere in Chicago

$–$$ **Reza.** This cavernous dining room with varnished wood tables and a large window overlooking the street is a major Andersonville brunch scene. The Middle Eastern, Mediterranean, and Persian menu emphasizes vegetarian fare such as the *maust museer* (a tangy yogurt with shallot and dill, served with pita bread), but lamb and chicken are available, too. *5255 N. Clark St., ☎ 312/561–1898.*

$ **Heartland Cafe.** This Rogers Park compound—which includes an exotic beer bar, a general store that sells left-wing books and health food, a dining room, and a vast front patio—has long been a fixture of Chicago's countercultural scene. The menu is varied, offering lentil burgers, grilled rainbow trout, sandwiches, quesadillas, and breakfast until 3 PM. The crowd is all over the map, from activists to grungers to healthniks. *7000 N. Glenwood Ave., ☎ 312/465–8005.*

Coffeehouse Culture

Even before Chicago's coffee bar invasion reached its current fever pitch, artsy **Cafe Voltaire** (3231 N. Clark St., ☎ 312/528–3136) was staging poetry readings, exhibiting local art, and serving espresso and light munchies (foccacia pizzas, roasted-garlic pâté). Abstract hand-painted tables and brown vinyl seats that appear pilfered from a greasy spoon lend a funky air. Less artsy than other neighborhood hangouts, **Coffee Chicago** (2922 N. Clark St., ☎ 312/327–3228; 3323 N. Clark St., ☎ 312/477–3323) is clean, almost upscale, and usually filled with pretty people. These are the types who have their own espresso makers at home but come out anyway to hobnob with pals. The innovative **Halsted Street Digital/Audio Cafe** (3641 N. Halsted St., ☎ 312/325–2233), in a converted garage, sells used CDs and tapes in addition to coffee and snacks.

Kopi Café (5317 N. Clark St., ☎ 312/989–5674), in Andersonville, sells coffee, travel books, and Asian and New Age jewelry and arts and crafts to an offbeat crowd. In front is a groovy no-shoes parlor with cushions and carpeting. The "kitchen sink" cookies really do contain almost every imaginable ingredient. The enormous **Urbus Orbis** (1934 W. North Ave., ☎ 312/252–4446) occupies a converted Wicker Park warehouse with a big, central coffee bar and a scattering of plush leatherette chairs. Acid jazz fans mingle with Beat Generation wannabes. The theater next door is generally hopping with some kind of performance.

Saugatuck and Douglas, Michigan

For price ranges, *see* Chart B at the front of this guide.

$$$ **Toulouse.** In addition to having a major gay following, Toulouse is one of the finest restaurants in western Michigan. Parisian show posters line the walls of the candlelit, antiques-filled dining room. The food is delicious, from the vegan platter of pear-stuffed cabbage rolls with bell pepper-infused beurre blanc to the fresh walleye pike with lemon caper butter. The place to go for a special occasion—but sometimes tough to get a table on weekends. *248 Culver St., ☎ 616/857–1561.*

$$–$$$ **Café Sir Douglas.** The restaurant of the main gay hangout, the Douglas Dunes Resort, Café Sir Douglas has the look and feel of a standard hotel dining room with its wall-to-wall carpeting, jewel tones, and potted plants. In good weather you can dine on a covered patio. The Continental and American food is dependable, if not especially memorable. Fresh fish is your best bet. *333 Blue Star Hwy., Douglas, ☎ 616/857–1401.*

$$ **Chequers.** This festive place could pass for an English pub in the Cotswolds—it's warmly lighted and filled with British bric-a-brac and a big crowd quaffing pints of imported ales and stouts. Appropriately, the menu offers fish and chips, shepherd's pie, and bangers and mash as well as salads and sandwiches. *220 Culver St., ☎ 616/857–1868.*

$–$$ **Marro's Italian Restaurant.** With a long, attractive bar that zigzags along one wall and rows of windows looking across the street to Lake Kalamazoo, this rambling pizza-and-pasta house is a lively place to hang out. *147 Water St., ☎ 616/857–4248.*

$ **Loaf & Mug.** This is a homey, old-fashioned storefront deli with a vast array of hefty sandwiches (several of them vegetarian), a nice selection of wines, and friendly service. Pastrami on rye is a favorite. Breakfast and lunch only. *236 Culver St., ☎ 616/857–2974.*

$ **Pumpernickles.** This airy bakery is popular for breakfast and lunch, or grabbing picnic supplies for the beach. It's on a bustling corner in the heart of downtown Saugatuck, a good place for people-watching. Has a big gay following. *202 Butler St., ☎ 616/857–1196.*

$ **Uncommon Grounds.** This is about the only establishment downtown that greets patrons with a big, friendly rainbow flag over the front door—so you know you're very welcome. The staff is chatty, the coffees delicious, and the carrot cake especially tasty. The sunny deck out front is nice for ogling passers-by. *127 Hoffman St., ☎ 616/857–3333.*

SLEEPS

You won't find many minimalist, avant-garde places in old-fashioned Chicago. Jumbo cookie-cutter convention hotels prevail downtown; north of the Loop, around Michigan Avenue, you'll find a mix of stately high-end hotels and smaller European-style boutique establishments. All over town, traditional American and European antique furnishings and sedate color schemes are the rule.

Staying in the Loop means putting up with traffic noise and the trek to Lakeview's nightlife. The farther north you go above the Chicago River, the quieter the neighborhood and the shorter the distance to Lakeview. North of North Avenue, options are limited to three inns run by the extremely gay-friendly Neighborhood Inns of Chicago syndicate—these offer outstanding value and warm, personal service (*see below*).

For price ranges, *see* Chart A at the front of this guide.

Hotels

Greater Downtown

⚓ Plush to the nth degree, the **Four Seasons** is where you stay when you want to be treated like the owner of the hotel you're staying in. The staff is so attentive and personable that it's almost disconcerting. Rooms are fitted with Italian marble and handcrafted woodwork. A fancy shopping mall occupies the building's lower floors. *120 E. Delaware Pl.,* ☎ *312/280–8800 or 800/332–3442. 343 rooms. $$$$*

⚓ Sleek and refined, the Japanese-owned **Hotel Nikko** invites serenity throughout. After a back-breaking day of shopping along nearby Michigan Avenue, there's nothing more soothing than a stroll through the granite-and-black-lacquer lobby, which overlooks an ethereal rock garden. Rooms come with either American contemporary or traditional Japanese furnishings and marble baths. Nary a dust bunny in sight. *320 N. Dearborn St.,* ☎ *312/744–1900 or 800/645–5687. 421 rooms. $$$$*

⚓ Big, brash, and bustling, the **Hyatt Regency** has all the warmth of an immigration processing center. But if anonymity is your thing, you'll like it here. The location on Wacker Drive is convenient to Loop and Near North attractions and shopping, and the rooms are clean and contemporary. Very gay-friendly. *151 E. Wacker Dr.,* ☎ *312/565–1234 or 800/233–1234. 2,019 rooms. $$$$*

⚓ Chicago's **Ritz-Carlton,** which is actually a Four Seasons property, is a true stunner, perched on the floors above the high-end Water Tower Place shopping center. The atmosphere is not as stuffy as some other luxury properties in the city; afternoon tea is served in the airy, 12th-floor atrium lobby, and rooms have Chippendale-style armoires and stately wing chairs. Pretty tough to top. *160 E. Pearson St.,* ☎ *312/266–1000 or 800/691–6906. 431 rooms. $$$$*

⚓ The **Sutton Place Hotel** is a top choice of performers, models, and European jet-setters. Rather atypical in Chicago, the rooms have state-of-the-art entertainment centers (with VCRs, TVs, CD players, and radios) and a crisp black, white, and gray color scheme. Many have original Robert Mapplethorpe photos, too. *21 E. Bellevue Pl.,* ☎ *312/266–2100 or 800/810–6888. 247 rooms. $$$$*

⚓ So much attention is heaped upon the Italianate swimming pool at the **Inter-Continental** that people sometimes forget that this sumptuous two-building complex is a hotel. The pool section was built in 1929 as part of the chichi Medinah Athletic Club and later converted into a hotel (with the rooms decorated in Old World style). The other half was a hotel known as the Forum, which Inter-Continental purchased and overhauled a few years ago (with rooms done in a more contemporary vein and offered at slightly lower rates). *505 N. Michigan Ave.,* ☎ *312/944–4100 or 800/628–2112. 844 rooms. $$$–$$$$*

⚓ Just below Lincoln Park, in the tony Gold Coast residential neighborhood, the **Omni Ambassador East** is closer to New Town than most downtown properties yet still within walking distance of Michigan Avenue shopping. This intimate and courtly '20s hotel is furnished with an eclectic mix of reproductions of 19th-century antiques and newer pieces. The Pump Room restaurant is a favorite gathering spot of celebrities and bigwigs. *1301 N. State Pkwy.,* ☎ *312/787–7200 or 800/843–6664. 274 rooms. $$$–$$$$*

⛅ The **Swissôtel** may be the only property in any major American city that offers golf privileges (Dinah Shore fans may tee off at the Illinois Center Golf Course and Driving Range, next door). Guest rooms are plenty large and have marble baths. They also have doorbells, which will no doubt impress your callers. The 43rd-floor health club and pool have unbelievable skyline views. *323 E. Wacker Dr.,* ☎ *312/565–0565 or 800/637–9477. 636 rooms. $$$–$$$$*

⛅ The **Ambassador West,** across the street from the Omni Ambassador East, has similar, European-style ambience. But rooms are smaller and furnished in more basic style. Still, it's hard to beat the location and the price. *1300 N. State Pkwy.,* ☎ *312/787–3700 or 800/300–9378. 219 rooms. $$–$$$*

⛅ Free newspapers, Continental breakfast, and complimentary limo service to the Loop and Michigan Avenue make the sedate yet cozy '30s **Claridge Hotel** a Gold Coast bargain. Rooms are on the small side but tastefully decorated. *1244 N. Dearborn Pkwy.,* ☎ *312/787–4980 or 800/245–1258. 168 rooms. $$–$$$*

⛅ With doubles often going for well under $150 a night and a location just a couple of blocks from the Art Institute, the mammoth **Palmer House Hilton,** dating from the 1890s, is the Loop's top value. The lobby is impossibly ornate—note the 21 ceiling murals by Louis Rigal. Though room decor is ho-hum, there's plenty of space to kick back and relax. *17 E. Monroe St.,* ☎ *312/726–7500 or 800/445–8667. 1,669 rooms. $$–$$$*

⛅ The **Raphael** is one of those less-talked-about gems that locals recommend to visiting friends; most guest quarters have separate sitting rooms anchored by long, comfy chaise longues. Pets are accepted, too—unusual at big-city hotels. In the center of Magnificent Mile shopping. *201 E. Delaware Pl.,* ☎ *312/943–5000 or 800/821–5343. 172 rooms. $$–$$$*

⛅ A converted 1927 apartment building near the Magnificent Mile, the **Talbott** is a great choice if you're staying a while—rooms have full kitchens. Small and secure, it's popular with women. *20 E. Delaware Pl.,* ☎ *312/944–4970 or 800/825–2688. 147 rooms. $$–$$$*

North

⛅ A few blocks south of New Town is the **Comfort Inn–Lincoln Park,** a surprisingly bright, well-decorated motel that boasts its own parking lot. Continental breakfasts, and a friendly staff. *601 W. Diversey Pkwy.,* ☎ *312/348–2810 or 800/727–0800. 71 rooms. $–$$*

⛅ The deceptively named **Days Inn Near North** is actually *far* north, but that's fine if you want to be close to Boys' Town. It's a clean, low-key place with a strong gay and lesbian following. *646 W. Diversey Pkwy.,* ☎ *312/525–7010 or 800/329–7466. 121 rooms. $–$$*

⛅ Right below the Belmont Street El stop is the rambling old **City Suites,** one of the three Neighborhood Inns. It's not fancy—the decor leans toward old-fashioned wallpaper and reproduction antiques—but the place has loads of character and draws a wide range of guests, from visiting grunge rock bands to gays and lesbians who want to be steps from the bar scene. Room service is handled by Ann Sather (*see* Eats, *above*) next door. *933 W. Belmont Ave.,* ☎ *312/404–3400 or 800/248–9108. 45 rooms. $*

⛅ The **Park Brompton Inn** is an affordable, European-style hotel close to Lincoln Park and the lakeshore. Rooms are furnished with reproduction English antiques, and many of the spacious suites have refrigerators, microwaves, and wet bars. A member of the Neighborhood Inn group. *528 W. Brompton St.,* ☎ *312/404–3499 or 800/727-5108. 29 rooms. $*

☎ The most charming of the three Neighborhood Inns, the **Surf Hotel** sits on a quiet side street just steps from North Broadway's bars and restaurants. Rooms are long and narrow, fitted with spotless modern baths and reproductions of 19th-century French antiques. *555 W. Surf St., ☎ 312/ 528–8400 or 800/787–3108. 55 rooms. $*

Saugatuck and Douglas, Michigan

For price ranges, *see* Chart B at the front of this guide.

☎ An immense Queen Anne on the edge of downtown Douglas, **Kirby House** is one of the region's most striking properties with its five fireplaces, myriad stained-glass windows, and fine oak detailing. There's a pool and sundeck in the back. Don't miss the big breakfast. *294 W. Center St., Douglas, ☎ 616/857–2904. 7 rooms. Mixed gay/straight. $$–$$$*

☎ The lesbian-operated **Lighthouse Motel**, within walking distance of the Douglas Dunes disco, is pleasant and affordable. *130th St. and Blue Star Hwy., Douglas, ☎ 616/857–2271. Mixed gay/straight. 30 rooms, 26 with bath. $$*

☎ The **Moore's Creek Inn** occupies a rambling white 1873 farmhouse close to downtown. Each room has a theme, from Walt Disney memorabilia to teddy bears, and each mixes newish pieces with a smattering of antiques. Host Clif Taylor is helpful and knows a lot about the area. *820 Holland St., ☎ 616/857–2411 or 800/838–5864. 4 rooms. Mixed gay/straight. $$*

☎ The stately, brown clapboard **Newnham Suncatcher Inn** welcomes everyone but is especially popular with lesbians and same-sex couples traveling with children. The hosts treat guests like old friends, yet you're given plenty of privacy. Hot tub, pool, and sundeck are out back. *131 Griffith St., ☎ 616/857–4249. 7 rooms. Mixed gay/straight. $$*

☎ A five-minute drive from Oval Beach and Saugatuck's shops and restaurants, the rambling, 14-acre **Douglas Dunes Resort** is the region's gay ground-zero, with four bars, a restaurant, and 35 units ranging from cottages to motel rooms. Accommodations are clean and simple, with cable TV, air-conditioning, and private baths. Very friendly and well-run. *333 Blue Star Hwy., Douglas, ☎ 616/857–1401. 35 rooms. Mostly gay male/lesbian. $–$$$*

☎ One of the best values in the area is **Grandma's House B&B**, a grand Victorian on four secluded acres with all the amenities of a pricey resort. Public areas and guest rooms are comfortably furnished, and full breakfasts are served. There's a sundeck and hot tub (nudity permitted). The only drawback is the 10- to 15-minute drive from downtown shops and Oval Beach. *2135 Blue Star Hwy., Saugatuck, ☎ 616/543–4706. 5 rooms. Mixed gay male/lesbian. $–$$*

SCENES

Chicago has scads of chummy little neighborhood bars and several pockets of gay-friendly bars and clubs that are big with the grunge and alternative arts set. You'll also find warehouse discos, frisky strip joints, intimate piano bars, and everything in between. Despite the fact that the thriving gay nightlife strip in New Town is mostly male, Chicago has a better scene for lesbians than most cities. There's a terrific dyke disco and three smaller video bars. In addition, women are welcome and do hangout, to some degree, at places like Roscoe's, the Vortex, and the Gentry.

Risqué club gear and disco duds are occasionally seen on Halsted Street, but more common are collared shirts, dressy denims, and other casual sportswear. Compared with smaller Midwest cities such as St. Louis and

Milwaukee, Chicago's bar scene may seem a tad standoffish, but the gay community is still disarmingly forward and friendly. Bar greetings will seldom be met with an East Coast–style snarl or a West Coast–style glance over your shoulder. There is a perceptible ease. Still, if you're from either coast and can't stop raving about your home city, you can expect to be pilloried and stoned.

Bars and Clubs

Lakeview and New Town

Berlin. This plain-looking single-level club, a couple of blocks west of Halsted's main bar strip, was Lakeview's premier gay disco until Vortex and Spin began attracting crowds. Now its popularity varies from night to night: On weekends it gets good crowds after midnight; early in the week you're apt to see tumbleweeds rolling across the floor. You'll find a compact dance area on the left, a long video bar to the right, pink lighting, and predictable music—there's absolutely nothing wrong with it but there's nothing special about the place either. *954 W. Belmont Ave., ☏ 312/348–4975. Crowd: mixed m/f; racially diverse; under 35.*

Buck's Saloon. This is a throwback to the kind of snazzy, old-fashioned bar you might have expected to find in Chicago in the '20s. Though its layout is similar to that of Little Jim's, up the street, the mood and decor are totally different. Here, guys stand around chatting and dropping quarters in the old jukebox. Big windows allow those inside and out to ogle each other, and high ceilings and warm lighting make the place inviting. *3439 N. Halsted St., ☏ 312/525–1125. Crowd: mostly male; all ages; down-to-earth, chatty, casual; goatees, flannel shirts, and denim; a real neighborhood crowd.*

Cell Block. One of the best features of this leather-and-Levi's bar is the facade of huge one-way windows. You get a great view of the guys strolling along Halsted Street without their knowing you can see them—it's especially fun to watch them fix their hair in the reflection of the window. Inside is a large bar with several big video screens, lots of neon beer signs, and a pool table. Has fetish nights from time to time. *3702 N. Halsted St., ☏ 312/665–8064. Crowd: male, mostly over 30; lots of leather and some Levi's; some uniforms, bears and big daddies; butch and hard-core.*

Charlie's. Alas, the city's main country-western dance club, a comfy and friendly place with a neighborhood feel, is too small and more male-oriented than similar establishments in other cities. There's a little video bar off to one side, a little dance floor in the center, and a few rows of seats behind that. *3726 N. Broadway, ☏ 312/871–8887. Crowd: 80/20 m/f; 30s and up; neat mustaches and sideburns; blue denim and flannel shirts, a few 10-gallon hats; low-key.*

Gentry on Halsted. The Boys' Town branch of downtown's popular suits bar successfully brings a touch of formality to dressed-down Halsted (though you'll do fine in jeans and a T-shirt). The mood is civil but convivial. When there's no live piano music or a cabaret show, pop music hums in the background. You can sit at the long bar or on black bar stools surrounding dainty, candlelit cocktail tables. The ubiquitous exposed brick and indirect lighting round out the decor. This is definitely a place you could bring your mom to—there's even valet parking. *3320 N. Halsted St., ☏ 312/348–1053. Crowd: 80/20 m/f; over-35 with exceptions; a few suits, plenty of sweaters and khakis; artsy but coifed.*

Little Jim's. Of Halsted bars, this seems the most designed toward guys looking to pick up company for the evening—video screens showing porn and the tight quarters put everyone in a pretty willing mood. It's just a long room with a bar on one side and a long wall on the other—you lean against one side and wait for someone to walk over and punch your dance card. *3501 N. Halsted St., ☎ 312/871–6116. Crowd: male; diverse in age but leaning at mid-20s to late 30s; lots of professional oglers, touchy-feely in a rough sort of way.*

Manhole. Chicago's major leather disco is a large, rambling place with many theme nights, usually on weekends: strip shows performed by notable porn stars, "lights out" get-togethers, and underwear parties. *3458 N. Halsted St., ☎ 312/975–9244. Crowd: mostly male; mid-20s to late 30s; lots of leather and Levis but anyone dressed-down will fit in; butch.*

The North End. This is a spacious video bar, the largest attribute of which is a massive trophy case. It's not a dive but not especially glamorous either. You'll find a lot of guys playing pool here, and the North End also hosts the local mirth and girth group. *3733 N. Halsted St., ☎ 312/477–7999. Crowd: male, mostly over 35; regular guys; laid-back; semicruisy.*

Roscoe's. For several years this guppie bar has been the most reliable spot on the Halsted bar row. There's always a crowd, and it's an easy place to mingle and meet. The first room, an old-fashioned saloon, has a large central bar and the usual video screens. Off the middle bar is an outdoor patio. Yet another bar, in back, has two pool tables and, next to it, a tiny but fun dance floor that doubles as a show space for drag acts and whatnot. *3356 N. Halsted St., ☎ 312/281–3355. Crowd: 85/15 m/f; mostly 20s, early 30s; clean-shaven; hair gel galore.*

Sidetrack. Chicago's classic stand-and-model video bar. Its chief asset is the stylish decor—most notably the sparkling chrome bar counters and handsome pressed-tin ceilings throughout. The first of its three rooms is large and open with a long L-shaped bar and lots of room to mingle. The cozy enclosed patio behind it has a handsome little garden and a small center bar—it's quieter here than inside. To your right as you head inside and up a few steps is a long platform overlooking the first bar, and off it, an elegant cocktail lounge with a few tables and lots of seating at the bar. There's a different genre of music video on different nights—Tuesdays are '80s New Wave, Wednesdays are oldies, and so on. *3349 N. Halsted St., ☎ 312/477–9189. Crowd: mostly male and under 35, plus a few straight young women; guppie, clean-shaven, some not-too-severe attitude; cruisy but with manners.*

Spin. These days, this laid-back, midsize disco is the tame alternative to the Vortex: neither as stylish, intense, nor urbane. Inside there are two distinct halves: The first is a long video bar with several TV screens and a raised platform with two pool tables and big windows overlooking the cruisy intersection of Belmont and Halsted; it's warmly decorated with sconces and fancy light fixtures and the noise level promotes conversation. The second half has a small dance floor with pink lighting, a great sound system, and a small bar. "Single Dollar Sundays," when all drinks go for a buck, are always a good time to come. *800 W. Belmont Ave., ☎ 312/327–7711. Crowd: 75/25 m/f; young, white; a mix of guppies and corn-fed queerburbanites; lots of jeans and button-down shirts.*

The Vortex. Chicago's leading gay disco, a typical warehouse space with black walls and an industrial look, appears small from the outside. But it's actually fairly sizable, although the dance floor is a bit tight. The first level is centered around a bar. Behind that is the main dance floor, and behind that is a larger bar with pool tables and some seating. At a small dance bar at the back of the second level, you're likely to hear disco classics and popular dance tunes (Madonna, Real McCoy, etc.); there's a small cruise bar in the middle and a balcony in front that encircles and overlooks the action below. *3631 N. Halsted St., ☎ 312/975–6622. Crowd: 80/20 m/f; racially mixed; young, gym bods; disco bunnies; a little attitude and a lot of style.*

Annex III (3160 N. Clark St., ☎ 312/327–5969) may be the only gay bar with a neon football helmet in the window—it's a place where "bears" like to sit around talking about Bears . . . and Cubs and Bulls and Blackhawks. **Big Daddies** (2914 N. Broadway, ☎ 312/929–0922) is a festive little tavern that shows adult films and gets a mostly bearish leather crowd, plus a few urban cowboys. Bathed in pink neon, **Dandy's** (3729 N. Halsted St., ☎ 312/525–1200) is a fun piano bar popular for karaoke; there's both bar and table seating. The **Lucky Horseshoe** (3169 N. Halsted St., ☎ 312/404–3169) has male strippers nightly and never charges a cover; it's the city's top venue for watching the boys show off their toys.

Andersonville Vicinity

Big Chicks. When you first enter this spot—one of Chicago's friendliest, most diverse bars—it feels like a nice neighborhood place with a few art deco touches. But then you notice the fantastic collection of local art on the walls. Further exploration reveals video screens, darts, a minipool table, a small patio, and a great vintage jukebox with every imaginable kind of music. Big Chicks is popular with all types, especially folks from the area's many gay and lesbian sports teams. If you're alone and looking to make friends or get to know a few locals, you won't find a more genuine, sincere bunch of barflies. *5024 N. Sheridan Rd., ☎ 312/728–5511. Crowd: mostly gay; mixed m/f; mostly 30s and 40s; racially diverse; convivial; dressed-down; not at all cruisy.*

Clark's on Clark (5001 N. Clark St., ☎ 312/728–2373) is a big, dark, minimalist space that attracts a mix of men and women to shoot pool and hang out. The **Eagle** (5015 N. Clark St., ☎ 312/728–0050), which is attached to a bathhouse, is entered through an alley. The dark decor is meant to conjure up a motorcycle garage; it's big with the hard-core leather crowd. **Numbers** (6406 N. Clark St., ☎ 312/743–5772), just north of Andersonville, is a popular place to catch strippers and drag performers.

For several years the hip, gay-friendly **Smart Bar** (3730 N. Clark St., ☎ 312/549–0203) has been catering to Lakeview's dance-a-holics—it's an intentionally grimy looking place that feels like a bomb shelter inside a medieval dungeon. Thrash, house, and industrial are usually coming out of the speakers. The lively **Speedball** (4833 N. Broadway, no ☎), near Argyle Street, has dance parties many nights—look for ads in the gay papers. It generally draws an under-25, rave-oriented crowd.

Greater Downtown

Gentry. If you think the trading's heavy at the Commodities Exchange, check out the cologne-dipped suits on Chicago's corporate bar strip, Rush Street. Handsome bartenders and cocktail waiters saunter about in tuxedo shirts with green bow ties. The main room has magnificent chandeliers, ruby-hued wallpaper, and a big central bar where execs sip martinis and nosh on butter crackers and cheese dip. A back room with a black-and-chrome motif has piano music nightly. Early in the evening, about 90% of the guys are in business attire—as the hours pass, things become less dressy. *712 N. Rush St., ☎ 312/664–1033. Crowd: 90/10 m/f, wide age range, clean-cut, movers and shakers, discreet gentlemen.*

One of the best places to catch drag acts is the **Baton Show Lounge** (436 N. Clark St., ☎ 312/644–5269), which has a mixed gay and straight following. It's almost touristy, but fun just the same.

Elsewhere in Chicago

Estelle's. Although none of the clubs in Wicker Park and Bucktown is exclusively gay, the artsy but mostly straight Estelle's has a definite fag following. The jukebox is captivating, with tunes by everybody from Billie Holiday to Billy Corgan. There's a pool table in back, a long bar along the side of the room, and a fish tank with the least exotic fish you've ever seen. The bartenders are aloof to the point of being unpleasant, but that's part of the charm. *2013 W. North Ave., ☎ 312/486–8760. Crowd: 80/20 straight/gay, mixed m/f, mostly twentysomething, too cool for words; guys in black leather, black jeans; women in granny dresses; everybody wears Doc Martens.*

Also in Wicker Park, there's a big dance loft, **Red Dog** (1958 W. North Ave., ☎ 312/278–1009), that's mostly straight and big with groovy alternateens, but gays and lesbians are welcome, especially on Monday. The highly queer-friendly **Artful Dodger** (1734 W. Wabansia, ☎ 312/227–6859) has strange, colorful drinks and a similar crowd. You can dance to rock and disco classics.

Shelter (564 W. Fulton St., ☎ 312/648–5500) is mostly straight but gay-popular much of the week; on Sunday its way queer and throbbing with dancers. The crowd is young and racially diverse, the decor minimal except for the zillion Lava lamps.

Most Chicago neighborhoods have at least one gay bar that draws local dykes as well as fags. In Rogers Park, it's **Charmers** (1502 W. Jarvis St., ☎ 312/465–2811). West of I–94 on Irving Park Road are a few others: **Lost & Found** (3058 W. Irving Park Rd., ☎ 312/463–9617), an old-fashioned pub; **Visions** (3432 W. Irving Park Rd., ☎ 312/539–5229), more of a sports bar with darts, pool, and a jukebox; and **Legacy 21** (3042 W. Irving Park Rd., ☎ 312/588–9405), a combination of the two.

Women's Bars

The Closet. Although this narrow, attractive video bar draws equal numbers of men and women most nights, it's thought of as a lesbian hangout. It's almost always packed with neighborhood types, jocks, and regular Joes. It has several TV screens, darts, a pool table, warm lighting, and an outgoing staff. Famous for its Bloody Marys on Sundays. *3325 N. Broadway, ☎ 312/477–8533. Crowd: mixed 60/40 f/m; mostly 30s and 40s; low-key; equally popular with couples and singles.*

The Other Side. This small, smoky, unmarked bar on an industrial stretch of Western Avenue has a small dance floor that plays classic dance tunes, as well as a few tables and chairs, video poker, and darts. It's low-key and draws a local bunch. Has some spicy female go-go dancers on certain nights. *3655 N. Western Ave., ☎ 312/404–8156. Crowd: female; mostly 30s and 40s; some leather and Levi's; butch.*

Paris Dance. This hopping lesbian disco, tucked away in a residential neighborhood a ten-minute walk north of Lakeview, is one of the city's most stylish nightclubs. A row of porthole-style windows punctuating the facade make it look like a giant ship. Inside, there's a large, neon-lit dance floor with a top-notch sound system. Guppies gravitate toward the bar at the right of the dance floor—a bright, elegant cocktail lounge with art deco touches. A decidedly more butch crowd favors the dark video bar to the left, with its pool table, darts, and booths. *1122 W. Montrose Ave., ☎ 312/769–0602. Crowd: mostly female; mostly 20s and 30s; racially mixed; well-heeled, collegiate.*

You can take a breather down the block from Paris Dance at **Off The Line** (1829 W. Montrose Ave., ☎ 312/528–3253), a quiet local watering hole.

On the Wild Side

All over town there are baths, strip clubs, video booths, and the like, similar to those in other large cities; the most popular are around Boys' Town and Andersonville.

The **Bijou** theater (1349 N. Wells St., ☎ 312/943–5397) has several levels and private rooms; the **Ram** (3511 N. Halsted St., ☎ 312/525–9528), another popular theater, is in the heart of Boys' Town. A few blocks away is the **Unicorn** (3246 N. Halsted St. ☎ 312/929–6081) bathhouse; you can also buy porn and erotica here. Adjacent to Andersonville's Eagle is **Man's Country** (5017 N. Clark St., ☎ 312/878–2069), another bathhouse, but with more of a leather scene.

Saugatuck and Douglas, Michigan

The only game in town is the **Douglas Dunes Resort** (333 Blue Star Hwy., Douglas, ☎ 616/857–1401); it has a sizable disco, a cocktail lounge and video bar, a huge fenced-in sundeck and bar with a large pool and lush foliage, and a piano cabaret. All kinds mingle—though the crowd is almost entirely gay and lesbian.

THE LITTLE BLACK BOOK

At Your Fingertips

AIDS Foundation of Chicago: ☎ 312/922–2322. **AIDS Hotline (statewide):** ☎ 800/243–2437 (within Illinois). **Chicago Black Lesbians & Gays:** ☎ 312/871–2117. **Chicago Women's Health Center:** ☎ 312/935–6126. **Cook County Department of Public Health AIDS Hotline:** ☎ 708/445–2437. **Gerber/Hart Gay and Lesbian Library and Archives:** 3352 N. Paulina St., ☎ 312/883–3003. **Horizons Lesbian and Gay Community Services:** 961 W. Montana St., ☎ 312/929–4357. **Lesbian Community Cancer Project:** ☎ 312/561–4662. **Saugatuck Area Business Association:** Culver and Butler Sts. (information booth), Saugatuck; ☎ 616/857–3133. **Saugatuck-Douglas Convention & Visitors Bureau:** Box 28, Saugatuck, MI 49453, ☎ 616/857–1701. **Women's Place Resource Center:** ☎ 312/553–9008.

Gay Media

The **Windy City Times** (☎ 312/935–1974) is one of the city's best gay and lesbian news weeklies, with strong national and local coverage. The arts and entertainment pages are especially well-written and insightful. **Gay Chicago Magazine** (☎ 312/327–7271) is an entertainment-oriented newsweekly. The monthly newspaper **Outlines** (☎ 312/871–7610) and its weekly pocket-size bar rag, **Nightlines,** are also helpful lesbigay resources. *Outlines'* lesbian coverage is especially strong; the same publisher also puts out the monthly **Blacklines** for Chicago's gay, lesbian, bisexual, and transgender community. **Gab** (☎ 312/248–4542) is a punchy, if irreverent bar 'zine with all of the latest on clubbing and sleazing around town.

The clearly gay-friendly **Chicago Reader** (☎ 312/828–0350) is a dense weekly feast of performing and fine arts coverage, left-leaning news, and other juicy tidbits. **New City** (☎ 312/243–8786) aspires to emulate the *Reader,* but with a dash more artiness.

BOOKSTORES

In its big, spiffy new premises, the city's most popular lesbigay bookstore, **People Like Us** (1115 W. Belmont Ave., ☎ 312/248–6363) now offers a small café and computer terminals (where you can surf the gay net) in addition to its extensive selection of fiction and nonfiction, periodicals, and cards and gifts. An Andersonville landmark for more than 15 years, **Women & Children First Bookstore** (5233 N. Clark St., ☎ 312/769–9299) has a vast array of women's titles, plus music videos and magazines.

Body and Fitness

Around the Loop, the seven-floor **Athletic Club Illinois Center** (211 N. Stetson, ☎ 312/616–9000) is terrific, well-equipped, and popular with the gay community. Lakeview's **Body Shop** (3246 N. Halsted St., ☎ 312/248–7717), next to the Unicorn bathhouse, is a cruisy fitness center. The **Chicago Sweat Shop** (3215 N. Broadway, ☎ 312/871–2789) draws a better mix of men and women for aerobics and Nautilus. Plenty of space for working those buns. **Quad's Gym** (3727 N. Broadway, ☎ 312/404–7867) and the **Chicago Health Club** (2828 N. Clark St., ☎ 312/929–6900) are also good.

6 *Out in Dallas*

IN JANUARY 1995, THE DALLAS CITY COUNCIL voted to add sexual orientation and marital status to the city's already fairly comprehensive employment nondiscrimination policy. Of course, votes like this occur regularly across the country, and as many pass as fail. In Dallas, however, the 9 to 5 outcome came as a surprise. This is a conservative—some might say uptight—city, and had the option to vote on this issue been extended to the city's general population, it might never have made it. It certainly wouldn't have passed by a margin of nearly 2 to 1.

It's easy to make fun of gay Dallas. The phrases "buttoned-down" and "starched-collar" are part of the regional gay vernacular; they're used self-referentially to describe this most image-conscious and fashion-enslaved breed of Texans. Gay Dallasites have difficulty wearing their sexual orientation on their sleeves; they tend not to cut loose outside gay-friendly arenas. With this recent vote, however, Dallas's gay community may have taught the rest of us a few things about politics and about how to work in subtle ways for slow, steady change. The original antidiscrimination policy had been presented before the council without any mention of sexual orientation. Because the City Manager would not add orientation to the policy, two council members (one of them openly gay) drafted the amendment. Shortly thereafter, several gay and lesbian activists contacted individual council members and persuaded them to vote for the amendment. It's interesting that the council members least predisposed to vote in favor were never contacted—in fact, they weren't apprised of the amendment until shortly before it was brought to a vote. By then, it was too late for these few vehemently antigay members to rally public support against the amendment. The rest, as they say, is history.

So in a city where the nationally celebrated gay men's chorus goes by the nonconfrontational (and more fashionable) name of Turtle Creek Men's Chorale, successful passage of a gay-positive policy was accomplished without widespread parading and picketing. As the then president of the Dallas Gay and Lesbian Alliance, Cece Cox, commented to the gay *Dallas Voice,* "We wanted to show them that we are reasonable people asking for reasonable things."

Reasonable discourse has long had its proponents—from Plato to Booker T. Washington. There are disadvantages to keeping such a quiet profile, however. Many in the gay community are kept closeted by Dallas society's unspoken long-standing rules. Coming out is tricky and frightening; fear of reprisal can be strong. Being gay in Dallas means walking a delicate balance and can often mean trying to be the darling of straight society and the darling of gay society simultaneously, which is an exhausting act to sustain over time. It's perhaps a manifestation of the schizophrenic nature of Dallas's closet that the heart of the gay community, Oak Lawn, rubs shoulders with the city's most fashionable neighborhoods, Turtle Creek and Highland Park. It's not as though the community steals away to a ramshackle "gay ghetto" far from the hubbub of city politics, commerce, and society. On the contrary, closeted gays dance, mingle, and eat right under the noses of their most conservative neighbors, within a stone's throw of the elaborate estates that dot Preston Road.

THE LAY OF THE LAND

Many who visit Dallas, besides the hordes of conventioneers who descend on the city weekly, come to visit the site where President John F. Kennedy was assassinated or to visit Jock and Miss Ellie's ranch. When it comes to big Texas cities, Houston is actually better for sightseeing and culture, and Austin is more scenic. For better or worse, Dallas is just a hodge-podge of neighborhoods, many of them worth driving through simply to admire homes and to do some shopping.

Oak Lawn/Turtle Creek/Highland Park

Dallas's so-called Uptown, which comprises the neighborhoods of Oak Lawn, Highland Park, Turtle Creek, and McKinney Avenue, is where many Dallasites eat, shop, and live, and where a good many of them work, too. This segment of the city is a rectangle north of downtown, roughly bounded to the south by the Woodall Rogers Freeway, to the east by the Central Expressway (I–75), to the north by Mockingbird Lane, and to the west by the Dallas North Tollway.

Oak Lawn is for the most part a young, middle-class gay enclave. The hub is Cedar Springs Road, which, from the intersection with Oak Lawn Avenue up to about Knight Road, is lined with either gay-owned or gay-supported restaurants, bars, and shops (the **Tom Thumb** grocery store just north of the bars on Cedar Springs is one of the nation's cruisiest). The intersection of Cedar Springs Road and Throckmorton Road, has come to be known as "the Crossroads" of Oak Lawn; the immediate surrounding area has a fairly strong mix of genders, races, looks, and ages, though on a Saturday night it's pretty well overrun with pretty young things on the prowl. The blocks immediately east, north, and west of the Crossroads are generally residential but no less gay.

The moneyed gay community extends south of Oak Lawn Avenue into posh **Turtle Creek,** but the bulk of condos and housing developments throughout Uptown have a good share of gays and lesbians living in them. Abutting all of this gayness to the north is swank **Highland Park,** Dallas's premier residential neighborhood—a land of perfectly manicured lawns and grand mansions. **Highland Park Village** (Mockingbird La. and Preston Rd.) has upscale clothiers and boutiques, plus several good restaurants. (Good luck finding a parking space.) **McKinney Avenue,** which is in eastern Uptown and runs more or less parallel to the Central Expressway, has been revitalized in recent years. Dozens of the city's trendiest restaurants are here, and a restored trolley provides access.

Knox-Henderson

In the northeast quadrant of Uptown, another resurgence of tony shops and restaurants has sprouted along Knox Street, which becomes Henderson Street once it crosses the Central Expressway. **Knox-Henderson** takes in **Travis Walk,** a small complex containing several gay-owned or gay-frequented restaurants and boutiques. Once you hit Henderson, you'll notice several antiques shops and galleries, and a few more places to eat. This whole section borders the southern edge of **Southern Methodist University,** and a good number of college types filter through this neighborhood.

Downtown and the West End District

Like so many cities, Dallas's downtown is almost derelict most evenings. Its dramatic, space-age skyline, however (nothing to sneeze at by day, either), is positively spectacular at night—many of its building framed with streaks of neon. There's a modest **Arts District** at the northern tip of downtown, near the base of McKinney Avenue, whose sights include the **Dallas Museum of Art** (1717 N. Harwood St., ☎ 214/922–1200), which has an esteemed collection of pre-Columbian art, and the stunning, I. M. Pei–designed **Morton H. Meyerson Symphony Center** (2301 Flora St., ☎ 214/670–3600), where the Turtle Creek Chorale performs regularly.

The **West End Historic District,** anchored by the **West End Market Place** (603 Munger Ave.), is a series of early 20th-century brick warehouses and factories that have been restored in recent years to accommodate more shops, bars, and restaurants. Though you hardly need to worry about crime, this is definitely the city's least gay-friendly entertainment district.

Just south of here is **Dealey Plaza,** the triangular patch of grass where thousands congregate every year to ponder the loss of President Kennedy on November 22, 1963. Across Elm Street, along which Kennedy's motorcade was moving, is the so-called **grassy knoll,** the site that has led so many to speculate about a second gunman. And at the northeast corner of the plaza and Houston Street is the legendary **Texas School Book Depository** (☎ 214/653–6666); on the sixth floor is a museum documenting all that is known about the assassination.

Deep Ellum

Follow either Elm or Main streets east from downtown, under the I–75 overpass, to about the 3000 block, and you'll come to **Deep Ellum** (that's "Deep Elm" with a slow Texas drawl), a haven for nonconformists and alterateens. Most of conservative Dallas warns to watch your wallet and your back while walking these streets. It can in fact be a tad spooky, but no more so than similar districts in other American cities. Once Dallas's first black neighborhood, Deep Ellum is now just a blizzard of low warehouses converted into clubs and eateries, plus a few tattoo shops and art galleries. Many exterior walls are painted with elaborate murals. This is not so much a gay community as an everything-goes community, but gays (especially young ones) frequent many of Deep Ellum's establishments—or should we say *anti*establishments.

GETTING AROUND

Outside of its compact downtown, most of Dallas is what a New Yorker or Chicagoan would call the suburbs. Every house has a yard; every commercial establishment is in a shopping center; and, not surprisingly, everybody gets around by car—people in Dallas don't use mass transit and they certainly don't walk. If you're spotted on foot along any street Uptown, drivers passing by will assume you're in trouble. Little of Dallas except the downtown is laid out in a grid, and roads often change names between neighborhoods. It's best to get a detailed map. Parking near the bars in Oak Lawn can be frustrating.

EATS

Dallas has an extremely sophisticated palate, with lots of trendy bistros dreaming up inventive contemporary creations. Yet you can also find more familiar comfort food—such pseudo-exotic delicacies as fajitas and *frozen* margaritas were invented here. Burgers and barbecues are also plentiful.

Most of the city's best restaurants just happen to be in the gayest neighborhoods—northwest of downtown and in the somewhat alternative Deep Ellum. You'll also find a slew of good eateries along the northern end of Belt Line Road. Oak Lawn—especially near the Galleria—is a trendy shopping and dining area that draws a rather well-to-do suburban crowd. Hotel restaurants are also quite good here: The dining room at the **Mansion at Turtle Creek** is one of the top two or three in the country, and the restaurants at the **Adolphus** and the **Hotel Crescent Court** are also outstanding.

The very gay-friendly chain of frou-frou Italian bistros, **Sfuzzi,** began in Dallas. Of its several locations in the city, the one at 2504 McKinney is most popular. Another Dallas-based chain, the Southern-style cafeteria **Black-Eyed Pea,** is also hot, the one at 3857 Cedar Springs Road being particularly gay. There are a number of so-so restaurants around the Crossroads, notably **Panda's** and the **Good Wok** (both Chinese, the former being the best better of the two), the **Thai Lotus Kitchen,** and **Jolly's Shrimp and Oyster Bar.**

For price ranges, *see* Chart A at the front of this guide.

Uptown and Oak Lawn

$$$$ **Mansion on Turtle Creek.** There's electricity in the air of this luxurious restaurant in the old Sheppard King mansion, a splendid structure whose circular lobby has a black-and-white marble floor. Renowned nationally is the food of chef Dean Fearing, whose inventions include tortilla soup and warm lobster salad with yellow tomato salsa and jicama salad. His style is complex, the food always astonishing; if your beloved is a foodie, don't miss this place. *2821 Turtle Creek Blvd.,* ☎ *214/559–2100.*

$$$$ **Old Warsaw.** Incongruously housed inside a rather hideous building with a siding of plaster and pebbles, this windowless spot has been one of the city's swankest and most formal French restaurants for years. Expect fine china and crystal, a piano-and-violin duo, and waiters in tuxedos—it's almost a bit retro. Save room (and money) for any of the lavish dessert soufflées. *2610 Maple Ave.,* ☎ *214/528–0032.*

$$$–$$$$ **Star Canyon.** This very popular dining room is in the upscale, gay-frequented Centrum Sports Complex. It's tough to get a table here, the service can be uppity, and some complain it's overrated. It's hard to argue, though, when the kitchen turns out phenomenal dishes such as red snapper on Texas jambalaya with *chilipiquin* aioli. *3102 Oak Lawn Ave., Suite 144,* ☎ *214/520–7827.*

$$–$$$ **Bombay Cricket Club.** In a small white mansion near the Hotel St. Germain and the Crescent Court, this elegant Indian restaurant differs from many in America: The decor is bright, crisp, and sophisticated, and the menu is impeccably authentic, with every kind of curry, tandoori, and *biryani* imaginable. Lots of veggie dishes, too. *2508 Maple Ave.,* ☎ *214/ 871–1333.*

$$–$$$ **Lombardi's.** This well-liked regional chain is a bit more upscale than Sfuzzi and its recipes are more authentic. The tables are decked with the requisite red-and-white checked tablecloths, the menu is in Italian, and veal is well represented. Very romantic. *311 Market St.,* ☎ *214/747–0322.*

$$–$$$ **Parigi.** Parigi is one of the most talked about Oak Lawn eateries. The marble tables, dainty wooden chairs, and lemon-yellow and pale-blue color scheme make for a chic atmosphere. The healthful bistro menu offers many

Dallas

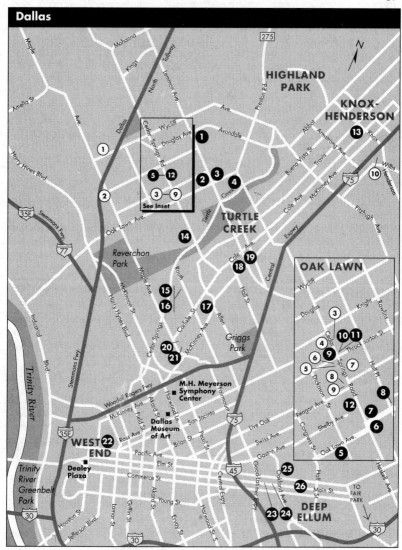

Eats ●
Bombay Cricket
Club, **21**
Bronx, **12**
Café Society, **13**
Cosmic Cup, **5**
Deep Ellem Cafe, **24**
Dream Cafe, **16**
Feed Bag, **18**
Gloria's, **1**

Hunky's, **10**
Java Jones, **7**
J. Pepe's, **15**
Lombardi's, **22**
Lucky's Cafe, **3**
Mansion on Turtle
Creek, **14**
Monica
Aca y Alla, **26**
Natura, **17**

Old Warsaw, **20**
Parigi, **8**
Sambuca, **23**
Spasso, **11, 19**
Star Canyon, **6**
Sweet Endings, **25**
That Special Blend, **9**
Yoli's, **2**
Zuzu, **4**

Scenes ○
Anchor Inn/Big
Daddy/Numbers, **3**
Brick Bar, **2**
Desert Moon, **10**
JR's, **6**
John L's, **1**
Moby Dick's, **4**
Round-Up Saloon, **7**
Sue Ellen's, **9**
Throckmorton
Mining Co., **5**
Village Station, **8**

whole-wheat pastas and delicious accents like shallot smashed potatoes and ginger-lime cream sauce. *3311 Oak Lawn Ave.,* ☎ *214/521–0295.*

$–$$$ Natura. You can't not like the entrance to this place—a pair of shockingly enormous artichoke sculptures guard the front door. With the menu comes a full nutritional analysis (calories, protein, fat, etc.) of each dish, which ranges from roast chicken and herb potatoes with field greens to grilled tuna wasabi. Gimmicky but good. *2909 McKinney Ave.,* ☎ *214/855–5483.*

$–$$ Bronx. For more than two decades the best of the gay restaurants at the Crossroads, the Bronx is still refreshingly inexpensive and untrendy. You come for the mom-style pot roast, London broil, omelets, and chicken cacciatore, and to chat with old friends. Should be called the Bronx Zoo on weekend evenings, though. *3835 Cedar Springs Rd.,* ☎ *214/521–5821.*

$–$$ Gloria's. Next to a dull T.G.I.F. on Lemmon Avenue, Gloria's is a noisy, cavernous, unromantic place with unfinished concrete floors and green plastic chairs. Nonetheless, the no-frills Mexican and South American menu is fiery and fresh, and the staff is outgoing. Yummy black bean dip. *4140 Lemmon Ave., Suite 102,* ☎ *214/521–7576.*

$–$$ J. Pepe's. Because it's in the trendy Quadrangle, the kitschy trappings of this crowded Mexican restaurant pass as stylish. The Tex-Mex is good (try the smoked brisket tacos), the margaritas better. Popular with power-lunchers. *Quadrangle, 2800 Routh St.,* ☎ *214/871–0366.*

$–$$ Lucky's Café. Lucky's is at its best late on weekend nights, especially as the bars are letting out. Of course, this is Dallas, so this diner is especially well-dressed, with art deco tables and chairs, a black-and-white tile floor, and judicious use of neon. The food is good but typical. *3531 Oak Lawn Ave.,* ☎ *214/522–3500.*

$–$$ Yoli's. The familiar A-frame exterior gives away that this was once an IHOP. Look closely though, and you'll notice that the pink trim on the roof is neon. This isn't a greasy pancake house anymore. Inside, the large fish tank anchoring the dining room tells you more about what Yoli's is famous for: Dozens of varieties of fish are served, all of the entrées under $10. *3827 Lemmon Ave.,* ☎ *214/521–9654.*

$ Dream Café. Dream Café is the place to go for breakfast anytime or for leisurely patio dining on a Saturday afternoon. There's always a great mix of people here, all of them longing for another crack at the Café's veggie-oriented menu. The buttermilk pancakes topped with ricotta are famous. Between bites, you can toss a frisbee to your dog or your date on the long green lawn out front. *Quadrangle, 2800 Routh St.,* ☎ *214/954–0486.*

$ Feed Bag. This ineloquently named restaurant with its red-and-white barn facade is a standout in its dull shopping center setting. Wagon wheels and farming equipment continue the theme inside. Feed Bag offerings are just a cut above fast food, but possibly even greasier—note that the BLT comes with six thick slabs of bacon. The cholesterol-laden burgers and fries are great. *Corner of Lemmon and McKinney Aves.,* ☎ *214/522–2630.*

$ Hunky's. A gay study in fast food on Cedar Springs Road's bar strip: Hunky waitrons skirt around tables of hunky patrons. They have the juiciest old-fashioned hamburgers here, but, in contrast to the Feed Bag (*see above*), none of the food is overly greasy. *4000 Cedar Springs Rd.,* ☎ *214/522–1212.*

$ Spasso. The branch of this local chain at Throckmorton and Cedar Springs is the gayest (and it's *quite* gay), but all of them serve the best pizza in Dallas—from traditional to white, with both mundane and exotic toppings. The dining room is warm and colorful, unusually nice for a pizza parlor. *3227 McKinney Ave.,* ☎ *214/520–6000; 4000 Cedar Springs Rd.,* ☎ *214/521–1141.*

$ ZuZu. In a swank shopping center is this ultrabright, cheerful place (part of a regional chain) where you order at the counter before plopping down into one of the festive little red chairs. The Mexican food is standard by Texas standards (which means stellar to everybody else); Mexican pizzas and margaritas are a highlight. *3848 Oak Lawn Ave., ☎ 214/521–1290.*

Deep Ellum

$$–$$$ **Monica Aca y Alla.** This is the best, and most festive, of Deep Ellum restaurants. Even yupsters in suits brave the neighborhood's eccentricities for the live music—mostly Latin-flavored jazz, salsa, and mambo—and feisty, somewhat Southwestern-inspired fare, from Mexican lasagna to pumpkin ravioli. *2914 Main St., ☎ 214/748–7140.*

$$–$$$ **Sambuca.** As bohemian—in a well-to-do sort of way—as it gets. The sign outside says MEDITERRANEAN CUISINE—JAZZ BAH, and that basically sums it up. The seats upholstered in faux-leopard skin are the highlight of the post-industrial interior. Dishes include couscous, pasta, salmon over spinach, and the like. The nightly jazz shows are renowned. *2618 Elm St., ☎ 214/744–0820.*

$$ **Deep Ellum Café.** Vietnamese chicken salad and crawfish enchiladas are a couple of the delicious, diverse dishes you can sample off this quirky menu. It's in a purposefully shabby redbrick building with teal and raspberry trim—not too cute, but artsy and innovative. *2706 Elm St., ☎ 214/741–9012.*

Coffeehouse Culture

Despite its somewhat pretentious name, **Café Society** (4514 Travis St., Suite 133, ☎ 214/528–6543) is inviting if not particularly offbeat. Its fine coffees, eclectic menu (Tex-Mex meets Provence), marble-and-tile floors, and antique furniture bring in a fairly well-heeled bunch. The dining room at the **Cosmic Cup** (2912 Oak Lawn Ave., ☎ 214/521–6157) is filled with crunchy, unconventional types perusing the small library of good-for-your-soul, New Age titles. A favorite dish is the "I hate eggplant" sandwich, which, inexplicably, requires that you eat a good bit of eggplant, along with basil, tomatoes, and mozzarella. Good juice bar. Cool and jazzy, with live music some nights, **Java Jones** (3211 Oak Lawn Ave., ☎ 214/528–2099) definitely collars Oak Lawn's collared-shirt crowd. It's the best spot for desserts in the neighborhood—scrumptious freshly made pastries and rich gelato. The sandwiches and pasta dishes are good, too. You wouldn't think the purple-haired and navel-pierced would bother with **Sweet Endings** (2901 Elm St., ☎ 214/747–8001), a cute little hangout in otherwise seedy Deep Ellum, but they seem to love it. Apparently the legendary cheesecake pulls them in. Despite its plum location midway between JR's and Moby Dick's (*see* Scenes, *below*), **That Special Blend** (4001A Cedar Springs Rd., ☎ 214/522–3726) leaves a bit to be desired in the way of atmosphere. And the cheap, white plastic lawn furniture outside doesn't help. Still, the boys and girls do linger here for hours, hoping to discover other new boys and girls.

SLEEPS

Dallas has plenty of outstanding options close to things queer. For this reason, even the stodgiest hotels are used to gay travelers, though discretion is always wise (this is Dallas, after all). Thanks to its popularity as a trade-show site, Dallas has from two to five outposts of just about every major hotel chain and a total of more than 40,000 hotel rooms. The most interesting and historic hotels (*not* the chains) offer travelers personal attention, individually designed rooms, and great restaurants—

though often at a price. The two small inns in the Oak Lawn area are very popular with the gay community.

For price ranges, *see* Chart A at the front of this guide.

Hotels

⊡ The finest downtown hotel is the grand, vintage 1912 **Adolphus**. A Beaux Arts beauty built by beer baron Adolphus Busch, the structure is widely admired by students of architecture. The only problem is that it's a good distance from the grooviest restaurants and nightlife. *1321 Commerce St.,* ☏ *214/742–8200 or 800/221–9083. 432 rooms. $$$$*

⊡ Arguably the top hotel in the country, the **Mansion on Turtle Creek** is a mere 15-minute walk to the Crossroads, has an absolutely amazing restaurant (reserve well ahead), a new state-of-the-art health club, and plush rooms in which no expense has been spared. *2821 Turtle Creek Blvd.,* ☏ *214/559–2100 or 800/527–5432. 141 rooms. $$$$*

⊡ A touch less exclusive, the **Hotel Crescent Court** is close to both downtown and Oak Lawn. It feels and looks like a European hotel, and rooms are spectacular (some are duplexes with lofts and glass dormers), all with Chanel bath amenities. If you stay here, be sure to have breakfast in the glitzy coffee shop. *400 Crescent Ct.,* ☏ *214/871–3200 or 800/654–6541. 216 rooms. $$$–$$$$*

⊡ It's only about 200 yards from the lobby of the stately, 1924 **Melrose** to most of the action on Cedar Springs Road and in Oak Lawn, and practically just across the street is the Centrum Sports Club (*see* The Little Black Book, *below*), at which guests have privileges. Rooms are nicely appointed, with ceiling fans and reproductions of antiques. *3015 Oak Lawn Ave.,* ☏ *214/521–5151 or 800/637–7200. 183 rooms. $$$*

⊡ Another more moderately priced historic property, the 70-year-old brick **Stoneleigh** is where Oliver Stone stayed while filming *JFK*. It's also close to Oak Lawn. It's convenient to many restaurants and home to the Dallas Press Club. *2927 Maple Ave.,* ☏ *214/871–7111 or 800/255–9299. 132 rooms. $$–$$$*

⊡ A bit farther afield but close to the Galleria shopping mall and Belt Line Road restaurants, the **Holiday Inn—Northpark Plaza** is just off I–75 and has an indoor pool and a decent fitness center. *10650 N. Central Expressway,* ☏ *214/373–6000 or 800/465–4329. 248 rooms. $$*

⊡ The best budget accommodation is the **La Quinta** across I–75 from Travis Walk, in the Knox-Henderson area. It's practically behind the Desert Moon bar (*see* Scenes, *below*). *4440 N. Central Expressway,* ☏ *214/821–4220 or 800/531–5900. 101 rooms. $*

Guest Houses and Small Hotels

⊡ The most luxurious of the city's small inns, the **Hotel St. Germain** is a turn-of-the-century house in southern Oak Lawn whose suites are all fitted with French and New Orleans antiques. Some of the elaborate touches include canopied featherbeds, rich tapestries, marble bedstands, balconies, fireplaces, and, in two suites, Jacuzzis. *2516 Maple Ave.,* ☏ *214/871–2516 or 800/683–2516. 7 suites. $$$$*

⊡ More affordable and attracting a mostly gay crowd, the **Inn on Fairmount** is still on a par with some of Dallas's top hotels in terms of both service and amenities. *3701 Fairmount,* ☏ *214/522–2800. 7 rooms. $$–$$$*

SCENES

Dallas's gay nightlife bubbles in small, dense pockets scattered throughout Uptown (mostly near Oak Lawn). The bars along the Crossroads are the most heavily frequented by visitors. Four of them, J.R.'s, Sue Ellen's, the Throckmorton Mining Co., and the Village Station, share the same owner, who throws a "Cruising the Crossroads" party on weekend nights: From 9 until 11, the four bars rotate for a half hour each, offering 50¢ well-drinks.

Dallas may be the only city in America where people actually dress up to go out for a beer. At Moby Dick's or Sue Ellen's, a collared shirt is almost a requirement. Outside of the Crossroads, places are more casual, particularly those clustered around Maple Avenue where it crosses below the Dallas North Tollway (most of these are leather), Fitzhugh Street where it's bisected by Travis and Cole avenues (neighborhood hangouts), and Lemmon Avenue just northwest of the Tollway (mostly local Latino bars).

In Deep Ellum, the major dance club, **Club One** (3025 Main St., ☎ 214/741–1111) is fairly straight, though gay-friendly, throughout the week; the queerest night is Friday. Likewise, most of Deep Ellum music clubs and restaurants have small to significant gay followings.

Anchor Inn/Big Daddy's/Numbers. These three bars make up what is essentially a long shopping center of gay drag and strip shows. The Anchor Inn has the strippers, and a loud, fun-loving crowd watching them; Big Daddy's has two drag shows nightly; and Numbers is just a watering hole. Because the compound is technically part of the Crossroads, you see a surprising number of suits and guppies strolling through here. *4024 Cedar Springs Rd., ☎ 214/526–4098. Crowd: male, generally older, raunchy, raucous.*

Brick Bar. Everything about the Brick Bar does seem to be brick. It's a brick-shape, painted-red brick building with glass brick windows. Most of the men have brick upper bodies—and, some would say, brick brains. The only collars you're gonna see around here are leather with silver spikes—although a certain number of preppy curiosity-seekers amble through most nights, usually in giggling gaggles. There's a good leather shop inside this labyrinthine complex, which is a short walk from a few other, slimier, leather bars. *4117 Maple Ave., ☎ 214/521–2024. Crowd: more leather than Levi's, all ages, mostly male, gruff but lovable.*

Desert Moon. The only gay bar in the up-and-coming Knox-Henderson neighborhood, this lesbian watering hole is a great alternative to the Crossroads. It's far less frenzied, and less of a scene, than Sue Ellen's, but still extremely popular. It's decorated with an array of festive colors—a bit like a Mexican restaurant—and has pool tables and a small stage for live music. There is country-western dancing here, but there's not a whole lot of space to kick up those heels. *5039 Willis Ave., ☎ 214/828–4471. Crowd: mostly female, mixed ages, friendly, laid-back, country-western.*

J.R.'s. Similar to Houston's J.R.'s, only this one is no longer the main stand-and-model venue—Moby Dick's has stolen that honor. Still, it's a splendid place aesthetically—a true "city" bar with high pressed-tin ceilings, brass bar fixtures, and high windows overlooking the Crossroads. Though not as happening as it once was, almost everybody pops in here before heading to one of its neighbors. Has a decent pub-food menu. *3923 Cedar Springs Rd., ☎ 214/380–3808. Crowd: 70/30 m/f, mixed ages, some suits, starched-shirt.*

John L's. What was once the place to find a date is now the place to take one. It's the city's prettiest and most popular gay cabaret and piano bar (it even has a strong straight following). The dim lighting and cozy seating give a soft, romantic feel. The entertainment, from your usual lounge singers to female impersonators, is top-notch (try to catch Coco, Miss Gay USA). *2525 Wycliff Ave.,* ☎ *214/520–2525. Crowd: diverse in age and gender, fat wallets and nice duds.*

Moby Dick's. Formerly a run-of-the-mill piano bar, Moby Dick's seems to have stolen the pretty-boy populace away from J.R.'s. Two floors are decked out with video screens; balconies allow bird's-eye cruising of those down below. And guys do cruise here, so relentlessly that it's rare that anyone lets his guard down long enough to meet somebody. The upstairs patio bar gives a little relief from the always-packed interior; from here you can admire the palm trees bedecked with Christmas lights out front. Great sound system; weak, pricey drinks. *4011 Cedar Springs Rd.,* ☎ *214/520–6629. Crowd: mostly male, buff and beautiful, starched-shirt, younger, a bit narcissistic.*

Round-Up Saloon. Though it may be the friendliest bar in the Crossroads, the Round-Up can still feel a bit intimidating, at least relative to other country-western bars. And perhaps because Dallas has a very good lesbian country-western club, the Desert Moon (*see above*), few women come here. It may not be the best place to *learn* how to two-step, but if you know what you're doing, join right in—these guys are good. The decor is typically Western (lots of wagon wheels). There's also a nice little room with pool tables off the main dance floor. Very welcoming staff. *3912 Cedar Springs Rd.,* ☎ *214/522–9611. Crowd: mostly male, starched-shirt, country-western, mostly in 20s and 30s, trying hard to be butch.*

Sue Ellen's. A terrific lesbian disco. In the heart of the Crossroads, this roomy club has a big dance floor, lots of booth seating, clear windows showing onto the street, and a patio out back that is packed on weekends (when it also gets its largest share of guys). The bar is well decorated and thoughtfully laid out—very conducive to chatting—and off the main room is a second section with pool tables and more seating. *3903 Cedar Springs Rd.,* ☎ *214/380–3808. Crowd: 80/20 f/m, guppies, younger, lots of lipstick and mousse.*

Throckmorton Mining Co. (TMC). Like other "Mining Companies," this one aims for a dark and forbidding leather look, but TMC is smack in the heart of the Crossroads, and it gets a lot of the same guys from J.R.'s, the Round-Up, and the Village Station. It is, nevertheless, dark, smoky, and devoid of ambience. One nice touch: peanuts served out of huge beer vats. *3014 Throckmorton St.,* ☎ *214/380–3808. Crowd: mostly guys, more Levi's than leather but some of both, a few guppies, lots of bears, wide mix of ages.*

Village Station. It's had other names, it's been burned to the ground, and at times it's been a fairly shaggy dive. Now rebuilt in concrete, it's more crowded. It's also much roomier inside than you might think (larger, some joke, than Dallas–Ft. Worth Airport): There's a room with go-go dancers, the neighborhood's nicest patio bar, and a stage for drag shows (some of the best in the country). Saturday nights are the most popular. Cover most nights. *3911 Cedar Springs Rd.,* ☎ *214/380–3808. Crowd: just about anybody who parties around the Crossroads; generally younger, male, and well dressed, but the many exceptions define the rules; significant racial mix.*

Two more bars close to the Crossroads are **Jugs** (3810 Congress St., ☎ 214/ 521–3474), a mid-size women's pool hall and dance club that's racially diverse, and the tiny **Side 2 Bar** (4006 Cedar Springs Rd., ☎ 214/528–2026), which is, oddly, in the middle of things, right next to Hunky's, and draws a cross-section of dykes and fags.

East of Oak Lawn, across Turtle Creek, Fitzhugh Avenue leads to a few spots popular primarily with older guys who find the Crossroads attitude a bit of a turnoff. Despite the fact that it's an unattractive bar in the Mr. M Foods shopping center, the male **Crews Inn** (3215 N. Fitzhugh Ave., ☎ 214/526–9510) is probably the most popular of the bunch. The slightly dreary **Hideaway Club** (4144 Buena Vista St., ☎ 214/559–2966), whose patio is lit with trillions of lights and colors, is the city's non-uppity piano bar (some women). **Pub Pegasus** (3326 N. Fitzhugh Ave., ☎ 214/559–4663), your quintessential neighborhood dive, has occasional piano entertainment, a lovely neon Pegasus sign inside, and friendly bartenders. **Zipper's** (3333 N. Fitzhugh St., ☎ 214/526–9519) features male strippers nightly.

Near the Brick Bar (*see above*) are several rough-and-raw bars: **Backstreet** (4020 Maple Ave., ☎ 214/522–4814) is right across the street from the Brick.

The only bar near downtown, the **Trestle** (412 S. Haskell St., ☎ 214/826–9988) is a gnarly hustler bar, which gets raided often, in a dicey neighborhood.

THE LITTLE BLACK BOOK

At Your Fingertips

AIDS Hotline: ☎ 214/263–2437. **AIDS Resource Center Hotline:** ☎ 214/559–2437. **AIDS Services of Dallas:** ☎ 214/941–0523. **Dallas Convention and Visitors Bureau:** 1201 Elm St., Suite 2000, 75270, ☎ 214/746–6677 or 800/232–5527. **Gay and Lesbian Community Center:** 2701 Reagan St., ☎ 214/528–9254. **Lesbian Visionaries:** ☎ 214/521–5342, ext. 844. **Oak Lawn Community Services** (referrals, counseling, and medical services): ☎ 214/520–8108.

Gay Media

Dallas has no shortage of gay papers, all of them quite useful and well-written. The **Dallas Voice** (☎ 214/754–8711) is a weekly news and entertainment magazine. **Maleman** (☎ 713/527–9111) is a gay-male, Houston- and Dallas-oriented bar rag. **This Week in Texas** (☎ 713/527–9111), an entertainment-oriented magazine covering the whole state, has plenty of stuff on Dallas. The **Texas Triangle** (☎ 713/871–1272) is a mostly news-oriented weekly newspaper. There's also a gay arts and news monthly for neighboring Tarrant County (Ft. Worth), the **Alliance News.**

Good mainstream resources include the **Dallas Observer** (☎ 214/757–9000), an alternative-scene arts-and-entertainment monthly; and the youthful **Met** (☎ 214/696–2900).

BOOKSTORES

The major lesbigay bookstore, **Crossroads Market** (3930 Cedar Springs Rd., ☎ 214/521–8919) is a busy place that has an extensive selection of lesbian and gay titles, plus gifts, cards, and porn mags. Just up the street, the **Lobo/After Dark Bookstore** (4008 Cedar Springs Rd., ☎ 214/522–1132) is basically an adult, gay-male bookstore with a few mainstream titles.

Body and Fitness

The **Crossroads Gym** (4001 Cedar Springs Rd., ☎ 214/522–9376) is an incredibly gay scene—some might argue that it's a better place to pick people up than to work out. Bigger and better is the renowned **Centrum Sports Club** (3102 Oak Lawn Ave., ☎ 214/522–4100).

7 *Out in Denver*

With Aspen

A FEW YEARS AFTER COLORADO RESIDENTS voted the controversial and antigay Amendment 2 into law, a relative calm has descended upon the community. As you walk down the streets of Colorado's largest city, visiting gay bars, chatting with locals, reading the gay papers, it's hard to believe things were in such a state of flux just a short while ago.

The passage of the amendment swiftly drew lines in Denver, in Colorado, and throughout the nation. A lawsuit was immediately filed on behalf of opponents to the amendment, which had called for an across-the-board ban on all local or statewide laws protecting persons against discrimination of employment, housing, and public accommodation on the basis of their sexual orientation. Within a couple of days, a comprehensive plan was put into place by both the local and national gay community calling for a boycott on travel to Colorado, and on purchasing goods or paying for services provided by Colorado companies.

The majority of those who voted in favor of the amendment stood ardently behind their decisions. How many of these persons would overtly condemn homosexuality is unclear. Much talk centered on the confusing language of the amendment, suggesting that a significant number of people may have voted as they had not intended. Others stood behind their decision to strike down what they perceived to be laws extending "special privileges" or "favoritism" to persons based on who they happened to be attracted to. Their common justification seemed to be: "I don't have any problem with what people do in their own bedrooms, but I don't feel these activities should earn them entitlements denied to the rest of us." Still others stood on the simple principle that the government has too much say in our day-to-day decision-making, and antidiscrimination ordinances, well-intended or not, contribute to the bureaucracy.

Why Amendment 2 passed is a difficult question. But the fact is the ruling has done more than draw indelible lines between gays and intolerant straights, between the religious right and the liberal left—it has drawn profound lines among different schools of thought *within* the gay community. The question of whether or not to boycott Colorado, for how long and how, created the most significant rift. Plenty of gays and lesbians took it upon themselves to cancel leisure trips to the state and, in extreme cases, to discontinue business with Colorado firms.

Ironically, had the cities of Aspen, Boulder, and Denver never passed laws protecting gays in the first place, nobody would have introduced legislation to repeal them, and the rest of us would never have needed to consider a boycott. There are a number of states in America that have never had to introduce an amendment similar to Colorado's, for the simple reason that no local antidiscriminatory laws exist to be repealed.

Though no official whistles had been blown, no gongs had sounded, the boycott of Colorado had fizzled out by 1994. As early as January 1993, when Colorado judge Jeffrey Bayliss placed a restraining order on the state preventing it from enforcing the amendment, many gays and lesbians resumed travel to Colorado. As the months passed and the amendment fell out of the spotlight, efforts to boycott the state were dropped by virtually everybody.

Did the boycott work? Again, the answer to this is hotly debated. Colorado had a booming ski season in 1993, thanks to heavy snowfall, so tourism was not significantly affected. A spokesperson for the Denver Convention and Visitors Bureau claimed that very few organizations canceled functions in 1993. However, the boycott did affect convention bookings for a few years down the road—many companies that had been considering Denver as a site in 1996 or 1997 chose other locations. There are plenty who claim the boycott was a success, if for no other reason than that it rallied widespread national support for quashing the amendment.

Unfortunately, while attention from those opposed to Amendment 2 had turned quietly to other controversies in other states, supporters of the amendment had been quietly preparing to defend it during its appearance before the U.S. Supreme Court in the fall of 1995. Of about 500 cases presented before the court during one session, the case known officially as *Evans vs. Romer* was chosen to be tried. The court's decision (due by July 1996) will have broad and serious ramifications on similar battles raging elsewhere. Do gays and lesbians have civil rights? Does Amendment 2 prohibit gays and lesbians from participating in the political process? Nine Supreme Court justices will decide—and the residents of Denver, gay and straight, are in agreement on one thing: It's gonna be a close one.

THE LAY OF THE LAND

Contrary to popular belief, Denver is not *in* the Rocky Mountains, but just east of them. True, it is a mile above sea level, but it is nonetheless flat as can be. Of course, immediately west of the city limits, the foothills of the Continental Divide begin their magnificent, sharp ascent. Barring poor visibility, the mountains are a constant fixture of Denver's western skyline.

As weather systems cross the Continental Divide west to east, dumping several feet of snow at a time, they reach Denver largely worn out and packing very little punch. For this reason, winters here are milder than in most northern U.S. cities, and though it snows often in late winter and early spring, the precipitation usually melts by midday. Denver has more than 300 sunny days annually, more than either Florida or southern California.

Like most flat cities, Denver is laid out largely in a grid pattern. Broadway is the major north–south axis, Colfax Avenue the major east-west one; the latter extends for miles in either direction, is lined with drab carpet stores and auto parts dealers, and may very well be the ugliest road in America. The northwest quadrant of the city is the most densely developed of the four, and it's where Denver started, when gold was panned in 1859 at the confluence of Cherry Creek and the South Platte River. The streets of this oldest section of Denver, though still in a grid plan, actually run at about a 45° angle to the rest of the city's streets. The other major thoroughfare in Denver, Speer Boulevard, runs diagonally through the city, for the most part straddling Cherry Creek.

Downtown

There are pockets of stunning Victorian and turn-of-the-century residential and commercial architecture throughout the city, but on the whole, Denver's facade is rather ordinary. The downtown skyline is punctuated by 16 skyscrapers, built mostly during the energy boom of the late '70s and early '80s.

Nevertheless, there's a fair amount to see downtown. Highlights include the estimable **Trianon Museum and Art Gallery** (335 14th St., ☎ 303/623–0739), whose strengths are 18th-century European paintings, decorative arts, and home furnishings; the **D&F Tower** (16th and Arapahoe Sts.), a 325-foot replica of the campanile of St. Mark's in Venice; and the new (1995) 10-story **Denver Public Library** (10 W. 14th Ave. Pkwy., ☎ 303/640–6200), a $64 million wonder with a three-story atrium crossed by pedestrian overpasses, turrets, and rotundas, and an art collection with originals by Thomas Moran, Frederic Remington, and Albert Bierstadt. (Denver has the most library-card holders per capita of any major U.S. city.)

In 1982, 16th Street was closed between Market Street and Broadway and transformed into a mile-long **pedestrian mall,** which, in 1995, was expanded two more blocks into LoDo (*see below*). Most of the shops and restaurants along here are on the touristy side, but it's an attractive commercial promenade. The hip boutiques and restaurants at Victorian **Larimar Square** (Larimar and 15th Sts.) are peopled with a more colorful, local crowd.

In 1995, when **Elitch Gardens** (☎ 303/595–4386) moved from the burbs to a 67-acre plot of land by the Platte River, Denver's downtown became the first in America to have its own major amusement park. Elitch's has all the usual rides and diversions, and once a year a "gay day" is held at the park, when legions of screaming queens cut loose aboard the *Twister II* roller coaster and other dizzying rides. A bad hair day is enjoyed by all.

Lower Downtown (LoDo)

Larimar Square marks the beginning of downtown's considerably more dapper sister, **LoDo,** which is bounded to the north by the train tracks, to the east by 20th Street, to the south by Market Street, and to the west by 14th Street. LoDo was Denver's original shipping and retail center, but as recently as 10 years ago, this section had been reduced to slums and abandoned brick warehouses. LoDo's comeback began when artists started converting these classic redbrick buildings into galleries and studios. A flood of restaurants, coffeehouses, and shops followed, but, as rents have risen, many of the fringe establishments have been pushed out in favor of more mainstream ventures and brew pubs. **Coors Field,** a stadium designed to replicate the quirky old ballparks of years past, is the home of baseball's Colorado Rockies.

Capitol Hill and Cheeseman Park

The residential neighborhood south and east of Capitol Hill (which is at the intersection of Colfax Avenue and Broadway) is the closest thing Denver has to a gay ghetto. It's bordered by Colfax Avenue to the north, York Street to the east, 1st Avenue to the south, and Broadway to the west.

The century-old, Federal Revival **State Capitol** (1475 Sherman St., ☎ 303/866–2604), Denver's centerpiece, is capped with a magnificent dome that was built with more than 200 ounces of gold leaf. Nearby are the **Colorado History Museum** (1300 Broadway, ☎ 303/866–3682), which traces the region's gold-mining past; the **Denver Art Museum** (100 W. 14th Ave., ☎ 303/640–2793), whose Native American holdings are the most extensive in the world; and the **U.S. Mint** (W. Colfax Ave. and Cherokee St., ☎ 303/844–3582), where you'll see money . . . lots of it.

Lovely **Cheeseman Park,** which is most easily accessed from Race Street, 9th Avenue, or 12th Avenue, is surrounded by a gradually gentrifying neighborhood of century-old homes. The Pavilion on the east side of the park has outstanding views of the mountains west of Denver (and a notoriously cruisy parking lot). Also part of the park is the **Denver Botanic Garden** (1005 York St., ☎ 303/331–4000).

Southeast of here, the **Cherry Creek Shopping District** is Denver's upscale playground for browsing and spending. There's the Cherry Creek Mall, at 1st Avenue and Milwaukee Street, which has all the usual high-end suspects, plus a little network of boutiques, eateries, and galleries north of 1st Avenue, opposite the mall, called Cherry Creek North.

Denver International Airport

Perhaps no airport in the world had been more anxiously awaited, more aggressively promoted, and more sharply ridiculed than **DIA (Denver International Airport),** which opened late and severely over budget in February 1995. Denverites yammer about it constantly, some with pride, others in horror. The airport is enormous. Its peaked Teflon roof is shaped to resemble the 34 peaks of the Rockies, its terminals are filled with high-end shops, and luggage (despite promises that DIA's baggage-transportation system is revolutionary) seems about as likely as it's ever been to be reunited on time with its rightful owner. In the end, DIA is an airport—little more, nothing less.

Boulder

The vibrant town of **Boulder** is about an hour's drive northwest of Denver, and if you have a free day, it's definitely worth a visit—perhaps even an overnight. A funky, eco-sensitive college community, Boulder is a cycling and hiking mecca, has as diverse and trendy a selection of shops and eateries as any Colorado city, and is extremely gay-friendly. A few good Boulder resources include the **Boulder Convention and Visitors Bureau** (2440 Pearl St., 80302, ☎ 303/442–2911 or 800/444–0447); **Word is Out** (1731 15th St., ☎ 303/449–1415), the lesbigay book, music, and gift shop; and **The Yard of Ale** (2690-C, 28th St., ☎ 303/443–1987), the popular gay and lesbian bar.

Aspen

Of the numerous ski resorts that straddle the Continental Divide, Aspen has the most striking setting and inhabitants. You'll be charmed by the grid of neatly preserved 19th-century buildings. You'll be blown away by the 360° curtain of 14,000-foot mountains. You'll be just as astounded by all the townspeople who are ever so tan, trim, and beautiful. The pages of *GQ* and *Vogue* spring to life here.

Unlike Vail, a synthetic creation of the 1960s, Aspen is a delightful Victorian mining town still crisscrossed by rows of redbrick shops and clapboard homes. Skiing is but one, albeit its most impressive, strength. Summer is lush with wildflowers and a perfect time to trade in your ski gear for hiking boots or to test your fly-fishing skills on the Roaring Fork and Frying Pan rivers. The season also brings major music, food, and dance festivals. Indeed, the recent boom in warm-weather tourism has caused "off-season" hotel rates to approach the levels of those in peak season.

Of the ski towns in Colorado, Aspen is the warmest in its embrace of gays and lesbians. It has had an antidiscrimination law on the books longer than any town in the state, and residents gay and straight have always railed vociferously against the infamous Amendment 2. Arguably the country's most famous lesbian, Martina Navratilova, calls Aspen home, and part-time Aspen resident Barbra Streisand was a loud proponent of the boycott. And although two other North American ski towns now hold them, Aspen is home to the original, the fantastic, the coolest (literally) homo gathering in the world, Gay Ski Week. Information on this event can be obtained by contacting the **Aspen Gay Community** (☎ 970/925–9249).

GETTING AROUND

Denver's Light Rail System will get you to and from some of the museums and tourist sights, as will the Cultural Connection Trolley. Neither of these systems is extensive, though. For public transportation throughout the metro area and even up to Boulder, you can use the city's Regional Transportation District bus system, but most visitors find it inconvenient and slow. Taxis are available by phone.

EATS

Denver is a solid dining city, with strong representatives of many ethnic cuisines and a blossoming New American scene. LoDo has a good number of trendy, youthful places, and Pearl Street, in South Denver, has recently attracted some hip restaurants. Like most western cities, informality is the rule—even at the fanciest restaurants. Several of the gay bars have restaurants, the best of which are **Charlie's** and the **Grand**.

Denver

For price ranges, *see* Chart B at the front of this guide.

$$$–$$$$ **Denver Buffalo Co.** Touristy, with its own gift shop, but fun and a genuinely Denver thing to do. The buffalo used in everything from buffalo chili to buffalo sausage are raised on a nearby farm, ensuring freshness. The top steak dishes are costly but delicious. Has some chicken and fish dishes, too, but, disappointingly, no buffalo ice cream. *1109 Lincoln St.,* ☎ *303/832–0880.*

$$$–$$$$ **Zenith.** A popular choice of movers and shakers, Zenith is cutting edge in both its contemporary look and creative Southwestern cuisine. Favorites include duck with cilantro and corn sauce and venison with caramelized apples. One of the few Denver restaurants where you'll want to dress fashionably, though not formally. *1750 Lawrence St.,* ☎ *303/820–2800.*

$$–$$$$ **McCormick's Fish House and Oyster Bar.** Part of the wonderful Oxford Hotel, McCormick's and the hotel's two bars have the best seafood menu in town. At happy hour, several items, including excellent fish tacos and clam chowder, are available for next to nothing. *1659 Wazee St.,* ☎ *303/825–1107.*

$$–$$$ **Greens.** Exposed brick, hardwood floors, and warm lighting help make Greens one of Pearl Street's most elegant and popular eateries. The moderately priced, vegetarian-oriented menu is outstanding, and there's also a long wine list. You can get a nice steak here, too, but the name of the place reveals what it does best. *1469 S. Pearl St.,* ☎ *303/744–1940.*

$$–$$$ **Sushi Den.** This is the place to go for fresh sushi, not to mention great Japanese steak and chicken dishes. It's set in a toasty dining room on Pearl Street, with exposed brick, high ceilings, contemporary hanging lights, and sleek furnishings. Very trendy. *1487 S. Pearl St.,* ☎ *303/777–0826.*

$$ **Wazee Supper Club.** This classic LoDo redbrick Victorian houses a popular pre-disco restaurant, where jazz is piped over the sound system and terrific pizzas and creative overstuffed sandwiches are served. Outstanding beer selection. Very gay. *1600 15th St.,* ☎ *303/623–9518.*

$–$$ **Basil's.** A hub of South Broadway's gay social scene, Basil's is equally popular with the rest of the city. Prices are low, the pasta is made fresh daily, and the staff is lively and outgoing. *30 S. Broadway,* ☎ *303/698–1413.*

Denver

$–$$ **City Spirit Cafe.** Pee Wee Herman would feel at home at this beer hall and pub decorated like his wacked-out Playhouse, with bright colors and crudely shaped furnishings. A mixed bag of students, alternateens, and artsy types comes here to munch on the cheap pasta dishes and grills. *1434 Blake St.,* ☎ *303/575–0022.*

$–$$ **Mercury Cafe.** It's hard to characterize the Mercury: It's equal parts café, coffeehouse, music hall, and theater. Something odd is always going on here, and many of the events and performers are gay-oriented. Crunchy, New Age cuisine—tofu, fish grills, salads—is served throughout the day. *2199 California St.,* ☎ *303/294–9258.*

$–$$ **Racine's.** Often referred to as "gay screams," which are all you'll hear during Sunday's chaotic brunches, Racine's is also a favorite for power breakfasts and filling lunches. The food is just a cut above standard diner offerings, the few Mexican choices being among the best. *850 Bannock St.,* ☎ *303/595–0418.*

$–$$ **Rock Bottom.** Though it was voted the best hetero pick-up spot by readers of a local Denver newspaper, Rock Bottom is fairly big with the gay community, too. It's one of several great local microbreweries, which are all the rage in Denver these days. Good pub grub, such as fish (salmon) and chips. *1001 16th St.,* ☎ *303/534–7616.*

$–$$ **Wynkoop Brewing Company.** A short walk from Coors Field baseball stadium, the Wynkoop is the most popular of the city's microbreweries— and probably the most gay-popular. It's a huge place with a varied menu, an upstairs pool hall, and a viewing area downstairs, where you can examine the vats. Older, mellower crowd. *1634 18th St.,* ☎ *303/ 297–2700.*

$ **Benny's.** Exceedingly gay and fun, Benny's outdoor patio and neon-signed indoor dining room are the places to dish about last night or plan for tonight. The food is good but the atmosphere brings in the crowds. *301 E. 7th St.,* ☎ *303/894–0788.*

$ **Blue Bonnet Cafe.** This distinctive art deco restaurant is a short distance from the frumpy South Broadway gay bars. Come here for the best and most healthful Mexican food in Denver (no lard is used) and great margaritas. Expect a line on weekends. *457 S. Broadway,* ☎ *303/778–0147.*

$ **Goodfriends.** This cheap and cheerful local tavern well east of downtown is a good spot for a meal if you're heading toward any of the bars along Colfax, or if you're simply looking for a place to eat and meet people. The staff is friendly, and lesbians and gays love it. Try the catfish, burgers, onion rings, or many veggie dishes. *3100 E. Colfax Ave.,* ☎ *303/399–1751.*

$ **Pasquinis.** Near B. J.'s Carrousel, this old-fashioned storefront pizza parlor has been a South Denver institution for many years (they also run the phenomenal Campagna's bakery down the street). There's often live music here. *1310 S. Broadway,* ☎ *303/744–0917.*

Coffeehouse Culture

A look at the young, bookish crowd at LoDo's **St. Mark's Coffeehouse** (1416 Market St., ☎ 303/446–2925) suggests roughly who Dan Quayle was referring to when he railed against America's intellectual elite. Cozy and warm with ragged exposed brick. **Java Creek** (287 Columbine St., ☎ 303/377–8902) is a good place to cool your heels after a day of shopping in Cherry Creek; this loud and colorful lesbian-owned coffeehouse has live music many nights, good food, and the usual impressive array of flavored drinks. **Full of Beans Espresso** (1 N. Broadway, ☎ 303/778– 1826) is a spare little coffee bar with good food in the heart of South Broadway's gay bar district. With blond Windsor chairs and a bright decor, it's uncharacteristically cheerful for the area. Try the turkey pesto sandwich.

Denver's premier people-watching coffeehouse, the **Market** (1445 Larimar St., ☎ 303/534–5140) has a lively patio out front devoted to this very activity. A real scene, drawing a sophisticated bunch. At the **Newsstand Cafe** (630 E. 6th Ave., ☎ 303/777–6060), you can buy a magazine (many gay titles), sip a *latte*, chat up your neighbor, order a turkey and provolone sandwich, and watch the buzz of pedestrian traffic outside on 6th Street. There are tables and counter stools along the window, but often you have to wait a bit for a seat.

Aspen

For price ranges, *see* Chart A at the front of this guide.

$$$$ **The Restaurant at the Little Nell.** This European-style hotel restaurant is perfect for special occasions, with its white linen napery, beautiful still lifes, oversize armchairs, and lots of orchids and crystal. Chef George Mahaffey offers what he calls American alpine cuisine—grilled tuna steaks, elk tenderloin, mustard-coated trout. *675 E. Durant St.,* ☎ *303/920–6330.*

$$$$ **Syzygy.** Of the many outstanding, expensive restaurants in town, trendy Syzygy is a hot spot for drinks, and a big to-do for dinner. With a sleek decor of peach and black, refined service, and an innovative menu that combines the best of Asian, Southwestern, and French cuisines, a meal here is a memorable way to cap off Gay Ski Week. *520 E. Hyman Ave.,* ☎ *970/925–3700.*

$$$–$$$$ **Renaissance.** If a special dinner is in order, consider this seductive stunner, an abstract take on a sultan's tent. Chef-owner Charles Dale honed his skills under New York City celebrity chef Daniel Boulud, and such dishes as striped bass with fennel-tomato marmalade and ravioli with pistachio pesto don't disappoint. *304 E. Hopkins St.,* ☎ *303/925–2402.*

$$$ **Kenichi.** Although the sushi bar here is a parade of glamorous ski bunnies, this establishment is celebrated as much for its fresh raw delicacies as for its pretty faces. The soft-shell crabs and spicy Japanese rack of lamb are also outstanding. *533 E. Hopkins St.,* ☎ *970/920–2212.*

$$–$$$ **Campo di Fiori.** Urbane, northern Italian bistro fare is generously represented in Aspen, and Campo di Fiori is the pick of the litter. Set in a small courtyard of upscale shops, this warmly lit café is the right spot for swapping ski tales or setting the tone for a romantic evening. The hearty risottos, such as the one tossed with brandy-flambéed shrimp, are recommended. *205 S. Mill St.,* ☎ *970/920–7717.*

$$ **Little Annie's.** In a town whose restaurants strive more for cosmopolitan flare than for ski bum sincerity, it's refreshing to stumble into this slightly divey, always toasty tavern decked with red-checked tablecloths and wood-paneled walls. Burgers, ribs, fresh brook trout, and lamb are the specialties—nothing fancy here. *517 E. Hyman Ave.,* ☎ *970/925–1098.*

$ **Alley Cafe.** It's a small town. All day you keep running into the object of your affection, but by the time you muster up the courage to ask dream date out for a bite, the bars have closed. What to do? Pop over to this minuscule café that brews Aspen's finest coffees and is open 24 hours. There are salads, soups, and sweets, too. *417 E. Hopkins St., Caribou Alley,* ☎ *970/544–0825.*

$ **Explore Bistro.** Tucked in the second-floor garret amid the stacks of Explore Books, this charming café has a great vegetarian lunch and dinner menu of pastas, sandwiches, and salads. *221 E. Main St.,* ☎ *970/925–5336.*

$ **Pour La France.** Happy, warm, and bright, Pour La France's big plate-glass windows capture the morning sunlight, and its fancy coffees, fluffy egg dishes, and flaky French pastries nourish the soul. For some people, a day on the slopes just can't happen without first fueling up here. There are good soups and sandwiches for lunch, too. *413 E. Main St.,* ☎ *970/920–1151.*

SLEEPS

Most of Denver's hotels are downtown or in LoDo, two of the most desirable neighborhoods for window-shopping, bar-hopping, and seeing the city. There are a few historic properties here, but for the most part, Denver's hotel selection is similar to what you'll find in other cities. Two good B&Bs are in the largely gay Cheeseman Park neighborhood, too.

Denver

For price ranges, *see* Chart B at the front of this guide.

Hotels

☏ Denver's best known luxury hotel, the **Brown Palace** is popular with celebrities and politicians. Built in 1892, the nine-story lobby alone is worth a peek: It's crowned with a stained glass ceiling. The formal rooms have a mix of turn-of-the-century and Art Deco decor. *321 17th St., ☏ 303/297–3111 or 800/321–2599. 230 rooms. $$$–$$$$*

☏ A more personable choice is the **Oxford Hotel,** built a year before the Brown Palace by the same designer. The Oxford's rooms are less sumptuous but no less authentically Victorian, and the splendid public areas really put this hotel above others—especially considering the rates. The Art Deco Cruise Bar, for example, should not be missed, and McCormick's Fish House and Oyster Bar is one of the best restaurants in town. The Oxford also has a great spa. *1600 17th St., ☏ 303/628–5400 or 800/228–5838. 81 rooms. $$–$$$$*

☏ Showing a few signs of wear, the 1966 **Warwick Hotel** is nonetheless a perfectly civilized downtown business hotel with large, plain but comfortable rooms. It's just a couple blocks from the Uptown Saloon, the Grand, and several good restaurants. Denver's Playboy Club used to occupy the top floor. *1776 Grant St., ☏ 303/861–2000 or 800/525–2888. 194 rooms. $$–$$$$*

☏ Without question, the **Comfort Inn Downtown** is the best bargain in the city. It used to be the modern half of the Brown Palace, which is practically next door, and has large, nicely furnished rooms. *401 17th St., ☏ 303/296–0400 or 800/221–2222. 229 rooms. $*

Guest Houses

☏ One of the more dramatic dwellings in Denver is the turreted stone-and-wood **Castle Marne,** a Romanesque mansion (1889) three blocks from Cheeseman Park. Rooms are ornately done with period antiques. *1572 Race St., ☏ 303/331–0621 or 800/926–2763. 9 rooms. Mixed gay/straight. $$–$$$$*

☏ Less impressive but equally inviting is the **Victoria Oaks Inn,** a restored turn-of-the-century Victorian mansion just across the street from Castle Marne. *1575 Race St., ☏ 303/355–1818 or 800/662–6257. 9 rooms. Mostly gay/lesbian. $–$$*

Aspen

Given the high cost and demand for rooms here, you may want to book through **Aspen Central Reservations** (☏ 800/262–7736), which can also arrange short-term rentals at private homes and condos.

For price ranges, *see* Chart A at the front of this guide.

Hotels

☏ The most charming high-end property is the renovated, historic **Hotel Jerome,** which was built at the height of the city's 1880s silver boom. Amenities and decor leave nothing to be desired, yet the hotel retains a warm, old-fashioned air, set by tiled fireplaces in public areas and authentic

Victorian papers, fabrics, and fixtures in the unusually big guest rooms. *330 E. Main St.,* ☎ *970/920–1000 or 800/331–7213. 93 rooms. $$$$*
☷ Though relatively new, the **Little Nell** is just as dignified as the Hotel Jerome; moreover, it's the only ski-in/ski-out property in town. A few standards here are gas fireplaces, down-filled sofas, and stunning marble baths. *675 E. Durant Ave.,* ☎ *970/920–4600 or 800/525–6200. 92 rooms. $$$$*
☷ Rooms don't come cheaply at the **Snowmass Lodge & Club,** which is a 10-minute drive from Aspen, but you can take advantage of the extensive facilities, including 11 tennis courts, a championship golf course—on which you can cross-country ski in winter—and a complete fitness center. The rooms are spacious and have decks or balconies that overlook the slopes. *Snowmass Club Cir., Snowmass Village,* ☎ *970/923–5600 or 800/525–0710. 76 rooms, 60 villas. $$$*

Inns

The **Hotel Lenado** (200 S. Aspen St., ☎ 970/925–6246 or 800/321–3457; 19 rooms; $$$) and the **Sardy House** (128 E. Main St., ☎ 970/920–2525; 14 rooms, 6 suites; $$$) are two outstanding small inns managed by the same company. The former has more of a lodge feel, the latter is done with ornate Victoriana. Both are centrally located and unabashedly romantic.

The handsome **Snowflake Inn** (221 E. Hyman Ave., ☎ 970/925–3221; 38 rooms; $$) has cheerfully furnished, cozy (yes, that means small) rooms and is outfitted with the three amenities that every tired skier must have: an outdoor, heated pool; a sauna; and a Jacuzzi. **Skier's Chalet** (233 Gilbert St., ☎ 970/920–2037 or 800/262–7736; 18 rooms; $–$$) is as close to Aspen's skiing action as any property in town, and it draws a young, fun-loving crowd.

SCENES

Denver

Denver is a tolerant city and some would say the gay bar scene has declined some, with more gay men and lesbians now heading out to the microbreweries, pubs, and other hangouts throughout LoDo and the rest of the city. Many of Denver's downtown clubs, especially those in LoDo, while not necessarily gay-oriented, are at the very least popular with gays and lesbians. Here are three of the best: **Rock Island** (1614 15th St., ☎ 303/572–ROCK) is in a historic redbrick Victorian, has great music, and pulls in a range of collegiate types, yuppies, and the like. The **Aqua Lounge** (724 E. 17th Ave., ☎ 303/832–3474), just down the street from the Grand, is a smaller club most popular with gays during Thursday's Car Wash Party, when the DJs spin several hours of vintage trash disco. **Industry** (1222 Glenarm Pl., ☎ 303/620–9554) is a typical warehouse bar that's especially gay on Thursdays; it's also famous for its unusual theme nights, such as leather or fetish parties.

Though Denver's primarily gay venues aren't as popular as they once were, there are still a ton of them. One pocket of action is in South Denver, along South Broadway. There are also a bunch of bars around Capitol Hill, out on East Colfax Avenue, and along trendy East 17th Avenue.

Midtowne Spa (2935 Zuni St., ☎ 303/458–8902) and the **Denver Swim Club** (6923 E. Colfax Ave., ☎ 303/321–9399) are gay bathhouses. The latter is the seedier of the two.

B. J.'s Carousel. One of the older bars in Denver, B. J.'s is a campy place with pink walls, Tiffany-style glass, '60s sconces and furnishings, pool tables, and a volleyball court out back. There's a light lunch and dinner menu, and there are shows on weekends. *1380 S. Broadway, ☎ 303/777–9880. Crowd: the old male guard—tried and true, beer-bellied and proud.*

Charlie's. With a large dance floor and great Western decor, Charlie's is the best two-stepping place in town. The wild and rowdy crowd is very open with strangers. Thursdays are especially popular. They also have a parlor room that serves light meals from 11 AM to 4 AM. *900 E. Colfax Ave., ☎ 303/839–8890. Crowd: 80/20 m/f, country-western crowd, mixed ages, lots of 10-gallon hats.*

Compound. Sunday nights at the Compound have become something of a tradition in Denver—even preppy boys sneak down here in their denim outfits. It's a midsize disco where you can let your hair down and have a scandalous time—you'll encounter little attitude and plenty of energy. Can be very trashy in a fun way. Tuesdays and Wednesdays are also popular. *145–149 S. Broadway, ☎ 303/722–7977. Crowd: men only, rough and rarin' to go; racially diverse; flannel shirts, gold chains, and goatees; mostly ages 25 to 35.*

Denver Detour. Though this is more a women's bar, it's owners and staff are always friendly to the boys. It's near the capitol and is worn and comfy, with an avid pool-shooting crowd and great live music many nights. It's a popular place to meet for drinks before heading out to the discos and country-western dance halls. *551 E. Colfax Ave., ☎ 303/861–1497. Crowd: 75/25 f/m, mostly thirtysomething, as butch as not, lively.*

Elle. Denver has a relatively high number of women's bars or clubs popular with both genders, and Elle is probably the most popular and mainstream of the bunch: an energetic dance bar that rocks on Thursday, Friday, and Saturday nights (the only nights it's open). *716 W. Colfax Ave., ☎ 303/572–1710. Crowd: mostly women, mostly under 35, fairly professional, hip.*

Flavors. The people here seem like the sort your mother may have warned you about—S&M fans and female impersonators with names like Chocolate Thunder Pussy. But, of course, when not exploring the outer reaches of human sexuality, most of Flavors's patrons do the usual nine-to-five thing. In fact, you never know who you're gonna see here, nor how they'll be dressed. Not for the closed-minded. The music changes nightly at this fetish bar: one night it's industrial, the next it's death rock, gothic, or techno. *1700 Logan St., ☎ 303/830–0550. Crowd: mixed gay/straight, kinky, game for just about anything.*

Footloose. This is Denver's gay-friendly sports bar. The decor is rather upscale—like a bar in the lobby of a business hotel. Half the space is a restaurant, the other half a bar with TV screens showing games. There are also a few seats out on the sidewalk. *102 S. Broadway, ☎ 303/722–3430. Crowd: mixed bag.*

Garbo's. Garbo's was the city's premier cabaret before the Grand stole much of its thunder. But this is still a great spot to catch a piano act or chat with friends. It's in an ugly, squat building several blocks south of the capitol; the bar room itself is dimly lit and geared toward sitting at tables more than standing and mingling. *116 E. 9th Ave., ☎ 303/837–8217. Crowd: mixed m/f, diverse in age, low-key.*

The Grand. Part of a new generation of gay bars, the relatively new Grand is supremely elegant, set inside a lovely old redbrick building with a huge stone fireplace and tall windows overlooking upscale 17th Avenue. This is where most guys—and some women—stop on their way home from work or on their way out to dinner. You might also consider eating here—there's a good selection of sandwiches, salads, steaks, and cute waiters in bow ties. Piano music inside; Cozy patio out back. *538 E. 17th Ave., ☎ 303/839–5390. Crowd: 80/20 m/f, professional, diverse in age but heavily thirtysomething, down-to-earth, some suits on weekends.*

Metro Express. Denver's only always-gay disco is in a one-level brick building with a view of the state capitol. It gets an older, wiser, mellower bunch than the mixed gay/straight warehouse discos downtown, but it's not particular exciting here. Just the same old dance tunes, night after night. The Friday-night strippers are popular. *314 E. 13th Ave., ☎ 303/894–0668. Crowd: mostly male, cruisy, white-bread, slightly clonish, mostly ages 25 to 40.*

DIVES AND NEIGHBORHOOD BARS

The South Broadway strip of bars includes several somewhat seedy, dark gathering spots: **Bandits** (255 S. Broadway, ☎ 303/777–7100) has mostly Marlborough men in their 30s and 40s and a few women. **Mike's/The Outlaw** (60 S. Broadway, ☎ 303/777–0193) is a bearish pool and darts hall and country dancing saloon all in one. **The Triangle** (2036 N. Broadway, ☎ 303/293–9009), for the serious leather crowd, has a big after-hours following and a notoriously frisky basement.

Other neighborhood bars include **Brick's** (1600 E. 17th St., ☎ 303/377–5400), a quiet, nondescript downtown men's bar with a good lunch and weekend brunch menu; the **Colfax Mining Company** (3014 E. Colfax Ave., ☎ 303/321–6627), a rough drinking hall; **Highland Bar** (2532 15th St., ☎ 303/455–9978), a no-nonsense spot in northwest Denver frequented mostly by women; **Ms. C's** (7900 E. Colfax Ave., ☎ 303/322–4436), which packs in the k. d. lang and Kathy Mattea wanna-bes; **Raven** (2217 Welton, no ☎), a dance club that's at its most popular on Saturday nights; **Three Sisters** (3358 Mariposa St., ☎ 303/458–8926), known affectionately as "Six Tits," is one of the longest running women's bars in the country; and **Ye'o Matchmaker Pub** (1480 Humbolt St., ☎ 303/839–9388), a seedy show bar known mostly for its lukewarm male and female strippers.

Aspen

Aspen, though teeming with nightlife opportunities, has no gay bars, except during Gay Ski Week, when the town appears to have no straight bars. Given the town's open, accepting mood, gay and lesbian visitors should feel comfortable just about everywhere—a quick survey of the crowd will often reveal one or two like souls.

Faced with outlandishly high rents, bars and clubs change hands and names almost seasonally, so it's difficult to guess which après-ski hangouts will be the hottest any given year. In recent years, **Club Soda** (419 E. Hyman Ave., ☎ 970/925–8154), a fast-paced disco, and mellower **The Tippler** (535 E. Dean St., ☎ 970/925–4977), which has long drawn a big scene, have been must-dos for gay nightcrawlers. Both, however, draw a predominantly straight crowd.

THE LITTLE BLACK BOOK

At Your Fingertips

Aspen Chamber Resort Association: 328 E. Hyman Ave., 81611, ☎ 970/925–5656. **Aspen Gay Community:** 970/925–9249. **Colorado AIDS Project:** ☎ 303/837–0166 or 800/333–2437. **Colorado Department of Health-AIDS Information Line:** ☎ 303/782–5186 or 800/252–2437. **Denver Convention and Visitors Bureau:** 225 W. Colfax Ave., 80202, ☎ 303/892–1112 or 800/888–1990. **Lesbian and Gay Community Center:** 1245 E. Colfax Ave., ☎ 303/831–6268.

Gay Media

Quest (☎ 303/722–5965) is a monthly features-oriented gay/lesbian magazine. *Out Front Colorado* (☎ 303/778–7900), a newspaper that covers the whole state, with an emphasis on Denver, comes out biweekly. *FM* (Fag Mag; ☎ 303/753–6969) is the city's nicely laid out weekly entertainment magazine. *H. Magazine* (☎ 303/722–5965) is a fairly skimpy gay/lesbian biweekly newspaper. Denver's gay-friendly arts and entertainment newsweekly is *Westword* (☎ 303/296–7744).

BOOKSTORES

Denver has both an excellent gay and lesbian bookstore, **Category Six Books** (1029 E. 11th Ave., ☎ 303/832–6263), and a great feminist one, the **Book Garden** (2625 E. 12th Ave., ☎ 303/399–2004). **Magazine City** (200 E. 13th Ave., ☎ 303/861–8249) has a broad selection of used and new magazines, newspapers, and books, many of them gay. Though mainstream, the four-story **Tattered Cover** (1st Ave. and Milwaukee St., ☎ 303/322–7727) is one of the largest bookstores in the country. Though there are no gay bookstores in Aspen, **Explore Books** (221 E. Main St., ☎ 970/925–5336) has a solid selection of gay, lesbian, and feminist books as well as a lively little café.

Body and Fitness

Very gay, but lacking the best equipment, is Denver's **Broadway Bodyworks** (160 S. Broadway, ☎ 303/722–4342).

8 Out on Fire Island

THE FIRE ISLAND EXPERIENCE—the gay one at least—begins outside two ramshackle ferry terminals in Sayville, Long Island. On virtually any summer weekend morning, island goers begin forming two distinct but, for the most part, harmonious camps.

On the left winds the line for the ferry to Cherry Grove—a hodgepodge of creatures representing every gender, age, race, and style. In hand are soiled canvas bags overflowing with sunflower-print beach towels, disposable cameras, and crinkled brown lunch bags. Under buttocks are decade-old Igloo beach coolers packed with canned light beer and 3-liter boxes of Almaden. Kinetic bandanna-collared mutts mingle playfully, much as their owners do. Dykes with tykes change diapers dockside. Drag queens trade dish. The occasional straight couple hops into line—perhaps they have gay friends in the Grove, or maybe they're just mixed up.

Next door winds the line for the ferry to the Pines—a curving band of chiseled bodies, mostly male, white, young, and wearing at least the appearance of money. Armani sunglasses sparkle in the sunlight. Some guys already have their shirts off, revealing a long off-season's pursuit of the perfect figure. Virtually all are done up in cutoff denim shorts and oiled work boots—a far cry from the spirit-stifling suits many of them endure five days a week, but a look that is no less dull and interchangeable. Many carry shopping bags from gourmet food shops like Zabar's and Dean & Deluca, along with cases of Sam Adams and creels of fruit and brie. Yellow labs and Jack Russell terriers wait patiently by their masters. The sight of each bronze Adonis bathing in the glow of the one standing before him is at once breathtaking, heartbreaking, and curious.

Almost simultaneously, the two ferries load up, set sail, and chug along a narrow river from Sayville into Great South Bay, then about 5 miles out to the north shores of Fire Island's two gay communities: to the east, the Pines; to the west, Cherry Grove. Alike in sexual orientation, they are separated only by a small forest and a strip of white beach. Aesthetically, socially, and, to some extent, ideologically, the gulf between them is much greater.

At the risk of generalizing, the Pines draws the more image- and beauty-conscious segment of the gay community. The perception is nicer digs, bigger pecs, fewer wigs, and hotter sex. Cherry Grove welcomes everybody else. It also contains none of the Pines's unfortunate narcissism. The advantages and disadvantages of each side are fairly obvious. Lesbians usually prefer Cherry Grove, where they make up nearly half the population. The Pines is mostly male.

A week in either place will permanently alter your sense of the world. The first time you hop off the boat in Cherry Grove or the Pines, and step into these tiny villages of narrow boardwalks, red wagons, and rainbow flags, you begin to feel as though you've just entered Willy Wonka's chocolate factory: An entire kingdom, just for me! Not in Provincetown, not in Manhattan's Greenwich Village, not in San Francisco's Castro are you so completely immersed in gay culture. For a moment the phrase "10 percent" loses all meaning, until you realize that this figure describes the segment of the population here that *isn't* gay.

In whichever community you decide to spend most of your time, try to allot at least a day to explore the other. They both have a great deal to offer. And if time allows, take the water taxi over to Ocean Beach, the section just west of Cherry Grove, just to remind yourself what straight people look like.

THE LAY OF THE LAND

In both communities, your feet are never actually permitted to touch the ground. Each "road" is nothing more than a wooden-plank boardwalk barely wide enough for two people to pass each other. **Cherry Grove** is the senior community of the two—it is both smaller-scale and less uniform in its architecture and ambience. Its primary organ is external: a long ferry dock that juts into Great South Bay from its north shore. The dock turns into the Grove's only true commercial thoroughfare, which twists its way south past the first east–west boardwalk (Bay Walk), around the Cherry Grove Beach Club, past Tulio's restaurant and disco, through the second east–west boardwalk (Atlantic Walk), by a couple more shops and a restaurant, before finally climbing down a set of wooden stairs to the sandy beach. Virtually every structure east or west of this curving spine is residential—anything from a sprawling contemporary gray-shingle triplex to a modest, white-clapboard Cape. The boardwalk layout is similar to a train track, with Bay and Atlantic walks acting as the two sides of the tracks, and about 20 short boardwalks running perpendicularly between them.

Aesthetically, Cherry Grove's character is playful, a tad rebellious, and decidedly queeny. As you saunter along the boardwalks perusing the sandy "yards" of its seaside retreats, you'll see rainbow windsocks, tatty pink flamingos, gaudy wind chimes, and gardens inhabited by gussied-up Barbie and Ken dolls. Crudely executed signs hang over many front doors, proudly proclaiming the often silly name of each domicile. Foliage-choked wooden fences fringe most every property, and trees and shrubs tower overhead, encouraged to grow unchecked—you're often forced to duck under or swerve around overgrown tree branches. The community has a sloppy, cluttered, yet luxuriant feel to it. In a world where co-op boards are known to forbid us from draping rainbow flags from our windows, or where condo developments are defined by their rigidly planned and flawlessly manicured flower beds and geometric hedges—where our desire to express ourselves is so frequently stifled—it's refreshing to wander through a village that has raised gay-tackiness and unkempt landscaping to a respectable, if not empowering, art form.

The neat and tony **Pines** suffers a bit at the hands of Cherry Grove's reverse snobbery. Its primary organ is internal: a long, narrow harbor bordered on the east bank by clusters of pines and on the west bank by about a dozen shops, a couple of restaurants, and the Botel Pines and Dunes Yacht Club. The ferry motors through the harbor and passengers debark at its base, a wooden-plank town square anchored by a central kiosk, which serves as a community bulletin board. Tied up to the docks fringing the harbor on both sides are dozens of enormous and expensive pleasure craft. Seaplanes land and take off on the bay just to the left of the harbor's mouth. Unlike Cherry Grove, business does not extend across the island to the ocean, but ends exactly where the harbor ends. Sitting on the dock you are consumed by the parade of tan hairless pecs and tight retro swimsuits—the kind you might have pictured Dick Diver wearing in *Tender Is the Night*. Everybody looks like a runway model. People sometimes make fun of these gaggles of gorgeous gay men. But it's hard not to admire them.

Away from the harbor, the Pines is largely a residential enclave of some 600 homes—vastly larger and more often male-occupied than the Grove's. Most of the homes are hulking and quite spectacular—gray, angular, and modern, they rise dramatically from the sand like abstract sculptures. You see skylights and porticos, pillars and cathedral ceilings, exposed beams and massive plate-glass windows. Many of the decks have hot tubs, and some even have full-size swimming pools. Like the homes of Cherry Grove, they are furnished with care and dedication; unlike the homes of Cherry Grove, they are furnished more often with taste and refinement.

Although it's unfair to make too much of the stereotypes that characterize these two communities, it's impossible not to notice them: On the one side are pretty boys with hard bodies; on the other are campy queens unencumbered by traditional notions of beauty and fun-loving lesbians of all ages and varieties.

To be fair, charity events are organized and attended by folks from both communities. Pines types like to eat at the Grove's restaurants. Grove types like to party at Pines bars. There is considerable mingling and little animosity—only good-natured rivalry—between the two. And then there is the one section of Fire Island that both geographically and spiritually connects the Pines to Cherry Grove, binds the pretty boys unmistakably to the campy queens. This section is called the **"Meat Rack."**

An undeveloped area of sand dunes, pines, shrubs, deer, and other beach flora and fauna, the area is administered by the National Park Service and spans about a mile between the two communities. It is one of the nation's most active cruise grounds, making it a cross between Mutual of Omaha's Wild Kingdom and the back room at New York City's Limelight. Whether you walk through here at noon on a Tuesday or at midnight on a Saturday, you're quite likely to encounter a few discreet (or not so discreet) encounters. Testimony to the Meat Rack's reputation, plastic shopping bags filled with condoms dangle strategically from gnarled tree branches (courtesy of Gay Men's Health Crisis). The maze of both clearly and vaguely marked trails is tricky, especially after dark. You enter from Cherry Grove by following either Bay Walk or Atlantic Walk east to the end. From the Pines you follow Coast Guard Walk west to its end. If you're heading in for a "good time," beware: That soft and fuzzy nose nuzzling at your belt buckle may be that of a white-tail deer foraging for dinner.

WHEN TO GO

The high season—when most businesses are open, the ferries run full swing, and the island is fully inhabited—is from roughly Memorial Day through Labor Day. Some hotels and businesses are open during all of May and September, even fewer in April and October. The ferries run only sporadically in these months. In winter, Fire Island is a ghost town, although the Dune Point rentals in Cherry Grove (*see* Sleeps, *below*) stay open year-round. If the Bay freezes, which it does every few winters, you're stuck here until it melts.

GETTING THERE

By Plane
If you're flying into Kennedy or LaGuardia airports, it's a pain to get out to Sayville. Your best bet is to rent a car. It's faster but more expensive to catch a connecting flight to MacArthur Airport, in Islip (☎ 516/467–3210), which is a short taxi ride from Sayville.

North American Flying Services (☎ 201/440–1941) can whisk you by helicopter from the East 23rd Street Marine Terminal in Manhattan to Fire Island Pines in 30 minutes. They take off anywhere from four to seven times a day; the cost: $135 one-way if you pay with cash, $145 on a card.

By Train and Bus
Long Island Rail Road (LIRR, ☎ 718/739–4200) trains depart regularly from New York City's Penn Station for Sayville—it's about a 90-minute ride. You might have to change trains; be sure to check with your conductor. Shuttle buses and group taxis to the ferry terminal meet almost every train and cost $2. If you're ever stuck at the station, call Colonial Taxi (☎ 516/589–7878).

Horizon Coach Islander's Club (☎ 212/255–8014 or 516/654–2622) runs buses from Manhattan to the ferry terminal Thursdays, Fridays, and Saturdays (cost: $20 one-way; $170 for a 12-trip ticket).

By Car
Once on Long Island, head east on the Long Island Expressway (LIE). Take exit 59 (Ocean Avenue South) to Sayville. Once in downtown Sayville, signs direct you to the ferry terminal. There's a huge parking lot across from the terminal; it costs $7 daily.

By Ferry
No matter how you get to Sayville, you'll need to take the ferry out to the island. The schedule is based on the LIRR train schedule, and boats run quite often: about every hour from 7 AM to midnight on Friday, until around 10:30 PM on Saturday and Sunday, and every couple of hours from 7 AM to 7 PM on weekdays. Call the **Sayville Ferry Service** (☎ 516/589–0810) for exact times. The round-trip fare is $10 for adults, $5 for kids under 12, and $3 for dogs. Discount commutation tickets are available.

If you miss the ferry and you're desperate to get across that day, call **South Bay Water Taxi** (☎ 516/665–8885). They'll charge anywhere from $100 to $150 for the first group of six people depending on the hour ($10 for each additional person).

GETTING AROUND

There are no paved roads and no automobiles in either Cherry Grove or the Pines—just miles of narrow boardwalk. It's an easy walk to and from any point within each community. Transporting heavy goods and groceries is done via shiny red wagon, the kind you dragged around as a kid. You can rent them near the ferry docks.

The trek between Cherry Grove and the Pines is not over boardwalk. You either walk along the beach, which fringes the entire Atlantic shore of the island, or scamper through the forest, which is laced with poorly marked paths that circuitously connect the two communities. The beach walk takes

20 to 30 minutes; the forest walk can take from 20 minutes to all day, depending on your navigating skills and several other factors.

Water Taxi

Getting around by water taxi is a way of life out here. Boats hold from a dozen to three-dozen passengers and make frequent stops at all Fire Island communities. The boats generally run from sunrise to midnight, but when the crowd warrants it, they continue to shuttle people between the Pines and the Grove until as late as 4 AM, when the last bars have closed. If you plan to stay out past midnight, call **Aqualine Water Taxi** (☎ 516/ 639–9190), which shuttles between Cherry Grove and Ocean Beach or **South Bay Water Taxi** (☎ 516/665–8885), which also services the Pines, or ask at the dock how late they're running. If there are enough of you in your party, they'll take a reservation. Be patient: You sometimes have to wait a while dockside. Once aboard, the ride between Cherry Grove and the Pines takes about 10 minutes; depending on the size of the boat, the number of people on board, and weather conditions, the jaunt can be anything from a picturesque glide across the bay to a nipple-hardening, gravity-defying ordeal that renders your precious hairdo a matted, salt-sprayed bird's nest.

Though the system is rather informal and is dictated largely by supply and demand, a few constants can be counted on: In the Grove, you catch the taxi at the foot of the ferry dock, just to the left as you're facing the mainland. In the Pines, you catch it on the dock just outside the Pines Pantry grocery store. The fare between the two is $4 per person; it's $7 from the Grove to Ocean Beach; $8 from the Pines to Ocean Beach. It is customary to tip a buck or two.

HELPFUL TIPS

There are no banks on Fire Island and no ATM machines, so bring all the cash you'll need. Most stores, however, do let you pay for merchandise with your ATM or credit cards. The Cherry Grove Beach Hotel allows you to get up to $200 with your ATM card at its front desk; there is an extortionist catch, though: You must apply $20 of however much you withdraw toward the bar at the Ice Palace Disco.

Staples such as groceries, hardware, and household goods cost anywhere from 20% to 50% more here than on the mainland, so stock up before coming. The **Pines Pantry** (Harbor Walk, ☎ 516/597-6200) and, in Cherry Grove, the **Associate Too** (Main Walk, ☎ 516/597-9210) are the two grocery stores. The former is better by far: It's twice as large, has a wonderful selection of produce, a fresh fish market and deli, and lots of exotic foods. There are two liquor stores in the Pines; both have a better selection than the one in Cherry Grove. Both communities have hardware stores and florists; the Pines has a pet supply store.

Never walk over the sand dunes. Each year, the fierce and greedy Atlantic Ocean steals precious tons of sand from Fire Island's beaches. Preventing erosion is an ongoing battle. In the Pines, where little foliage grows on the span of sand dunes that separates the homes from the beach, orange fencing has been set up to bolster the dunes and keep people off of them. Stay away from these fences.

Generally, Cherry Grove's beach is mixed lesbian and gay male, with more dykes to the west of The Dunes (Ocean and Lewis walks) restaurant. It's fine and quite popular to bathe nude. The "no-man's" stretch that abuts the Meat Rack, connecting the Grove to the Pines, gets more of the nudists. The Pines's beach is mostly male, but for some reason very few people here remove their suits. Swimming can be dangerous along the entire stretch, as currents are strong and violent; exercise caution.

Outside of the commercial areas, the boardwalks are not lit and are actually quite dark at night. Consider bringing a flashlight to prevent yourself from stumbling off a walkway and spraining your ankle on somebody's Flintstones garden diorama.

Fires are a major concern here, as most of the buildings and walkways are made of wood. Campfires here are prohibited, and cigarettes should be completely extinguished before you discard them. Do not toss them off the boardwalk or onto the beach.

Pets are common. If you bring your pet to Fire Island (many people do), you must have them on a leash at all times and you must clean up after them, or you'll be fined. Technically, it's against the law to have them on the beach, but the park service seems to overlook this if they're leashed. Best not to chance it.

EATS

Every entrée in every Fire Island restaurant costs about 20% more than it would in New York City, which is about 20% more than it would cost anywhere else. Why? Not necessarily because the food merits high prices. Figure that restaurateurs must earn every cent during the short-lived summer season, and that every morsel must be hauled over by boat from the mainland.

A few things to keep in mind: Cherry Grove has the best restaurants on the entire island—even straight people come here to eat. You're seldom permitted to tip with your credit card, so plan to have extra cash on hand. Typically, restaurant service here sucks: a bunch of kids trying to subsidize a summer on Fire Island—they party all night, sun themselves all day, and generally resent the time they must spend serving meals. Really, who can blame them? All told, considering the very limited resources in the way of personnel and ingredients, Fire Island's restaurants manage as well as can be expected. But dining is not a reason in itself to visit.

For price ranges, *see* Chart A at the front of this guide.

Cherry Grove

$$$$ Top of the Bay. The best of either community's restaurants. This second-floor dining room is half indoors, half in a covered porch that overlooks the ferry dock and Great South Bay. The staff is friendly and attentive—rare for Fire Island. There are always about a dozen specials, but consider also the fresh crab cakes, mussels, and all-you-can-eat prime rib on Thursday. *Dock Walk,* ☎ *516/597–6699.*

$$$ The Dunes. This beachfront restaurant (opened in 1995) offers a standard menu (seafood, pasta, chicken dishes, and hamburgers) and ocean views from the awning-covered dining porch. BYOB. *Lewis and Ocean Walks,* ☎ *516/597–6462.*

$$$ Tullio's. This outdoor restaurant, above the Mostro disco, has good but pricey American cuisine. Tables are on a deck, set around a central bar that's also a popular place to grab a beer during the day. It gets breezy up here, so be prepared. Dishes include grilled chicken with sautéed apples and onions and a stuffed lobster that weighs in at around $20. Service can be poky. *Ocean Walk,* ☎ *516/597–6888.*

$$–$$$ Suzy Wrong. Finally, Fire Island has a Chinese restaurant! It even has a cute, faggy name. Suzy is in the same building as Tullio's—just go up the stairs and through the porch; the restaurant is in the back, in a bright,

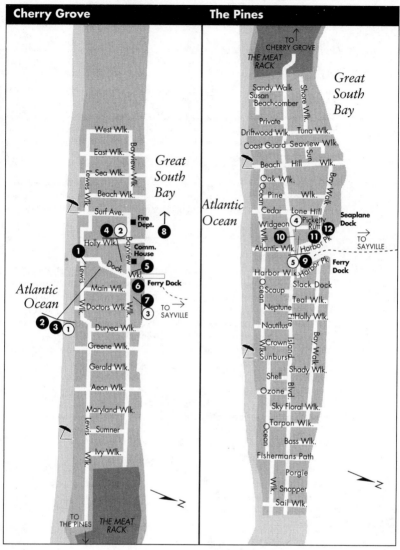

Cherry Grove | The Pines

Eats ●

Cherry Grove Pizzeria, **4**

Cherry Pit Restaurant, **7**

Cultured Elephant, **10**

The Dunes, **1**

The Encounter, **12**

Island Club Bistro, **9**

Island Mermaid, **8**

Michael's, **5**

Suzy Wrong, **3**

Top of the Bay, **6**

Tulio's, **2**

Yacht Club, **11**

Scenes ○

Cherry's, **3**

Ice Palace Disco, **2**

Island Club Bistro, **5**

The Mostro, **1**

The Pavillion, **4**

airy room. Prices are high for Chinese food: Shrimp in garlic sauce is $17, but some of the chow meins and lo meins are less than $10. *Ocean Walk,* ☎ *516/597–7037.*

$$ Cherry Pit Restaurant. Better known as a bar, Cherry's has a small indoor/outdoor dining area. Service is uneven but usually quite friendly. The food, which is crummy and overpriced, is basic, consisting of burgers, salads, fried appetizers, and sandwiches. Nice views of Great South Bay. *Bayview Walk,* ☎ *516/597–7859.*

$–$$ Michael's. A family-run diner with good, cheap grub and pleasant service with little attitude. There's seating inside or out—at little pink tables with white plastic chairs. Serves the usual hot dogs, fries, salads, a variety of egg dishes and a good lobster salad. It's open 24 hours on Saturday. *Dock and Bayview Walk,* ☎ *516/597–6555.*

$ Cherry Grove Pizzeria. Directly beneath the Ice Palace, this hole-in-the-wall parlor has about 15 outdoor tables with umbrellas; they serve slices, calzones, and heroes. Also a popular place to grab a quick breakfast. *Ocean Walk,* ☎ *516/597–6766.*

The Pines

$$$ Yacht Club. Part of the Botel complex, this is the island's largest restaurant, with plenty of indoor and outdoor seating. The food varies in quality: Some love it here, but it's a little overrated. The Caesar salad is the best on the island. Also stellar are the burgers, with a wide selection of toppings: sun-dried tomato and watercress, chili, feta cheese, etc. The grilled seafood entrées and steaks are less memorable. *Harbor Walk,* ☎ *516/597–6131.*

$$ Cultured Elephant. About as good as the Yacht Club and quite a bit cheaper, it's right on the dock—near the base of the harbor—with a deck overlooking passersby. Not gourmet but straightforward, with good gazpacho, burgers, blackened tuna steak, fried seafood platters, and grilled swordfish. *Harbor Walk,* ☎ *516/597–6010.*

$$ Island Club Bistro. This clean, cheerful spot—fresh flowers on the tables and natural white maple floors—serves a standard menu of salads, sandwiches, pizza, and chicken. Upstairs is a night club and flower shop. Takeout available. *Picketty Ruff Walk,* ☎ *516/597–6001.*

$ The Encounter. Small snack bar beside the Pines Pantry grocery store that sells frozen yogurt, ice cream, juices, and other goodies. No seating. *Harbor Walk,* ☎ *516/597–6211.*

Ocean Beach

$$$–$$$$ Island Mermaid. This is a great Italian restaurant in the family-oriented community of Ocean Beach, about a 15-minute ferry ride from the Grove and a 20-minute ride from the Pines. Best bets are the antipasto table, baked chevre, the seafood paella, and any of the pasta dishes. The best seats are on the dock overlooking the bay, but it gets chilly out here; dress warmly. The Mermaid is very gay-friendly and pays the return water taxi fare of every customer. *480 Baywalk,* ☎ *516/583–8088.*

SLEEPS

With the exception of Belvedere Castle, accommodations here are bare, simple, and functional. All are inordinately expensive, and if you're planning to stay a week it's economical to get a share. Space is limited (there are fewer than 200 rooms between the two communities), so you should book ahead at least a month for summer weekends; most places begin taking reservations on January 1. Two-night minimums are almost always enforced on weekends, as well as three- and four-day minimums on certain holidays.

For price ranges, *see* Chart A at the front of this guide.

Cherry Grove

🏠 One of the most inspired properties on the East Coast, the **Belvedere Guesthouse** is grandiose and crazy, patterned immodestly after a Venetian palazzo. Amid the statuary, domes, and terraces, the guest rooms are decorated individually with antiques and reproductions and plenty of quirky touches. There's a hot tub, a small but well-appointed gym, a roof deck with splendid views, and a main pool. *Bayview Walk,* ☎ *516/597–6448. 38 rooms. Gay male. $$$$*

🏠 Less refined but higher-energy is the **Cherry Grove Beach Hotel,** which, in addition to its guest quarters, comprises the Ice Palace Disco (*see* Scenes, *below*) and an enormous pool and sundeck. Rooms are small but clean with standard motel furnishings. It's the focal point of Cherry Grove, a true party hotel, and, frankly, your best bet if coming to Fire Island to get laid. *Bayview Walk,* ☎ *516/597–6600. 57 rooms. Mixed gay/lesbian. $$$–$$$$*

🏠 If the **Holly House** were a car, it would be a 1973 Volkswagen bus. This tan-stain, three-story building looks like Robinson Crusoe's tree house. With shaded decks and a quiet, secluded setting, this is perfect if you're trying to cool your jets for a week. Rooms are large, a bit musty, but quirkily done with knotty pine walls, exposed rafters, hanging plants, and bohemian '70s furnishings. Breakfast and a drink are included in the daily rate. *Holly Walk,* ☎ *516/597–6911. 4 rooms. Mixed gay/lesbian. $$–$$$*

🏠 The **Carousel Guest House** is the only B&B on the island; it's a small, simple, ranch structure that looks like an ordinary home. It's surrounded by gardens and backs up to the Cherry Grove Beach Club. Continental breakfast is included. *185 Holly Walk,* ☎ *516/597–6612. 11 rooms. Mixed gay/lesbian. $–$$*

🏠 **Dune Point** rents six units, which work either as weekend retreats or summer-long rentals and can accommodate from two to six people. Every unit is fully furnished and quite homey—it has the feel of a share in somebody's home. It's open year-round. *Lewis Walk,* ☎ *516/597–6261. Mixed gay/lesbian. $–$$*

The Pines

🏠 **Botel Pines and Dunes Yacht Club** is the only public accommodation in the Pines, and therefore a monopoly, and therefore lacking any motivation to make customers happy. It's in an ugly, three-story, white, cinder block monolith with blue-and-green trim. Nothing fancy—basically a Motel 6 anywhere but here. Not unlike the Cherry Grove Beach Club, except that here the staffers are bitchy and act like they're doing you a favor for checking you in. On the Harbor, some rooms overlook Great South Bay. *Harbor Walk,* ☎ *516/597–6500. 27 rooms. Mostly gay male. $$$$*

SCENES

This is definitely a party playground, especially on weekends when all the spots listed below are packed. The Pines's clubs draw an expectedly perfect-looking, clonish crowd. As somebody once described his first experience at a Pavillion tea dance: "I felt like I'd stepped into the middle of a gay joke." Cherry Grove's nightlife offerings are a bit less intense and are much more diverse, with good spots for the old, the young, the male, and the female. The complaint on this side is that you may meet new friends, but few of them are single.

Cherry Grove

Cherry's. There are two bars here. Inside, before you reach the dining area, is a small video bar that's usually not very crowded. Outside, under a red-and-white stripe awning, is a piano bar with a pool table and a small area for live entertainment—usually pop music or reggae, a cabaret on Thursdays. A nice spot to have a drink before hitting the discos. *Bayview Walk, ☎ 516/597–6820. Crowd: ages 20s to 80s, mixed genders, lots of regulars and here-for-the-week visitors, very friendly, laid-back.*

Ice Palace Disco. This is a long, rectangular disco with pool tables, video games, and a bar at one end; a stage in the center; and access to a deck that overlooks an outdoor pool. There's also a bar and porch at the front of the building, which overlooks the bay. On Saturday night the place really fills up; you'll see every kind of person in virtually every kind of outfit—even a small straight following has developed. Friday is popular, too, but it's fairly dead the rest of the week. The stage is the frequent site of impersonators, comedians, drag shows, and the famed Miss Fire Island Pageant, held every September. *Bayview Walk, ☎ 516/597–6600. Crowd: truly diverse in age, gender, and race; low attitude; plenty of energy; professional partyers.*

The Mostro. The patrons here always looks as if they've just stumbled out of a Halloween party. They *can* dance, however, and they'll kick your butt in pool. The dance floor is small, but the DJs are terrific—even when the crowds are meager. Will stay open as late as 6 AM if everyone is up for it, though liquor is cut off at 4. Gets more lesbians than any other bar on the island. *Ocean Walk, ☎ 516/597–7455. Crowd: mostly ages 30s and 40s, 60/40 f/m, offbeat and groovy, not cruisy.*

The Pines

Island Club Bistro. A small, smartly decorated second-floor bar and disco with a regulation-size pool table in perfect shape, bartenders whose packages are tied neatly in G-strings, a small dance floor that spins very hot music, a quieter outdoor terrace, and an even quieter piano bar. It's mellower and less snooty than the Pavillion. *Pickety Ruff Walk, ☎ 516/597–9592. Crowd: young but with many exceptions, 90% male, everything from pretty boys to hotshot entertainment-industry moguls.*

The Pavillion. Next to the Island Club. The only place on Fire Island that has the look and feel of an urban warehouse disco. It has a moderately large rectangular dance floor with one wall entirely of mirror—giving it the feel of a much larger club. Adjacent is a long, almost always packed, cruise bar. Upstairs, overlooking the harbor, is an L-shape outdoor balcony where tea dances are held early each evening. On weekends, the tea dances are impossibly crowded and getting from one end of the balcony to the other—let alone actually meeting somebody—is a tremendous feat. The tea dances are notoriously attitudy; late nights in the disco are less so—maybe because it's so dark and everybody's so wasted. Best sound system on island. *Fire Island Blvd., no ☎. Crowd: young, mostly male, gorgeous but homogeneous, stand-and-model, wired.*

THE LITTLE BLACK BOOK

At Your Fingertips

Coast Guard: ☎ 516/661–9100. **Community Manager:** Cherry Grove and Pines, ☎ 516/597–6060. **Doctor:** Cherry Grove, Doctor's Walk, ☎ 516/

597–6616; Pines, 577 Coast Guard Walk, ☎ 516/597–6160. **Fire:** Cherry Grove, use the alarm boxes along the boardwalks; Pines, ☎ 0.

BOOKSTORES

If reading is important to you, bring your own books or, on the way to the ferry, stop by **Runaway Bay Books** (10 Main St., Sayville, ☎ 516/589–9212), a full-service bookstore with a decent selection of lesbian and gay titles.

The **Pines Pantry** has a shelf of best-selling novels and gay erotic fiction, as well as gay newsmagazines (no porn) and a few major newspapers (*New York Times, USA Today*); the **Cherry Grove Grocery** has only the major newspapers.

Body and Fitness

The **Island Gym** (adjacent to the Botel, Pines) is open to members and guests (cost: $10 for a one-day pass, $45 for one week). It has a pool and sundeck and free weights under an awning. There's no fitness-training equipment.

9 *Out in Houston*

AS THE 1970s DREW TO A CLOSE, an oil boom vastly increased Houston's open coffers, and it seemed poised to become the most vibrant, prosperous city in the southern United States. Shimmering new skyscrapers rose one after another, and the ritzy western neighborhood of River Oaks witnessed the construction of one mammoth mansion after another. But the oil bust of the 1980s brought Houston quickly to its knees: The decade saw infrastructure crumble, businesses fold, and Houstonians flee for greener pastures. Only recently, since the early '90s, has the Bayou City begun to awaken from its economic doldrums.

Now, even though Houston is right back in the swing of things, residents seem somewhat humbled by the experience of the '80s. Neither cocky nor contrite, they act like people who have survived an economic tornado. Having lived through the '80s they can beat just about anything, but they also know how quickly the sky can come tumbling down again. They're very happy to have visitors, and they welcome you warmly, talk your ear off, show off the city's strengths, sheepishly acknowledge its weaknesses, and treat you to a very good time.

The plucky, gracious character you encounter in many native Houstonians has a lot to do with the hybridization of Western and Southern cultures. Situated at the confluence of the Oak and Buffalo bayous (what better marries the Wild West with the Deep South than the words "buffalo" and "bayou"?), at a point where the Gulf of Mexico is deep enough to serve as a turning basin for cargo ships, Houston developed during the middle part of this century into the most significant port city in the gulf. As such, it always had more commerce with the other Southern cities along the gulf than with the land mass of Texas to the west. Perhaps partly for this reason, many Houstonians think of themselves as southerners, not southwesterners.

As in most port cities, the population is quite diverse. There are many Cajuns and Creoles here, as well as significant numbers of Latin-Americans, Asians, African-Americans, and Greeks. The resulting mix of residents— outsiders once themselves—is very open to newcomers and visitors.

In the '70s, this spirit of tolerance helped to foster the growth of a new, nationally recognized gay ghetto—the downtown neighborhood of Montrose (the community at that time was notoriously large, loud, and lusty). It's still big and still the center of gay life in Houston. There is also a very conservative, macho element—reinforced in pockets by an indigenous brand of Texan-Latino machismo—and you may encounter disapproval or, at best, a cool, as-long-as-you-keep-it-to-yourself sort of attitude.

This same mix of cultural influences—Southern, Texan, Latin American—that shapes the character of the city also allows for some curious and colorful blends within the gay community itself. Houston has some of the liveliest drag scenes in America; weekly shows are staged at almost every bar in town. Many of these clubs also host weekly steak cookouts. In Houston, the two elements—the first very Southern and Latin American, the second very Western—mingle surprisingly well.

Regardless of what they wear to work each day, gay and lesbian Houstonians like to dress in denim or leather when they head out for a good time; you'll also see lots of cowboy hats and boots. If one gender is better represented among the city's well-dressed, well-heeled yuppies, it's women. Many of the city's gay male professionals left during the '80s. Emerging in their absence is an extremely effective lesbian community of entrepreneurs and professionals, who played as large a role as anyone in turning the city around.

THE LAY OF THE LAND

Houston, the fourth-largest city in the United States, is marked by striking contrasts. In many spots it looks as if time stood still in the late '70s. In other sections, rows of storefront windows are boarded over—victims of the economic downturn in the '80s. Then there are the pockets of Houston that have been developed in the '90s: the office buildings and swank shopping plazas. What's so odd is that these three urban visions appear in combination virtually anywhere you look. There is no zoning: Gleaming skyscrapers rub shoulders with vacant lots; the patio of the trendiest eatery sits across from a 20-year-old Jiffy Lube; and an avenue of stately Colonial Revival homes suddenly gives way to a tired lane of tenements and unkempt lawns. The trade-off from whatever aesthetic embarrassments arise from this highly unplanned urban landscape is Houston's air of accessibility. All cities regard themselves as melting pots; Houston can truly make this claim.

Montrose

Plenty of gays have settled into less-expensive areas such as the Heights, White Oak Bayou, and Old Sixth Ward, but **Montrose** is still the community's headquarters and commercial hub. The neighborhood is about midway between downtown and the Galleria, bounded to the west by Shepard, to the north by Allen Parkway, to the east by Bagby, and to the south by the Southwest Freeway (U.S. 59). Westheimer Road cuts east–west through its center; Montrose Boulevard divides the neighborhood north–south.

This is not a particularly swank area: Its streets are a hodgepodge of restored early 20th-century architecture along with more recent experiments in urban design—some tasteful, some not—particularly around Fairview and Pacific streets. You'd never know you're within a couple miles of downtown: The blocks resemble a dowdy, middle-class, Southern suburb. And, although some nice homes are close by, much of Montrose has an almost rural feel to it. Its cuteness quotient is on the low side, but it also lacks the attitude. Montrose is low-key and modest in every respect: an eclectic mix of guppies, leather aficionados, artists, professionals, and college students. Houston's outgoing and welcoming nature is more than evident here.

On the western outskirts of Montrose along Westheimer Road, from roughly the 1500 block to the 2300 block, is a popular **antiques row.** On the eastern side of the area (the blocks just south of Westheimer Road and east of Montrose Boulevard) is the **Westmoreland Addition.** In the absence of zoning, Houston does have a number of "deed-restricted" neighborhoods; these are essentially planned—and sometimes gated—communities. The Westmoreland Addition, plotted in 1902 on a 12-block grid and consisting of hundreds of midsize to enormous late-Victorian and Colonial Revival homes, is one of the prettiest.

The district's top cultural sights include the **Menil Collection** (1515 Sul Ross St., ☎ 713/525–9400), with works by Warhol, Léger, Picasso, Braque, Matisse, and a building designed in 1987 by Renzo Piano. Near this eclectic and esteemed art museum is the nearby **Rothko Chapel** (1409 Sul Ross St., ☎ 713/524–9839). The 14 large-scale Rothko paintings here were commissioned specifically for the chapel. They are among the last important pieces he struggled to complete before his untimely suicide in the early '70s. There is a peaceful reflecting pool and plaza, punctuated by Barnett Newman's sculpture, *Broken Obelisk*.

Downtown

Walk through downtown on a sultry summer day, and you won't see a soul—it's as though a neutron bomb silently wiped out the population. Houston has managed its oppressively crummy climate by linking every major hotel and office building with a 6-mile network of underground tunnels.

Houston's downtown is unusually dense. The entire contemporary skyline fits into a relatively compact pocket of office towers—it looks as though you could toss a lasso over the whole lot of them. The most striking of them all is I. M. Pei's 75-story **Texas Commerce Tower** (600 Travis St.), whose observation deck is definitely worth a visit. Dallas is always cited as the state's major design center, but Houston is no slouch: The visual arts and architecture receive tremendous attention here. Despite all its shimmer and shine, however, there's little to do downtown, and activity dwindles at night and on weekends, when all the suits have scooted. The only exception is the impressive **theater district,** concentrated up near the Buffalo Bayou around the intersection of Texas and Smith streets. Both **Market Square** and **Allen's Landing,** site of the city's first settlement, are near here. In addition to some touristy restaurants and bars, there are a number of historic buildings in the vicinity. One, the old **Rice Hotel** (Main St. and Texas Ave.), is infamous: President Kennedy spent the final night of his life here; vacant since 1977, it's in sore need of restoration.

Sam Houston Park, near where Lamar runs into Bagby, is literally in the shadows of downtown. With a fascinating collection of historic buildings moved here from other sites in Houston, the park offers an impression of the city's mid-19th-century beginnings; one-hour tours are available (☎ 713/655–1912).

Just northwest of the park, across I-45, is the **Old Sixth Ward Historic District,** Houston's oldest residential neighborhood. Many gays and lesbians have migrated here in recent years, attracted by the challenge of restoring small, relatively affordable, Greek Revival and Victorian cottages. Kane Street and Washington Avenue are two of the most picturesque streets.

Museum District/Texas Medical Center

To the surprise of many visitors, Houston is the most culturally endowed city in the Southwest and the Deep South, with a fine symphony orchestra, opera, and ballet, as well as outstanding museums. The **Museum District,** a loosely defined rectangle south of downtown, is bisected diagonally by Main Street and borders the northern tip of neatly landscaped **Hermann Park.** Among the must-sees here are the highly regarded **Museum of Fine Arts** (☎ 713/639–7300; highlights: 18th-century, Italian and Spanish Renaissance, impressionism); the **Contemporary Arts Museum** (☎ 713/526–3129; highlights: changing exhibits, which have featured Miro, Calder,

Sophie Calle); the **Houston Museum of Natural Science** (☎ 713/639–4600; highlights: 25,000-square-foot butterfly and tropical rain forest, 2,500 sea shells, space station exhibits, the Burke Baker Planetarium); and the **Holocaust Museum** (☎ 713/789–9898), which opened in March 1996 with a sculpture garden, a memorial area, changing exhibits, and a theater in which oral histories are movingly rendered. The south end of Hermann Park leads to the **Texas Medical Center,** an area comprising several hospitals, hotels, and the beautiful campus of **Rice University.**

River Oaks and the Galleria

This section west of downtown and Montrose (follow Westheimer Rd.) is often referred to simply as **Uptown.** It takes in the **Galleria** shopping district and the **Post Oak** neighborhood of newer homes, hotels, and office buildings. The Galleria is made up of three mammoth shopping malls packed with every upscale boutique known to humankind. It's fun to simply sit in the parking lot and listen to the fever-pitched chirping of car alarms being activated and deactivated by their owners. Between Uptown and Montrose is **River Oaks,** Houston's snazziest residential neighborhood, and **Memorial Park,** which is the closest thing the city has to a gay cruising ground. If you hang around in the latter you run the risk of being mugged or bumping into former president George Bush in jogging shorts (it's up to you to decide which is the more terrifying prospect).

Longtime resident Miss Ima Hogg—heir to a vast fortune and bearer of quite possibly the most embarrassing name in human history—left the public her magnificent River Oaks home, **Bayou Bend** (1 Westcott St., ☎ 713/639–7750; reservations required), which sits on a scenic curve in the Buffalo Bayou. Inside is one of the world's most priceless collections of decorative arts and Early American painting.

The Heights

At the turn of the century, Northern Houston, a.k.a. **the Heights** (from Montrose, follow Waugh Dr. several miles until it crosses the White Oak Bayou and becomes Heights Blvd.), was the city's first streetcar suburb. It gradually lost status, and many of the area's grand Victorians were torn down to provide space for low-income housing. Now it's largely a working-class Latin American neighborhood, broken up here and there by a few pockets of artsy bohemianism. Dribs and drabs of hip young fags are settling in this relatively inexpensive, if not especially cheerful, neighborhood.

The best area for exploring is along **West 19th Street** (from Heights Blvd., head west on 11th St. for several blocks; turn right onto Rutland and continue north for a few more blocks), where there's a concentration of antiques and consignment shops, galleries, furniture restorers, and restaurants.

Galveston

Galveston Island became a resort destination around the turn of the century. It has all the gaudy seaside attractions and amusements of the Jersey Shore or Mississippi Gulf. For general tourism information, contact the **Galveston Island Convention and Visitors Bureau** (2106 Seawall Blvd., 77550, ☎ 409/763–4311 or 800/351–4237). There are two gay clubs here: **Evolution** (2214 Mechanic St., ☎ 409/763–4212) and **Kon-Tiki** (315 23rd St., ☎ 409/763–6264).

GETTING AROUND

With its maze of freeways and clotted two- and four-lane roads, Houston can be a frustrating place to drive during the workday. Westheimer Road is both narrow and overused, particularly in the Montrose district.

Nevertheless, an automobile is your best weapon here. You'll need one to get from your hotel to any of the good bars and restaurants, and though downtown is walkable, you'll do best to spend as little time there as possible. The city has the third-largest cab fleet in America, and drivers are consistently helpful and reliable.

EATS

Virtually all the restaurants in Montrose have a gay following, and a few qualify as established hangouts. The swank River Oaks neighborhood and the Galleria shopping district farther west are both also quite gay-friendly.

Thanks to its Southern, Cajun, Southwestern, Mexican, and Latin-American accents, Houston is a food lover's city. And although all of those regional cuisines are known for heavy and/or spicy fare, you'll also find plenty of light contemporary cuisine as well, especially in River Oaks and around the Galleria.

Many of the bars serve good, basic pub grub, and most have a weekly "steak out," to which you can bring your own meat—generous sides of slaw and baked beans are usually provided. These are a great deal of fun, and outsiders are always welcome. Although a few of the city's many Mexican restaurants are reviewed below, a couple have a major gay following on certain days. **Cafe Adobe** (2111 Westheimer Rd., ☎ 713/528–1468), for instance, is big with lesbians and gays on Sunday afternoons and with gay men on Mondays; **Ninfa's** (2704 Navigation St., ☎ 713/228–1175) in East Houston cranks queer on Sunday afternoons.

For price ranges, *see* Chart B at the front of this guide.

$$$$ **Cafe Annie.** This fancy Galleria restaurant is to Houston what Spago is to L.A., so consider it only for special occasions and reserve well ahead for weekends—it's where the stars dine when in town. Innovative Southwestern-inspired dishes include grilled quail with red-chile vinaigrette and snapper with crab, avocado, and tomatillo salsa. *1728 Post Oak Blvd.,* ☎ *713/840–1111.*

$$$–$$$$ **Churrascos.** Though mired in a poorly designed shopping plaza that never has enough parking, Churrascos is one of the hottest spots in the city. Hanging plants, bamboo, dark-wood beams, and clean white walls lend an elegant air and set diners up for fine Latin American cuisine. *2055 Westheimer Rd.,* ☎ *713/527–8300.*

$$$–$$$$ **La Griglia.** In the chichi, art deco River Oaks Center shopping district, La Griglia is part of a local syndicate of exceptional, though pricey, Italian bistros. The design is as impressive as the food: a cavernous dining room painted with a dazzling array of colors; huge, copper air ducts rising from behind the bar to the ceiling; and columns spackled with colorful chunks of mosaic. *2002 W. Gray St.,* ☎ *713/526–4700.*

$$–$$$$ **Carrabba's.** A major bastion of yuppiedom, this dining room is large, loud, crowded, and festive—there's lots of standing and modeling. The Italian menu shows off such specials as pancetta-wrapped quail and a delightful minestrone. *3115 Kirby Dr.,* ☎ *713/522–3131.*

$$–$$$$ **La Strada.** La Strada's "Great Bilini Bash" puts this place in serious competition with Ruggles (*see below*) for the best Sunday brunch award. With a more sophisticated mood and a more serious menu, La Strada serves fine—if slightly trendy—Italian dishes at dinner, including several good steak, chicken, and fish grills. The staff is plenty fey and friendly. The kind of place that'll get you in the mood for bar-hopping later on. *322 Westheimer Rd.,* ☎ *713/523–1014.*

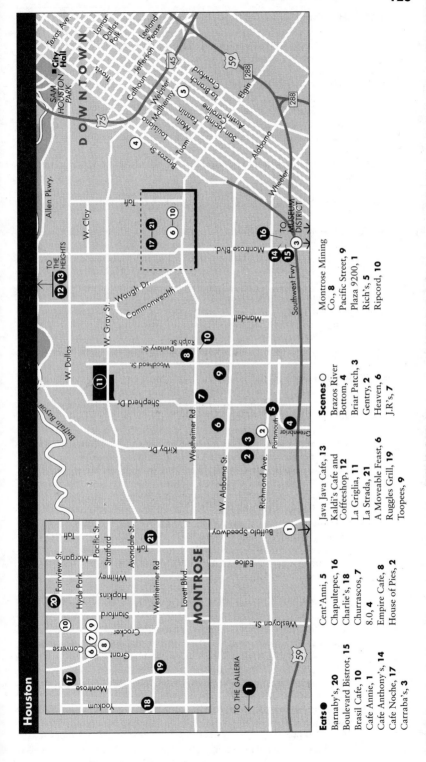

Houston

DOWNTOWN

MONTROSE

Eats ●
Barnaby's, **20**
Boulevard Bistrot, **15**
Brasil Cafe, **10**
Cafe Annie, **1**
Cafe Anthony's, **14**
Cafe Noche, **17**
Carraba's, **3**

Cent'Anni, **5**
Chapultepec, **16**
Charlie's, **18**
Churrascos, **7**
8.0, **4**
Empire Cafe, **8**
House of Pies, **2**

Java Java Cafe, **13**
Kaldi's Cafe and Coffeeshop, **12**
La Griglia, **11**
La Strada, **21**
A Moveable Feast, **6**
Ruggles Grill, **19**
Toopees, **9**

Scenes ○
Brazos River Bottom, **4**
Briar Patch, **3**
Gentry, **2**
Heaven, **6**
J.R's, **7**

Montrose Mining Co., **8**
Pacific Street, **9**
Plaza 9200, **1**
Rich's, **5**
Ripcord, **10**

$$–$$$ Boulevard Bistrot. Almost too neat and dapper for shaggy Montrose, the Bistrot sits on a promenade of boutiques and has a bright, airy dining room in which steak, pastas, grilled chicken, salmon, flounder, and other tempting possibilities are jazzed up with the latest New American preparations. *4319 Montrose Blvd.,* ☎ *713/524–6922.*

$$–$$$ Cafe Anthony's. Yet another spot on Montrose Boulevard with designer pizzas on its menu (though they *are* excellent), Cafe Anthony's is actually distinguished by its fine contemporary seafood dishes. The setting is cheerful, with walls of floor-to-ceiling windows and a wooden deck outside overlooking the homo-happy sidewalk. Draws a fairly young crowd. *4315 Montrose Blvd.,* ☎ *713/529–8000.*

$$–$$$ Cafe Noche. Not your ordinary Tex-Mex eatery but a very festive Mexican restaurant with a somewhat daring chef (note the portobello mushroom fajitas). It's best to dine in the mercilessly adorable courtyard out front; a foliage-choked, black-iron gate hides the mundanity of Montrose Boulevard. *2409 Montrose Blvd.,* ☎ *713/529–2409.*

$$–$$$ Cent'Anni. Houston has no shortage of Italian bistro-style dining, much of it overpriced; Cent'Anni delivers the goods without bankrupting you. Despite its dull shopping center venue, the dining room is elegant, with trompe l'oeil walls made to capture the setting of an Italian piazza. The traditional menu delivers with rich shrimp primavera, designer pizzas, and fine wines. Very romantic. *2128 Portsmouth,* ☎ *713/529–4199.*

$$–$$$ 8.0. The perfect spot if you have a case of the funky munchies: Everything at "eight-oh" is a bit off the wall—including the abstract murals. The eclectic menu pitches black beans and rice, olive burgers, chilis, jerk chicken, and other Southwestern- and Caribbean-inspired fare. *3745 Greenbriar St.,* ☎ *713/523–0880.*

$$–$$$ Ruggles Grill. Ruggles is highly popular with the queer community. People come because of the colorful (and pretty) staff and the Italy-meets-New Mexico menu, which presents such clever creations as red-snapper-and-crab chowder, and black-bean pasta. The Sunday brunch is legendary. *903 Westheimer Rd.,* ☎ *713/524–3839.*

$ A Moveable Feast. Maybe a bit too politically correct (the good-for-you sandwiches are blessed with such perky sobriquets as the "happy burger," owing, one suspects, to the fact that no cows were made unhappy in creating them), this sunny veggie restaurant and market serves far more than piles of alfalfa sprouts. They have a long list of salads and sandwiches, plus some delicious cakes and pies. *2202 W. Alabama St.,* ☎ *713/528–3585.*

$ Barnaby's. This tatty, down-home diner notable for its rainbow-flag chimney and facade painted with legions of yellow, blue, and red stars is as close to Montrose's main bar district as you can get. Has a loyal local following—especially at breakfast. *604 Fairview St.,* ☎ *713/522–0106.*

$ Chapultepec. A popular Montrose hangout, Chapultepec is a cut above most Tex-Mex places in the area—great salsa, chili *rellenos,* and margaritas that'll purse your lips. The best seating is out on the festive but noisy tiled front porch. Open 24 hours. *813 Richmond Ave.,* ☎ *713/522–2365.*

$ Charlie's. There are no pretensions at this big ole diner, just droves of big ole fags—and rather butch ones at that. A bit perfunctory on decor (the Tiffany-style lamps are a standout), and the food is just so-so—but there isn't a better place to dish with your friends on Westheimer. *1100 Westheimer Rd.,* ☎ *713/522–3332.*

$ Empire Cafe. An old gas station along Westheimer Road's antiques row has been transformed into one of the slickest, hippest cafés in Houston. Heavenly offerings include the boutique pizzas, hearty frittatas, and a breakfast of hot polenta with honey-cream and toasted almonds. Cute, curved dining room with high ceilings and funky hanging lamps. *1732 Westheimer Rd.,* ☎ *713/528–5282.*

$ House of Pies. This circa-mid-'60s pie diner has, for much of its tenure, been referred to affectionately as "House of Guys." It's open 24 hours and is especially busy after the bars close. Everything is no-frills (meat loaf is a typical special); whatever you do, *do* choose something from their long, long list of freshly baked pies. Tacky and proud of it. *3112 Kirby Dr., ☎ 713/528–3816.*

Coffeehouse Culture

The crunchiest of local coffeehouses, the **Brasil Cafe** (2604 Dunlavy St., ☎ 713/528–1993) is also an art gallery. You can dine in the tree-shaded courtyard, enjoying such healthful dishes as mesquite-smoked turkey sandwich, hummus, or *baba ganoush*. There are also dozens of vegetable and juice blends on tap. **Kaldi's Cafe and Coffeeshop** (250 W. 19th St., ☎ 713/802–2246), a large antiques emporia-cum-restaurant, prints its daily menu on brown paper bags plastered to the walls. The food itself is somewhat more sophisticated—sandwiches and salads with plenty of gourmet ingredients. Very boho, with poetry readings and open-mike nights. Though it's not really near anything, **Java Java Cafe** (911 W. 11th St., ☎ 713/880–5282) is probably the gayest coffeehouse in the Heights. It's inside a shop that sells flowers, antiques, balloons, plants, and gifts. The horrid Liquid Drano–blue roof, vinyl booths, and Formica tables at **Toopees** (1830 W. Alabama St., ☎ 713/522–7662) put it on the aesthetic plane of your average Denny's, but there is a pleasant, arbored courtyard off the side of the building. They serve good, simple diner food, and have a major gay following.

SLEEPS

Houston's hotel scene is characterized by typical chain properties. Most are downtown or out by the Galleria (Montrose is directly between these two neighborhoods); a smaller, third cluster is in and around the Texas Medical Center. The advantages of the Galleria neighborhood are its luxe shopping and dining and its location away from the daytime bustle and nighttime desolation of downtown.

For price ranges, *see* Chart B at the front of this guide.

Hotels

Near Downtown

🏨 The intimate **Lancaster** is one of only two hotels in Houston that could be said to possess historic character and European charm. A restored 1926 gem, it's equidistant from the theater and financial districts. *701 Texas Ave., ☎ 713/228–9500 or 800/231–0336. 93 rooms. $$$–$$$$*

🏨 The Lancaster's only competitor for charm and style, the **Wyndham Warwick** is a newer, slightly less extravagant property just south of downtown in the Museum District. The Warwick has exquisite public areas and a strong homo following. *5701 Main St., ☎ 713/526–1991 or 800/822–4200. 308 rooms. $$–$$$$*

🏨 The top business choice downtown is the towering **Hyatt Regency,** whose rooms have balconies looking out over a 30-story atrium. *1200 Louisiana St., ☎ 713/654–1234 or 800/233–1234. 959 rooms. $$–$$$*

🏨 The best economy choice within a short drive of Montrose is the **Allen Park Inn,** a fairly typical motor lodge that's cleaner than most and has a nice pool and exercise room. *2121 Allen Pkwy., ☎ 713/521–9321. 249 rooms. $–$$*

Near the Galleria

🖼 The former Remington Hotel is now the exclusive and expertly managed **Ritz-Carlton Houston,** the hostelry of choice for world leaders and celebrities. It's very close to Montrose and has a fabulous rooftop swimming pool and sundeck. *1919 Briar Oaks La.,* ☎ *713/840–7600 or 800/241–3333. 232 rooms. $$$$*

🖼 Long-term guests and couples traveling together should consider the **Guest Quarter Suites–Galleria West,** whose two-bedroom suites with kitchens are a particularly good value. *5353 Westheimer Rd.,* ☎ *713/961–9000 or 800/222–8733. 335 suites. $$–$$$*

🖼 A frequent host of gay and lesbian events, the **Westin Oaks** rises 21 stories directly above the Galleria Mall. Rooms are large and contemporary. *5011 Westheimer Rd.,* ☎ *713/960–8100 or 800/228–3000. 406 rooms. $$–$$$*

Guest Houses and Small Hotels

🖼 Madonna stays at **La Colombe d'Or,** a 1920s 21-room mansion that has been meticulously restored with every detail considered. Each suite has a private dining room and is decked with a collection of regionally and internationally acclaimed art. *3410 Montrose Blvd.,* ☎ *713/524–7999. 5 suites, 1 penthouse. Mixed gay/straight. $$$$*

🖼 On a homier—and much more affordable—scale is the **Lovett Inn,** the former home of a Houston mayor and the most popular choice of gays and lesbians for several years now. Rooms are done with a tasteful mix of antiques and reproductions, and in back, a pool and hot tub are given privacy by rows of box hedges. All of Montrose's bars and restaurants are within walking distance. *501 Lovett Blvd.,* ☎ *713/522–5224 or 800/779–5224. 6 rooms. Mostly mixed gay male/lesbian. $–$$*

🖼 The **Montrose Inn** is the area's most affordable choice, a clean but characterless spot in the heart of Montrose. It's a fairly social place. *408 Avondale St.,* ☎ *713/520–0206 or 800/357–1228. 7 rooms. Gay male. $*

SCENES

Houston has no shortage of bars—about 30 of them—most small and catering to a local crowd. Montrose is the major hub for nightlife and partying, though there are a few bars downtown and scattered around in other parts of the city.

The main cluster of Montrose bars is in a somewhat ordinary-looking residential area just east of Montrose Boulevard and north of Westheimer Road. Most of the major venues here—Heaven, the Ripcord, J. R.'s, and Pacific Street—are patronized predominantly by men. There really is no single dyke district. The Plaza 9200 complex in southwest Houston, however, just inside the Loop (I–610), has a largely female following.

Houston bar culture has a raw, gritty character that somehow draws together the city's two strongest (though not mutually exclusive) factions of bar goers: fans of leather and fans of drag. Many Montrose bars still look a lot as they did 15 years ago—they're dimly lit, the walls are coated with chipped paint, the windows are shuttered, the floors are covered with grubby linoleum.

All bars stop serving liquor at 2 AM. The Montrose Mining Co. and the Ripcord, however, serve coffee and soft drinks until 4 on Fridays and Saturdays. After-hours clubs pop up frequently; they open, close, and move so rapidly it's impossible to review them, so ask around.

Brazos River Bottom (BRB). BRB has been hopping for many years and is a great place to go if you're new in town. It has a good-size bar and offers two-stepping and line-dancing most nights, lessons on Tuesdays and Thursdays. On Sundays hundreds cram in here for what's arguably the best steak night in town. *2400 Brazos St., ☎ 713/528–9192. Crowd: more men but very woman-friendly, good mix of ages and types.*

Briar Patch. The city's main piano bar, this is a nice place to take a date, get to know locals, and get away from the intensity of Montrose—it's a 10-minute drive to the south. It gets a bit campier here during the drag shows. The only problem is the soft pink lighting: It gives everybody a Pepto-Bismol complexion. Often thought of as a "wrinkle bar," but lots of young guys like it here, too. *2294 Holcombe St., ☎ 713/665–9678. Crowd: mostly male, generally older, chatty.*

Gentry. This is a terribly popular spot when work lets out and closet cases need a fix of gaiety before heading home to the family. Despite that reputation, it's a convivial, elegant bar—feels like a very proper social club. *2303 Richmond Ave., ☎ 713/520–1861. Crowd: mostly ages 30s to 50s, many older guys preying upon the younger ones, lots of suits and ties.*

Heaven. This is the city's best small disco. The lighting and sound system are outstanding, and huge video screens abound. A second cruise bar off to the side is quieter—a good place to dish. Used to be a more uptight, clonish crowd, but lesbians and Latinos have thankfully livened up the mix and loosened things up. Watch for the 50-cent drink specials on Sundays. Cover many nights. *810 Pacific St., ☎ 713/521–9123. Crowd: mostly under 30; diverse in race and gender; some stand-and-model, more urban than preppy, plenty of disco bunnies.*

J. R.'s. Like its namesakes in Dallas and Washington, J. R.'s is the quintessential fern bar of the '90s, with hanging plants, Tiffany-style lamps, wood paneling, brick archways, brass bar fixtures, and lots of nooks and corners for standing around and ogling. A flagstone floor leads through an archway to the Santa Fe bar and patio, which is decorated with Navajo tapestries and fake cacti; the patio has a great dyke following on Sunday afternoons. *808 Pacific St., ☎ 713/521–2519. Crowd: like a J. Crew fashion show with a few cowhands thrown in; young, professional, on the prowl; mostly guys but lesbian-friendly.*

Montrose Mining Co. Typical of other "Mining Companies" around Texas, this one tries to be the major leather bar, but actually gets more of a mix of guys; for instance, it's host to Houston's "bear of the month" contests. It's extremely dark (they should hand out flashlights at the door) and kind of dingy inside, but there's a nice patio off the back. Gets a little more mainstream late on weekends, when it's open after hours. *805 Pacific St., ☎ 713/529–7488. Crowd: men only, very butch (hairy chests and faces, some leather but more denim), ages 30 and up, strong racial mix.*

Pacific Street. Some say it's just a quieter, less interesting version of its neighbors on the same street (J. R.'s and Montrose Mining Co.); others say it's more fun than either of them. It does have a nice little dance floor and a great balcony overlooking all the action on Pacific Street. There's also a good game room with pool, pinball, and video games. *710 Pacific St., ☎ 713/523–0213. Crowd: mostly male, a lot like Heaven's with some of the Mining Co.'s guys thrown in.*

Plaza 9200. The ownership of this giant '70s complex in southwest Houston, which used to be a tacky shopping center, is emphatic about not wanting Plaza 9200 to be called a lesbian bar. Nevertheless, the majority of its patrons are women. It's a big place with plenty to do and very little attitude, but it's also a bit of a haul from Montrose and lacks some of that neighborhood's cheerful hustle and bustle. Within its dowdy walls are several bars: **Ms. B's,** which looks like a Howard Johnson's cocktail lounge circa 1976, is a conversation/cruise bar (open every night but Mon.). **The Ranch** is a popular country-western dance bar (open Tues. and Thurs.–Sat.; lessons on Tues.). **XTC**, a disco, draws a great mix of ages and genders; TVs and TSs tend to find it very comfortable here as well (open Fri. and Sat.). There's also a patio open anytime any of the bars are. *9200 Buffalo Speedway,* ☎ *713/666–3356. Crowd: mostly women though men are welcome; very diverse in age and race, dressed-down.*

Rich's. A short drive from Montrose, Rich's is *the* downtown warehouse disco; it's only open Thursday to Saturday. It has a big dance floor and an outstanding sound system. Friday's retro disco theme is the best of the three nights; Saturday is a bit too crowded—though it's still the place to be seen, so most everyone makes an appearance. *2401 San Jacinto,* ☎ *713/759–9606. Crowd: 80/20 m/f, younger disco bunnies and club kids.*

Ripcord. A true leather bar, with the traditional, mind-numbing black decor and dim lighting (a few preppy boys sneak in here for a look every once in a while). It's set in a tan, windowless compound in the heart of Montrose's bar territory. *715 Fairview St.,* ☎ *713/521–2792. Crowd: mostly men; somewhat older; leather, Levi's, and uniforms.*

DIVES IN MONTROSE

Bacchus II (2715 Waughcrest St., ☎ 713/523–3396) is a dark and smoky dyke bar; Wednesdays are the most crowded. **Club 403** (403 Westheimer Rd., ☎ 713/523–0030) is a male bar set in a dilapidated, wood-frame house that looks a bit like a bait-and-tackle shop. **Cousins** (817 Fairview St., ☎ 713/528–9204) is the home of Houston's drag organization. **E/J's** (2517 Ralph St., ☎ 713/527–9071), a big bar just off Westheimer's antiques row, is best known for its lively patio grill, nasty but beloved Saturday night drag shows, and the E/J's Mug Club (you buy a mug and they keep it there for you). **Mary's** (1022 Westheimer Rd., ☎ 713/527–9669) is one of the oldest bars in town and can get lively from time to time. If Flannery O'Connor were to design a gay bar, it would look like **Past Times** (617 Fairview St., ☎ 713/529–4669), a low gray house that's spare, trashy, dark, smoky, dirty, and looks almost abandoned; it also has a terrible sound system. The **Venture-N** (2923 S. Main St., ☎ 713/522–0000), actually just east of Montrose, is home to four leather-and-Levi's clubs, and gets more of the motorcycle crowd than the Ripcord or Mining Co. (*see above*); can get very frisky in here late at night.

Club Houston (2205 Fannin St., ☎ 713/659–4998) is the city's male bathhouse, with lockers, video rooms, tanning beds, an outdoor pool, and workout equipment.

THE LITTLE BLACK BOOK

At Your Fingertips

AIDS Foundation Houston Hotline: ☎ 713/524–2437. **Greater Houston Convention and Visitors Bureau:** 801 Congress Ave., 77002, ☎ 713/227–3100 or 800/446–8786. **Gay and Lesbian Switchboard:** ☎ 713/529–3211. **Hate Crimes Hotline:** ☎ 713/529–9615. **Montrose Clinic:** ☎ 713/520–2000.

Gay Media

Houston has no shortage of gay papers, all of them quite useful and well-written. *Out Smart* (☎ 713/520–7237) is a monthly news and entertainment magazine, *Houston Voice* (☎ 713/529–8490) is a weekly, and *This Week in Texas* (☎ 713/527–9111) includes plenty of stuff on Houston. The *Texas Triangle* (☎ 713/871–1272) is the news-oriented weekly newspaper. *Maleman* (☎ 713/528–6253) is the gay-male bar rag (also covers Dallas).

Good mainstream resources include the **Houston Tribune** (☎ 713/862–9603), an upbeat arts monthly that covers mostly events and happenings in western Houston, including Montrose; **Public News** (☎ 713/520–1520), a vaguely counterculturist newsweekly; and the ubiquitous **Houston Press** (☎ 713/624–1400), the major arts and entertainment weekly.

BOOKSTORES

Crossroads Market (111 Westheimer Rd., ☎ 713/942–0147) has both mainstream and lesbigay titles; it's rather upscale and literary. **LOBO Books** (1424-C Westheimer Rd., ☎ 713/522–5156) has some gay and lesbian titles (and an especially good selection of used titles), though it's decidedly more male-oriented and carries adult videos. **Inklings** (1846 Richmond Ave., ☎ 713/521–3369) has the best selection of feminist and lesbian titles. Of the three stores, this one comes closest to serving as the hub and resource center of the gay and lesbian community.

Body and Fitness

The big cruising and buffing grounds, for both men and women, is the **Fitness Exchange** (3930 Kirby Dr., ☎ 713/524–9932), a huge, well-equipped health club. Smaller, far less of a scene, and more personal and user-friendly, is **Body Balance** (2425 Sunset Blvd., ☎ 713/520–9916).

10 Out in Key West

KEY WEST IS LIKE AN ENTIRE ISLAND of goofy great-uncles and eccentric great-aunts. With a mood that is equal parts American, Caribbean, and bacchanalian, this small city takes great delight in failing to fit in with the rest of the world. In keeping with the town's quirkiness, the most cherished annual event here is Fantasy Fest, a weeklong celebration of all that is wacky and wicked. The Fantasy Fest of 1993 was the least successful in Key West's history, something that just about everyone blamed on the festival's theme that year, "Lost in the Sixties." Quipped one local, "For most of us here, Lost in the Sixties isn't fantasy, it's reality. It felt pretty much like any other week in Key West."

Indeed, although Key West has for decades resisted traditional mores, it was during the '60s that the fringes of society began moving here and in the mid-'70s that gay guest houses began opening in rapid succession. For at least a decade, there were sporadic clashes between the new guard of gayification and the conservative, in some cases homophobic, old guard. Real estate prices rose dramatically, making it tough for slackers to move in.

Whatever tensions between gays and straights existed during these years, they were certainly no worse than those in major American cities and even in other gay resort towns. What is significant, however, is how little tension exists today. The occasional tourist who ambles off a visiting cruise ship or out of one of the city's many cheap motels is met with stern disapproval by locals if caught behaving rudely toward the gay population. Residents realize that gays and lesbians were responsible, in part, for as much as 75% of the restoration of Key West's historic district, and that we account for a tremendous cut of the city's tourism revenue.

Nineteenth-century New England seafarers built a number of the town's clapboard conch (pronounced "conk") houses, many of which are still standing. Subsequent waves of immigrants included persecuted Bahamians, Cuban cigar makers, and anybody with a reason to take flight from the mainland—from bootleggers to run-of-the-mill scofflaws. Wrecking, the salvaging of goods from ships smashed against Key West's dangerous coral reefs, was a popular occupation here for many years.

In 1912, railroad magnate Henry Flagler connected Key West and all of the Florida Keys to the mainland by building the Overseas Railroad, giving the city a second vital boom. But the Depression, followed by a tremendous hurricane in 1935, snuffed out the town's good fortune until 1938, when a highway was built on top of the old rail bed, again linking Key West with the mainland. The navy, which had taken advantage of the island's strategic position at various times, especially during the Civil War, became a major economic power through the '40s, as did tourism and the ever-popular cigar industry.

Through the past half-century, the town has boomed, then tapered off, then boomed again. At the height of the period of gay tourism and development, the AIDS epidemic struck Key West and ended the lives of many who had settled here. The epidemic also motivated a wave of gay men already diagnosed with AIDS to move here to continue their battle to survive. By the mid-'80s, the town's orgiastic reputation had given way to the stark reality of the disease. According to longtime resident Jerry Frantz, a man who has acted as a "buddy" to 24 young gay men with AIDS—and who has watched each of them die—Key West still retains an extremely high AIDS-stricken population, but the rate of new persons diagnosed with the virus has finally begun to subside.

Walk through the town today, and you'll notice a spirited camaraderie not just among gay men, but among lesbians and gays, and among straights and gays. Certainly 15 years ago, the older gay guard had less regard for lesbians. This is changing steadily, and today at many guest houses you'll find both genders mingling and hot-tubbing in harmony. However, the lesbian residential population still lacks an equal say in the machinations of the gay community. Only one lesbian-operated guest house and a handful of lesbian-owned businesses have opened here.

There is a mischievous gleam in the eyes of most Key Westers. If you spend a week here, you'll leave feeling as though you've befriended half the community. That sounds hokey, but it's true.

Everybody in Key West has mourned the death of several close friends to AIDS. The constant zaniness and off-color humor, the nonstop joking, the love of all that is odd, new, and foreign—this is Key West's long "black sheep" history at work. But it is just as much a by-product of the daily struggle to feel hope and happiness in the face of much grieving.

THE LAY OF THE LAND

There's enough sightseeing here for the most avid walkabout to kill a couple of days exploring, though most visitors come here just to lounge around and sunbathe. Best daytime game plan: Rent a bike or scooter and wander—without a map or a guidebook. You can't not discover an engaging sight, a quirky neighborhood, an amusing insight. Key West is all very interesting and colorful and relatively safe.

Duval Street and Environs

By day, the touristy buzz of **Duval Street** is worth braving if only to observe its diversity: groovy middle-age executives with ponytails and Rolexes; children with ice cream–smeared cheeks; husbands fresh off the cruise ships, dodging furtively in and out of gay peep-show parlors; blue-haired matrons picking voraciously over floral muumuus and seashell jewelry; rippled butch boys in white T-shirts and denim cut-offs snapping photos of themselves and each other every 50 feet.

The rule on Duval Street seems to be that the smaller the street number (numbering begins at Mallory Square on the north end), the greater the incidence of homophobia. At the north end of Duval are several of the more touristy Key West attractions, among them the predictable **Ripley's Believe It or Not Museum** (527 Duval St., ☎ 305/293–9686) and the somewhat more interesting **Wreckers Museum** (322 Duval St., ☎ 305/294–

9502), which details the city's history of wrecking and contains 18th- and 19th-century antiques.

Many of the gay bars and gay-popular restaurants are on or just off Duval south of Fleming Street. There are also dozens of gay-owned and/or gay-popular shops along this stretch, including the **Annex** (705 Duval St., 305/296–9800), which sells swimwear, lotions, gay magazines, and club-kid fashion; **Fast Buck Freddies** (500 Duval St., ☎ 305/294–2007), a full department store of glitz and camp; **In Touch** (715 Duval St., 305/292–7293), which sells cards and gifts; and **Goldsmith Jewelers** (335 Duval St., 305/294–1243), one of the nation's foremost gay and lesbian custom jewelers. You might also head a block east from Duval to **Fausto's Food Palace** (522 Fleming St., ☎ 305/296–5663; also 1105 White St., ☎ 305/294–5221), an extremely cruisy grocery store and the only one downtown—it's a good place to stock up the pantry of your rental. The T-shirt logo proudly proclaims: *You Can't Beat Our Meat.*

At night, Duval Street takes on the feel of New Orleans's Bourbon Street, without the immense crowds and the fear of crime: Music blares out of open-air bars, and everybody bounces around jovially.

Parallel to Duval one block west is **Whitehead Street,** a mostly residential avenue with two great museums. The **Ernest Hemingway House** (907 Whitehead St., ☎ 305/294–1575), in which the author wrote the majority of his life's work, contains original furnishings. Milling around the property are dozens of cats; virtually every home in Key West has three stinky, inbred cats—here they're actually a part of the attraction. Across the street is the 92-foot-tall **Lighthouse Museum** (938 Whitehead St., ☎ 305/294–0012), which includes the 1880s house in which the keeper lived, plus a few exhibits. It's worth climbing the 98 steps to the tower, which affords magnificent views of town and of the cute guys sunbathing around the pool of the Lighthouse Court guest house, next door. At the southern end of Whitehead, where it intersects with South Street, is a marker that incorrectly labels the spot the **Southernmost Point** in the United States—it is actually the southernmost point accessible to civilians; the true location is within Key West's navy base.

Mallory Square and Front Street

Front Street and **Mallory Square** are at the north end of Duval Street. This is the least gay and the most touristy part of Key West. Every night vendors, street artists, and tourists rub shoulders during Mallory Square's sunset celebration. The **Conch Tour Train** (☎ 305/294–5161) departs daily from the square, carrying mostly bored-looking cruise ship passengers, each wearing a bright green sticker on his or her breast—supposedly so the ship authorities can keep better tabs on them but more likely to identify them to shop owners as prospective suckers. The trains do give a nice overview of the island, and the narration is usually quite lively.

A few attractions near the square include the **Key West Aquarium** (1 Whitehead St., ☎ 305/296–2051) and the **Mel Fisher Maritime Heritage Society Museum** (200 Greene St., ☎ 305/294–2633), which contains treasure and artifacts recovered in 1985 from a pair of 17th-century Spanish galleons that sank 40 miles offshore during a hurricane.

Historic District

The blocks bounded on the west by Duval Street, on the north by Caroline Street, on the east by White Street, and on the south by Truman Avenue loosely constitute Key West's historic district. Many of the gay guest houses are here, and plenty of other restored cottages and homes bear examining. This is also where many of Key West's famed gay artists have lived, including Tennessee Williams (at 1431 Duncan St.), Jerry Herman, and the guy who wrote the "plop, plop, fizz, fizz . . ." jingle for Alka-Seltzer.

Beaches and Bushes

The **Dick Dock,** at the south end of Reynolds Street, juts rigidly into the Atlantic and is popular with gay sunbathers. It was circumcised a few years back when a ferocious storm passed through Key West. This area is extremely cruisy; guys hang around the dock and the sidewalk behind the tennis courts, across the street, at all hours. Note, however, that the dock is officially closed at night. Other popular sunbathing spots, for both gay men and lesbians, are the deck at the **Atlantic Shores Beach Club** (*see* Scenes, *below*) and the beach at **Ft. Zachary Taylor State Historic Park** (follow the signs from Southard St., ☎ 305/292–6713), which tends to draw more locals than tourists.

The **Salt Ponds** near the airport have long been a haven of cruising. It's a network of paths and underbrush and is frequented all day and night, though these days by a mostly local band of guys. Backing up to the Salt Ponds is **Little Hamaca Park,** which is also pretty cruisy. Both spots are sometimes patrolled by police.

GETTING THERE

If you book a couple months ahead, the airfare to Key West from Miami isn't much more than the fare from your original destination to Miami—sometimes it's the same. The most you'd pay on the spot is $200 round-trip. Airlines include American Eagle, Comair, USAir Express, Gulf Stream (in partnership with United) and, only from Naples, Cape Air. Greyhound comes into town twice weekly, but this is a long ride, and, when you consider how cheap car rentals are out of Miami, it makes more sense to drive. Heading to Key West on a Friday or back to the mainland on a Sunday can take five or six hours; other times expect a three- to four-hour drive.

GETTING AROUND

Though considered a lousy city to drive in, Key West has slow but not impossible traffic. In high season, parking can be tough. It's best to look on a side street in the historic area—a 15-minute walk from Duval Street. A fleet of pink taxis serves the island.

Although most everything in town is walkable, the most popular forms of transportation are bicycles, which are available for nominal rental fee from most guest houses, and mopeds, which you can rent from a bunch of places, including **Keys Moped & Scooter** (523 Truman Ave., ☎ 305/294–0399) and **Moped Hospital** (601 Truman Ave., ☎ 305/296–3344).

WHEN TO GO

Key West is as seasonal as the rest of Florida, with tourism slowing dramatically in summer. Although July and August can swelter at times, it's actually no more unbearable here than in much of the country; there are always cool breezes off the water. The humidity is always high, and the island is subject to quick passing rain showers at any time, but generally you can expect warm sunny days year-round. High season is October through April.

The annual **Fantasy Festival** (last week of October) is to Key West what Mardi Gras is to New Orleans; it's a crowded, crazy, wonderful time to visit, but if you're interested, book rooms at least six months ahead. Other popular times include the **Gay Arts Festival** (late June), **Women in Paradise** (a.k.a. women's week, mid-July), and the **Key West Theatre Festival** (late Sept.-early Oct.). Christmas and New Year's are also popular times.

EATS

For a seasonal tourist town, Key West is above average from a culinary standpoint. The recent influx of cruise ships to Key West has ensured the survival of the town's many tacky, dull, and overpriced restaurants—most of them along the northern end of Duval Street and around Mallory Square. The worst of these offer bleak all-you-can-eat buffets, but just as many worthy options are nearby. To be safe, don't eat anywhere that hasn't been recommended to you by at least a couple of reliable sources.

Key West is as much a Caribbean island as a tiny Florida town, and the phrases "Floribbean" and "Key West regional" are bandied about at some of the more inventive eateries. This blend of culinary cultures results in creations like conch minestrone or pan-seared grouper with mango chutney. In general, the emphasis is on fresh seafood and tropical fruits and vegetables, including avocado, carambola (star fruit), and papaya. Key West is much closer to Cuba than to the Florida mainland, and the connection to that island's heritage is kept alive in several good Cuban restaurants.

Every restaurant in Key West is ostensibly gay-friendly. Restaurants geared to the cruise ship crowd and other easily shocked factions of the tourism trade form an exception to this rule, however; in these establishments you and your companion may stand out.

For price ranges, *see* Chart A at the front of this guide.

$$$$ **Cafe des Artistes.** This formal, diminutive dining room definitely has flare: crisp white napery, a black-and-white-checkered floor, and smooth, varnished wood—plus some of the best local art of any area restaurant. The food is French, but these chefs throw in the odd local touch: Lobster flambéed in cognac with shrimp in saffron butter, mango, and basil is a specialty. *1007 Simonton St., ☎ 305/294–7100.*

$$$$ **Louie's Backyard.** Though the service can be blatantly snotty, Louie's oceanfront dining room is one of the most inviting in town. The Latin American- and Caribbean-influenced menu is pretty fab, too—sample dishes are grilled Black Angus steak with smoked chili red wine sauce served with corn relish, and grilled smoked salmon served with sweet soy wakame salad with shiitake mushrooms—but if this all seems like more than your wallet can handle, at least drop by the back porch for drinks, to watch the sun set slowly over the Gulf of Mexico. *700 Waddell Ave., ☎ 305/294–1061.*

$$$-$$$$ **Square One.** A departure from Key West's predominant laid-back tropical look, Square One is a cosmopolitan restaurant done in a bold green-and-white color scheme, with white table linen and fine china. The regional cuisine includes such inventive fare as pistachio-encrusted chicken or yellow-tail snapper in annatto oil with plum-tomato chutney, Latin pesto, and plantain chips. Very gay and very trendy. *1075 Duval St., ☎ 305/296–4300.*

$$$ **Cafe Marquesa.** This is the island's top purveyor of Key West cuisine, which fuses New American, Floridian, and Caribbean fare. Typical is the grilled shrimp with roast banana and red curry sauce, sweet potato fritters, and mango relish. You dine in a light, airy dining room with local art and views directly into the open kitchen. *600 Fleming St., ☎ 305/292–1244.*

$$-$$$$ **Mangoe's.** One of Duval Street's true places to be seen, Mangoe's is typically brimming with colorful sorts. The designer pizzas, composed salads, pastas, and grills—all with nouvelle Floribbean touches—are commendable. It's easy to spend a few hours with friends over dinner on the cool, breezy patio. The only downer is the uneven service. *700 Duval St.,* ☎ *305/292–4606.*

$$–$$$ Antonia's. This Italian standby burned in a fire in 1995 but was expected to reopen in spring of 1996. It's pricey for what it offers. You'll find innovative pasta, veal, and chicken dishes: veal with shiitake mushrooms, fontina cheese, and marsala wine, for example, or meunière sauce with pine nuts. *615 Duval St.,* ☎ *305/294–6565.*

$$–$$$ Croissants de France. This can be anything from a simple French bakery to a slightly formal conch-Continental eatery, depending on what you're looking for. The crepes are a mainstay, as is the Greek salad. The more upscale entrées like beef bourguignon and seafood risotto are always top-notch. Try for a table in the lush garden to the side of the building. *816 Duval St.,* ☎ *305/294–2624.*

$$–$$$ Dim Sum. This sophisticated, 15-table alley café is one of the most striking restaurants in town. You dine beneath a high-peaked bamboo roof with paddle fans, amid authentic Oriental art in lacquer frames. The spicy Pan-Asian cuisine is terrific, from piquant eggplant and tofu to an Indian three-curry naan platter, to the stir-fried fresh catch of the day. *613½ Duval St.,* ☎ *305/294–6230.*

$$–$$$ La-Te-Da. The new owners of La-Te-Da have worked hard to improve its Continental cuisine. The tables outside by the pool and the fountains are intimate, and perfect for a romantic tête-à-tête. There are often waiters working in drag, and during the occasional prix-fixe theme nights, the staff provides campy cabaret entertainment. Great brunches. *1125 Duval St.,* ☎ *305/296–6706.*

$$–$$$ Pepe's Cafe and Steak House. Dating back to 1909, Pepe's is the oldest restaurant on the island. Naked-lady murals and historical anecdotes on the menus successfully capture Key West's colorful history of debauchery and pirating. It's a true institution known more for its atmosphere than its food and service, both of which can be spotty. Stick to the steak and oyster dishes; the fresh catches of the day are often a bit fishy. *806 Caroline St.,* ☎ *305/294–7192.*

$–$$ Mangia Mangia. The slogan here is "pasta to the people," a philosophy reflected by the one-track-mind menu of many varieties of heavenly homemade pasta, and by the fair prices. This reliable restaurant is set in a painstakingly preserved building with a lovely garden and redbrick patio in back—away from the crowds and noise of Duval Street. More than 300 choices on the wine list. *900 Southard St.,* ☎ *305/294–2469.*

$ Camille's. You'll need luck and persistence to get a seat at this little storefront bistro most nights, but the delightfully dishy atmosphere and down-home comfort food are worth the struggle. Expect the usual sandwiches, chicken fingers, and chilled salads—plus some great breakfasts. *703½ Duval St.,* ☎ *305/296–4811.*

$ Court Cafe at the Lighthouse Court. The crowd consists largely of gay men staying at the rather frisky Lighthouse Court resort (the café overlooks the pool), but everyone is welcome here, and it's a fine place to make friends and savor a cheap breakfast or lunch. A simple but solid menu of burgers, homemade potato salad, tuna sandwiches, quiche, etc. *902 Whitehead St.,* ☎ *305/294–9588.*

$ El Siboney. This zero-atmosphere place is the Cuban answer to Deep South barbecued-ribs joints. You eat at rickety tables with plastic tablecloths and paper napkins, feasting on such Havana specialties as conch chowder, garlic chicken, stuffed shrimp and crabs, *platanos,* and a sweet flan to top it off. The best Cuban food in town. *900 Catherine St.,* ☎ *305/296–4184.*

$ The Half Shell Oyster Raw Bar. This is exactly what you expect to find next to one of the busiest marinas in Key West, a simple shanty that serves

Key West

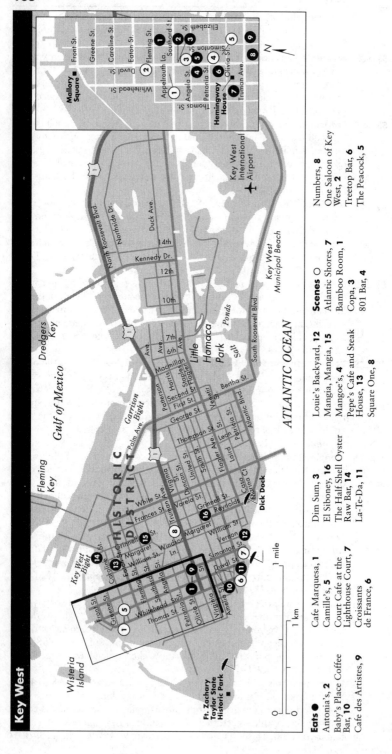

Eats ●

Antonia's, **2**
Baby's Place Coffee
Bar, **10**
Cafe des Artistes, **9**

Cafe Marquesa, **1**
Camille's, **5**
Court Cafe at the
Lighthouse Court, **7**
Croissants
de France, **6**

Dim Sum, **3**
El Siboney, **16**
The Half Shell Oyster
Raw Bar, **14**
La-Te-Da, **11**

Louie's Backyard, **12**
Mangia, Mangia, **15**
Mango's, **4**
Pepe's Cafe and Steak
House, **13**
Square One, **8**

Scenes ○

Atlantic Shores, **7**
Bamboo Room, **1**
Copa, **3**
801 Bar, **4**

Numbers, **8**
One Saloon of Key
West, **2**
Treetop Bar, **6**
The Peacock, **5**

up hours-old fresh oysters, stone-crab claws, and the like. The fried oyster sandwich is as good as any in New Orleans, too. Rows of shellacked picnic tables allow views of the maritime action. *Land's End Marina,* ☎ *305/294–7496.*

Coffeehouse Culture

Key West has only one gay-popular coffeehouse—one that lacks the sort of chic poseurs of South Beach and the brooding artiness of Seattle and San Francisco. **Baby's Place Coffee Bar** (1111 Duval St., ☎ 305/292–3739) is just a fun-loving, urbane little spot where locals gather to gossip and sip coffee.

SLEEPS

There is no shortage of rooms, but certain seasonal events make bookings tight. As with Provincetown or Palm Springs, the gay guest house network here is tremendously well developed, and choices abound. Most of the mainstream guest houses here are completely gay-friendly, too, but lack the convivial mood of the all-gay establishments. The bulk of the guest houses—gay and straight—are either in the heart of downtown, along Duval, Whitehead, or Simonton streets, or in the historic district several blocks east of downtown. The latter accommodations are usually the quietest and most secluded—but nowhere are you too far from the action.

Key West has plenty of great hotels as well, but at any large resort you're paying as much for the extensive staff and facilities as you are for your room. Consequently, comparably furnished and spacious rooms at most guest houses cost from 60% to 80% less than rooms at resorts.

For price ranges, *see* Chart A at the front of this guide.

Hotels and Motels

⊡ Though large and impersonal, the historic **Marriott Casa Marina** is the most sumptuous chain resort on the island. Built with the money of Henry Flagler's railroad empire, this 13-acre, 1921 resort is set on its own point, about 15 minutes from lower Duval Street. Sunday brunch is a big deal here. *1500 Reynolds St.,* ☎ *305/296–3535 or 800/626–0777. 311 rooms. $$$$*

⊡ The **Pier House Resort,** just off Mallory Square, is unaffordable for most mortals. Whirlpool baths, CD players, VCRs, and other over-the-top touches are among the unusual features. There's also a beloved but overpriced restaurant and a full health spa and fitness center. *1 Duval St.,* ☎ *305/296–4600 or 800/327–8340. 142 rooms. $$$$*

⊡ The striking, seven-story **La Concha Holiday Inn** dates from 1926 and is the tallest structure in town (views from the rooftop lounge are amazing). The rooms are quite large, have period reproductions, and are occasionally let go at low rates if you call at the right time. *430 Duval St.,* ☎ *305/296–2991 or 800/745–2191. 160 rooms. $$$*

⊡ The **Key Lodge Motel** is a standard motel with a gay following and a prime location—it's as cheap a motel as you'll find on Duval Street, though still no bargain. *1004 Duval St.,* ☎ *305/296–9915 or 800/458–1296. 22 rooms. $$*

⊡ The **Atlantic Shores Motel,** site of the popular oceanfront bar and grill of the same name, has been given a postmodern makeover in the past year. It's still a simple motel, albeit Key West's gayest one. *510 South St.,* ☎ *305/296–2491 or 800/526–3559. 71 rooms. $–$$*

Guest Houses

☐ Of the many mainstream but gay-friendly guest houses in town, the **Marquesa Hotel** is the most luxurious. Rooms in the original 1884 restored property have the most character, with Queen Anne antiques and marble details. The service is first-class. *600 Fleming St., ☎ 305/292–1919 or 800/869–4631. 27 rooms. Mostly straight. $$$–$$$$*

☐ One of the best smaller guest houses, and the oldest exclusively gay one in town, the **Curry House** is presided over by friendly innkeeper Carl Cordes and has always had a major following with Europeans. Rooms of this 1890 house are clean and bright, with hard date-palm walls, floral or paisley valances and bedspreads, but small baths. Out back is a big, curvaceous pool. *806 Fleming St., ☎ 305/294–6777 or 800/633–7439. 9 rooms. Gay male. $$$*

☐ **Alexander's** is a tad less sumptuous than the nearby Brass Key (*see below*) but no less inviting—with fragrant bougainvillea and other tropical flowers in abundance, several sundecks, tropical furnishings, and clean tiled bathrooms, some of which are shared. The main 1910 house has been flawlessly restored, and several units were added two years ago. *1118 Fleming St., ☎ 305/294–9919 or 800/654–9919. 16 rooms. Gay male/lesbian. $$–$$$$*

☐ Qualitatively similar to the Brass Key, **Big Ruby's** nevertheless offers a wholly different experience. Though secluded, it's sleek and contemporary, and only a block off Duval Street. It also seems to cater a bit more to disco bunnies. Rooms are spacious, spotless, and bright; the few that accommodate two couples are a relative bargain. The owners' three adorable miniature dachshunds, Clayton, Roseanna, and Maude, follow guests around everywhere. *409 Appelrouth La., ☎ 305/296–2323 or 800/477–7829. 17 rooms. Mostly gay male. $$–$$$$*

☐ Hotelier Michael MacIntyre's knowledge of first-rate accommodations (he has worked for the Ritz-Carlton chain) shows at his **Brass Key Guesthouse.** This duo of immaculate yellow clapboard buildings with glistening corrugated metal roofs has the most elegant rooms of any gay property here, with tropical-print quilts, high-quality colonial reproductions, and clean, modern baths. Every detail has been thought of—from a small basket of snacks left in your room to a generous evening cocktail party held nightly around the hot tub. *412 Frances St., ☎ 305/296–4719 or 800/932–9119. 15 rooms. Gay male/lesbian. $$–$$$$*

☐ If you're here to meet men and the quality of your accommodations is of minimal importance, consider the **Island House,** which also sells $10 day-memberships. The largest guest-house pool on the island is here; you will also find a sauna, Jacuzzi, and a house-wide clothing-optional policy. If you keep your eye on the naked men lying around the pool you may not notice the chipped paint and rotting wood—this place is quite shabby and surprisingly costly. When a door is left open at night, however, all sorts of interesting creatures have been known to amble in. Open 24 hours is the video room with communal seating and boxes of Kleenex laid about strategically—apparently, they show a lot of sad movies in here. A poor man's Lighthouse Court. *1129 Fleming St., ☎ 305/294–6284 or 800/890–6284. 34 rooms. Gay male. $$–$$$$*

☐ The reputation of the **Lighthouse Court** has risen in recent years, thanks to new owners. It's still every bit as social, with its own reception lounge-cum-video bar, a maze of lushly landscaped decks, one of the busiest hot tubs in town, a nice exercise room, and the most rooms of any guest house compound. Rooms are large and clean, but spare. The location is terrific, near downtown but on a quiet street, snug below the Lighthouse. *902 Whitehead St., ☎ 305/294–9588. 42 rooms. Gay male. $$–$$$$*

⌖ The **Mangrove House** is a smart, small, yellow Bahamian house with thin white columns and a perfectly restored tin roof. It's a quietly elegant, low-key property. *623 Southard St.,* ☎ *305/294–1866 or 800/294–1866. 4 rooms. Gay male. $$–$$$$*

⌖ The owners of the Oasis (*see below*) also run the considerably more upscale and quieter **Coral Tree Inn** across the street. From the antiques-filled lobby to the four-poster beds to the lovely redbrick patio and pool out back, this 1892 house is the superior of the two, and rates are only about 20% higher. Guests at either house have rights to the public rooms and swimming pools of both. *822 Fleming St.,* ☎ *305/296–2131 or 800/362–7477. 11 rooms. Gay male. $$–$$$*

⌖ A bit smaller than but offering a similar experience to the that of the Lighthouse Court, the **Oasis** has three buildings and two swimming pools with plenty of decking and a diverse, outgoing crowd. Rooms are a comfy hodgepodge, all with paisley bedspreads, sofas, and somewhat utilitarian wooden furniture; some have private bath. *823 Fleming St.,* ☎ *305/296–2131 or 800/362–7477. 20 rooms. Gay male. $$–$$$*

⌖ If staying at an all-female house is a priority, you have but one choice, the **Rainbow House,** a nicely laid-out former cigar factory (circa 1886) that's neither fancy nor substandard—just a good solid guest house with beautiful sundecks and a pretty heated pool. Some say it's pricey for what it is, but in fact, the rates are in keeping with those at other guest houses in town. *525 United St.,* ☎ *305/292–1450 or 800/749–6696. 25 rooms. Lesbian. $$–$$$*

⌖ New owners took over the **Eaton Lodge** in May 1995 and completely overhauled the rooms within its historic 1880s frame just off Duval Street. They have also added a pool. Though baths are modern, every other aspect of the decor—from the old hardwood floors to the many antiques, Bahama ceiling fans, and original architectural details—harks back several decades. They also rent a neighboring bungalow that easily sleeps six. *511 Eaton St.,* ☎ *305/292–2170 or 800/294–2170. 14 rooms. Mixed gay/straight. $$*

⌖ Next door to the Oasis, the equally social **Coconut Grove** has three buildings, most with functional, tropical decor (lots of rattan and wicker) and rooms in a variety of configurations, accommodating from one to six guests. The evening cocktail hour here is one of the better ones in town. A highlight is the roof deck, which is one of the highest points in the historic district. *817 Fleming St.,* ☎ *305/296–5107 or 800/262–6055. 20 rooms. Mostly gay male, lesbians welcome. $–$$$$*

⌖ A dependable, reasonable choice that caters to a somewhat more mature crowd is **Colours,** a striking Victorian mansion close to the bars on Appelrouth Lane. *410 Fleming St.,* ☎ *305/294–6977 or 800/934–5622. 12 rooms. Mostly gay male/lesbian. $–$$$*

⌖ The **Knowles Guest House** is a restored 1880s conch house with original floors, an antiques-filled parlor, and small but clean rooms. This is one of the homier guest houses in town, and there's a wealth of tropical greenery and a pretty Jacuzzi out back. *1004 Eaton St.,* ☎ *305/296–8132 or 800/352–4414. 5 rooms. Mostly gay male/lesbian. $–$$*

⌖ If you're on a budget but wish to be in the historic district, consider the **Nassau House** whose new owners are wonderful guys, but whose rooms are a bit ramshackle. Renovations are underway, and some units have been spruced up. *1016 Fleming St.,* ☎ *305/296–8513. 8 rooms. Mixed gay/straight. $–$$*

⌖ The **Tropical Inn,** across from the 801 Bar, is a historic conch house; some of the neat but standard rooms have balconies overlooking Duval Street. *812 Duval St.,* ☎ *305/294–9977. 7 rooms. Mixed gay/straight. $–$$*

Rentals

The price of rentals in Key West has shot up in the past 10 years, but for a group of six to eight, a weeklong stay in a fairly luxurious place still costs a fraction of what they'd have to pay staying as couples at one of the better guest houses. Two-, three-, and four-bedroom accommodations in high season start as low as $900 a week but average between $1,800 and $2,400; off-season you can find a small weekly rental for $650 to $700. Two of the better gay-friendly sources are **Greg O'Berry Real Estate** (701 Caroline St., 33040, ☎ 305/294–6637 or 800/654–2781) and **Key West Realty** (1109 Duval St., 33040, ☎ 305/294–7368 or 800/654–5131).

SCENES

The nightlife scene in Key West is slightly perplexing. That such a small community should have so many bars (eight) is most surprising, particularly when you consider that at least a dozen of the guest houses have late-afternoon cocktail hours and bar set-ups around the pool. But of course, if you're in Key West to socialize, bar-hopping is another way to mingle with locals as well as with out-of-towners staying at other accommodations. In no other destination in America, by the way, are locals more likely to introduce themselves to complete strangers in a bar. This is a terribly forward community, with none of the body-glorification or standoffishness of some gay resorts. Also, Key West draws a considerably older median crowd (largely ages 35 to 55) than South Beach.

Most of the bar activity is on or just off Duval Street, from about Appelrouth Lane to Olivia Street. Weeknights, except during major weeks for tourism, are typically quiet at all of these bars, with Fridays and Saturdays the only times you can count on big crowds.

Atlantic Shores. This is Key West's essential "sun and be seen" bar—an outdoor deck, pool, and dock jutting into the Atlantic Ocean from a motel complex on South Street. Both boys and girls lie here all day, often nude. A second wave of patrons arrives later in the day to watch the sun sink gracefully below the horizon, and by the time darkness has arrived, the Atlantic Shores is empty. There's a snack bar with good burgers and sandwiches. Sunday's "tea by the sea" dances are legendary. *511 South St., ☎ 305/296–2491. Crowd: diverse, mixed m/f.*

Bamboo Room. This puny dive with mint green walls has stiff, cheap drinks, a pool table, a great jukebox, a campy staff, and usually anywhere from three to 13 guys yucking it up. *422 Appelrouth La., ☎ 305/294–2655. Crowd: 80/20 m/f, kind of a loopy bunch.*

Copa. Once a theater, it became the town's largest disco. Alas, in August 1995, it burned to the ground. A new, industrial-strength disco with many levels is under construction and, at press time (fall 1995), was slated to open in February 1996. *623 Duval St., ☎ 305/296–8521.*

801 Bar. Some locals are known to pop into the open-air 801 Bar as often as three times a day to catch up with friends and throw around a little gossip. The smaller bar in the back gets the town's only leather contingent, though all are welcome, and the upstairs bar has a stage, where everything from drag shows to live music are performed. *801 Duval St., ☎ 305/294–4737. Crowd: 75/25 m/f—more mixed on second floor; local, colorful, outgoing, drunk.*

Numbers. Numbers is a short walk from downtown and, oddly, shares most of the building it's in with Key West's straight strip club (there are separate entrances from outside). All in all, it's a pretty uninspired strip joint. *1023 Truman Ave.,* ☎ *305/296–0333. Crowd: if you like strippers. . . .*

One Saloon of Key West. What used to be more of a leather bar has gradually become the town's standard cruise bar and small disco. The South Beach disco set tends to favor the Saloon, though few locals bother with it. It's not a big place; the dance floor is a fraction of the size of the Copa's old one. *1 Appelrouth La.,* ☎ *305/296–8118. Crowd: mostly male, young by Key West standards, a bit stand-and-model, touristy.*

The Peacock. Because it's on a stretch of Simonton Street traversed by few tourists, some fear this neighborhood bar may not survive. It has been developing a loyal following, though, and it draws more women than most of the other bars; that alone sets it apart and may keep it going. The interior is brightly decorated—lots of black and silver, and there's pool, pinball, and videos. *900 Simonton St.,* ☎ *305/296–9230. Crowd: very mixed m/f, low-key.*

Treetop Bar. The owners of the La-Te-Da spruced things up a couple of years ago, and the Treetop—a once-venerable Key West institution that had been on the decline—has been back in rare form ever since. Less of a dive than most of the local bars, it's still not the sort of place that could ever leave you feeling under-dressed or out of place (the friendly bar staff deserves at least part of the credit for this). It's a cute space with a pitched roof, soft pop music, ceiling fans, French windows, and a great marble bar. *La-Te-Da Guest House, 1125 Duval St.,* ☎ *305/296–6706. Crowd: mixed m/f, older, quieter, upscale, a good mix of locals and visitors.*

THE LITTLE BLACK BOOK

At Your Fingertips

AIDS Help Hotline: ☎ 305/296–6196 or 800/640–3867. **General gay/lesbian crisis and referral help line:** ☎ 305/296–4357. **Key West Business Guild (gay):** Box 1208, 33041, ☎ 305/294–4603. **Key West Chamber of Commerce (mainstream):** ☎ 305/294–2587. **South Florida AIDS Network:** ☎ 305/585–7744.

Gay Media

There are no specifically gay newspapers, but the monthly *Southern Exposure Guide* (no phone) is a good source for gay and lesbian travelers.

BOOKSTORES

One of the best bookstores in town, **Caroline Street Books** (800 Caroline St., ☎ 305/294–3931), is in the Red Doors Building, a restored 1868 house that was a brothel as recently as 25 years ago (there are several other interesting shops here as well). This bookstore has an excellent selection of gay and lesbian books and magazines, books by or about local authors (Hemingway, Tennessee Williams, etc.), and other good literature. You'll also find a small selection of books as well as cards and gay novelties at the **Leather Master** (418A Appelrouth La., ☎ 305/292–5051).

Body and Fitness

The larger resorts and a couple of the larger gay guest houses have fitness centers, but most gay men and lesbians work out at **Club Body Tech Health & Fitness** (1075 Duval St., ☎ 305/292–9683); prices of weekly memberships are extremely reasonable.

11 *Out in Las Vegas*

IN LAS VEGAS YOU ALWAYS HAVE TIME and you always have money. From the perspective of the casinos—and they essentially dictate every city rule, ordinance, and law—it's imperative that their patrons always have the time and the money to gamble. Only if the typical visitor to Las Vegas spends at least a couple of hours a day gambling will the casinos—and therefore the city—turn a profit.

Making sure you have money is the easier imperative to satisfy, especially in today's computerized world. Cash machines are placed strategically throughout the city, in bars, convenience stores, and—most important—in the casinos themselves, where you can also get a cash advance on your credit card. The cost of lodging, dining, and entertainment is kept as low as possible, so that you will feel comfortable—almost obligated—to spend the money you've "saved" on other typical vacation expenses on the slot machines and gaming tables instead.

Remember, while you're busy devouring obscenely large plates of food and living it up, the casino has gingerly snuck its hand into your back pocket. Does this mean Las Vegas rips people off? Not necessarily. For some, Las Vegas represents America's greatest bargain. For others it is a long, deluded road to bankruptcy or job loss or alcoholism. For most people, it is a fair exchange: You will spend, per day, about what you would on any other vacation, and you will leave having had just as good a time. Even by Las Vegas standards, these are pretty good odds.

Providing visitors with enough time to gamble has been a more challenging and rather ingeniously solved problem. You have only so many hours in the day. You want to eat, shop, perhaps visit a casino's theme park, or go bowling, rest, hit a couple of bars, maybe work out or take a swim. At some point you have to get snacks or a soda at the store. And you must leave eventually, probably via the airport or train station. With all that, are you really going to have enough time to gamble?

The answer is yes, and here's how: Not only are the casinos open 24 hours, but so are most of the shops, restaurants, convenience stores, bars, bowling alleys, and gyms. Even the wedding chapels are open all night. Furthermore, different forms of gambling—usually slot machines and video poker tables—are located in most of these places. You are never far from some form of gambling. At the minimart, the airport, most bars—wherever you look, there are slot machines. At the Robin Hood restaurant in Excalibur's Medieval Village, you are given keno cards to play while you eat; all eyes remain fixed on the red digital keno board. The socializing at the table revolves around the board; you never have to stop gambling. . . . Ever.

The planners of Las Vegas have created what is basically America's first timeless city. Day blends imperceptibly into night; casinos have no windows or clocks to remind you where you are, how long you've been here, and whether other obligations might exist. It's escapism in one of its most alluring forms: You leave the rest of life behind and play games all day with little piles of pretty plastic chips. The reality, that these chips represent real money, is kept hushed.

Perhaps the greatest example of timelessness in Las Vegas is the striking trompe l'oeil ceiling above the Forum Shops at Caesars, which are laid out to resemble an ancient Roman city. The ceiling is painted to look like the sky, and the lighting changes slowly but constantly so that one hour the city appears dark, an hour later it appears light. It all happens so subtly that it's difficult to notice it. Spend a few hours here and the distinction becomes meaningless—you actually lose track of how many "days" have passed you by.

And the same can be said for Las Vegas as a whole. There's no hurry to finish your game, because whatever you're planning to do after you leave the casino, it will still be there, open and crowded, whenever you arrive.

This is a city everyone should see at least once. There is a region in the mind of each of us—a repository of sorts—in which we pile our self-indulgent tendencies, imprudence, garish tastes, lasciviousness, and extravagant desires. Las Vegas is dedicated exclusively to this region of our brain. It's impossible to drive the length of Las Vegas Boulevard—this broad avenue lined with glowing monuments to gambling, drinking, and eating—without being impressed. The colors, the vibrancy, the synthetic nature of Las Vegas are fascinating.

The region has never had an especially gay following. Although in theory just as many gay people gamble as straight people, you seldom hear the city mentioned among the nation's most popular gay destinations. But as the makeup of this town has begun to include an influx of transplants—most of them from California and many of them lured by the low cost of living, predictably moderate weather, and job opportunity— an active, though relatively small, gay community has emerged. No one comes expecting much in the way of gay culture. The arts community is virtually nonexistent, and the University of Nevada–Las Vegas offers less of a bohemian, intellectual buzz than other large universities. So as the general population grows exponentially, the gay population grows proportionally. Lesbians and gays also move here with some trepidation, unsure just how out to be and sometimes unwilling to invest a great deal in the gay community when their stay may be brief (many of the jobs are short-term).

Nevertheless, many gay newcomers to Las Vegas were used to gay bars, coffeehouses, enlightened political laws, and general tolerance—and they're not about to creep back into the closet. During the past couple of years, this inflow of movers and shakers has led to many positive political changes. Both candidates for governor in 1994 courted the gay community with fund-raisers, the state's antisodomy law was repealed in 1993, and the culinary union—which represents the bulk of the casinos' dining employees—now prohibits discrimination on the basis of sexual orientation. Most of the big casinos have added sexual orientation to their antidiscrimination policies, and the rest are expected to join them soon. Las Vegas is a tremendously progressive city, not necessarily in terms of where it is in relation to other major cities, but definitely in terms of what it has accomplished in so little time.

THE LAY OF THE LAND

Las Vegas has none of the trappings of urbanity. The airport is right off the southern part of the Strip, about as close to downtown as can be. There is virtually no mass transit and no need for it. People drive instead of walk. There really aren't any neighborhoods. Las Vegas is flat and spread out, lacking perspective and volume. Hotels and casinos rise above the strip much as the red and green markers do on a Monopoly board.

Las Vegas, of course, *is* a sight. And it's at its most spectacular at night, preferably from a distance. For a cool nighttime view, drive south along the Boulder Highway (U.S. 93/95) and, after about 15 minutes, you'll reach the crest of the first hill south of Las Vegas, in Henderson. Pull off at any exit to admire the immense glow behind you—there may not be a brighter tract of land anywhere in the world. And this view is all the more eerie because Las Vegas is surrounded entirely by pitch-black desert.

This city so rich in kitsch is essentially devoid of historically and culturally significant points of interest. The precious and much heralded **Liberace Museum** (1775 E. Tropicana Ave., ☎ 702/798–5595) is the one exception. This giddy tribute to the late entertainer is set inside a small one-story building that looks as though it might once have housed a Chinese fast-food restaurant. Inside the museum are photos, costumes (including Lee's beloved Czar Nicholas uniform), mannequins, and pianos (one was played by Chopin, another by Gershwin). A small gift shop sells, among other colorful mementos, Liberace soap and ashtrays.

If you have more time for museum-hopping, you can schedule visits to the **Guinness World of Records Museum** (2780 Las Vegas Blvd. S, ☎ 702/792–3766) and the **Imperial Palace Automobile Museum** (3535 Las Vegas Blvd. S, ☎ 702/731–3311), which counts among its more than 200 vintage autos Adolf Hitler's 1939 Mercedes-Benz touring sedan.

Downtown
If there is any area of town with an urban feel, it's downtown. Formerly the hub of Las Vegas nightlife, it went through a stage of decline for many years and has only recently been cleaned up in places. There are sidewalks here, and you can walk around, but few people seem to leave their cars behind.

A major Las Vegas phenomenon is the dense abundance of pawnshops, and most of the popular ones are downtown. Try the **Ace Loan Company** (215 North 3rd St., ☎ 702/384–5771) or **Stoney's Loan and Jewelry** (126 S. 1st St., ☎ 702/384–2686). These brokers serve a valuable purpose in a town where financial crises occur with disturbing frequency.

Wedding Chapel Row
Bette Midler and Richard Gere are just two celebrities alleged to have exchanged vows (not with each other, thankfully) along Las Vegas's handy little Wedding Chapel Row, which is along Las Vegas Boulevard between Sahara Avenue and Charleston Boulevard. Liberal divorce and marriage laws were instituted in Nevada in 1931 in an attempt to lure tourists. The laws have never changed, so today a man and a woman can get hitched faster than you can fry an egg. As for same-sex unions, while gay weddings are not legally sanctioned by the state of Nevada, **Susan L. Thompson** (☎ 702/258–0157), an ordained minister and licensed therapist, does perform lesbian and gay commitment ceremonies/holy unions. She will conduct the event at your choice of locale, including your hotel (both Bally's and Harrah's welcome same-sex weddings).

The Strip

The Strip is Las Vegas Boulevard from about Hacienda Avenue north to about Sahara Avenue. Along this six-lane road are most of the newest casinos. With casino development still rampant, more properties are being planned for the blocks east of the Strip out to about Paradise Road.

Casinos

Most of us come to Las Vegas for the casinos, of which there are dozens, ranging from spectacular compounds inspired by theme parks to shaggy dives that date from the early '50s. If you're a gambler, consult a general guidebook dedicated solely to Las Vegas gaming. If you're not, consider visiting two or three casinos just to marvel at their splendor. Below is an entirely random sampling of high and low points:

Caesars Palace. Great restaurants, the only truly luxurious hotel rooms, a terrific shopping gallery, and a sophisticated atmosphere have made Caesars the most popular casino among gay travelers. The casino itself has two wings—one for high rollers, the other for low-stakes gamblers. Where other compounds tire you with neon and bright lights, Caesars's Ancient Rome theme incorporates marble columns, archways, and plush design elements. Really a cut above the rest. *3570 Las Vegas Blvd. S,* ☎ *702/731–7110.*

Circus Circus. The owner of Luxor and Excalibur, Circus Circus has always courted gay business. Their casinos also tend to encourage low-budget families with lots of tots. Hordes of them are lured here by an "under the big top" circus show and, above the casino, a games-packed midway/observation balcony from which kids can watch their parents gamble away their college tuition. *2880 Las Vegas Blvd. S,* ☎ *702/734–0410.*

Excalibur. From the outside, this sister property to the Luxor appears fantastic—an acid-induced tribute to King Arthur that from any vantage point looks like a giant pink-and-blue cartoon. The clientele, however, is mostly leisure suit–clad parents with children, and lesbians and gays may feel conspicuous. On the other hand, the showroom regularly features an intriguing, if kinky, jousting tournament. *3850 Las Vegas Blvd. S,* ☎ *702/597–7777.*

Flamingo Hilton. There are two reasons not to miss the Flamingo: history and a charming sense of charmlessness. Bugsy Siegel introduced Las Vegas to a "classy" gambling scene by opening the Fabulous Flamingo almost 50 years ago. He was exterminated shortly after the Flamingo opened, and as the decades passed, the casino's sophistication waned. Its appeal always depended upon America's relationship with pink flamingos, once symbols of elegance and flair, later the stuff of trailer-park decorating and, more recently possessing a certain retro appeal. Today the Flamingo Hilton is back in style—entirely in spite of itself. *3555 Las Vegas Blvd. S,* ☎ *702/733–3111.*

Golden Nugget Hotel and Casino. Most of the downtown casinos are rough-hewn predecessors of the fabulous wonderlands that dominate the Strip. But the Golden Nugget, taken over by Steve Wynn a couple of decades ago, still recalls the days when downtown Las Vegas drew high rollers. Though visitors are spared the radioactive glow of neon, there is more than enough gold inside to compensate: gold elevators, pay phones, slot machines, and a 63-pound nugget said to be the world's largest. *129 Fremont St.,* ☎ *702/385–7111.*

Luxor. A sleek pyramid rising high above the Strip, the Egyptian-themed Luxor emits a laser straight into the sky. But this ray, unfortunately, is gobbled up by the searing glow of every other light in Las Vegas and is barely visible. The structure itself is without lights, so you cannot see it well after dark. The interior is nondescript and offers little diversion beyond gambling. Allegedly, the Luxor is cursed due to having trivialized—in its decor—the sacred tradition of Egyptian pyramids. Further speculation is that the laser is costing too much, the hotel occupancy is dangerously low, and the building itself is sinking several feet annually. It certainly *seems* cursed. *3900 Las Vegas Blvd. S, ☎ 702/262–4000.*

MGM Grand Hotel and Theme Park. The theme alone should explain the MGM's appeal to the gay community: It is a homage to *The Wizard of Oz*. This is the world's largest casino and perhaps Las Vegas's leading attraction. Among the restaurants are the highly gay-friendly Coyote and Wolfgang Puck cafés. A truly spectacular 33-acre theme park is housed within this small city of four emerald-green hotel towers, re-creating Hollywood back lots and buzzing with rides and attractions. *3799 Las Vegas Blvd. S, ☎ 702/891–1111.*

Lake Mead

About 40 minutes southeast of town is the gay beach at **Lake Mead.** Head east on Lake Mead Boulevard out of north Las Vegas. Continue past Hollywood Boulevard. Wind through the desert about 5 miles until you reach a stop sign. Turn left and head north toward Overton; 4.8 miles later, make a right onto the 8-mile marker road.

GETTING AROUND

You'll need a car to get around, but rentals are cheap and the streets are idiot-proof, laid out generally in a grid pattern. Las Vegas Boulevard (a.k.a. the Strip up to about Sahara Ave.) is the main north–south route; it's bisected by several major east–west roads, Tropicana, Flamingo, Desert Inn, and Sahara being the most central. Attractions, bars, and restaurants are generally close to one another, so cab fares never run high. You don't hail cabs on the street, but you can easily find them at hotels and at the airport.

EATS

Well, if you must eat, choose carefully. There are virtually no gay-oriented dining options and few decent restaurants. Of the more than 800 eateries, only a couple dozen rise above the crowd. Generally, the best *and* the worst restaurants are in casinos. Avoid the buffets and any restaurant in a low-stakes casino: The food served at these spots is cafeteria-quality, fattening, and bland. Although the buffet at the **Golden Nugget** is a cut or two above any others, it's still nothing to write home about and a bit more expensive. The best casino restaurants are those at the Caesars Palace Hotel and Casino and the Forum Shops at Caesars.

For price ranges, *see* Chart B at the front of this guide.

In the Casinos

$$$$ **Palace Court.** Many say the Bacchanal Romanesque feast at Caesars Palace is the ultimate Las Vegas dining experience, but male guests are massaged by "wine goddesses" before dessert, which can be embarrassing or annoying. A better option, still at Caesars, is the refined Palace Court, an authentic fine dining establishment with white-glove service, fine china, and a superb Continental menu. *Caesars Palace, 3570 Las Vegas Blvd. S, ☎ 702/731–7731.*

$$$–$$$$ **Spago.** Probably the best New American grub you'll find in Las Vegas, this outpost of the famous Los Angeles restaurant—presided over by celebrity chef Wolfgang Puck—is part of the Forum Shops at Caesars. There's an open-terrace café with lighter fare and views of the Romanesque streetscape, and there's an elegant formal dining room inside. *Forum Shops at Caesars, 3570 Las Vegas Blvd. S, ☎ 702/369–6300.*

$$–$$$$ **Coyote Café.** This offshoot of the eponymous Santa Fe restaurant has two parts: the more exclusive and more private Grill Room and the lively and more casual Cantina, which has a bar and is open to the tumult of the casino. The decor of both sections is Southwestern, and the menu emphasizes this region as well: you'll find chili rellenos alongside the steak, tuna, and crab cakes. The largest selection of tequila in the state. *MGM Grand Hotel, 3805 Las Vegas Blvd. S, ☎ 702/891–7394.*

$$$ **Antonio's.** This terrific restaurant is popular with locals, who come for the well-prepared, filling Northern Italian entrées and desserts. Small, with marble walls, murals, and crystal chandeliers, it doesn't feel like a hotel restaurant. (For a more upscale dining experience in the same hotel you may wish to investigate Fiore.) *Rio Suites Hotel and Casino, 3700 W. Flamingo Rd., ☎ 702/252–7777.*

$$ **Bertolini.** Formerly Lombardi's. Many locals recommend that you skip Spago (just down the Roman promenade) and head here instead. It's cheaper, and the food is just as tasty. Pizza, pasta, and other dishes, all with contemporary touches, come in large portions. Seating in the courtyard is noisy, as it's adjacent to the huge Roman fountain. Be sure to sample the wonderfully authentic gelato, which is available to go. *Forum Shops at Caesars, 3570 Las Vegas Blvd. S, ☎ 702/735–4663.*

$–$$ **California Pizza Kitchen.** Las Vegas offers two versions here of this popular national chain, renowned for its designer pizzas and healthy salads. The one downtown at the Golden Nugget is best, as the one in the Mirage restaurant is too loud and too close to the casino action. *Mirage, 3400 Las Vegas Blvd. S, ☎ 702/791–7111; Golden Nugget, 129 E. Fremont St., ☎ 702/385–7111.*

$ **Café Roma.** An ideal spot for hefty, inexpensive portions of comfort food, the kind you find at a good diner. There's an American menu 24 hours, a Chinese menu after 5 PM. *Caesars Palace, 3570 Las Vegas Blvd. S, ☎ 702/731–7731.*

Outside the Casinos

$$–$$$ **Z'Tejas.** Outposts of this outstanding contemporary Southwestern restaurant have been popping up in Texas, Arizona, and Nevada. Aside from such traditional regional dishes as Sonoran stuffed shrimp, Southern and Cajun influences are evident in the likes of blackened snapper in banana-pecan sauce. Very trendy and gay-friendly. *3824 S. Paradise Rd., ☎ 702/ 732–1660.*

$$ **Culturati Café.** This is kind of an urban, hip T.G.I.F. with a noisy covered patio and an equally animated, high-ceiling dining room with minimalist decor. Selections include designer pizzas, angel-hair pasta with veggies, and towering *muffuletta* sandwiches (round loaves of Italian bread filled with ham and other cold cuts, cheese, and an olive salad). *2570 S. Decatur Ave., ☎ 702/227–8080.*

$–$$ **Alias Smith and Jones.** Just your basic 24-hour tavern with burgers and no-frills American food in a warm, chatty atmosphere. It's got a fairly gay following because lots of performers from Vegas shows show up here after work. *541 E. Twain Ave., ☎ 702/732–7401.*

$–$$ **Citibank Park.** This shopping center, a short drive from the Strip, the airport, and several gay bars, has a slew of decent restaurants, all reasonably priced. It's sort of an unplanned food court. The best of the bunch is the chain favorite, **Ruth's Chris Steak House** (☎ 702/791–7011), which has outstanding steaks and the antique-style ceiling fans, hanging lamps, and celebrity photos required to give the place an old-fashioned Gay '90s feel. Other eateries here include **Beijing Restaurant** (Chinese,

148

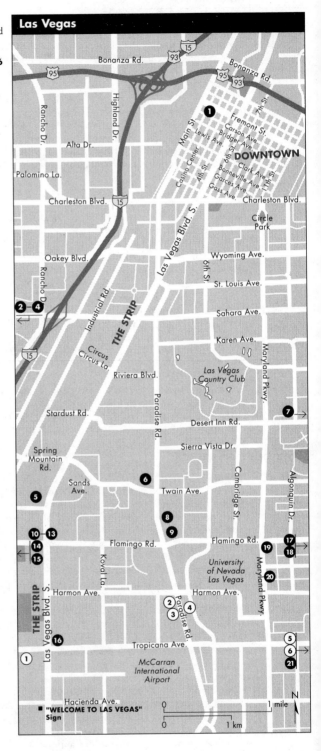

Las Vegas

☎ 702/737–9618); **Café Milano** (Northern Italian, ☎ 702/732–2777); **Hakase** (Japanese, ☎ 702/796–1234); **Marrakesh** (Moroccan, ☎ 702/737–5611); **Paradise Bistro** (American comfort food, ☎ 702/791–5161); **Park Deli** (New York–style sandwiches, ☎ 702/369–3354); **Shalimar** (Indian, ☎ 702/796–0302); and **Yolie's Steakhouse** (Brazilian, ☎ 702/794–0700). *3900 Paradise Rd.*

$–$$ Viva Mercado. This family-run eatery is hands down the best Mexican restaurant in town, and despite a location well west of the Strip, everyone who cares about good cooking makes it a point to come here. Small and always packed, it has potent margaritas, powerful salsa, and perfectly cooked Mexican dishes, including a wide variety of vegetarian and seafood options. *6182 W. Flamingo Rd.,* ☎ *702/871–8826.*

$ Blueberry Hill. This is Las Vegas's cross between Denny's and IHOP, and though there are branches all over the city, the one at Maryland Parkway and Flamingo Road teems with fags after the bars close. Though all meals are available, the greasy, sweet, fattening platters of blueberry pancakes with bacon and fried eggs are the best—and breakfast is served around the clock. *Maryland Pkwy. and Flamingo Rd.,* ☎ *702/696–9666; Sandhill St. and Flamingo Rd.,* ☎ *702/433–9999.*

$ Wild Oats. Las Vegas's contribution to crunchy, environmentally sensitive cuisine is set *way* west on Sahara Avenue—though a second location is set *way* east on Flamingo Road. Within this cavernous, bright complex are a full grocery store with a vast array of prepared salads, grains, cheeses, and other organic offerings, and a café, done in a wood-grain, cafeteria motif and serving millet, veggies-and-sprouts sandwiches, and all sorts of healthy things. *6720 W. Sahara Ave.,* ☎ *702/253–7050; 3455 E. Flamingo Rd.,* ☎ *702/434–8115.*

Coffeehouse Culture

Albion Used Books and the Daily Grind Espresso Bar (2466-G E. Desert Inn Rd., ☎ 702/792–9554) is not exactly what you'd expect a mile off the Strip: They sell newspapers from around the country; they have stacks of used, hardcover books in great condition; and they have an amazing selection of sheet music along with a piano from which tunes occasionally emanate. **Café Copioh** (4550 S. Maryland Pkwy., ☎ 702/739–0305), Las Vegas's contribution to Eurobohemian style and atmosphere, is very popular with the gay community and UNLV students. You'll find lots of soulful, pensive academics chatting about Proust and the Pet Shop Boys. Best snack food: the gooey pizza bagels. A regular slate of poetry readings and musical performances livens things up at **Cafe Espresso at Borders Books** (2323 S. Decatur Blvd., ☎ 702/258–0999). The yuppiest, starched-shirt types saunter into this elegant little café after completing their literary purchases. The sandwich and dessert menu is stellar. Although **Jitters** (2457 E. Tropicana Ave., ☎ 702/898–0056) has the best food of any coffeehouse in Las Vegas and is arguably the most gay-frequented, this strip-mall establishment lacks warmth, with its bright lighting, black floor, and Mondrianesque color-scheme. You can get sandwiches, jalapeño tuna melts, and sweets—all served by a nice staff.

SLEEPS

There are no shrinking violets on the Las Vegas hotel horizon. Even the Motel 6 is enormous with streaks of neon. Nine of the world's 10 largest hotels are here, with the MGM Grand topping the list. When gambling was the city's only draw, hotel rooms were made drab and unpleasant, with the hope of keeping guests out of their rooms and glued to the slot machines. As the '90s have seen a more family-attractive, theme park–oriented approach to Las Vegas tourism, hotel rooms have quickly been worked into shape, providing guests with all the amenities and perks you'd expect at any solid city accommodation.

It is still the land of hotel bargains, but not, as some suspect, because the supply outweighs the demand. In fact, with major conventions in town every other week and a steady inflow of tourists even on weekdays, you're wise to book a room several weeks ahead. Rooms are cheap here simply because hotel/casino compounds make their money almost solely on gambling revenue, and the more they tie up your expendable income on hotel rooms and food, the less you'll be able to wager at the tables.

For price ranges, *see* Chart B at the front of this guide.

🏨 When the Tom Cruise character in *Rain Man* sought the best room in Las Vegas, he chose one at **Caesars Palace,** the Rolls-Royce of the city's hotels. With great restaurants and a chic shopping mall attached, Caesars is worth the splurge. *3750 Las Vegas Blvd. S, ☎ 702/731–7110 or 800/634–6661. 1,600 rooms. $$$–$$$$*

🏨 The **Alexis Park Resort Hotel** is the only business hotel in town, devoid of casino action, bright lights, neon, and entertainment. *375 E. Harmon Rd., ☎ 702/796–3300 or 800/582–2228. 500 suites. $$$*

🏨 Of any hotel in town, **Harrah's** has done the most for the gay community, actively courting our business and donating money to bring the AIDS quilt to Las Vegas. Built during the aesthetically challenged early '70s, the hotel is somewhat garish. But you'll always be made to feel at home here. *3475 Las Vegas Blvd. S, ☎ 702/369–5000 or 800/634–6765. 1,713 rooms. $$$*

🏨 Arguably the best all-around hotel and casino in terms of value, ambience, size, and offerings, the Steve Wynn–produced **Mirage** has a rain forest abundant with tigers, dolphins, sharks, and more than 3,000 tropical plants. Siegfried and Roy are the house entertainment. *3400 Las Vegas Blvd. S, ☎ 702/791–7111 or 800/627–6667. 3,049 rooms. $$$*

🏨 The **Golden Nugget Hotel** has the feel and look of a ritzy, Victorian, city hotel and is the only truly decent accommodation downtown. Such details as white marble, etched glass, and bordello-red carpets leading to the lobby account for the Nugget's glitter. *129 E. Fremont St., ☎ 702/385–7111 or 800/634–3454. 1,911 rooms. $$–$$$*

🏨 The perfect place to act out that freakish "Surrender, Dorothy!" fantasy you've been bottling up for years, the **MGM Grand** has more than 5,000 rooms in four emerald-green, Wizard of Oz–theme towers. This is actually a vast entertainment megaresort that comprises, among other things, the world's largest casino, nine restaurants, an enormous swimming pool, a complete day-care center, and a 33-acre amusement park. *3799 Las Vegas Blvd. S, ☎ 702/891–1111 or 800/929–1111. 5,005 rooms. $$*

🏨 The **Sahara Las Vegas** has for years featured Kenny Kerr's you've-got-to-see-it-to-believe-it "Boy-lesque" act, an over-the-top drag extravaganza that draws all the sisters. It's otherwise a very ordinary Strip hotel. *2535 Las Vegas Blvd. S, ☎ 702/737–2111 or 800/634–6666. 2,036 rooms. $$*

🏨 The **Hacienda Hotel and Casino,** a somewhat low-key but clean complex, is one of the southernmost hotels on the Strip. *3950 Las Vegas Blvd. S, ☎ 702/739–8911 or 800/634–6713. 1,200 rooms. $–$$*

🏨 The world's only cool **Motel 6** has a big pool, neon, and nearly 900 rooms. Once you wedge yourself inside your tiny cell, however, you'll realize that the size and decor are pretty much the same as that of rooms in every other Motel 6. It *is* a bargain, though. *195 E. Tropicana Ave., ☎ 702/798–0728. 877 rooms. $*

SCENES

In terms of gay nightlife, Las Vegas is often said to be a younger sibling of Los Angeles: lots of cliques and lots of posing—just smaller. Its relatively low gay population is a drawback for residents, most of whom quickly get to know each other. But if you're an out-of-towner, it isn't a terribly difficult place to find conversation in a bar. Outsiders strolling into the cruiser spots might as well be wearing a NEW MEAT sign on their backs, considering all the attention they're given.

Compared to Los Angeles, Las Vegas is rather lacking in good discos. Both the Gipsy has its following, but it's extremely small compared with clubs in other cities. Really the best place to dance here is Backstreet, a country-western bar with an excellent dance floor. There is no gay nightlife district, but the more popular bars are in southern Las Vegas, near the airport.

Most places don't get going until well after midnight, when many actors, blackjack dealers, and waiters are through with their shows or shifts. Keep in mind that most bars are open 24 hours and that Las Vegas has extremely liberal liquor laws, so beer and liquor busts and other great drink specials are rampant just about every night of the week.

Bars and Nightclubs

Angles. The city's classic cruise bar. It's mid-size and has plenty of slots, diverse music spanning a couple of decades, a fireplace, and some comfy armchairs and ottomans. Most people pop in here before heading next door to the Gipsy dance club. The bar in back, which is also mid-size and very nicely decorated, used to be the dyke bar, Lace; it remains so unofficially, but the two bars are now fully attached and accessible to each other, so to some extent you'll see either gender in either place. Note that Lace is the only bar in town with an air hockey table. *4633 Paradise Rd., ☎ 702/791–0100. Crowd: mostly male in front room, mostly female in back room; fairly clean-cut, gym types, a touch of attitude, mostly ages 20s and 30s.*

Backstreet. The nicest bar in town, where bar hands and customers work hard to make everyone feel welcome. It's in southwest Las Vegas—somewhat tricky to get to. You can come and cruise here, strike up a conversation after a long day, meet regulars, or just dance—and they're *good* here. Two-step lessons are given Thursday nights, 7 to 9. Good lighting and attractive western decor. *5012 S. Arville Rd., ☎ 702/876–1844. Crowd: 60/40 f/m, starched-shirt cowboys, all ages, zero attitude.*

The Buffalo. The bare-bones decor and setting—a large rectangular room with a dirty black linoleum floor, lots of trophies, and three pool tables—makes the popular Buffalo the kind of bar just about anyone will feel comfortable in. The crowd mingles quite well and is chatty and spirited. *4640 Paradise Rd., ☎ 702/733–8355. Crowd: mostly male, most diverse in Las Vegas with townies, students, hustlers, older guys, jocks, video poker addicts; a mild leather-and-Levi's.*

The Eagle. Compared with other Eagles, this one is extremely laid-back and down-to-earth. Has the usual black walls and dark lighting. Customers shuttle between here and Texas, next door. *3430 E. Tropicana Ave., ☎ 702/458–8662. Crowd: mostly guys in late 20s to early 40s; soft-core leather following, more white T-shirts and denim, fair number of beards/mustaches.*

Gipsy. This is the only dance club for the young set, UNLV students, and guppies. And though it's small with an even smaller dance floor, the music is terrific, the bartenders friendly, and the atmosphere vibrant. There's a cruisy video bar off to one side, which is a good spot to fill your dance card. Cover most nights. *4605 Paradise Rd.,* ☎ *702/731–1919. Crowd: mixed m/f, very young, cute and relatively attitude-free.*

Texas. Adjacent to the Eagle, this former storefront is a cross between a tame leather bar and a rough-edge cowboy bar. There's no dance floor, but they do have a great country-western jukebox. It's smaller and friendlier than the Eagle, ruby red inside with lots of ropes, antlers, and other cowboy paraphernalia hanging about. *3430 E. Tropicana Ave.,* ☎ *702/456–5525. Crowd: most of the same guys you find at the Eagle; a country-western, leather-and-Levi's bunch.*

Neighborhood Bars and Dives

The **Backdoor Lounge** (1415 E. Charleston Blvd., ☎ 702/385–2018) is seedy but loveable. **Badlands Saloon** (953 E. Sahara Ave., ☎ 702/792–9262) is a decent country-western alternative to the spiffier Backstreet. **Faces Lounge** (701 E. Stewart St., ☎ 702/386–7971) is exclusively lesbian, very butch.

THE LITTLE BLACK BOOK

At Your Fingertips

Aid for AIDS of Las Vegas Hotline: ☎ 702/474–2437. **Gay and Lesbian Community Center of Southern Nevada:** 912 E. Sahara Rd. (behind Bertha's furniture store), ☎ 702/733–9800. **Las Vegas Chamber of Commerce:** 711 E. Desert Inn Rd., Las Vegas, NV 89109, ☎ 702/735–1616. **Las Vegas Convention and Visitors Authority:** 3150 Paradise Rd., Las Vegas, NV 89109, ☎ 702/892–0711. **Nevada AIDS Project:** ☎ 702/593–2380. **Rape Crisis Line:** ☎ 702/366–1640.

Gay Media

The monthly **Las Vegas Bugle** (☎ 702/369–6260), the main lesbian and gay news and entertainment magazine, is quite substantial. Its cousin, the **Bugle Night Beat** (same ☎), has classifieds and pages of phone-sex ads. **Odyssey Magazine** (☎ 800/463–9773), best known as the main bar rag in San Francisco and Hawaii, recently started publication here. The community also has a free **Lambda Business Directory** (☎ 702/593–2875), a list of members of the Lambda Business Association. And, at Get Booked bookstore (*see below*) you can pick up the **Women's Yellow Pages of Southern Nevada** (☎ 702/362–6507), which has no lesbian-specific information but plenty of resources for women.

Arts and entertainment papers include **Scope** (☎ 702/256–6388), a gay-friendly monthly; **Spinzo** (☎ 702/594–3981), which covers Las Vegas's gradually emerging underground music and film scene; and the **Las Vegas New Times** (☎ 702/871–6780), which is similar to *Scope*.

BOOKSTORES

Though tiny, **Get Booked** (4643 Paradise Rd., ☎ 702/737–7780) is the best overall lesbian and gay bookstore in the Southwest. It's open until 2 AM on Friday and Saturday (midnight otherwise), has a friendly staff, and is in the same shopping center as the bars Angles, Lace, and Gipsy (*see* Scenes, *above*). The selection of lesbian and gay titles is strong; you'll also find gay videos and porn mags (nothing hard core), many gifts, and the most comprehensive selection of gay-related literature for Mormons. Of mainstream bookstores, the **Borders Bookstore** (2323 S. Decatur Ave., ☎ 702/258–0999) has one of the better selections of lesbian and gay materials; it also has a cruisy little coffee shop, **Espresso,** on the premises.

Body and Fitness

As an alternative to using a hotel gym, which in Las Vegas typically charges a great deal even to guests, you can sweat at **Gold's Gym** (3750 E. Flamingo Rd., ☎ 702/451–4222), which has a very strong lesbian and gay following and is one of the nation's largest gyms. It's open daily, 24 hours.

12 *Out in Los Angeles*

With Laguna Beach

LOS ANGELES'S GAY AND LESBIAN POPULATION—especially in that trendy homo haven, West Hollywood—is one of the most image-conscious around. Your status is established by (in no particular order) the make of your car, the style of your hair, the cost of your clothing, the source of your mineral water, the shape of your nose, the location of your home, the breed of your dog, the influence of your agent, and the tone of your body. This fixation with superficial qualities permeates every segment of the community, whether you're involved directly with the entertainment industry or not.

Being gay, insofar as it shapes your image, can define your role in Los Angeles society. The film industry, for example, though producing more gay-theme movies than ever before, still does not encourage its gay stars to live openly so. Although a few lesser-known personalities such as Amanda Bearse and Dan Butler have come rather triumphantly out of the closet, the biggest names continue either to deny being gay or to insist that it's not anyone's business. Those who come to L.A. hoping to be discovered face the difficult decision about how coming out may affect their image and, therefore, their livelihood.

Given this atmosphere, it's not surprising that discussion here of the politics, psychology, and sociology of sexual orientation is fairly minimal. In the city's gay and lesbian magazines and newspapers, the emphasis is squarely on nightlife, the arts, and health and fitness. Politics take a back seat. (And with nearly constant 72°F weather and the seductive proximity to ocean, mountains, and desert, would you really expect much introspection?)

Nonetheless, the city has an outstanding track record when it comes to gay-related fund-raising, particularly with regard to AIDS causes. The gay-and-lesbian road to acceptance within Washington's political circle has been paved largely with L.A. dollars. People also forget that Los Angeles, over time, has played a significant role in the gay rights movement. In 1950, local activist Harry Hay, a communist and teacher of Marxist principles, organized the International Bachelors Fraternal Orders for Peace and Social Dignity, committed to unifying, educating, and empowering homosexuals. Hay's chief concern was addressing the antigay attacks that were a trademark of the McCarthy hearings. In 1951, the group was renamed the Mattachine Society. After one founding member, Dale Jennings, was arrested for allegedly picking up an undercover cop in a park, the society pooled its legal resources and fought back. The case was ultimately dismissed, albeit on a technicality, and publicity about the battle spread, leading to the formation of new Mattachine branches in several American cities.

In the late '60s, Bill Rand and Dick Michaels established *The Advocate,* which has become North America's most widely read gay and lesbian periodical. Impetus behind the magazine was the brutalization they suffered while and after being arrested during a police raid of the Melrose bar they were visiting. And in 1969, the gay-embracing Metropolitan Community Church, which now has hundreds of congregations, was founded in Los Angeles by a young minister named Troy Perry. Meetings were initially held in a variety of locations, but by 1970 the church had a permanent home and busloads of visitors were attending.

All in all, Los Angeles may be the least appreciated city in America. It has been the site of some of the nation's most infamous recent legal battles, from the O. J. Simpson spectacle to the sensational Menendez case to the Rodney King trial, whose verdict fueled several days of intense rioting. A major flood, earthquake, fire, or combination thereof ruptures L.A.'s infrastructure every year or two. It doesn't actually cost much more to live here than it does in New York or San Francisco. But the likelihood that your home and your belongings will eventually be destroyed by either natural or human forces adds what you might call a futility surcharge to everything you purchase.

Despite the beating that the city's image has taken over the past decade, you can't overlook the fact that people are always talking about L.A. It's a pacesetter where fashion and entertainment trends are concerned. And if some outsiders scoff at Los Angeles, few can keep from talking about it.

As a visitor, you'll find as many gay-popular diversions here as just about anywhere. Culturally, the city's offerings continue to improve rapidly, with new museums opening regularly. There are celebrities to gawk at, and the scads of struggling models and actors wandering around also provide a constant supply of eye candy. And there's that buzz you get while cruising along Wilshire Boulevard with the top down or crawling through posh Beverly Hills admiring homes of the stars. Such a sybaritic world may not be conducive to direct political action, but it makes for one hell of a vacation.

THE LAY OF THE LAND

You can roll a bowling ball along the sidewalk of Santa Monica Boulevard on a weekday afternoon without hitting anybody. In Los Angeles, you must have a car—you will be required to drive on even the shortest errands. There is a downtown, but it's not the city's spiritual center (there isn't one)—and even there, few people walk the streets. Los Angeles is a cluster of neighborhoods, but, oddly, not one of them has a true hub—a definitive commercial core where folks congregate, eat, and shop. Without people walking its sidewalks and without one or a series of centers, L.A. feels vast and even a little empty (unless you're sitting in traffic on the Santa Monica Freeway—then it feels quite full).

The reach of greater Los Angeles is tremendous, but orienting yourself isn't impossible. The community due northwest of downtown is Hollywood and gay-popular Silver Lake. Farther west is West Hollywood (the densest concentration of the region's gays and lesbians), followed by the monied Beverly Hills, Westwood, Brentwood, Bel Air, Pacific Palisades, and Santa Monica. North of the hills that hem in these northern Los Angeles enclaves is the San Fernando Valley, whose major towns include Universal City, North Hollywood, Studio City, Burbank, and Van Nuys. Northeast of downtown is the San Gabriel Valley, where you'll find the relatively conservative, upper-middle-class communities of Pasadena, San Marino, and Pomona. West of downtown, along the Pacific Ocean, are a string of beach communities: In the north are swank Malibu and Santa Monica; moving south are Venice, Marina Del Rey, Manhattan Beach, Redondo Beach, and Long Beach—the southern towns tend to be working-class suburbs with few tourist attractions.

Downtown

Once a commercial and cultural center, downtown lost popularity shortly after World War II and has only recently begun to rebound. If you're only visiting for a few days, touring downtown should not be a priority, but there are a few notable attractions.

The heart of downtown is centered just southeast of where the Hollywood and Harbor/Pasadena freeways converge, by Grand Avenue and Temple Street. This section's most significant cultural site is the leviathan **Music Center** (1st St. and N. Grand Ave., ☎ 213/972–7211), a complex of three performance spaces, where you can catch a variety of opera, music, drama, and ballet events. The largest venue, the **Dorothy Chandler Pavilion,** often hosts the Academy Awards. Just south of here is the impressive **Museum of Contemporary Art** (250 S. Grand Ave., ☎ 213/626–6222), whose holdings include works by Mark Rothko, Jackson Pollock, and many others. Also in this vicinity is **City Hall** (200 N. Spring St.), which you'll recognize from the opening credits of television's *Dragnet,* and the Spanish Mission–style **Union Station** (800 N. Alameda St.), which you'll recognize from many, many movies.

Downtown's north–south commercial spine is **South Broadway,** which is crammed with fairly mundane stores from about 1st to 9th streets. Note the impressive 1893 **Bradbury Building** (304 S. Broadway), one of the city's most striking examples of Victorian architecture. Also check out **Grand Central Market** (317 S. Broadway, ☎ 213/624–2378), a loud, frenetic, international amalgam of food markets, where you'll find some highly unusual produce.

Two of the city's Asian communities are downtown. **Little Tokyo** is east of South Broadway, bounded by Temple Street, Alameda Avenue, 4th Street, and Los Angeles Street. North of the Hollywood Freeway, **Chinatown** is bounded by Yale, Bernard, and Ord streets, and Alameda Avenue. Most of the shopping in Chinatown is on **North Broadway.** While neither of these neighborhoods are good places for bargains—especially Little Tokyo—if you muscle your way through the mobs of tourists, you'll find some great restaurants and unusual imported goods.

Just southeast of Chinatown, **El Pueblo de Los Angeles Historic Monument** (Visitors Center: 622 N. Main St., ☎ 213/628–1274) is a 44-acre urban park preserving many of L.A.'s oldest structures. This is said to be the site of the city's first settlement (1781). Dozens of food and crafts stalls line cobbled, pedestrians-only **Olvera Street,** and Spanish colonial folk-dancing is held at the **Plaza** daily at noon.

Hollywood

Though the word "Hollywood" is synonymous with glitter and glamour, the area has faded to the point of seeming sleazy and dowdy. Standing at the fabled corner of **Hollywood and Vine,** it's hard to imagine movie moguls and starlets moving along these streets. Faded or not, Hollywood is still where America's film industry began, and many vestiges of its "Golden Era" still remain.

To the northeast, above Beachwood Canyon, is the immense HOLLYWOOD sign, whose 50-foot letters have graced the horizon for more than 70 years. You can't visit the sign, but you can tour a number of museums and sites—some tacky, others engaging—along Hollywood Boulevard. The most popular attractions include the **Hollywood Wax Museum** (6767 Hollywood Blvd., ☎ 213/462–8860); the **Hollywood Guinness World of Records Museum** (6764 Hollywood Blvd., ☎ 213/463–6433); and **Ripley's Believe It or Not** (6780 Hollywood Blvd., ☎ 213/466–6335). Hollywood Boulevard itself is a museum of sorts, as the beloved **Walk of Fame** runs from Highland Avenue to Vine Street. There are also theaters, studios, and other famous buildings here, including the **Capitol Records Building** (1756 N. Vine St.), which is shaped like a stack of 45s; the **Pantages Theater** (6233 Hollywood Blvd.), which from 1949 to 1959 was site of the Academy Awards ceremonies; and **Mann's Chinese Theater** (6925 Hollywood Blvd., ☎ 213/464–8111), where more than 160 stars have had their handprints or footprints preserved in cement. Also, check out the lively **Hollywood Farmer's Market** (Ivar St., just below Hollywood Blvd.), which is held on Sunday. Its exotic-food stalls, crafts-and-antiques vendors, and music performers draw thousands of curious onlookers.

If you head up Highland Avenue, you'll pass one of the world's great concert arenas, the **Hollywood Bowl,** whose parking lot is the site of the **Hollywood Studio Museum** (2100 N. Highland Ave., ☎ 213/874–2276).

Silver Lake

Roughly defined by the I–5, the Pasadena Freeway, the Hollywood Freeway, and Vermont Avenue, **Silver Lake** is, following West Hollywood, the city's second-largest gay and lesbian neighborhood. The standard joke is that Silver Lake has been an up-and-coming community for the past 30 years; when it will officially and come is anybody's guess. Los Angeles first expanded east to west, with places like Silver Lake and neighboring Echo Park developing earlier than the beach communities. Silver Lake was never densely populated; its hilly, parklike terrain might remind you more of Seattle than of Southern California.

During the '50s much of the city's homophile political and social activity took place here, both in homes and at neighborhood bars (which were constantly raided by the police). The first Mattachine Society meeting was held at Harry Hay's Cove Avenue home (the avenue overlooks Silver Lake, which is actually a reservoir). Early activists such as Jim Kepner, Chuck Rowland, and Bob Hill lived here, and about five or six gay bars have been in the area (in one form or another) since the late '50s.

Far stronger than the presence of homosexuals is that of Hispanic-Americans: They've been settling here since the '60s. Many gay and lesbian Hispanic-Americans live in these parts. They also party here as there are several gay-Hispanic bars and discos. Koreans also make up a fair share of Silver Lake's mix. Unfortunately, gay bashing has been a problem in the area. A rash of such incidents in the early '90s spawned neighborhood street patrols. They successfully restored a sense of safety, but be cautious here at night.

Although the old homes perched along the winding, hilly streets provide great (albeit somewhat perilous) car touring, Silver Lake has few sights. Look for Frank Lloyd Wright's **Hollyhock House** (4800 Hollywood Blvd., ☎ 213/662–7272); its design mimics the hollyhocks planted on the grounds—note the moat surrounding the living-room fireplace.

Just north of Silver Lake and east of Hollywood, there are a few noteworthy attractions. **Griffith Park Observatory and Planetarium** (Los Feliz Blvd. and Vermont Ave., ☎ 213/664–1191) is where James Dean, Sal Mineo, and Natalie Wood formed their tragic love triangle in *Rebel Without a Cause*. The observation area and the park are among the cruisiest (and most heavily policed) spots in Los Angeles. Next door is **Forest Lawn Memorial Park–Hollywood Hills** (6300 Forest Lawn Dr., ☎ 213/254–7251), where you'll find impressive bronze and marble statuary, and the grave sites of celebrities ranging from Errol Flynn to Liberace.

West Hollywood and the Wilshire District

Once the modest, rather forgettable little town of Sherman, the independent city of **West Hollywood** is often considered the gayest city in America, and you can explore the main streets on foot. This stylish, trendy community has many cutting-edge shops, restaurants, and clubs.

Sherman was incorporated in 1895 as a major railroad center. The Pasadena and Pacific Railway Company ran tracks along what is now Santa Monica Boulevard; the main rail yard, around which town life revolved, was on the site of what is now the Pacific Design Center. Many of the old bungalows that line West Hollywood's residential streets were built in the early part of this century to house railway workers.

West Hollywood remained a working-class community until World War II; some gentrification took place in the '50s and '60s, and retirees and Russian immigrants began to settle here. At the same time, the film industry was booming next door in Hollywood, and many set designers, make-up artists, wardrobe hands, and other behind-the-scenes workers moved here. A decorating and fashion industry grew around the intersection of Melrose Avenue and Robertson Boulevard, as skyrocketing rents in nearby Beverly Hills pushed all but the most established designers into West Hollywood.

From its earliest days, West Hollywood was a major nightlife center. Because it fell outside the jurisdiction of the oppressive L.A. Police Department, strip clubs and peep shows opened along Santa Monica Boulevard, and gay bars ran little risk of being raided. Anyone whose lifestyle or interests ran against the accepted norm felt comfortable here. Not only gays but many film celebrities and rock stars had West Hollywood addresses by the '60s. The most dramatic surge in the gay population occurred in the '70s, when Santa Monica Boulevard truly became a nightlife mecca.

The city of West Hollywood was officially incorporated in 1983. The first mayor was openly lesbian, and many of the councilpersons were gay, too. Today there are few homosexuals in city politics, but West Hollywood remains tolerant and gay-friendly—the gay community center here is larger than the new city hall. As you amble along, you'll see signs of West Hollywood's three different, though not mutually exclusive, groups: gay, Russian, and elderly.

Santa Monica Boulevard is one of the gayest streets in the world. Most of the action is concentrated between Doheny Drive, which is the boundary between Beverly Hills and West Hollywood, and La Cienega Boulevard. There are gay hangouts along Santa Monica clear out to La Brea Avenue. In addition to the many gay-popular shops, you might stop by the **Eight Muses Art Gallery** (8713 Santa Monica Blvd., ☎ 310/659–2545), one of the city's foremost gay and lesbian art spaces.

Just south of Santa Monica Boulevard, the **Mazur Collection** (626 N. Robertson Blvd., ☎ 310/659–2478) is one of the nation's only lesbian-history archives. The collection was begun in 1981 in Oakland and brought to West Hollywood by two local activists, Bunny MacCulloch and the late June Mazur. In this three-room archive you'll find stickers, mugs, newspaper clippings, buttons, and license plates—all with sapphic slogans. There's a substantial T-shirt collection and hundreds of books, including quite a few misguided psychological studies and some intriguing old pulp novels with wicked portrayals of lesbian love. In the same building is the **Gay and Lesbian International Archives** (☎ 310/854–0271), although parts of that collection were slated to move at press time (winter 1995).

Since the '30s, the hippest, rowdiest nightclubs have lined **Sunset Boulevard** (a.k.a. Sunset Strip) from Doheny Drive to Fairfax Avenue. Running north of and parallel to Santa Monica Boulevard, the Strip is a touristy, glitzy, rather straight section of West Hollywood, but most of its clubs and restaurants are gay-friendly. The best place for sidewalk strolling— and celebrity spotting—is Sunset Plaza, a swank stretch of shops and outdoor restaurants.

The high-end fashion and retro home-furnishings shopping drag, **Melrose Avenue** runs parallel to and below Santa Monica Boulevard. On L.A.'s answer to Rome's Via Veneto meshed with New York's Madison Avenue, you'll find unique boutiques that offer everything from avant-garde clothing to futuristic eyewear to kitschy furniture. Coffeehouses and "like the latest" happening restaurants also abound. At the western end of Melrose is the striking, Cesar Pelli–designed **Pacific Design Center** (8687 Melrose Ave., ☎ 310/657–0800), which has 200 showrooms packed with furniture, textiles, and interior-design accessories. Buying goods here is limited to interior designers, architects, and set designers, but, with persistence, you can get in. Shopping is definitely encouraged at the nearby **Beverly Center** (Beverly and La Cienega Blvds., ☎ 310/854–0070).

South of here, along **Wilshire Boulevard,** is a rich stretch of land called **Miracle Mile;** it runs from La Brea to Fairfax where the gorgeous, gold-columned May Company store dominates the intersection. Curson Avenue intersects Wilshire at the site of the **La Brea Tar Pits,** from which more than 100 tons of Pleistocene fossil bones have been excavated. They're displayed in the **George C. Page Museum of La Brea Discoveries** (5801 Wilshire Blvd., ☎ 213/936–2230). The five-building **Los Angeles County Museum of Art** (5905 Wilshire Blvd., ☎ 213/857–6000) occupies the same lot as the tar pits. It has comprehensive costumes and textiles exhibits; outstanding Indian and Southeast Asian art galleries; an estimable collection of Japanese paintings, sculpture, ceramics, and lacquerware; and two dramatic sculpture gardens. Just steps away is the **Craft and Folk Art Museum** (5800 Wilshire Blvd., ☎ 213/937–5544). The **Carole & Barry Kaye Museum of Miniatures** (5900 Wilshire Blvd., ☎ 213/937–6464), which houses hundreds of miniature-scale models of people, important architectural sites, and the like, and the new **Petersen Automotive Museum** (6060 Wilshire Blvd., ☎ 213/930–2277) are also nearby.

For more scenery and art, head for the downtown museums and galleries on Wilshire, 3rd Street, or Beverly Boulevard East, driving through the luxurious Hancock Park neighborhood along the way. (When the lanes start to wind at 3rd or Beverly, you're in the area for sure.) Many of the large mansions were built for Hollywood producers and directors in the early days of the film colony. Overlooking the golf course and reservoir are several tall deco-style apartment buildings. Mae West made her home here. It's Old Hollywood without the media madness: Hancock Park exudes wealth, character, and well-landscaped charm—less the "new money" feel of Beverly Hills.

Beverly Hills and Westwood
Now's your chance to buy a map of the stars' homes and putter around looking for the abodes of Shirley Jones, Elke Sommer, or Dick Van Patten. Yes, more celebrities—and has-beens—live in **Beverly Hills, Brentwood,** and **Bel Air,** than any community on the planet. Many of the homes are close to the road; when they're not gated, you can get a good look at them. The main sights are the pseudo-palaces and, south of Santa Monica

Boulevard toward Wilshire, the unbelievably chichi shops along **Rodeo Drive.** The one cultural sight in this high-rent district is the **Museum of Tolerance** (9786 W. Pico Blvd., ☎ 310/553–8403). Next door to the Simon Weisenthal Center, this new museum uses a fascinating array of interactive exhibits to explore issues of prejudice and injustice.

To the west is **Century City,** consisting mainly of executive office towers and the **Century City Shopping Center & Marketplace** (10250 Santa Monica Blvd., ☎ 310/277–3898).

Known mostly as the home of the **University of California at Los Angeles** (UCLA), **Westwood** is a haven of yuppies and collegiate types, with a thriving café culture on Wilshire Boulevard.

Venice and Santa Monica

From the '30s till the '50s, the section of **Santa Monica** just south of where Wilshire Boulevard hits the Pacific Coast Highway was known as Queer Alley. Today, you'd never know that this beach suburb—which is primarily straight, white, and professional—was an early bastion of gay society. Queer Alley was a land of bathhouse culture, cruising, and nude sunbathing. Just off the beach, a huge gay bar, the Tropical Village, drew everybody from navy men to closeted celebrities to resident authors Christopher Isherwood and Stephen Spender. With encroaching gentrification and police crackdowns, the area lost its gay popularity by the '60s.

Where San Vincente Boulevard hits the ocean you'll find **Will Rogers State Beach** (15800 Pacific Coast Hwy., ☎ 310/394–3266), L.A.'s gay and lesbian tanning salon. South of here is **Santa Monica Pier;** it and the small stretch of Broadway a few blocks east are lined with arcades, gift shops, and colorful, if touristy, amusements. The area's increasingly artsy side is represented by the **Santa Monica Museum of Art** (2437 Main St., ☎ 310/399–0433). Designed by Frank Gehry it frequently has exhibits of up-and-coming artists. **Main Street,** from Pico Boulevard to the Venice border, has unique shops, groovy galleries, and tourist eateries.

North of Santa Monica, in the wealthy, cliff-side enclave of **Malibu,** is the **J. Paul Getty Museum** (17985 Pacific Coast Hwy., ☎ 310/458–2003), a 38-gallery re-creation of a 1st-century Roman villa that contains one of the nation's foremost collections of Roman and Greek antiquities. Parking is limited, so you must reserve a spot for your car at least a week in advance. Taking the bus here and walking up the hill to the entrance is possible but time consuming. In 1997 much of the collection will be moved to the new J. Paul Getty Center in Brentwood.

South of Santa Monica, hippies, yuppies, retirees, beatniks, in-line skaters, and slackers mill about **Venice**'s boardwalk and the streets nearby. Second-hand clothing stores, piercing and tattoo parlors, health food stores, and outdoor markets line the streets near the beach. You'll also find some of the region's most important modern art galleries. Brimming with kitsch and bits of pop history, Venice has about the same irresistible appeal as a 1973 Dodge Dart.

San Fernando Valley

Usually called simply "the Valley," this expanse of bedroom communities northwest of Los Angeles has long been picked on for typifying everything that is boring, bland, and banal about suburbia. A decade ago the movie *Valley Girl* lampooned the region, and the stereotype never really died. On the other hand, if image-conscious L.A. starts to wear on your nerves, you might enjoy a visit to the Valley: Though less glamorous, it's far less snooty.

Just over the Hollywood Hills, by way of Laurel Canyon Boulevard is **Studio City,** which is heavily populated with gay industry types. East of Studio City, **Universal City** and **Burbank** have long been home to major television and film studios. **Universal Studios Hollywood and CityWalk** (100 Universal Pl., Universal City, ☎ 818/508–9600), a 420-acre theme park and working studio, is the most spectacular; you can tour the sets of dozens of famous movies and TV shows. You can also visit **Warner Brothers Studios** (Hollywood Way and Olive Ave., Burbank, ☎ 818/954–1744) and **NBC Television Studios** (3000 W. Alameda Ave., Burbank, ☎ 818/840–3537), where *The Tonight Show* is taped.

San Gabriel Valley

Northeast of Los Angeles, **San Gabriel Valley** has more cachet and a more conservative demeanor than its neighboring valley to the west. Here you'll find small but posh, old-moneyed **Pasadena,** which is most famous for its **Tournament of Roses Parade** and the **Rose Bowl** football game, held each New Year's Day. You can spend a day or two tooling around this city, admiring the eclectic architecture and verdant landscapes. There are numerous boutiques and cafés in **Old Town,** a trendy eight-block stretch of restored turn-of-the-century buildings bordered by Pasadena Avenue, Arroyo Parkway, and Walnut and Green streets. To the east is the **Pacific Asia Museum** (46 N. Los Robles Ave., ☎ 818/449–2742), which is filled with art and collectibles from Asia and the Pacific Islands. West of here are the **Norton Simon Museum** (411 W. Colorado Blvd., ☎ 818/449–6840), whose outstanding art collection includes several Rembrandts, Goyas, Degas, Monets, Picassos, and Van Goghs; and the dramatic **Gamble House** (4 Westmoreland Pl., ☎ 818/793–3334), one of the most noteworthy examples of Craftsman-style architecture in the country. A must-see in this area is the **Huntington Library, Art Gallery, and Botanical Gardens** (1151 Oxford Rd., ☎ 818/405–2100) in nearby San Marino.

Laguna Beach

The beautiful seaside community of **Laguna Beach** has long been a popular spot for vacationing gays and lesbians. This lively, progressive city (it elected the nation's first openly gay mayor in 1983) is about 60 miles south of Los Angeles, in the heart of the so-called California Riviera. Often referred to as SoHo by the Sea, the area began attracting artists in the early 1900s. Today, Laguna Beach and the towns north and south of it along the ocean—Newport Beach, Corona Del Mar, Laguna Niguel, Dana Point—have loads of art galleries and studios, high-end clothiers and tony boutiques, great restaurants, and Mediterranean-inspired resorts. There are festivals and exhibitions held throughout the year; call the **Laguna Beach Chamber of Commerce** (☎ 714/494–1018) for details.

Laguna Beach is scenic and ritzy. Rising above the Pacific Coast Highway, which runs north–south through the community paralleling the sandy beach, are dramatic cliffs covered with a dense canopy of homes—reminiscent of the French and Italian rivieras. Downtown, where Broadway intersects the highway, there's a popular boardwalk and beach where locals and tourists laze in the sun, the peace interrupted only by the occasional ring of a cellular phone. Yuppies abound. Many art galleries and antiques shops are within walking distance of the town's center. The queer presence is low-key and discreet; only a few businesses have specifically gay followings. In this sophisticated seaside community, however, everyone is tolerated, especially if they have a bit of money and a yen for buying art. Culture and good taste permeate the air. The **Laguna Moulton Playhouse,** an outstanding community theater, was established here in 1920.

A five-minute drive south of Broadway, where Mountain Road and Calliope Street intersect with the Pacific Coast Highway, you'll find the region's only concentration of gay-popular businesses. The anchor is the **Coast Inn** (*see* Sleeps, *below*), which has a large bar and disco and a gay and lesbian beach behind it.

GETTING AROUND

Driving won't be a nightmare if you are prepared: Listen to traffic reports, keep a detailed map by your side—the best are made by Thomas Brothers—and plan your travel to avoid rush hour. Streets are broad and parking garages and lots are easy to find (although you're often forced to deal with the so-called convenience of valet parking). Parking in West Hollywood can be difficult; try the lot at the **Pacific Design Center** (use the entrance off San Vincente, between Melrose and Santa Monica Blvds.). The cost is reasonable, especially in the evening, and the lot is open until 2 AM.

Mass transit is not a practical option. In a pinch, you can call a cab; it's unlikely you'll be able to hail one on the street.

EATS

Restaurateur Wolfgang Puck, often credited with single-handedly upgrading the city's culinary reputation, is one of several chefs who started a local culinary revolution by using fresh California produce with international spices, condiments, and other goodies. There are countless Mediterranean bistros and New American restaurants, most with postmodern decor and menu descriptions that defy syntax and challenge comprehension. Still, it's just as easy (and often cheaper) to find enormous steaks, fresh burritos, outstanding sushi, every imaginable treatment of tofu, and, possibly the most satisfying cheeseburgers in the nation.

The gayest places you'll find are in West Hollywood, especially along Santa Monica and Sunset boulevards. West L.A., from Beverly Hills to the Pacific Ocean, is a mecca for culinary explorers, though few of the establishments have specifically gay followings. The Valley and the southern coastal communities have fewer offerings for committed foodies, but you won't go hungry: There are plenty of drive-through fast-food chains along the expansive boulevards. Downtown is quiet at night; the best dining, including some terrific seafood, is available to the north in Chinatown. Silver Lake has excellent taquerias and a few greasy spoons that are worth a look. Hollywood has several film-industry watering holes, but many of these survive on name alone.

People eat early in Los Angeles, so don't set out for a fancy dinner much past 9:30. On the flip side, this is a major breakfast town; producers, agents, and, sometimes, actors rise early to cut deals over eggs.

For price ranges in both Los Angeles and Laguna Beach, *see* Chart A at the front of this guide.

West Hollywood

$$$–$$$$ **Cafe La Bohème.** Formal for West Hollywood, La Bohème is truly operatic in its proportions; the dining room is anchored by a huge fireplace and has high ceilings, flowing velvet drapes, and other over-the-top furnishings. The completely incongruous California menu also offers Mediterranean (try the pasta *pescatore*) and Asian flavors. Seared tuna sashimi is a signature dish. *8400 Santa Monica Blvd.,* ☎ *213/848–2360.*

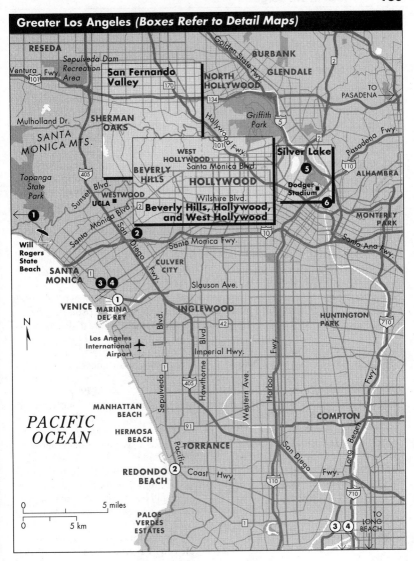

Greater Los Angeles (Boxes Refer to Detail Maps)

Eats ●

Apple Pan, **2**
Astro Family
Resaurant, **5**
Dandelion Cafe, **4**
Granita, **1**
Mon Kee, **6**
Van Gogh's Ear, **3**

Scenes ○

Babylon, **2**
Ripples, **4**
Roosterfish, **1**
Silver Fox, **3**

$$$–$$$$ **Eclipse.** With a dining room designed by Claude Monet's grandson and a kitchen presided over by a former Spago maître d', Eclipse has a lot going for it. The inventive Mediterranean food is stellar. Try the fish of the day, which is displayed at your table, dabbed with olive oil, baked whole in the kitchen, and then served with your choice of sauces. *8800 Melrose Ave.,* ☎ *310/724–5959.*

$$$–$$$$ **Le Dôme.** This Sunset Strip brasserie is a culinary fixture. It's popular with the rich and famous who like its dark, clubby atmosphere. The straightforward Continental dishes include veal ossobuco, Belgian hare, and what may well be the best steak tartare in town. *8720 Sunset Blvd.,* ☎ *310/659–6919.*

$$$–$$$$ **Matsuhisa.** What looks like a plain Japanese storefront restaurant is actually the city's best sushi house. You'll be astounded—and a little intimidated—by the 40-page menu of innovative specialties, including shrimp in a fiery pepper sauce and sea-urchin tempura wrapped in a shiso leaf. *129 N. La Cienega Blvd.,* ☎ *310/659–9639.*

$$$–$$$$ **Morton's.** Run by the son and daughter of steak-house veteran Arnie Morton (as in Morton's of Chicago), this upscale hangout has a busy industry scene. Try the juicy red steaks, the lime chicken, or the tender veal chops, and keep your eyes and ears open for the real dishing. *8764 Melrose Ave.,* ☎ *310/276–5205.*

$$$–$$$$ **Spago.** What would the food scene in L.A. be like if Spago had never opened? It's frightening to imagine. The designer pizzas, risottos, and meat grills are sublime. But you may decide that, if the maître d' deigns to seat you at a decent table, Spago is more a place to see and be seen than a truly cutting-edge restaurant. *114 Horn Ave.,* ☎ *310/652–4025.*

$$–$$$$ **Cicada.** Every dish here is organic, healthful, and wonderful. The grilled swordfish in wasabi sauce is a typical offering. Price and presentation make it a celebrity stop. *8478 Melrose Ave.,* ☎ *213/655–5559.*

$$–$$$ **Benvenuto.** Believe it or not, this charming restaurant was once a recording studio. People now come to dine on the shady terrace, hemmed in by gardens, vines, and hedges. The food is Italian: traditional pastas, outstanding designer pizzas, heavenly *tiramisù*. Has a big lesbian following. *8512 Santa Monica Blvd.,* ☎ *310/659–8635.*

$$–$$$ **Book Soup Bistro.** Attached to a popular bookstore, the bistro is a full sit-down restaurant where you're as free to pop in for coffee and dessert as you are for a full meal—maybe a salad Niçoise or a bowl of cioppino. Call ahead for info on book signings—to avoid the crowds or to line up for an autograph. *8800 Sunset Blvd.,* ☎ *310/657–1072.*

$$–$$$ **Café d'Etoile.** You could take a first date to this casual, intimate restaurant, and you would both feel fine in jeans. Favorite dishes from the eclectic menu are coquilles St. Jacques, English bangers and mash, and won-ton chicken. *8941½ Santa Monica Blvd.,* ☎ *310/278–1011.*

$$–$$$ **Checca.** Known for its nightclub, which gets going around 10:30 most nights and is extremely gay friendly, Checca is also a fine Italian restaurant. The inventive pasta dishes, including the penne alla Checca (with olive oil, onions, tomatoes, mushrooms, basil, garlic), are always fresh and deftly prepared. *7323 Santa Monica Blvd.,* ☎ *213/850–7471.*

$$–$$$ **La Masia.** Live music, a great tapas bar, and the warm, Spanish countryhouse theme make La Masia a popular place for dinner or drinks. The saffron-infused paella and the mushroom *relleno* are excellent. *9077 Santa Monica Blvd.,* ☎ *310/273–7066.*

$$–$$$ **Melrose Place.** No, this fashionable restaurant near Melrose Avenue's fine shopping is not affiliated with the TV show. It's just a chic spot for sipping cocktails over fine, relatively affordable Pacific Rim cuisine. You might start with shrimp-and-chicken dumplings, before moving on to an *ahi* tuna with ginger-garlic soy sauce. Very romantic patio. *650 N. La Cienega Blvd.,* ☎ *310/657–2227.*

$$–$$$ **Petit Four.** This quaint Tuscan and Provençal restaurant has a natty interior with a peach-and-green color scheme, dainty bentwood chairs, and soft lighting—understated and elegant. About 15 varieties of pasta are offered as well as such light dishes as a cold poached-salmon salad. *8654 Sunset Blvd.,* ☎ *310/652–3863.*

$$–$$$ **Talesai.** Duck curry and tiger prawns in a piquant garlic sauce are two dishes that have earned this upscale, art-filled Thai restaurant considerable kudos. *9043 Sunset Blvd.,* ☎ *310/275–9724.*

$$ **Bossa Nova.** Lauded for its spicy servers and spicy Brazilian food, Bossa Nova is the place to go for rich steaks or lime chicken with black beans. Request the patio for extra equatorial ambience. *685 N. Robertson Blvd.,* ☎ *310/657–5070.*

$$ **Caffe Luna.** This cozy, mellow bistro in the Melrose District is great for intimate conversation; you can't say the same for most of its neighbors. The food packs plenty of punch, though, from the signature *zuppa rustica* (tomato and vegetable soup) to the filling vegetarian lasagna. *7463 Melrose Ave.,* ☎ *213/655–8647.*

$$ **Caioti.** The chef at this Hollywood Hills café trained under Wolfgang Puck and may have bettered the master in creating memorable pizzas. Options range from wild mushrooms, gorgonzola, sausage, basil, and pine nuts to shrimp with Thai spices. *2100 Laurel Canyon Blvd.,* ☎ *213/650–2988.*

$$ **Chin Chin.** Part of a famed contemporary chain of outstanding Chinese restaurants, this trendy branch has plenty of outdoor seating and nearby window shopping. The sweet-and-sour orange chicken and the Cantonese dumplings are good choices. *8618 Sunset Blvd.,* ☎ *310/652–1818.*

$$ **Hugo's.** Power breakfasts have long been associated with this venerable purveyor of carbo-packed morning food; try pumping up with sweet pumpkin pancakes. At night, the noisy, cavernous dining room serves less-inspired Italian food, such as jumbo shrimp scampi and chicken piccata. The portions are huge—day or night. *8401 Santa Monica Blvd.,* ☎ *213/654–3993.*

$$ **La Petit Bistro.** This bistro has moderately priced French food and is close to Santa Monica's gay scene. Mussels *marinière,* braised lamb shank with couscous, and chicken sautéed with mushrooms and honey vinaigrette are among the better dishes. *631 N. La Cienega Blvd.,* ☎ *310/289–9797.*

$$ **Olvera.** Sunday brunch here is a leisurely affair that's like attending one of L.A.'s fabulous pool parties—only there's no pool. You dine on the patio or inside by the fireplace of what was once John Barrymore's home. Either spot is romantic. A mix of Mexican, Continental, and American dishes, such as tequila shrimp pasta or apricot chicken, prevail. Formerly Butterfields. *8426 W. Sunset Blvd.,* ☎ *213/656–3055.*

$–$$ **Figs.** The popular choice for dykes who lust for plain, old-fashioned home cooking, Figs feels like a neighborhood tavern; it's unpretentious, but not a dive. In addition to traditional chicken-fried steak and blackened pork chops, you can sample such unusual dishes as rigatoni with white beans in marinara sauce. *7929 Santa Monica Blvd.,* ☎ *213/654–0780.*

$–$$ **Marix Tex-Mex.** Marix doesn't serve the world's greatest Mexican food, but it's a certifiable gay hangout; the patio is especially popular on weekend afternoons. *Huevos chipotle,* seviche, and chicken-fried steak are among the better offerings. Festive, but expect service with a sneer. *1108 N. Flores St.,* ☎ *213/656–8800.*

$ **Ben Frank's.** Hideously fabulous or fabulously hideous? It's hard to say. This 24-hour diner is in an angular '50s-style building that's reminiscent of an IHOP. The food is ordinary, but the round-the-clock parade of mod chicks, blue hairs, corporate types, and fashion plates provides diversion. *8585 Sunset Blvd.,* ☎ *310/652–8808.*

$ **French Quarter Market.** Despite the New Orleans decor—wrought iron green-and-white filigree, hanging plants, and a terrace under a turquoise-and-

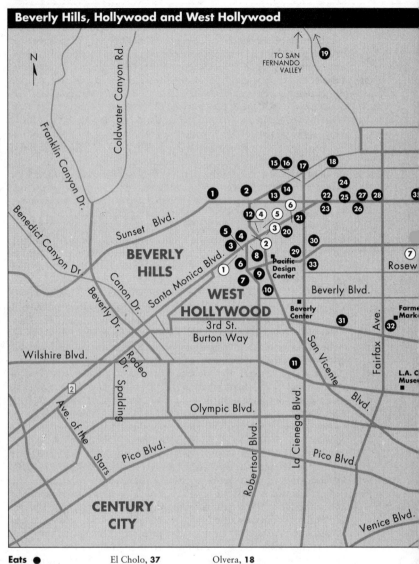

Eats ●

The Abbey, **8**
Basix, **25**
Ben Frank's, **17**
Benvenuto, **21**
Book Soup Bistro, **13**
Bossa Nova, **6**
Buzz Coffee, **26**
Cafe La Bohème, **23**
Café d'Etoile, **4**
Caffe Luna, **34**
Caioti, **19**
ChaChaCha, **38**
Checca, **35**
Chin Chin, **16**
Cicada, **33**
Eclipse, **7**

El Cholo, **37**
Figs, **28**
French Quarter
Market, **27**
Hamburger
Heaven, **5**
Hugo's, **22**
Jerry's Deli, **10**
Kokomo, **32**
La Masia, **3**
La Petit Bistro, **29**
Le Dôme, **14**
Little Frida's, **20**
Marix Tex-Mex, **24**
Matsuhisa, **11**
Melrose Place, **30**
Morton's, **9**

Olvera, **18**
Petit Four, **15**
Six Gallery, **12**
Spago, **2**
Talesai, **1**
Who's on Third, **31**
Yukon Mining Co., **36**

Scenes ○

Axis/Love Lounge, **1**
Mickey's, **4**
Mother Lode, **3**
The Palms, **6**
Rage, **2**
Revolver, **5**
Spike, **7**

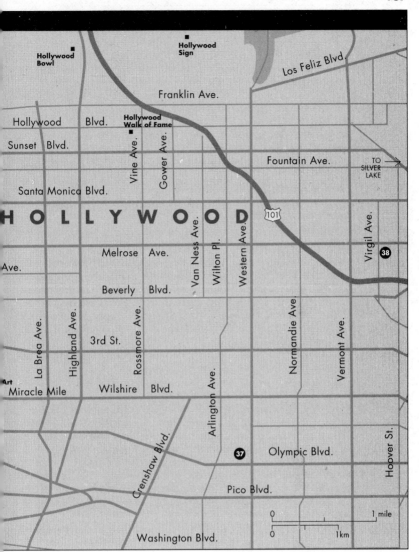

Hollywood
Bowl

Hollywood
Sign

Los Feliz Blvd.

Franklin Ave.

Hollywood   Blvd.   Hollywood
Walk of Fame

Sunset   Blvd.

Vine Ave.

Gower Ave.

Fountain Ave.

TO
SILVER
LAKE

Santa Monica Blvd.

H O L L Y W O O D   101

Ave.

Melrose   Ave.

Van Ness Ave.

Wilton Pl.

Western Ave.

Virgil Ave.

38

Beverly   Blvd.

La Brea Ave.

Highland Ave.

Rossmore Ave.

3rd St.

Normandie Ave.

Vermont Ave.

Art
Miracle Mile

Wilshire   Blvd.

Arlington Ave.

Crenshaw Blvd.

Hoover St.

37   Olympic Blvd.

Pico Blvd.

0   1 mile

0   1km

Washington Blvd.

pink awning, the food is upscale diner-style—from French-dip sandwiches to baked orange roughy. Sunday brunch is fun and cruisy: party people, weekend lovettes, and disco refugees repair here; during the week it's a neighborhood dinner spot. *7985 Santa Monica Blvd.,* ☎ *213/654–0898.*

$ Hamburger Haven. A dumpy red shack across from the Abbey (*see* Coffeehouse Culture, *below*), the Haven is noted for its burgers, Polish sausage, and corn on the cob. The front terrace overlooks the busy intersection of Robertson and Santa Monica. *8954 Santa Monica Blvd.,* ☎ *310/659–8774.*

$ Jerry's Deli. This New York–style deli, famous for its chicken soup, is actually better than the much hyped Canter's Deli. It's open 24 hours and always serves huge fresh sandwiches and salads. *8701 Beverly Blvd.,* ☎ *310/289–1811.*

$ Yukon Mining Co. A major post-club scene, this beloved greasy spoon is open 24 hours. Expect standard diner food—fried chicken and the like. *7328 Santa Monica Blvd.,* ☎ *213/851–8833.*

Elsewhere

$$$–$$$$ Granita. If you're looking for a night on the town away from the bustle of the city, Wolfgang Puck's (no, that name won't go away) Granita is a good bet, visually striking and tucked in tony Malibu. The decor is seaside surreal, with blown-glass light fixtures and tiles with bits of embedded seashell. Puck emphasizes seafood in his usual array of creative pizzas, light pastas, and grills. *23725 W. Malibu Rd. (in Malibu Colony Plaza), Malibu,* ☎ *310/456–0488.*

$$–$$$ Cha Cha Cha. This place is often overlooked because of its dicey location in Silver Lake. Yet such inventive Caribbean fare as shrimp in a hot *negro* sauce or a starter of black-bean sweet tamales is worth the drive. *656 N. Virgil Ave., Silver Lake,* ☎ *213/664–7723.*

$ Apple Pan. Don't let anyone tell you otherwise: You'll find L.A.'s best burger at this '40s joint. Although the menu is short (they don't even offer shakes here), you'll at least find fries and fresh-baked pies. There are often long lines for a quick, perfect bite around the horseshoe-shape countertop. *10801 W. Pico Blvd., Rancho Park,* ☎ *310/475–3585.*

$ Astro Family Restaurant. People come to this gay-popular Silver Lake diner after the bars close—as much to eat as to see the hostess, who looks a bit like Alice Ghostly and is usually clad in an inspired and gaudy outfit. *2300 Fletcher Blvd., Silver Lake,* ☎ *213/663–9241.*

$ Dandelion Cafe. Take a walk on the beach and then dine on the shaded patio of this popular café. Big hearty breakfast offerings include sourdough French toast; for lunch there are fajitas and burgers. *636 Venice Blvd., Venice Beach,* ☎ *310/821–4890.*

$ El Cholo. The neighborhood around L.A.'s oldest Mexican restaurant (established 1928) has declined, but the outstanding no-frills fare hasn't (greencorn tamales are a specialty). *1121 S. Western Ave., Los Angeles,* ☎ *213/734–2773.*

$ Kokomo. The best—and gayest—of several restaurants at the popular open-air farmers' market, Kokomo offers diner classics with New American touches. Break the fast with *huevos rancheros* (with smoked tomato salsa), stargaze a little, and return later for a turkey burger and mocha shake. *6333 W. 3rd St., Fairfax,* ☎ *213/933–0773.*

$ Mon Kee. Cheap and simple, with plenty of Formica and fluorescent light, Mon Kee is one of Chinatown's best restaurants. The fish is fresh, the sauces zesty, and the portions huge. *679 N. Spring St., Chinatown,* ☎ *213/628–6717.*

Coffeehouse Culture

The Abbey (692 N. Robertson Blvd., West Hollywood, ☎ 310/289–8410) is *the* gay coffeehouse. Sit cozily inside amid faux-opulent statuary, fountains, and chandeliers, or outside in a courtyard filled with terra-cotta statues and anchored by a gaudy fountain of cast-iron flamingos. Most of West Hollywood and its visitors wind up here at some point on a Saturday night; the food is good, too.

A big breakfast crowd heads to **Basix** (8333 Santa Monica Blvd., West Hollywood, ☎ 213/848–2460) for a full meal or for the rich coffees; the Cal cuisine is healthy and affordable. **Buzz Coffee** (8200 Santa Monica Blvd., West Hollywood, ☎ 213/650–7742) has light sandwiches, heavy desserts, great coffees, and a strong gay following. **Little Frida's** (8730 Santa Monica Blvd., West Hollywood, ☎ 310/854–5421), which is named for artist Frida Kahlo, is often more packed with stylish dykes than the bars and clubs. Faithfully, the decor is strictly Kahlo reproductions and collectibles. In the back there's a pool table and a patio for scoping.

The **Six Gallery** (8861 Santa Monica Blvd., West Hollywood, ☎ 310/652–6040) is a chic, postmodern coffeehouse that's known for it's nonfat cheesecake—only in L.A. **Van Gogh's Ear** (796 Main St., Venice, ☎ 310/314–0022) is the gay-beach coffee bar; it's known for its all-you-can-eat Sunday buffets, and it's open all night. **Who's on Third** (8369 W. 3rd St., West Hollywood, ☎ 213/651–2928) is a contemporary option that gets a mix of straights and gays.

Laguna Beach

$$$ **Kachina.** This inventive restaurant has flavorful, beautifully presented, contemporary Southwestern fare. Typical are the honey-braised mesquite-grilled pork with a chipotle cream sauce, charred rare ahi tuna served on a sweet corn pudding with bean ragout and tomatillo sauce, and the hand-wrapped lobster tamale with jicama-and-squash salad. *222 Forest Ave.,* ☎ *714/497–5546.*

$$–$$$ **Renaissance.** With great northern Italian food at reasonable prices, Renaissance is a solid dinner option. Try the clams simmered in white wine with herbs and garlic for starters; follow them with rib-eye pepper steak grilled to order. This is also a cozy place for coffee and dessert, and there's live music many nights. *234 Forest Ave.,* ☎ *714/497–5282.*

$$ **The Cottage.** Although it's touristy these days, the Cottage has been a major see-and-be-seen dining spot for years. The straightforward Continental cuisine is competently prepared—charbroiled lamb with herbs, olive oil, and thyme sauce is a favorite. There are many pastas, too. Sunday brunch is wildly popular. *308 N. Pacific Coast Hwy.,* ☎ *714/494–3023.*

$$ **Royal Thai.** This gay-popular Thai restaurant near the gay bars has a greenhouse-style dining room and a redbrick patio whose serenity is marred by traffic from the busy road nearby. Some excellent dishes include the green chicken curry and the charbroiled beef grill in a spicy sauce. *1750 S. Pacific Coast Hwy.,* ☎ *714/494–8424.*

$$ **Tortilla Flats.** The Puerto Vallarta–inspired murals (remember that the Tennessee Williams play was set there), gurgling fountains, terrace seating, and ocean views have earned this restaurant a loyal following. The Cal-Mex dishes (cheese enchiladas, tamales, chili rellenos) are delicious. *1740 S. Pacific Coast Hwy.,* ☎ *714/494–6588.*

$ **Penguin Cafe.** This charming '50s-style diner is a dependable spot for breakfast and lunch. A few Mexican specialties dot a menu that's otherwise heavy on burgers, fries, malts, and other American standbys. *981 S. Pacific Coast Hwy.,* ☎ *714/494–1353.*

SLEEPS

Location is the most important consideration in choosing an L.A. accommodation. There are only a few establishments within walking distance of West Hollywood's club scene, and most of them are pricey. Nearby Hollywood has scads of places, but many are cheap-looking motels in questionable quarters. West Los Angeles has lovely rooms and exorbitant prices. Downtown isn't a long drive from West Hollywood, and it's close to the Silver Lake restaurants and bars, but most of the lodgings are overpriced, characterless business hotels. For economical, low-key, clean lodging, small hotels and guest houses are best. Also, consider staying in the San Fernando Valley, where most of the hotel franchises have properties, and prices are generally lower than in L.A. proper.

For price ranges in both Los Angeles and Laguna Beach, *see* Chart A at the front of this guide.

Hotels

Downtown Vicinity

⊞ The 1923 **Biltmore** is a piece of movie-industry history; its public areas and guest rooms have been used for the filming of dozens of Hollywood classics—the ballroom was shot as the capsized ship's dining room in the *Poseidon Adventure*. Unlike other grandes dames, the Biltmore has aged gracefully and the rooms, though a bit small, are still lavish. *506 S. Grand Ave., ☎ 213/624–1011 or 800/245–8673. 683 rooms. $$$–$$$$*

⊞ The **Wyndham Checkers,** which opened in 1923, is as historic as the nearby Biltmore but more intimate. Rooms have marble baths and are loaded with Asian and European antiques. *535 S. Grand Ave., ☎ 213/624–0000 or 800/996–3426. 188 rooms. $$$–$$$$*

⊞ Though the **Orchid Hotel**'s rooms are plain, this '20s budget lodging has plenty of character. *819 S. Flower St., ☎ 213/624–5855. 63 rooms. $*

West Hollywood and Beverly Hills

⊞ The posh **Hotel Nikko** is close to the best Beverly Hills shopping and dining, has its own renowned Pacific Rim restaurant, and is decorated in the contemporary Japanese style for which the chain is known. Rooms have VCRs and CD players as well as a traditional soaking tub. *465 S. La Cienega Blvd., ☎ 310/247–0400 or 800/645–5687. 304 rooms. $$$$*

⊞ The discreet, 12-story **Beverly Prescott** is popular with gay and lesbian tourists and business travelers and is situated on a hill overlooking Beverly Hills and Century City. Rooms are large, contemporary, and have balconies. *1224 S. Beverwil Dr., ☎ 310/277–2800 or 800/421–3212. 139 rooms. $$$–$$$$*

⊞ One of several popular all-suite properties in West Hollywood, **Le Montrose** is just off the Strip and close to the bars on Santa Monica Boulevard. Rooms are huge, with fireplaces, kitchenettes, and private balconies. Enjoy amazing views of the skyline from the rooftop pool and hot tub. *900 Hammond St., ☎ 310/855–1115 or 800/776–0666. 125 rooms. $$$–$$$$*

⊞ The rooms at low-key **Le Parc** have gas fireplaces, TVs and VCRs, and large sunken living rooms. There's also an on-site health club. This boutique hotel is on a quiet residential street, close to the bars. *733 N.W. Knoll Dr., ☎ 310/855–8888 or 800/578–4837. 154 rooms. $$$–$$$$*

⊞ The **Mondrian,** a distinctive cube, is famous for its red, blue, and yellow Mondrianesque facade and the millions of dollars of contemporary art scattered throughout. The picture windows in the large rooms afford expansive city views. There are frequent celebrity sightings in the lounge. *8440 Sunset Blvd., ☎ 213/650–8999 or 800/525–8029. 224 rooms. $$$–$$$$*

⊞ The **Hyatt on Sunset** is often dubbed the rock 'n' roll hotel because music-industry luminaries—from Little Richard to the Doors—have encamped here. Amenities are standard, but there's a spectacular rooftop pool and sundeck with views of Hollywood Hills and downtown. *8401 Sunset Blvd., ☎ 213/656–1234 or 800/233–1234. 262 rooms. $$$*

⊞ The **Ramada West Hollywood** may be the most gay-popular mainstream hotel in America: It's in the heart of the bar district and has a sleek art deco look and a cruisy pool and sundeck out back. Most of the stylish, spacious suites have sleeping lofts; all have kitchenettes. *8585 Santa Monica Blvd., ☎ 310/652–6400 or 800/845–8585. 135 rooms, 40 suites. $$–$$$$.*

⊞ One of the area's better values is the old **Hollywood Roosevelt,** where the first Academy Awards ceremony was held. It had become a neglected dump by the mid-'80s, before it was purchased and converted into a terrific property. The poolside cabana rooms are romantic. *7000 Hollywood Blvd., ☎ 213/466–7000 or 800/950–7667. 470 rooms. $$–$$$*

⊞ The **Holloway Motel** is a clean, affordable, gay-friendly property in the heart of the gay entertainment strip. *8465 Santa Monica Blvd., ☎ 213/654–2454. 23 rooms. $*

Points West

⊞ The posh **Hotel Bel Air** might have the strongest star-following of any property in the city. It's a full resort with a fabulous pool and fitness center and lush gardens. Rooms are secluded, impeccably decorated, and ridiculously expensive. *701 Stone Canyon Rd., Bel Air, ☎ 310/472–1211 or 800/648–4097. 92 rooms. $$$$*

⊞ The fancy **Ritz-Carlton** looms oddly over Marina Del Rey's contemporary skyline, looking something like a Georgian-style armoire surrounded by plastic beach chairs. A stay here is a breezy respite from any hint of action; rooms have panoramic marina views and all that Ritz-Carlton comfort. If nothing else, stop by for the over-the-top Sunday brunch. *4375 Admiralty Way, Marina Del Rey, ☎ 310/823–1700 or 800/241–3333. 306 rooms. $$$$*

⊞ Reminiscent of a tony San Francisco boutique hotel, the **Century Wilshire** is an intimate, warmly furnished property near UCLA. Rooms are spacious and have kitchenettes. *10776 Wilshire Blvd., West Los Angeles, ☎ 310/474–4506 or 800/421–7223. 99 rooms. $$–$$$*

⊞ The **Pacific Shore** hotel is a block from the Santa Monica beach, a long but scenic walk or short drive to the gay section. Rooms are bright, simple, and the price is right. *1819 Ocean Ave., Santa Monica, ☎ 310/451–8711 or 800/622–8711. 168 rooms. $$*

⊞ If you want to escape from the pace of West Hollywood, consider the intimate **Mansion Inn** near Venice's boardwalk. Rooms at this European-style property have most of the amenities of larger properties, cost far less, and have a great deal of charm. *327 Washington Blvd., Venice Beach, ☎ 310/821–2557 or 800/828–0688. 43 rooms. $–$$*

Guest Houses and Small Hotels

⊞ Couples should consider the romantic **Grove Guesthouse,** a small cottage in West Hollywood with a kitchen, TV and VCR, separate living room, and a pool with a hot tub. *1325 N. Orange Grove Ave., West Hollywood, ☎ 213/876–7778. 1 cottage. Mixed gay male/lesbian. $$*

⊞ The **San Vicente B&B Resort** is the quintessential California gay guest house—complete with buffed and in-the-buff men lying around a pool and foliage-choked lanai. Rooms and cottages have tasteful contemporary furnishings and kitchenettes. The rates are extremely fair. *845 San Vicente*

Blvd., West Hollywood, ☎ *310/854–6915. 14 rooms, 3 cottages. Mostly gay male. $–$$*

▣ The women-owned **Country Comfort B&B** is an affordable spot popular with both lesbians and gay men. Rooms are eclectically furnished, some with antiques; you'll find a hot tub, a video library, a full breakfast, and evening refreshments. It's in Anaheim (20 minutes or an hour to West Hollywood, depending on traffic), close to Disneyland. *5104 E. Valencia Dr., Orange,* ☎ *714/532–4010. 3 rooms. Mixed gay male/lesbian. $*

Laguna Beach

There are a variety of resorts, motels, and guest houses in and around Laguna Beach. The knowledgeable folks at the gay-owned **California Riviera 800** (☎ 714/376–0305 or 800/621–0500) reservation service can find accommodations from Santa Barbara to San Diego, although they specialize in this area.

▣ Although it's stuffy, costly, and a 15-minute drive from downtown Laguna Beach, the **Ritz-Carlton Laguna Niguel** is a stunning resort. Perched atop a 150-foot cliff, it commands panoramic ocean views. Rooms have museum-quality furnishings and marble baths; the service is discreet and attentive. A golf course, fitness center, spa, and pool complete the fantasy. *1 Ritz-Carlton Dr., Dana Point,* ☎ *714/240–2000 or 800/241–3333. 393 rooms. Mostly straight. $$$$*

▣ Not as over-the-top luxurious as the Ritz-Carlton, the **Surf & Sand Hotel** is still one of Southern California's cushiest resorts, and it's a short walk from Laguna Beach's three gay bars. Rooms have balconies that overlook the ocean and casual yet elegant furniture. There are two first-rate restaurants and a large pool and deck. *1555 S. Pacific Coast Hwy.,* ☎ *714/497–4477 or 800/524–8621. 160 rooms. Mostly straight. $$$–$$$$*

▣ The cheerful, mainstream **Best Western Laguna Brisas Spa Hotel** has a good reputation in the gay and lesbian community. Rooms are done in cool pastels; they're big, comfortable, and have ocean views. Each bath has a king-size whirlpool spa. *1600 S. Pacific Coast Hwy.,* ☎ *714/497–7272 or 800/624–4442. 65 rooms. Mostly straight. $$–$$$*

▣ The straight-owned, extremely gay-friendly **Casa Laguna B&B** is an enchanting Spanish Mission–style compound with spectacular ocean views, lush gardens and courtyards, and a sprawling pool and sundeck shaded by banana and avocado trees. The varied accommodations include a 1,360-square-foot mission house with two fireplaces that sleeps six, a small romantic cottage, and 19 smaller units. *2510 S. Pacific Coast Hwy.,* ☎ *714/494–2996 or 800/233–0449. 21 rooms. Mixed gay/straight. $$–$$$*

▣ The large, motel-style **Capri Laguna Inn** is one of the better values in the area and is near the gay bars. Rooms are spacious, and most have ocean views. There's a heated pool on the top deck, and the beach out back is a short walk from the gay section in front of the Coast Inn down the street. *1441 S. Pacific Coast Hwy.,* ☎ *714/494–6533 or 800/225–4551. 42 rooms. Mostly straight. $–$$$*

▣ A full-service gay resort for more than 30 years, the **Coast Inn** sits right on the beach and has bars; a restaurant; and clean, comfortable rooms. The fanciest have private sundecks, fireplaces, and wet bars, but you can get simple accommodations with ocean views for as little as $60. Though all kinds of guys stay here, the place attracts gay porn stars and other buffed L.A. types. It's definitely popular among single guys. *1401 S. Pacific Coast Hwy.,* ☎ *714/494–7588 or 800/653–2697. 23 rooms. Mostly gay male. $–$$*

SCENES

L.A.'s nightlife scene extends well beyond the clubs clustered along Santa Monica Boulevard in West Hollywood. For many, these dozen-or-so establishments are the only places worth hitting. Fair enough: If you're in search of glitzy gay Los Angeles, West Hollywood is the hub. It's where you'll find the "industry" crowd—aspirants of all shapes and sizes—and it's where most gay tourists party. The area is popular with lesbians as well as gay men, but it's undoubtedly dominated by the male bar scene. This stretch can seem cold and intimidating, particularly if image isn't everything to you.

Bars stop serving liquor at 2 AM, but many stay open as late as 4. When the bars in West Hollywood close, the blocks between San Vincente and Robertson, on the north side of Santa Monica Boulevard, turn into one big cruisy sidewalk party. Ask around about after-hours clubs or private parties: The crowd is fairly convivial—and tanked—at this point. Some of the overflow spills into the 24-hour supermarket, **Pavillions** (8969 Santa Monica Blvd.), down the block—an excellent time to do your shopping.

L.A.'s gay community is more stratified by class than that of other cities—there isn't a lot of play between the guppie bars of West Hollywood and the mostly working-class clubs in nearby communities. For enlightening bar crawls, explore San Fernando Valley, Silver Lake, and the beach communities—from Venice Beach to Long Beach. Silver Lake has one of the country's strongest Latino-and-leather scenes. Bars downtown and in Hollywood tend to be divey and sometimes dangerous. The Valley bars have a suburban feel and are very down-to-earth. The beach bars, which are predominantly white and, the farther south you go, working-class, epitomize Southern California's laid-back personality. In the neighborhood bars of Long Beach and the Valley, check your attitude at the door.

Bars and Small Clubs

West Hollywood

Axis/Love Lounge. These two clubs are joined but have separate addresses and different parties each night. Inside are several bars on different floors, plenty of places to sit and get cozy, and a room with pool tables. Twice a week, usually Thursday and Sunday, under-21-year-olds are allowed inside. The crowd is generally mixed gay men and lesbians, but a couple times a week dykes rule. Go-go boys and girls frequently perform, and theme nights feature all types of music, including new wave, hi-NRG, tribal, rock, and Latin house. *Axis: 652 N. La Peer Dr., ☎ 310/659–0471. Love Lounge: 657 N. Robertson Blvd., ☎ 310/659–0472. Crowd at both: varied but usually under 30; mixed racially; mixed m/f.*

Mickey's. At first, Mickey's seems the same as Rage, which is just down the street. There's a bar in front, a dance floor in back, and lots of room for posing and cruising. Plenty of people float between the two clubs, but Mickey's has an older, more outgoing and diverse crowd. Women come here more than to the neighboring guys clubs. Outstanding drink specials. *8857 Santa Monica Blvd., ☎ 310/657–1176. Crowd: 80/20 m/f; mostly 20s and 30s; gym boys; greater racial mix than neighboring bars.*

Mother Lode. This low-key bar is famous for its Sunday beer blasts but is always a great place to shoot pool or meet friends. It's a compact, warm tavern with brass light-fixtures, polished wood trim, and ornate cast-iron street lamps. *8944 Santa Monica Blvd., ☎ 310/659–9700. Crowd: mostly male; late 20s to late 30s; jeans and flannel shirts; low-key, on the make.*

Rage. Among guppies and gym boys, Rage is the most popular nightly gay disco in L.A. It's a midsize club with seating and standing room in the front bar and on the sidewalk out front. The disco has the usual accoutrements (pulsing lasers, strobe lights, a mirror ball), and off to one side there's a small video lounge where boys exchange vital statistics between stints on the dance floor. *8911 Santa Monica Blvd.,* ☎ *310/652–7055. Crowd: 85/15 m/f; young; stand-and-model, shirtless muscle boys; high energy, high attitude.*

Revolver. L.A.'s definitive pretty boy bar—redolent of cologne, sculpting gel, and Marlboro cigarettes—is friendlier than you might think. You enter through a pair of oddly imposing brass gates. Inside a half dozen video screens play campy film and music clips. The usual suspects are more often more interested in the monitors than the cruising. Squeeze your way to the smaller video bar in back—it's more conducive to chatting and an easier place to get a drink. Staff is cute and personable. *8851 Santa Monica Blvd.,* ☎ *310/659–8851. Crowd: mostly male; young; guppies and Twinkies; buffed and bronzed.*

Spike. A harder-action crowd hangs at the Spike, east of Guppie Land where Santa Monica Boulevard begins to turn seedy. Collared shirts appear in spurts at this leather-and-Levi's club, especially on weekends after 2 AM when this is one of the few places still going (though it serves only coffee and soda). The long, narrow bar has three rooms, all dimly lit and minimally decorated. There's a pool table and a bar in the front room and pinball machines in the middle one; the back room opens onto a screened-in patio heated by an open-pit fire. *7746 Santa Monica Blvd.,* ☎ *213/656–9343. Crowd: male; mostly thirtysomething; some leather but has drawn more of a jeans and T-shirt bunch in recent years; fairly butch.*

OTHER OPTIONS

Sneeringly nicknamed the "Mold Coast," the **Gold Coast** (8228 Santa Monica Blvd., ☎ 213/656–4879) is a cruisy, neighborhood cocktail lounge that draws a mostly thirtysomething, dressed-down crowd. A cavernous disco of indirect lighting and mirrored walls, **Numbers** (8029 Sunset Blvd., ☎ 213/656–6300) is L.A.'s upscale hustler bar. **Rafters** (7994 Santa Monica Blvd., ☎ 213/654–0396) is a sleepy video bar that's big with country-western fans. **Trunks** (8809 Santa Monica Blvd., ☎ 310/652–1015) is the neighborhood sports bar.

Hollywood

On Saturday nights, especially after midnight (it's open after hours), the serious dancing and drug scene centers around **Probe** (836 N. Highland Ave., ☎ 213/461–8301), a South Hollywood disco about midway between West Hollywood and Silver Lake. Tuesday and Friday are gay at the largely Latin and African American **Circus Disco** (6655 Santa Monica Blvd., ☎ 213/462–1291). **Mugi** (5221 Hollywood Blvd., ☎ 213/462–2039) is a cocktail bar with a strong Asian following and a great campy drag show on Thursday.

Silver Lake

Cuff's. The only visible decor in this dark one-room hangout are a few pilfered street signs and a toilet seat that hangs over the bar. The place's tough, blue-collar image seems just that: an image. Many suits-by-day come here to act out their butch fantasies and meet dangerous-looking guys. It's the kind of bar where the hunk in the leather harness turns out to be your accountant. Cuff's is jam-packed on weekends (when it's open till 4 AM) and lively the rest of the week. *1941 Hyperion Ave.,* ☎ *213/660–2649. Crowd: male; 20s to 40s; gruff, horny; lots of leather and denim.*

Detour. Not as intense as the nearby Gauntlet II, Detour is a leather bar with a fairly broad following. You're more likely to find West Hollywood strays here than elsewhere in Silver Lake. It's a divey bar cast in faint pink-and-red lighting and set inside a brown building just off Santa Monica

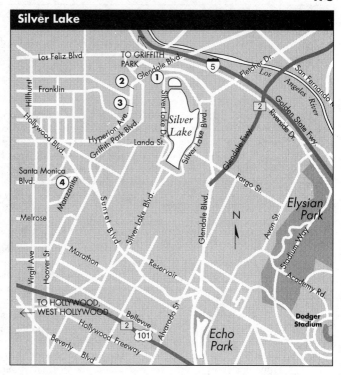

Silver Lake

Boulevard. *1087 Manzanita St., ☎ 213/664–1189. Crowd: male; mostly 30s and 40s; mix of leather and Levi's; working-class.*

Houston's. Home of the best martini in Silver Lake, Houston's is a handsome little piano bar and cocktail lounge bedecked with carpeting, elegant sconces, amber lighting, and neatly framed show posters. Friendly; a good place to meet people if you're new in town. *2538 Hyperion Ave., ☎ 213/661–4233. Crowd: 75/25 m/f; older; laid-back.*

Woody's Hyperion. At Silver Lake's middle-of-the-road disco, the crowd is rough-edged and down-to-earth. But Woody's isn't nearly as seedy as other neighborhood clubs. There's a small bar up front, a pool table off to one side, and a fairly large dance floor. Popular place to dance, cruise, or just hang out. *2810 Hyperion Ave., ☎ 213/660–1503. Crowd: 80/20 m/f; mixed Latino and Anglo; neighborhood crowd with a smattering of those from farther afield; diverse in age; friendly, unpretentious; some grunge and alternative; dykes in boots and bras.*

OTHER OPTIONS

The **Gauntlet II** (4219 Santa Monica Blvd., ☎ 213/669–9472) is a hardcore, leather-and-uniform place in an unmarked gray building; lots of neon beer signs, a pool table, and rugged bartenders. The **Faultline** (4216 Melrose Ave., ☎ 213/660–0889) is similar. Primarily a Latino club, **Le Bar** (2375 Glendale Blvd., ☎ 213/660–7595) welcomes everybody and has terrific music, friendly bartenders, and hot strippers. The **Silver Lake Lounge** (2906 Sunset Blvd., ☎ 213/663–9636) is a crowded, cruisy neighborhood club with an almost exclusively Latino crowd.

Downtown

Catch One (4067 W. Pico Blvd., ☎ 213/734–8849) is a big dance club with a fairly young but racially diverse crowd of men and women. **Score** (107 W. 4th St., ☎ 213/625–7382) is a mostly Latino dance club.

Pasadena

Two popular options are **Encounters** (203 N. Sierra Madre Blvd., ☎ 818/792–3735), which draws a local, mostly male crowd for dancing, pool, darts, and cruising; and **3772** (3772 E. Foothill Blvd., ☎ 818/578–9359), which has country-western music and gets an even mix of men and women.

San Fernando Valley

Apache. This stand-and-model disco and video bar has a small dance floor and is crowded on weekends, especially after hours. The decor is not memorable but perfectly comfortable—lots of cheap wood-paneling—and there's a small patio off to the side. Guys who find West Hollywood to be a tease like it here, where everyone is looser. It's a major pick-up scene: easy to bed, easy to rise. *11608 Ventura Blvd., Studio City, ☎ 818/506–0404. Crowd: 80/20 m/f; young, aspiring guppies; Valley boys too lazy to wander over the hills.*

Oasis. Although the Valley's gay nightlife is often dissed, Oasis may be the coziest, friendliest place in greater L.A. Behind the dull, white-concrete facade is a classy little piano bar with nightly entertainment, a well-lit pool room, and a cheerful patio. It fills up many nights with an appealing, approachable crowd. *11916 Ventura Blvd., Studio City, ☎ 818/980–4811. Crowd: 80/20 m/f; mostly ages 30 and up; mellow, boys and girls you can take home to the family.*

Oil Can Harry's. It's been around for almost 30 years and continues to be L.A.'s best gay country-western dance club—popular with men and women of all ages. The attractive interior has lots of video screens, a large central dance floor, and bars at both ends. There are two-stepping lessons on weekends. *11502 Ventura Blvd., Studio City, ☎ 818/760–9749. Crowd: 70/30 m/f; all ages; gets more non-Valley types than other area bars; insatiable country-western line dancers; very outgoing and fun.*

OTHER OPTIONS

Bullet (10522 Burbank Blvd., North Hollywood, ☎ 818/760–9563) is one of several dreary neighborhood bars in an industrial neighborhood. There's a nice little patio in back, but the inside bar is pitch black and smoke-filled; getting from the front to the patio is like trying to escape from a burning airplane. **Escapades** (10437 Burbank Blvd., North Hollywood, ☎ 818/508–7008) is a casual tavern with a long bar, lots of dartboards, pinball, a tiny dance floor, and two pool tables. For a while, people stole the balls from the pool tables, so now, before they issue you a rack of balls, you have to leave your driver's license with the bartender as collateral. Nice.

Gold 9 (13625 Moorpark St., Sherman Oaks, ☎ 818/986–0285) is a peculiar neighborhood bar, with a rowdy, older crowd; if you're a stranger in these parts, just about everybody in this bar will notice you—and will introduce themselves. In definitively drab Reseda, **Incognito** (7026 Reseda Blvd., Reseda, ☎ 818/996–2976) is your only option; inside is a small dance floor with mirrored walls, a room with a couple of pool tables, and a cozy video bar. A mix of straights and gays come to see the rather tired but funny female impersonators at the **Queen Mary** (12449 Ventura Blvd., Studio City, ☎ 818/506–5619), a large show lounge with a wide stage and plenty of seating. Although not as widely known as Oil Can Harry's, the country-western **Rawhide** (10937 Burbank Blvd., North Hollywood, ☎ 818/760–9798) bar is worth a visit: It has a popular Sunday beer blast, a couple pool tables, roadhouse-inspired decor, and an extremely friendly staff.

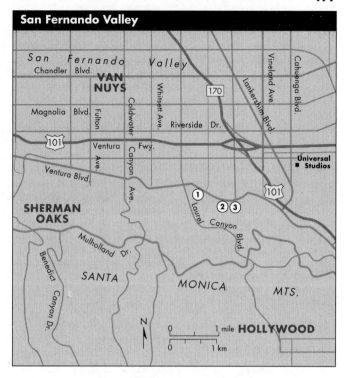

San Fernando Valley

The Beaches and Points West

Babylon. This large dance club and lounge draws big local after-work and weekend crowds. A central bar and a room with a couple of pool tables keep people occupied till the music starts. It doesn't open its arms wide to strangers, but on the dance floor everyone blends in. *2105 Artesia Blvd., Redondo Beach,* ☎ *310/371–7859. Crowd: 85/15 m/f; all ages, some racial mix; working-class surfer set; a bit cliquey.*

Roosterfish. This cement building on a funky Venice street is painted a frightening bright aqua that's tempered only by a patch of glass brick. Inside, it's a dive with character: a small bar with Tiffany-style lamps, a linoleum floor, bits of memorabilia, a pool table, pinball machines, and a large patio out back. By day, the crowd is local; at night—especially on weekends—Metallica fans, Barbra fans, and poetry slammers all squeeze in for a little peace, love, and understanding. Unpredictable but always engaging. *1302 Abbot Kinney Blvd., Venice Beach,* ☎ *310/392–2123. Crowd: 80/20 m/f; the most diverse in L.A.; popular with aged hippies, retired surfers, and disenchanted West Hollywooders.*

Long Beach

Ripples. This two-story shack across from the beach has great views of the ocean and is usually the best game in town on weekends. It's what you'd imagine a gay California beach bar to be: filled with laid-back beach queens and a few dykes. It's not big, but there's lots to do. On the top level is a disco that plays popular dance music and classic disco. The ground floor has a piano bar and plenty of seating on one side and a cruise bar and pool tables on the other. Note the lovely dolphin sculptures along the roofline. *5101 E. Ocean Blvd.,* ☎ *310/433–0357. Crowd: 80/20 m/f; mostly under 35; mix of locals and out-of-towners; lots of bleach-blond surf bums with ponytails; laid-back.*

Silver Fox. Happy hours at this upscale video bar are packed—it's not as happening later, but it's one of the most comfortable bars for visitors to Long Beach. The Fox is well lighted and decorated with maroon carpeting, chrome, mirrors, and white Christmas lights. Stand at the bar or sit at one of the many tables to watch music videos on two huge screens. *411 Redondo Ave.,* ☎ *310/439–6343. Crowd: 80/20 m/f; all ages; guppies, lots of suits after work.*

OTHER OPTIONS

One of Long Beach's more serious leather clubs is **Bulldogs** (5935 Cherry Ave., ☎ 310/423–8228), which is open after hours. The **Executive Suite** (3428 E. Pacific Coast Hwy., ☎ 310/597–3884) cocktail lounge and disco is popular with both men and women; a somewhat older crowd. **Floyd's** (2913 E. Anaheim St., ☎ 310/433–9251) is the area's country-western dance club. Come to the **Mineshaft** (1720 E. Broadway, ☎ 310/436–2433) for the cheap drink specials; it draws a young, denim-and-flannel crowd. **Wolf's Den** (2020 E. Artesia Blvd., ☎ 310/422–1028) is a leather, uniform, and western bar, not unlike its namesakes in Palm Springs and San Diego.

Women's Bars and Hangouts

Many of the bars mentioned above, though predominantly male, have strong lesbian followings, especially the Axis/Love Lounge, the Executive Suite, Mickey's, Oil Can Harry's, Ripples, and Woody's Hyperion. Also, Little Frida's (*see* Coffeehouse Culture, *above*) is always packed with a swinging bunch.

Girl Bar. This glamorous party is thrown at several places; call the information line (☎ 213/460–2531) or check the gay rags for details. In recent years, Girl Bar has been held on Friday at **Axis** (*see above*) and on Saturday at the **Love Lounge** (*see above*). Every so often, the Girl Bar is held poolside at a fancy hotel on Sunset Boulevard, often the Mondrian or the Argyle. These parties draw a modest (often closeted) celebrity following. *Crowd: mostly mid-20s; hot, stylish, sophisticated; lively, cruisy; lots of bisexuals.*

The Palms. This pubby bar in the heart of West Hollywood isn't as cruisy as the Girl Bar parties but is more open to out-of-towners than some neighborhood dyke bars. There's plenty of seating and standing room; the back section has pool tables, and off that is a deck. The dance floor is large, and there's a rocking jukebox, a DJ some nights, and live bands from time to time. On Wednesday night drinks cost a buck, and this is the place to be. Sunday's beer blast is also popular. *8572 Santa Monica Blvd.,* ☎ *310/652–6188. Crowd: 80/20 f/m; highly diverse in age and race; some guppies, some working-class; lipstick, butch—kind of a catchall.*

OTHER OPTIONS

The **Cobalt Cantina** (4326 Sunset Blvd., ☎ 213/953–9991), a trendy Mexican restaurant in Silver Lake, has a women's party on Wednesday night and a strong lesbian following at all times. They recently opened a branch in West Hollywood, too. In the Valley, friendly, local **Club 22** (4882 Lankershim Blvd., North Hollywood, ☎ 818/760–9792) has a small patio, a pool table, and a dance floor. The **Oxwood Inn** (13713 Oxnard St., Van Nuys, ☎ 818/997–9666) gets an older, suburban crowd (it's nicknamed "Menopause Manor"). **Rumors** (10622 Magnolia Blvd., North Hollywood, ☎ 818/506–9651) is a dark, smoky bar that has the feel of one of those women-in-prison B movies from the '50s.

In Long Beach, **Que Sera Sera** (1923 E. 7th St., ☎ 310/599–6170) is a lesbian beach bar, drawing a diverse bunch for dancing to either DJ's choice or live music. Much rowdier is **Club Broadway** (3348 Broadway, ☎ 310/438–7700), a butch pool hall with a local following.

On the Wild Side

Sex clubs and bathhouses change often—read the bar rags. A couple standbys: **Basic Plumbing** (1924 Hyperion Ave., ☎ 213/953–6731), a popular Silver Lake bathhouse, and the infamous—in a good way—**Zone** (1037 N. Sycamore Ave., Hollywood, ☎ 213/464–8881) sex club.

Laguna Beach

Boom Boom Room. The rambling four-bar complex at the Coast Inn is packed, especially on weekends, with tan, toned bodies. The front room has a large central bar; two pool tables; and such embellishments as a pressed-tin ceiling, glass brick, and hurricane shutters. A small room with a pool table connects this bar to the one at the rear, which has a fabulous 8-foot-long tropical fish tank and soft amber lighting. Off this is the dance bar; it's tiny but the music is good. *1401 S. Coast Hwy., ☎ 714/494–7588. Crowd: 75/25 m/f; age varies, but tends to be under 35 on weekends; lots of yuppies; touristy, well-heeled; occasionally some attitude but fairly down-to-earth.*

Little Shrimp. This convivial piano bar consistently has talented entertainers. The interior is brightly lit and has too many mirrors; head for the patio, which is bedecked with festive Christmas lights. Serves decent Cal-Mex and American food. *1455 S. Coast Hwy., ☎ 714/494–4111. Crowd: 60/40 m/f; mostly ages 30s and up; laid-back; lots of locals; settled dykes.*

Main Street. With red-leatherette smoking chairs and a mock Tudor interior, Main Street doesn't look like a typical beach bar. The crowd, however, is Southern California all the way: fun-loving, chatty, and bleach blond. People often sing up a storm around the piano. *1460 S. Coast Hwy., ☎ 714/494–0056. Crowd: 70/30 m/f; a bit older and less touristy than at the Boom Boom Room, but otherwise similar.*

Newport Station. This loud, high-energy, warehouse-style nightclub is a 15-minute drive from Laguna Beach in unpretentious Costa Mesa. Has pool tables and a large dance floor. Nontouristy alternative to Laguna Beach clubs. *1945 Placentia Ave., 714/631–0031. Crowd: mostly male; young; mixed racially; low attitude; Orange County club kids.*

THE LITTLE BLACK BOOK

At Your Fingertips

AIDS Hotline of Southern California: ☎ 800/922–2437. **Audre Lorde Lesbian Health Clinic:** ☎ 213/993–7570. **Community Outreach & Education Project for Women:** ☎ 213/993–7448. **Gay and Lesbian Community Center of Long Beach:** ☎ 310/434–4455. **Gay and Lesbian Community Center of Los Angeles:** ☎ 213/993–7400. **Gay and Lesbian Community Center of Orange County:** ☎ 714/534–0961; info hotline: ☎ 714/534–3261. **Gay and Lesbian Community Center of South Bay:** ☎ 310/379–2850. **Gay Men's Activities Hotline:** ☎ 213/993–7444. **Laguna Beach Chamber of Commerce:** 357 Glenneyre Ave., 92652, ☎ 714/494–1018. **Laguna Beach Community Clinic:** ☎ 714/494–9429. **Los Angeles Chamber of Commerce:** 350 S. Bixle St., 90017, ☎ 213/580–7500.

Gay Media

Edge Magazine (☎ 213/962–6994) provides comprehensive bar and restaurant coverage and has a health-and-fitness bent; it's full of beefcake, chatty, and hard to escape. *Frontiers* (☎ 213/848–2222) is based in West Hollywood and has news and entertainment features on all of

Southern California. The *Gay & Lesbian Times* (☎ 619/299–6397) is based in San Diego and also has information on all of Southern California—it's not as strong on L.A. coverage as some, but it's good for Laguna Beach. *Nightlife* (☎ 213/462–5400) is a fairly standard biweekly entertainment rag with good men's and women's coverage.

Female FYI (☎ 310/657–5592) and *LA Girl Guide* (☎ 310/390–3979) are small, handy guides to lesbian nightlife and fun. The monthly *Lesbian News* (☎ 310/392–8224) magazine is one of the most substantial lesbian publications in the country, with comprehensive coverage of Southern California and lots of interviews and news.

The free alternative papers are *L.A. Weekly* (☎ 213/465–9909) and the smaller *LA Village View* (☎ 310/477–0403).

BOOKSTORES

The city's major lesbigay bookstore is **A Different Light** (8853 Santa Monica Blvd., ☎ 310/854–6601), which is in the heart of West Hollywood's gay entertainment area. **Unicorn Bookstore** (8940 Santa Monica Blvd., ☎ 310/652–6253) has a more modest array of titles, but a good selection of videos, greetings cards, and gifts. The best selection of porn videos and magazines is at **Drake's** (7566 Melrose Ave.).

For women, L.A. has two excellent stores: **Page One Books** (1200 E. Walnut St., Pasadena, ☎ 818/796–8418), which also has a good selection of women's music, and the **Sisterhood Bookstore** (1351 Westwood Blvd., Westwood, ☎ 310/477–7300).

A couple of independent bookstores with good, queer stock are **Book Soup** (8818 Sunset Blvd., ☎ 310/659-3110) and the **Midnight Special Bookshop** (1350 3rd St. Promenade, Santa Monica, ☎ 310/393–2923), which is strong on leftist titles.

Body and Fitness

In West Hollywood, the **Sports Connection** (8612 Santa Monica Blvd., ☎ 310/652–7440) is one of the gayest gyms on the planet—a major workout and cruise scene for men and women. To work out here, you must know a member or be staying at a hotel with privileges (many in the area have them). The **World Gym West Hollywood** (8560 Santa Monica Blvd., ☎ 310/659–6630) nearby does not impose such restrictions and has extensive facilities. In Hollywood, try **Gold's Gym** (1016 N. Cole Ave., ☎ 213/462–7012); in Silver Lake, the **Body Builders' Gym** (2516 Hyperion Ave., ☎ 213/668–0802). All are lesbian-friendly, but if a women-only environment is a priority, consider the **L.A. Women's Gym** (3407 Glendale Blvd., ☎ 213/661–9456) in Silver Lake.

13 *Out in* Nashville

AS YOU TRAVEL THROUGH THE SOUTH and listen to gay people's assessments of their hometowns, a recurring theme emerges: every city—Charlotte, Chattanooga, Columbia, Birmingham, Jackson, Memphis—considers itself to be the buckle of the Bible Belt, and despite this (or more likely because of it), every city boasts a close-knit, defiant, though small gay community.

If you consider regions of the country on the basis of their tolerance of homosexuality, the South, because of its consistently antigay state laws and identification with the religious right, scores low marks. And so it is with considerable trepidation that many gay men and lesbians, especially when traveling as couples, approach a state like Tennessee and a city like Nashville.

To be sure, you'd be wise as a gay couple to conduct yourself differently in Nashville than you might in Key West or West Hollywood. Nashville has no gay ghetto, no street where you're likely to see an unusually high homo-presence. If you wish to avoid confrontation, you should, as you would in 98% of America, behave discreetly.

Symbols of gay pride—rainbow jewelry, flags, bumper stickers, T-shirts with gay logos—and open acts of affection between same-sex couples are common even in such southern climes as New Orleans and Atlanta, but not in Nashville. In the former two cities, you feel a certain strength in numbers, that if your statement or behavior provokes a negative response, others will (you hope) jump to your defense. Nashville is too small to permit high levels of openness.

But compared with Memphis or Columbia or Jackson, you get the feeling that you could walk arm-in-arm with your girlfriend down 2nd Avenue without provoking much of a reaction, that you and your boyfriend could check into the Opryland Hotel without the clerk batting an eyelash. It *feels* safe in Nashville to be gay, but you can't help reminding yourself, "This is a conservative Southern city, and I'm not sure there are any other gay people around me, and isn't country music all about straight people drinking and fighting . . . ?"

In fact, Nashville is quite tolerant. The presence of 16 universities contributes to this general tolerance of sexual, as well as religious and ethnic, diversity. Nashville is peopled with educated men and women. The presence of higher education also keeps a steady flow of twentysomethings passing through town.

What might surprise you is that Nashville's history as Music City USA has contributed just as much, in certain respects, to gay tolerance. Although country music has never made strong overtures to gay audiences, Nashville's lavishly choreographed country music shows have long attracted gays to work on them as dancers, chorus singers, stagehands, and behind-the-scenes staff. By the mid-'80s, many country musicians had become aware of the contribution gays had made to Nashville, although few acknowledged them publicly.

Attitude about sexual orientation began to change in Nashville with both the advent of cable TV and the publicity of AIDS. Cable TV put rock-oriented MTV and the country-oriented Nashville Network a couple of channels apart on many TV screens. A third music network, VH1, soon emerged, bridging pop and country and showing videos from both markets. Country artists like Garth Brooks, Lyle Lovett, and Mary Chapin Carpenter dabbled with folk and rock, and popular country star k. d. lang released an album of pure pop songs while simultaneously coming out as a lesbian. (Rumors continue to fly concerning the orientation of at least a couple more country stars.) Country music merged more and more with the considerably more gay-friendly forces of rock, folk, and New Wave.

The AIDS virus ravaged every gay community, including Nashville's, and a number of country music stars—most notably Brooks and Kathy Mattea, devastated by the loss of friends and crew, responded with fundraising, as well as consciousness raising. To say country music has "gone gay" would be a gross overstatement, but Nashville continues to witness changes.

The simultaneous emergence of Branson, Missouri, as a major competitor for country music tourism has actually fueled Nashville's transformation into a sophisticated and more open-minded city. There now appear to be two distinct camps of country-western entertainment: Nashville appeals to a broader, younger, hipper crowd; Branson pulls in an older, more traditional, and more conservative segment. These two camps overlap and blend in many ways, but gays are far more welcome in Nashville than in Branson.

Two recent events in Nashville illustrate this progress. The down-home, Nashville-based restaurant chain, Cracker Barrel, was criticized harshly in recent years for its alleged policy of dismissing openly gay and lesbian employees. The company has not only backed down on this policy, it quietly gave money to Nashville's AIDS walk in 1994, and several Cracker Barrel employees participated in the march. That same year, the Gay Softball World Series was slated to be held in Nashville, a move that raised the hue and cry of many in the community. Many major local businesses, however, fronted by the Nashville Chamber of Commerce, pushed for the city to welcome the players enthusiastically, and the tournament went on as planned. Infamous antigay activist Fred Phelps (known throughout the South for crashing the funerals of people dead of AIDS) promised a war and showed up for the tournament to protest it—nobody joined him. The world's still waiting for a lesbian love story or a film about showstopping drag queens that's scored by Nashville's country music elite. Don't hold your breath . . . but don't rule it out either.

THE LAY OF THE LAND

The narrow Cumberland River meanders tortuously through metro Nashville, clipping the eastern edge of downtown, where it changes course from north–south to east–west, before turning north–south once again out by Opryland USA (a 15-minute drive from downtown). In central Nashville, numbered roads run north–south; the avenues are west of and parallel to the Cumberland, the streets east of and parallel to it.

Downtown

Downtown Nashville, other than what is historic, is a bit ordinary; it could be any capital city in any state. But for the controversial twin-spired **South Central Bell building,** built in 1994, which reminds many of Batman's pointy-eared logo, little about the skyline stands out. Downtown is set around the courtly Greek Revival **capitol building** (Charlotte Ave., ☎ 615/741–2692), which is perched atop the highest hill in Nashville. Behind here, beyond the north face of the hill, a long mall and reflecting pool are under construction in anticipation of the state's 1996 bicentennial; many events will be staged on the mall and around the capitol. To the south stand a few noteworthy samples of late 19th- and early 20th-century architecture. Nearby is the **Tennessee State Museum** (505 Deaderick St., ☎ 615/741–2692), which traces the state's history, and the beaux arts-style **Hermitage Suite Hotel** (231 6th Ave. N, ☎ 615/244–3121), which is where, in 1920, suffragists and antisuffragists from around the country encamped while debating the ratification of the 19th Amendment (women's right to vote). The Tennessee Legislature sided with the suffragists, and so ended a dark chapter of America's political process. A block over, **5th Avenue** was the site throughout the '60s of numerous civil rights demonstrations, the success of which inspired like movements throughout the South. Just off 5th, between Union and Church streets, is a restored turn-of-the-century arcade of boutiques and simple eateries—it's usually packed at lunchtime with office dwellers out for some fresh air and a quick bite.

A few blocks east, toward the Cumberland, is Nashville's old Market Street, now **2nd Avenue,** where a long row of redbrick Victorian warehouses was rescued from neglect in the 1980s and converted into restaurants, music clubs, brew pubs, and specialty shops. **Broadway** between 3rd Avenue and the river has a similar feel, and a few good antiques shops. **First Avenue** is lined on one side with the backs of 2nd Avenue's buildings; across the street is **Riverfront Park,** a long brick promenade with views across the murky Cumberland of the industrial east bank. At the top of the park, just below where Church Street intersects 1st Avenue, is a reproduction of the settlement's first outpost, **Fort Nashborough,** the original of which was four times bigger. The revitalization of this area has been a tremendous success, and though many of the attractions are predictable tourists haunts (the Hard Rock Cafe, Hooters, etc.), this is a boisterous, festive neighborhood for wandering on weekend nights.

On 5th Avenue, between Broadway and Commerce Street, stands the **Ryman Auditorium** (116 5th Ave. N, ☎ 615/254–1445), within whose walls country music transformed Nashville into Music City USA. The ornate Ryman was built in 1892, and was initially the site of crowded religious revivals. Within a couple of decades it had been converted into a concert hall, where Enrico Caruso, Isadora Duncan, Martha Graham, Charlie Chaplin, Mae West, the Ziegfeld Follies, and many others performed.

In the meantime, the National Life and Accident Insurance Company had begun a radio station, WSM (for "We Shield Millions"), which presented a weekly Barn Dance on Saturday evenings. In 1927, prior to one such broadcast, announcer George Hay segued from a performance of the New York Opera to the night's barn dance by joking, "Folks, for the past hour we've been listening to music taken largely from the Grand Opera. Well ya'll just sit right back, because from now on, you're gonna hear the Grand Ole Opry."

The name stuck and the Opry passed through a few venues before settling into the Ryman Auditorium in 1943, where it would remain until 1974. That year it moved to its current locale, the Grand Ole Opry House, on the banks of the Cumberland River. The Ryman was shut down for a couple of decades before undergoing a complete refurbishment in 1994, which has turned it once again into a major concert hall for a diverse lineup of nationally known music acts; there's also a museum chronicling the Ryman's history.

Music Row

Not to be confused with the Opryland section of Nashville, **Music Row** (Demonbreun St. exit off I-40, ☎ 615/256–1639) is the hub of the city's country music recording industry. The neighborhood is just southwest of downtown, where 16th Avenue intersects Demonbreun Street. You can actually tour **Studio B,** where everyone from Elvis to Dolly Parton has made records, or cut your own demo—for a small fee—at **Recording Studios of America** (☎ 615/254–1282), which is part of the popular **Barbara Mandrell Country Museum** (1510 Division St., ☎ 615/242–7800), notable for its great gift shop and a full replica of Mandrell's bedroom. There are a few more attractions here that will probably get a rise out of the most loyal country music fans, including the **Hank Williams Jr. Museum** (1524 Demonbreun St., ☎ 615/242–8313), the **Car Collectors Hall of Fame** (1534 Demonbreun St., ☎ 615/255–6804), and the **Country Music Wax Museum and Mall** (118 16th Ave. S, ☎ 615/256–2490). Even if you're not a fan of the genre, however, you might enjoy a tour through the **Country Music Hall of Fame and Museum** (4 Music Sq. E, ☎ 615/256–1639), which abounds with photos, costumes, instruments, and memorabilia.

West End Avenue and Belle Meade

Beyond Music Row, if you follow Broadway southwest until it turns into **West End Avenue,** you'll pass several of the city's schools and medical facilities, including **Vanderbilt University,** and discover many of the city's best restaurants and shops—the kinds of places popular with students. Also along West End is the city's most memorable site, **the Parthenon** (West End and 25 Aves., ☎ 615/862–8431), a detailed replica of the one that sits above Athens. Built for the city's 1897 centennial, the Parthenon is set in a neatly landscaped park and houses a small collection of American painting and *Athena Parthenos,* a 42-foot-tall statue.

West End eventually leads into the ritzy neighborhood of **Belle Meade,** where many of Nashville's celebrities and politicians reside. There are a couple of mansion-museums in this region, including the Greek Revival **Belle Meade Plantation** (5025 Harding Rd., ☎ 615/356–0501), once the site of a 5,300-acre thoroughbred breeding farm, and **Cheekwood** (1200 Forrest Park Dr., ☎ 615/356–8000), a 1925 Georgian-style house on whose grounds you'll find the **Tennessee Botanical Gardens & Museum.**

Opryland USA

This 120-acre **theme park** (2808 Opryland Dr., via Briley Pkwy., ☎ 615/889–6611) is Nashville's most popular attraction, a complete amusement park and country music entertainment compound, with 70 live shows and 30 rides. It's twice the size of Disneyland and nearly as popular. No matter how enlightened Nashville has become over the years, it's still safe to assume that Opryland, though it employs many gays and lesbians, is not a particularly inviting setting for homosexuals to let loose and be themselves. Admission to the park is $25 per person, too, so you really have to want to subject yourself to this.

On the other hand, touring the grounds of America's most heavily booked hotel, the **Opryland Hotel** (2800 Opryland Dr., ☎ 615/889–1000) is free and extremely entertaining. A massive American flag looms over the hotel's entrance, which leads to a busy lobby filled with thick, plush armchairs that are typically filled with thick, plush guests. For such an enormous facility, it's surprisingly tasteful—done with reproduction antiques, white-brick, and a gurgling fountain in virtually every public area. The hotel surrounds a series of glass-enclosed courtyards that abound with lush greenery, waterfalls, carp-filled ponds, fern-decked paths, and fountains. Hundreds of camera-toting guests mill around in leisure suits, taking in this spectacular scene. It's just a huge hothouse of traditional American values. Though a bit hokey and overwrought, the Opryland Hotel is no less spectacular for it.

The **Grand Ole Opry** (2804 Opryland Dr., ☎ 615/889–3060) is still the hottest ticket in town, and has been infused in recent years with a slick roster of today's talents, including Vince Gill, Marty Stuart, Travis Tritt, Alison Krauss, Hal Ketchum, Patty Loveless, and many others.

Metro Nashville

Attractions throughout greater Nashville range from the historic to the outlandishly commercial. Among the former, Andrew Jackson's homestead, **The Hermitage** (4580 Rachel's La., Hermitage, ☎ 615/889–2941) is the most impressive, with its 28,000-square-foot museum, the original mansion, and many gardens. Among the latter, Johnny Cash's shrine to country music, the **House of Cash** (700 Johnny Cash Pkwy., Hendersonville, ☎ 615/889–2941), contains many of his personal mementos.

GETTING AROUND

Nashville's downtown is walkable, but only a fraction of the city's notable restaurants, bars, and sights are in this section. Buses are impractical and taxis are worthwhile only in a pinch; it's best to use a car. Garages are cheap and plentiful downtown, and parking is easy elsewhere.

EATS

Of small, inland, southern cities, Nashville has the best culinary reputation. The influx of music celebrities and politicians puts the price of dinner at Nashville's best places nearly as high as in L.A. and New York City, but there are plenty of cheap family-style eateries, too. Barbecue is popular throughout the South, and Nashville is no exception, but the residents of no southern city east of Texas are as fond of steak as Nashvillians. The two best local steak house chains are **Longhorn Steaks** (110 Lyle Ave., ☎ 615/329–9195, plus four other locations; $$–$$$) and **Outback Steakhouse** (3212 West End Ave., ☎ 615/385–3440, plus three other locations; $$–$$$). Also consider the branches of the nationally renowned **Ruth's Chris Steakhouse** (204 21st Ave. S, ☎ 615/320–0163; $$$–$$$$) and **Morton's of Chicago** (641 Church St., ☎ 615/259–4558; $$$$).

For price ranges, *see* Chart B at the front of this guide.

$$$$ **Arthur's in Union Station.** Less pretentious than your typical high-end French restaurant, Arthur's is supremely elegant—set in the meticulously restored Union Station and replete with polished silvers, fine china, and formal linens. The wait staff verbally presents each night's seven-course menu, which might include chateaubriand with béarnaise sauce, tomato-basil soup, and rich bananas Foster, for which Arthur's is deservedly well known. *1001 Broadway,* ☎ 615/255–1494.

$$$$ **Mario's.** The place to go if your goal is to dine among country music glitterati and hot shot politicos. Mario's serves authentic Northern Italian food— veal medallions with roasted peppers and fontina cheese, duck marsala,

Unfortunately, the delicious pasta dishes come only as starters, making Mario's a bit of a wallet-buster. *2005 Broadway,* ☎ *615/327–3232.*

$$$$ **106 Club.** As Nashville's gay nightlife lacks a true piano bar, the sophisticated 106 Club—done in the style of a 1920s supper club—often draws a big gay crowd around its elegant, black, baby grand piano. New American favorites include free-range chicken with pasta primavera. A very good value. *106 Harding Pl.,* ☎ *615/356–1300.*

$$$$ **Wild Boar.** Conspicuous consumption is the name of the game in this faux European hunting lodge with an award-winning wine list (more than 15,000 bottles). Original art worth $2.5 million hangs on the walls; on the tables are rack of venison with seared foie gras and other luxurious fare, some prepared tableside. Take money. *2014 Broadway,* ☎ *615/329–1313.*

$$$–$$$$ **F. Scott's.** Chef celeb Emile Labrousse—a Nashville legend—lovingly manages the inventive menu at this flashy art deco spot in the tony Green Hills shopping district. Sample the mushroom terrine with shallot vinaigrette, baby greens, and berries; or grilled lamb chops with flageolet beans and braised endive. Impressive wine list. *2210 Crestmoor,* ☎ *615/269–5861.*

$$$–$$$$ **Merchants.** A $3 million restoration of this 1892 brick building, a former hotel, has given Nashville one its most cosmopolitan restaurants. The three levels have high ceilings and windows, and spectacular architectural details. The first floor offers the grill, which has a lighter, less expensive menu. Very fine dining is to be found on the third floor, with white table clothes, freshly cut flowers, and subdued light. The seafood dishes—like grouper in corn husks with poblano butter and grilled corn pico de gallo—are the standouts on the New American menu. *401 Broadway,* ☎ *615/254–1892.*

$$$–$$$$ **Mère Bulles.** Part of 2nd Avenue's big comeback, Mère Bulles is a place to meet for wine, listen to jazz, and dine on fine Continental fare amid clear river views. Specialties include the asparagus salad, escargots tossed with angel hair pasta, and shrimp and scallops in a walnut pesto. The old-fashioned brass-and-mahogany bar is a favorite gathering spot. *152 2nd Ave. N,* ☎ *615/256–1946.*

$$$ **The Mad Platter.** This is the city's most gay-identified restaurant with serious food, set in a quiet historic neighborhood north of the capitol. It's a quirky place; one wall of the dining room is lined with shelves of old books. The California-inspired cuisine is anything but quaint, however, with such bold selections as sesame-marinated sea bass and red snapper with an orange-pineapple-poblano sauce. *1239 6th St.,* ☎ *615/242–2563.*

$$–$$$ **Blue Moon.** In West Nashville, a 20-minute drive from downtown, the Blue Moon is the only waterfront restaurant in town; it has a long dock jutting into the Cumberland. Lots of good seafood and other traditional American dishes. Very romantic. *525 Basswood Ave.,* ☎ *615/352–5892.*

$$–$$$ **Bound'ry.** Part of a strip of trendy collegiate hangouts off West End Avenue, the Bound'ry is set in a striking, pumpkin-color stucco-and-wood frame addition to an old redbrick house; the dining room and bar are bright and airy, with French doors opening onto the street. An array of exotic tapas is offered, such as Oysters Mary (Louisiana oysters deep fried in cornmeal and served with horseradish cocktail sauce). Entrées include such dishes as paella and polenta steak. *911 20th Ave. S,* ☎ *615/321–3043.*

$$–$$$ **Sunset Grill.** Popular with university types, this postmodern, whimsical dining room is just off the Vanderbilt campus. For such creative, filling dishes, the prices are terrific: The rosemary chicken is less than $10. Also reasonable are grilled vegetables with spinach-basil pesto, turkey mignon, and "angel shrooms" (pasta and mushrooms). Entrées are half price after 10. *2001 Belcourt Ave.,* ☎ *615/386–3663.*

Eats ●

Arthur's in Union Station, **4**
Blue Moon, **7**
Bongo Java, **14**
Bound'ry, **11**
F. Scott's, **15**
Houston's, **10**
Jamaica, **12**
The Mad Platter, **16**
Mario's, **2**
Merchants, **5**
Mère Bulles, **6**
106 Club, **8**
Rio Bravo Cantina, **9**
Sunset Grill, **13**
12th and Porter, **1**
Wild Boar, **3**

Scenes ○

Chez Collette, **3**
The Chute Complex, **6**
Connection, **5**
The Gaslight, **2**
Ralph's, **4**
Roxy's, **7**
World's End, **1**

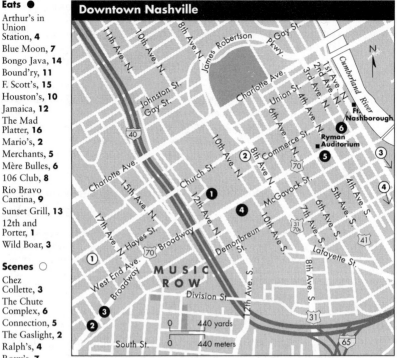

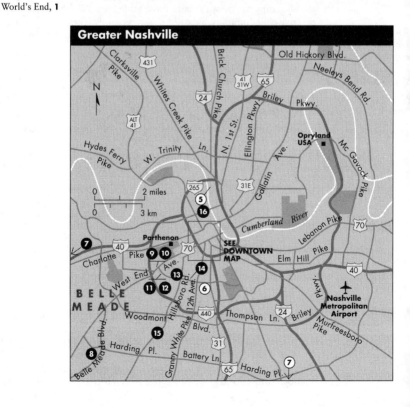

$$ **Houston's.** This is one of Nashville's premier power-lunching spots—the dining room, with its exposed brick, dark wood paneling, gas lamps, and brass, is always jammed with business sorts. Portions of Southern-inspired American fare are huge, from the bountiful salads and pastas to the sides of fries and couscous. Can be a bit loud. *3000 West End Ave.,* ☏ *615/269–3481.*

$$ **Jamaica.** The chipped, red corrugated roof of this somewhat dingy-looking West Indian-style building near 19th and Broadway prepares you for the Caribbean-influenced menu within. You dine amid colorful saltwater aquariums on outstanding jerk chicken, lamb, snapper, plantains, and other island staples. Gets a funky crowd. *1901 Broadway,* ☏ *615/321–5191.*

$–$$ **Rio Bravo Cantina.** This bright terraced Mexican restaurant near the Parthenon is the yuppie hangout of choice on weekend afternoons. The food is pretty standard—though the margaritas and the guacamole are both unusually fresh. Flirtatious staff; pretty straight crowd. *3015 West End Ave.,* ☏ *615/329–1745.*

$ **12th and Porter.** There are a few hip music clubs that double as restaurants around this industrial intersection just west of downtown—a miniature version of Atlanta's Little Five Points. Some of the best food and music are found in the all-black, minimalist interior of this turquoise-and-salmon brick building. Good designer pizzas and pastas. *114 12th Ave. N,* ☏ *615/254–7236.*

Coffeehouse Culture

In a turn-of-the-century house, **Bongo Java** (2007 Belmont Blvd., ☏ 615/385–5282) is large, bright, and contemporary. Local artists display their art not only on the walls but on the table tops. Healthy dishes such as vegetable chili, hummus, avocado-and-tuna sandwiches, as well as pastries, compliment the wide array of coffees. This is a great place to meet locals.

SLEEPS

Nashville's selection of hotels is typical of other small business cities: Only the Opryland Hotel stands out. All of the major chains are represented and none are any more gay-popular than any other. Hotels are generally in three areas: downtown, which puts you within walking distance of several good restaurants and shopping; the Opryland area; and West End Avenue, which puts you near Music Row, Vanderbilt, and Belle Meade. There is one gay-oriented guest house.

For price ranges, *see* Chart B at the front of this guide.

Hotels

🏨 The **Loew's Vanderbilt Plaza Hotel,** on West End Avenue, slightly removed from downtown, is a sleek, luxurious property with dark cherry furniture, a slick white lobby, and first-rate service. This is the top business hotel in the city. *2100 West End Ave.,* ☏ *615/320–1700 or 800/336–3335. 340 rooms. $$$–$$$$*

🏨 For proximity to Opryland attractions there's no better choice than the **Opryland Hotel,** the gargantuan compound built around a 2-acre glass-walled conservatory. *2800 Opryland Dr.,* ☏ *615/889–1000. 1,891 rooms. $$$–$$$$*

🏨 The centrally located 25-story **Stouffer Renaissance** has high-end reproduction antiques and great views, but is attached to a convention center and is a bit of a zoo at times. *611 Commerce St., ☎ 615/255–8400. 673 rooms. $$$*

🏨 The turn-of-the-century **Union Station,** the former railroad terminal, is full of character. The lobby contains the station's original clock and furnishings, and the restaurant, Arthur's (*see* Eats, *above*), is one of the best in the city. *1001 Broadway, ☎ 615/726–1001 or 800/331–2123. 136 rooms. $$–$$$*

🏨 One of the better deals downtown is the historic **Hermitage Suite Hotel,** an all-suite hotel with elegant period reproductions; it's just steps from the capitol. *231 6th Ave. N, ☎ 615/244–3121 or 800/251–1908. 120 rooms. $$–$$$*

🏨 The **Ramada Inn,** which is just across the street from Opryland, has perfectly gracious rooms at a good value. *2401 Music Valley Dr., ☎ 615/ 889–0800 or 800/228–2828. 307 rooms. $–$$*

🏨 Another option on West End Avenue is the **Hampton Inn Vanderbilt,** a bright, contemporary, six-story motel with unusually large rooms for such low rates. *1919 West End Ave., ☎ 615/329–1144 or 800/426–7866. 171 rooms. $*

Guest Houses and Small Hotels

🏨 The ragged but comfortable **Savage House Inn** is directly above the gay Gaslight cocktail and piano lounge and the Towne House restaurant, a small Southern-style luncheonette. This is the only Victorian town house still standing downtown, and, with its eclectic smattering of antiques and bric-a-brac, it still feels a bit like the rooming house it was during the mid-1800s. This is a perfectly suitable budget choice, but rooms and baths are slightly threadbare. *165 8th Ave., ☎ 615/254–1277. 6 rooms. Mixed gay/straight. $–$$*

SCENES

For a small city, Nashville has an unusually varied and popular gay nightlife. Here you will find two decent lesbian bars, three popular gay discos, plus a straight one with a gay following—the **Underground** (176 2nd Ave. N, ☎ 615/742–8909), which draws a mostly alternative, collegiate bunch. There's also a terrific gay and lesbian restaurant-cruise bar in the heart of downtown. Where some cities have 25 or 30 small, interchangeable neighborhood bars, Nashville has only a few noteworthy bars, but each possesses a distinct personality. This is not to call Music City USA a premier spot for gay nightlife—the universities and employees of Opryland keep the bars lively on weekends, but Sundays through Thursdays are pretty sleepy.

Chez Collette. Come if only to examine the extensive collection of bras hanging from the several chandeliers. Chez Collette is a trip—sort of a dykey French burlesque. Proprietress Collette, who still retains her thick native French accent, greets all and can even be heard to belt out a tune or two on karaoke night. Photos of celebs and bar regulars coat the walls, and one section of this brightly decorated and lighted lounge is furnished with long wooden tables and chairs, as though it's a family-style restaurant. *300 Hermitage Ave., ☎ 615/256–9134. Crowd: female, stylish, loud, festive, diverse in age.*

The Chute Complex. The Chute might remind you of those catch-all suburban gay bars that must offer a little of everything—dancing, a patio, a sports bar, a piano bar, a restaurant—to satisfy all types and all tastes. Indeed, before Connection opened, this was the major club in metro Nashville for many years. It's in a dumpy old multipurpose office building in an uninspired neighborhood a 10-minute drive south of downtown. The main room has a bar and a mid-size dance floor, off of which is the Trophy Room, a sports bar with the requisite pubby look. Off that room is an unusually pleasant patio with iron lawn furniture. Through a separate entrance beside the front door is the Silver Stirrup, a new, clubby-looking piano bar that used to be the city's only gay bookstore, but which now presents a nondescript menu of traditional American dishes. The staff is extremely chatty. *2535 Franklin Rd., ☎ 615/297–4571. Crowd: totally diverse, mixed m/f; all ages, looks, and styles.*

Connection. Few would guess that the largest gay club in America—at 40,000 square feet—would be in Nashville, but here it is, a few miles east of town in an industrial neighborhood across the Cumberland River. The parking lot looks as if it could accommodate about 1,000 cars; inside are five bars, a restaurant, a showroom with well-known female impersonators, and the best-looking bar hands in Nashville. What's more, the club is new, clean, intelligently laid out, and well-decorated. Some big-city club impresarios could learn a thing or two from the folks who run this gay amusement park (and handle a similar operation in Louisville, Kentucky). No matter what your taste in music, in this club you can always cut loose: There's often two-stepping on the smaller dance floor in the lounge, and high energy dancing in the enormous warehouse-style arena. *901 Cowan St., ☎ 615/742–1166. Crowd: 75/25 m/f, diverse, but tending to be under 35.*

The Gaslight. Attached to the historic Savage House Inn, the Gaslight exudes a brand of French Quarter charm with its ornate chandeliers, gilt frame mirrors, and overstuffed armchairs. It's a great space, completely absent of attitude and contemporary atmosphere. There's also a stage up front on which drag shows are occasionally presented, and live piano music many nights. *167½ 8th Ave. N, ☎ 615/254–1278. Crowd: 80/20 m/f, mostly mid-30s and up, local crowd, down-to-earth, some couples.*

Ralph's. Though small, this is the city's main lesbian dance bar, just south of downtown. It's always jumping around happy hour, and lots of women come before heading out to dance elsewhere. There are plenty of tables and chairs and a pool table, and the decor could best be described as contemporary American roadhouse. Check the bar rags for upcoming live music performances—they usually happen three or four times monthly. *515 2nd Ave. N, ☎ 615/256–9682. Crowd: 75/25 f/m, mixed ages, working class, neighborhoody, a few cowboy hats, some baseball caps, no attitude.*

Roxy's. This is Nashville's disco with a kick, run by the mother of one of the Roxy's celebrated *male* impersonators—although female ones perform here, too. These cross-dressing men and women always pack a huge crowd—they're some of the best dancers in the South, and some of them are more stunning in drag than even the slickest patrons. There's always a theme here, from the drag shows to karaoke to country line dancing. Roxy's has also had a few rave parties, all of which have gone very well. It's wackier here than at the Chute, more intimate than at Connections, but the 20-minute drive from downtown is a turnoff for some. *4726A Nolensville Rd., ☎ 615/333–9010. Crowd: 60/40 m/f, varied and colorful—from blue-haired alternateens to dykes on bikes to drag queens.*

World's End. Though it's the closest thing Nashville has to an afterwork, stand-and-model video bar, the World's End is not exactly any of these things—it just happens to attract that crowd with a popular pub-style American menu (burgers, grilled chicken, omelets); a long, old-fashioned bar; a large patio up front; and great alternative rock, grunge, and such. The food is decent, but many come simply to toss back a few drinks after work, shoot the breeze, and shed the day's stresses. There are booths along one wall and huge, colorful murals throughout. Good place to go before hitting the discos. *1713 Church St.,* ☎ *615/329–3480. Crowd: mostly gay, mixed m/f, young, lots of yuppies mixing with college students, low-key.*

There are two largely local bars south of town, not far from the Chute: The **Crazy Cowboy II** (2311 Franklin Rd., ☎ 615/269–5318) draws mostly, as the name suggests, crazy cowboys into its long, dark bar packed with video games and neon signs; **Ynonah's Station Saloon** (1700 4th Ave. S, ☎ 615/251–0980), out by the fairgrounds, bills itself a sports bar but feels more like a leather bar.

THE LITTLE BLACK BOOK

At Your Fingertips
AIDS Hotline: ☎ 800/845–4266. **Gay and Lesbian Community Center:** 703 Berry Rd., ☎ 615/297–0008. **Nashville Convention and Visitors Bureau:** 161 4th Ave. N, 37203, ☎ 615/259–4700. **Positive Voice:** ☎ 615/259–4866, ext. 128.

Gay Media
Nashville has a tiny gay and lesbian newspaper, ***Xenogeny*** (☎ 615/228–6572), which comes out weekly. There's also an equally slim statewide gay and lesbian newsweekly, ***Query*** (☎ 615/259–4135), which is based in Nashville.

BOOKSTORES
There is no specifically gay/lesbian bookstore in the area—or in Tennessee, for that matter—but the three-story **Davis-Kidd Booksellers** (Grace's Plaza in Green Hills, 407 Hillsboro Rd., ☎ 615/385–2645) has a good selection of gay and lesbian titles.

Body and Fitness
No gym is considered to be a major gay scene, but you'll feel perfectly at home working out at the huge **Centennial Sportsplex** (222 25th Ave. N, ☎ 615/862–8480).

14 *Out in New Orleans*

I MAGINE SIFTING THROUGH YOUR HOUSE in search of every dust-covered bottle of cleaning agent, paint, grease, lubricant, cooking oil, and flavor enhancer. Now imagine tossing into a bowl a tablespoon of every solution you discovered. Then envision sitting back and watching the ingredients mix and settle and boil and bubble. In creating New Orleans, the Grand Architect of our Universe conducted just such an experiment. And yet somehow, though it is at times prone to operational meltdowns and violent explosions—and its infrastructure decays as though consumed by an invisible toxic sludge—New Orleans is the most magical city in North America, if not the world.

The "Crescent City," the "Big Easy," the "northernmost coast of Central America"—New Orleans is forever nicknamed, forever picked on, and forever adored and abhorred by both natives and tourists. Nearly 300 years of French, Spanish, African, Caribbean, Irish, Choctaw Indian, Italian, Slavic, Acadian, and Anglo immigrants have mixed and settled and boiled and bubbled here. The experiment has been conducted not in a temperate, dry land with plenty of elbow room and four distinct seasons to steady tempers. No, New Orleans is a patch of swamp fringed on one side by an enormous lake and on the other by a mighty river. Humidity rarely drops below 60%, and even in the dead of winter, temperatures often rise into the mid-sixties and rarely dip to below freezing. In summer, forget it.

The hot, sultry climate does little to encourage efficiency and hard work. A common stereotype suggests that people here take their time and quit work early and laze around a good bit of the day. And with all that time on their hands, they think of new ways to amuse themselves. They eat and drink and party and listen to music. Some New Orleanians, however, would say simply that they balance their capacities to work and play better than most folks.

Whichever the case, this predisposition to revelry is most apparent during Carnival, the pre-Lenten festival that reaches fever pitch on Mardi Gras (a.k.a. Fat Tuesday), the day before Ash Wednesday. New Orleans hosts the largest and craziest of Mardi Gras celebrations in the United States. (A little-known fact about the city's history foreshadowed these festivities: French-Canadian explorer Pierre Le Moyne, who named this region Pointe du Mardi Gras, first set foot on land here on March 3, 1699, that year's Fat Tuesday.) Though parties and balls commence on January 6 (Twelfth Night) and continue through the big day, festivities really get hopping on the two weekends before Ash Wednesday. It's an official holiday here, and virtually everybody but the police, who try desperately to preserve order, comes out to celebrate. (If you're planning ahead: In 1997 Ash Wednesday is on February 11; in 1998, February 24.)

Whatever has shaped this city's bawdy character, New Orleans has long been a city of sin. And because homosexuals have traditionally felt welcome in such environs, the city as a whole has tolerated us for as long as just about any in America. Countless gay writers and artists have called the Big Easy home during the past century (most notably Tennessee Williams), and certainly Mardi Gras has long been perceived as a highly gay event.

In many American cities, the gay community has been accepted by the straight community first as a political force—as men and women fighting for their rights—then later as a social force. And furthermore, interaction between gays and straights in most cities has occurred under the most mundane circumstances—working in the same offices, living in the same apartment buildings, riding the same buses. In New Orleans, gay men were first accepted—if not celebrated—as a social force, as colorful decorations at the city's many wild parties. A gay man was typically stereotyped to be an eccentric bachelor uncle with fey mannerisms, a silver tongue, and a penchant for cross-dressing. The gay lifestyle has been, until recently, accepted as yet another outlandish aspect of life in New Orleans—particularly during Carnival.

Through the '80s, as the number of gay krewes (secret societies that hold parties and processions during Mardi Gras) marching in the parades decreased, owing partly to the death of so many gay men to AIDS, New Orleans slowly began to think of its gay residents as real people living real lives. Gays, and finally lesbians, began wielding more political clout and showing more interest in activism (current mayor Marc Morial is extremely gay-supportive). In 1992, when an ordinance was passed protecting persons from discrimination on the basis of gender, race, ethnicity, religion, or sexual orientation, the precarious relationship between Mardi Gras tradition and tolerance of diversity came to a boil. Most of the anger emanated from krewes that had always comprised white men (some of them even excluded Jews). The issue was never an overtly gay one, but it did force the city to examine its attitudes about all minorities. And several of the most famous krewes, rather than cave in to the perceived meddling of outsiders, have since ceased marching at Mardi Gras.

Nevertheless, New Orleans remains a playful city, and the residents by and large regard gay people as loyal defenders of the city's unofficial motto: "*Laissez les bons temps rouler*" (Let the good times roll). Come to the Big Easy, any time of year, looking for a good time, and there's no question you'll have one.

THE LAY OF THE LAND

Relative to other cities its size, New Orleans is rather unsafe. Just in terms of statistics, it's extremely dangerous—it has the nation's highest murder rate, a police force riddled by incompetence and corruption (though it's working hard to improve itself), rampant drug use, and poverty lingering around most every street corner. The city poses little threat to the average tourist, however (most murders here are related to domestic violence or drug use). As is the case in most big cities, it's necessary to follow a few common-sense rules and to be aware of what districts and neighborhoods are less safe and when. The Quarter itself, especially up around Rampart Street, is somewhat crime infested, so it's best to travel in groups (especially at night); plan ahead to figure out how to get where you're going and avoid any street or situation that arouses even the slightest sense of uneasiness. You are always a potential target here, especially if walking around drunk, beleaguered, and horny (never cruise here for sex).

The streets of the **Quarter** and the **Garden District** are elegant and charming. They show off some of the nation's finest examples of late-18th-century and 19th-century residential architecture. And yet, to the surprise of many first-time visitors, they are neither cute nor sparkling. This is not an amusement park but a real, financially troubled, working city. It looks and feels a bit like Martinique's capital, Fort de France, or any number of semitropical Third World cities. And, hopefully, in the highly unlikely event that New Orleans suddenly becomes a financially viable metropolis, it will remain as lovingly unkempt and craggy as it has been for centuries.

French Quarter

New Orleans may be the only major city in America whose primary entertainment district is equally frequented by gays and straights, locals and tourists. Virtually every restaurant in the French Quarter (a.k.a. Vieux Carré, which here is pronounced voh-*cair*-eeh) is gay-popular, as is every hotel and, assuming none of your fellow patrons are homophobic, bar or music venue. The only general rule, however, if your ultimate aim is to mingle among the Quarter's hordes of homos, is that St. Ann Street acts as something of a dividing line between the predominantly straight *lower* French Quarter and the gay *upper* one. (In a typically frustrating manner, New Orleanians have named the upriver half of the French Quarter the "lower" one, and vice versa.) Particularly with regard to **Bourbon Street,** just about every establishment between Canal and St. Ann overflows with gaudy signage, noise, and the usual tourists, frat boys, sorority girls, and more than a few "Bubbas" from points intolerant. Once you cross St. Ann Street, however, you'll encounter two of the city's three most popular gay clubs, Oz and the Bourbon Pub; a block later you'll discover the third one, Café Lafitte.

Decatur Street is a better walking thoroughfare than Bourbon; it's less frenetic and more diverse, still touristy, but home to some good, cheap eateries and quirky shops. Just off Decatur is the entrance to **Jackson Square,** the historic center of the French Quarter, a lovely park laid out in a classic sun pattern, with walkways emanating from the central circle. Behind the square is the stunning late-18th-century **St. Louis Cathedral.** William Faulkner once resided at **624 Pirate's Alley,** which is one of two alleys that cuts beside the cathedral between Chartres and Royal streets. To the left of the Square as you face it are the **Pontalba Apartments,** in which Sherwood Anderson once resided. Also right around the corner, at 632 St. Peter Street, is the house (now private) in which Tennessee Williams lived, and where he penned *A Streetcar Named Desire.*

From here you're close to the many antiques shops and galleries along **Chartres** and **Royal** streets; the noises, sights, and sounds of the open-air **French Market,** which is filled with shops, restaurants, and a wonderful farmer's market where just about every local spice and ingredient is sold daily; and an array of historic house-museums, including the **Beauregard-Keyes House** (1113 Chartres St., ☎ 504/523–7257), the **1850s House** (523 St. Ann St., ☎ 504/568–6968), and the **Gallier House** (1132 Royal St., ☎ 504/523–6722). Across from the entrance to Jackson Square are steps leading to the Mississippi River and the **Woldenberg Riverfront Park,** which is a relaxing place to explore day or night—and not a bad spot for making eye-contact with whomever strolls into your view. The river itself is muddy and somewhat industrial, although historic riverboats are often docked alongside the park.

Faubourg Marigny

The neighborhood just downriver from the Quarter—across lovely, tree-shaded Esplanade Avenue—is Faubourg (French for suburb) Marigny, which, because of its high concentration of gays and lesbians, is often dubbed "Fagburg" Marigny. Here elegant, old French colonial buildings stand neck and neck with new stucco atrocities. Some are falling down; others have been restored. Nearer the Quarter, from about Elysian Fields—south of Burgundy and north of Chartres—you see more rainbow flags than anywhere else in the city. But every kind of person owns a piece of this neighborhood: black and white, old and young, gay and straight. It, and the section just upriver from the Quarter, now the Central Business District (CBD) but originally Faubourg St. Mary, are often said to have been America's first suburbs, having been settled during the first decade of the 19th century as a result of the Quarter's overcrowding.

Even inexpensive (by national urban standards) Faubourg Marigny has become too costly for some people hoping to restore a cheap, run-down French West Indian cottage or modest Greek Revival "mansion." The next neighborhood downriver, known either as Bywater or Faubourg Washington, is now being swallowed by a new wave of settlers, many of them gay, salvaging a few more chunks of a city still reeling from the effects of a post–World War II "white flight" that left New Orleans's most elegant homes tattered and uninhabitable.

The Central Business District

Modern New Orleans—the skyscrapers, the Superdome, the Civic Center, many contemporary hotels, and most of the city's corporate life—centers on the literally centralmost patch of streets that spans roughly from the river up to I–10, between about Canal Street and the I–90 overpass. There are some prime examples of early 20th-century commercial architecture in and around where Perdido Street intersects with Loyola Avenue, but this district looks like any other city's downtown and offers little to the visitor.

The most appealing span of this area is Julia Street, between roughly St. Charles Avenue and the river. Now dubbed the **Warehouse District,** this formerly industrial section has become the center of New Orleans's emerging, somewhat avant-garde, arts scene.

Uptown

From Canal Street, you can take the streetcar along **St. Charles Avenue** for several miles clear out to Carrollton Avenue, where the river once again bends in a northerly direction before leaving the city for good. The tour along here takes in countless house-museums, churches, and the exteriors of some beautiful private homes; such landmark establishments as the **Commander's Palace** restaurant (1403 Washington Ave., ☎ 504/899–8221) and the classic **Pontchartrain Hotel** (2031 St. Charles Ave., ☎ 504/524–0581); the sprawling **Audubon Park and Zoo** (6500 Magazine St., ☎ 504/861–2537); **Loyola** and **Tulane universities;** and the courtly **Garden District.** To see the stately homes and gardens that give the Garden District its name and allure, alight at the Washington Avenue streetcar stop and walk a block down Washington to Prytania Street. Follow Prytania back toward the Quarter all the way to First Street (about five blocks), and you'll pass the most spectacular of the homes.

Running roughly parallel to and about seven blocks down closer to the river from St. Charles Avenue is **Magazine Street,** which, from about Felicity Street heading upriver to Audubon Park, is the city's outstanding antiques and art gallery row. If you're serious about this endeavor, skip the Quarter and spend your day wandering along here amid the furniture restorers, "junque" dealers, and other bric-a-brac vendors.

GETTING AROUND

Locals simply don't use such silly and dated directional cues as "east," "west," "south," and "north," so once you finish reading this, put away your compass and forget about such trivial matters. New Orleans is a swath of land that's sandwiched between enormous Lake Pontchartrain (whose shore runs east–west, forming the city's northern boundary) and the tortuous, murky Mississippi River (whose shore curves around the city—hence the nickname, the "Crescent City"—but for all practical purposes forms the city's southern boundary).

Canal Street bisects the city, running northwest from the river to Metarie Road, then turning and running due north to the lake. Anything below Metarie Road and to the left of Canal Street is considered Uptown. Uptown streets are, paradoxically, named South. Once they bisect Canal Street, they're considered Downtown and named North. The region just Downtown (or downriver) from Canal, on the river side, is the French Quarter.

The Quarter is laid out in a grid, the upriver boundary of which is Canal Street, the lake side boundary North Rampart Street, the river side boundary the Mississippi River itself, and the downriver boundary Esplanade Avenue. Got all that?

Roads in these parts are pocked and poorly paved; driving into New Orleans leaves you feeling as though you've just ridden in on a horse. Park your car at the hotel and walk, take taxis, or ride the streetcar around town. Once you're in the Quarter or the Faubourg Marigny, you can get to most of the important sights in either neighborhood on foot. The historic **St. Charles Avenue streetcar** can take you as far Uptown as you need to go (from the Quarter, pick it up at the corner of St. Charles Avenue and Canal Street; fare $1.25). Cabs are a nuisance, especially at night; although they're metered, cabbies will try to trick you, leave you short of your destination, or, on a whim, refuse to take you certain places. Get good directions ahead of time, and make your wishes clear to your cab driver.

EATS

The distinction between Cajun and Creole cuisine is lost on many visitors. They are quite different, as any expert on local cuisine will stress, but to the untrained palate the distinction is not especially important. Bear in mind only that very few New Orleans restaurants actually draw on legitimate Cajun recipes (K-Paul's, with its blackened fish and meats, fried crawfish tails, and sweet potato–pecan pie is the most famous purveyor—and true Cajuns would still never serve their families much of what K-Paul's passes off as the real thing). For authentic Cajun fare, you must head to the sultry southwest Louisiana towns of Lafayette, New Iberia, and thereabouts.

Though Cajun cooking owes its roots exclusively to the Acadian-settled areas of Louisiana, Creole cooking has evolved throughout the Deep South, the Carolinas Low Country, and the Caribbean, influenced largely by French, Spanish, African, and Native American traditions. Those famed New Orleans restaurants you've been hearing about for decades (Antoine's, Galatoire's) specialize chiefly in Creole techniques, not Cajun ones. With Creole cooking, expect rich cream and butter sauces (Cajuns traditionally favored lard, because dairy products were too costly) and a menu that's equal parts tame (souffléed potatoes, trout meunière, lamb in béarnaise sauce) and exotic (spicy andouille sausage, saffron-infused bouill-abaisse, smoked soft-shell crab). To be sure, there's plenty of crossover in New Orleans between both styles of cuisine. Gumbos from seafood to okra appear often in both Cajun and Creole restaurants. And in New Orleans, Creole, Cajun, and soul influences are found in every variety of food—from Asian to Italian to, especially, New American (or Nouvelle Creole, as it's sometimes called here), giving the city a tremendously varied culinary scene.

That said, a few things can be counted on at most every New Orleans eatery: unbelievably high quality and freshness of ingredients (even at the tourist traps), rather easygoing (i.e., slow) but congenial service, outstanding coffee (always chicory-laced) and desserts, and stellar seafood. That every dish here is hot and spicy is something of a myth. Towering *muffuletta* sandwiches (Italian bread with cold cuts, ham, mozzarella, and green olives) are never incendiary. Other food is consistently well-seasoned, but only a few traditionally hot dishes (gumbo, jambalaya, étouffée, blackened tuna) need be avoided if fire is your enemy. Most tables are set with bottles of Tabasco and other pepper sauces.

For price ranges, *see* Chart A at the front of this guide.

The French Quarter

$$$$ Antoine's. Oysters Rockefeller was invented here in the 1880s, as was, many argue, New Orleans's marriage of fine French and regional Creole cuisine. Antoine's is set in a former Quarter rooming house and is the longest-running show in town, having opened more than 150 years ago. It's pricey, formal, and a bit overrated, but it's a must-do for many. *713 St. Louis St.,* ☎ *504/581–4422.*

$$$–$$$$ Galatoire's. Nearing its first century of operation and showing no signs of slowing down—the place is packed on weekends—Galatoire's is chic and elegant. The dining room is done in polished brass, bentwood chairs, and crisp white napery; the long, traditional French-Creole menu has such notables as Creole bouillabaisse and fried oysters and bacon in a pastry shell. *209 Bourbon St.,* ☎ *504/525–2021.*

$$$–$$$$ Mr. B's Bistro. Setting this updated Creole menu apart from others is the generous use of hickory grilling, which imparts a special flavor to such standbys as barbecue shrimp. Has some great pasta dishes, too. The dining room is loud and vibrant. *201 Royal St.,* ☎ *504/523–2078.*

$$$ Café Sbisa. On funky Decatur Street, a few blocks down from the crowds of Jackson Square, this is where Tuscan-Provence meets Cajun-Creole. You might sample, for instance, the rack of lamb in a sauce of Creole mustard with rosemary, or tuna in a delicious crawfish beignet. The dining room is elegant, but in good weather sit in the patio out back. *1011 Decatur St.,* ☎ *504/522–5565.*

$$$ Nola. Noted local chef Emeril Lagasse serves up his rich, lusty fare in casual surroundings at this Quarter favorite. Try the pasta with sautéed eggplant and smoked-tomato-and-Parmesan sauce, and the apple-buttermilk pie with cinnamon ice cream. *534 St. Louis St.,* ☎ *504/522–6652.*

$$–$$$$ G&E Courtyard Grill. This Decatur Street favorite seems more San Francisco than New Orleans, with plenty of brass, exposed brick, and varnished wood, and a California-inspired New American menu that is nevertheless loaded with local influence: The crisp Caesar salad has flash-fried oysters; the grilled Louisiana shrimp are almond-pepper encrusted. *1113 Decatur St.,* ☎ *504/528–9376.*

$$–$$$$ K-Paul's Louisiana Kitchen. While we wait for some gay-savvy entrepreneur to open "Roux-Paul's" Louisiana Kitchen, many of us shall continue to stand in long, long lines for a chance to dine at this hallowed restaurant run by portly celebrity chef, Paul Prudhomme. This is Cajun fare—blackened everything-under-the-sun, spicy gumbos, fried crawfish tails. The service generally stinks. *416 Chartres St.,* ☎ *504/524–7394.*

$$–$$$ **Bayona.** Not exactly what you'd expect in the Quarter. Bayona's cuisine is eccentric, almost overwrought, but delectable. Salmon in white wine paired with sauerkraut is a classic that's done to perfection here. The building is a quaint, late-1800s Creole cottage, but the dining room is contemporary and refined, with dried flowers and neatly matted photographs. *430 Dauphine St.,* ☎ *504/525–4455.*

$$–$$$ **Irene's Cuisine.** This is the best kept secret in the Quarter; a simply outstanding, gay-frequented hole-in-the-wall you would expect tucked off a side street in Florence. The decor and food are traditional Italian: Chianti bottles hanging about and chicken marsala or veal-and-mozzarella-stuffed manicotti on the plates. There's a great, moderately priced wine list. The staff is friendly, even flirtatious. *539 St. Philip St.,* ☎ *504/529–8811.*

$$–$$$ **Petunia's.** This very gay *crêperie* beside the Round Up (*see* Scenes, *below*) is in a cute, pink stucco building with green shutters. The dining room is softly lit, and the tables, on which fresh flowers are arranged, are covered with pink linen. The Creole and Continental menu has everything from hearty jambalaya to seven types of enormous crepes, including one filled with ratatouille, shrimp, and crab meat. *817 St. Louis St.,* ☎ *504/ 522–6440.*

$–$$ **Acme Oyster House.** For oysters on the half-shell, not to mention po'boys and red beans and rice, Acme Oyster House is the best of the bunch—a no-frills cafeteria with linoleum floors, a great jukebox, and very low-key service. *724 Iberville St.,* ☎ *504/522–5973.*

$ **Clover Grill.** A very noisy collection of pretty boys, leather hunks, hungry dykes—all chowing on such greasy comfort food as burgers and fries and the like. It's across from Café Lafitte and is open all night. *900 Bourbon St.,* ☎ *504/523–0904.*

$ **Coops.** Locals always seem to outnumber tourists at this small, pubby hangout on Decatur Street. Coops serves a vast array of domestic and imported beers and big portions of inexpensive Creole and Cajun food— thick crab cakes, shrimp remoulade, hot gumbos. The crowd verges on bohemian. *1109 Decatur St.,* ☎ *504/525–9053.*

$ **La Madeleine.** This is one of the Quarter's most popular breakfast hangouts. The lines to get in on a weekend morning can be daunting, but the aroma of French pastries, breads, and brioches emanating from the wood-burning oven keeps everybody going. Light lunches and dinners are available, too, and most tables look out onto Jackson Square. *547 St. Ann St.,* ☎ *504/568–9950.*

$ **St. Ann's Café and Deli.** This is the Quarter's gay deli, catering especially to the young, pierced crowd. Served here are about 20 kinds of sandwiches, several pizzas, and delicious breakfasts. It's the perfect place to stop on your way home from barhopping, and it's right across the street from Good Friends bar. Very cruisy. *800 Dauphine St.,* ☎ *504/529–4421.*

New Orleans has a much-heralded reputation for great sandwiches, everything from oyster and shrimp po'boys to thick deli sandwiches to classic muffulettas. In the Quarter, try **Café Maspero** (601 Decatur St., ☎ 504/ 523–6250) for gargantuan chili burgers, turkey sandwiches, and the like; **Johnny's Po'boys** (511 St. Louis St., ☎ 504/524–8129) for, you guessed it, outstanding po'boys made on the softest French bread and "dressed" with pickles, tomatoes, and lettuce; or **Central Grocery** (923 Decatur St., ☎ 504/523–1620) for those foot-in-diameter muffulettas.

Faubourg Marigny

$$–$$$ **Bayou Ridge.** Wonderful for several reasons—moderate prices, a big gay following, cozy ambience—Bayou Ridge is near the base of tree-lined Es-

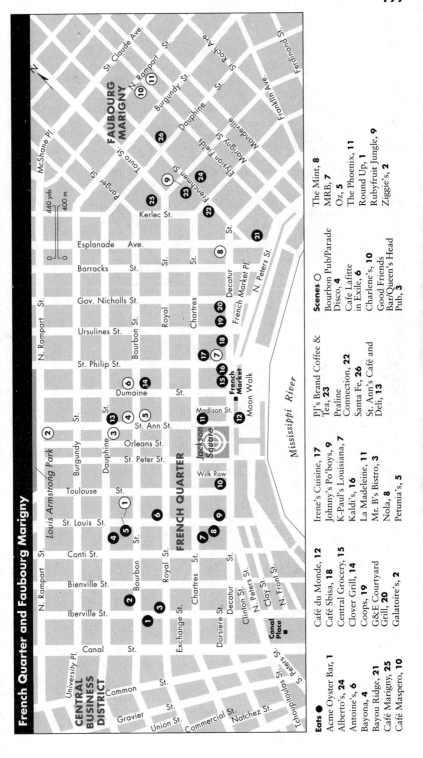

French Quarter and Faubourg Marigny

CENTRAL BUSINESS DISTRICT

FAUBOURG MARIGNY

FRENCH QUARTER

Louis Armstrong Park

Jackson Square

French Market

Moon Walk

Wilk Row

Mississippi River

Canal Place

Eats ●

Acme Oyster Bar, **1**
Alberto's, **24**
Antoine's, **6**
Bayona, **4**
Bayou Ridge, **21**
Café Marigny, **25**
Café Maspero, **10**

Café du Monde, **12**
Café Sbisa, **18**
Central Grocery, **15**
Clover Grill, **14**
Coops, **19**
G&E Courtyard
Grill, **20**
Galatoire's, **2**

Irene's Cuisine, **17**
Johnny's Po'boys, **9**
K-Paul's Louisiana, **7**
Kaldi's, **16**
La Madeleine, **11**
Mr. B's Bistro, **3**
Nola, **8**
Petunia's, **5**

PJ's Brand Coffee &
Tea, **23**
Praline
Connection, **22**
Santa Fe, **26**
St. Ann's Café and
Deli, **13**

Scenes ○

Bourbon Pub/Parade
Disco, **4**
Cafe Lafitte
in Exile, **6**
Charlene's, **10**
Good Friends
Bar/Queen's Head
Pub, **3**

The Mint, **8**
MRB, **7**
Oz, **5**
The Phoenix, **11**
Round Up, **1**
Rubyfruit Jungle, **9**
Ziggie's, **2**

New Orleans

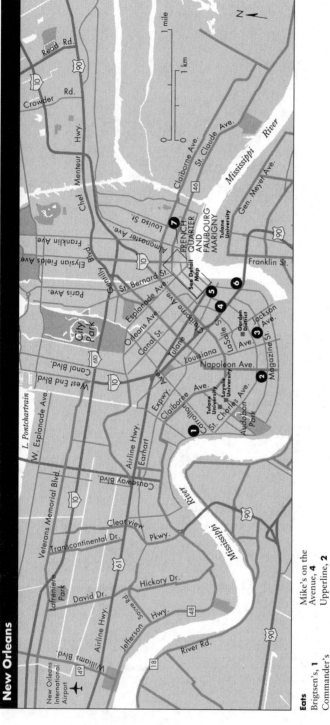

Eats

Brigtsen's, **1**
Commander's Palace, **3**
Emeril's, **6**
Feelings Café, **7**
Graham's, **5**
Mike's on the Avenue, **4**
Upperline, **2**

planade Avenue. Among the better nouvelle-inspired Creole dishes are chicken roulade with brie, roast garlic, spinach au jus; and ancho-pepper barbecue shrimp with rosemary buttermilk biscuits. *437 Esplanade Ave.,* ☎ *504/949–9912.*

$$–$$$ Feelings Café One of the essential gay restaurants in New Orleans, though a long walk or short cab ride east of the Quarter, Feelings is set in an old, white stucco building at the corner of Franklin and Chartres streets. It's best known for its Sunday brunches, but has a decent Continental menu at every meal. *2600 Chartres St.,* ☎ *504/945–2222.*

$$ Santa Fe. This Tex-Mex eatery overlooking quiet Washington Square is in a white, 19th-century building with a fiery red door. It's very un–New Orleans, with Southwestern furnishings and whitewashed walls, and a totally nonlocal menu of chilis, nachos, and the like. *801 Frenchmen St.,* ☎ *504/944–6854.*

$–$$ Praline Connection. As the Praline Connection has become a bit more touristy in recent years, alas, the food has become milder—but it's still mouthwatering. This even blend of soul and Creole cuisine always hits the spot. Whatever you order, save room for the rich bread pudding or any of the pralines sold in the sweets shop next door. *542 Frenchmen St.,* ☎ *504/943–3934.*

$ Alberto's. Colorful, funky, and teeming with queens many nights, Alberto's is one of Faubourg's best restaurants, serving great pasta, poultry, and seafood at away-from-the-Quarter prices. The stuffed pastas usually have Creole touches—maybe crawfish or shrimp. Very romantic and unfettered by tourists. *611 Frenchmen St.,* ☎ *504/949–5952.*

Elsewhere

$$$$ Commander's Palace. Several national magazines and restaurant surveys have named this the top eatery in New Orleans and one of the top 10 in America. The menu draws on a variety of non-Creole cultures, resulting in such elaborate fare as poached oysters in a cream sauce with caviar, and the renowned turtle soup. In the Garden District. *1403 Washington Ave.,* ☎ *504/899–8221.*

$$$–$$$$ Emeril's. The esteemed chef Emeril Lagasse worked at Commander's Palace before he opened his own fine dining establishment. Emeril's captures the spirit of the artsy, postmodern Warehouse District, with generous use of burnished metals, abstract art, brick-and-glass walls, and an open, noisy dining room. The food also manages to challenge tradition, offering New American takes on Creole dishes—maybe a corn crepe topped with Louisiana caviar or sautéed crawfish over jambalaya cakes. *800 Tchoupitoulas St.,* ☎ *504/528–9393.*

$$$–$$$$ Mike's on the Avenue. Chinese, Japanese, Thai, Southwestern, and Creole sensibilities inform the extravagantly flavorful cuisine of Mike's gay chef and coowner Michael Fennelly (he also did the bright paintings on the walls of the two big dining rooms). Oysters grilled on the half shell come with a Korean barbecue sauce, spring rolls come filled with crawfish and shredded vegetables. Yum. *628 St. Charles Ave., the Lafayette Hotel,* ☎ *504/523–1709.*

$$$ Brigtsen's. This restaurant occupies a simple uptown cottage that dates from the turn of the century. But, since the eponymous chef is one of the most innovative practitioners of modern South Louisiana cooking, the food is anything but simple: Note the stunning cream of oysters Rockefeller soup, the robust duck dishes, the intense gumbos, and the incredible banana ice cream. *723 Dante St.,* ☎ *504/861–7610.*

$$$ Graham's. One of the hottest restaurants in the city, this CBD dining room is stark, from the bare, curtainless, arched windows to the flat white walls and bare black tabletops. The beautifully presented food provides all the color and texture. Try the duck lacquered with chicory coffee and oranges, the seared yellowfin tuna glossed with lemon-and-star-anise marmalade, or, for dessert, the surprising sweetened polenta, topped with mascarpone. Noisy. *200 Magazine St., the Pelham Hotel,* ☎ *504/524–9678.*

$$–$$$ **Upperline.** One of the few restaurants that is gay-popular, has serious food, *and* is outside the Quarter. Some of the creative Creole dishes here include grilled fish of the day with roasted pecans, and quail with jambalaya. A short drive uptown from the Quarter, Upperline is set in a rustic cottage with an art deco-inspired interior and plenty of paintings and local art. *1413 Upperline St.,* ☎ *504/891–9822.*

Coffeehouse Culture

One late-night New Orleans tradition that even the most stubborn individualist should conform to is enjoying café au lait and beignets at **Café du Monde** (French Market, Decatur and St. Ann Sts., ☎ 504/525–4544), an immense, open-air hangout overlooking Jackson Square. It's the perfect way to finish off a night of barhopping and debauchery. **Café Marigny** (1913 Royal St., ☎ 504/945–4472), in a cute old house smack in the middle of Faubourg, is about the gayest of them all. There are plenty of leaflets and flyers around telling of upcoming events. **Kaldi's** (941 Decatur St., ☎ 504/586–8989), in a turn-of-the-century building, draws a fairly artsy, intellectual bunch; it's best to grab a cappuccino and sit over by one of the huge windows overlooking busy Decatur Street. **PJ's Brand Coffee & Tea** (634 Frenchman St., ☎ 504/949–2292) attracts a somewhat bookish, fairly yuppie crowd that's a little mellower than what you'll encounter in the Quarter.

SLEEPS

With a steady rise in the tourism and convention trade and the sudden presence of casinos, hotel rooms in New Orleans have become horribly scarce and overpriced during Mardi Gras, the Jazz Festival, most of December, and most fall weekends. Summer is always low season. But, in general, hotel rooms cost far more year-round than they did just five years ago.

The hotels in the Quarter all have fairly strong gay followings, as do many of the guest houses. The section of the Garden District nearest Canal Street has less expensive—but no less characterful—older hotels that are operated by national chains (Ramada, Quality Inn, etc.). The Central Business District is quiet and spooky on weekends and at night—first-time visitors might avoid hotels in this area.

This is a great city for B&Bs, but again, because hotel rates are on the rise, guest houses here tend to charge quite a bit for what you get in return. Many of the best gay-friendly or gay-operated guest houses are listed below, but just as many are small (often renting out just one or two rooms) and don't book directly to the public. To find them, call the gay-staffed **French Quarter Reservation Service** (☎ 504/523–1246). If an establishment's gay quotient is less important to you, the mainstream **Bed & Breakfast, Inc.** (☎ 504/488–4640 or 800/729–4640) also has a wide range of accommodations throughout the city, from low-end to luxury.

For price ranges, *see* Chart A at the front of this guide.

Hotels

French Quarter

▣ The **Bourbon Hotel,** which is just off St. Ann Street, has the gayest clientele of any major city hotel, with a few rooms directly overlooking the fun at Oz and the Bourbon Pub. The interior is brighter and better kept but less charming than that of the Royal Sonesta. *717 Orleans St., ☎ 504/ 523–2222 or 800/521–5338. 211 rooms. $$$–$$$$*

☷ Tennessee Williams was quite fond of the century-old **Monteleone Hotel,** whose busy baroque facade is memorable, to say the least. Rooms are somewhat less inspiring and the mood is stuffy, but the Monteleone exudes charm like no other. *214 Royal St., ☎ 504/523–3341 or 800/535– 9595. 635 rooms. $$$–$$$$*

☷ In the eyes of many, the elegant but mammoth **Royal Sonesta Hotel** is *the* place to stay in the Quarter. It encompasses an entire block, and rooms have wonderful wrought-iron balconies overlooking either the streets or the lush courtyard. *300 Bourbon St., ☎ 504/586–0300 or 800/766–3782. 532 rooms. $$$–$$$$*

☷ The Best Western's **Inn on Bourbon Street** is in the heart of Bourbon Street's vibrancy (and noise). With a charming courtyard and pool, and reproduction antiques throughout, it looks and feels nothing like a typical Best Western. It also has huge, individually decorated rooms and many personal touches (ironing boards and blow-dryers in each room). *541 Bourbon St., ☎ 504/524–7611 or 800/535–7891. 186 rooms. $$–$$$$*

☷ **Le Richelieu** is a terrific deal. It's in the Quarter but close to Faubourg Marigny. *1234 Chartres St., ☎ 504/529–2492 or 800/535–9653. 86 rooms. $–$$*

Outside the Quarter

☷ If you seek authentic Old World charm, the contemporary **Windsor Court** may disappoint; more in the style of a Ritz-Carlton and a 15-minute walk from Jackson Square, it's nevertheless one of the most sumptuous accommodations in America, and its public rooms and restaurants are the best of any New Orleans hotel. *300 Gravier St., ☎ 504/523– 6000 or 800/262–2662. 322 rooms. $$$$*

☷ The gracious **Fairmont Hotel** celebrated its 100th birthday in 1993 with a $22-million renovation—it now looks better than ever. The hotel comprises three connected buildings, each containing large guest rooms with down pillows, bathroom scales, and other thoughtful touches. *123 Barrone St., ☎ 504/529–7111 or 800/527–4727. 735 rooms. $$$–$$$$*

☷ If you're willing to traipse several blocks from the Central Business District, **Le Pavillon** offers one of the better values in the city—it's a classic 1905 hotel with ornate chandeliers in the lobby and high-ceilinged bedrooms. *833 Poydras St., ☎ 504/581–3111 or 800/535–9095. 227 rooms. $$–$$$*

☷ A solid affordable favorite is the Lower Garden District's mutibuilding **Prytania Park Hotel,** which is in a bland but fairly safe location. The nicest rooms are in the 1834 town house. *1525 Prytania St., ☎ 504/524– 0427 or 800/862–1984. 62 rooms. $$*

☷ The best of the mid-range chain motels is the **Ramada Hotel-St. Charles** a few blocks up from the Prytania Park Hotel. It has extremely large rooms and is a short streetcar ride from the Quarter. *2203 St. Charles Ave., ☎ 504/566–1200 or 800/443–4675. 140 rooms. $–$$*

Guest Houses and Small Hotels

All of the properties listed below cater to a mixed gay and straight clientele.

☷ Celebs, and others who can afford to, choose the flawlessly appointed **Melrose Mansion Hotel,** a restored Victorian mansion whose rooms are done in period antiques and whose baths have marble whirlpool tubs or Jacuzzis. *937 Esplanade Ave., ☎ 504/944–2255. 8 rooms. $$$$*

▣ It's less heralded than some, but the quite gay-frequented **Hotel de la Monnaie** is also luxurious, with enormous one- and two-bedroom suites complete with kitchenettes and sofa beds. It's ideal for two, or even three, couples traveling together. *405 Esplanade Ave., ☎ 504/947–0009. 53 rooms. $$$–$$$$*

▣ **The Frenchmen** is a dramatic salmon-color complex of buildings with a lovely brick courtyard and pool in back and Victorian decorating in the rooms. It's very gay, very charming, and just across the street from the Mint nightclub. *417 Frenchmen St., ☎ 504/948–2166 or 800/831–1781. 27 rooms. $$–$$$*

▣ The truly fabulous, gay or straight, favor the **Lafitte Guest House,** a ritzy Victorian town house just steps from several bars. Rooms are individually decorated with antiques, long flowing drapes, and Oriental rugs; many have fireplaces. *1003 Bourbon St., ☎ 504/581–2678 or 800/331–7971. 14 rooms. $$–$$$*

▣ The warm and chatty Danner family runs the **Olivier House Hotel,** which has long had a European following owing to its intimacy, kitchenettes in many suites (some of which are split-level), and odd touches like a gurgling fountain in one room. *828 Toulouse St., ☎ 504/525–8456. 42 rooms. $$–$$$*

▣ One of the classiest gay-popular guest houses in the Quarter, the **Ursuline Guest House** is within minutes of the most popular bars; has a friendly, informative staff; and is set in a charming, historic 18th-century house with working gas lamps out front. Many of the rooms open onto a brick courtyard with wrought-iron furniture. *708 Ursulines St., ☎ 504/525–8509 or 800/654–2351. 13 rooms. $$*

▣ A block over from Lafitte Guest House, similar but simpler accommodations can be had at the **Bon Maison Guest House,** an 1840 town house. The most romantic rooms are behind the house in what were once slave quarters. *835 Bourbon St., ☎ 504/561–8498. 5 rooms. $–$$*

▣ Two blocks north of Rampart and up Esplanade Avenue, in a borderline neighborhood, the courtly **Rathbone Inn** is nonetheless a terrific spot. Behind its handsome, white, two-story, Greek-Revival facade are several simply but tastefully decorated rooms. *1227 Esplanade Ave., ☎ 504/524–3900 or 800/776–3901. 15 rooms. $–$$*

▣ There's a friendly (and disproportionately gay) staff at the **Rue Royal Inn,** which was built in 1830 as a private home and is now a small, somewhat modest hotel, notable for its quirky decor, kitchenettes in many rooms, and proximity to Jackson Square. The courtyard units, though small, are among the city's top bargains. *1006 rue Royal, ☎ 504/524–3900 or 800/776–3901. 17 rooms. $–$$*

▣ Though Ursulines is a charming street, even north of Rampart, where things get a little dicey, the walk along here to the **New Orleans Guest House** is a bit unsettling at night. However, this lovely, old, pink-stucco house, decorated graciously, has plenty of parking and is still only a 10-minute walk from Bourbon Street. *1118 Ursulines St., ☎ 504/566–1177 or 800/562–1177. 4 rooms. Mixed gay/straight. $–$$*

SCENES

All of those wanton tales you've heard from bleary-eyed buddies returning from the Quarter overfed, oversexed, and poised on the brink of liver failure, well, they're all true. Every one of them. The majority of the gay bars here are open 24 hours. What's perhaps even more astounding is that several of them stay crowded—or at least moderately populated—all 24 of those hours. Happy hour is held commonly from 5 until 9—

each evening and then again in the morning. Drinks are cheap at all times; during happy hour, they're practically given away.

Gay New Orleanians party constantly but not seriously. There is little room here for the stand-and-model set, for posing beefcakes, and the like. It's a friendly, disheveled, often dumpy scene. All of these places are unabashedly cruisy, and despite even the blurriest stupor, the average bar attendee remains shockingly polite, good-natured, and flirtatious.

Most of the touristy bars are right in the heart of the Quarter, though a few are farther over in Faubourg Marigny. North Rampart Street is also a strip of "neib" (i.e., dilapidated, sparsely utilized) bars. It's a dicey thoroughfare, especially at night, and you shouldn't wander along here alone. Nevertheless, no matter how scary the bar's appearance (to say nothing of the crowd's), you will just about always be made to feel welcome. There's a great mix of lesbians and gay men at the more popular bars except for the rough-and-rowdy Phoenix and the ol' boys'–oriented Café Lafitte.

Bars

Bourbon Pub/Parade Disco. This and Oz, across the street, are the premier bars in the city, and plenty of people move back and forth between them. The crowd here is more diverse on weeknights and during the afternoon, but on a Friday night it's almost exclusively young, guppie, stand-and-model types. It's nice here because there's no cover in the Pub, and hurricane doors open onto Bourbon Street, allowing patrons to party in the street, too. The bar itself is huge and takes up a good bit of the room—it's always a tight squeeze. The Parade Disco (directly above the Pub) is only open on weekends and has a cover. The dance floor has several doors leading onto the exterior wraparound balcony, which is a good perch from which to gawk at the crowd across the way at Oz. Fairly typical dance music. *801 Bourbon St.,* ☎ *504/529–2107. Crowd: mostly male in the Pub but more mixed in the Disco; cruisy, touristy.*

Cafe Lafitte in Exile. Lafitte's is the grandfather of gay bars—you may even spot a few grandfathers in here. But you'll see just about every other type, too, from club kids on their way up to Oz and Parade to leather bears heading the opposite way toward the Phoenix. It's usually crowded on both floors, with more mingling around the first floor cruise bar, and a somewhat more cliquey crowd upstairs either playing pool or sitting around the bar. Sexual activity is not unheard of upstairs, and guys sometimes neck on the wraparound balcony overlooking Bourbon Street. A good place to let your hair down. Friendliest bartenders in New Orleans. *901 Bourbon St.,* ☎ *504/522–8397. Crowd: mostly male, mostly ages 30s to 50s, fairly butch, Levi's and T-shirts, cruisy.*

Charlene's. The city's catch-all dyke bar, Charlene's is in a pale-yellow corner building across Elysian Fields from the Phoenix. It has shows, dancing, pool tables, and plenty of space to mingle and chat. Charlene herself is a local institution, and the bar has a major following. Some of the younger lesbians tend toward Oz and the Parade Disco, so the crowd is often a bit older. It's still packed on weekends. *940 Elysian Fields Ave.,* ☎ *504/945–9328. Crowd: 90/10 f/m, mixed ages, diverse.*

Good Friends Bar/Queen's Head Pub. Though basically a neighborhood bar, Good Friends overlaps somewhat with the nearby more frenetic Oz and the Bourbon Pub, drawing a healthy cross-section of locals and visitors. Despite its cement floor, the place is fairly homey, with wood-paneled walls, fireplaces, and vases with neon floral designs shooting out of them. Upstairs is the Pub, a congenial clubby space with hunter green walls, darts, and incredibly friendly bartenders. More women frequent the pub, and late on weekend nights it's crowded and diverse. *740 Dauphine St.,*

☎ *504/566–7191. Crowd: 80/20 m/f, mostly 30s and 40s, guys/gals next door, low-key.*

The Mint. This stately turn-of-the-century building has wonderful architectural details such as elaborate moldings and tile floors. It's one of the Quarter's favorite off-the-wall show bars, and though predominantly gay, draws plenty of straight onlookers. The bartenders are cute and sweet, and the variety of drag acts, comedy shows, and cabarets is wonderful. *504 Esplanade Ave.*, ☎ *504/525–2000. Crowd: 80/20 gay/straight, mixed m/f, all ages, many tourists, curiosity seekers, outgoing, fun-loving, loud.*

MRB. But for a great courtyard out back, MRB is a somewhat ordinary cruise bar—mostly local on weekdays, more popular on weekends. The strip shows are well-attended and quite wild. *515 St. Philip St.*, ☎ *504/586–0644. Crowd: mostly male, mostly 30s and 40s, a bit ribald, loud, mustachioed.*

Oz. Since it opened in 1993, Oz has been the Bourbon Pub's biggest rival, drawing a similar clientele but far more lesbians. It has a small dance floor encircled by a magnificent wrought-iron balustraded balcony that's perfect for people-watching and cruising. Outside is an equally impressive balcony with good views across Bourbon Street to Parade's balcony. There are plenty of places to sit and mingle; it's a great space—great music, too. This is the best overall bar in town, marred only by the snotty attitude of most of the bartenders and bouncers. *800 Bourbon St.*, ☎ *504/593–9491. Crowd: mixed m/f, young, somewhat stand-and-model, energetic.*

The Phoenix. The "anything goes" scene here is surprising considering the Phoenix's setting: a cute, fire-engine red clapboard house with cornflower blue trim. Inside is another story: a dark, seedy room that's only slightly more inviting than the inside of somebody's garage. The crowd is wound up and wild. The back stairs lead to something akin to a back room. *941 Elysian Fields Ave.*, ☎ *504/945–9264. Crowd: male, hardcore leather, bears, motorcycle types, rough-and-ready.*

Rubyfruit Jungle. What opened as a lesbian bar a couple of years ago has become increasingly mixed because of its popular two-stepping nights. It's one of the nicer bars in Faubourg Marigny and makes a refreshing dancing alternative to Oz. Very low on attitude. *640 Frenchmen St.*, ☎ *504/947–4000. Crowd: 75/25 f/m, mixed ages, lots of country-western types.*

Ziggie's. This is the best of North Rampart's half-dozen dumpy neighborhood bars, having added an entire two-stepping dance floor in 1995 and giving the interior brand-new wood siding, bar stools fashioned out of saddles, and other country-western touches. The staff is outgoing and funny. *718 N. Rampart St.*, ☎ *504/566–7559. Crowd: a total mixed bag, drag-friendly, colorful.*

Dives in the Quarter

Though it shares its name with one of Marilyn Monroe's earlier films, **Bus Stop** (542 N. Rampart St., ☎ 504/522–3372) reminds you more of Monroe's final project, *The Misfits*. It has a long bar, great photos on the walls, and a chatty staff. The frighteningly low-budget **Corner Pocket** (940 St. Louis St., ☎ 504/568–9829) may be the only strip bar in America where the go-go dancers must provide their own music by dropping quarters into the jukebox. **Footloose** (700 N. Rampart St., ☎ 504/523–2715) has a drag shows some nights but is otherwise rather sleepy. Most guys hang out at the tiny **Golden Lantern** (1239 Royal St., ☎ 504/529–2860) to watch soaps on TV, though tourists sometimes pop in here on the way out of or home to their hotels. **Jewel's Tavern** (1207 Decatur St., ☎ 504/524–5598) is, despite a hot location on touristy Decatur St., a dive except during Sunday's popular beer blast. The pitch-black **Rawhide** (740 Burgundy St., ☎ 504/525–8106) has pool tables, slot machines, a cute little fireplace, continuous porn, and a fairly rough crowd. **Round**

Up (819 St. Louis St., ☎ 504/561–8340), the city's only true country-western bar, lacks a dance floor and a personality but has a good juke-box. **TT's** (820 N. Rampart St., ☎ 504/523–9521) is pretty skeevy and known for its bartop strippers who have an affinity for heavy metal music. **Wild Side** (439 Dauphine St., ☎ 504/529–5728) is the most bizarre bar in town, with a tired jukebox, lots of video games and pin-ball, and scads of societal dropouts trading makeup tips and dish. The mostly African-American **Wolfendale's** (834 N. Rampart St., ☎ 504/524–5749) is fairly crowded on weekends but a bit quiet the rest of the time.

Dives in Faubourg Marigny

Big Daddy's (2513 Royal St., ☎ 504/948–6288), one of the cutest neigh-borhood bars in the city, is popular with both men and women; it has big clear windows looking out onto the street, an attractive bar, and rain-bow flags. **Another Corner/Boots** (2601 Royal St., ☎ 504/945–7006), across the street from Big Daddy's, is in a great old building; it has high ceilings, antique ceiling fans, a long bar of red vinyl stools, and a mag-nificent balcony around the exterior. The invitingly named **Friendly Bar** (2301 Chartres St., ☎ 504/943–8929) lacks atmosphere and is set in an unfriendly mint green building with glass brick windows. It attracts a fairly mixed male/female crowd.

Music Clubs

Of course, nightlife here revolves quite a bit around music. Consider any of the following spots for a great time. Café Istanbul and Checkpoint Char-lie's have fairly gay followings—the rest draw a typical cross-section of New Orleans visitors.

Café Istanbul (534 Frenchmen St., ☎ 504/944–4180) is an eccentric, shabby-looking, Middle Eastern–decorated club with every kind of music imaginable, from swing to salsa. You can eat, drink, listen to alternative rock and blues, cruise, and do your laundry at **Checkpoint Charlie's** (501 Esplanade Ave., ☎ 504/947–0979)—right off the main room is a com-plete coin-operated laundry. For a taste of authentic Cajun dancing in a somewhat homo-unfriendly environment, stop by **Mulate's** (201 Julia St., ☎ 504/522–1492). **Pete Fountain's** (2 Poydras St., ☎ 504/523–4374) masterful Dixieland jazz is presented several nights a week on the third floor of the New Orleans Hilton. **Preservation Hall** (726 St. Peter St., ☎ 504/522–2841), though certainly very touristy, is worth visiting to hear jazz. And finally, be sure to see who's headlining at **Tipitina's** (501 Napoleon Ave., ☎ 504/897–3943 or 504/895–8477), the former base of the late R&B pianist Professor Longhair and the regular home of im-portant national and local acts.

THE LITTLE BLACK BOOK

At Your Fingertips

AIDS Hot Line: ☎ 504/944–2437 or 800/992–4379. **Greater New Or-leans Tourist and Convention Commission:** 1520 Sugar Bowl Dr., 70112, ☎ 504/566–5068 or 504/566–5031. **Lesbian and Gay Community Cen-ter of New Orleans:** 816 N. Rampart St., ☎ 504/522–1103. **New Or-leans AIDS Coalition:** The Boswell Center, 704 N. Rampart St., ☎ 504/524–3488.

Gay Media

The two gay newspapers, **Ambush** (☎ 504/522–8049) and **Impact** (☎ 504/944–6722), are both issued biweekly and offer the usual news and entertainment coverage.

Gambit (☎ 504/486–5900) is the alternative arts and entertainment weekly, and *Offbeat* (☎ 504/522–5533) has excellent coverage of the local music scene.

BOOKSTORES

The city's cute gay and lesbian bookstore, the **Faubourg Marigny Bookstore** (600 Frenchmen St., ☎ 504/943–9875), is a 10- to 15-minute walk from the Quarter. It's a low-key place (less a center of the community than such stores in other cities) and has a vast selection of books, compact discs, and porn magazines and a somewhat limited selection of other gay periodicals. More recently, **Gay Mart** (808 N. Rampart St., ☎ 504/523–6005) opened in the Quarter and sells some books and magazines, as well as freedom rings, flags, cards, and gifts.

Of mainstream chain stores, the **Bookstar** (411 N. Peters, ☎ 504/523–6411) in the Quarter is very gay-friendly and has a huge selection of gay and lesbian titles plus gay periodicals.

Body and Fitness

The main gay health club (beer is sold here, so their dedication to fitness is questionable) is **Club New Orleans** (515 Toulouse St., ☎ 504/581–2402). Guys do work out here, in the legitimate sense, but it's also a bathhouse with lockers and rooms available.

15 *Out in New York City*

IF YOU'VE LIVED MOST OF YOUR LIFE outside a large, tolerant city, you may be overwhelmed by Manhattan's gay goings-on. At any time of day or night there's something to explore: a café abuzz with chatter, a disco throbbing with sweaty bodies, the opera, performance art, galleries, Broadway or any other street pulsing with color. For many visitors, New York is the first place they'll eat in a restaurant that is predominantly staffed and patronized by gays. For a lot of women, a trip to the Clit Club on a Friday is equally novel, dancing in the company of hundreds of screaming, jumping, sweating fellow dykes. You feel perpetually like the proverbial kid in a candy shop—with more sights to see than there are hours in the day, more treats to buy than you may be able to afford. If you fail to spend significantly more here than you anticipated, pat yourself on the back. It isn't easy.

In his *Gay New York*, a rich account of homosexual culture prior to World War II, author George Chauncey demonstrates that Manhattan's gay culture was never quiet and hidden. There was a lively gay subculture in the bawdy Bowery during the 1890s and in Greenwich Village, Harlem, and Times Square into the 1920s. Elaborate drag balls attended by both gays and curious straights were major to-dos during the late '20s and early '30s.

Eventually, gays' high visibility spawned an unprecedented backlash, which began in the late '30s and peaked during the '50s. Yet during this period, when the community was forced underground in a way that it had never been before, several homophile organizations began rallying for gay rights. This nascent gay activism culminated in 1969 with the Stonewall riots: In the wee hours of June 28, police raided (a common practice in this era) a small Greenwich Village gay bar called the Stonewall Inn. Bar goers defied cops, and the rioting lasted several days. Now, every year, thousands of gays and lesbians stroll by the Stonewall, remembering that before 1969, homosexuals could not congregate publicly without fear of police harassment.

Today's New York City is a largely tolerant place for gays and lesbians. The gay community is diverse, creative, and highly visible throughout the city, particularly in the Village, Chelsea, and Hell's Kitchen and on the Upper West Side. State congressman Tom Duane, a Chelsea resident, is openly gay. City politicians recognize the power of the gay community, and to a varying extent, its needs. Anonymous testing for the HIV virus is easily available, and scores of young men from other communities travel hundreds of miles to New York City clinics to get it. Annual pride parades draw bigger crowds every year, turning all of Manhattan into a gay and lesbian mixer; the warmest, loudest cheers are for the gay and lesbian police officers among the marchers. For that matter, the straight officers patrolling the procession are famous for their civility.

No matter what your sexual orientation, New York is no paradise. It's easy to be put off by the traffic, the panhandling, the noise, and the high cost of visiting. New York is served by virtually every airline and is within 25 miles of three major airports; but they're expensive, inconvenient, and time-consuming to get to. There are tens of thousands of hotel rooms—priced at rates that are the highest in the nation. Much that there is to see, do, and experience comes with a high price tag—and a long line. One moment New York is exciting, raw, and full of opportunity; the next it is chaotic, dirty, and draining.

Yet residents bite the bullet and take it all in stride. They bristle when outsiders disparage the city they call home, even as they joke about their long-term dysfunctional relationship with it. And you can be sure they wouldn't live anywhere else.

THE LAY OF THE LAND

When most people refer to New York City they're usually talking about Manhattan, which contains most of the city's popular attractions, restaurants, and hotels. It's also the gayest of the city's five boroughs. The Bronx is immediately north and east of Manhattan, across the Harlem River (it's the only borough that's part of the mainland). Queens, the largest borough, lies east of Manhattan, across the East River. To the southeast of Manhattan (south of Queens) is Brooklyn. Due south of Manhattan, across the Verrazano Narrows, is Staten Island, which hugs the shore of New Jersey.

Central Park is Manhattan's geographical center. Depending on who you are and how you see life, any of several neighborhoods might be considered Manhattan's spiritual center. For most visitors, it's Midtown, which begins just south of Central Park. North of Midtown are the Upper West and East sides, and above them Harlem. Below Midtown are, in descending order, Chelsea and Gramercy Park, the East and West villages, SoHo and Little Italy, Tribeca and Chinatown, and finally, at the southern tip of the island, Lower Manhattan, also known as the Financial District.

North of 14th Street the city's streets form a regular grid pattern. Consecutively numbered streets run east and west (crosstown), while the broad avenues, most of them also numbered, run north (uptown) or south (downtown). The chief exceptions are Broadway (which runs on a diagonal from East 14th to West 79th streets) and the thoroughfares that hug the shores of the Hudson and East rivers. Below 14th Street, streets are crooked and crazy—running every which direction—and named or numbered.

Lower Manhattan

Though few people live in **Lower Manhattan,** it is New York City's financial center, and it's home to several popular attractions. Encompassing the southern tip of the island, this densely developed pocket of crooked streets has several of the city's most important skyscrapers, including the 16-acre **World Trade Center** (☏ 212/323–2340), which begins at the intersection of Vesey and Church streets. For the highest vantage point in the city, head to the 107th floor of **2 World Trade Center.** South of here is sprawling Battery Park, from which ferries (☏ 212/269–5755) leave for both the **Statue of Liberty** (☏ 212/363–8340) and **Ellis Island** (☏ 212/363–3200). Two of the most memorable attractions in America, both can be mobbed on weekends.

Virtually all of the original Colonial architecture in Lower Manhattan has been built over, but a few relics stand, including the **Fraunces Tavern** (54 Pearl St., ☎ 212/425–1778), a former home that dates from 1719 and now houses a period-furnished museum, a restaurant, and a bar. The blocks north of here comprise **Wall Street's** Financial District, and aren't especially exciting with the exception of the grandiose neoclassical **New York Stock Exchange** (20 Broad St., ☎ 212/656–5165). You'll have to visit on a weekday if you want to see any trading action.

North of the financial district and just south of the **Brooklyn Bridge** (the crossing of which, if you have an hour to spare, makes for a delightful stroll) is the 11-block **South Street Seaport Historic District,** an urban entertainment complex jammed with shops and restaurants. At night, the bars here are taken over by rowdy, straight tourists.

SoHo and Tribeca

If the East Village is where struggling artists thrive, **SoHo** ("*south of Houston* Street") and **Tribeca** ("the *Triangle below Canal* Street") are neighborhoods to which many artists gravitate after becoming successful. Both areas were slums of derelict warehouses and factories until a couple of decades ago, when artists and preservationists began to recognize the practical and aesthetic value of SoHo's rich concentration of Victorian cast-iron architecture. Most popular between Broadway and 6th Avenue and between Houston and Canal streets, today's (surprisingly straight) SoHo is packed with high-end galleries and clothiers, home-furnishing stores, and see-and-be-seen eateries.

Southeast of Soho are **Little Italy** and **Chinatown;** to the southwest, concentrated around the intersection of Greenwich and Harrison streets, is the recently trendified **Tribeca,** where Robert De Niro has established his **Tribeca Film Center,** and where several chic restaurants and shops are located.

Greenwich Village

You may have heard that **Greenwich Village**—referred to by most New Yorkers simply as "the Village"—is no longer the official center of the city's gay community. Yes, life in this historically gay ghetto has definitely changed. The onset of AIDS, the neighborhood's 1980s real-estate boom, and the growing influx of straight tourists and rowdy teens have discouraged new generations of gays from settling here and have driven away some gay-owned businesses. And yes, a huge number of gays have discovered Chelsea to the north, and a smaller contingent has moved to the East Village. But the West Village's anchor, Sheridan Square, is nevertheless still mighty pink.

Generally, when people are speaking of Greenwich Village as a gay ghetto, they're really referring to the **West Village**—the maze of quaint, crooked streets west of 6th Avenue and extending between 14th and Houston streets to the Hudson River. The central part of Greenwich Village, whose hub is **Washington Square** (5th Ave. at W. 4th St.), is mostly the domain of **New York University,** which is not to say it isn't festive to explore: jazz clubs, coffeehouses, and funky shops line the area's main commercial drags—most notably Bleecker Street and the narrow lanes off it.

In the West Village, however, you really notice the gay presence. The neighborhood is much more diverse than it was a decade ago, when it was still largely the province of young, white, upwardly mobile, gay men. As you move west along **Christopher Street** from **Sheridan Square** (7th Ave. S at W. 4th St.), you'll notice that most bars cater to an older, slightly rougher crowd. Christopher Street is still alive with gay shops and still a tad tawdry.

Once you cross **Hudson Street,** you'll enter the city's main gay African-American and Hispanic entertainment district. The streets south of Christopher and east of Hudson have in recent years become a significant lesbian community and playground. Throughout the entire West Village, there is great variety in age, race, class, and, yes, even sexual orientation.

If you don't mind the crowds, which can be excessive on weekends, the neighborhood continues to be one of the city's best for sidewalk strolling. **Seventh Avenue South** has dozens of cafés, small theaters, and cabarets—most of them with a strong mix of gay and straight patrons. Both **West 4th Street** and **Bleecker Street** are lined with romantic bistros, antiques shops, and lovely restored homes. **Hudson Street** has dozens of gay-oriented shops and hangouts.

Wherever you walk, you're retracing the footsteps of an entire century's worth of prominent artists who lived and played here, beginning with Henry James and Walt Whitman and extending to Mikhail Baryshnikov, Gregory Hines, and Susan Sarandon. Poet Hart Crane grew up and lived on these streets. Willa Cather and her companion Edith Lewis spent time together in a boarding house on Washington Square, as did Stephen Crane, Theodore Dreiser, Sinclair Lewis, and many other indigent idealists. Dylan Thomas took his last swig of booze at the White Horse Tavern on Hudson Street. Edna St. Vincent Millay and Eugene O'Neill worked together at the Provincetown Playhouse on MacDougal Street. Iconoclastic artist Marcel Duchamp was spotted on several occasions wandering around in drag. And beat poet Allen Ginsberg penned much of his verse while living here. There is not a neighborhood in America that can claim such a history of association with creative figures.

The East Village

If Chelsea has threatened Greenwich Village's reputation as Manhattan's gay mecca, the **East Village** has threatened its sister neighborhood's reputation as the city's Bohemia. Young, avant-garde artists can no longer afford the West Village. But the East Village, which begins at 4th Avenue (called The Bowery south of East 4th Street) and extends east between 14th and Houston streets to the East River, has emerged as a hotbed of alternative culture. **St. Marks Place** (the name of 8th Street east of 4th Avenue) is jammed with divy bars, funky shops, and cheap restaurants, as are **1st** and **2nd avenues** and **Avenue A.** As you continue east, past **Tompkins Square Park**—a site of frequent confrontations between the city and the homeless and their defenders—the East Village begins to look grimier, although avenues B and C get nattier every day.

The East Village couldn't be summed up easily as either gay or straight, as you'll find plenty of both types sauntering along its streets. The common denominator here is nonconformity although some complain that the neighborhood's countercultural tendencies are so uniform, everybody winds up looking much the same anyway. You'll stand out if you're wearing anything made by Banana Republic; though a branch of The Gap opened on St. Marks Place a couple of years ago (much to the chagrin of locals), thrift shops are still the clothing outlets of choice. The East Village has become a bit too fancy for many extremists, who continue to move east and south, chased by a tidal wave of gentrification.

Chelsea

As recently as a decade ago, few visitors to Manhattan knew of **Chelsea,** although for quite a bit longer this neighborhood immediately north of the West Village has been residentially popular with gays. Bordered by 5th Avenue to the east, 23rd Street to the north, the Hudson River to the west, and 14th Street to the South, Chelsea had been a mundane lower-

and middle-class white and Hispanic neighborhood for many decades before its gayification.

Several gay discos and leather bars had been doing business for years in what had been the industrial westernmost reaches of Chelsea, and in the mid-'80s a few trendy restaurants, shops, and bars opened along 8th and 7th avenues—joining the neighborhood's established symbol of high-end fashion, **Barneys** (106 7th Ave.). But now, **8th Avenue** has eclipsed Christopher Street as the hip gay thoroughfare. The street's older bodegas and dry goods shops have quickly been snapped up by gay entrepreneurs, who have converted them into new eateries, coffeehouses, gyms, and gay-themed shops. New York's major lesbigay bookstore, **A Different Light** (*see* Bookstores, *below*), relocated here from the West Village in 1994; several superstores, including **Barnes & Noble** and **Bed, Bath, and Beyond,** established branches along **6th Avenue;** and a few gay bars opened near the intersection of 6th Avenue and 18th Street.

The major sight in Chelsea are the legions of Chelsea Boys—a term that's either disparaging or affectionate depending on who's using it. The stereotypical Chelsea Boy—today's gay clone—sashays up and down 8th Avenue in a white T-shirt, blue-denim cut-offs, and oiled work boots, showing off the chiseled body perfected by months of pumping iron.

The neighborhood's major eyesore, its run-down but rather fascinating piers, are on the verge of becoming Chelsea's most significant attraction. A $60 million **Chelsea Piers** redevelopment project, launched in 1994, calls for the conversion of the derelict piers along the West Side Highway between 17th and 24th streets into a 1.7 million-square-foot sports and entertainment complex, with a golf-driving range, in-line and ice-skating rinks, indoor jogging tracks, a 10,000-square-foot rock-climbing wall, a marina, Manhattan's largest TV and film studio, and several restaurants. At press time, portions were open to the public. Now one of Manhattan's hottest neighborhoods, Chelsea is rapidly becoming too costly for many people, and gayification is quickly spreading north above 24th Street, to the neighborhood of Clinton.

The Flatiron District and Environs

Named for the distinctive Renaissance-style **Flatiron Building** (5th Ave. at 23rd St.), the **Flatiron District**—east of 5th Avenue between 14th and 23rd streets—is a chichi enclave of ornate, early 20th-century apartment and office buildings now housing a slew of media-related industries, artists' lofts, and design studios. The most interesting streets are **Broadway** and **5th Avenue** south of 23rd Street.

Walking south along Broadway will lead you past New York's favorite home-furnishings emporium, **ABC Carpet & Home** (888 and 881 Broadway, at 19th Street), and, two blocks farther, into the formerly hideous but now hopping **Union Square.** On Monday, Wednesday, Friday, and Saturday, a couple of dozen farmers from upstate New York operate a delightful **Greenmarket** at the northwest corner of the square. This is a terrific spot for sunning and people-watching. North and east of here is the city's most anglophilic sight, **Gramercy Park** (Lexington Ave. at E. 21st St.). This tiny, dapper city park and most of the grand town houses surrounding it date from the 1830s; unfortunately, only residents are furnished with a key to the park.

Midtown

New York City's second major commercial district is **Midtown,** which is defined by most people as the area north of 34th Street (although some would argue that Midtown extends to 23rd Street), south of 59th Street, and between Broadway and the East River. **Rockefeller Center,** which takes in 19 buildings between 5th and 7th avenues and 47th and 52nd streets, anchors the neighborhood. The center's tallest tower, the 70-story **GE Building,** looms above the popular Lower Plaza, whose trademark ice-skating rink is open from October through April; the rest of the year, it becomes an open-air café. In December the plaza is decorated with an enormous live Christmas tree. **Radio City Music Hall** (6th Ave. at 50th St., ☎ 212/247–4777), also a part of Rockefeller Center, is where you'll find the Rockettes chorus line. A few other well-known Midtown buildings include Philip Johnson's "Chippendale" **Sony Building** (Madison Ave. at 55th St.); the **Seagram Building** (Park Ave. between 51st and 52nd Sts.), Mies van der Rohe's prototype for contemporary office towers; and the unique and magnificent Art Deco **Chrysler Building** (Lexington Ave. at 42nd St.). For a view of it all, take the elevator to the 102nd floor of the **Empire State Building** (350 5th Ave., ☎ 212/736–3100).

Fifth Avenue between 50th and 59th streets has long been the city's most respected shopping corridor—**Bergdorf Goodman, Saks Fifth Avenue, Steuben,** and **Tiffany's** (which has never served breakfast) are a few notables. **Fifty-seventh Street** from Lexington Avenue west to Broadway has several more high-end shops, many galleries, **Carnegie Hall** (W. 57th St. at 7th Ave., ☎ 212/247–7800), and, more recently, a number of touristy theme restaurants including **Planet Hollywood** and the **Hard Rock Cafe.** For a diversion, tour the huge **F.A.O. Schwarz** toy store (5th Ave. at 58th St.), which has an entire section devoted to Barbie and Ken dolls. Despite the fact that Ken is clad in earrings, a tank top, and hot pants, a company spokesperson insists that the doll is not gay. Perhaps he's bi-curious.

Though Midtown hardly oozes with character, it is home to a few important attractions. The **Museum of Modern Art** (MOMA, 11 W. 53rd St., ☎ 212/708–9480) has six floors of some of the world's most talked-about pieces. As its name indicates, MOMA's exhibits emphasize modern artistic movements, from impressionism/postimpressionism onward. Cezanne, Gaugin, Picasso, Miró, and Chagall are all represented here. The relationship between **St. Patrick's** (5th Ave. at 50th St.) and the gay community is at best a tenuous one, but you'll be hard-pressed to find a more breathtaking cathedral both inside and out. The Beaux Arts **New York Public Library** (5th Ave. at 42nd St., ☎ 212/930–0800) is one of the most stunning examples of this style, as is the imposing **Grand Central Terminal** (Park Ave. at 42nd St.). Farther east, the **United Nations Headquarters** (1st Ave. at 46th St., ☎ 212/963–7713) gives some of the city's more engaging tours.

The Theater District and Hell's Kitchen

It's almost unheard of to pass through New York City without taking in a show. The most popular options in the **Theater District** are in a 10-block stretch of Broadway between Times Square (7th Ave. at 42nd St.) and 53rd Street. Good seats at major shows run from $45 to $75 and can be hard to come by; first call or visit the house box offices, who know the schedule and seating arrangement. You can also book through **Tele-Charge** (☎ 212/239–6200) or **TicketMaster** (☎ 212/307–4100), both of which add a few dollars' surcharge, or through any of several ticket brokers, who may mark up tickets by as much as 100% but often have last-minute seats to the hottest shows (scan the major newspapers or check with your hotel concierge for the brokers). If you're an adventurous soul and a bit short on funds, drop by the **TKTS booth** (47th St. and Broadway, ☎ 212/768–1818; cash only), a discount, same-day clearinghouse where tickets to both major and lesser-known shows often go for as little as half price. Generally, the booth is open from about four hours before most performances until show time, but lines can be long. There's also an excellent little pocket of Off-Broadway theaters a few blocks west of Times Square on 42nd Street (between 8th and 9th avenues), and another cluster of diverse venues in Greenwich Village.

Times Square is the city's neon focal point. The views are astonishing and should be experienced at least once for their sheer vibrancy. New Yorkers actually spend little time here; restaurants and shops are overpriced and the area riddled with porn shops, panhandlers, and prostitutes. (It's where you'll find most of the city's gay strip shows and adult theaters.) Major plans are under way to reinvent the neighborhood.

Hell's Kitchen, the semiresidential area from 34th Street north to 57th Street and from about 8th Avenue west to the Hudson, is home to many Theater District performers and other employees. It's a sketchy neighborhood, especially the farther west you go, but in the last decade its popularity has skyrocketed, particularly among gays in search of affordable housing.

South of Times Square, where Broadway cuts through the intersection of W. 34th Street and 6th Avenue, is the somewhat crowded and characterless **Herald Square,** which is nevertheless notable as the home of **Macy's,** the nation's largest retail store.

Central Park

New Yorkers need their parks. Without **Central Park** and its 843 acres of make-believe countryside, the city would simply dry up. It is both a mirage, in that it gives the illusion of endless meadows, dense forests, and serene lakes, and a real urban oasis, in that it contains comfy lawns, wooded trails, and small ponds.

If you were to run screaming through Central Park every night at midnight with money hanging out of your pockets, at some point, somebody would probably mug you—maybe even kill you for making so much noise. If you wander through by day and keep your wits about you, nobody will bother you.

Most nonresidents are unfortunately unaware of the dozens of wonderful things there are to do and see in the park. Here is a random sampling of activities you might try if you need a break from shopping and museum-hopping: Feed the many ducks bumbling around the **pond** (enter from E. 59th St.); sun among the throngs of queens—and straights—who take over **Sheep Meadow** (enter at W. 67th St.) on warm days; rollerblade, cycle, or jog along the several miles of winding park road (which is closed to auto traffic weekdays 10 AM–3 PM and 7–10 PM, and on weekends and holidays); rent a rowboat at the **Loeb Boathouse** ($10/hr, ☎ 212/517–4723) and paddle yourself and a date around the **lake** (enter at W. 77th St.), site of the magnificent Bethesda Fountain; catch a free summer production of **Shakespeare in the Park** (☎ 212/539–8500) at the enchanting, open-air **Delacorte Theater** (enter at W. 81st St.); or, in winter, rent ice skates and glide for a while around **Wollman Memorial Rink** (enter from Central Park S at 6th Ave., ☎ 212/396–1010).

There is really only one section that most New Yorkers approach at all times with caution, this being the **ramble,** a tortuous tangle just north of the **lake** and just south of the **79th Street Transverse** (the easiest access is via **Bow Bridge**). The main reason people are spooked by this section is that it's a notorious cruising ground for gay men. *You* may actually *like* this section.

Upper East Side

The antithesis of hip, the Upper East Side is where 19th-century industrialists and dignitaries built their mansions, and it's where many of today's wealthiest folks continue to nest. There are few establishments here that cater specifically to homosexuals—the few gays who live here tend to be older, male, and well-off (confirmed bachelors, as the saying goes). Between 79th and 96th streets and from Lexington Avenue to the East River, the Upper East Side is a popular address for straight yuppies just out of college.

Madison Avenue from 59th to 79th streets is where you'll find the high-end fashion boutiques, including **Gianni Versace, Givenchy, Vera Wang, Nicole Miller, Giorgio Armani,** and dozens of others. **Lexington Avenue** has fewer of the big names but is rather posh as well. Antiques shops are well-represented on both avenues. Closer to Midtown are two of the city's most popular department stores, **Barneys** (Madison Ave. at 61st St.) and **Bloomingdale's** (1000 3rd Ave.). The funk factor around here is nonexistent, but if you're looking for what is conventionally considered to be top-drawer, head to the Upper East Side. Wide, ritzy, and residential **Park Avenue** runs parallel to Lexington and Madison avenues and is what, on *Green Acres,* Lisa (Eva Gabor) trades for a life of agrarian enchantment on her husband Oliver's (Eddie Albert's) farm. What on earth was she thinking?

Between 79th and 104th streets, **5th Avenue** is New York's Museum Mile. A pleasant, compact stretch of territory, it would take about a month of daily viewing to exhaust the neighborhood's options. Few visitors walk in this direction without a visit to the **Metropolitan Museum of Art** (5th Ave. at 82nd St., ☎ 212/535–7710), which has the largest collection of art in the Western Hemisphere. But other worthy attractions include the **Frick Collection** (1 E. 70th St., ☎ 212/288–0700), a diverse survey of the masterworks assembled by coke-and-steel baron Henry Clay Frick; the **Whitney Museum of American Art** (945 Madison Ave., ☎ 212/570–3676), which sponsors major changing exhibits alongside its own small but esteemed permanent collection; Frank Lloyd Wright's controversial wedding cake, the **Guggenheim Museum** (1071 5th Ave., ☎ 212/423–3500), which houses modern painting and photography; the **Cooper-Hewitt Museum** (2 E. 91st St., ☎ 212/860–6868), the former home of Andrew Carnegie and current home of thousands of works in metal, glass, textile, and many more media; the relatively modest **International Center for Photography** (1130 5th Ave., ☎ 212/860–1777); and the unique **El Museo del Barrio** (1230 5th Ave., ☎ 212/831–7272), which is the nation's leading authority on Latin American art and culture. There are also two historical museums of note: the **Jewish Museum** (1109 5th Ave., ☎ 212/423–3230), which documents more than four millennia of Judaic culture; and the **Museum of the City of New York** (1220 5th Ave. at 103rd St., ☎ 212/534–1672).

Upper West Side and Columbia University

After the Village and Chelsea, New Yorkers typically think of the **Upper West Side** as the city's third major gay neighborhood. You'll see plenty of same-sex couples, both male and female, but rainbow flags are rare and the homos here harder to distinguish from the hets. Historically, the area has always been pleasant and middle-class, and over the past 20 years it has attracted increasing numbers of academics, actors, and artists along with advertising, public relations, and publishing types. Upper West Siders are apt to be either artists who pay the bills with ordinary white-collar jobs or professionals who maintain their sanity with artistic hobbies. The sun always seems to shine up here: There's good shopping, proximity to Central Park, and excellent housing in the form of both older town houses and handsome apartment buildings. It's a relatively good neighborhood in which to raise children (or pets). So why isn't it every

New Yorker's cup of tea? Maybe because it's not particularly offbeat, because it's a tad provincial. (People sometimes joke that the *New York Times* ought to be renamed the *Upper West Side Times;* the paper's liberal views but Milquetoast manner so typify the neighborhood.)

The Upper West Side is bound on the east by Central Park, on the south by 59th Street, and on the west by Riverside Park, which fronts the Hudson River. Not everybody agrees on a northern boundary, though most feel it extends all the way up to the northern edge of Columbia University's campus (near 125th St.).

This is a terrific walking neighborhood, especially in the following areas: **Broadway** from Columbus Circle at 59th Street clear to 125th Street is loaded with everything from tiny boutiques to major chain stores, plus dozens of restaurants and movie theaters. Food lovers should check out **Zabar's** (at 80th St.), **H & H Bagels** (at 80th St.), **Citarella's** fish and meat market (at 75th St.), and **Fairway Market** (at 74th St.). **Columbus Avenue** from 66th Street up to 86th has a slew of cute, yuppified, though overrated, cafés, plus a few good clothiers and design shops. **Amsterdam Avenue,** which parallels Broadway and Columbus through much of the neighborhood, is home to a mix of fun and dull shops, slick restaurants and generic groceries, straight pick-up bars and surly dives; it's best between 72nd and 86th streets. Both **West End** and **Riverside avenues,** above 72nd Street, are worth ambling along to see the many shining examples of late-19th-century and early 20th-century residential architecture. **Central Park West,** from Columbus Circle to about 96th Street, is lined with beautiful, often ostentatious, apartment houses (including the Dakota at 72nd Street, where John Lennon lived and outside of which he was shot).

The **Lincoln Center** complex (Broadway between 62nd and 66th Sts., ☎ 212/875–5000) comprises the Metropolitan Opera House, the New York State Theater, Avery Fisher Hall, the Guggenheim Bandshell, the Juilliard School for music and theater, Alice Tully Hall, and the Walter Reade Theater. The performing arts anchor of Manhattan, its geometric 1960s architecture is loved by many, despised by a few. It's difficult, however, to stand at night in the central court, admiring the compound's dazzling spotlit fountain and the Met's trademark Chagall paintings, some of the largest oil-on-canvas artworks in the world, and not feel a tingle in your toes.

The Upper West Side's only must-see museum is the immense **American Museum of Natural History** (Central Park West, between 77th and 81st Sts., ☎ 212/769–5920) with its adjacent **Hayden Planetarium.** Give yourself at least a full day here to explore.

Riverside Park is often overlooked in favor of that larger park a few blocks over, but Olmsted and Vaux laid out this one, too. And because of its river views and modest scale, many New Yorkers prefer it.

On both Broadway and Amsterdam Avenue at 116th Street, iron gates mark the entryway to the campus of **Columbia University,** the only Ivy League school in New York City. Across the street is **Barnard College,** the esteemed women's institution. At the nearby **Cathedral of St. John the Divine** (1047 Amsterdam Ave., ☎ 212/316–7540), a work-in-progress that when finished will be the world's largest cathedral, there's a moving National AIDS Memorial. Also, in the cathedral's Saint Saviour Chapel, is Keith Haring's final work, a three-panel plaster altar.

Harlem and Environs
Around the turn of the century, African-Americans began settling into **Harlem,** a country village that had become a suburb of apartment houses

and brownstones. For the next 30 years, Harlem buzzed with jazz clubs, literary salons, and outrageous parties, and ever since then it's been a mecca for African-American and Hispanic-American culture. Harlem extends north from 110th Street to about 145th Street. One of the most interesting sights is a handsome set of town houses known as **Striver's Row** (W. 138th and W. 139th Sts., between 7th and 8th Aves.), where many of Harlem's middle-class professionals once lived—as well as musicians W. C. Handy and Eubie Blake. Major cultural attractions include the **Studio Museum in Harlem** (144 W. 125th St., ☎ 212/864–4500), which contains historic art and photos depicting the neighborhood; the fully restored **Apollo Theatre** (253 W. 125th St., ☎ 212/749–5838); and the **Schomburg Center for Research in Black Culture** (515 Lenox Ave., ☎ 212/491–2200). Hailing a cab up here is especially difficult late at night. It's best to phone for one—try **Harlem Cab Co.** (☎ 212/663–8080).

At the northern tip of Manhattan, in **Washington Heights,** is one of New York City's most enchanting attractions, **The Cloisters** (take either the A train to 190th St. or the M–4 bus from Madison Ave. below 110th St., from Broadway above it; ☎ 212/923–3700). Atop a hill overlooking the Hudson River are five authentic monastic cloisters and a 12th-century chapter house, which were moved here from France and Spain. There's much to see, including the Metropolitan Museum of Art's medieval collection, but you might come simply to read under a tree or picnic with friends.

Brooklyn

Four neighborhoods in Brooklyn—**Brooklyn Heights, Cobble Hill,** and **Carroll Gardens** (which are strung together), and **Park Slope** (across the Gowanus Canal from the others)—have become increasingly popular with gay men and especially lesbians over the past two decades. Even if you're only in Manhattan for a short spell, consider spending an afternoon wandering over here.

Brooklyn Heights (take the 2, 3, 4, 5, M, N, or R train to Borough Hall) has long been a fashionable place to live—its more than 600 19th-century buildings are now commanding rents comparable to those found in many parts of Manhattan. For some funky shopping and several good restaurants, walk along **Montague Street** from Court Street to the **Promenade,** a several-block-long narrow park that runs high above the run-down ferry district and affords amazing views of Lower Manhattan. From here, residential Clinton and Henry streets and commercial Court Street lead south through **Cobble Hill** and then **Carroll Gardens.** The latter is Brooklyn's Little Italy, full of great food shops.

Park Slope (take the 2, 3, D, F, or Q train to 7th Ave.) is now a popular lesbian hood; check out the restaurants, coffeehouses, and shops along 7th Avenue. The nicest homes, most of which date from the late 19th century and remain relatively affordable, are within a couple of blocks of the western border of **Prospect Park.** This 526-acre Olmsted-Vaux creation is a great place to blade, jog, or cycle, and it's the site of the **Brooklyn Public Library** (☎ 718/780–7700), the 52-acre **Brooklyn Botanic Garden** (☎ 718/622–4433), and the 1897 **Brooklyn Museum** (☎ 718/638–5000), which in most American cities would qualify as the top attraction but is often overlooked by Manhattanites.

GETTING AROUND

Manhattan is really big, but it's easy to navigate. Walking is one of the best forms of transportation. To play it safe, stick to major avenues and broad, busy cross-streets, and take cabs late at night. If in doubt, check with a local to be sure that the most obvious route is the safest.

The subway, which is cheap, and safe for the most part, is the quickest way to get uptown from downtown (and vice versa) and your best bet for exploring the outer boroughs (except Staten Island). You can get a free map at most token booths, or route information by calling 718/330–1234. Buses are brighter and cleaner than subway cars, but they're exceptionally slow. They are a convenient option if your goal is to get straight across town (that is, from west to east or east to west)—most of the subway lines run north-south. Both buses and subways are mobbed at rush hour; unnecessary travel should be suspended at this time if you don't want to stand for 40 minutes with somebody's elbow jammed against your kidney.

Maybe one in a hundred cab drivers will mess up your trip, intentionally or not. The rest of the time, cabs are an efficient, if sometimes hair-raising, way to get around—and they're indispensable late at night. Hail *only* those *yellow* cabs with the *center panel* of their rooftop signs *lighted* by sticking your *right* arm out *calmly* at a *right* angle (you're not dancing the hokeypokey!). Fares are comparable to those in most American cities, but because taking cabs is highly addictive, you may spend all of your money on them.

New York City's crime rate is actually lower than that of many American cities; where violent crime is concerned, it doesn't even rank among the worst 20. And most residents of Manhattan are very tolerant of gays. Nevertheless, for some morons, the sight of two boys or girls schmoozing on a street corner—even in the Village—is an invitation to start trouble. It's a cliché, but exercise common sense and you'll be fine. Plan a course before setting out, look as if you know where your going, and don't hesitate to ask a respectable (i.e., stylish, sexy) passerby for advice.

EATS

In San Francisco and New Orleans, it's difficult to find a bad meal. Despite the fact that there are 12,000 options, in New York, it's pretty easy to strike out, even if you choose one of the city's best-known eateries. Many of the "in" restaurants, however, truly are outstanding, and, contrary to popular belief, most treat John Doe from Dubuque as well as celebrities and regulars. So if you're dead set on experiencing one of the city's *name* restaurants, by all means do so. But if your goal is simply to find good food, you don't need to stand in line or make reservations, nor must you shell out more than $20 per person—even for a three-course dinner.

In addition to the restaurants reviewed below, consider strolling along some of the city's important "restaurant rows." For a good meal in the Theater District, try the diverse grouping of eateries along **46th Street** between 8th and 9th avenues. In east Midtown, **2nd Avenue** from 45th to 60th Street has a variety of ethnic spots; this is due largely to the closeness of the United Nations. **Lexington Avenue** on the East Side has dozens of affordable pubs and bistros, as does **Amsterdam Avenue** on the Upper West Side, between 72nd and 86th streets (avoid those on the same stretch of Columbus Avenue—they're costlier and no better).

Downtown, Chelsea's **8th Avenue** has tons of fair-to-decent, gay-popular bistros, and in the Village, **West 4th** and **Bleecker** streets, between 6th Avenue and Hudson Street, have some of the city's most romantic cafés. In the East Village, **East 6th Street,** between 2nd and 1st avenues, is lined with cheap Indian restaurants. See-and-be-seen types typically infest the eateries on **West Broadway** in SoHo. The intersection of **Mulberry and Spring streets** is the heart of Little Italy; just south of here, along **Mott Street,** are many of Chinatown's best restaurants.

In Brooklyn Heights, head to **Atlantic Avenue** between Court and Hicks streets for great Middle Eastern food; and to **Brighton Beach Avenue,** near Coney Island, for the city's best Russian food. In Queens, the intersection of **Broadway and 31st Street** (take the N train to Broadway) is a hub of Greek tavernas.

For price ranges *see* Chart A at the front of this guide.

Below Houston Street

$$$–$$$$ **Nobu.** You may recognize the name if you've been to L.A., where the extraordinary young chef, Nobu Matsuhisa, has revolutionized Japanese cuisine. Nobu came to Manhattan in 1995, and you still may need to reserve a month ahead. What's all the fuss? Sublime clam skewers, okra tempura, soft-shell crab rolls, and many other delectables. *105 Hudson St., ☎ 212/219–0500.*

$$$ **Zoë.** Get a little gussied up before strutting into this cavernous loft to sample the dazzling world-beat cuisine. A light option is the grilled-portobello-mushroom sandwich with smoked-onion-and-rosemary aioli or go for one of the many fish grills or designer pizzas. *90 Prince St., ☎ 212/966–6722.*

$$–$$$ **Odeon.** Hmmm . . . the Formica, the linoleum floor, the elegantly downcast neighborhood. It's rather easy to see where Florent, in the West Village (*see above*), received its inspiration. Odeon, however, has been around longer—and the food is superior, or, at the very least, more consistent. The menu emphasizes French bistro cooking, though Asian and Middle Eastern influences are apparent as well. Try grilled salmon with tomato-and-basil vinaigrette and sliced fennel and asparagus. *145 W. Broadway, ☎ 212/233–0507.*

$$–$$$ **Trattoria Amici Miei.** On the border of SoHo and Greenwich Village, Amici Miei isn't especially cutting edge or trendy but the variety of pasta, grilled fish, and chicken dishes, the vast wine list, the cheerful service, and the festive ambience make it a downtown favorite. Very romantic. *475 W. Broadway, ☎ 212/533–1933.*

$ **Big Wong.** This is one of the best of the many, affordable, BYOB holes-in-the-wall in Chinatown. No ambience, no pizzazz—just spicy, barbecue spare ribs and other solid Chinese standbys. Gotta like the silly name, too. *67 Mott St., ☎ 212/964–1452.*

$ **El Teddy's.** El Teddy's really does have the best margaritas in New York: tart, potent, and huge. The Mexican food is a cut above the ordinary; there's always a nice, smoky, roasted-corn soup and a few excellent seafood grills. The campy, over-the-top decor is a plus. *219 W. Broadway, ☎ 212/941–7070.*

Greenwich Village

$$$$ **One If By Land, Two If By Sea.** Moon-eyed couples have been known to fall hopelessly in love here amid the heady fragrance of beef Wellington, the soft tinkle of piano keys, and the warm glow of flames emanating from four fireplaces. Then the check comes. In a quaint, 18th-century carriage house just off Sheridan Square (the former home of dueling statesman Aaron Burr). *17 Barrow St., ☎ 212/228–0822.*

$$–$$$ **Grange Hall.** The noisy, well-heeled crowd and elegant Art Deco decor belie what is actually, from a culinary standpoint, one of the Village's simplest, down-home dining experiences. Such entrées as herb-crusted organic chicken or lamb roast can be matched with items from a long list of hearty vegetable sides like rosemary potatoes or crunchy green beans. *50 Commerce St., ☎ 212/924–5246.*

$$-$$$ **Indochine.** This hot and celebrity-studded spot has the city's most imaginative Cambodian and Vietnamese food. Try such zesty creations as fried chicken stuffed with rice vermicelli, bean sprouts, carrots, lemongrass, and diced chicken; or shrimp in a sauce of tamarind, pineapple, and tomato. Palm fronds combine with dark-green banquettes to create a lush, tropical mood. *430 Lafayette St., ☎ 212/505–5111.*

$$-$$$ **Marys.** The charming, compact dining room with its gilt mirrors, ornate chandeliers, and other period details captures the ambience of a late-19th-century, city town house. The wonderful New American cuisine is, however, anything but old-fashioned. Would be a nice place to come out to your parents (after they've settled the bill). *42 Bedford St., ☎ 212/741–3387.*

$$-$$$ **Paris Commune.** This narrow storefront bistro near Hudson Street is noted for its country-French brunches and romantic candlelit dinners. A glass of Calvados before the fire really takes the edge off a day of trying on leather kilts. Rough-hewn floors, one wall of exposed brick, and unfinished dark-wood tables add to the cozy feel. The no-nonsense French menu offers the likes of grilled loin of pork with a fruit compote and calves' liver with capers and shallots. *411 Bleecker St., ☎ 212/929–0509.*

$$-$$$ **Universal Grill.** Quite possibly the West Village's merriest gay eatery, it's tucked in a tiny, amber-lit brick box on the corner of historic Leroy and Bedford streets and histrionic 7th Avenue South. Trashy '70s background music sets the tone for the gregarious wait staff's antics—a birthday celebration here is deliciously embarrassing, a wonderful way to horrify your favorite shrinking violet. The cuisine is American with a Continental drift; try the corn-and-sage soup, followed by tender, pan-fried brook trout with lemon-caper butter. *44 Bedford St., ☎ 212/989–5621.*

$$ **Fannie's Oyster Bar.** Elegantly shoddy, and authentically New Orleans, Fannie's thrives on this quaint but seedy stretch of Washington Street. The dining room is minuscule, so prepare to rub elbows with your neighbors; downstairs is a funky bar with live jazz many nights. Try starting with mouthwatering raw oysters, followed by the eye-watering étouffée. *765 Washington St., ☎ 212/255–5101.*

$$ **Orbit.** The embodiment of lesbian chic, Orbit is just up the street from the dyke bar Crazy Nanny's; the crowd is usually pretty mixed, about 60/40 female/male. The menu is eclectic—everything from fried plantains to pan-seared salmon to designer pizzas (of the latter, the Nonna—with roasted garlic, black olives, sun-dried tomatoes, and goat cheese—is a trusty choice). Very cute down-to-earth wait staff. In good weather a sidewalk table is the perfect place to split a bottle (or two) of wine. *46 Bedford St., ☎ 212/463–8717.*

$-$$ **Brother's Bar-B-Q.** If you're all alone in the big city, plunk yourself down at the long, crowded counter and enjoy the retro, greasy-spoon ambience: This North Carolina–style barbecue is so authentic it's scary—like stepping inside the movie *Deliverance*. Only, if you look around, the place is filled with bookish NYU types and foreign film fans. Heavenly ribs, fried chicken, cornbread. *225 Varick St., ☎ 212/727–2775.*

$-$$ **Caribe.** This brash, lively Caribbean restaurant, in the heart of the bistro-heavy West Village, has hot pink walls and palm trees overhead. The velveteen *callaloo* soup (made with seafood and the West Indian root vegetable, dasheen), is authentically rendered; other favorites are curried goat and the salt-fish stew. To cleanse the palate, order a fat little bottle of Red Stripe beer. *117 Perry St., ☎ 212/255–9191.*

$-$$ **David's Pot Belly.** This 1953 Village dinosaur is a bit worn but always comfy. The Pot Belly is known for its variety: Choose from among roughly 75 items in creating your own omelette, pizza, hamburger, or crepe; possibilities include apples, corned-beef hash, barbecue sauce, chutney, tahini, grits, gravy, guacamole, fried chickpeas, and about 15 varieties of cheese.

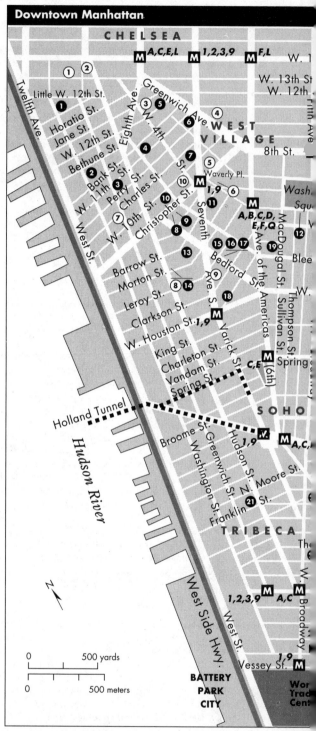

Downtown Manhattan

Scenes ○
The Bar, **12**
Bijou Theater, **11**
Boiler Room, **13**
Cake, **17**
Crazy Nanny's, **9**
Crowbar, **16**
Cubbyhole, **3**
Dick's Bar, **10**
Henrietta Hudson, **8**
J's Hangout, **2**
The Lure, **1**
The Monster, **6**
Rubyfruit Bar, **7**
Stonewall, **5**
Tunnel Bar, **14**
Uncle Charlie's, **4**
Wonder Bar, **15**

(There are less eccentric toppings, too, for you earthlings.) *94 Christopher St.,* ☎ *212/242–8036.*

$–$$ Florent. Well off the beaten asphalt path, Florent is in the heart of the West Village's cobblestone, but definitely not quaint, meat-packing district. Despite its shimmering shell of stainless steel, Formica bar and tabletops, red vinyl stools, and gummy linoleum floor, this is not your typical diner; the all-night pageant of drag queens and assorted merrymakers attests to that. As for the food—skirt steaks, boudin noir, escargot, goat cheese—it's the cheapest taste of Paris this side of the Atlantic. *69 Gansevoort St.,* ☎ *212/989–5779.*

$–$$ Greenwich Café. Formerly a dumpy diner, it was transformed in '95 into a smart, sophisticated 24-hour bistro. The mostly Mediterranean menu ranges from veal couscous to an array of salads. *75 Greenwich Ave.,* ☎ *212/255–5450.*

$–$$ Hudson Feed & Grain. A hopping, tiny adjunct to Henrietta Hudson's lesbian bar, the Feed & Grain's cozy storefront dining room looks much as it might have a century ago, with rough wood floors and brick walls. Dishes are grainy indeed; garbanzos, wheatberries, barley, and the like are used along with fresh vegetables and herbs to make a diverse and delicious array of salads, stews, roasts, and casseroles. Intimate and low-key, it's a great place to meet people. *438 Hudson St.,* ☎ *212/924–3347.*

$–$$ Manatus. Manatus is informal, affordable, quick, warmly decorated, open 24 hours, decidedly gay, and smack in the heart of the West Village. As upscale diner fare goes, it isn't bad—but come more for any of the above reasons. *340 Bleecker St.,* ☎ *212/989–7042.*

$ Benny's Burritos. The neighborhood's all-natural burrito boom seems finally to be tapering off these days, and as the smoke clears, one of the older institutions is still cranking right along (the long lines are a drag). Many varieties of foot-long burritos are offered, plus a memorable black-bean chili. *113 Greenwich Ave.,* ☎ *212/727–0584. East Village: 93 Ave. A,* ☎ *212/254–2054.*

$ Dojo. If you find yourself indigent and overfed on the final night of your vacation in New York, you might consider slumming alongside legions of poor college students for some of the cheapest, healthiest, sit-down fare in the city. Most of the dishes are meatless, several of them flavorless—the carrot cake, however, is both rich and tasty. *14 W. 4th St.,* ☎ *212/505–8934. East Village: 24 St. Mark's Pl.,* ☎ *212/674–9821.*

East Village

$$–$$$ Circa. This very *in* restaurant draws the famous, the upper crusty, and the fashion-conscious to eat and party. In addition to a seasonally changing menu and brick-oven-baked pizzas, there are often DJs and dancing or theme fetes. A sliver of glamour in the grungy East Village. *103 2nd Ave.,* ☎ *212/777–4120.*

$$–$$$ First. Striking decor, enticing New American cuisine, and delectable wines combine at this bar-eatery for a chic, uniquely New York experience. Request a seat at one of the large booths, and pretend you're at the Stork Club circa 1940. *87 First Ave.,* ☎ *212/674–3823.*

$$ Boca Chica. One of the most popular, festive restaurants in the East Village, sassy and spirited Boca Chica offers a broad sampling of Latin-American and Caribbean dishes, from jerk chicken to Cuban sandwiches. And there's dancing and live music, to boot. *13 1st Ave.,* ☎ *212/473–0108.*

$$ Marion's. This is a great place to take a first date: It's fun, filled with models, surprisingly lacking in attitude, and the kitchen always delivers good, reasonably priced, northern Italian and Provençal cuisine. Best martinis in the neighborhood. *354 Bowery,* ☎ *212/475–7621.*

$–$$ Avenue A Sushi. A narrow, somber little restaurant that without the tables and chairs would look like one of the East Village's gay bars, Avenue A is tops for Japanese food and fresh sushi. Try to make it to happy hour (5:30–7:30 Mon.–Fri.), when 16-ounce glasses of several upscale beers are a buck a piece. *103 Ave. A, ☎ 212/982–8109.*

$–$$ **Global 33.** This futuristic-looking tapas bar is a great place for East Village people-watching. Munch on fried codfish and potato pancakes or roast beets and baked chèvre, sip a classy martini (accompanied by the shaker), and enjoy the show. *93 2nd Ave., ☎ 212/477–8427.*

$–$$ **Old Devil Moon.** The eclectic collection of folk art and antiques give this cozy restaurant an air of organized chaos. The straightforward Southern-style menu (steak, fried chicken, catfish platters) is punctuated by somewhat daring dishes (Oaxaca shrimp with garlic and chiles). *511 E. 12th St., ☎ 212/475–4357.*

$–$$ **Pisces.** People have voiced surprise over the success of this tony seafood house on the edge of Alphabet City; perhaps it's evidence of the neighborhood's gentrification, or just proof that even counterculturists demand good food. The diverse menu of fresh seafood is terrific—especially fennel-fried calamari with marinated tomatoes or delicate grilled tuna. *95 Ave. A, ☎ 212/260–6660.*

$ **Stingy Lulu's.** This Formica fantasyland is a popular spot to grab a bite after the bars close. On weekend nights a DJ spins tunes to the delight of a stylishly indigent crowd. Good, no-frills diner food. *129 St. Mark's Pl., ☎ 212/674–3545.*

$ **Three of Cups.** Cozy in an almost yuppie-ish way, this wood-fired-pizza parlor serves thin-crust pies with dozens of great toppings. Nice salads, too. Exposed brick, wooden booths, and amber lighting impart a cheerful ambience. *83 1st Ave., ☎ 212/388–0059.*

$ **Yaffa Café.** Your bohemia barometer should peak upon strolling into this funky basement restaurant on St. Mark's Place. Lesbian grungettes are commonplace, as are green-haired boys with pierced extremities. The largely vegetarian menu is cheap. It's open 24 hours. *97 St. Mark's Pl., ☎ 212/674–9302.*

Chelsea

$$$ **La Lunchonette.** Some of Chelsea's tastiest French food is served inside this unprepossessing restaurant, set amid a bunch of auto repair shops on lower 10th Avenue. Inside is a toasty nest of dark woods, exposed brick, and rich colors. Specialties include lamb couscous, lobster bisque, and a rich cassoulet. *130 10th Ave., ☎ 212/675–0342.*

$$$ **Zucca.** Having opened just as western Chelsea and the new piers are attracting an increasingly well-heeled bunch, Zucca has plenty of style and excellent regional chow to match. Diffused lighting and contemporary furnishings create a mood of updated elegance. Some of the most interesting dishes are pumpkin soup with goat cheese and chives, and pan-roasted guinea hen with wild rice and pan jus. *227 10th Ave., ☎ 212/741–1970.*

$$–$$$ **Claire.** One of the first Chelsea restaurants to cultivate a gay following, Claire specializes in "Floribbean" fare (conch chowder, farfalle with crawfish tails), insouciant (i.e., slow) service, and tropical-hue decor. *156 7th Ave., ☎ 212/255–1955.*

$$ **Food Bar.** A beacon on Chelsea's avenue of the buffed and bronzed, the squeaky-clean Food Bar could pass for one of Princeton's tony supper clubs, except that here the homosexual camaraderie is entirely aboveboard. The New American food—herb-crusted trout, roast-chicken sandwiches, penne with sun-dried tomatoes—is sometimes okay, sometimes lousy, but always affordable. Sit in its cruisy bar and ogle for the price of a drink. The gayest restaurant on the avenue. *149 8th Ave., ☎ 212/243–2020.*

$$ Rocking Horse Café. The Rocking Horse serves inventive Mexican fare, such as mussels steamed in a smoky chipotle sauce, in a smart if somewhat cramped dining room. Several varieties of fresh-fruit margaritas are offered, and the chips and salsa are unusually good. *182 8th Ave.,* ☎ *212/ 463–9511.*

$$ Viceroy. The trendy Mediterranean fare provides some of the best meals on the avenue. The service is generally competent, and the scenery is not bad either: a beautiful setting replete with polished brass and varnished wood, and a handsome crowd. *160 8th Ave.,* ☎ *212/633–8484.*

$–$$ Bright Food Shop. In this sparsely decorated turn-of-the-century luncheonette that looks like an Edward Hopper painting come to life, don't expect mundane diner fare: The menu offers several inexpensive but lavish marriages of East Asian and Mexican food, such as *Moo Shu Mex,* an enchilada stuffed with about a dozen ingredients and topped with hot Thai peanut sauce. The everything-but-the-kitchen-sink cooking is sometimes overwrought but always eye-opening. *218 8th Ave.,* ☎ *212/243–4433.*

$–$$ Eighteenth & Eighth. Despite a recent expansion, everybody's favorite neighborhood hangout is as cramped as ever. Big plates of straightforward, high-carbo chow keep the gym queens coming; plenty of women, too. The day's grilled salmon special is always a good bet. Long lines. *159 8th Ave.,* ☎ *212/242–5000.*

$–$$ Empire Diner. Having starred in Madonna videos and Hollywood movies, the Empire Diner seems to feel it's earned the right to charge $10 for turkey sandwiches. Still, this slick, chrome, '30s diner is usually enjoyable—many dishes, including grilled pesto tomatoes, aren't bad, and there's lovely sidewalk seating in summer. A block from 12th Avenue bars and clubs. *210 10th Ave.,* ☎ *212/243–2736.*

$ Bendix Diner. Despite rather uneven service and food, hordes of gays and lesbians congregate here for cheap eats and people-watching. The standard diner menu is enlivened with several pseudo-Thai dishes (satays, chicken in ginger). Challah-bread French toast is a favorite for brunch. *219 8th Ave.,* ☎ *212/366–0560.*

The Flatiron District and Gramercy Park

$$$ Mesa Grill. No wallflower, the Mesa Grill is dressed in flamboyant colors and fabrics, and its cavernous dining area is always abuzz (often too much so). The contemporary Southwestern cuisine packs quite a punch as well: blue-corn-coated salmon cakes with pineapple-and-tomatillo salsa, and shrimp paired with a roasted garlic-corn tamale are two of the kitchen's delightful concoctions. *102 5th Ave.,* ☎ *212/807–7400.*

$$–$$$ The Coffee Shop. Don't let the name fool you: You won't find donuts or white ceramic cups and saucers, though there is a small coffee bar off to one side. Models and wannabes flock here like drag queens to a makeup sale at Macy's. They booze it up at the large main bar and schmooze it up over such consistently well-prepared dishes as latkes with applesauce or coq au vin. In summer, the Coffee Shop operates a chic open-air café in Union Square's colonnade. *29 Union Sq. W,* ☎ *212/243–7969.*

$$–$$$ Union Square Café. It's among the top restaurants in town (reserve a month ahead), yet dinner for two can be had for under $60. And although its New American bistro fare has been mimicked by competitors, the Café does it best. Typical is a heavenly risotto with spinach, prosciutto, and sage. Servers, though highly professional, are generally cheerful and fun. In summer try for a seat outside looking toward Union Square. *21 E. 16th St.,* ☎ *212/243–4020.*

$ Republic. With its red star insignia calling to mind Chairman Mao, this Asian restaurant has taken Union Square by tsunami. The place is spacious and airy, unique in New York. Cheap, tasty, filling fare is prepared before your eyes. Try the spicy coconut chicken or the *pad thai* (rice noodles, shrimp, squid, sprouts, egg strips, and garlic). *37 Union Sq. W,* ☎ *212/627–7172.*

Above 34th Street

$$$$ Aureole. To dine at this member of the city's culinary royalty, you need to reserve well in advance. On the other hand, ordinary Joes are not routinely shuffled away to a table in Siberia. This is New American cuisine with an Asian kick: Pan-seared yellowfin tuna with ginger-sesame glaze is typical. Wear something natty. *34 E. 61st St.,* ☎ *212/319–1660.*

$$$$ Lespinasse. This sumptuous dining room at the snazzy St. Regis Hotel is stellar in every regard. If the one you love is a foodie, you won't find a better setting for romance amid the crystal, silver, and pale brocade. The cuisine of chef Gary Kunz, who came to New York by way of Switzerland and Singapore, is subtle, refined, and idiosyncratic. *2 E. 55th St.,* ☎ *212/339–6719.*

$$$–$$$$ The Post House. To sample the thickest, juiciest rib eyes and sirloins in the city, you're going to have to brave the straight-and-narrow environs of the Upper East Side—and you're going to have to spend a bundle. Seasoned beefeaters won't settle for less, but don't come expecting to find a pink triangle welcome mat outside the door—discretion is advised. *28 E. 63rd St.,* ☎ *212/935–2888.*

$$$ China Grill. The high-powered tête-à-têtes you see here look like scenes from *The Firm*—which means the casually clad may feel out of place. But if you're looking for a world-class meal that's both convenient to Midtown offices and the Theater District, don't miss the excellent, contemporary, Pacific Rim cooking here. A favorite is the grilled squab with caramelized black-vinegar sauce and shiitake-rice cake. *60 W. 53rd St.,* ☎ *212/333–7788.*

$$$ Dāwat. True, it's more expensive than the curry houses on East 6th Street, but then owner Madhur Jaffrey—a celebrated author and TV personality in Britain—cooks, decorates, and serves with the highest standards. The menu doesn't lack for tandoori specialties, but such unusual selections as Cornish game hen with fiery green chilies are worth bearing in mind. It's next door to the Townhouse Restaurant. *210 E. 58th St.,* ☎ *212/355–7555.*

$$–$$$ Josephina. Set along a row of rather uneven Lincoln Center restaurants, Josephina is almost always good and sometimes stellar. The emphasis is on Continental fare, such as herb-crusted St. Peter's fish with roasted vegetables. There's also always a three-part appetizer sampler. The front dining room, which looks onto Broadway, is more intimate than the noisy one in back. *1900 Broadway,* ☎ *212/799–1000.*

$$–$$$ Tout Va Bien. This is one of the city's best-kept secrets. Tables of this basement brasserie are jammed together, and straightforward renderings of coq au vin and crispy-domed crème brûlée are offered. About half of the patrons and all of the staff appear to be French ex-pats. Nothing trendy, not the least bit affected, and for an hour or two, you're in Paris. *311 W. 51st St.,* ☎ *212/974–9051.*

$$–$$$ Townhouse Restaurant. Run by the owners of the nearby Townhouse and Julie's bars (*see* Scenes, *below*), the Townhouse Restaurant is the only true gay-dining venue north of Chelsea—and the only one in New York where suits and ties are common. Lobster-crab cakes and rack of lamb are the sort of Continental dishes you can expect here. A tad stuffy. *206 E. 58th St.,* ☎ *212/826–6241.*

$$ Zarela. Riotously loud, small, and crowded, Zarela is a lesser-known standout among east Midtown's many clonishly corporate restaurants. You won't find the usual Americanized Mexican standbys here; instead, ex-

228

Eats ●

Bendix Diner, **12**
Big Cup, **13**
Bright Food Shop, **14**
Café Elsie, **2**
China Grill, **3**
Claire, **20**
The Coffee Shop, **24**
Dawat, **7**
Eighteenth and
Eighth, **16**
Empire Diner, **10**
Food Bar, **18**
Kaffeehaus, **19**
La Lunchonette, **11**
Lespinasse, **4**
Mangia, **5**
Mesa Grill, **21**
Republic, **22**
Rocking Horse Café, **15**
Tout Va Bien, **1**
Townhouse
Restaurant, **6**
Union Square Café, **23**
Viceroy, **17**
Zarela, **8**
Zucca, **9**

Scenes ○

Barracuda, **15**
The Break, **13**
Bump! at the
Palladium, **22**
Champs, **20**
Cleo's, **2**
Club Edelweiss, **1**
Club 58, **3**
The Eagle, **8**
Julie's, **4**
King, **17**
Load, **19**
M Bar, **6**
Mike's, **11**
Rawhide, **16**
Rome, **12**
Roxy, **10**
Sound Factory Bar, **21**
The Spike, **9**
Splash, **18**
The Townhouse, **5**
Twilo, **7**
Unicorn, **14**

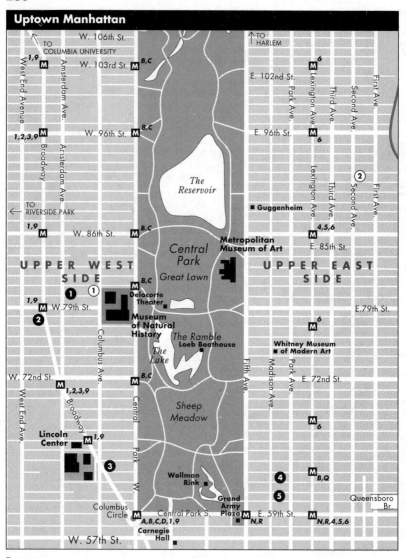

Uptown Manhattan

W. 106th St.

TO COLUMBIA UNIVERSITY

1,9

W. 103rd St.

B,C

E. 102nd St.

6

West End Avenue

Amsterdam Ave.

Broadway

TO HARLEM

Park Ave.

Lexington Ave.

Third Ave.

Second Ave.

First Ave.

1,2,3,9

W. 96th St.

B,C

E. 96th St.

6

The Reservoir

2

TO RIVERSIDE PARK

Guggenheim

1,9

W. 86th St.

B,C

Metropolitan Museum of Art

4,5,6

E. 85th St.

Lexington Ave.

Third Ave.

Second Ave.

First Ave.

UPPER WEST SIDE

Central Park

Great Lawn

UPPER EAST SIDE

1

1

B,C

Delacorte Theater

1,9

W. 79th St.

2

Columbus Ave.

Museum of Natural History

The Ramble

Loeb Boathouse

The Lake

E. 79th St.

6

Whitney Museum of Modern Art

W. 72nd St.

B,C

Fifth Ave.

Madison Ave.

Park Ave.

E. 72nd St.

1,2,3,9

West End Ave.

Broadway

Sheep Meadow

6

Lincoln Center

1,9

3

Central Park W.

Wollman Rink

4

B,Q

5

Columbus Circle

Central Park S.

Grand Army Plaza

E. 59th St.

Queensboro Br.

A,B,C,D,1,9

N,R

N,R,4,5,6

Carnegie Hall

W. 57th St.

Eats ●

Aureole, **5**

Café Monaco, **1**

Josephina, **3**

La Caridad, **2**

The Post House, **4**

Scenes ○

Toolbox, **2**

The Works, **1**

pect such sophisticated fare as red-snapper hash or sautéed shrimp with jalapeños, cilantro, and coconut. *953 2nd Ave.,* ☎ *212/644–6740.*

$–$$ **Mangia.** Trying to find a decent, affordable lunch in Midtown is nearly impossible, and although Mangia is a bit pricier than your average deli, the quality and variety of food is on par with a first-rate restaurant. Dozens of Euro-style sandwiches (such as chèvre, sun-dried tomatoes, and watercress on a baguette) are available, and there's also an amazing all-you-can-eat antipasto buffet. *16 E. 48th St.,* ☎ *212/754–0637.*

$ **Café Elsie.** Just a homey, gay-popular hole-in-the-wall that's perfect if you're searching for cheap, hearty grub before or after taking in a show. Soups, salads, and potpies are among the offerings. *358 W. 47th St.,* ☎ *212/765–7653.*

$ **Café Monaco.** This bright café (close to the Upper West Side's only popular gay bar, The Works) stands out for its delicious French munchies. The grilled calamari is a standout; there are also dozens of rich pastries. *421 Amsterdam Ave.,* ☎ *212/873–3100.*

$ **La Caridad.** There are several good Cuban-Chinese restaurants in Manhattan, found by Chinese who emigrated to Cuba to build its railroads This no-frills place often has long lines, but when you sit down to a plate of shrimp-fried rice, black beans, and sweet plantains, you'll understand the attraction. *2199 Broadway,* ☎ *212/874–2780.*

Coffeehouse Culture

Kaffeehaus (131 8th Ave., ☎ 212/229–9702), with its marble tables, pressed-tin ceiling, velvet banquettes, and dark-wood paneling, captures the mood of a traditional Viennese café. Racks of periodicals, rich coffees and desserts, and such filling fare as Wiener schnitzel and vegetable strudel with an herb sauce keep the crowds happy. The first true gay (as in cruisy) coffeehouse in Chelsea, the **Big Cup** (228 8th Ave., ☎ 212/206–0059) is a wonderful alternative to the sometimes sullen bar scene. A mix of armchairs and diner-style tables and chairs are set in such a way that you almost can't help but chat with the cute caffeine addicts seated around you. Avoid the crappy food, though.

The phrase "strike a pose" might have been coined at the ultrastylish **Caffe Rafaella** (134 7th Ave. S, ☎ 212/929–7247), an antiques-filled coffeehouse with amazing desserts and some of the coolest and hottest (we don't mean temperature) sidewalk seating in the Village. Indirect lighting and exposed brick may make the **Original Espresso Bar** (82 Christopher St., ☎ 212/627–3870) seem too precious for gritty Christopher Street, but the coffees here are rich and delicious.

There are four coffeehouses at the intersection of MacDougal and Bleecker streets; avoid all of them in favor of **Caffé Reggio** (119 MacDougal St., ☎ 212/475–9557) just up the street. Not all that gay but a good perch from which to watch the world go by. In the East Village, **Limbo** (47 Ave. A, at 3rd St., ☎ 212/477–5271) has all the ingredients of Bohemia, good sandwiches, board games, and plenty of gay staff.

SLEEPS

New York City's hotels are unbelievably costly. Though the steep room taxes have been slashed, it's hard finding basic accommodations for less than $100 a night. Operating expenses are high, so even though occupancy rates may be lower than elsewhere, rates are unlikely to drop soon. This doesn't mean you can't convince a hotel operator to cut you a break, or that you won't find some outstanding specials by perusing the travel sections of major newspapers.

Most major hotels are in Midtown or the nearby Theater District. There aren't a lot of options in gay neighborhoods, but the few rooms available in Greenwich Village and Chelsea, and on the Upper West Side are comparatively affordable; if you can live without full-scale amenities, the several B&Bs listed below are an attractive alternative to Midtown's dreary convention hotels.

For price ranges, *see* Chart A at the front of this guide.

Hotels

Upper East Side

⌕ If you must be a kept man, try to be kept at the **Lowell,** New York's most dignified, intimate transient address. This 1926 hotel, where Noel Coward once resided, is decorated with a magnificent mix of Art Deco and Second Empire antiques, and some rooms have wood-burning fireplaces. Just a few blocks from the Townhouse bar. *28 E. 63rd St.,* ☎ *212/838–1400 or 800/221–4444. 65 rooms. $$$$*

⌕ For 50 years, the **Barbizon** was a women's residential hotel (Candace Bergen and Grace Kelly both stayed here). KLM Airlines took over in the mid-'70s and converted this handsome neo-Gothic hotel into one of the best bargains in the city. Rooms are small and simple, but the public areas retain the hotel's historic charm. *140 E. 63rd St.,* ☎ *212/838–5700. 345 rooms. $$–$$$*

Upper West Side

⌕ Thanks to major renovations over the past few years, the **Radisson Empire,** which overlooks Lincoln Center, has evolved into one of the city's most elegant hotels. Rooms are small but have VCRs, CD players, and other high-end amenities. *44 W. Broadway at 63rd St.,* ☎ *212/265–7400. 368 rooms. $$–$$$*

⌕ Though its rooms are a bit musty and worn, the dirt-cheap **Excelsior** has a terrific location—across the street from the Museum of Natural History, and the popular bar, The Works. Friendly staff. *45 W. 81st St.,* ☎ *212/362–9200 or 800/368–4575. 150 rooms. $–$$*

⌕ Rooms and health club facilities are a bit dowdier than at the Vanderbilt Y (*see* Midtown East, *below*), but the **West Side YMCA** has a great location—it's steps from Lincoln Center and Central Park and close to the most direct subway lines to Chelsea and the West Village. *5 W. 63rd St.,* ☎ *212/787–4400. 539 rooms. $*

Midtown East

⌕ The controversial, nearly blank lower facade of the **Four Seasons** fails to reveal that this is truly one of the world's most splendid hotels. Above the Grand Foyer's 33-foot ceiling and Magritte and Kandinsky paintings are 52 floors of pure luxury—huge rooms with English sycamore furniture and all-marble baths. *57 E. 57th St.,* ☎ *212/758–5700. 370 rooms. $$$$*

⌕ Want to splurge? You won't be disappointed by the **St. Regis,** one of the city's classic Beaux Arts buildings, whose guest rooms are decorated sumptuously with Louis XV–style pieces. Be sure to see the famed Maxfield Parrish mural in the King Cole Bar. *2 E. 55th St.,* ☎ *212/753–4500 or 800/759–7550. 365 rooms. $$$$*

⌕ Steps from the United Nations, the splendid Art Deco **Beekman Tower** is not cheap, but because all of its rooms are full suites, and some have private balconies and patios, it's a relative bargain for four travelers willing to share a suite (they start at just over $200). *3 Mitchell Pl.,* ☎ *212/ 355–7300 or 800/637–8483. 171 rooms. $$$–$$$$*

⌕ The least known—but to many rock and film stars the best—of Ian Schrager's trendy properties, **Morgans** thinks of itself as more of a discreet home away from home than a hotel; there's not even a sign outside the door. Rooms are futuristic, monochromatic, even bleak—and many have Mapplethorpe photos in them. *237 Madison Ave.,* ☎ *212/686–0300 or 800/334–3408. 112 rooms. $$$–$$$$*

🏨 Get past its drab exterior and the **Beverly** emerges as one of the best deals in Midtown. Most of the midsize rooms have been redecorated recently and have walk-in closets, although the bathrooms are dinky. Great location. *125 E. 50th St.,* ☎ *212/753–2700 or 800/223–0945. 187 rooms. $$–$$$*

🏨 The best of the city's Y's, the **Vanderbilt YMCA** has a convenient Midtown location. The tiny bare rooms accommodate from one to four persons. The health club is popular, and there's an above-average cafeteria. *224 E. 47th St.,* ☎ *212/756–9600. 430 rooms. $*

Midtown West

🏨 The mammoth, gaudy **Marriott Marquis** is Times Square's landmark hotel. It comes complete with a revolving 46th-floor rooftop restaurant and midsize rooms done with chain-hotel furnishings and colors. Theater divas will appreciate the location. *1535 Broadway at 45th St.,* ☎ *212/398–1900 or 800/843–4898. 1,877 rooms. $$$$*

🏨 Of 5th Avenue's top-of-the-line hotels, the **Peninsula** is the warmest and the most romantic. Unlike the Plaza, or even the Pierre, the Peninsula has a human scale and courteous but unstuffy staff. The three-floor, rooftop health club and spa with a terrace bar is spectacular. *700 5th Ave.,* ☎ *212/247–2200 or 800/262–9467. 250 rooms. $$$$*

🏨 Popular with New Yorkers for its Round Bar and 44 restaurant, the **Royalton Hotel** is a favorite roost for visiting fashion, film, and publishing moguls. The most celebrated of Ian Schrager's three properties, the Royalton's dramatic rooms are notable for their cushioned window seats, working fireplaces, and spacious, curvaceous bathtubs. *44 W. 44th St.,* ☎ *212/869–4400 or 800/635–9013. 168 rooms. $$$$*

🏨 The 52-story, postmodern **Millennium Broadway** will remind you of the Paramount and Royalton hotels; its contemporary rooms have gray, black, and white color-schemes and deco touches. *145 W. 44th St.,* ☎ *212/768–4400 or 800/622–5569. 629 rooms. $$$–$$$$*

🏨 The minuscule rooms at the ultrachic **Paramount** would be inhuman but for designer Phillippe Starck's clever touches, such as the quirky, conical, stainless-steel sinks. The lobby bar is a parade of professional and amateur poseurs. Many singles are $99. *235 W. 46th St.,* ☎ *212/764–5500 or 800/225–7474. 600 rooms. $$–$$$*

🏨 The **Ramada Milford Plaza** is often remembered for its disturbingly perky jingle, in which the Plaza is lauded as the "lullaby on Broadway." In fact, it's a noisy, convention hotel usually teeming with high school kids. The price and location are perfect, however. *700 8th Ave.,* ☎ *212/869–3600. 1,300 rooms. $–$$*

East Below 34th Street

🏨 Staying at the **Gramercy Park Hotel** gets you access to the otherwise exclusive Gramercy Park, but it's also a lovely restored hotel in its own right (Stanford White once lived here) with cheerful rooms, a quiet location, and a stylish bar. *2 Lexington Ave.,* ☎ *212/475–4320. 500 rooms. $$*

🏨 The **Carlton Arms** is the strangest—and possibly the cheapest—hotel in Manhattan. Though lacking such mundane amenities as phones and TVs (and the towels are threadbare), rooms are enlivened with some of the freakiest, kitschiest murals and paintings you'll ever see. *160 E. 25th St.,* ☎ *212/684–8337. 54 rooms. $*

🏨 Only slightly more serious than the nearby Carlton Arms, the **Gershwin** is a converted Greek Revival with funky art, brightly colored bare-bones rooms, and a lively, youthful following. *7 E. 27th St., ☎ 212/545–8000. 160 rooms. $*

West Below 34th Street

☵ Since the objective of staying in Greenwich Village is to spend as little time as possible in your hotel room, it shouldn't bother you that the **Washington Square Hotel's** rooms are unmemorable (though they're entirely pleasant). What's more important is that the staff is knowledgeable and helpful, and that you're only steps from the action. *103 Waverly Pl., ☎ 212/777–9515 or 800/222–0418. 160 rooms. $–$$*

☵ The much-hyped **Chelsea Hotel** is lovable for its history: Tennessee Williams, Joni Mitchell, Vladimir Nabokov, and many other luminaries have lived here; Edie Sedgwick and Dylan Thomas died here; and Sid Vicious killed Nancy Spungeon here—before killing himself. It's close to things gay and rooms are cheap; it's also a dump. *222 W. 23rd St., ☎ 212/243–3700. 300 rooms. $*

Below Houston

☵ The sleek, minimalist **Millennium** is the best hotel in the Financial District. Rooms have contemporary furnishings; those above the 40th floor have incredible views of the Hudson and East rivers. Although it's downtown, the Millennium is no farther from the Village and Chelsea than are Midtown hotels. *55 Church St., ☎ 212/693–2001 or 800/835–2220. 561 rooms. $$$$*

☵ In the heart of Chinatown, the **Holiday Inn Downtown** has small, clean rooms, a friendly staff, and one of the city's strongest gay followings. *138 Lafayette St., ☎ 212/966–8898. 223 rooms. $$–$$$*

Guest Houses and Small Hotels

The **New York B&B Reservation Center** (☎ 212/977–3512) is a gay and lesbian reservation service that can find you accommodations in any of 80 hosted and unhosted apartments throughout the city. Rates range from $60 to $150.

☵ The **Chelsea Pines Inn,** the best-known gay accommodation in the city, is equidistant from Village and Chelsea attractions on an albeit drab stretch of 14th Avenue. This 1850 town house is run by a helpful staff and has small but pleasantly furnished rooms and a quaint (by Manhattan standards) garden out back. It's a great deal. *317 W. 14th St., ☎ 212/929–1023. 21 rooms. Mostly gay male. $*

☵ The **Colonial House Inn** is set in a historic town house on a spiffy tree-lined street in Chelsea; rooms are attractively decorated, and there's a terrific, roof sundeck. *318 W. 22nd St., ☎ 212/243–9669 or 800/689–3779. 20 rooms. Mixed gay male/lesbian. $*

☵ With a great location at the northern tip of the West Village, the **Incentra Village House** is a popular choice. Rooms in these adjoining Victorian town houses have fireplaces; some have kitchenettes. Though cheaper than a hotel, rooms here are among the costliest of area guest houses. *32 8th Ave., ☎ 212/206–0007. 12 rooms. Mixed gay male/straight. $*

SCENES

For all of its glamour and panache, New York City's gay nightlife is surprisingly accessible. Contrary to sensationalist rumors, getting into hot discos does not typically require being dressed or looking a certain way—you just have to be willing to pay a $10 to $20 cover. And although it's easy to find attitude at the more popular bars, Manhattan's bar goers are a fairly approachable lot. One reason for this is the city's constantly high number of tourists and business travelers—there are always plenty of fresh faces. Also, visitors in town for a short stay are more likely to start up a conversation in a bar. And New Yorkers, who tire quickly of meeting other New Yorkers, usually respond cheerfully to such overtures.

Another nice thing about New York's gay nightlife is the sheer variety. There are at least four or five choices for every brand of gay bar, from leather to piano to stand-and-model to Gen-X to neighborhood. Several smaller gay discos are open seven nights a week, and an equal number of megasize dance clubs have gay nights once or twice a week. The only form of gay bar that's sorely lacking in New York City is country-western; for some reason there is no full-time two-stepping club in a city that's full of transplanted southerners and westerners.

The only negatives about the city's gay bars are that most are too small and cramped—an unavoidable effect of the city's high real-estate costs. Newer clubs are both larger and more cleverly decorated than their predecessors. Still, the average New York City gay bar is a midsize, all-black, dimly-lit room with three or four homoerotic photos on the walls and precious little room for mingling.

Bars and Small Clubs

Greenwich Village

The Lure. This is the only leather club that enforces a dress code. Well, at least on weekends. The list of do's and don'ts is about as long as *The Communist Manifesto,* and at least as interesting. For instance, you may wear a jockstrap; you may not wear knickers. You may wear rubber rain gear; you may not wear clothing whose scent has been enhanced by a fabric softener. You may wear military gear; you may not dress in drag (it's not clear what happens to you if you're dressed as a female Navy cadet). The bar is cavernous, crowded, and anchored by a dentist chair. During the week there are theme nights, such as Wednesday's Pork, when a DJ presides over S&M demonstrations, half-price drinks, and other wholesome fun (which, oddly, does not include dancing). *409 W. 13th St., ☎ 212/741–3919. Crowd: male, all ages; serious leather; bears; butch-chic.*

The Monster. You'll either love or hate this Sheridan Square institution. Upstairs the tone-deaf gather and sing around the piano; downstairs the rhythm-impaired gyrate in a campy, pitch-black disco (and that's coming from someone who loves it). Leave your attitude at the door. *80 Grove St., ☎ 212/924–3558. Crowd: mostly male, very diverse in age and race; strong Latin following; cruisy, outgoing, fun.*

Stonewall. An odd mix of curious tourists and down-to-earth locals ensure that this place stays refreshingly untrendy and free-spirited. Here you can channel the spirits of our brothers and sisters who rioted for our rights on this very spot (well, actually, the original Stonewall Inn was a couple doors down). The pool table gets more action than most of the patrons, though lonely hearts can pile into the snug little room in the back to view videos into the wee hours. *53 Christopher St., ☎ 212/463–0950. Crowd: mostly male, diverse in ages; local, down-to-earth.*

Uncle Charlie's. The video bar of all video bars until the opening a few years ago of Splash. The turnout is highly uneven—sometimes heavy; others as few as three or four guys. Choose from among three bars, browse the video screens, or try to break into a game at the popular pool table. If you do get someone's phone number, be sure to ask for the area code; chances are it's not 212. *56 Greenwich St., ☎ 212/255–8787. Crowd: mostly male, fairly young, suburban guppie, lots of out-of-towners expecting the wild scene of years past.*

OTHER OPTIONS

There are quite a few sleepy, local bars in the West Village, each with a small but fiercely loyal following: **Boots & Saddle** (76 Christopher St., ☎ 212/929–9684) and **Ty's** (114 Christopher St., ☎ 212/741–9641) get more of a leather-and-Levi's crowd; **Two Potato** (143 Christopher St., ☎ 212/255–0286) and **Keller's** (384 West St., ☎ 212/243–1907) are popular with African-Americans; and the **Hangar Bar** (115 Christopher St., ☎ 212/627–2044), **Nuts & Bolts** (101 7th Ave., ☎ 212/620–4000), and **Pieces** (8 Christopher St., ☎ 212/929–9291) are friendly but rather dated-looking video bars. A couple of others are so scary as not to warrant recommendations; another, **Julius** (159 W. 10th St., ☎ 212/929–9672), though a bit of a dump, has been a gay, West Village landmark for a century according to some—history fans might want to check it out. Be sure to chat up the regulars, many of whom remember what New York was like a century ago.

East Village

The Bar. Some people joke that the East Village has only one bar—it just has seven different locations. Indeed, the other spots reviewed in this section are quite similar to The Bar: tiny, intentionally downcast, dressed in black, and blessed with an amazing jukebox (mostly rock/punk/grunge—from Pink Floyd to Elastica) and a slightly worn pool table. Although the cruise factor is fairly high, many people come here just to socialize with friends or relax after a long day. Thursday through Saturday non-locals arrive in great numbers, but most of the guys here live within a few blocks. May be closing. *68 2nd Ave., ☎ 212/674–9714. Crowd: mostly male, ages range from NYU boys to thirtysomethings; somewhat alternative, racially mixed; lots of black jeans, goatees; a bit of an edge.*

Boiler Room. One of the neighborhood's more recent gay hangouts, after suffering through its first hundred days of solitude, it's become a hot scene for grungiqueers and their admirers. Numbers swell on Saturdays. It's not all that different from the other bars around here except for three things: enticing drink specials (Sunday through Thursday you can get pints of beer for $2 to $2.50); dykes are most welcome every night and have the run of the place on Sundays; and in two corners of the bar are several plush armchairs and sofas that make it possible to hold your very own salon. (Bias warning: This is the author's favorite hangout.) *86 E. 4th St., ☎ 212/254–7536. Crowd: 75/25 m/f; same crowd as at the Bar but more women.*

Cake. The pleasant lighting; couches for sitting and chatting; dark, cozy basement; and offbeat jukebox are all draws at this mellow hangout on the fringes of the East Village. Still a little quiet at press time (it opened in August 1995), the place has loads of potential. *99 Ave. B, ☎ 212/505–2226. Crowd: local, young, and hip.*

Crowbar. There are different theme-dance parties here most nights, with Friday's **1984** being the most engaging; that's when this fabulous club pulses robotically to Wham, Duran Duran, Men Without Hats, and other New Wave syntho-trash from the mid-'80s. This club swelters inside, the dance floor is cramped and tiny, the two bathrooms are dank and subject to long lines, and the sound system is ear-splitting—but somehow it's impossible to have a bad time here. It helps that the bartenders are so cute and cheerful, and a recent renovation saw the addition of a larger coat-check in back and some table-seating off of the dance floor. Very downtown. *339 E. 10th St., ☎ 212/420–0670. Crowd: 85/15 m/f, young; somewhat mixed racially; friendly, sweaty, hip.*

Dick's Bar. When the Boiler Room and the Bar get overrun with visiting Chelsea boys, locals retreat to this narrow, dark, and somber space, their own divy turf bar. The jukebox has the most delightfully obscure tunes—

lots of "greatest hits" compilations by bands you never realized had any hits. The T-shirts bearing Dick's tasteless logo make nice Christmas gifts. *192 2nd Ave., ☎ 212/475–2071. Crowd: 80/20 m/f, young; local, very alternative—lots of baggy jeans, dyed hair, pierced eyelids.*

Tunnel Bar. The least interesting but cruisiest bar in the neighborhood. Same formula as the rest but no pool table. *116 1st Ave., ☎ 212/777–9232. Crowd: mostly male but otherwise diverse; relatively old for this area—some guys over 30!*

Wonder Bar. A little campier and homier than the others in this part of town, the Wonder Bar is a tiny cocktail lounge with lots of seating, both at tables and at the long bar—there's not much standing around unless it's crowded. Music videos and porn flicks are shown on a *big* video screen in back. Used to get a funkier crowd but now seems a tad mundane. The women who come here appear to be straight. Wednesdays and Sundays there's an itzy-bitzy back room. *505 E. 6th St., ☎ 212/777–9105. Crowd: 80/20 m/f, generally young but a few latter-day hippies; low attitude, very anti–pretty boy.*

Chelsea

Barracuda. The front and back halves of this bar are full of nooks and crannies. Take your cue at the pool table or people-watch from one of the funky '50s-style couches. Thursday night you'll find a groovin' DJ and a talent show hosted by the fabulous drag queen, Mona Foot. Having opened in 1995, the Barracuda has become Chelsea's hottest bar. Only drawbacks: tight layout and too few bathrooms. *275 W. 22nd St., ☎ 212/646–8613. Crowd: mostly male; stylish; a few stray East Village guys; mostly ages 20 and early 30s.*

The Break. Used to be more like Splash and the Works, but since a few other guppie and musclehead bars have opened in Chelsea, the Break has become a bit more rough-and-tumble; it's even been drawing a few banjee boys and leather men. Nevertheless, a good number of Chelsea stand-and-model types pop in here from time to time, especially when good drink specials are offered. Until midnight (in good weather) you can escape from the otherwise cramped, hot bar into a snazzy patio in back. *232 8th Ave., ☎ 212/627–0072. Crowd: mostly male, mid-20s to mid-30s; fairly local; aggressively cruisy.*

Champs. In most cities, the gay sports bars have TV screens showing a variety of sporting events, a few pennants and trophies scattered around, and lots of regular Joes drinking beer and rooting for local teams. Champs calls itself Manhattan's sports bar but features none of the above elements. It's basically just Splash with a dance floor and lots of glitzy decorating touches such as marble bathrooms and a wall of mini-TV screens showing vintage clips of football players in tight uniforms. There's a punching bag, too. It's kind of silly—not a single queen here knows the difference between a javelin and a hockey stick—but the place is quite crowded every day of the week. *17 W. 19th St., ☎ 212/633–1717. Crowd: Same as Splash, but with even more guys checking in gym bags.*

The Eagle. Much more hard-core than the Spike nearby but not as hip as the Lure, The Eagle is serious about three things: drinking, glaring, and shooting pool. Lean against the pool table, and you'll lose a finger. A nice place to break in those chaps you got for Valentine's Day. *142 11th Ave., ☎ 212/691–8451. Crowd: male, thirtysomething and older; lots of leather and some Levi's.*

King. This bar opened in 1994 and immediately pissed everybody off by charging a cover and throwing around a lot of attitude. They seem to have stopped charging the cover except for a couple of nights when they have big dance parties, but the crowds are still sparse—nobody is quite sure how to characterize this place. It's nicely decorated and has three floors:

The first is a regular cruise bar, the second is a dance floor, and the top floor is only open certain nights and tries (often unsuccessfully) to attract back-room action. *579 6th Ave., ☎ 212/366–5464. Crowd: mostly male, kind of a blend of the crowds at Champs, Splash, and The Break.*

Mike's. New York had high hopes for this natty 1993 addition to the kinky intersection of 14th Street and 9th Avenue. But so far, despite cheap drinks, gregarious bartenders, two walls of floor-to-ceiling French windows, a campy jukebox, and a long, elegant trapezoidal bar, it hasn't caught on. Maybe someday it will get rolling; in the meantime, a small band of regulars continues to take advantage of Mike's many attributes. *400 W. 14th St., ☎ 212/691–6606. Crowd: 70/30 m/f, mostly ages 35 and up; down-to-earth; some racial mix, a few drag queens.*

Rawhide. Not the place to show off your bright, white Calvins, or your Gap anything—this is the only Chelsea bar away from 12th Avenue that has any serious edge to it. It's just a small, dark room with pool, pinball, and a divy feel. The Rawhide's most distinctive feature is a vent above the front door that blows several cubic tons per second of nasty exhaust onto pedestrians passing in front of it. The beer blasts on weekend afternoons are pretty popular. *212 8th Ave., ☎ 212/242–9332. Crowd: male, mostly thirtysomething and up; some leather and Levi's; musta-chioed, a pretty ornery bunch.*

Rome. Appropriately, the walls of this new Chelsea club are adorned with inlaid marble, the bar is covered with tile mosaics, frescoes abound, and the go-go dancers wear little Roman legion outfits. And, owing to a layout that would make any of the ancient engineers proud, Rome is spacious and airy. *290 8th Ave., ☎ 212/249–6969. Crowd: mature, sedate muscle boys; kind of upscale for Chelsea.*

The Spike. Once the ultimate parade of black leather, chains, and Levi's, the Spike's bark is now quite a bit worse than its bite (which disappoints). There are a couple of rooms, all done with the requisite butch motorcycle look, but most guys here are regular old Chelsea fags looking for something a little seedier than the Break but not yet ready for a full-on leather bar. Saturday nights are best. *120 11th Ave., ☎ 212/243–9688. Crowd: male, mostly ages 25 to 35; some leather but more Levi; a few guppies.*

Splash. The staggering popularity of this bar is due as much to its size as to anything else: It dwarfs the competition. This is a classic stand-and-model club with several bars, a ratty pool table in back, lots of step-seating, tacky tables made out of surf boards, and several video screens of varying sizes. The urge to merge is Splash's raison d'être. A simple "Come here often?" will usually do it; sometimes you don't even have to say anything. The opening of nearby Champs in 1994 took away some business, so Splash added a dance area downstairs. The go-go shows are popular—the dancers perform in translucent shower cubicles. *50 W. 17th St., ☎ 212/691–0073. Crowd: mostly male, young to middle-aged; cute, dapper; lots of out-of-towners.*

Above 34th Street

Cleo's. This is a good spot to grab a drink before or after catching a Broadway show. It's the only nonsleazy gay bar near Times Square. *656 9th Ave., ☎ 212/307–1503. Crowd: male, older; laid-back, friendly, mixed racially.*

Club Edelweiss. If she or he or it exists, you'll find her or him or it at this fun-filled circus in Hell's Kitchen. This has a tag as simply a transvestite and transsexual club, but everybody is welcome—and there's always some wild people-watching. Just don't stand around staring like an idiot—mingle! There are two levels, several lounges and bars, and two dance floors. *578 11th Ave., ☎ 212/629–1021. Crowd: all ages, races, genders; low attitude.*

Club 58. This is the only gay New York City club with any substantial Asian following. This two-tiered basement club has dated decor, mediocre music, and unfortunately rarely draws much of a crowd. *40 E. 58th St.,* ☎ *212/308–1546. Crowd: mostly male, ages 30 to 70; about a quarter Asian; many suits.*

M Bar. At this Midtown cocktail lounge there aren't as many suits as at the Townhouse, but it's still upscale. Note the zebra-print wall covering, abundance of mirrors, slick homoerotic photography, and postindustrial furniture. There are three levels: One is a dance floor; another a quiet, intimate bar; and still another a bustling lounge. *256 E. 49th St.,* ☎ *212/935–2150. Crowd: male, lots of older gentlemen in suits, a smaller faction of young guys.*

Toolbox. Prior to the 1994 opening of this somewhat generic video bar, the Upper East Side had no gay nightlife. The Toolbox certainly helped fill the void, but unless you live or are staying nearby, there's little reason to trek all the way up here. It's a one-room bar with a minuscule, tinsel-backed stage for go-go dancers, a pool table, lots of miniature rainbow flags, and a sadly dated selection of pop music. *1748 2nd Ave.,* ☎ *212/427–3106. Crowd: mostly male, generally under 35; neighborhood types; cruisy.*

The Townhouse. On good nights, it's like stepping into a Brooks Brothers catalogue—cashmere sweaters, Rolex watches, distinguished looking gentlemen—and it's surprisingly festive. On bad nights, you bump into your sister's husband, and he's cruising your boss's son (a lot of these suits have never been out of the closet). Decor seems to recall a stately Philadelphia hunt club, although the nasty plaid carpeting is somewhat more reminiscent of a suburban Elk's Club. Not as business-oriented as some, though you might still see a few "transactions" going down. It can get a little stuffy in here—most of the fun guys seem to congregate in the back of the largest room, around the piano. The waiters are stunning. *236 E. 58th St.,* ☎ *212/754–4649. Crowd: mostly male; upscale crowd, lots of suits, may be the only bar in Manhattan where ascots are still fashionable.*

The Works. Gay men who typically suffer nose bleeds north of 23rd Street still flock religiously to this Upper West Side institution for the Thursday night $1 margaritas (be careful, they're strong and taste like powdered lemonade mixed with paint thinner) and Sunday beer blasts ($6 for all you can siphon). Monday through Wednesday the crowd is quieter and mostly local (a good place to play pool); weekends see a little more bridge-and-tunnel action. Whatever the night, there are always a few boys who look like J. Crew models, and the rest of the crowd at least dresses like them. It's a long narrow place with dim lighting, black walls, lots of video screens, and zero ambience. More manageable than Splash. *428 Columbus Ave.,* ☎ *212/799–7365. Crowd: mostly male and under 35, guppie, stand-and-model, very cruisy, lots of attitude; a mix of collared shirts and muscle T's with a few suits thrown in.*

Clubs

Several of the spots listed below are straight discos that have gay parties once or twice a week. The nights are liable to change at any moment and the cover charges range from $8 to $20. The descriptions given of the crowds below apply only to the gay nights.

Bump! at the Palladium. Sunday night's Bump! used to be one of the most exciting dance parties in the city, but since its reinvention at the Palladium it has lost some of its luster. The Palladium, with its old theater seats, is a great place to talk, and there's a cozy little lounge in the back. *126 E. 14th St.,* ☎ *212/473–7171. Crowd: see Saturday nights at the Roxy, above.*

Roxy. Probably no gay party is better known than the all-out buff-boy parties held every Saturday at the Roxy—although if you really want to experience something wonderfully different, come on a Tuesday for gay roller-skating. This humongous danceteria has all the traditional disco trappings—strobes, disco balls, and a fantastic sound system pumping the latest house music. Upstairs is a smaller dance floor (featuring retro-disco) with views of the main one down below. At the Tuesday roller-skating parties you can rent skates if you don't have your own; on these nights, the crowd is much more diverse and friendly. *515 W. 18th St.,* ☎ *212/645–5156. Crowd: mostly male, young; hunky and attitudy, professional party creatures.*

Sound Factory Bar. Not to be confused with the recently closed warehouse disco of the same name, the cramped Sound Factory Bar is a pure disco that plays deep and industrial house music most nights—you come here to dance and show off your gym bod. The dance floor is upstairs along with a couple of crowded bars; downstairs is an only slightly quieter spot that's better for lounging or chilling. Although you can enter only until 4 AM, the dancing usually continues for a long while after. It's open Tuesday and Thursday through Saturday. *12 W. 21st St.,* ☎ *212/206–7770. Crowd: male, young; racially mixed; lots of tortoise-shell pecs, either too wired or too snotty to make conversation.*

Twilo. Stepping into this huge glam-filled club, formerly the Sound Factory, is like stepping into to the 21st century. The multicolor, odd-shape, flashing lights and the first-class sound system are almost extraterrestrial. Blast off is at 11 PM; although admission is a hefty $20, for a heady dance trip, Twilo's is worth it. *530 W. 27th St.,* ☎ *212/268–1600. Crowd: mixed on Fri.; mostly gay on Sat.; always good looking and into serious dancing.*

OTHER OPTIONS

The Tunnel (220 12th Ave., ☎ 212/695–8238) has a huge, mixed gay/straight party on Saturdays—the crowd progressively faggier as the night goes on, is glowing pink by morning. **Webster Hall** (125 E. 11th St., ☎ 212/353–1600), a huge club big with straight, bridge-and-tunnel kids, no longer has a specific gay night, but it's almost always pretty gay-friendly.

Women's Bars

Crazy Nanny's. The biggest dyke bar in the city is painted a striking shade of purple, so you can't miss it. Downstairs there's a video bar that gets rocking only on weekends. Upstairs is a sizable dance floor with a DJ booth and an invariably big crowd sashaying away. Off of that is a no-frills lounge with a bunch of benches against the wall. There's also an extremely popular pool table. Nanny's doesn't get going till pretty late, usually after midnight. *21 7th Ave. S,* ☎ *212/366–6312. Crowd: mostly women (men only with female friends), young; about half African-American and Latino; cruisy; boisterous, fairly working-class; lots of diesel dykes, downtown vagabonds, Sinead O'Connor wannabes, backwards baseball caps.*

Cubbyhole. This sleepy fern bar has bright green walls and windows looking out onto lively 12th Street. It's a nice place to chat with old friends or to sit around watching the tube. The kind of place where you'll bump into your high school phys ed teacher. Formerly D. T. Fat Cats. *281 W. 12th St.,* ☎ *212/243–9041. Crowd: mostly women, mostly over 35; low-key, casual.*

Henrietta Hudson. This is a cozy corner bar with attractive weathered-wood paneling, hardwood floors, and a classic old-fashioned bar—the whole place feels like an old ale house. The small bar up front is usually packed on weekends. A jukebox plays middle-of-the road dance and pop tunes. Long lines to the bathroom. *438 Hudson St.,* ☎ *212/924–3347.*

Crowd: 85/15 f/m, mostly ages 20s and 30s; white-bread, friendly, down-to-earth; fairly professional.

Julie's. This classy, lively, popular bar is on the same upscale block as the Townhouse restaurant (*see* Eats, *above*). Upon entering you're at a long bar with stools, beyond which is a small standing area that opens into a larger (but still compact) dance floor. It's decorated like somebody's parlor, but the stuffiness stops there: The staff is friendly and outgoing; the patrons outgoing if not downright wild (especially late in the evening). *204 E. 58th St., ☎ 212/688–1294. Crowd: mostly women, mid-20s to late-30s; well-heeled, professional, lots of stylish duds and expensive coifs.*

Rubyfruit Bar. This upbeat restaurant has a popular cocktail bar and is in the heart of Hudson Street's dining and nightlife action. Has become increasingly lesbian over the past couple of years. *531 Hudson St., ☎ 212/929–3343. Crowd: mostly female; otherwise diverse.*

Lesbian One-Nighters

Though it's held only on Friday nights, the **Clit Club** (432 W. 14th St., ☎ 212/529–3300) is the hottest dyke party in the city—a feast of boots and bras. Gorgeous go-go girls work the sweaty dance crowd upstairs; downstairs there's a crowded lounge where you'll find a lot of dykes cruising and flirting and many more getting rather hot and heavy. Very young, hip crowd. Women only.

It's **No Man's Land** at the Boiler Room (*see* East Village bars, *above*) on Sunday. This party draws an alternative bunch—lots of retro granny dresses and beads. Despite the name, gay men are welcome, too.

Juicy (Buddha Bar, 150 Varick St., ☎ 212/255–4433), on alternating Sunday nights, draws together the most stylish bunch of lesbians and bisexual women in the city (Naomi Campbell is said to pop in from time to time)—plus a few chic fags. All night a gorgeous gaggle of go-go girls dances on platforms in the center of the room—in another room there's a pool table and plenty of space for mingling.

Sundays at Cafe Tabac (232 E. 9th St., ☎ 212/674–7072) draws a slightly younger—more hip but less elegant—bunch than Glamourpussy. The L-shape bar is open for women on Sunday. There's a pool table, lots of mingling, and decent house music—although there isn't really much room to dance.

A lot of the regulars you see at Julie's attend the popular roving parties organized by **Shescapes** (☎ 212/645–6479).

Lend Me Your Ears . . .

Piano cabarets are a strength of the West Village, and they make a lovely, low-key venue for chatting with old friends or first dates, or for gently breaking your straight friends and family in to gay culture. Most popular are the cozy **Five Oaks** (49 Grove St., ☎ 212/243–8885), which is a bit shaggy but entirely lovable; **Marie's Crisis** (59 Grove St., ☎ 212/243–9323), which is extremely shaggy—even dumpy—and almost lovable; **Rose's Turn** (55 Grove St., ☎ 212/366–5438), which is the coziest and queerest of all; and **Eighty-Eights** (228 W. 10th St., ☎ 212/924–0088), which has top-notch performers in its upstairs cabaret (a cover is usually charged) and a laid-back piano scene downstairs. Though not strictly gay, this is one of the warmest and most colorful piano bars in the city. On Saturday nights, drop by the downstairs lounge to hear the owner and a gaggle of what appear to be unemployed Broadway singers belt out several hits from *The Sound of Music*. Equally charming, more popular (but also a bit cramped) is the famous **Duplex** (61 Christopher St., ☎ 212/255–5438), which has cabaret shows and stand-up comedians and a tiny, cozy little bar upstairs. Here also, the crowd is mixed gay and straight.

Pegasus (119 E. 60th St., ☎ 212/888–4702) is a stylish cabaret bar around the corner from Barneys Midtown. Up front is a terrific, friendly little bar—in back is the piano. It's all smartly decorated, and gets an older, classy crowd. In the Theater District, right along Restaurant Row, is little **Don't Tell Mama** (343 W. 46th St., ☎ 212/757–0788), a mixed gay/straight piano bar and cabaret featuring some outstanding acts.

Nontraditional Parties

Two local organizations regularly hold great parties outside of the traditional club scene. During the school year, Columbia University's gay student alliance presents the **Columbia Gay Dance** (Earl Hall, Broadway and 116th St., ☎ 212/629–1989) on the first Friday and third Saturdays of every month. The entry fee and three cans of beer cost less than the average club cover, and the music is decent (local DJs from popular gay clubs alternate). The crowd is two-thirds college-age, the rest wishing they still were; it's about three to one male to female. Definitely not your typical college dance!

The least snobby and most inviting parties in Manhattan are the infectious dances held at the **Lesbian & Gay Community Center** (208 W. 13th St., ☎ 212/620–7310). A diverse, outgoing crowd and surprisingly good music make this place a winner.

Movable Fetes

For details on Manhattan's numerous circuit parties, call the **Saint-at-Large** (☎ 212/674–8541).

Some long-running dance gatherings include the very gay danceathon, **Milk** (☎ 212/629–1911; Mon.); **Sugar Babies** (☎ 212/777–6800; Mon.), an esteemed, deep-house party that's been hot for several years now; **Clubhouse** (☎ 212/726–8820; Wed.), a trash-disco and fairly mainstream house party held at Hollings (215 W. 28th St.); **Gotham Rodeo** (☎ 212/570–7399; Sat.), one of the city's only gay and lesbian two-stepping and country line-dancing get-togethers; and **Café con Leche** (☎ 212/819–0377; Sun.), a charged, Latin dance party with a particularly mixed gay/straight crowd.

A few urbane, stylish salons include **Bar d'O** (29 Bedford St., ☎ 212/627–1580; Tues., Sat.–Sun.), which is big with admirers of drag; **Jackie 60** (432 W. 14th St., ☎ 212/677–6060, Tues.), a carnivalesque freak show out to shock the masses with performance art and both planned and spontaneous acts of mayhem; **Nation** (50 Ave. A, ☎ 212/473–6239; Fri.), a bohemianized soul and funk party in the East Village; and **Salon Wednesdays** (219 2nd Ave., ☎ 212/533–2860; Wed.), an I'm-too-slick-for-words, drag-hosted mixer at the chic restaurant, Flamingo East.

The most distinctive weekly event is **Squeezebox,** which is held Fridays at Don Hill's in SoHo (511 Greenwich St., ☎ 212/334–1390). Here an ensemble of drag queens burns up the stage (they're actually very talented musicians) with high-decibel renderings of both classic and original rock, punk, and heavy metal tunes. In between acts, favorite metal songs from the past are pumped over the sound system. This is a must-do for queer metalheads, but it's a kick for just about anybody. Lots of good old-fashioned slam-dancing. The crowd is about two-thirds male, and two-thirds queer, with lots of glam queens, Metallica T-shirts, grungers, latter-day punks, and the like.

On the Wild Side

Despite anything you may have heard about a crackdown on bathhouses, sex clubs, X-rated movie houses, video booths, and all-around debauchery, there is far more sleaze in New York City than can possibly be catalogued here. Look to the fag rags for the full story.

In Times Square, the **Gaiety** (201 W. 46th St., ☎ 212/391–9806) is without question the best place to watch male strippers—it does, after all, feature some of the boys you may have·seen in Madonna's book, *Sex*. This place draws a diverse—actually rather upstanding—crowd, and the shows often include some of the adult-film industry's better known performers.

Bijou Theater. For some reason, New York's most action-packed playground of sleaze is never written up in publications. And what's more, there's no telephone number and no sign on the front door. Word gets around, though, because after the East Village bars close, this place gets pretty busy. A $10 cover entitles you to the full run of this basement complex, which comprises a few fairly well-lighted lounges, a bar that distributes free soda and Oreo cookies, a small adult video theater (be careful, the seats come unhinged easily), and a few dark corridors with some private rooms. The Bijou is not very carefully monitored, but one of the lounges is a shrine to safe-sex education and AIDS awareness. *82 E. 4th St., no ☎. Crowd: male, mostly under 35; down-to-earth but adventuresome.*

J's Hangout. Everyone seems to refer to this as a sex club, but relatively few guys come here exclusively, or even peripherally, for this purpose. Most just come because it's one of the few places without loud music that's open after the bars close—it operates from 11 PM to 11 AM, but nobody with any self-respect arrives before 3 AM. *675 Hudson St., ☎ 212/242–9292. Crowd: male, butch; varied in age but mostly older.*

Load. Inside this Chelsea hot spot is a long corridor with rest rooms and a large, dark room that's cordoned off by hanging curtains. While the music plays, so do the boys. *36 W. 17th St., ☎ 212/243–3425. Crowd: young and on the prowl.*

Unicorn. Plenty of fun is only $10 and a turnstile away in this porn video and magazine store. On the ground floor there is a video arcade; downstairs there are more video booths, little rooms with video screens, and a large dungeon space. *277C W. 22nd St., ☎ 212/924–2921. Crowd: young; lots of guys from the Barracuda, next door.*

THE LITTLE BLACK BOOK

At Your Fingertips

AIDS Hotline: ☎ 718/768–0221. **AIDS Resources Hotline:** N.Y.C. Dept. of Health, ☎ 212/447–8200. **Bisexual Information and Counseling Service:** ☎ 212/496–9500. **Community Health Project:** ☎ 212/675–3559. **Lesbian and Gay Community Services Center:** 208 W. 13th St., ☎ 212/620–7310. **Lesbian Switchboard:** ☎ 212/741–2610. **New York Convention and Visitors Bureau:** 2 Columbus Circle, 10019, ☎ 212/397–8222 or 212/484–1200. **New York City Police Department Liaison to the Lesbian and Gay Community:** ☎ 212/374–2366.

Gay Media

New York City has two excellent weekly bar rags, **Homo Extra** (*HX*, ☎ 212/627–0747), which is black-and-white, and **Next** (☎ 212/627–0165), which is color. Both are produced by club promoters and used to advertise their own events, but they have detailed and helpful listings on all bars and gay-popular restaurants. Neither gives very much information about lesbian venues, though *HX* does a slightly better job. **Sappho's Isle** (☎ 516/676–7909), though published in the suburbs, is a much better lesbian source for news and events concerning New York City.

The city's only true gay-and-lesbian newsweekly, **New York Native** (☎ 212/627–2120), is rather lame considering all of the fine papers produced in cities much smaller than this one. You might also check out **MetroSource** (☎ 212/691–5127), a quarterly directory of community businesses with articles and entertainment coverage, too. **Body Positive** (☎ 212/566–7333) is an excellent resource for persons affected by HIV and AIDS. **Christopher Street** (☎ 212/627–2120) is an arts-and-entertainment-oriented magazine.

BOOKSTORES

Since moving into bright and spacious new digs in Chelsea, **A Different Light** (151 W. 19th St., ☎ 212/989–4850) has become one of the country's best lesbigay bookstores; it now has a great little café, too. Though it's tiny, the **Oscar Wilde Bookstore** (15 Christopher St., ☎ 212/255–8097) has been serving the community since 1967; in addition to books, it sells lots of gay jewelry and gifts. **Creative Visions** (548 Hudson St., ☎ 212/645–7573) stands in the little space A Different Light vacated; it has a limited number of titles and a small coffee bar. Next door is **Gay Pleasures** (☎ 212/255–5756), one of the city's best purveyors of gay and lesbian erotica, porn, and various odds and ends. The sugary-named **Rainbows and Triangles** (192 8th Ave., ☎ 212/627–2166), though not exactly a bookstore, has tons of gay cards, gifts, CDs, magazines, and a few books.

A few mainstream bookstores worth checking out are the **Biography Bookshop** (400 Bleecker St., ☎ 212/807–8655), which has a number of gay and lesbian biographies and diaries; the **Strand** (828 Broadway, ☎ 212/473–1452), with its eight miles of shelves of used books; and **Hotaling's News** (142 W. 42nd St., ☎ 212/840–1868), which carries daily newspapers from hundreds of cities around the world, plus a vast selection of magazines.

Body and Fitness

There are a zillion good places to work out in Manhattan, and just about all of them, except for the **New York Health and Racquet Club** and **Equinox** chains, have strong gay followings. Your best deal will be had at either of the following branches of the **YMCA:** the Vanderbilt (224 E. 47th St., ☎ 212/756–9600), which gets the most corporate crowd; and the McBurney branch (215 W. 23rd St., ☎ 212/741–9210), which is in Chelsea, but because it's such a dreary facility gets a sort of dreary crowd. Also in Chelsea is the **David Barton Gym** (552 6th Ave., ☎ 212/727–0004), where pretty boys work out (once they've attained an already perfect body by working out for a few years at some lesser gym); the **Chelsea Gym** (267 W. 17th St., ☎ 212/255–1150), which has been the city's gayest— and cruisiest—gym for more than a decade; and the fairly new **American Fitness Center** (128 8th Ave., ☎ 212/627–0065), a huge, clean facility that's popular with gay men and lesbians. The crowd at **Better Bodies** (22 W. 19th St., ☎ 212/929–6789) is more serious and less chatty than at other gyms. It has a wide array of equipment and plenty of space.

16 *Out in Palm Springs*

IT WAS IN THE 1930s THAT WELL-TO-DO Hollywood types first discovered Palm Springs's virtues as a resort. And if you drive the couple of hours it takes to get here from either Los Angeles or San Diego, you'll see what attracted them. As you weave along I–10 through the Coachella Valley, patches of green become rare, and tawny mountain peaks begin to dominate the barren landscape. Once you come around the last few bends in the road on your final approach to Palm Springs and behold the miles of lush, green golf courses, lawns, and gardens (all fed by the region's prolific springs), you'll understand the appeal of this treasured oasis.

From the city's beginnings, gay people have maintained a steady if discreet presence here, but only in the early '70s did a specifically gay resort open. In the early '80s several more followed, as did some bars and gay-owned shops and restaurants, and in the late '80s, development boomed as Palm Springs emerged as one of the most exclusive getaways in America. In the last few years, however, tourism—gay and straight—has leveled off, which is bad for innkeepers, but good for tourists who are finding rates here a little easier to take than they were a few years back. The region's popularity as a gay destination doesn't appear to be in jeopardy, but overbuilding and overspeculation, coupled with the emerging popularity of northern Arizona and New Mexico, suggest that the city's growth and appeal is not without limit. On the other hand, the area buzzes with a higher charge of sexual energy than any other gay resort in the western half of the country. Palm Springs may always remain popular with at least gay society's bon vivants.

It's difficult to appreciate much of what makes this region so breathtaking—the beauty of the mountains and the high desert—from town. Palm Springs and its neighboring communities—Cathedral City, Rancho Mirage, Palm Desert, and Indio—are densely settled and somewhat insulated from the surrounding wilderness. Zoning restricts the use of neon and electric signs, and keeps buildings below five stories. Nevertheless, you'll encounter a fair number of bland, windowless shopping centers and condos next to the lovely hacienda-style homes and resorts.

None of these towns has a viable geographic center that reins in the sprawl and provides visitors with a recognizable hub, with the possible exception of Palm Springs's own small village green. The sweltering heat may be responsible. Locals spend a lot of time indoors, and in every shopping plaza and structure, aesthetic appeal seems to have taken a back seat to keeping people cool.

That said, Palm Springs is slow-paced and casual most of the year; only during winter does the place become markedly more lively and diverse. Certain aspects of the city's gay scene are as image-conscious and party-driven as L.A.'s, but Palm Springs is chiefly a place to unwind, lie in the buff around the pool, and catch up with old friends.

THE LAY OF THE LAND

Most gay resorts are in the southeastern part of town, a section framed by Ramon Road to the north, Sunrise Way to the east, South Palm Canyon Drive to the west, and East Palm Canyon Drive to the south. Most gay-oriented businesses are here as well, though some are scattered around town. Most bars, many gay restaurants, and a few gay resorts are in the next town over, **Cathedral City,** which you reach by continuing southeast out of Palm Springs on East Palm Canyon Drive. This town's activity is concentrated in a small quadrant defined by Perez Road to the north and west, Cathedral Canyon Drive to the east, and East Palm Canyon Drive to the south.

Downtown Palm Springs
North Palm Canyon Drive, the city's commercial spine, used to have the shopping cachet of Beverly Hills's Rodeo Drive, but it's become considerably more pedestrian. Many boutiques specialize in the sorts of keepsakes and gaudy glitter-wear of other sunny resort towns. There aren't many gay-oriented shops, except in a small stretch centered around the gay-popular men's clothier **R&R Menswear** (333 N. Palm Canyon Dr., ☏ 619/320–3007). These include **Sophia's** (326 N. Palm Canyon Dr., ☏ 619/320–7551), a souvenir and T-shirt shop; and **Craig & Craig Booksellers** (333 N. Palm Canyon Dr., ☏ 619/323–7379), which, though not a lesbigay bookstore, has a great selection of used books (including many first editions) and lots of titles covering Hollywood's film industry. A bit north of here is a deliciously tacky '50s furniture store, the **Village Attic** (798 N. Palm Canyon Dr., ☏ 619/320–6165), which has a selection of kidney-shape and molded-plywood furniture.

For a phenomenal view of the desert, take the quick hop on the **Palm Springs Aerial Tramway** (☏ 619/325–1391) to the peak of Mt. San Gorgonio. To get to the base, follow Tram Hill Road from downtown's Highway 111 about 3½ miles. The 20-minute tram ride takes you to an elevation of about 8,500 feet and allows views of up to 75 miles.

Farther Afield
The leading attraction in the vicinity are the **Indian Canyons** (end of S. Palm Canyon Dr., ☏ 619/325–5673), which are about 5 miles south of Palm Springs. Here you can visit four of the several canyons inhabited for centuries by Agua Caliente Indians. You'll find the foundations of ancient dwellings, pictographs, and a wealth of fascinating hiking trails.

Should you have a more serious yearning for a good hike or scenic drive, spend a day at the half-million-acre **Joshua Tree National Park,** which is an hour from Palm Springs on Route 62. Information can be obtained from the **Oasis Visitor Center** (74485 National Park Dr., Twentynine Palms, 92277, ☏ 619/367–7511). Joshua Tree comprises parts of two deserts, the higher Mojave—which is studded with the distinctive trees for which the park is named—and the lower, and somewhat less interesting, Colorado Desert (carpeted with wildflowers in spring). Hiking, rock climbing, and mountain biking are among the many draws. The park's 40-mile road has dozens of scenic overlooks and interpretive signs.

GETTING THERE

Palm Springs is a straight, though sometimes congested, shot down I–10 from Los Angeles, and an only slightly longer and more convoluted drive from San Diego. Las Vegas and Phoenix are also within a half-day's drive. There's ample public transportation by plane, bus, and train.

GETTING AROUND

You'll need a car. There are few walkable neighborhoods, and most shops are in shopping centers and malls. Virtually all the gay establishments are in Palm Springs and Cathedral City.

WHEN TO GO

It's a fiery hell here much of the year. You'll be assured again and again by locals that "it's a dry heat" and that your blood begins to thin within days, but 110°F is still 110°F—this is a typical high from late May through early October. These months are, not surprisingly, Palm Springs's slowest, but it's a great time to find hotel bargains; just pace yourself and drink plenty of fluids. The most crowded and expensive times to visit are late November (when the gay rodeo comes to town), Christmas, and late March through April. The hottest and most celebrated lesbian party in America occurs during the week of the **Dinah Shore LPGA Championship** (late March or early April)—book months ahead if you don't want to miss this legendary event. February through late March is cool and slightly less crowded—a great time to visit.

EATS

The dining landscape is dominated by traditional Italian restaurants, steak houses, fast-food restaurants, and pubs. Some of the nicer hotels have good food (notably the Ritz-Carlton), but this is still largely a retirement community, so most of the cuisine is comparatively tame and old-fashioned. Most of the restaurants with strong gay followings are in Cathedral City.

For price ranges, *see* Chart B at the front of this guide.

Palm Springs

$$–$$$ **Billy Reed's.** The nice thing about this Palm Springs institution is that lunch entrées can be ordered all day, and they're just as good as, and quite a bit cheaper than, the dinner fare. The place looks like an old brothel, has plenty of spunk, and has a roster of entertainers who appear as impersonators of your favorite stars. The traditional American food is perfectly good but unspectacular. *1800 N. Palm Canyon Dr.,* ☎ *619/325–1946.*

$–$$ **La Tacqueria.** This airy, inexpensive Mexican restaurant in the heart of Palm Springs has dozens of veggie dishes, build-your-own tacos, and oversize platters of fresh food. It's one of the best options in town for south-of-the-border specialties. There are two other branches in Palm Desert. *125 E. Tahquitz Way,* ☎ *619/778–5391; 72–286 Hwy. 111, Suite J5, Desert Palm,* ☎ *619/776–8240.*

$ **Elmer's Pancake and Steak House.** The specialties of this low-budget, no-frills pseudo-Denny's pretty well sum up the strengths of Palm Springs restaurants: good old American standbys. The food truly is good, and the people-watching is even better. *1030 E. Palm Canyon Dr.,* ☎ *619/327–8419.*

248

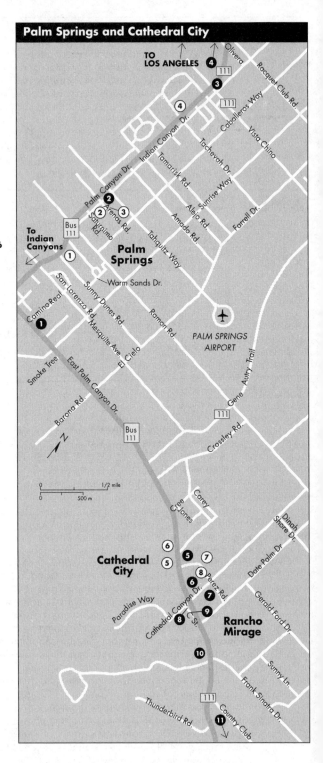

Palm Springs and Cathedral City

Cathedral City

$$$–$$$$ **The Wilde Goose.** The rare Cathedral City restaurants that draws celebrities down from Palm Springs, this pricey, classy spot serves stellar Continental fare (the '80s decor could use some updating, though). Five varieties of duck (plus a chilled duck salad), several wild game dishes, and decent lobster are usually offered. *67–938 Hwy. 111,* ☎ *619/328–5775.*

$$–$$$$ **Shame on the Moon.** One of the more cheerfully decorated restaurants in Cathedral City, this sleek bistro successfully follows the popular L.A. dining room recipe of track lighting, black furniture, and white walls. The traditional Continental fare throws out few surprises, but is consistently good—favorites include pasta bolognese, medallions of pork, and fresh seafood with pasta. *69–950 Frank Sinatra Dr., just off Hwy. 111, Rancho Mirage,* ☎ *619/324–5515.*

$$–$$$ **Richard's.** In a squat, pink brick building, Richard's feels like a cocktail lounge and steak house straight out of the '70s. The dark dining room has lots of heavy furniture and a long bar with red vinyl seats. The straightforward Continental cuisine—grilled eggplant, salmon piccata with lemon and capers—is ordinary but reliable. Piano entertainment nightly. Very old-school gay. *68–599 Hwy. 111,* ☎ *619/321–2841.*

$ **KC's.** In a new shopping center by the police station, KC's is a festive luncheonette with cheerful maroon and blue-green tablecloths and attractive Southwestern photos on the walls. They serve great comfort food—Oriental chicken salad, burgers, good Cajun fries, and tasty crab melts. Has a diverse and very gay following. *68–625 Perez Rd.,* ☎ *619/ 324–7044.*

$ **The Red Pepper.** Opened by the same folks who own the Red Tomato (*see below*), this restaurant is a big hit with the gay community. The menu is similar to that of its sister eatery. *36650 Sunair Pl.,* ☎ *619/770–7007.*

$ **The Red Tomato.** This pizza parlor whose name celebrates juicy red tomatoes is actually best known for garlicky white pies. But all types of pizzas are baked to perfection, and the crowd always includes a few cute queens. *Hwy. 111 at Van Fleet St.,* ☎ *619/328–7518.*

Coffeehouse Culture

Jeremy's Cappuccino Bar and Beer Haus (*61597* Twentynine Palms Hwy., at Sunset, ☎ 619/366–9799) might be the only legitimate piece of funk in the desert (it's actually several miles from Palm Springs up by Joshua Tree National Park). A great spot for cheap caffeinated or alcoholic drinks, Jeremy's also has lots of veggie sandwiches, bagels, and snacks. Occasional live rock music, too.

SLEEPS

When it comes to service and in-room amenities (and the friendliness of innkeepers), Palm Springs is like no other gay vacation hub in the country. A resort generally won't survive here without at least one pool, a misting machine (indispensable on sundecks, especially from May through October), new furnishings, large guest rooms, and in most cases, VCRs in all rooms along with an extensive adult video library. On the other hand, although resorts are consistently plush and clean, the quaintness factor of Key West or Provincetown is totally absent. If you have an aversion to chrome and mirrors, you may have difficulty with Palm Springs. Finally, this is the most hormonally charged resort scene on the planet, and hence, at least in season, not the ideal destination for a quiet, romantic retreat. Social butterflies will find plenty of opportunity to flutter their wings.

While much of the gay dining and nightlife is in Cathedral City, about two-thirds of the area's gay resorts are in two clusters just south of Palm Springs's commercial district. The more upscale resorts are in the **Warm Sands** area, and the older and more affordable properties are another ½ mile south of here in the **San Lorenzo** area. The remaining third of the properties are scattered among Palm Springs and Cathedral City, many of them along Highway 111. In general, you should be able to get a perfectly nice one-bedroom unit with a kitchen and a pool view, for $80 to $100 in season, as little as $60 the rest of the year. For lower rates, hit one of the cheaper chains along Highway 111.

Very few gay resorts have a mix of men and women, and only two are specifically for lesbians. This means that in high season a good number of dykes wind up at mainstream resorts, most of which are extremely gay-friendly. Some of the best are below.

For price ranges, *see* Chart B at the front of this guide.

Mainstream Resorts and Motels

⌂ Small, secluded, and popular with Hollywood personalities who wish to avoid the crowds of a full-scale resort, the **Ingleside Inn** has antiques-filled rooms and a popular restaurant. *200 W. Ramon Rd.,* ☎ *619/325–0046 or 800/772–6655. 30 rooms. $$$$*

⌂ The palatial **La Quinta Hotel Golf and Tennis Resort,** a revered compound of Spanish-style casitas, has been hosting celebrities since 1926. Frank Capra once lived on the grounds, and Greta Garbo was a frequent guest. In addition to having the top golfing facilities in the area, La Quinta has 25 swimming pools, 35 hot tubs, and 30 tennis courts. *49–499 Eisenhower Dr., La Quinta,* ☎ *619/564–4111 or 800/598–3828. 640 rooms. $$$$*

⌂ The **Ritz-Carlton Rancho Mirage** is where the monied queens are most likely to roost. Rooms are fairly ordinary for a luxury resort, but the property's location in the foothills of the Santa Rosa Mountains affords guests spectacular views. *68–900 Frank Sinatra Dr., Rancho Mirage,* ☎ *619/321–8282 or 800/241–3333. 240 rooms. $$$$*

⌂ The centrally located **Wyndham Palm Springs,** the site of many gay conventions and gatherings, has gracious and expansive grounds and pools and is within walking distance of Palm Springs's three gay bars. The staff here is attentive and friendly, and rooms are large and brightly furnished. *888 E. Tahquitz Canyon Way,* ☎ *619/322–6000 or 800/822–4200. 568 rooms. $$$*

⌂ Always a safe bet is the clean, new **Courtyard by Marriott.** *1300 Tahquitz Canyon Way,* ☎ *619/322–6100 or 800/321–2211. 149 rooms. $–$$*

⌂ If you're on a budget and want to be within walking distance of downtown, pick the no-frills **Roadway Inn.** Rooms are small and dreary, but the crowd is young and usually congregates around the two pools. *390 S. Indian Canyon Dr.,* ☎ *619/322–8789. 107 rooms. $*

⌂ A shorter drive from Cathedral City, the **Travelodge** is another good budget option; its rooms are larger than those at the Roadway, and it's very popular with gays and lesbians. *333 E. Palm Canyon Dr.,* ☎ *619/327–1211 or 800/578–7878. 169 rooms. $*

Gay Resorts and Guest Houses

Warm Sands

⌂ The **Atrium, Mirage, and Vista Grande Villa** make up a complex of guest houses that has a reputation for fun-loving, wild, and horny guys. Nudity certainly isn't required around the grounds, but it's as common here as at any other property in town. Also, all rooms have VCRs and there's a library of more than 200 adult films. Guests can wander freely among the three properties, whose grounds are gussied up with some fairly campy touches—waterfalls, Flintstones-inspired lagoons, pink flamingos. Rooms are clean and bright but otherwise not memorable. *574 Warm Sands Dr.,* ☎ *619/322–2404 or 800/669–1069. 20 rooms. Gay male. $$–$$$*

The sprawling, three-year-old **Desert Paradise** has one of the nicest pools in town, giving it the feel of a truly first-rate resort. The rooms are furnished in contemporary style; all have VCRs with plenty of movies to choose from. Appeals to a younger crowd. *615 Warm Sands Dr.,* ☎ *619/320–5650 or 800/342–7635. 12 rooms. Gay male. $$–$$$*

☷ Howard Hughes, in a bid to woo Elizabeth Taylor, built **El Mirasol** in 1940 for the actress's mother. In 1974 it was opened as the first gay resort in Palm Springs, and although many newer and fancier properties have bloomed around it, El Mirasol still retains a good bit of charm. The grounds are full of native trees, fountains, and beautiful gardens (all visited by dozens of exotic birds), and there are two bright pool areas. Rooms are simply furnished, but all have kitchens. *525 Warm Sands Dr.,* ☎ *619/327–5913 or 800/327–2985. 15 rooms. Mostly gay male. $$–$$$*

☷ If only every resort in Palm Springs were as efficiently and thoughtfully run as **Hacienda En Sueno,** one of the town's oldest gay properties. Each room has a kitchen, and three on-site pantries are stocked with booze, soft drinks, and hundreds of different foods—simply sign for what you want. This system reflects the management's overall philosophy—they truly want to show you a good time. Of the guest rooms, the front ones with red-tile floors are the nicest, but all rooms are large. Two pools. *586 Warm Sands Dr.,* ☎ *619/327–8111 or 800/359–2007. 7 rooms. Mostly gay male. $$–$$$*

☷ Of the more social resorts, the neatly landscaped **InnTrigue** is the most tasteful and down-to-earth. It's run by, and seems to attract, a genuinely nice, though fairly young, bunch of guys. Having so many rooms puts the place somewhere between a guest house and a small hotel. All of the rooms are poolside (there are two pools) and all have microwaves; the efficiencies are nice for long stays. *526 Warm Sands Dr.,* ☎ *619/323–7505 or 800/798–8781. 28 rooms. Gay male. $$–$$$*

☷ The **Whispering Palms** isn't everybody's cup of tea, but it has developed a loyal following over the years—mostly frisky guys 35 and older who are comfortable wandering around in the buff. Rooms have outlandish tropical decor; each has a kitschy glow-in-the-dark diorama mounted above the door. There's a small (some might say intimate) pool in back with a small bar. *545 Warm Sands Dr.,* ☎ *619/327–6413 or 800/669–9276. 7 rooms. Gay male. $$–$$$*

☷ The adobe-style **Inn Exile** is a pale blue low rise with a striking Spanish-tile roof. The rooms are a bit more basic than most in this neighborhood, but the staff is very friendly, and the guests are young and pretty. There's also a small gym with erotic photos on the walls and a "social room" called the Gang Way—that should tell you something. *960 Camino Parocela,* ☎ *619/327–6413 or 800/962–0186. 15 rooms. Gay male. $$*

☷ If you want a kitchen and dining area in your room, the **Sago Palms** is one of the best deals in town. It's just a block from the properties on Warm Sands Drive, on a quieter street. The low number of rooms means there's never a huge crowd around the pool or in the small gym. Rooms have an eclectic array of Sears-type furnishings, but they're clean and fairly large; the one suite has a fireplace. *595 Thornhill Rd.,* ☎ *619/323–0224 or 800/626–7246. 6 rooms. Gay male. $$*

☷ A good, solid option, the **Alexander Resort** is not as fancy or sleek as some of the other resorts in the neighborhood, but the owners are friendly, the rates are decent, and many rooms have kitchens. Several also have unusual art deco showers. *598 Grenfall Rd.,* ☎ *619/327–6911 or 800/448–6197. 8 rooms. Gay male. $–$$*

San Lorenzo Road

☷ Though it's not especially attractive from the street, the **Triangle Inn** is the nicest resort on San Lorenzo. Rooms are quite sumptuous, with such creature comforts as CD players and extensively equipped kitchens. Many of the suites have two bedrooms. *555 San Lorenzo Rd.,* ☎ *619/322– 7993 or 800/732–7555. 9 rooms. Gay male. $$–$$$$*

☷ One of the few exclusively all-women guest houses in the area, **Delilah's Enclave** is a clean, charming house with Southwestern decor. It's surrounded by parklike grounds on which you'll find a sizeable swimming pool, a Jacuzzi, and a barbecue area. Half the rooms have full kitchens; the other half are for "bachelorettes." Pets are welcome. *641 San Lorenzo Rd.,* ☎ *619/325–5269. Lesbian. $$*

☷ **Camp Palm Springs** is a modern motel-style guest house with peculiar L-shape pillars bracketing the building's facade. Rooms have standard furnishings but come in varied configurations (it's good for three or four guys traveling together). A few rooms are themed: The Taos Townhouse has some Southwestern pieces; the Key West Studio has a suitably tropical theme. From the nightly cocktail parties to the continual frolicking around the pool, it's always abuzz with activity. *722 San Lorenzo Rd.,* ☎ *619/322–2267 or 800/793–0063. 20 rooms. Gay Male $–$$$*

☷ **A Place in the Sun** is a squat complex of converted apartments with an unusually expansive courtyard, neatly kept gardens, a lattice-shaded porch overlooking the pool, and neat little bungalows with white Spanish-style tile roofs. There aren't many luxe amenities in the rooms, but this is a good economical choice. *754 San Lorenzo Rd.,* ☎ *619/325–0254 or 800/779–2254. 16 bungalows. Mixed gay/straight. $–$$*

☷ There isn't anything that sets the run-of-the-mill **Avanti** above other properties in town. It has a standard pool, reasonably large rooms (some with kitchens), VCRs and TVs, and either private or shared baths. Very casual. *715 San Lorenzo Rd.,* ☎ *619/325–9723 or 800/572–2779. 14 rooms. Gay male. $–$$*

Elsewhere in Palm Springs

☷ Owned by the same people who run the El Alameda and Casablanca (*see below*), **Abbey West** is a luxury gay resort in the heart of Palm Springs; the sleek, art deco rooms are named after celebs (Bogart, Bergman, Garbo), average nearly 500 square feet, and have kitchenettes and modem hookups. The grounds are beautiful and there's a bar on the premises. *772 Prescott Circle,* ☎ *619/320–4333 or 800/223–4073. 17 rooms. Mostly gay male. $$$–$$$$*

☷ Rooms at the **Casablanca** have a softer, more traditional look than at the other Harlow Club properties, but they're just as luxurious. This place is also smaller and more intimate. Otherwise, the atmosphere and amenities are quite similar to the other two. *2095 N. Indian Canyon Rd.,* ☎ *619/320–4333 or 800/223–4073. 12 rooms. Mostly gay male. $$$–$$$$*

☷ The discreet, high-end **El Alameda** is the only men-only property within the Harlow Club group of luxury gay properties. Consequently, things are a bit more active here, and nudity on the sundeck is more common than at the others. Each room comes with a chilled bottle of chardonnay and snacks. *175 El Alameda,* ☎ *619/323–3977 or 800/223–4073. 15 rooms. Gay male. $$$–$$$$*

☷ The **Bee Charmer,** one of the most charming women's resorts you'll find, is clean and attractive, with a striking bronze-tile roof and a very private, enclosed pool. First-floor rooms have tile floors, upstairs rooms are carpeted, and all have bright tropical decor. *1600 E. Palm Canyon Dr.,* ☎ *619/778–5883. 13 rooms. Lesbian. $$*

⌂ Next door to the Bee Charmer, the **Smoke Tree** has been serving lesbians for more than a decade but now caters to a mixed clientele. Not quite as dapper as its neighbor, it's nonetheless quite an attractive option. The grounds are lushly landscaped, and the large, carpeted rooms are clean and comfy—many have quilts and wicker furniture; five have full kitchens. The pool, whirlpool, and sunning area are surrounded by fruit trees. *1586 E. Palm Canyon Dr.,* ☎ *619/323–2231. 11 rooms. Mixed gay/straight. $$*

⌂ One of the newer gay resorts in the desert, the **Canyon Club Hotel** offers plenty of value—and it's a short walk from downtown shopping and restaurants. Rooms have typical motel furnishings and completely surround a pool and sundeck. *960 N. Palm Canyon Dr.,* ☎ *619/322–4367 or 800/295–2582. 32 rooms. Gay male. $–$$*

Cathedral City

⌂ Behind the Target shopping center and Camelot Amusement Park, the **Desert Palms Inn** is a lively gay resort with a fairly rambunctious following of men and women. The café and bar are popular enough to draw nonguests, and the Inn stays busy year-round. The perfect spot for those who like to party. Rooms are like those of any inexpensive chain motel, but the pool and sunning area are quite nice. *67–580 E. Palm Canyon Dr.,* ☎ *619/324–3000 or 800/801–8696. 29 rooms. Mixed gay/lesbian. $–$$*

⌂ One of the West Coast's largest gay resorts, **The Villa** is a secluded, shady spot run by friendly guys. Only a few hundred yards from the Desert Palms Inn, the Villa draws a somewhat older and more laid-back bunch. Rooms are bright and spacious, and the rates here are lower than at comparable properties on Warm Sands Drive. *67–670 Carey Rd.,* ☎ *619/328–7211 or 800/845–5265. 44 rooms. Mostly gay male. $–$$*

SCENES

In general, the high-season club scene here is not unlike that at Fire Island, Key West, or Provincetown: The biggest discos are packed with every kind of guy and a smaller contingent of women, and each season, specific establishments become *the* places to haunt at particular times of the day or night. In the above-mentioned resorts, many of these bar-scene rituals—like the popular tea dances on open decks—at least partially take place in scenic spots out of doors. In Palm Springs, however, most of the dancing and socializing goes on indoors; outdoor patios typically have very little ambience.

Another reason that the club scene here isn't quite as festive as in some of the oceanside resorts is that lodgings are so extremely social and often quite luxurious—there's little need to party elsewhere. Many of the properties throw cocktail parties and have lively lounges and ample social areas.

Club Palm Springs (68–449 Perez Rd., Cathedral City, ☎ 619/324–8588) is the area's only 24-hour bathhouse.

Palm Springs

J. P.'s Bar. If it weren't for the heat in Palm Springs, this would be a leather bar. Instead Levi's and T-shirts are the norm (no L.A. twinkies here). You'll also find pool tables and a video bar with a big-screen TV. Occasionally there are live performances by singers or dancers, and a dance floor is in the works. *1117 N. Palm Canyon Rd.,* ☎ *619/778–5310. Crowd: mostly male, otherwise diverse.*

Rainbow Cactus Café. A piano bar whose peach walls are festooned with an odd mix of Christmas lights and Native American art, this lively spot is a great alternative to the high-energy dance clubs in Cathedral City. It's across the street from the Streetbar. *Arenas Rd. at Indian Canyon Dr., ☎ 619/325–3868. Crowd: 80/20 m/f, mostly older guys, strong local following.*

Streetbar. Many of the guys staying at resorts near Warm Sands Drive (a short walk away) drop in here for a beer or two before heading to the larger clubs in Cathedral City. It's a small, simple, neighborhoody video bar with pool and pinball; there's also a nice little terrace out front on the sidewalk. Strippers perform on Saturday nights. *224 E. Arenas Rd., ☎ 619/320–1266. Crowd: as local as any area bar, low-key, mostly male.*

Tool Shed. Described in its own ads as a "working man's bar," the Tool Shed is very reminiscent of the no-nonsense bars you find in Long Beach or parts of Phoenix. It's a rather grim, dark little place with a small loyal following. *600 E. Sunny Dunes Rd., ☎ 619/320–3299. Crowd: male, blue-collar, some leather, lots of facial hair, guys trying to look rough.*

Cathedral City

C. C. Construction Co. You'll sometimes find country-western on the smaller of the two dance floors here, while the other usually has disco. There are three bars and a patio out back, but the latter can get a little smelly since it's opposite the loading docks of several neighboring warehouses. The smaller dance floor and bar are open after hours (until 3) on Fridays and Saturdays; there are pool tables here and it's a better spot for chatting. *68–449 Perez Rd., ☎ 619/324–4241. Crowd: mostly male, all ages but generally on the young side, some leather, some cowboys, mostly disco bunnies.*

Choices. After the C. C. Construction Company, this is the area's largest disco. It has a large dance floor, a game and pool area, and a large but dull patio outside. The crowds here might have a slightly softer edge than at some of the other clubs, but you'll find most visitors include Choices on the mainstream bar-hopping circuit. *68–352 Perez Rd., ☎ 619/321–1145. Crowd: very diverse, many more women than at C. C. Construction but otherwise similar.*

Delilah's Nightclub. The sole lesbian bar in the area, Delilah's opened in 1994. On weekends, L.A. lesbians mingle with the locals and party to high-energy house music. Sunday is devoted to country music, and Monday night features football (after all, this is a dyke bar). Inside the colors are warm and inviting, and there are pool tables and video games. *68–657 Hwy. 111, ☎ 619/324–3268. Crowd: mostly lesbian but otherwise diverse.*

Wolf's Den. You might expect the Den to be in some dark, cozy bunker, but it's actually a big, modern club in a tacky shopping center (it looks as if it once might have been the home of a discount carpet store). Tall, blackened plate-glass windows surround the exterior, and the owners have done their best to create a dark, macho place. With leather such a big deal in Arizona and southern California, it's taken seriously here—although guppies are never frowned upon. If you need a proper outfit, check out the on-site leather shop. The Den also has one of the nicer outdoor patios. *67–625 E. Palm Canyon Dr., ☎ 619/321–9688. Crowd: lots of leather, leatherette, Levi's, and tank tops; ages 35 and up.*

THE LITTLE BLACK BOOK

At Your Fingertips

AIDS Assistance Program: ☎ 619/325–8481. **Desert Business Alliance (gay):** ☎ 619/324–0178. **Desert Woman's Associations:** ☎ 619/363–7565. **Palm Springs Desert Resorts Convention and Visitors Bureau:** 69–930 Hwy. 111, Suite 201, Rancho Mirage, 92270, ☎ 619/770–9000 or 800/417–3529.

Gay Media

Palm Springs has several gay publications—all of them decidedly male-oriented. The most comprehensive and popular gay and lesbian entertainment magazine is the **Bottom Line** (☎ 619/323–0552), which comes out twice a month. The biweekly **Star Magazine** (☎ 619/323–0552) is similar but has broader coverage of the region. Done in a black-and-white newspaper format, **Mega Scene** (☎ 619/327–5178), more a newspaper than a magazine, is another option.

At **Between the Pages,** (214 E. Arenas Rd., ☎ 619/320–7158) you can sip a cappuccino at the espresso bar while you peruse one of the many gay-oriented books this store offers. **Crown Books** (333 S. Palm Canyon Dr., ☎ 619/325–1265) has a solid selection of gay and lesbian titles. Although it's an adult bookstore, **Perez Books** (68–366 Perez Rd., Cathedral City, ☎ 619/321–5597) has a few nonporn publications (such as *The Advocate*).

Body and Fitness

Many of the guest houses have small gyms. The gayest health club in town is **Gold's Gym** (4070 Airport Center Dr., ☎ 619/322–4653).

17 *Out in Philadelphia*

With New Hope

FOR A CITY OF 1.6 MILLION PEOPLE, Philadelphia appears, at first glance, to lack the sort of scene evident in other large metropolises. There are but a dozen gay bars; recent gay pride parades have been short and quiet; civil rights protests are few and far between; and nowhere—not even in Philly's tiny four-square-block "gay district"—are you likely to see a sizable presence of lesbians and gays.

Bounce this observation off locals, and you'll hear a variety of reactions. Some say that though the lesbian/gay population has mushroomed over the past three decades, there's a paucity of the queers between the ages of 25 and 35, who are often the most visible segment of a gay community. A local bartender put the lack of political spark more simply: "Too many generals and not enough troops."

Others say that if you live in Philly there's a good chance you grew up here, came out here, and see little reason to rock any boats. You may still live at home or near your family and old friends, and being gay is a somewhat incidental aspect of your life. Accordingly, Philadelphia lacks a real gay ghetto; instead the community is spread thinly through the metro area. It could be that the mellowing of the community here is simply a sign that, in terms of civil rights and general acceptance, gay life is relatively agreeable.

New York, Los Angeles, and San Francisco weren't the only cities to foster a pre-Stonewall homophile movement. In August 1960, New York City's Mattachine Society held a meeting in the affluent Philadelphia suburb of Radnor; the police got wind of this unsavory cabal and arrested 84 people, most of them men, for showing gay-theme films. The organizers' aim had been to establish a Philadelphia chapter of the society; they soon succeeded, and in the mid-'60s, according to local gay-historian Marc Stein, Philadelphia emerged with "the most militant female and male wings of the national homophile movement." Stein also recalls that Philadelphia was a city in which lesbians and gay men worked closely together (conflicts notwithstanding) to further their collective goals. In fact, the earliest Mattachine and Janus (a related group) societies were lesbian-led, even when membership was mostly male. The lesbian Daughters of Bilitis soon became a major force in Philadelphia, and Janus shifted into a male-oriented political group and publisher of *Drum,* one of the nation's first magazines of defiant gay politics and soft-core porn.

From 1965 through 1969, each July 4 was marked at Independence Hall by lesbian- and gay-rights protests. In 1975, the state of Pennsylvania became the first governmental body in the world to establish a committee to address the concerns of sexual minorities. A year later, as America celebrated its bicentennial, Pennsylvania became the first state to establish a Gay Pride Month.

Nineteen seventy-eight saw the formation of the Philadelphia Lesbian and Gay Task Force, which has steered the city's government, media, and educational institutions into becoming the most tolerant in the nation. In 1980, the city aired the nation's first public-service gay-rights TV announcements. The Task Force guided passage of the 1982 Philadelphia Fair Practices Act, which has secured gays the right to fair employment, housing, and public accommodation. The task force has also rallied the city's broadcast and print media into positive coverage of lesbians and gays.

A police-civilian review board was put in place in 1991 to cut gay bashers out of police ranks, and all officers now receive gay-sensitivity training. In 1994 a rainbow curriculum—the most comprehensive of its kind—was established for the city's public schools, kindergarten through 12th grade. There are lesbians and gays working at senior levels in the mayor's office (which has its own sexual minorities task force), on virtually every city commission, and for many of the city's most influential newspapers and radio and TV stations.

Many societal wrongs have been righted here. But the fight continues for the legislation of public and private sector same-sex-couple employment benefits. Activists keep hot on the heels of Mayor Ed Rendall, who is viewed by some as gay-friendly only when the mood strikes him. And putting the rainbow curriculum into practice provides a brand-new challenge: funding. All these programs take money, and Philadelphia has little of it to burn.

This is a land where enlightened policies are passed left and right, but logistics and lack of funding hamper implementation; where tolerance is high but where pride and unity inside the community may have subsided. Some like it; some don't. Say what you will, Philadelphia may just hold the vision of America's gay future.

THE LAY OF THE LAND

The part of the city most visitors see, downtown (a.k.a. Center City), is less defined by neighborhood monikers than other major metropolises. Basically the visitor-friendly rectangle runs east–west from the Schuylkill to the Delaware rivers (streets are numbered, going high to low toward the Delaware) and north–south from around Race to South streets. In the northwest, Fairmount Park and the Art Museum areas are also touristy.

The Business District and City Hall

The business district, on and just south of Market Street between 20th and 8th streets, offers some of the city's best upscale shopping, highlighted by the **Shops at Liberty Place** (16th and Chestnut Sts.), the **Shops at the Bellevue** (Broad and Walnut Sts.), and **Hecht's** (12th and 13th Sts., at Market St.)—formerly the famed Wanamaker's Store. Walnut Street, between Rittenhouse Square and the Bellevue, has more of the same. By night, this area is rather deserted and spooky; avoid it. Walnut and Sansom streets, especially, are major thoroughfares for hustlers and muggers.

Looming 542 feet above the intersection of Broad and Market streets, the **City Hall** (☎ 215/686–1776) took 30 years (1871–1900) to build and is today the largest and most stunning city hall in America. The Philadelphia Fair Practices Act, one of the country's earliest gay civil rights amendments, was passed here in 1982. Nearby is the **Masonic Temple** (1 N. Broad St., ☎ 215/988–1917), a marvelous 1868 structure that draws from seven architectural styles—Corinthian, Ionic, Italian Renaissance, Norman, Gothic, Oriental, and Egyptian. The rest of this area belongs to an array of attractive and not-so-pretty office buildings, including the deco-inspired 63-story **One Liberty Place** (1650 Market St.), the first city building to rise above the City Hall. Two blocks north, stop by the massive High Victorian Gothic **Pennsylvania Academy of the Fine Arts** (Broad and Cherry Sts., ☎ 215/972–7600), a somewhat grandiose structure built in 1876 by world-renowned local architects Frank Furness and George Hewitt. The late-19th-century artist Thomas Eakins, who is believed to have been gay, was the Academy's director until the 1880s, when his insistence on using nude models in coed classes cost him his job. A few blocks east is the leviathan **convention center,** and north of here is the city's small but lively **Chinatown.**

Rittenhouse Square

A great spot for lounging around on the grass and a relatively safe place for same-sex couples, the ritzy and sophisticated Rittenhouse Square (between 18th and 19th Sts. at Walnut St.) is near some outstanding small museums and beautiful architecture. City-planning guru and historian Jane Jacobs has called Rittenhouse Square the most successful urban park in the United States; indeed, it remains picturesque, socially diverse, relatively safe, and at least partially unsullied by post–World War II architecture. The Square was also quite the pick-up spot a couple of decades ago but is now largely devoid of such endeavors.

Off the Square's southeast corner are the recently condoized **Barclay Hotel,** the **Philadelphia Art Alliance,** and the **Curtis Institute of Music** (1726 Locust St., ☎ 215/893–5261), where the likes of Samuel Barber, Leonard Bernstein, Anna Moffo, and Ned Rorem studied. Walking south a block you'll hit possibly the best-preserved row of homes in the city, on **Delancey Street.** Along here, the **Rosenbach Museum and Library** (2010 Delancey Pl., ☎ 215/732–1600), a Victorian town house, has more than 130,000 manuscripts, 25,000 rare books, and an incredible collection of antiques. The two Rosenbach brothers (one was gay) were the nation's leading antiquarian book collectors at the turn of the century.

Fairmount Park and the Schuylkill River

From the corner of 16th and Arch streets, the Benjamin Franklin Parkway runs diagonally toward Fairmount Park, passing first through **Logan Circle,** which is actually a lovely—and sometimes quite cruisy—square anchored by a Calder-designed fountain (1920). This area, which deviates from William Penn's original grid plan, was meant—with its expansiveness, stately mansions and museums, and trees and statuary—to recall the Champs Elysées. Some of the many notable museums along here include the **Franklin Institute** (20th St. and Benjamin Franklin Pkwy., ☎ 215/448–1200), the city's science museum; the **Academy of Natural Sciences** (19th St. and Benjamin Franklin Pkwy., ☎ 215/299–1020), with its dinosaur exhibit; and the stellar **Auguste Rodin Museum** (22nd St. and Benjamin Franklin Pkwy., ☎ 215/563–1948). The **Philadelphia Museum of Art** (26th St. and Benjamin Franklin Pkwy., ☎ 215/763–8100) is wonderful for several reasons: its imposing Greek architecture and 10 landscaped acres; its contemporary collection, with many works by Picasso, Braque, and Matisse as well as a number of post–World War II artists; its outstanding Marcel Duchamp collection, which includes renditions of his *Nude Descending a Staircase* (the "nude," people often overlook, is male); and a fine collection of Eakins's photos and paintings of young, virile men crewing and boating on the Schuylkill River (in many of them you'll recognize the old rail bridge that still spans the Schuylkill up a short way near the Girard Avenue Bridge). North of the Museum, **Fairmount Park** has a number of picturesque gardens, mansions, and walkways.

Just about anywhere three queens are caught tanning together is immediately dubbed "Judy Garland Memorial Park"—virtually the entire east bank of the Schuylkill River has earned this distinction. Most popular for both sunning, and at night, cruising, is the **Schuylkill River Park** (where Spruce, Pine, and Lombard Sts. meet the river). It's also quite busy along the Schuylkill from below the Philadelphia Museum of Art through Fairmount Park, from Boathouse Row to roughly East Park Reservoir. By day these areas are safe for strolling and contemplating nature, but note that on weekends Boathouse Row can be overrun with boisterous crew boys.

The Gay District

This small rectangle runs east–west from Juniper to Quince streets (which are actually tiny little alleys that run parallel to 13th and 12th streets and down to the gayest of Philly's alleys, Camac Street) and north–south from Walnut to Pine streets. In the 19th century, Camac (pronounced cuh-*mack*) Street, a small enclave of historic redbrick mews (or trinities, as they're known here), was the area's red-light district. It eventually became the site of several artists' clubs and small theaters, and a commercial—though not especially residential—gay scene grew up around it. In the heart of the district, gay-male club fashion and accessories are proffered at **Surfaces** (206 S. 13th St., ☎ 215/546–5944), located conveniently down the block from Woody's nightclub (*see* Scenes, *below*), where most of this stuff is worn.

As you walk west from here along Pine Street (a.k.a. Antiques Row), which is probably the safest street to traverse late at night, things continue to be fairly gay through Rittenhouse Square and all the way out to the Schuylkill River.

East of the gay district, to about Washington Square but south of Walnut Street, is also pretty safe for gays. In this region you'll find Jewelers' Row, the nation's oldest and most prestigious diamond district, which takes in about a one-block area bounded by Sansom, 8th, Chestnut, and 7th streets. There are nearly 400 jewelers and artisans here, including **Today's Male** (104 S. 8th St., ☎ 215/922–5178), which specializes in gay custom pieces.

South Street

This is Philadelphia's leading oddity—a funky, commercial area southeast of Washington Square and bounded east–west from about 7th to Front Street and north–south from Lombard to Catherine Street. The closest thing the city has to an alternative or grunge scene, it's marked by dozens of gay-owned shops and eateries, and it's where many of the city's major gay hangouts opened. During the 1970s and '80s, city planners threatened to raze South Street for a highway overpass. Real-estate prices plummeted, and such institutions as Giovanni's Room, the Painted Bride (a famed lesbian/gay-frequented art space), and the original gay community center opened here (all have since moved). It might also owe something of its gay incarnation to having been, in Colonial times, one of the nation's first theater districts—just outside the original city limits, it was beyond the reach of anti-theater ordinances. And so now it's a mix of alternateens slinking between body-piercing parlors and the Gap, locals (many of them gay), and a somewhat uneasy blend of straight and gay tourists. Gay couples often mistake South Street as another gay district, which, especially on weekends, it is not. A somewhat rowdy suburban crowd seeps in here on Friday and Saturday nights, and same-sex displays of affection are ill-advised. Exercise caution, and you'll be fine.

People like to joke about the neighborhood just south of here, Queen Village. Despite its name, it's not particularly queeny, and some would say it's grown a bit decrepit. However, it was named in the 18th century after Sweden's Queen Christina, who, it will interest some to know, was said to be a lesbian.

The Old City
The most touristy section of the city, it's east of the business district and north of South Street. Many Old City sights are part of **Independence National Historical Park** (3rd and Chestnut Sts., ☎ 215/597–8974). These attractions are usually free and open daily 9–5. Most famous is the **Liberty Bell Pavilion** (Market St., between 5th and 6th Sts.), the glass-enclosed site of America's beloved—and cracked—2,000-pound bell. Across Chestnut Street is the early-18th-century **Independence Hall** (Chestnut St., between 5th and 6th Sts.), where the Second Continental Congress met in 1775, the Declaration of Independence was adopted in 1776, the Articles of Confederation were signed in 1778, and the Constitution was adopted in 1787. Forever a symbol of liberty and independence, it was the site of the city's first major civil rights demonstrations (which included the concerns of lesbians and gays) every July 4 from 1965 through 1969. Nearby is **Old City Hall,** where the U.S. Supreme Court convened until 1800 and where Emma Goldman, one of the nation's first gay-rights advocates, was imprisoned briefly early in this century. Other major sights in the vicinity are the **First Bank of the United States** (3rd and Chestnut Sts.), the nation's oldest such institution; the Parthenon-inspired **Second Bank of the United States** (420 Chestnut St.), which contains an unparalleled collection of political portraiture; **Independence Square** (between 5th and 6th Sts. and Chestnut and Walnut Sts.), where the Declaration of Independence was first read publicly on July 8, 1776; the first meeting place of the U.S. Congress, **Congress Hall** (6th and Chestnut Sts.); the home of early flag-fashion maven **Betsy Ross** (239 Arch St., ☎ 215/627–5343); and the **United States Mint** (5th and Arch Sts., ☎ 215/597–7350), the largest in the world.

Penn's Landing
City father William Penn debarked in 1682 at a spot that is today the 37-acre historical park known as **Penn's Landing** (on the Delaware River a few blocks east of Independence Park, ☎ 215/923–2060). Here you'll find shops, hotels, and condos; an amphitheater that hosts major concerts and festivals; the newly relocated **Philadelphia Maritime Museum;** several historic ships and homes; and the **Riverbus** across the Delaware to Camden, New Jersey, home to the **New Jersey State Aquarium** (1 Riverside Dr., ☎ 609/365–3300). The Camden–Philadelphia connection is also a notorious site of gay controversy: In the early 1950s, the Bishop of Camden flipped out upon learning that a new bridge spanning the Delaware would be named after former resident Walt Whitman—a noted deviant. Despite a completely offensive antigay offensive, the Catholic Church failed to sway public opinion. You can visit the **Walt Whitman House** (330 Nickel Blvd., ☎ 609/964–5383), where the poet lived during the 1880s and entertained a number of kindred spirits, including Thomas Carpenter, Oscar Wilde, and Thomas Eakins.

The Outskirts
Outside downtown, a few residential neighborhoods have become quite lesbian in recent years—namely the Germantown and Mt. Airy regions, northwest of City Center. Another area that's becoming increasingly popular with gay men is the West Philadelphia neighborhood

near the University of Pennsylvania; it runs east–west from about 38th to 50th streets and north–south from about Market Street to Baltimore Avenue.

New Hope

As compared with other gay-popular resorts in the northeast, New Hope is less a place to see and be seen, and more a restful hideout for week-ending couples. Fire Island and Provincetown have for years cultivated a tea-dance atmosphere—nonstop sunning, mingling, cruising, and gossiping. They are urban resorts, in that you needn't switch gears when visiting from the city. New Hope, though blessed with two discos and several trendy restaurants, breezes along at a laconic pace. This small, riverside hamlet is a mere hour from Philadelphia and 90 minutes from New York City, but the tempo of either city is absent here.

Few come to New Hope with a pack-a-week-into-a-day mentality. On the contrary, it's a bit of a challenge to keep busy for seven straight days, which suggests part of the appeal. Most visitors come for two to four days, but if you are looking to spend a week somewhere, and you require a full slate of daily diversions, don't rule out New Hope just yet. This is prime day-tripping territory.

Like the Russian River in California, New Hope is that rare breed of gay resort that's neither fringed by ocean nor surrounded by desert. In fact, the terrain and appeal of both communities are similar. Each is set in a verdant river valley traversed by winding rural roads. You can sun for a few hours back at the inn and tour downtown on foot in an afternoon, but you'll need to strike out by car or bicycle to appreciate the region's strengths—its history, country manors, antiques shops, and sylvan vistas.

Formerly the territory of Lenni-Lenape Indians, New Hope was settled in 1700 by a British family and developed quickly into a major Delaware River ferry crossing, linking the York Road stagecoach route with New Jersey, thereby connecting New York City with Philadelphia. By the Revolutionary War, the town had changed names from Wells Ferry to Canby's to Coryell's Ferry. Throughout 1776, General George Washington and his ragged troops had suffered a series of setbacks at the hand of British General Cornwallis and his Hessian mercenaries, forcing the weary Americans from New York City west through New Jersey over the Delaware River and into Pennsylvania. As he retreated across the river, Washington had all boats removed from the Jersey shore, preventing the British from following him, and the tired, dispirited patriots encamped for several weeks at Coryell's Ferry, licking their wounds and regrouping. On Christmas Night, Washington executed his unlikely, and now legendary, sneak attack. He and his troops rowed down the icy Delaware from Coryell's Ferry to McConkey's Ferry (now called Washington's Crossing), where they crossed the river (the scene immortalized in Emanuel Leutze's unforgettable painting), marched to Trenton, and sacked the garrison of startled, hungover Hessians. A young Lieutenant James Monroe, later the nation's fifth president, led a squadron of 50 militia to block the Hessians from retreating to Princeton. New Hope's place in American history was now secure.

Throughout the 1700s, lumber, flaxseed, grist, and other mills had been erected along Ingham Creek, a spur of the Delaware River, which parallels Mechanic Street. In 1790 a fire burned most of the mills, inspiring owner Benjamin Parry to build a new millworks, dubbing it the New Hope Mills. The name stuck, and so did New Hope's prosperity. In 1832 the Delaware Division Canal was laid through town; the railroad soon followed.

Ironically, though New Hope's commercial success earned it railroad tracks, by the end of the 19th century rail transportation had destroyed the town's commercial livelihood. Simply being on the Delaware River was no longer of strategic value, and transport along the canal, which closed in 1931, was no longer profitable. Better commercial routes opened throughout the northeast, and New Hope's mills and factories gradually shut down, leaving behind a sleepy, picturesque town, which, like the Brandywine River valley southwest of Philadelphia, began attracting a small colony of landscape painters, among them Daniel Garber, William Lathrop, and Edward Redfield. The area continued to draw artists and writers, many of them from New York City, including Dorothy Parker, S. J. Perelman, Oscar Hammerstein, Moss Hart, and Pearl Buck.

The increasingly gay presence in town was precipitated here, as it was in similarly low-key Ogunquit, Maine, by the opening of an important regional theater, the Bucks County Playhouse, in 1939. Built in the rustic shell of Benjamin Parry's old 18th-century grist mill, the theater brought New Hope a regular summer tour of actors and stagehands. A good many of them settled here for at least part of the year, and their presence continues today—as does the tremendous success of the playhouse, the nearby S. J. Gerenser Theatre, and the New Hope Performing Arts Festival, held annually at several locations throughout July and August.

New Hope itself is tiny—roughly 1 square mile of preserved 18th- and 19th-century buildings, most of them now inns, restaurants, shops, and private homes. Locals often refer to the three or four miles south, west, and north of town as New Hope, but this land falls technically in Solesbury Township, which is part of Bucks County—defined by a 10-mile-wide corridor, which begins just 20 miles northeast of Philadelphia and takes in those towns bordering the Delaware River from Morrisville north to Riegelsville. Across the river from New Hope is the New Jersey county of Hunterdon.

Though you'll see same-sex couples wandering about and notice the occasional rainbow flag hanging in a couple of shops, New Hope doesn't look or feel especially like a gay resort. **Main Street** runs north–south parallel to and between the river and the canal; it's lined with shops and eateries—some more historic than others. In addition to crafts and antiques shops and several galleries, you'll also find an outpost of **Zipperhead** (102 South Main St., ☏ 215/862–2393), the noted purveyor of shock clothing, magenta hair dye, and body-piercing paraphernalia based on South Street in Philadelphia, and **Grown Ups** (2 East Mechanic St., ☏ 215/862–9304), a tiny boutique proffering lingerie, risqué novelties, and a few porn videos. There's just enough edge in New Hope to keep things from getting dull. There are also a few campy shops on Mechanic Street, notably **Ember Glo** (27 West Mechanic St., 215/862–2929), which sells rainbow flags and wind socks, kitschy bric-a-brac, incense, and gay jewelry and cards.

Running perpendicular to Main Street are **Mechanic, Ferry,** and **Bridge** streets, all of which are lined with more historic buildings. At the corner of Main and Ferry streets, the 1784 **Parry Mansion** (☏ 215/862–5148), built by the founder of the New Hope Mills, contains decorative arts and furnishings from the late Colonial through late Victorian eras. For a detailed tour of the village's many sites, pick up a copy of *The Walking Tour of Historic New Hope,* published by the New Hope Historical Society and available at the Information Center.

Bucks County

From New Hope, the rest of **Bucks County** is perfect terrain for exploring with or without a map. For a detailed description and history of every town in Bucks and Hunterdon counties, check out *The Area Guide Book* ($3.50), which is sold at the New Hope Information Center. Area highlights include the **Washington Crossing Historic Park** (☎ 215/493–4076), which is set on two properties, 2 and 7 miles south of New Hope, respectively, on Route 32. Continue south and you'll reach the well-preserved town of **Yardley**, once a Delaware River hub of shad hauling, and still a great place to cast a line. North of town, it's a gorgeous drive along the river, where you'll pass through the towns of **Lumberville, Point Pleasant, Tinicum,** and **Bridgeton.** The **Lumberville General Store** preserves the tradition of buying groceries, stamps, and hardware at the same shop— and they make great sandwiches.

Inland, in lower Bucks County, you might spend the afternoon touring **Pennsbury Manor** (☎ 215/946–0400), in Morrisville, William Penn's 40-acre (it was originally 8,400 acres) estate on which stands the original Georgian mansion and many outbuildings. Just west of New Hope, U.S. 202, which is lined with antiques shops through **Lahaska,** leads to the touristy (at times overly so) **Peddlar's Village,** a 42-acre village of some 70 restaurants, middle-end specialty shops and boutiques, and crafts shops. Continuing west on U.S. 202, you'll pass several more picturesque towns, including **Buckingham, Doylestown,** and **Chalfont.** Doylestown, the county seat, is the largest town in the region and is where James Michener grew up. There are more than 1,200 buildings here in the downtown historic district; contact the **Central Bucks Chamber of Commerce** (115 W. Court St., Doylestown, 18901, ☎ 215/348–3913) for information. Just north of here, another town of literary significance, **Perkasie,** is site of the **Pearl S. Buck Home** (520 Dublin Rd., ☎ 215/249–0100).

GETTING AROUND

In Philadelphia, drive to Center City, park in a garage, and don't touch your car again until you leave. The city is small enough to manage on foot, or at worst by cab. Cars on the street get vandalized, stolen, or towed away. Unfortunately, overnight parking in a garage is usually $18 to $22.

Cabs are easy to hail during the day, when they seem to crawl all through Center City. A ride across town shouldn't run you more than $5. At night, as bars are closing, you might have to phone for one. Try **Quaker City Cab** (☎ 215/728–8000). You don't need public transportation downtown; it's really for running between Philly and the burbs.

EATS

Philadelphia may be the only city in America where all of the gay bars have restaurants. The majority serve traditional American food, most of it recently paroled from storage freezers; none could survive solely on culinary merit. The Venture Inn, Westbury Bar, and Raffles are the best regarded, and all of them have their adherents. Only one, Rodz, is reviewed below, since, in a city of exceptional cuisine, this section focuses on those eateries whose raison d'etre is just that: eating.

French cuisine is the star; Le Bec-Fin, Chanterelles, and Deux Cheminées are often cited among the nation's top 20, and they're all gay-popular. Many of the hotels—the Four Seasons, the Rittenhouse, the Hotel Atop the Bellevue, and the Penn's View Inn—have terrific restaurants, though none is especially gay. Also noteworthy, but again not very gay, are the many fine spots in Chinatown and the traditional Italian kitchens of South Philadelphia. As for outstanding gay eats, the two principal regions are the South Street neighborhood and the several blocks south and east of Rittenhouse Square.

For price ranges, *see* Chart A at the front of this guide.

Center City

$$$$ **Deux Cheminées.** Probably the gayest of the stellar restaurants: The non-pareil French cuisine of award-winning American chef Fritz Blank is served in an elegant Frank Furness town house. The rack of lamb with truffle sauce is legendary. Prix fixe only: Dinner is $68. *1221 Locust St.,* ☎ *215/790–0200.*

$$$$ **Striped Bass.** Fresh seafood and nothing but. This local culinary star stands out for its setting in the original First National Bank of Philadelphia building, a dramatic space with mahogany ceilings, marble pillars, and an exhibition kitchen. But the main kudos go to the innovative cuisine. The menu changes daily, but there's always a full selection of caviar. *1500 Walnut St.,* ☎ *215/732–4444.*

$$$$ **Susanna Foo.** In Philadelphia's priciest Chinese restaurant, a renovated former steak house hung with a fortune in native art, Chinese food gets a contemporary twist. Eight Treasure Quails, a favorite, has Chinese sausage, lotus seeds, and sweet rice; even fortune cookies stand out: They're chocolate-dipped. *1512 Walnut St.,* ☎ *215/545–2666.*

$$$–$$$$ **Café Nola.** Signature dish: popcorn shrimp. Signature beverage: the prima margarita. Also check out the great oyster bar and many mouthwatering New Orleans–style dishes. Heavy, dark-wood furniture, a tile floor, floral lamp shades, filigree ironwork, and a dark-green pressed-tin ceiling lend a Garden District–cum–art-deco elegance. *328 South St.,* ☎ *215/627–2590.*

$$$ **Bistro Bix.** Inside a 1920s Deco building, this French-Italian bistro has a very casual ambience and a simple, straightforward menu: pasta, fish, poultry. The bar has 10 beers on tap and a special selection of bourbons and Irish whiskeys. On the weekends live jazz swings this joint. Very gay. *114 S. 12th St.,* ☎ *215/925–5336.*

$$–$$$ **Astral Plane.** You know it's gay-operated the minute you walk in the door— a parachute wafts against the ceiling overhead, the walls are ruby-color, there's clutter and Victoriana everywhere, and it's dark. The New American food (e.g., orange roughy with a piquant tomato-cilantro salsa) is outstanding. The Sunday brunch has a make-your-own-Bloody-Mary bar. Very romantic. *1708 Lombard St.,* ☎ *215/546–6230.*

$$–$$$ **Café Einstein.** One of the few Old City eateries with a gay following, the Café glows with a wood-burning stove and shows off original paintings on its walls. It was formerly a Colonial blacksmith shop. The food is contemporary Continental: linguine with sun-dried tomatoes and spinach, for example. Very popular are the live-jazz dinners on Sunday evenings. *208 Race St.,* ☎ *215/625–0904.*

$$–$$$ **Circa.** In what was originally a bank building—the high ceilings lend an airy, classical ambience to the dining room—you can feast on such elaborate Mediterranean creations as salmon osso buco, which is served with sea scallops, risotto, and asparagus doused with tomato broth. On Friday and Saturday evenings Circa becomes a gay dance club playing music that concentrates heavily on '70s disco. *1518 Walnut St.,* ☎ *215/545–6800.*

$$–$$$ **Judy's Cafe.** People go on and on about Judy's, which is packed every night with lesbians, gay men, fabulously hip straight people, and gourmands. The staff is mostly gay and extremely welcoming; the New American cuisine is great—especially the seafood. Consider rainbow trout panfried with a nut flour–caper sauce or cornmeal-crusted oysters with corn-and-poblano relish. The interior has a minimalist feel, and a decidedly political crowd congregates most evenings around the bar. *3rd and Bainbridge Sts.,* ☎ *215/928–1968.*

$$–$$$ Waldorf Café. You'll find great American and Continental dishes in this small brick house with a blue awning and an elaborately carved gray cornice. Try the sautéed wild mushrooms in cognac sauce or the osso buco with white wine. Background jazz and vintage photos set a refined tone. Queer as can be on Saturday night. *20th and Lombard Sts.,* ☎ *215/985–1836.*

$$–$$$ Warsaw Cafe. The heavy Eastern European fare can really weigh you down, but that doesn't seem to keep even the most body-conscious stand-and-model types from overdosing on beef Stroganoff and borscht. *306 S. 16th St.,* ☎ *215/546–0204.*

$$ Tapioca. A hole in the wall that seems to exist exclusively by word of mouth—you never see it written about or advertised. The tiny dining room has mint-green walls and tables and black vinyl bar stools. Waiters are known for dishing with and at customers. And the food will remind you of grandma's––authentic, home-style Pennsylvania fare. Breakfast and lunch only. BYOB. New owners took over in '96 and may rethink the name and menu. *1743 South St.,* ☎ *215/735–2463.*

$–$$ Montserrat. The grunge waitpersons have lots of pierced body parts and can get a little ornery, but Montserrat serves tasty, inexpensive, and healthy grub—from veggie grinders to gourmet pizzas to a variety of stir-fries. You can get half orders of most dishes. Can be quite lesbian-chic. *633 South St.,* ☎ *215/627–4224.*

$–$$ Opera Cafe. Lesbian-owned, with a strong dyke following, Opera Cafe is unassumingly set in an ugly stucco building, but it has a sleek black-and-white checkered floor and simple, crisp furnishings. The healthful, Italian-influenced menu has creative salads, veggie pastas, and several refreshing selections from the juice bar. *1940 Pine St.,* ☎ *215/545–3543.*

$–$$ Reading Terminal Market. Granted, this is a major tourist spot; it's also a great place to sample spicy dishes and ogle spicy passersby. For a century the Market has shown off food ranging from local produce to exotic dishes from around the world. Choose from among 80 stalls, 25 of which have seating and ready-to-eat food. *12th and Arch Sts.,* ☎ *215/922–2317.*

$–$$ Rodz. Though the traditional American cuisine here (lots of chicken, veal, and steak) is the best of Philly's gay bars, you still come more for the atmosphere and the affordability. Choose from a few dining rooms plus a terribly romantic roof deck with city views. The Sunday brunch draws a particularly convivial crowd. Female-friendly but mostly gay men. *1418 Rodman St.,* ☎ *215/735–2900.*

$ Cheap Art Cafe. The name refers to the changing exhibits of the works of local artists. This 24-hour modern American diner has the standard burgers and cheese steaks as well as health-conscious updates like garden vegetable burgers and pasta with eggplant and mushrooms. In gay Valhalla, this is a place to be seen late on weekends. *260 S. 12th St.,* ☎ *215/735–6650.*

$ Latimer Deli. In addition to being your classic Jewish deli—good for take-out sandwiches or eating in the no-frills dining area—Latimer also has dinner specials that draw on the cuisine of other regions, such as the Middle East or Mexico. Very popular with the gay community. *255 S. 15th St.,* ☎ *215/545–9244.*

$ Taco House. The intimate confines here almost beg you to walk over and say "hi" to that cute thing sitting all alone, fresh from a book-buying binge at nearby Giovanni's Room. The decor is quaint: bare-wood tables, red-and-blue chairs, amber lighting, and exposed brick. Expect simple and basic Mexican fare—nothing special. *1218 Pine St.,* ☎ *215/735–1880.*

Philadelphia

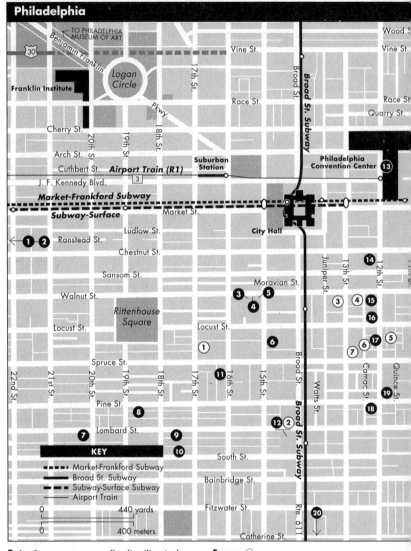

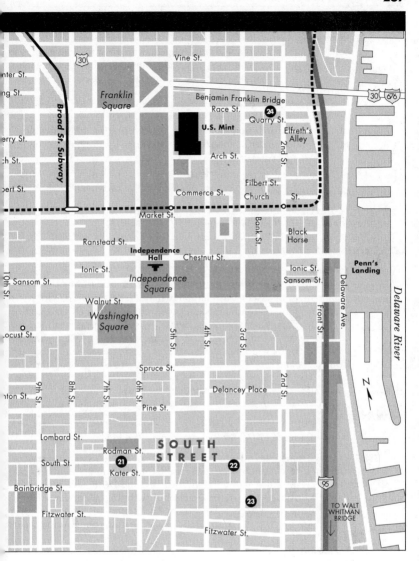

Outside City Center

$$$ **White Dog Café.** This bric-a-brac–filled brownstone may be the best restaurant in University City, and it's popular with academics and the area's active lesbian and increasingly gay-male community. Excellent vegetarian dishes, whole-grain breads, and an emphasis on regional, farm-fresh ingredients. *3420 Sansom St.,* ☎ *215/386–9224.*

$$ **Goat Hollow.** In the residential and very lesbian enclave of Mt. Airy, northwest of City Center, Goat Hollow is a woman-operated restaurant in a restored building on a picturesque street. A big pull is the wide selection of tap and imported beers. Food tends toward grilled seafood dishes, bountiful salads, and pasta dishes. *300 W. Mt. Pleasant Ave.,* ☎ *215/242–4710.*

$ **Melrose Diner.** *Not* a gay restaurant (so ogle any cute patrons at your own risk), but a true big-hair-and-bangles institution in a working-class South Philly neighborhood, a sea of CHECKS CASHED signs and pawnbrokers. It's best to come after the bars let out, but either drive (there's a small lot) or take a taxi. *1501 Snyder Ave.,* ☎ *215/467–6644.*

Coffeehouse Culture

Millennium Coffee (212 S. 12th St., ☎ 215/731–9798), the unofficial homo coffee shop of Philadelphia, is right beside Afterwords, the unofficial lesbian-and-gay newsstand. In addition to the tables in front (good for people-watching) and in back (good for people-chatting), there's a nice coffee bar midway (good for people-meeting). The staff is friendly and unpretentious. Gay-friendly **More Than Just Ice Cream** (1143 Pine St., ☎ 215/574–0586), which has a take-out area and a cute café with wrought-iron chairs and tables, is right next to Giovanni's Room bookstore. In addition to ice cream and a limited range of coffees, you can get great soups and sandwiches and outstanding apple pie.

New Hope

For price ranges, *see* Chart B at the front of this guide.

$$$$ **La Bonne Auberge.** This is one of the finest, though priciest, French restaurants in a region known for such establishments. Thin scallops of veal with a cream sauce and morel mushrooms, and Dover sole sautéed in butter with capers are two of the typically delicate, by-the-book haute French dishes. Best to come Wednesday or Thursday for the four-course table d'hôte, which is a great deal. *Village 2 off Mechanic St.,* ☎ *215/ 862–2462.*

$$$ **The Raven.** If you're intent on having a somewhat formal dinner in a predominantly gay atmosphere, the several classy, darkly lit dining rooms at the Raven are your best bet. The Continental American menu is dependable, if predictable, though you'll find a few unusual offerings, such as roast duck with a tangy blueberry-peach chutney. There's a small tavern in back. *385 W. Bridge St.,* ☎ *215/862–2081.*

$$–$$$ **The Cafe.** In tiny, rural Rosemont, New Jersey, a 15-minute drive from New Hope, you'll be surprised to see a rainbow flag hoisted high above the town's only eatery, which looks and feels like a 1940s general store, with hardwood floors and mismatched wooden chairs. The two women running this place are among the area's most talented chefs, preparing a great variety of dishes—pasta with blue cheese and walnuts, Tunisian sesame eggplant, a peasant omelet with sour cream and caviar—with an emphasis on farm-fresh ingredients. *Junction of Rtes. 519 and 604, Rosemont, NJ,* ☎ *609/397–4097.*

$$–$$$ **Karla's.** Karla's is a gay-popular place downtown, attracting a colorful bunch of theater workers and gallery owners. Choose among eating on the open terrace with marble-top tables, on the glassed-in porch, or in the formal, intimate dining room with hanging plants, lace curtains, and a cloudy-sky ceiling. A mix of formal and casual fare, from St. Peter's fish with red potatoes to pâté to steak fajitas. *5 W. Mechanic St.,* ☎ *215/862–2612.*

$$ The Landing. Popular with New Hope's many day-trippers and shoppers, the Landing is a red clapboard tavern on the river. The brick patio offers views clear across to Lambertville and hosts a friendly, if aggressive, posse of ducks. Try the turkey chili or red bean hummus. *22 North Main St.,* ☎ *215/862–3558.*

$–$$ Fran's Pub. This, and Richard's, next door, are two of the town's better pizza-and-pasta joints—very informal, catering to the many alternateens dashing in and out of Main Street's few grunge-sensible shops. Looks and feels like a roadhouse. *116 South Main St.,* ☎ *215/862–5539.*

$ Wildflowers. The small, traditional dining room of this old clapboard house near the corner of Main and Mechanic lacks atmosphere. Scoot through to the back terrace, however, and you'll find a delightful, shady, brick terrace overlooking Ingham Creek. Old-fashioned Pennsylvania cooking, such as baked ham and meat loaf. *8 W. Mechanic St.,* ☎ *215/ 862–2241.*

SLEEPS

Of Philadelphia hotels popular with lesbians and gays, about a third are top-of-the-line luxury hotels, which derive about 75% to 85% of their revenue from midweek business travelers; at many of these you can get good deals on weekends. Another popular option is the Holiday Inn Midtown, from which you can pretty much smell the essence of libido wafting off Woody's dance floor, 50 feet away across Walnut Street. There are also a few gay-oriented guest houses (covered below), a number of drab convention hotels (not covered below), and several touristy accommodations near Independence Park (a couple are covered below).

Philadelphia

For price ranges, *see* Chart A at the front of this guide.

Hotels

▦ Cunard Cruise Line reopened the esteemed **Bellevue Hotel** in 1989. New owners have since turned down the stuffiness a few notches, although chaps and spurs at afternoon tea are still no-no's. On the premises are three floors of the city's toniest shops and a terrific fitness center. *1415 Chancellor Ct., at Broad and Walnut Sts.,* ☎ *215/893–1776 or 800/221–0833. 170 rooms. $$$$*

▦ The **Four Seasons,** built in 1983, is the city's most expensive hotel, and justly so. The Fountain Restaurant is one of the nation's best. *1 Logan Sq.,* ☎ *215/963–1500 or 800/332–3442. 371 rooms. $$$$*

▦ The **Rittenhouse** is about as gay-oriented a luxury hotel as you're going to find: In addition to employing many gay staff and participating in AIDS fund-raisers, it has a concierge with information on gay bars and restaurants. The Rittenhouse treats all its guests like old friends, and movie buffs will appreciate its having hosted the cast of *Philadelphia* during filming. *210 W. Rittenhouse Sq.,* ☎ *215/546–9000 or 800/635–1042. 98 rooms. $$$$*

▦ The **Ritz-Carlton** rises 15 stories above a chichi shopping mall, and it's close to Rittenhouse Square and the gay district. *17th and Chestnut Sts.,* ☎ *215/563–1600 or 800/241–3333. 290 rooms. $$$$*

☎ Centrally located, the sleek and contemporary **Doubletree** is a fair-priced option. The fitness center is good, rooms are among the largest in town, and the hotel's accordionlike facade allows guests some unusual city views. *Broad and Locust Sts., ☎ 215/893–1600. 427 rooms. $$$*

☎ Though packed with tourist families, the **Holiday Inn Independence Mall** is very gay-friendly. *4th and Arch Sts., ☎ 215/923–8660 or 800/843–2355. 371 rooms. $$$*

☎ An older apartment building–cum-hotel, the **Warwick** completed a $5 million renovation in 1992 and now rivals any city hotel for European-style charm and elegance. *1701 Locust St., ☎ 215/735–6000 or 800/523–4210. 225 rooms. $$$*

☎ The **Comfort Inn Penn's Landing** is not a gay-oriented hotel and is in a noisy spot, but it is one of the cleanest mid-price hotels in town. *100 N. Christopher Columbus Blvd., ☎ 215/627–7900 or 800/228–5150. 185 rooms. $$–$$$*

☎ When there are gay events in town, the 30-year-old **Holiday Inn Express Midtown** is wall-to-wall homos. It's steps away from the gay district (and several steamy adult theaters) and has friendly employees. *1305 Walnut St., ☎ 215/735–9300 or 800/465–4329. 164 rooms. $$–$$$*

☎ The budget **Travelodge,** down near Veteran's Stadium and the Spectrum, is a clean, simple place in a safe but rather inconvenient South Philadelphia neighborhood. You'll get free parking, a free shuttle to and from the airport, and very gay-friendly service. *2015 Pensrose Ave., ☎ 215/755–6500. 204 rooms. $*

Small Hotels and Guest Houses

☎ The **Society Hill Hotel** is in a converted 1832 longshoreman's house with a smattering of antiques along with brass beds and lamps; it's a good value. The outdoor cafe has a cozy bar that overlooks a park. Jazz piano is played from Tuesday through Saturday. *301 Chestnut St., ☎ 215/925–1394. 12 rooms. Mixed gay/straight. $$–$$$*

☎ Built in 1769 by a prominent physician, the **Thomas Bond House** has been meticulously restored to capture the flavor of Colonial Philadelphia. Authentic touches include marble fireplaces and four-poster Thomasville beds. *129 S. 2nd St., ☎ 215/923–8523. 12 rooms. Mostly straight. $$–$$$*

☎ Two brothers opened the **Abigail Adams,** a small seven-story hotel right in the gay district, in 1994. They and offer one of the best bargains in town. The rooms are quite large and clean, though rather plain. *1208 Walnut St., ☎ 215/546–7336. 32 rooms. Mostly straight. $–$$*

☎ **Antique Row Bed & Breakfast.** Affordability is the name of the game at this comfortable and charming Euro-style B&B. Full breakfast. *341 S. 12th St., ☎ 215/592–7802. 6 rooms. Mixed gay/straight. $*

New Hope

For price ranges, *see* Chart B at the front of this guide.

Hotels

☎ Among hotel options in New Hope, the **Inn at Lambertville Station** has the most character. It's just across the river from New Hope, by the bridge. Rooms are extremely homey, with antiques and reproductions, and great river views. *11 Bridge St., Lambertville, NJ, ☎ 609/397–8300 or 800/524–1091. 45 rooms. $$$–$$$$*

☎ Less interesting but clean and friendly are the **Best Western of New Hope** (Rte. 202, ☎ 215/862–5221 or 800/465–4239; 159 rooms; $–$$) and the **New Hope Motel** (400 W. Bridge St., ☎ 215/862–2800; 28 rooms; $). The latter is a short walk from the gay clubs.

Small Hotels and Guest Houses

⛉ **Back Street Inn** is a modest 1750s house full of tasteful country antiques and set on one of the most beautifully landscaped properties in town. Includes an intimate pool area. *144 Old York Rd., ☏ 215/862–9571 or 800/841–1874. 7 rooms. Mixed gay/straight. $$$*

⛉ A 10-minute drive from downtown, the **Lexington House,** parts of which date from 1749, gives you the chance to experience a gay B&B on 7 serene acres in the country. Authentically, though simply, furnished, the Lexington's most notable feature is the stone foundation of an old barn that has been artfully transformed into a pool, surrounded by lush gardens and a flagstone terrace. *6171 Upper York Rd., ☏ 215/794–0811. 6 rooms. Mixed gay male/lesbian. $$$*

⛉ A magnificent country inn in the tiny village of Erwinna, **Evermay on the Delaware** is run by Fred Cresson and Ron Strouse, the latter a gourmet chef—one seven-course prix fixe dinner is included. This stately 1720 manor is impeccably restored; many rooms face the river, and all have air-conditioning. Two-night minimum if you arrive on Saturday. *River Rd., Erwinna, ☏ 610/294–9100. 16 rooms. Mostly straight. $$–$$$$*

⛉ The most charming downtown accommodation, the **Wedgewood Inn** consists of a bright blue 1870 Victorian clapboard house, an adjacent 1830 Classical Revival stone-and-plaster house, and a nearby small Victorian that's used mostly in conjunction with conferences. Wedgewood pottery, of course, is placed everywhere, along with lavish Victorian antiques. *111 W. Bridge St., ☏ 215/862–2570. 18 rooms. Mostly straight. $$–$$$$*

⛉ On a stretch of the Delaware Canal, just north of town, the romantic **Inn at Phillips Mill** is a former grist mill, later the home of landscape painter William Lathrop, and now a first-rate French eatery famous for its rich desserts. Rooms are small, but decorated with a cheerful mix of dried flowers, country and folk antiques, and original art. *2590 N. River Rd., ☏ 215/862–2984. 5 rooms and a cottage. Mostly straight. $$–$$$*

⛉ The **Woolverton Inn** is a 1792 stone manor with a dramatic high mansard roof, set on several pastoral acres with an old stone barn, a carriage house (with several guest rooms), and apple and oak trees everywhere. One of the loveliest settings in the valley—romantic and secluded. *6 Woolverton Rd., Stockton, NJ, ☏ 609/397–0802. 11 rooms. Mostly straight. $$–$$$*

⛉ Just down busy Bridge Street a half mile from Raven Hall, the **Fox & Hound** is an 1850s stone-and-stucco house with a mansard roof. Period antiques fill the rooms, and there's a pretty patio outside. *246 W. Bridge St., ☏ 215/862–5082 or 800/862–5082. 5 rooms. Mixed gay/straight. $–$$$*

⛉ West of downtown, near the gay bars, the **Raven Hall** (also know as the Ravenwood B&B) is the only true gay guest house, although it feels more like a small motor lodge. Rooms, most of which have private baths, are basic and set in a colonial-style dark blue building, which is a new addition to the original structure. Very social. *385 W. Bridge St., ☏ 215/862–2081. 17 rooms. Mostly gay male. $–$$$*

SCENES

Philadelphia

Barflies and conversationalists adore Philadelphia's small but extremely convivial bar scene. Twentysomethings, poseurs, and lonely hearts hate it, generally dubbing Woody's the only "real" game in town. There are about a dozen bars, nine of which are set in the gay district. Two of the other three bars, 247 and the Post, fall between the gay district and Rittenhouse Square, a few blocks over. Rodz is about four blocks south of here on 15th Street. On a good night, you could hit all 12 places.

Other than these, several of the gay-friendly restaurants around South Street—notably Judy's and Café Nola—have active little bars, particularly in the early evening. Also downtown, Circa is a great restaurant with a dance floor that's popular on Fridays and Saturdays with gays and lesbians.

What you'll find in Philadelphia, as opposed to virtually every other major city in America, is that nobody can remember when a gay bar last opened or closed. Things don't change here. The crowds are consistently chatty, older, local, and relatively uninterested in playing musical beds. Bartenders and patrons will strike up a conversation with strangers. Since all these places serve food, a clubby, tavernlike atmosphere prevails. To the visitor from bigger cities, it will seem quiet—but you'll be made to feel right at home.

Each of these establishments, of course, has its own edge. Woody's is the only true stand-and-model bar-disco. And there's a popular after-hours hangout, the 24 Club. There are also roving lesbian and gay parties, two regionally famed AIDS benefits (the Blue Ball each fall, White Heat each spring), and a few straight clubs with occasional gay events or at least gay followings. Gay events here are typically impromptu and sometimes unadvertised except for flyers posted at Giovanni's Room and some of the bars.

A group called **Queer Slut Cafe** (no ☎) organizes lesbian parties from time to time at various venues, but these events are only advertised by flyer. Check the bulletin board at Giovanni's Room to see if anything is up.

Though based in southern New Jersey, **Ladies for the 80s** (☎ 609/784– 8341) sponsors lesbian parties at dance clubs and bars throughout the region. Depending on the venue, the turnout can be incredible. Generally, the hottest dance parties are those held at the 24 Club. There's almost always some event on the first Saturday of the month, and other fetes pop up from time to time. Call to get on the mailing list.

New Hope
Though sneeringly called "No Hope" by city folk disheartened by New Hope's low-key nightlife, the community supports two relatively large discos and a small gay tavern—a busier scene than you'll find in Rehoboth Beach, Delaware. On weekends, especially in spring and fall, your odds of meeting friends and having a blast are actually very good. Other times, the crowds are mostly local and quite cliquey. Obviously, experiences will differ from night to night, depending on the crowd, but the bar regulars in town aren't famous for making strangers feel welcome. All three clubs (described below) are within walking distance of each other.

Bars and Nightclubs

Philadelphia
Bike Stop. Once an exclusively leather (some would argue leatherette) bar, the Bike Stop added two upper floors a couple of years ago. The second level is a true sports bar with a big trophy case, a baseball or hockey game going most nights, and pinball, pool, and darts. On the third floor is a midsize disco (open Fri. and Sat.) that's become gradually more popular with both lesbians and gay men. *206 S. Quince St., ☎ 215/627–1662. Crowd: leather-and-Levi's and mostly mixed-age male on first floor, more diverse on upper levels.*

Raffles. Everyone is made extremely welcome here by the outgoing bartenders and friendly patrons, who frequently erupt into sing-alongs in the popular restaurant on the main floor. Downstairs is a game room. Very casual. Only the decor is uninspired. *243 S. Camac St., ☎ 215/545–6969.*

Crowd: 70/30 m/f, mixed ages, theater/piano types of varying talent, zero attitude.

Rodz. It's popular for many reasons: a good restaurant, a romantic roof deck with city views, and a classy piano bar. Most nights the several bars draw a down-and-dirty crowd of regulars who come pretty much for the banter. Attached is an after-hours dance spot, **Club Tyz**, for which membership is required (you must be sponsored by a current member). Tyz has a dance floor on the top floor, and on the lower floor, called Bottoms, there are pool tables and pinball machines. Weekly events, such as Jock Strap Night, change monthly. *1418 Rodman St., ☎ 215/735–2900. Crowd: mostly male but women-friendly, a mixed bag.*

24 Club. Since it's open until 5 AM, this very hot disco is the *only* place to go when the clubs have closed and the adrenaline is still pumping. There's no alcohol (patrons seem to find other ways to keep a buzz going), it costs $25 to join (membership is good for a year), and you must be introduced to become a member. Best bet: Hang out till closing at Woody's, and with enough persistence you'll meet somebody who belongs. Some events and some Sundays are open to nonmembers. *204 S. Camac St., ☎ 215/735–5772. Crowd: very young, mixed genders and races.*

247 Bar. In a city seemingly unhindered by backward thinking, it's surprising that 247 was raided recently for showing porn videos in the basement. Oddly, the vice squad paid no attention to the upstairs go-go dancers, who have a reputation for displaying their goods rather aggressively. This complex has several rooms and floors, and though none allow sexual activity, the atmosphere is steamy. Some reports of hustlers. Gets a rush after midnight. *247 S. 17th St., ☎ 215/545–9779. Crowd: male, some leather-and-Levi's, mixed ages.*

Westbury Bar. A terrific neighborhood hangout that's been the Cheers of the gay district since 1987. There's a pinball machine, a great jukebox, and a bright decor of exposed brick and comfy booths. It's a great place to meet friends before heading elsewhere, or just to grab soup and a sandwich. Bartenders are gregarious when it's not too busy. *13th and Spruce Sts., ☎ 215/546–5170. Crowd: 80/20 m/f, local, mixed-age, fairly mixed racially, very friendly.*

Woody's. This is easily Philadelphia's most popular club, the first—and often the only—place out-of-towners head to. The very people who complain about the scene, the attitude, and the conformity of its clientele hang out here night after night. Its two levels have a fairly large disco (expanded a couple years ago); two video bars; and a room with tables, chairs, and a long bar. You can barely move on weekends—which keeps things frisky. Tuesday and Sunday there are two-stepping lessons. Best dance night: Wednesday, when under-21s are admitted for a $3 cover—more women come then, too. The downstairs video bar is friendlier than the upstairs one. *202 S. 13th St., ☎ 215/545–1893. Crowd: mostly white, guppie gym types, largely male.*

These spots have a quieter and more local following:

Once a popular disco, **Key West** (207 S. Juniper St., ☎ 215/545–1578) is now big only on weekends. **The Post** (1705 Chancellor St., ☎ 215/985–9720) is known for its colorful bar staff and Sunday go-go boys. **Uncles** (1220 Locust St., ☎ 215/546–6660) is popular with players on Philly's outstanding lesbian and gay softball teams. The **Venture Inn** (255 S. Camac St., ☎ 215/545–8731) is in a historic old tavern and also happens to be the oldest gay bar in town.

New Hope

Cartwheel. New Hope's largest club, the Cartwheel draws huge crowds on weekends and has an enormous parking lot to prove it. Things don't usually get going here until midnight, when everybody comes over from the other two bars, the restaurants, the theater, and neighboring towns—even Philadelphia. Inside are several bars plus a large dance floor. *Junction of Rtes. 202 and 179, ☎ 215/862–0880. Crowd: very mixed m/f, all ages but generally youngest crowd in town.*

The Prelude. This is a typical resort disco and dining complex, with several rooms and something for everyone, from the pleasant little fern bar up front to a small dining room set inside a greenhouse to a mid-size dance floor. It's traditionally been better known as a restaurant than as a club; many patrons come here first for drinks, then head over to the Cartwheel (*see above*). *408 York Rd., ☎ 215/862–9494. Crowd: more local and generally older, but otherwise similar to that of Cartwheel, above.*

Raven. There are three good times to come here: during the afternoon to lie out by the pool, in the early evening for predinner drinks, or later for after-dinner drinks in the small, amber-lighted tavern. The Raven has an extremely loyal local following. Bartenders are a touch attitudy. *385 W. Bridge St., ☎ 215/862–2081. Crowd: mostly male, locals and hotel guests, over 35.*

THE LITTLE BLACK BOOK

At Your Fingertips

AIDS Information Network: ☎ 215/575–1110. **Community AIDS Hotline:** ☎ 215/985–2437 or 800/985–2437. **Gay and Lesbian Counseling Service Hotline:** ☎ 215/732–8255. **Gay and Lesbian Switchboard:** ☎ 215/546–7100 (Sun.–Tues. 7 PM–10 PM, Thurs.–Sat. 6 PM–11 PM). **Gay, Lesbian, Bisexual Events Line:** ☎ 215/898–8888. **New Hope Tourism Information Center:** 1 W. Mechanic St., 18938, ☎ 215/862–5880 or 215/862–5030. **Penguin Place:** 201 S. Camac St., ☎ 215/732–2220 (the lesbian, gay, and bisexual community center). **Philadelphia Community Health Alternatives:** ☎ 215/545–8686 or 215/735–1911. **Philadelphia Convention and Visitors Association:** 1515 Market St., Suite 2020, 19102, ☎ 215/636–3300. **Philadelphia Lesbian and Gay Task Force Anti-Violence and Discrimination Hotline:** ☎ 215/772–2005. **Philadelphia Visitors Center:** 16th St. and John F. Kennedy Blvd., 19102, ☎ 215/636–1666 or 800/321–9563. **Women Organized Against Rape Hotline:** ☎ 215/985–3333. **Women's Switchboard:** ☎ 215/564–5810.

Gay Media

Philadelphia's main lesbian/gay newspapers are the weeklies *Au Courant* (☎ 215/790–1179), which began in 1982, and *Philadelphia Gay News* (☎ 215/625–8501), which began in 1976. The city's free women's monthly, *Labyrinth* (☎ 215/546–6686) is not gay per se, but has much lesbian-oriented coverage. The bimonthly newsletter "**LesBurbia**" (Box 293, Montgomeryville, PA 18936, no ☎) is geared more toward the suburbs but has some city-relevant lesbian information. The "**Gay Guide to Philadelphia**" ($2 at Giovanni's Room [*see* Bookstores, *below*]) is a fold-out pamphlet with a bulleted map and a directory of many gay establishments.

City Paper (☎ 215/735–8444) is the gay-friendliest of the arts and entertainment newspapers; *Welcomat* (☎ 215/563–1234), its competitor, is also helpful.

The city's (and one of the nation's) largest, **Giovanni's Room** (345 S. 12th St., ☎ 215/923–2960; call for a catalogue) is in the southeast quadrant of the gay district. It has two floors of lesbian and gay titles. It's also the region's only substantial source of feminist material, both gay and non-gay. There are several community bulletin boards, a wide range of periodicals, and a relatively tame but extensive selection of pornography. The staff is extremely helpful and has a real knack for finding out-of-print, import, or hard-to-find titles. **Afterwords** (218 S. 12th St., ☎ 215/735–2393) has a tiny but nonetheless gay-oriented selection of books and is comparable to Giovanni's Room in its lesbian and gay periodicals, post-cards, and greeting cards. It also carries magazines and newspapers of every type from around the world as well as lots of gifts and T-shirts. It's open late.

There are a couple of good independent bookstores in New Hope, including **Farley's** (40 South Main St., ☎ 215/862–2452), which has a small lesbian/gay section, and the **Book Gallery** (19 W. Mechanic St., ☎ 215/862–5110), which has a strong selection of feminist and gay/lesbian titles.

Body and Fitness

The **12th Street Gym** (204 S. 12th St., ☎ 215/985–4092), in the gay district, is the city's queerest gym, very guppie and good for both women and men. Much less of a scene but perfectly gay-friendly and nicely appointed is the **Rittenhouse Square Fitness Club** (2002 Rittenhouse Sq., ☎ 215/985–4095).

18 *Out in Phoenix*
With Sedona and Jerome

ARIZONA REMAINED A TERRITORY of the United States longer—for nearly 150 years—than any of the first 48 states. Perhaps for this reason, the state, and its capital city, Phoenix, still possess a distinct distrust of federal government, external control, and any initiative that might be construed as a threat to civil liberty. Phoenicians have traditionally rebuked attempts at zoning, antidiscrimination laws, and pollution controls. The city is highly contemporary and yet it's also the last stronghold of the western frontier. It's like Los Angeles dressed in cowboy boots.

Though it was a frontier town, Phoenix is no longer geographically rugged. Its spectacular setting, fringed by mountains and high desert, has been transformed over the past four decades into flat miles of tract housing and strip malls. The mountains invite a thick cloud of smog to envelop the valley on most afternoons. It's the ninth largest city in the country, but it lacks a center—even a downtown. Every square on its grid seems as important—or unimportant—as every other.

The city is often compared with Los Angeles because of its geography, as both are driving cities in dry climates (Phoenix rests in the world's second driest desert—only the Sahara has lower humidity). But the cultural influence of southern California is strong, too. As opposed to virtually every other territory west of the Mississippi, Arizona has been settled more by folks moving from the Pacific than by those moving from the East Coast. Californians were the earliest Americans to move to Phoenix in great numbers, beginning in the 1870s. Today, Phoenix still takes its cues, and many of its new residents, from southern California—its dining, shopping, and nightlife scenes consistently inspire comparisons with Los Angeles.

A major difference between the two is that in Phoenix the grocery clerk will stop checking items long enough to smile and say hello. Or the bus driver will pause long enough to offer directions. People move here typically for job opportunity—greater Phoenix is the third-largest silicon valley in the country—but also to escape from the rudeness and fast-pace mentality of other big cities.

Phoenix's mid-20th-century population boom is often attributed to the invention of air-conditioning. Indeed, in the early years, the hot weather kept year-round residents from settling here in large numbers. Back then, fashionable Europeans and Americans came for a taste of the Wild West—the chance to watch the rodeo world championships, to shop for Indian crafts and jewelry, and to live on a dude ranch. On the hottest summer nights, you encamped on your lawn or inside screened gazebos.

In the '30s, air-conditioning became practical and relatively affordable. Most Phoenicians installed these heavenly devices, and living here comfortably, year-round, became a reality. Nonetheless, even after air-conditioning made its debut, the population grew little through World War II, hovering around 50,000. What actually spurred the valley's population explosion was the wartime installation of the Luke Air Force Base. Thousands of young men and fewer women discovered the city, and many returned here after the war. Simultaneously, the aviation industry set up shop, becoming a forerunner to hundreds of cutting-edge technological interests that would dominate the commercial landscape for the next half century.

Phoenix's population grew to 600,000 by the mid-'70s and has swelled to more than a million today; three-fourths of the state's population lives in greater Phoenix. As a result of the recent boom, what you almost never meet in this city is a native Phoenician. Hispanics are the most heavily represented of the city's ethnic minorities, which only account for about 20% of the population—very low compared with other cities near Mexico. People come here in search of a fresh start or a stopover between careers. During the last decade, 200,000 people moved here annually, and another 150,000 moved out. Many were retirees, but many more were young, white professionals.

Already a city hostile toward big government, Phoenix has witnessed a massive intake of senior citizens and upwardly mobile, but transient, technocrats. The result is a deeply conservative votership. The city has never been especially sympathetic to the plight of minorities, sexual or racial—Arizona's former governor, Evan Mechem, made it his first official act to repeal the state's Martin Luther King Jr. holiday.

Perhaps the most popular brand of Phoenix conservatism is that made famous by another former governor, Barry Goldwater, whose libertarian views espouse a somewhat benevolent live-and-let-live philosophy. Himself a surprisingly open defender of the gay community (he has a warm relationship with an openly gay grandson), Goldwater has nonetheless been unable to sway popular opinion significantly in favor of gay rights initiatives. At best, you can count on the average conservative Phoenician to believe that consensual acts that occur in the privacy of people's homes are nobody else's business. Actually pushing through an antidiscrimination policy has yet to fly, however, because to most libertarians such a measure represents one more way in which the government operates with too heavy a hand.

The transiency of Phoenicians has made it difficult for the gay community to stay focused politically, and even socially. Until November 1995 this was the largest city in the country without a full-scale gay and lesbian bookstore, and it's still one of the largest without any particular gay ghetto—or even a strip of gay bars. It would help, of course, if residents walked the streets more, but this is the sort of place where you drive 50 feet to buy a pack of gum. The diffusion of gays and lesbians does have the effect of keeping every section of town somewhat tolerant: No matter what block you decide to settle on, you're likely to have a few gay neighbors.

Adamantly opposed to interference, Phoenicians have created their own paradise, one that rolls along according to the laws of nature rather than the laws of constitutional democracy. There are drawbacks, such as unchecked pollution and the city's disjointed, formless landscape. And as free enterprise and capitalism have reigned, corruption has flowered. The lack of rules gives the city a *Lord of the Flies* mentality, which has brought out the best and the worst in every Phoenician.

THE LAY OF THE LAND

As the policeman shouts to a mob of rubberneckers in every low-budget cops-and-robbers film ever made: "Move along folks . . . there's nothing to see here!" Indeed, the country's third-largest silicon valley, for all of its shops, spas, and good restaurants, boasts little in the way of sight-seeing. Remnants of pre-1900 Phoenix are rare. Though you'll pass by a few interesting examples of 20th-century architecture, most do not merit a second glance. And though you'll discover a smattering of museums and galleries, few of them compares with the best of what you might find in cities of comparable size.

The city is, like Las Vegas, sprawling and flat. Streets are straight, geo-metric, and broad. Some homes are fronted by short, scrubby plots of yellow-green grass, but most have "desert landscaping," a gracious eu-phemism for what are often motley arrangements of dirt, rocks, and cacti. A building boom began in the early 1950s and flourished extensively through the 1960s and '70s. The resultant miles and miles of drab low rises and whitewashed shopping centers tell the story.

Some of the best sights in the state are within a two-hour drive of Phoenix; see Sedona and Jerome (*below*) and the Tucson chapter for more.

Downtown

The **East End** of downtown, bounded roughly by Van Buren to the north, 7th Street to the east, Madison Street to the south, and Central Avenue to the west, has been revitalized and contains several noteworthy sights. **Heritage Square,** where 7th and Adams streets intersect, is lined with re-stored turn-of-the-century homes, including one of the few remaining Vic-torians in the city, **Rosson House** (6th and Monroe Sts., ☎ 602/262–5071), of which tours are available. Several other homes on the south side of the square are open for touring. A couple blocks northwest, the con-temporary, Aztec-influenced Mercado contains the small but estimable **Museo Chicano** (1242 E. Washington St., ☎ 602/257–5536) on its sec-ond floor, a museum devoted to art depicting Hispanic culture.

If you drive up Central Avenue several blocks, you'll see the shiny new Phoenix and its many shiny new skyscrapers. A bit dull, it nevertheless contains two museums worth visiting. The **Phoenix Art Museum** (1625 N. Central Ave., ☎ 602/257–1222), at the corner of Central and Coro-nado Road, houses a substantial number of 19th-century European paint-ings and an outstanding American West collection, with works by Remington, O'Keeffe, and many others. Two blocks north, at the corner of Monte Vista Road, is the superb **Heard Museum** (22 E. Monte Vista Rd., ☎ 602/252–8840), a 1928 traditional adobe house containing the nation's top collection of Native American art and artifacts.

Camelback Road and Greater Phoenix

In central Phoenix, around Camelback Road and Central Avenue, you will find many an excuse to spend money. **Park Central Mall** (Central Ave. and Earll Dr., ☎ 602/264–5575) is the oldest and probably gayest of any shopping mall in Phoenix. It's not at snazzy as some of the newer ones, but it has some great gay-friendly shops, such as **International Consign-ment World,** an emporium of all that glitters (some of which is gold), in-cluding antiques, home furnishings, gourmet items, and other gifts.

Northern Phoenix, where it is crossed by Camelback Road and Lincoln Drive, has the more expensive real estate, shopping, and dining. The ut-terly stupendous **Biltmore Fashion Park** (24th St. and Camelback Rd., ☎

602/955–8400) is where many a diva whiles away her Saturday afternoons, gazing at such high-end boutiques as Polo and Gucci.

Points west of downtown are mostly middle-class suburbs; points south, lower-class suburbs. To the east of downtown is a mix—seedy around the airport and in most of Phoenix south of Thomas Road and east of 51st Street, but pleasant once you cross the Salt River and enter the enclaves of Mesa (now the third-largest city in Arizona) and Tempe. East of Phoenix but north of Thomas Road takes you into Scottsdale, the ritziest of area communities.

In Phoenix, the closest you'll come to a gay district is the stretch of rectangle bounded by 7th Avenue to the west, Indian School Road to the south, 7th Street to the east, and Bethany Home Road to the north. But as noted earlier, it's not a big area for sightseeing—it's just where many of the city's lesbians and gays live and the bulk of the bars are.

Scottsdale

A cross between Beverly Hills and Santa Fe, Scottsdale has hundreds of high-end arts and crafts galleries and specialty shops. It is as uniformly comfortable for lesbian and gay visitors as any part of metro Phoenix. Though conservative, locals tend to mind their own business and shouldn't be too freaked out by same-sex couples strolling arm in arm. In a sophisticated, upscale community such as this, the laws of morality are superseded only by the laws of discretion: They may not approve of us in Scottsdale, but they're too refined to notice us and certainly too polite to comment.

The **Scottsdale Fashion Square** (Scottsdale and Camelback Rds., ☎ 602/990–7800) is an enormous, fancy mall, but *the* place to be seen is definitely the **Borgata** (6166 N. Scottsdale Rd., ☎ 602/998–1822), a Renaissance-style compound supposedly designed to resemble a beautiful Italian village. Just south of the Fashion Square, **5th Avenue** curves northeast from Indian School Road up to Scottsdale Road, lined with clothiers, jewelers, boutiques, and, behind the Common Ground coffeehouse, the yuppyish gay bar BS West. More touristy but still brimming with great shopping is **Old Town Scottsdale,** which is at its best along Main Street between Brown Avenue and 70th Street (Scottsdale Road crosses Main Street midway).

The one nonshopping must-see is **Taliesin West** (114th St. and Cactus Rd., ☎ 602/860–8810 or 602/860–2700), the historic winter home of Frank Lloyd Wright, where he kept a studio and his school in the desert. Tours of the grounds only are available daily.

Tempe

One of the few areas of sidewalk culture is in Tempe, about a 20-minute drive east of central Phoenix, in the heart of Arizona State University's (ASU's) campus. Thanks to its influx of academics and students, gays feel very comfortable walking around the campus. And Mill Street, which runs just north of University Drive, has dozens of funky shops, restaurants, and hang-outs, none specifically gay-oriented, but most quite gay-friendly.

Sedona

With an increasing number of lesbian and gay travelers seeking alternatives to the somewhat intense scenes in Palm Springs and Provincetown, quiet, colorful Sedona has developed a particularly strong following, particularly among lesbians and New Agers, who recognize the region as containing some of the Earth's most significant vortices (energy centers).

Sedona has definitely succumbed some to the vagaries of zoneless development—such as the rapidly expanding sea of shops hawking T-shirts and pets rocks. And skeptics snicker, insisting that the town is made up of matured hippies who have traded in their Volkswagen buses for $40,000 Range Rovers. Balancing what some would call negatives, however, are Sedona's rippling, azure creeks, precious Indian ruins, dark green patches of pine forest, and majestic red rock cliffs.

The easily accessed wilderness, which has drawn artists and filmmakers here for decades, makes Sedona one of the loveliest settings in Arizona. Opportunities to learn about crystals, soothsaying, healing, and Native American lore abound, but just as many visitors come to hike, sun, or play golf and tennis at the handful of first-rate resorts.

In terms of mood, Sedona is clearly—but quietly—open to gay tourism. Though the terms New Age and gay-friendly aren't necessarily interchangeable, tolerance is the rule. Nonetheless, Sedona is a typically conservative Northern Arizona town; the gay community is discreet, if not closeted, especially for men. There's no disco, gay or straight, no gay bookstores or gay community organizations. It is rather a straight vacation destination with an increasingly gay and lesbian following. And it's the perfect, relaxed retreat for a romantic interlude.

Sedona is made up essentially of three neighborhoods, which are loosely separated by the intersection of AZ 179 and Highway 89A. The area off Highway 89A west of the intersection is **West Sedona;** it's the least touristy of the three and where most locals do their shopping and hang out. It's also where more of the gay-oriented eateries are located (Troy's, Heartline, Sedona Bar and Grill). The area off Highway 89A east and north of the intersection is **Uptown,** where most of the touristy shops and motor lodges are. The stretch of AZ 179 south of the intersection is the least neighborhood-identified of the three, but after the road crosses Oak Creek it's sometimes referred to as **Bell Rock** and, a mile or two later, you actually enter the village of **Oak Creek.** This whole region is characterized by upscale shops, many of the town's newer homes, and a couple more resorts and restaurants.

You won't get bogged down by museums here, and you shouldn't plan to spend much time inside. That is unless shopping is your game, in which case you shouldn't miss the stunning **Tlaquepaque** (pronounced tuh-*lah*-cuh-*pah*-cuh) complex (AZ 179, ☎ 602/282–4838), a rambling, southwestern-style village of upscale studios, where more than 100 artists, including jewelers, painters, sculptors, and potters, sell their goods.

Among outdoor diversions, the dinner horse ride down to a creekside, led by the lesbian-owned **Kachina Stables** (Hwy. 89A and Lower Red Rock Loop Rd., ☎ 602/282–7252), is one of the most memorable experiences. Kachina can also do custom tours and group events, and though they cater to all, you'll find they have as gay a following as any in town.

Several companies give jeep tours, including **Pink Jeep Tours** (☎ 602/282–5000), **Sedona Adventures** (☎ 602/282–3500), and **Sedona Red Rock Jeep Tours** (☎ 602/282–6826); they're all reliable. All these tours start at about $20 per person, per hour.

Excursions from Sedona

Flagstaff is, unfortunately, known as that small city where most people spend the night in cheap motels before seeing the Grand Canyon. It's just 27 miles north and contains a few notable sights, including the **Museum of Northern Arizona** (☎ 602/774–5211), which contains an outstanding collection of Native American arts and crafts and historical exhibits;

and the **Coconino Center for the Arts** (☎ 602/779–6921), with arts exhibits, musical performances, and workshops, each dedicated to different aspects of Western America, from Native American history to the contemporary cowboy's lifestyle. The most dramatic site here is the **Arizona Snowbowl** (☎ 602/779–1951; ☎ 602/779–1950 for ski information), which is a popular ski area in winter and offers a tram ride to a height of 11,500 feet in summer.

The South Rim of the **Grand Canyon National Park** (☎ 602/638–7888; entry $10 per carload or, if arriving by public transport, $4 per person) is 110 miles northwest of Sedona and truly worth the drive—even if just to crane your neck over the ledge, feel that shiver shoot down your spine, and turn back again to Sedona. Spring through fall it's a tourist-laden nightmare, but no one can say this site is overrated.

Jerome

Jerome is smaller, less developed, and less expensive than Sedona. Accessible via a spectacular and tortuous drive up Highway 89A from the little desert town of Clarkdale, it's a mile above sea level and offers clear views of northern and central Arizona across the Verde Valley, including Sedona's red rocks and Flagstaff's snow-capped San Francisco Peaks.

Copper was king here for three-quarters of a century, beginning in 1876, when a copper camp was begun, clinging to the precipitous side of dramatic Cleopatra Hill. By 1929, 2,350 miners along with about 13,000 other smelters, gamblers, bootleggers, saloon keepers, prostitutes, entrepreneurs, and preachers lived more or less harmoniously here; the hodge-podge of early residents comprised an array of ethnic backgrounds.

Fires ravaged the town again and again, but it was always rebuilt. After too many uncontrollable blazes charred Jerome's 88 miles of subterranean tunnels, the town junked underground mining for the safer open-pit style, which was accomplished by dynamiting the hills. This caused buildings to rumble, shake, and in the case of the town jail, slide downhill 225 feet across the road from its original site.

Labor upheavals and uncertain copper prices put an end in 1953 to the town's mining operations. The population dwindled to about 50 stalwarts by the late 1950s, before counterculturists created a second boom here through the '60s and '70s.

Today's Jerome is a haven of aging hippies, writers, artists, musicians, historians, and shopkeepers numbering roughly 600 to 700 year-round. Though increasingly touristy, a tolerant mind-set prevails today, and the snobbery one frequently encounters in Sedona is frowned upon in quirky Jerome. The thing to do here, basically, is walk around. The town consists primarily of two streets, whose wonderfully offbeat shops and galleries can be visited in about two hours.

GETTING AROUND

You will need a car in **Phoenix;** nothing is within walking distance here. Virtually every thoroughfare, from two-lane road to eight-lane freeway, runs either east–west or north–south. Within the city limits, north–south roads are numbered, fanning out from Phoenix's commercial spine, Central Avenue. Every north–south thoroughfare to the east is a "street" (the major ones being 7th, 16th, 24th, and 32nd streets); each one to the west is an "avenue" (the major ones being 7th, 19th, 24th, and 35th avenues).

Major east–west roads are named. Following either Indian School or Camelback roads east will lead you into Scottsdale.

Public transit is of little use to visitors. Taxis are okay in a pinch but are unregulated and usually very expensive. Find out what the ride will cost before getting in.

From Phoenix it's roughly a two-hour drive to either **Sedona** or **Jerome** (there's no train or bus service). Take I–17 north to Route 260 for Jerome (just follow the signs from here to Highway 89A) or to Route 179 for Sedona. From Flagstaff, take Highway 89A through the Oak Creek Canyon to Sedona (27 miles). To reach Jerome from Sedona, take Highway 89A about 30 miles through the Verde Valley and the towns of Cottonwood and Clarkdale.

Tiny **Sedona Airport** (in West Sedona) handles on-demand charter flights from Phoenix on **Scenic Airlines** (☎ 520/282–7935); the cost is $195 for a three-passenger plane each way.

EATS

Plenty of restaurants in Phoenix have a gay following, or at least welcome the gay community. There are dozens of trendy, inventive, California-inspired restaurants, and some of Southwestern cuisine's major names either began their culinary careers here or have lately opened restaurants in town.

The bulk of the excellent restaurants is along Camelback Road in Phoenix, in any of the commercial areas of Scottsdale, and at the many great resorts. The best of the latter include the Latilla Room at the Boulders (New American), Mary Elaine's at the Phoenician (New American), Orangerie at the Arizona Biltmore (classic French), and the Restaurant at the Ritz-Carlton (New American). Only three of the city's top restaurants advertise regularly in gay publications, those being Eddie's Grill and Goldie's 1895 House (reviewed below).

Many of the gay bars serve brunch (Charlie's and Wink's are the best), have a limited menu of blah American food, or serve bar snacks. Some of the gayish coffeehouses have great sandwiches and salads. Also, most of the restaurants on 7th Avenue between the 4000 and 6000 blocks have gay followings.

For price ranges in Phoenix, Scottsdale, and Sedona, *see* Chart A at the front of this guide; for Jerome, *see* Chart B.

Phoenix

$$$$ **Christopher's and the Bistro.** A charming New American bistro and a striking, formal French restaurant with beautiful linen and silver share an open kitchen that turns out impeccable French fish and veal dishes. If you care about food, be sure to try one or the other. *2398 E. Camelback Rd.,* ☎ *602/957–3214.*

$$$$ **Vincent's.** The place to be seen—whether you're gay or straight—is presided over by Vincent Guérithault, often thought of as the founder of contemporary Southwestern cuisine. Here, sophisticated French techniques transform regional ingredients into such creations as crab cakes with avocado salsa, or duck tacos. Has a very "L.A." feel—and valet parking, too. *3930 E. Camelback Rd.,* ☎ *602/224–0225.*

$$$–$$$$ **RoxSand.** Here is the city's most outrageous restaurant, characterized by larger-than-life decor and true culinary chutzpah. The playful, if risky, menu borrows from all cultures where food reigns supreme: France,

Thailand, Jamaica, Greece, Mexico. Let your hair down and dive in to a plate of rice tamales stuffed with curried lamb, simmered in peanut sauce. *2594 E. Camelback Rd.,* ☎ *602/381–0444.*

$$–$$$ **Avanti.** This notable Italian mainstay has a fairly gay following (despite the Charlton Heston photo in the lobby). The striking art nouveau decor sizzles and sparkles, with its black-and-white checkered floor, zebra-stripe banquettes, and *lots* of chrome. It's somebody's idea of chic L.A.—and the relatively affordable food—osso buco, cioppino—is good and filling. *2728 E. Thomas St.,* ☎ *602/956–0900.*

$$–$$$ **The Beef Eaters.** Since 1961 this exercise in Elizabethan affectation has been catering to wealthy executives and their pretty "nieces" and "nephews." The decor is done to recall an English Tudor hunting lodge, and goes way over the top. Prime rib is sliced tableside, and the duck *à l'orange* is famous. *300 W. Camelback Rd.,* ☎ *602/264–3838.*

$$–$$$ **Eddie's Grill.** Typically in Phoenix, the snazziest places to eat are in modern office buildings. Eddie's, the most gay-frequented of the city's hot-shot restaurants, is in such a compound. The Mediterranean-meets-the-Southwest menu shows off such fare as shrimp sauced with a mix of lime juice, olive oil, peppers, cilantro, and mustard. *4747 N. 7th St.,* ☎ *602/ 241–1188.*

$$–$$$ **Timothy's.** This cute, white, creeper-covered cottage spouts live jazz and sophistication as well as any club in Greenwich Village. It's very respected, drawing a hip-by-Phoenix-standards pack of bon vivants. The food is good, too, with hearty sandwiches (try smoked mozzarella on focaccia) and moderately priced entrées (check out the great blue-corn-crusted sea bass). *6335 N. 16th St.,* ☎ *602/277–7634.*

$$ **Christo's.** No surprises at this elegant, slightly formal Italian restaurant with Greek undertones. But for the strip-mall location, you'd think you were eating in something straight out of *The Godfather.* The service is attentive, the decor refined, and the veal, shrimp, chicken, and daily fresh-catch specials delicious. *6327 N. 7th St.,* ☎ *602/264–1784.*

$$ **Goldie's 1895 House.** This brick painted lady wrapped in shades of lavender, purple, and white is memorable, if not for its food, then for its frilly Victorian decor and its chatty, characterful staff. The traditional American menu throws out the odd surprise—such as roast duck in a pomegranate-walnut sauce—but consists mostly of suitably prepared standbys. Very gay-friendly. *362 N. 2nd Ave.,* ☎ *602/254–0338.*

$$ **Options.** An Internet Media room is one of the draws at this French-Italian spot. Monday is *Ab Fab* night, Wednesday is reserved for campy movies, and on Thursday you can laugh between courses or drinks at the "Hysterical (comedy) Hour." *5111 N. 7th St.,* ☎ *602/263–5776.*

$$ **Such Is Life.** By day this is an outstanding Mexican restaurant, using fine Guadalajaran preparations and ingredients; by night it's a decent but less memorable Spanish restaurant. Best Mexican dish is the chicken Maya, shredded morsels in a piquant *achiote* sauce. *3602 N. 24th St.,* ☎ *602/ 955–7822.*

$ **Beulah's.** Famed for its Jewish pizza (topped with corned beef, sauerkraut, and swiss cheese), among other seemingly unappetizing offerings. This is the city's gay—or at least bohemian—pizza parlor. The Chinese pizza has veggies in a teriyaki sauce. Huge deli sandwiches and smoothie fruit shakes, too. *2022 N. 7th St.,* ☎ *602/252–5303.*

$ **Denny's.** Unless you've spent the past decade sealed snugly in a mason jar, you know what to expect from Denny's: cheap, cholesterol-laden breakfasts and fat-soaked meat-loaf dinners around the clock. After the bars close, this Denny's swells with bitchy and butchy queens. *16 E. Camelback Rd.,* ☎ *602/266–9868.*

$ **Munch a Bagel.** Northeastern types will feel right at home in this famed deli and bagelry, a short drive from many of the gay bars. Walk in, take

284

Eats ●

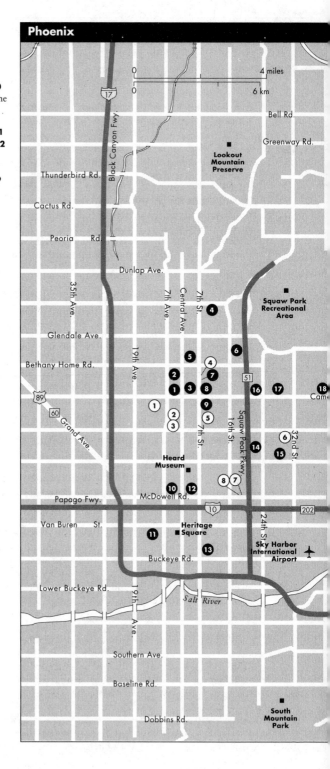

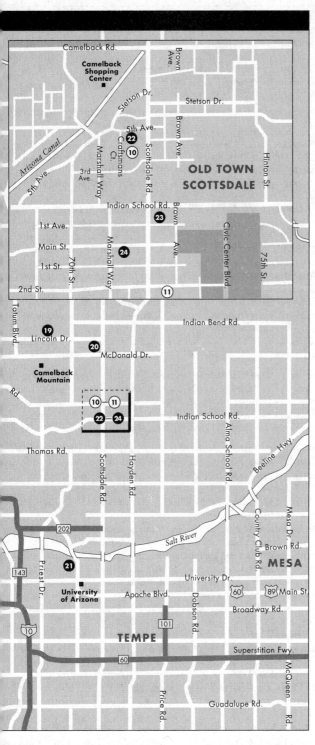

a number, and order a bagel piled high with lox. In the bright, airy room next door are plenty of tables and neatly framed photos on the walls. Best bagels in town, and great kosher meats. *5114 N. 7th St.,* ☎ *602/264–1975.*

$ **Shorty'z.** A tiny, gay-popular lunch and breakfast spot in a brick building on 1st Street, just north of downtown. The foot-long chili cheese dog is a work of art. *801 N. 1st St.,* ☎ *602/253–1985.*

Scottsdale

$$$–$$$$ **El Chorro Lodge.** Snug between Mummy and Camelback mountains in northern Scottsdale is this posh girls' school turned elegant eatery. The classic dinner entrées—chateaubriand, rack of lamb—are always great, but El Chorro is best known for its lavish Sunday brunches on the festive patio. *5550 E. Lincoln Dr.,* ☎ *602/748–5170.*

$$–$$$ **Café Terra Cotta.** After a day of gallery hopping at the ritzy Borgata shopping center, consider diving into a reasonably priced contemporary-Southwestern meal at this outpost of the famed Tucson restaurant. A typically inventive dish is the pork tenderloin *adobado* with black beans and apricot-basil pesto conserve. *6166 N. Scottsdale Rd.,* ☎ *602/948–8100.*

$$–$$$ **Malee's Thai Gourmet.** It's on gallery-studded Main Street, in Old Town Scottsdale, and has a very queeny following. Maybe its specialty dish, the flaming Cornish hen (it's marinated in a variety of spices and stuffed with ground chicken, water chestnuts, carrots, potatoes, and peas) accounts for this. Has a few flaming waiters, too. *7131 E. Main St.,* ☎ *602/947–6042.*

Coffeehouse Culture

Coffeehouses are *huge* here, precious oases in a desert of insipid shopping centers and somewhat lowbrow neighborhood bars. Yeah, and maybe they're a bit elitist, too. Phoenix's caffeine rag, **Java** (☎ 602/966–6352) comes out monthly and contains pensive essays, frothy diatribes, and gushing odes inspired by the rich, aromatic elixir.

Bean Tree. A funky coffeehouse with a small library of trashy novels, a wall of gray brick, another of yellow plaster, and plenty of red, purple, and silver trim. There's also an outdoor covered patio with lots of greenery and post-industrial silver chairs and small tables (stylish but hardly comfy). Wonderful salads, sandwiches, and soups. *7818 N. 12th St., Phoenix,* ☎ *602/906–0406.*

Coffee Plantation. In the heart of ASU's campus is this major student hangout. It's mostly straight but suitably academic, hip, and homo-friendly. A counter with stools lines the huge front window overlooking Mill Street, which may be the only engaging people-watching avenue within a 50-mile radius. The lively interior is done with Caribbean blues, peaches, yellows, and other tropical hues, and the coffee brewers work inside a little Caribbean-style shanty (granted, the Third World preciousness is a trifle glib). Great sandwiches. *680 S. Mill St., Suite 101, Tempe,* ☎ *602/829–7878.*

Common Ground. The gayest and grooviest coffeehouse in the area, this one tucked away on a courtly pedestrian mall off Scottsdale's swank 5th Avenue. Here amid colorful regional art, suave, politically correct, New Agers sip espresso and solve world problems. Favorite dishes include the garlic-chicken sandwich and veggie focaccia. There are also lots of yummy desserts to finish you off. *7125 E. 5th Ave., Scottsdale,* ☎ *602/970–4746.*

Jamaica Blue. This cozy, compact coffeehouse in Scottsdale's Old Town Pueblo shopping center has a couple of nooks with end chairs and sofas, live jazz many nights, and dozens of long-haired, urbane types in cowboy gear. A nice place to while away one of Arizona's rare rainy nights. *4017 N. Scottsdale Rd., Suite 104, Scottsdale,* ☎ *602/947–2160.*

Orbit Espresso. Hands-down the best coffeehouse in Phoenix and one of the best anywhere. The food and drinks are as good as at other coffeehouses, but Orbit has the added attractions of outstanding live music (jazz, mambo, folk) nightly and even a small dance floor. It has a cute patio overlooking a fountain, lots of art on the walls inside, exposed air ducts, high ceilings, and warm lighting. The crowd mixes well—you'll be comfortable alone or in a large group. A perfect alternative to loud bars. *40 E. Camelback Rd., Suite 102, Phoenix,* ☎ *602/265–2354.*

Willow House. You'll spot everybody here: lesbians with kids, grungers, students, gay bikers. In addition to being a full deli and coffee joint, the Willow House sells odd jewelry, T-shirts, and gifts. It has the best-attended poetry readings in the city (Thurs. evenings). *149 W. McDowell Rd., Phoenix,* ☎ *602/252–0272.*

Sedona

$$–$$$ **Heartline Cafe.** This is an outstanding, somewhat trendy spot with plenty of gay staff and an extremely loyal following. Track-lighting, ceiling fans, and wood trim and beams create a romantic, cozy ambience, especially in winter. The menu offers a somewhat eclectic array of pasta, vegetarian, and grilled-meat selections, and just about every dish packs a little punch, thanks to an infusion of Southwestern spices and ingredients. *1610 W. Hwy. 89A,* ☎ *520/282–0785.*

$$–$$$ **Sedona Grill and Bar/Samba Cafe.** Somewhat new on the scene, the Bar and Grill has quickly become the place many of the lesbian and gay wait staff go following their own shifts. It's open until 1 AM, and there's live music most nights. The rather traditional American menu shows off pastas, grills, and plenty of filling comfort foods. Quite chic for this otherwise sleepy town. Live entertainment. *2123 W. Hwy. 89A,* ☎ *520/282–5219.*

$$–$$$ **Takashi.** Locals rave about this fine Japanese restaurant, which offers such delicacies as soft-shell crab tempura-style, chicken wrapped with nori, and beef, chicken, and salmon teriyaki. There's also a vast sushi bar. *465 Jordan Rd.,* ☎ *520/282–2334.*

$$–$$$ **Troy's.** This is probably the most gay-frequented restaurant in town. Behind the smoked-glass facade of this shopping-center storefront lurks one of the most dramatic, outrageous dining rooms in northern Arizona—it's almost a bit campy. Most prominent is a tall, room-length mural depicting a serene oceanscape with clouds jostling overhead. The innovative New American menu almost always lives up to the daring setting. *2370 W. Hwy. 89A, No. 10,* ☎ *520/282–3532.*

$–$$ **El Rincón.** Set in the fascinating Tlaquepaque shopping complex, this Mexican restaurant has plenty of atmosphere: beam ceilings, arches, festive carpeting. The hearty Sonoran cuisine is good but unspectacular—lots of cheese and beans and somewhat heavy sauces. *336 South Hwy. AZ 179, Suite No. A–112,* ☎ *520/282–4648.*

Jerome

$$$ **House of Joy.** Many appetites have been satisfied in this historic house, once a popular bordello. Perhaps as a tribute to its sordid history, the two dining rooms are strung with red lights. Dinner is the only meal served here, and only on weekends—you *must* make a reservation, well in advance. The traditional Continental fare is excellent, but the ambience is the real draw. *Hull Ave., off Main St.,* ☎ *520/634–5339.*

SLEEPS

Phoenix, or technically Scottsdale, is known for its luxury resort scene, an industry that developed shortly after the turn of the century, owing to Phoenix's clear, dry climate. As you drive along Camelback Road into Scottsdale and then north up Scottsdale Road, you'll see that virtually every American chain has a resort outpost here. Most of them are quite good; the standouts are listed below.

Otherwise, Phoenix is just your typical business city, with all the usual corporate hotels and motor inns. There are two gay bed-and-breakfasts, one of which welcomes the general public, too; the other is gay-male exclusively.

Because you won't be walking much of anywhere here, it makes little sense to stay somewhere on the basis of its proximity to nightlife. Nowhere in Phoenix are you more than a short drive from the popular bars and restaurants. If you stay in Scottsdale, expect a 20- to 30-minute drive to the gayish Phoenix intersection of 7th Avenue and Camelback Road—but remember that there are a couple of gay nightspots and some outstanding restaurants in Scottsdale, too.

For price ranges in Phoenix, Scottsdale, and Sedona, *see* Chart A at the front of this guide; for Jerome, *see* Chart B.

Phoenix and Scottsdale

Hotels

⊞ The eight-year-old, 11-story **Phoenix Ritz-Carlton** is across the street from the Biltmore Fashion Square. Inside its otherwise contemporary sand-color Southwestern facade are things Old World and elegant—from British paintings to bone china. *2401 E. Camelback Rd.,* ☎ *602/468–0700 or 800/241–3333. 281 rooms. $$$$*

⊞ A memorable beacon along downtown's otherwise unmemorable skyline, the **Hyatt Regency Phoenix** is famed for its rotating rooftop restaurant and glass elevators. It's the top business hotel in Phoenix and has a nice pool and health club. *122 N. 2nd St.,* ☎ *602/252–1234 or 800/233–1234. 712 rooms. $$$–$$$$*

⊞ The **Holiday Inn Crowne Plaza** is gay-friendly, has lots of cute, young staff, and is a short drive from most of the 7th Avenue and Street bar action. *100 N. 1st St.,* ☎ *602/257–1525 or 800/465–4329. 533 rooms. $$$*

⊞ If you want to be fewer than 5 miles from every important section of metro Phoenix, stay at the **Embassy Suites Airport West,** whose rooms each have a microwave, fridge, and wet bar. *2333 E. Thomas Rd.,* ☎ *602/957–1910 or 800/362–2779. 183 suites. $$–$$$*

⊞ The vastly improved **Wyndham Metro Center** had been the tatty Hotel Westcourt until December 1994. It's a 15-minute drive north of downtown on I–17, on the outskirts of the massive Metro Center Mall and Castles 'n' Coasters Amusement Park. *10220 N. Metro Pkwy. E,* ☎ *602/997–5900 or 800/858–1033. 284 rooms. $$–$$$*

⊞ The most popular hotel in Phoenix with the gay community, the **Ramada Hotel in Camelback** is close to 7th Avenue; it has a nice heated pool and whirlpool and among the best rates in town. *502 W. Camelback Rd.,* ☎ *602/264–9290. 166 rooms. $–$$*

⊞ Scottsdale's best value is the **Motel 6,** which is within walking distance of area shops, and has a palm-shrouded pool. Not a good choice, though, if you plan on spending much time in your room. *6848 E. Camelback Rd.,* ☎ *602/946–2280. 122 rooms. $*

Resorts

🏨 The **Arizona Biltmore** is where the old money nests: sleeping soundly below gold-foil ceilings; surrounded by teak furniture; dreaming about tennis, golf, eating, sunning, and all the other activities this charming location affords. *24th St. and Missouri Ave., North Phoenix,* ☎ *602/955–6600 or 800/950–0086. 502 rooms. $$$$*

🏨 Actually 12 miles north of Phoenix in the aptly named town of Carefree, **The Boulders** has the most dramatic setting of area resorts, hidden behind massive—you guessed it—boulders. Rooms are in pueblo-style casitas with patios and kiva fireplaces. *34631 N. Tom Darlington Dr., Carefree,* ☎ *602/488–9009 or 800/553–1717. 136 units. $$$$*

🏨 You deserve to stay at **The Phoenician,** the priciest property in town, because you're currently paying a little something each year to repair part of the disaster that helped build it: Charles Keating's notorious savings-and-loan scandal. Everything exists here on a grand, lavish scale, almost to the point of being overdone. But hey, if swimming in a pool inlaid with mother-of-pearl excites you, it's worth shelling out the big bucks. *6000 E. Camelback Rd., Scottsdale,* ☎ *602/941–8200 or 800/888–8234. 580 rooms. $$$$*

🏨 The **Doubletree Paradise Valley Resort** is a tad less luxurious than the famed Biltmore and Phoenician and quite a bit more affordable. There's an excellent health club, two meandering pools, and tennis, but only fair dining. *5401 N. Scottsdale Rd., Scottsdale,* ☎ *602/947–5400 or 800/996–3426. 387 rooms. $$$*

Bed-and-Breakfasts

🏨 The gay-operated **Westways Private Resort Inn** is one of the most exclusive B&B resorts in America, and certainly the poshest in Phoenix. The 5,000-square-foot Spanish Mediterranean–style villa in northwest Phoenix was built in 1983 and has six sumptuous rooms. A favorite feature is the 40-foot heated pool. *Box 41624,* ☎ *602/582–3868. 4 private "casitas." Mixed gay/straight. $$$*

🏨 The considerably more affordable **Arizona Sunburst** is a somewhat basic B&B, with a pool and a clothing-optional hot tub. It's run by a couple of terrific guys who know plenty about the area dining and nightlife. *6245 N. 12th Pl.,* ☎ *602/274–1474. 7 rooms. Gay male. $*

Sedona

Resorts and Hotels

🏨 **Enchantment,** nestled brilliantly in secluded Boynton Canyon, has the best setting. It was built as a tennis resort, and appeals more to the sports enthusiast than to the New Age traveler. *525 Boynton Canyon Rd.,* ☎ *520/282–2900 or 800/826–4180. 162 rooms. $$$$*

🏨 The extremely gay-friendly **Los Abrigados Resort** is likewise quite luxurious. It's near the Tlaquepaque shops, so it's less secluded than Enchantment, but it has spectacular accommodations, each with separate living areas, stocked wet bars, and balconies; some have fireplaces and whirlpools, too. *160 Portal La.,* ☎ *520/282–1777 or 800/521–3131. 172 suites. $$$$*

🏨 The top value is the **Quality Inn–Kings Ransom,** whose rooms have great views of the red rocks in the distance. There's also a beautiful pool and deck in back, and a Jacuzzi. *Hwy. 179,* ☎ *520/282–7151. 81 rooms. $$*

Guest Houses

🏨 **The Lodge at Sedona** combines the intimacy of a B&B with the privacy and professional service of a small luxury inn. It has smartly done bedrooms and warmly decorated common rooms with fireplaces, and it offers a full gourmet breakfast. *125 Kallof Pl., ☎ 520/204–1942 or 800/619–4467. 13 rooms. Mostly straight. $$–$$$$*

⊡ The simpler **Cozy Cactus B&B,** one of the gay-friendliest B&Bs in town, is run out of a 1983 ranch-style house whose rooms each have a different theme (the Wyeth Room, for instance, has reproductions of Andrew Wyeth works). *80 Canyon Cir., ☎ 520/284–0082 or 800/788–2082. 5 rooms. Mostly straight. $$*

⊡ **Paradise Ranch** is women-only and offers a full gamut of spiritual programs, including psychic readings, crystal healings, and a sweat lodge. *135 Kachina Dr., ☎ 520/282–9769. 1 guest house. Women. $$*

Jerome

⊡ In a small residential neighborhood off Main Street called Upper Hogback, the **Cottage Bed and Breakfast** is a 1917 house that can be rented for a party of up to six or split into two separate bedrooms that share a bath (each has its own entrance). It's a modest place with unrivaled views of the Verde Valley. *747 East Ave., ☎ 520/634–0701. 2 rooms. Mixed gay/straight. $–$$*

⊡ The **Jerome Inn** is an authentic boomtown relic (circa 1899) smack in the middle of Main Street. It has been nicely but simply restored, and rooms have fluffy down quilts and pillows, a few antiques, pedestal sinks, and dried-flower arrangements. *309 Main St., ☎ 520/634–5094 or 800/634–5094. 8 rooms. Mostly straight. $*

SCENES

The high number of bars is a measure of Phoenix's love of barhopping; on the other hand, the majority of them are small neighborhood haunts. Enter a typical bar, and you'll learn quickly that at least half the customers patronize it regularly. This isn't the sort of city lesbians and gays flock to in search of glitzy, spectacular nightclubs and all-night cruise grounds. Phoenix is down-to-earth, meat-and-potatoes, largely blue-collar or, more recently, silicon-valley-employed. These are regular guys and gals who go out to socialize, play darts and pinball, shoot pool, get drunk, and holler and laugh.

Most bars are of the dress-down genre, with only a few exceptions (Bananas, BS West, Ain't Nobody's Bizness) emulating the stylish clubs of West Hollywood. At the snazzier places, you won't see trendy club gear so much as you will flannel or cowboy shirts; crisp, clean blue jeans; and nice leather belts—everything pressed and tucked in.

At just about every other bar, Western wear is king, followed by leather, Levi's, T-shirts, and simple duds. At most of these places, a business suit or dressy-casual sportswear will be met will cold stares. In general, the bars here are low on attitude but quick to perceive well-dressed outsiders as possessing attitude, whether they do or not.

There is no section with an especially high concentration of gay bars, and very few are within walking distance of one another. This means, unfortunately, that you must drive from place to place—and given Phoenix's outrageous drink specials, this makes driving while intoxicated a deadly temptation. Know also that streets in Phoenix are heavily patrolled by police cruisers.

Bars close at the annoyingly early hour of 1 AM, although three in the area are open after hours (the dance clubs, the Works and Trax, and the bar Bananas, which is adjacent to the Metro Dance Factory). No alcohol is served at these places after 1; just coffee and soft drinks.

Outside of those in California, Phoenix is the smuttiest city west of the Mississippi. You'll have no trouble at all finding pornography—there are adult bookshops, gay and straight, all over the city. And they are some of the cleanest and consumer-friendliest such stores in the country—especially the local chain, **Castle Boutique** (5501 E. Washington St.; 300 E. Camelback Rd.; 8802 N. Black Canyon Hwy.; 8315 E. Apache Tr.).

Phoenix and Scottsdale

Bars and Nightclubs

Ain't Nobody's Bizness. This is the largest women's bar in Phoenix as well as one of the nicest. It plays top-40 music, has a dance floor, and bands occasionally perform on weekends. *3031 E. Indian School Rd.,* ☎ *602/224–9977. Crowd: mostly lesbian but men-friendly, mostly under 40, generally professional, guppie, well-heeled.*

BS West. This is the preppiest gay bar in metro Phoenix. On Scottsdale's fancy 5th Avenue, behind the Common Ground coffeehouse, most guys here are in suits (especially weeknights) or dressy jeans and cotton shirts on weekends. The look is, a rarity for Phoenix, distinctly non-Western. There are two levels to this amber-lit, festive little video bar, and a nice patio with seating out front. Has a tiny dance floor. Where nice boys go to pick up nice boys. *7125 E. 5th Ave.,* ☎ *602/945–9028. Crowd: 90% male, cute, guppie, friendly, uniform, white.*

Charlie's. One of the best country-western bars in the Southwest, this enormous two-stepping dance club and cruise bar is near the corner of 7th Avenue and Camelback Road and draws a pretty butch crowd—guys who trade in their business suits for 10-gallon hats before heading out for a night on the town. Always a great, loud, friendly bunch—and lots of tight jeans. Dance lessons are given regularly, as are volleyball lessons—Charlie's has a court and regularly puts on tournaments. Has the best Sunday brunch of any gay bar. *727 W. Camelback Rd.,* ☎ *602/265–0224. Crowd: 95% male and white, 100% smartly dressed country-western, all ages.*

Club Kaos. This dance club throws theme parties every other weekend. On Thursdays Latin house and salsa tunes are spun ($2 Coronas); hard house is offered on Fridays (cheap well drafts in the early evening); and on Saturdays it's typical dance and house music. *1810 E. McDowell Rd.,* ☎ *602/929–1770. Crowd: young, upscale.*

Desert Rose. This relatively new bar has quickly become the second-most-popular dyke venue in town. It's well lit and nicely decorated, with a decent-size dance floor, on which two-stepping lessons are given Wednesday and Thursday nights. The Sunday night $2 steak-fry is always a big crowd-pleaser. *4301 N. 7th Ave.,* ☎ *602/265–3233. Crowd: mostly women but men welcome with their dyke friends, mixed ages, Western attire, more butch than lipstick, mostly white.*

The Eagle. Though the name Eagle is synonymous with leather in most cities, the owners of the Phoenix Eagle realized the city already had too many such establishments and have opened a gay sports bar, complete with pool, darts, and satellite and cable TV screens showing major sporting events. More than 90 different domestic and imported beers are available. Tuesday is ladies' night. Oh, and did we mention it's the only gay bar in Phoenix with shuffleboard? *4531 N. 7th St.,* ☎ *602/285–0833. Crowd: mostly male but women welcome, diverse in age; baseball caps, T-shirts, and jeans.*

Foster's. The crowd at Foster's depends almost entirely on the night of the week. Wednesday's drag shows are popular but not too cruisy. Sunday's Trash Disco party is legendary and usually packed with horny retro queens. And any time they advertise nickel drafts, you can count on a full house. The dance floor is small but well done, with good lighting and sound systems. A great place for out-of-towners looking to meet cute, down-to-earth locals. Cover some nights. *4343 N. 7th Ave.,* ☎ *602/263–8313. Crowd: 75/25 m/f, mostly mid-20s to late 30s, cruisy but relatively free of attitude, boy/girl next door.*

Metro Dance Factory/Bananas. Bananas is a clean, bright video bar with a salmon-and-teal color scheme and a small bar, plus a huge patio outside. Has friendly bartenders, no cover, and is open every night. On weekends, it's open until 3 AM but cuts off the booze at 1 AM. The adjacent **Metro Dance Factory** is only open Thursday through Saturday, and only then until 1 AM. Though the guys who dance here are the hottest in Phoenix, they know it and can be somewhat unapproachable. The music is always the latest house, techno, and dance mixes. Saturdays are best; Thursdays are quiet. *4102 E. Thomas Rd.,* ☎ *602/224–9457. Crowd: mostly male with a few straight women, guppies and pretty boys, poseurs, collared shirts and pressed denim, young.*

TRAX. TRAX is best known as one of Phoenix's three after-hours clubs. Other times, expect a fairly rough urban disco with excellent music, from industrial to retro disco. The interior is typical warehouse-style, with a large dance floor. The parking lot is shared with the straight Latino dance club—a topsy-turvy blend. In a rough neighborhood. Opens at 6 on Saturday mornings. *1724 E. McDowell Rd.,* ☎ *602/254–0231. Crowd: mostly male, young to mid-30s, mixed racially and ethnically, some leather, lots of jeans and T-shirts.*

Wink's. Maybe the only gay bar in Phoenix where you'd feel comfortable with your parents. Wink's is an intimate sit-down sort of bar in a festive little gray-brick building with a green musical note painted on the exterior. The crowd is diverse and chatty. Entertainment runs from your usual lounge lizards doing Billy Joel covers to female impersonators to some extremely talented piano acts. There's a decent bar-food menu, and both Saturday's submarine lunch buffet and Sunday's brunch are popular. *5707 N. 7th St.,* ☎ *602/265–9002. Crowd: 70/30 m/f, disco bunnies on their night off, suits, cowboys, lipstick lesbians, octogenarians, drag queens, bears, and piano-bar flies.*

The Works. This is the largest, loudest, and trendiest club in metro Phoenix (it's on the outskirts of Old Town Scottsdale). Not only is the techno, industrial, and alternative music the best you'll find in the Southwest, but the Works also has two huge dance floors and its own swimming pool. Furthermore, it's open until 3 (4 on weekends)—so everyone winds up here at some point. It's technically only "alternative" on Thursdays, but dykes and fags are always welcome and usually present. Wednesday is also a big gay night. Gets a lot of breeders on weekends, but everybody seems to get along fine. If dancing is your thing, it's actually better than the Metro—but not as cruisy. *7223 E. 2nd St., Scottsdale,* ☎ *602/946–4141. Crowd: from 10% to 90% gay, depending on the night; young; mixed genders; some grunge and alternateens but just as many guppies and club kids.*

DIVES AND SMALL BARS

The best leather bar is **Harley's 155** (155 W. Camelback Rd., ☎ 602/274–8505), which gets very crowded on weekends.

Two smaller lesbian options are the **Incognito Lounge** (2424 E. Thomas Rd., ☎ 602/955–9805), a roadhouse along East Thomas that's especially popular with Hispanic lesbians, and **Nasty Habits** (3108 E. McDowell Rd., ☎ 602/267–8707), where men are welcome, especially on Thursdays (but they'd do well to abide by the local customs: Most of the women here are bigger and stronger than they are.

Centrally located and drawing a mostly local crowd are **Apollo's** (5749 N. 7th St., ☎ 602/277–9373); the **Country Club** (4428 N. 7th Ave., ☎ 602/264–4553), a wilder and ramshackle piano/bar; and **Johnny Mc's Irish Pub** (138 W. Camelback Rd., ☎ 602/266–0875), which, until November 1994 was the leathery Cattleman's Exchange but has been extremely popular since going shamrock.

Two popular neighborhood bars in the southeastern part of town are the **Pumphouse** (4132 E. McDowell Rd., ☎ 602/275–3509), a dark bar with three pool tables, a filthy gray linoleum floor, and zero ambience, but good music; and, out by the airport, the **Nu Towne Saloon** (5002 E. Van Buren, ☎ 602/267–9959), the city's oldest gay bar, and, thanks to some great discount-drinks parties, the easiest place to get laid on Sundays and Tuesdays.

Saunas and Bathhouses

The **Fantasyland Motel** (2922 E. Van Buren St., ☎ 602/267–7898) is not really a bathhouse but is basically a gay, hourly-rate motel on scummy Van Buren near the corner of 29th Street, a stretch crawling with hookers and "all-nite girlie" shows. Entering the forbidding driveway of this long, dingy, brick motel goes against any sane person's better instincts. The notorious sauna, **Flex** (1517 S. Black Canyon Hwy., ☎ 602/271–9011), recently received a long-needed makeover and now features the latest in bathhouse amusement: rooms with waterbeds, a complete gym, pool, videos, and a massage therapist. This is the best-known such establishment in the state, having served the community for more than 20 years.

Sedona and Jerome

Sedona is a town virtually without any nightlife scene, excepting a few predominantly straight bars. Lots of gay men and lesbians head over to the **Sedona Grill and Bar** (*see* Eats, *above*), and on many nights you'll find a mixed crowd at the town's top music venue, **Red, Rock & Blues** (1730 W. Hwy. 89A, ☎ 520/282–1655). Toward the end of the 19th century, Jerome was home to about 25 wild and tawdry saloons. Today there are only two, but they are no less wild or tawdry: The more popular is the **Spirit Room** (Main St., ☎ 520/634–5792), a dark western bar that's touristy by day, and hootin' and hollerin' late into the night; there's live music here regularly. Down the street, **Paul and Jerry's Saloon** (206 Main St., ☎ 520/634–2603) offers more of the same, minus the live music and plus a couple of pool tables.

THE LITTLE BLACK BOOK

At Your Fingertips

Arizona AIDS Info Line: ☎ 602/234–2752, TTY 602/234–0873. **Arizona AIDS Project:** ☎ 602/265–3300. **Community AIDS Council:** ☎ 602/265–2437. **Concilio de Latino Salud:** ☎ 602/506–6787. **Information and Referral Line:** ☎ 602/263–8856. **Jerome Chamber of Commerce:** Box K, 86331, ☎ 520/634–2900. **Lesbian and Gay Community Switchboard (Valley of the Sun Gay and Lesbian Community Center):** ☎ 602/234–2752. **Lesbian Resource Project:** ☎ 602/266–5542. **Phoenix and Valley of the Sun Convention and Visitors Bureau:** 1 Arizona Center, Suite 600, 85004, ☎ 602/254–6500. **Sedona-Oak Creek Chamber of Commerce:** 331 Forest Rd., Sedona 86336, ☎ 520/282–7722. **Sexual Assault Recovery Institute:** ☎ 602/235–9345.

Gay Media

Echo (☎ 602/266–0550) is a biweekly gay and lesbian news and entertainment magazine. Similar is the newspaper, the ***Western Express*** (☎

602/254–1324). "**Transformer**" (☏ 602/973–5682) is a thin bar and re-sources pamphlet. And **X-Factor** (☏ 602/266–0550) is Arizona's gay-male adult entertainment biweekly. All of the above are free and found at many bars and adult bookstores.

The local arts and entertainment paper, the **Phoenix New Times** (☏ 602/271–0040) is about the only mainstream paper willing to scrutinize the city's conservative politics.

BOOKSTORES

The absence of a gay bookstore is a major blemish on Phoenix's homo landscape. The main store at ASU, **Changing Hands** (Mill St. and 5th Ave., Tempe, ☏ 602/966–0203), has an excellent selection of gay titles and nonporn mags, plus strong sections on feminism, Native American culture, psychology, and all academic matters. Also, try **Obelisk Books** (24 W. Camelback, Unit A, ☏ 602/266–2665) in Phoenix.

There are a few gay-oriented gift and card shops in town, including the **Freedom Company** (1722 E. McDowell Rd., right by the bar TRAX); **Ganeymede Rising** (5534 N. 43rd Ave., right by the bar J. C.'s Fun One); and **Unique on Central** (4700 N. Central Ave., Suite 105, ☏ 602/279–9691), which recently opened a coffeehouse and has been slowly adding gay and lesbian books and magazines.

Body and Fitness

If you find yourself craving a workout in Sedona or Jerome, you're out of luck; the only exercise you'll get is turning over the price tags in all those art galleries. In the greater Phoenix area, however, you can pump, pedal, treadmill, swim, steam, and bake at all hours. **Fitness Planet** is gay-friendly, and offers full gym facilites in five locations (240 W. Indian School Rd., Phoenix, ☏ 602/274–0800; 3202 E. Greenway Rd., Phoenix, ☏ 602/482–6600; 43rd Ave. and Indian School Rd., West Phoenix, ☏ 602/245–2511; 7303 E. Earll Dr., Scottsdale, ☏ 602/941–0800; and 1425 W. 14th St., Tempe, ☏ 602/894–2281). All are open around the clock seven days a week. **Fitness West** (1505 E. Bethany Home Rd., Phoenix, ☏ 602/248–8920) also has all the right machines as well as steam, sauna, pool, and cold plunge facilities. It also honors memberships in AHA-, IHRFA-, and ITFA-affiliated clubs nationwide. The club is open 24 hours Monday to Thursday, until 10 PM on Friday, and 5 AM to 10 PM weekends.

19 *Out in Portland*

PORTLAND IS XENOPHOBIC. It is the largest city in a state whose former governor, Tom McCall, came up with the slogan "Come visit us, but please don't stay." It will never be a place visitors converge upon in large numbers, or one that scads of people aspire to move to.

Here's why: Nobody in this city seems to have the slightest interest in Portland's *being* big. Since the hippie-dippie '60s, civic leaders have been obsessed with land use. While other American cities grew both horizontally and vertically, Portland created massive urban growth boundaries (a.k.a. greenbelts) within a couple of miles of the city center, and instituted height restrictions on Downtown buildings.

There have been other curious moves. Portland put forth measures that capped the number of parking spaces Downtown—it's almost impossible for a developer to get permits to put up a new garage. How are you going to attract visitors to Portland if you don't give them a place to put their cars? Then there's the issue of freeways. Back in the early '50s, Robert Moses, that beloved, big-city planner from back East, paid a visit to Portland. Locals asked the wizard of urban design how to improve the city. The good Mr. Moses responded graciously—and with foresight: He instructed city officials to tear down outmoded wharves and factories fringing the Willamette River and make room for an elevated highway. Decades later, what does the city do? It tears down this handy expressway and replaces it with a waterfront park and promenade. Are people supposed to walk into town?

Okay, by now you may have detected that Portland, crazy as it sounds, actually enjoys its small scale; the planners envisioned the city this way. Consider that Portland and Seattle looked and felt similar at one time. Each existed on an intimate scale, wore a fairly old-fashioned facade, and was a maze of seedy streets populated by rough-edged characters. Portland's scale has not changed. Its facade of cast-iron dinosaurs is interrupted occasionally by gleaming, glass-and-concrete towers, but none is higher than 36 stories and only a handful are higher than 20. Portland's streets remain, well, if not exactly seedy then populated by plenty of curious characters.

Seattle, meanwhile, has actively sought and earned international status. In many ways Seattle's expansion is impressive—it is still a lovely green city with a strong environmental record and plenty to recommend itself. It is certainly more cosmopolitan than Portland. But there are very few Portlanders—you could probably count them on one hand—who would trade their gritty, insular world for Seattle's. In Portland, you'll find a half-million people perfectly content with small-town living.

A half-million people? Small-town living? A paradox, you say? Perhaps in some spots Portlanders are forced to accept at least small-*city* living. Downtown, though it has parks and greenery, is clearly an urban space—but one with a human feel. It has a grassy, 12-block boulevard; several largely intact historic districts; and no prospect of growth—physically or geographically. There's a river on one side and mountains on the other three. Bordering the commercial sections—and just a short walk away—are residential neighborhoods such as Nob Hill, not looking the slightest bit urban. Across the river, Portland does sprawl, in a sense, for miles to the east. But these right-angled suburban streets, though uniform, are not bland. You'll find several dozen cohesive neighborhoods on this side of the river, each with a distinct personality, ethnic makeup, and style of architecture. Many of these neighborhoods will look alike from the window of a passing automobile, but if you get out, walk around, and talk to people, you will discern many flavors.

Curiously, Portland does not have a gay neighborhood, yet there seems to be a smattering of gay households in just about every section of town. Many live in Nob Hill in the northwest. A slightly more bohemian and more lesbian contingent live in Hawthorne in the southeast. But these are not predominantly gay enclaves.

Counterculturists have long been attracted to the seclusion, serenity, and rugged individualism of both Oregon and Portland. But the region's and the city's small-town mentality have also fostered a certain distrust of outsiders. It's not that Portlanders are especially unconventional or conventional, but that they act—and react—from a gut level, uninfluenced by outside forces. You will have little success imposing your beliefs on the people of this city: Liberals can't be told to soften their views or moderate their opinions; conservatives are equally inflexible.

This means that both homosexuals and ethnic minorities in Portland find themselves in a somewhat precarious position. They do possess a certain strength in numbers. But local hatemongers, such as white supremacist Tom Metzger and homophobe Lon Mabon, have found secure and visible platforms from which to spew their bile. Specifically, Oregon has faced antigay ballot wars—headed by Mabon—since 1992, the year Colorado's infamous Amendment 2 was passed. Similar measures in Oregon have failed in popular elections, but never by a wide margin. And although Portland itself is more tolerant than the rest of the state, you're more likely to witness flagrant acts of intolerance here than you are in many larger American cities. In Portland, prevailing political and intellectual agendas, no matter how broad-minded, can't prevent the loose cannons around town from taking aim.

It's the sort of city where people like Kevin Kelly Keith can be seen in a pickup truck outfitted with placards bearing antigay slogans. He parks his four-wheel pulpit in high-visibility areas, and sits in a chair mounted on the roof, overseeing the discomfort and anger he has provoked. Of course, Portland is also a city with people like Billie Lou Kahn. Ms. Kahn, a 52-year-old lesbian, once stumbled upon the controversial pickup truck, ran inside the variety store outside of which it was parked, bought a can of black spray paint, and covered Mr. Keith's hateful placards with a slogan of her own: "Ignorance Kills."

THE LAY OF THE LAND

The heart of Portland is just below the confluence of the Columbia and the Willamette (pronounced wuh-*lamm*-ett) rivers. The Columbia is the border between Washington and Oregon; from it, the Willamette twists in a southerly direction, bisecting the city center. Portland is divided into four directional quadrants; the river being the north–south spine and Burnside Street being the east–west spine.

The commercial heart of the city lies in the part of southwest Portland that's nearest the axis of Burnside Street and the river. The northwest quadrant is also heavily developed near the river. Both sections contain Portland's oldest neighborhoods, and both give way to steep, posh, suburban hills outside the city center. Across the river the terrain is flat, the streets gridlike for miles, the homes and businesses newer, the population mostly lower and middle class. Though there's less to do on this side of the river, visitors to Portland will find good reason to explore both sides.

Downtown

Portland has an eye-pleasing, though unspectacular, Downtown. The skyline is varied in height, color, and shape, and blocks are small. The bases of all buildings are built out to the sidewalk, and their ground floors are required to have display windows. There's a fairly consistent blend of office towers, apartment buildings, retail spaces, hotels, and restaurants; in the mix, high-end boutiques border pawn shops, trattorias sit beside burger joints, and postmodern boxes rise above cast-iron Victorians. Park Avenue, for 12 blocks, is marked by a green median of century-old trees. There are also several fountains, some parks, and an abundance of statuary. Portland's city center is a planner's dream—a bona fide, living neighborhood. The streets are busy with nine-to-fivers all day, and they remain lively into the evening, when a flood of teens, Gen-Xers, and thirtysomethings descend upon the music clubs, cafés, and coffeehouses.

Downtown's boundary is perfectly clear: Burnside Street to the north, the river to the east, and curving I–405 to the south and west. Along the river, the **Tom McCall RiverPlace Promenade** stretches for 2 miles, providing a scenic venue for cycling, jogging, blading, and sunning. Just in from the waterfront, from about Taylor to Morrison Street, is the six-block **Yamhill Historic District,** a rectangle of classic Italianate, cast-iron buildings that date from the early 1870s.

Brown baggers spend their lunch hours at **Pioneer Square,** a tidy redbrick plaza at the intersection of Yamhill Street and Broadway. Around this central point cluster many of Downtown's high-end chain stores, such as **Nike Town** (930 S.W. 6th Ave.), an unabashedly commercial tribute to the Portland-based maker of athletic wear; **The Galleria** (921 S.W. Morrison St.), an indoor mall with 50 stores; and **Pioneer Place** (700 S.W. 5th Ave.), also an indoor mall, with 70 shops.

South of Pioneer Square, along Broadway and Park Avenue, is a concentration of the arts, including the **Portland Center for the Performing Arts** (S.W. Broadway and S.W. Main St., ☎ 503/248–4335), the **Portland Art Museum** (1219 S.W. Park Ave., ☎ 503/226–2811), and the **Oregon Historical Center** (1200 S.W. Park Ave., ☎ 503/222–1741). North of Pioneer Square, bounded by 4th and 11th avenues and Oak and Yamhill streets, is the **Glazed Terra-Cotta Historic District,** whose early 20th-century architecture is characterized by ornate griffins and sculptures.

The Pearl District

Just west of the Glazed Terra-Cotta Historic District is Portland's **Pearl District;** it contains the city's tiny, gay entertainment mecca, the commercial spine of which is **Stark Street.** Though bar-studded Stark Street is slightly seedy—it will remind you of San Francisco's Polk Street—it's fairly safe and is a short walk to most of Downtown's major hotels and Nob Hill's restaurants and shopping. The rest of the Pearl District, which begins around Park Avenue and follows Burnside and Flanders streets west toward Nob Hill, is a haven of vintage clothing, used-record, and book shops. Most famous is **Powell's City of Books** (1005 W. Burnside St.); its several rooms of used and new books take up a full block. The store's Anne Hughes Coffee Room is a great place for *lattes* and butter cookies—and a fine spot for cerebral cruising.

Old Town and Chinatown

Though they're still spiritually part of Downtown, these districts north of Burnside Street, **Old Town** and **Chinatown,** both have their own flavor. Actually, this oldest commercial part of town begins with the **Skidmore Historic District,** which comprises the blocks immediately south and west of the Burnside Bridge. Buildings are a mix of cast iron and glazed terra-cotta, and though many are restored, the area retains a skid row atmosphere. You'll find some music clubs, restaurants, and galleries in these parts, too. On Ankeny Street, just in from Front Street, is the dramatic **Skidmore Fountain,** which dates from 1888. On weekends from March through December, the square surrounding the fountain is the site of the **Portland Saturday Market** (open Sundays as well), where more than 300 vendors sell food, junk, collectibles, and a rather quirky array of goods.

Continue north above Burnside to find Old Town's many eateries and restaurants, plus several of the city's divy gay bars. This neighborhood is also somewhat in a state of transition, as is Chinatown just to the west; its striking **ceremonial gate** stands at the intersection of Northwest 4th Avenue and Burnside Street.

Nob Hill

Though it's without any gay bars, **Nob Hill** is one of Portland's prime spots for gay eats and shopping. Named in the 1880s for the eponymous neighborhood in San Francisco, Portland's version isn't anywhere near as posh, but it has some of the finest Victorian houses in the city. There are two commercial strips, **Northwest 23rd** and **Northwest 21st streets.** Both, from about Burnside north to about Thurman Street, are replete with alternative-minded and -looking students, plus plenty of yuppies, gay men and lesbians, feminists, and aging hippies. Of the two, 23rd Street is the most upscale, but 21st Street has the better restaurants.

Southwest

Southwestern Portland is a hilly neighborhood of twisting roads and Colonial Revival mansions—some of the most valuable real estate in the city. **Council Crest Park,** at the peak of a hill, is the highest point within city limits; elevation is 1,000 feet above sea level. The panoramic view takes in everything from the skyline to Mt. St. Helens in the distance, and the green lawn is a wonderful place to lie in the sun.

West of Downtown, off U.S. 26, the city's century-old **Washington Park Zoo** (4001 S.W. Canyon Rd., ☎ 503/226–7627) sits in the middle of 322-acre **Washington Park,** which is crisscrossed by several trails so wooded you'd never know you're only a couple of miles from the city center. On the opposite side of the park, reached via Burnside Street, is the city's **International Rose Test Garden** (400 S.W. Kingston Ave., ☎ 503/823–3636). Portland is nicknamed the City of Roses, owing to its mild climate, and since 1907 its leading, must-attend affair has been the Portland Rose Festival. This 4-acre, terraced garden has 10,000 bushes with more than 400 varieties of roses. Just above the test garden is a 5½-acre **Japanese**

Garden (611 S.W. Kingston Ave., ☎ 503/223–4070). Another popular attraction near Washington Park is the **Pittock Mansion** (3229 N.W. Pittock Dr., ☎ 503/823–3624), a grandiose 1909 restored mansion filled with art and antiques.

Hawthorne and Sellwood

Though Portland is visibly not as gay a city as Seattle or San Francisco, it has one of America's strongest feminist and lesbian communities. The **Hawthorne District,** in the southeast quadrant, is the most concentrated lesbian neighborhood, but it's home as well to countless liberal-minded sorts, both young and old. Both **Southeast Stark** and **Southeast Belmont streets,** which actually run a bit north of the Hawthorne District, hold a share of the area's coffeehouses, boutiques, and music clubs. But the main commercial stretch is **Hawthorne Boulevard,** which first becomes interesting around 15th Avenue, peaks in funkiness between 30th and 40th avenues, and quiets down above 50th Avenue. A grittier version of Nob Hill, the Hawthorne District is a great place for Sunday brunch, browsing in bookshops and galleries, and listening to poetry readings and folk bands over coffee.

If you take Route 99E south for several miles, you'll reach the **Old Sellwood Antique Row;** it runs along **Southeast 13th Street,** between Bidwell and Sherrett streets. This community of wood-frame Victorians was annexed by Portland in 1893 and contains more than 50 great antiques shops.

Elsewhere

There are two additional major attractions at opposite ends of Portland. Several miles east of Downtown, lies the 62-acre **Grotto** (corner of N.E. 85th Ave. and Sandy Blvd., ☎ 503/254–7371), a tranquil parcel of fir trees and lush trails. You can take an elevator to the top of a 130-foot cliff to meditate in the interdenominational **Marilyn Moyer Chapel.**

In northwest Portland you'll find the largest wooded municipal park in the country, the 5,000-acre **Forest Park.** You can bike or hike along 70 miles of trails, where you may spot one of the park's many black bear and elk.

Gay Beaches

The most popular beach, **Rooster Rock State Park** (a.k.a. Cock Rock, ☎ 503/695–2261), lies 20 miles east of the city on Route 84 in scenic Columbia Gorge. The gay section is to the right, along the river, about a half-mile up. Closer to the city, the nude beach at **Sauvies Island** is about 8 miles northwest on U.S. 30. Parking for the gay section is at the end of Reader Road.

GETTING AROUND

A section comprising Downtown, up to Hoyt Street and then bound by I–405 and the Willamette River, is known as Fareless Square in transit lingo: Within this 300-square-block area, Tri-Met bus and MAX light rail-travel are free; outside it, public transportation is still fairly affordable. Portland's efficient and user-friendly mass transit system notwithstanding, visitors really don't have much reason to use it: It's not especially difficult to navigate Downtown streets, and attractions in Downtown and on Nob Hill are mostly within walking distance, anyway. You'll probably need a car to get to the southwestern hills and the Hawthorne District.

EATS

Heavy immigration from many Asian countries is as common here as it is in other Pacific Northwest cities, but Portland's strong Mexican, East-

300

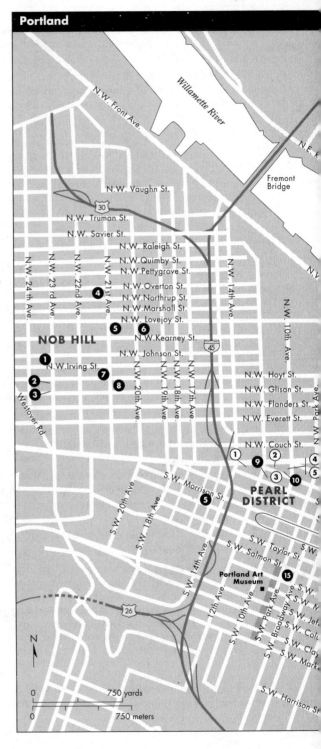

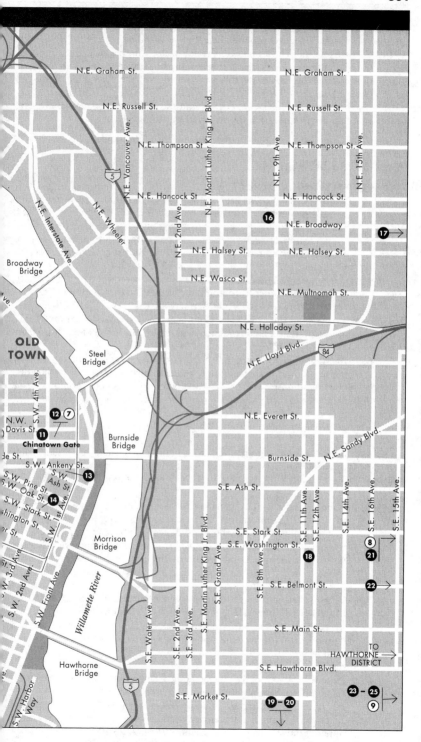

ern European, German, and Irish communities are unusual. The diversity shows in its variety of ethnic eateries. Contemporary Pacific Northwest cuisine is also popular here, but down-home, traditional restaurants are the rule. The dining scene is not flashy. Another real plus is the variety of seafood, from both freshwater and saltwater sources. If a gay atmosphere is important to you, eat at one of the several gay bars with restaurants—these places are usually affordable, but the food hardly memorable. Otherwise, virtually all the city's top restaurants are gay-friendly, but none has an extremely gay following.

For price ranges, *see* Chart B at the front of this guide.

West of the Willamette

$$$–$$$$ **Wildwood.** The hottest purveyor of Pacific Northwest cuisine in 1995, Wildwood is typically trendy: earthy hues, curvy chairs and tables inside, and postmodern metal furniture out on the patio. It succeeds in being a place where you'll look good in stylish duds. The menu changes often, but has featured such winners as corn-and-saffron soup with roasted pepper puree, and seared halibut with risotto, Romano beans, and tomato vinaigrette. *1221 N.W. 21st Ave.,* ☎ *503/248–9663.*

$$$ **Couch Street Fish House.** Near Chinatown and several of the gay bars north of Burnside, Couch (pronounced "Cooch") Street is one of the best restaurants in town. It's in a century-old, cast-iron building that oozes history and ambience. The Continental-style seafood is always fresh, some of it local (Chinook salmon) and some from farther afield (live Maine lobster). *105 N.W. 3rd Ave.,* ☎ *503/223–6173.*

$$$ **The Heathman Restaurant.** In a showcase kitchen at the center of the dining room, chef Philippe Boulot whips up such masterpieces as boletus-mushroom-dusted swordfish (with potato, coriander confit of carrot, and Amontillado sherry sauce) and roasted Northwest fallow venison wrapped in applewood-smoked bacon with bourbon-glazed acorn squash and huckleberry sauce. *Heathman Hotel, 1001 S.W. Broadway,* ☎ *503/ 241–4100.*

$$–$$$ **Café des Amis.** A romantic place to take a first date, this elegantly appointed French restaurant on Nob Hill has reasonably priced country-French fare, like fillet of beef with garlic and port sauce. *1987 N.W. Kearney St.,* ☎ *503/295–6487.*

$$–$$$ **Hobo's.** This is the city's one upscale gay restaurant, and it's so popular that lots of straight movers and shakers come here, too. With a classy lounge and piano bar, Hobo's has the feel of a big gay supper club. The two-tiered dining room has exposed brick walls and formal white linen—you'll see a lot of suits in here most nights, and a somewhat older, gentrified crowd. The menu concentrates on steak and seafood. *120 N.W. 3rd Ave.,* ☎ *503/224–3285.*

$$–$$$ **Zefiro's.** The heavy gold curtains, white linen, and black chairs give it the feel of a Shriner's Hall, but Zefiro's serves trendy Mediterranean fare. You can order a fairly traditional Greek salad, but more typical are such exotic dishes as grilled Chinook salmon with Thai tamarind curry, served with jasmine rice and green and yellow beans. *500 N.W. 21st Ave.,* ☎ *503/226–3394.*

$$ **Papa Haydn.** One of the more yuppified hangouts on Nob Hill, this cheerful storefront restaurant is famous for its weekend brunches. For lunch during the week there are overstuffed sandwiches—try the Gruyère and Black Forest ham; for dinner, tasty entrées such as chicken marinated in apple brandy appear on the menu. *701 N.W. 23rd Ave.,* ☎ *503/228– 7317; also 5829 S.E. Milwaukie St.,* ☎ *503/232–9440.*

$–$$ **Gypsy Cafe.** Though the kitschy '50s-diner decor is a bit overdone (think funky lamps and retro colors), the Gypsy serves up great traditional comfort fare, much of it with a twist. You can get the eggs Benedict, for instance, the usual way or vegetarian, with spinach and tomatoes. There's a narrow, sunny patio off to the side. *625 N.W. 21st St. at Irving St.,* ☎ *503/796–1859.*

$ **Dan & Louis Oyster Bar.** This simple fish house in the Skidmore Historic District has been run by the same family since 1919. In addition to the tasty raw oysters, you can sample a rich oyster stew, clam chowder, and several seafood platters. There are two dining rooms, each with unassuming wood tables and walls covered with decorative dinner plates. *208 S.W. Ankeny St.,* ☎ *503/227–5906.*

$ **Huber's.** With vintage clocks, cash registers, mahogany paneling, and stained glass, this famed Downtown sandwich shop probably doesn't look exactly the way it did when it opened in 1879, but it sure does look old. Such filling creations as roast turkey and baked ham come with generous sides of coleslaw and all the fixings. *411 S.W. 3rd Ave.,* ☎ *503/228–5686.*

$ **Pizzacato.** This chic little pizzeria's pies are available with any number of different toppings. Lamb sausage, prosciutto, and eggplant are a few popular options; you can also choose from a wide assortment of foccacia sandwiches. It's on a popular street corner and you can sit outside on black wrought-iron furniture while enjoying an optimum crowd-ogling experience. *505 N.W. 23rd St.,* ☎ *503/242–0023.*

$ **The Roxy.** This high-ceiling study in Formica is Pearl District's 24-hour gay-meets-grunge diner. On any given night you'll see big hair, pierced extremities, muscle queens, leather, drag, you name it. It's liveliest after the bars close, so expect a wait. Good sandwiches and egg dishes—a specialty is the Soylent Green omelet (spinach, mushroom, cheddar cheese). *1121 S.W. Stark St.,* ☎ *503/223–9160.*

$ **Suriya Thai Cuisine.** This is an extremely inexpensive Thai restaurant around the corner from Stark Street's gay bars. The decor is spare, the curries fiery, the service friendly. *1231 S.W. Washington St.,* ☎ *503/228–5775.*

East of the Willamette

$$–$$$ **La Catalana.** This gay-popular Catalan restaurant is one of the most romantic in eastern Portland, filled with hand-painted ceramics and objets d'art. Fresh bass and trout are specialties here, as is the appetizer of mussels on the half shell with spinach mousse. *2821 S.E. Stark St.,* ☎ *503/232–0948.*

$–$$ **Chez José.** You're as likely to find a mom and dad with a zillion children as you are a posse of muscle queens in this cavernous Mexican restaurant with a festive patio out back. In addition to the usual south-of-the-border fare, the menu shows off shrimp in a tangy honey-chipotle sauce and squash enchiladas with a spicy peanut sauce. The management is very active in charity work. *2200 N.E. Broadway,* ☎ *503/280–9888.*

$$ **Westmoreland Bistro.** Many diners hear about this place from part-owner Caprial Pence's PBS cooking show, and dishes featured on the show highlight the eclectic regional menu: warm spinach salad with dried cherry dressing, beef tenderloin with arugola pesto, ginger-peach upside-down cake. *7015 S.E. Milwaukie St.,* ☎ *503/236–6457.*

$ **Brite Spot.** A HoJo-esque breakfast and lunch spot in the heart of the funky Hawthorne District, Brite Spot is across the street from the Crow, a gay leather bar. The food is filling and fatty, the way it's supposed to be. The attached **Space Room** is a bizarre, alternateen-infested cocktail lounge with tacky intergalactic murals and lots of Naugahyde. *4800 S.E. Hawthorne Blvd.,* ☎ *503/235–6957.*

$ **Garbanzo's.** This falafel bar in Hawthorne has a big dyke following. You can eat in the shaded courtyard or in the airy dining room. Good veggie burgers, hummus, tahini, and salads. *3433 S.E. Hawthorne Ave.,* ☎ *503/239–6087; also 2074 N.W. Lovejoy St.,* ☎ *503/227–4196.*

$ Saigon Kitchen. For the best spring roll in Portland, head over the Broadway Bridge to this bustling, informal Southeast Asian restaurant. The salted calamari is popular, too, and there's a long list of Thai stir-fry noodle dishes with a variety of accompaniments. The service is so quick it verges on frantic. *835 N.E. Broadway,* ☎ *503/281–3669.*

Coffeehouse Culture

The brash and beatnik **Cafe Lena** (2239 S.E. Hawthorne Blvd., ☎ 503/238–7087) has newspaper clippings and photos of Billie Holiday, Lenny Bruce, and other performers on the walls, disco music blaring when there aren't poetry readings being staged, and great sandwiches (try the Birkenstock, a baguette with pesto mayo, veggies, and provolone). The **Rimsky-Korsakoffee House** (707 S.E. 12th Ave., ☎ 503/232–2640) has no sign out front and is staffed by smart-ass waitrons (the bad service is intentional—apparently somebody's idea of a marketing gimmick). The desserts are delicious though, and there's live folk music most nights. **Utopia** (3220 S.E. Belmont St., ☎ 503/235–7606) is another gay-popular spot for great coffee and desserts in the Hawthorne District.

There are a couple of Starbucks branches on Nob Hill, but the best spot for java is **Coffee People** (533 N.W. 23rd St., ☎ 503/221–0235), a tiny place with counter seating along the wall and front windows. They don't serve real food, but you can get great ice cream, shakes, and other sweets.

SLEEPS

Portland has several outstanding, European-style hotels, most in century-old buildings and all within a short walk of the Pearl District's gay bars. Several of these places are high-end, but three excellent ones charge as little as $60 nightly. All the major chain hotels are also represented in Portland.

For price ranges, *see* Chart B at the front of this guide.

Hotels

▦ Portland's grande dame is the 1912 **Benson Hotel.** Its lobby is one of the most stunning of any city hotel; guest rooms are less fancy but perfectly charming, with much of the original architectural details and such touches as crystal chandeliers. *309 S.W. Broadway,* ☎ *503/228–2000 or 800/426–0670. 287 rooms. $$$–$$$$*

▦ Before the 1909 Governor Building was converted into the posh **Governor Hotel,** its gutted interior starred as the home of a raffish posse of ne'er-do-wells and their Faginesque leader in the film *My Own Private Idaho.* You won't recognize it now: Murals in the lobby depict scenes from Lewis and Clark's Columbia River expedition, public rooms have dark mahogany detailing and a lodgelike rusticity, and the guest rooms are sumptuous and softly lit. The restaurant, Jake's Grill, has fine American cuisine. *6119 S.W. 10th St. at Alder St.,* ☎ *503/224–3400 or 800/554–3456. 100 rooms. $$$–$$$$*

▦ The **Hotel Vintage Plaza,** which was fully restored in 1991, is one of the loveliest properties in the Pacific Northwest. Every night in the lobby, the Plaza holds a complimentary wine reception, meant to capture the ambience of Oregon's wine country. The rooms are large and done in warm colors; 17 have hot tubs. *422 S.W. Broadway,* ☎ *503/228–1212 or 800/243–0555. 107 rooms. $$$*

The 1908 **Imperial Hotel** is full of character and as good a budget option as you'll find in any major city. It looks and feels nearly as nice as the luxury hotels that neighbor it, and though it lacks some of the business services and amenities, it's nevertheless a classy property with spacious rooms. *400 S.E. Broadway, ☎ 503/228–7221 or 800/452–2323. 136 rooms. $–$$*

Mallory Hotel (1920s) is a dependable, affordable choice just a 10-minute walk from the gay bars on Stark Street. It's run by the same folks who own the Imperial—rooms here are similarly clean and cheerful. It's popular; book well in advance. *729 S.W. 15th St., ☎ 503/233–6311 or 800/228–8657. 144 rooms. $–$$*

Steps from the popular gay bars, the **Mark Spencer Hotel** looks unsavory from the outside but is surprisingly clean and comfortable inside. It's basic and dirt cheap; rooms come with walk-in closets and kitchens. *409 S.W. 11th Ave., ☎ 503/224–3293 or 800/548–3934. 102 rooms. $*

This **Motel 6** in southeast Portland puts you close to the Hawthorne District. *3104 S.E. Powell Blvd., ☎ 503/238–0600. 69 rooms. $*

Guest Houses and Small Hotels

On swank King's Hill, which looms just above Downtown, the grand, turn-of-the-century **MacMaster House** offers a terrific option instead of staying Downtown. The rooms have a romantic mix of antiques and reproductions, and four have fireplaces. The full breakfast is quite good. *1041 S.W. Vista Ave., ☎ 503/223–7362. 7 rooms. Mixed gay/straight. $–$$*

The gay-operated **Sullivan's Gulch B&B** is in a modest but charming residential neighborhood across the Willamette. Rooms in this pretty, 1904 Colonial Revival are comfortably furnished; the hosts are friendly and knowledgeable. *1744 N.E. Clackamas St., ☎ 503/331–1104. 4 rooms. Mixed gay male/lesbian. $*

SCENES

Portland has a scruffy bar scene. You'll see plenty of beards and flannel shirts, hiking boots and Doc Martens. You'll also see much of the Northwest's grunginess, plus a fair number of Deadheads. If you have fantasies about butch outdoorsy types and working-class heroes, you'll find lots of attractive possibilities. (By the way, men who cut down trees in the forest are called loggers, *not* lumberjacks.) If you're even the least bit friendly, you'll have no trouble meeting people here. The bars draw a down-to-earth, affable crowd. At most of them there's at least a decent mix of lesbians and gay men.

Oddly enough, the most popular bars west of the Willamette are on Southwest Stark Street, and the most popular bars on the east side are on Southeast Stark Street. Otherwise, these two neighborhoods have absolutely nothing in common. Several other bars are located north of Burnside Street, in the Old Town district, but these are mostly neighborhood dives.

Bars and Clubs

Boxx's/The Brig. In the same building as the Panorama disco and the Fish Grotto seafood restaurant, these two connected bars are Portland's most popular hangouts. What tiny stand-and-model scene exists in this city, you'll find it here. However, it's still a fairly laid-back place. You enter through Boxx's, which is a very typical, nicely decorated video bar with lots of high cocktail tables and plenty of room for posing, mingling, and playing video poker. A hallway leads to The Brig, which on one side has a pool table and a few tables and on the other has a long bar overlooking a small, sunken, cement dance floor. There are railings surrounding it, which you can lean on and watch everybody wiggle, but the space is strangely grim—as though the designers had in mind the recreation room of a nuclear fallout shelter. The bartenders are very sweet and friendly. *1035 S.W. Stark St.,* ☎ *503/226–4171. Crowd: 75/25 m/f; mostly under 35; some guppies; clean-cut by Portland standards; fairly cruisy.*

Choices. This is a chummy neighborhood pub east of the river that's predominantly lesbian but welcomes all types. It's a large, contemporary, brightly lit place with two pool tables, a rockin' jukebox, a small dance floor, darts, and a couple of large-screen TVs. Very outgoing staff. *2845 S.E. Stark St.,* ☎ *503/236–4321. Crowd: mostly gay, 80/20 f/m; all ages; all types, fairly local.*

The Crow. This relatively new club in the Hawthorne District aims for a sleazy atmosphere and pulls it off rather well. It's a skinny room with a corrugated-metal bar, bartenders in leather gear, and dark lighting. And yet, there are some surprisingly festive touches, such as crow's feet painted on the ceiling, a small elevated lounge area with campy furniture, and a genuinely cheerful beer garden in back. It's really a great bar, and you never know who you're going to find inside. *4801 S.E. Hawthorne Blvd.,* ☎ *503/232–2037. Crowd: 80/20 m/f; lots of leather; mixed ages—from Gen-Xers to grampas.*

Eagle. Portland has a good leather scene, and the Eagle is where you'll find the most intense action. It's a fairly spacious place, but with several rooms. On the first floor there's a dark cruise bar, next to which is a smaller room with a pool table. Upstairs there's an open interior balcony: a cozy aerie more conducive to conversation. In addition to the strong leather presence, you're apt to see some guys in creative uniforms—an Eagle Scout was spotted in here recently. *1300 W. Burnside St.,* ☎ *503/241–0105. Crowd: male, mostly mid-20s to late 30s; mostly leather but some denim.*

Embers. This Old Town fixture was *the* hot young disco for quite some time, but in the past couple of years it's begun to slide downhill. The main reason to come now is to catch one of the drag shows, held in the main disco on a long stage. The front room is a dreary video lounge. *110 N.W. Broadway,* ☎ *503/222–3082. Crowd: mostly gay, mixed m/f; all ages and races; loud and disorderly; some hustlers.*

Hobo's. Known more as a restaurant (*see* Eats, *above*), this huge steak house and lounge on the edge of Chinatown has piano music nightly. *120 N.W. 3rd Ave.,* ☎ *503/224–3285. Crowd: 80/20 gay/straight, mixed m/f, all ages.*

Panorama. It opened in 1994 with the aim of becoming Portland's first same-sex superclub, but despite being in the same overwhelmingly gay complex that houses Boxx's and The Brig, the crowd has always been at least 50% straight. For some reason conflicts have arisen on many occasions as a result of this mix. It's still a good place to dance, but the tension between straights and gays pretty much kills the cruise factor. The crowd is also unbelievably young—lots of rebellious kids from the burbs. If you're comfortable with all this, you shouldn't find the place menacing, but Panorama is not for everybody. On the plus side the decor is inventive and quirky, with a dark, lively dance floor, one room with a bar and lounge chairs, and another done up with Moroccan-inspired furnishings, booth seating, and tall white columns. On weekends it's open until 4. *341 S.W. 10th St.,* ☎ *503/226–4171. Crowd: 50/50 gay/straight; mixed m/f; extremely young; serious dancers, poseurs; lots of spiked hair, shaved heads, body piercing.*

Scandals. This is the mellowest of Southwest Stark Street's several bars, a casual tavern with big windows looking onto the street. There's a long bar, video games, and plenty of diversions inside; many people here seem to know one another. Very friendly. *1038 S.W. Stark St., ☎ 503/227–5887. Crowd: mostly male; blue-collar, older; regular guys, local.*

Silverado. Were it not in the heart of the Pearl District's gay entertainment section, this would be just another tacky hustler bar with bad strippers. Instead, it's all that and so much more. You enter an oddly configured room with a long bar up front. Across from that is a small stage for the gangly strippers, with a counter and seats around it, so that lascivious old men can rest both their asses and their highballs while still being close enough to the action to stick dollar bills in as many waistbands as possible. In the far corner is a small dance floor, where a DJ spins mostly dated disco. The lighting here has a florid pink tint that makes everybody's denim appear acid-washed—or maybe it's just that everybody's denim *is* acid-washed. Off the main bar there's a small dining room with booths and a ship's wheel on the wall. *1217 S.W. Stark St., ☎ 503/224–4493. Crowd: mostly male; chickens and chicken hawks; racially mixed; a few drag queens; overall quite sleazy but kind of fun.*

Neib Bars

C.C. Slaughter's (1014 S.W. Stark St., ☎ 503/248–9135) is Portland's country-western dance hall, but it's not as lively or exciting as some you'll find in other cities—it's also mostly male. **Darcelle XV** (208 N.W. 3rd Ave., ☎ 503/222–5338) is famous among both gays and straights for its elaborate drag revues—it has strippers on other nights. The **Dirty Duck** (439 N.W. 3rd Ave., ☎ 503/224–8446) is a dirty old pub in an industrial area, with a strong contingent of leather bears. The **Fox and Hound** (217 N.W. 2nd Ave., ☎ 503/243–5530), in the Old Town district, is a gay pub with sandwiches and burgers, a popular karaoke scene, and a saucy crowd of locals. **Starky's** (2913 S.E. Stark St., ☎ 503/230–7980) is a terrific, clean, warm lounge in eastern Portland with a popular restaurant (serving the usual pub fare)—both men and women are welcome.

THE LITTLE BLACK BOOK

At Your Fingertips

Lesbian Community Project: ☎ 503/223–0071. **Oregon AIDS Hotline:** ☎ 503/223–2437 or 800/777–2437. **Portland Oregon Visitors Association:** 3 World Trade Center, 97204, ☎ 503/275–9750.

Gay Media

Just Out (☎ 503/236–1252) is the biweekly gay and lesbian newspaper. Just across the Columbia River from Portland, the small city of Vancouver, Washington, has a monthly gay and lesbian newspaper, *Vancouver Voice* (☎ 360/737–9879).

There are several left-leaning arts and entertainment papers in town, including *PDXS* (☎ 503/224–7316) and the *Rocket* (☎ 503/228–4702), which are biweekly papers with an emphasis on the local music scene. *Willamette Week* (☎ 503/243–2122) has the most comprehensive coverage, however, and is extremely pro-gay.

BOOKSTORES

Portland does not have a lesbigay bookstore, but **Twenty-Third Avenue Books** (1015 N.W. 23rd Ave., ☎ 503/224–5097) has a better selection of gay titles. **In Other Words** (3734 S.E. Hawthorne Blvd., ☎ 503/232–6003) has an extensive selection of feminist and lesbian books and videos, plus many good children's titles. This is also a great place to find resources and social opportunities for both straight women and lesbians. **It's My Pleasure** (4258 S.E. Hawthorne Blvd., ☎ 503/236–0505) is a fun, lesbian-oriented sex boutique with books, magazines, and movies. The enormous **Powell's City of Books** (1005 W. Burnside St., ☎ 503/228–4651) has an amazing selection of used titles, including a large lesbian and gay section.

Body and Fitness

The **YWCA** (1111 S.W. 10th Ave., ☎ 503/294–7420) is a clean, well-appointed gym and swim center that's extremely dyke-positive. The downtown **Gold's Gym** (N.W. 13th Ave. and N.W. Irving St., ☎ 503/222–1210) is popular with both gays and straights.

20 Out in Provincetown

AMERICA'S ORIGINAL GAY RESORT, Provincetown developed as an artists' colony at the turn of the century. A young artist and entrepreneur named Charles Hawthorne, charmed by the town's seclusion and magnificent setting, founded the Cape Cod School of Art, one of America's first open-air academies.

By 1916 the town's once vibrant fishing industry had slowed, and its whaling industry had died. But a half dozen art schools had opened; the Provincetown Art Association had staged its first exhibitions; and a small band of modernist theater folk—notably the young Eugene O'Neill and Edna St. Vincent Millay—had begun to produce plays on a small wharf in the town's East End.

The Provincetown Players, under the leadership of O'Neill, Kenneth Macgowan, and Robert Edmund Jones, essentially became America's first theater company. After a year in Provincetown the players moved to New York City's Greenwich Village, which had already become a gay ghetto. This kinship contributed partially to the early flourishing of Provincetown's gay community. By then, tourism had become a major source of revenue, and local homes had begun letting rooms to the hundreds of writers, painters, and other artists who were drawn to the town's thriving arts community.

Over the next few decades, many leaders of our country's artistic and literary movements spent time in Provincetown, including journalist and communist John Reed and painters Marsden Hartley, Charles Demuth, Edward Hopper, Max Ernst, Hans Hofmann, Robert Motherwell, Jackson Pollock, and Mark Rothko. Such writers as Truman Capote, Tennessee Williams, Norman Mailer, and John Dos Passos visited. Although traditional artistic styles continued to appear in Provincetown, the town was identified increasingly for its outrageousness—its willingness to flout convention.

By the 1960s the town had become a haven for anyone whose artistic leaning, political platform, social manifesto, or sexual persuasion was subject to persecution elsewhere in America. Provincetown, a hotbed of counterculture, naturally nurtured one of the country's most significant gay communities.

Today Provincetown is as appealing to artists as it is to gay and lesbian, as well as straight, tourists. The awareness brought by the onslaught of AIDS combined with the increasing tolerance of sexual diversity has turned the town into the most visibly gay community in America, excepting the Pines and Cherry Grove in Fire Island and possibly Key West.

It's significant that Fire Island is geographically isolated from the rest of the world, and both Provincetown and Key West are at the tips of their respective landmasses. Isolation was and is a major reason artists settle in Provincetown. Only now, few gays and lesbians rush off to P'town to dabble in the arts—being, acting, thinking, and living an openly gay lifestyle, whether for a few days or year-round, has become reason enough to come here.

THE LAY OF THE LAND

The two main streets in town are **Commercial Street,** which runs east–west the length of the harbor front, and **Bradford,** which runs parallel, a block inland. Dozens of short roads run between the two. The West End takes in those points west of about Central Street; the East End takes in points east of about Washington Street. Many of the town's main basic services and stores, such as grocery stores, laundromats, and the like, are on Shank Painter Road, which runs north–south between Bradford and Route 6, which is the main highway into town. The three-fourths of town above Route 6 encompasses the national seashore property.

Much of Bradford Street is on higher ground than Commercial, and from some homes along here you're afforded a view all the way down and around the Cape to Truro and Wellfleet to the east, and Hyannis and Brewster to the south.

Gay-oriented businesses line Commercial Street. To name but a few, **Silk and Feathers** and **Modifino** are both very popular with lesbians for trendy clothing; **All American Boy** is tops with the guys. **Hirsheldons** and **Northern Lights** are great for leather goods. **Provincetown Sandals** makes outstanding custom-designed leather sandals. **Pride's of Provincetown** sells gay cards, jewelry, and paraphernalia, and **Womencrafts** has lesbian jewelry, books, music, and crafts.

There are only a few notable tourist sights in town, most significantly the 252-foot-tall **Pilgrim Monument** (☎ 508/487–1310), commemorating the landing of the Pilgrims in 1620. At its base is a museum that contains exhibits and artifacts of Colonial Provincetown and pieces from an 18th-century pirate ship, *Whydah,* which sank off local shores. Another source of local history is the **Provincetown Heritage Museum** (Monument Hill, ☎ 508/487–0666), formerly the Center Methodist Episcopal Church, whose grand dwelling dates to 1860. Exhibits here show replicated rooms and shops in Provincetown as they might have existed during the 18th and 19th centuries. The **Provincetown Art Association and Museum** (460 Commercial St., ☎ 508/487–1750) houses a permanent collection of more than 1,500 works and mounts exhibitions year-round.

Outdoor Diversions

The **Cape Cod National Seashore** (for information, contact Marconi Station, Rte. 6, S. Wellfleet, 02663, ☎ 508/349–3785) extends for about 40 miles, from Chatham, at the Cape's outer elbow, to Provincetown; there's a visitor center at **Race Point Beach** (☎ 508/487–1256), which has trail maps and park rules. More than three quarters of P'town is administered by the seashore; this land includes more than 7 miles of pristine, paved bike trails; several dunes and forest walking trails; and two beaches: **Race Point,** which is on the northern side of town and gets more wind and rougher waters, and **Herring Cove,** which is in the west end and, to the far left, has a crowded gay beach (nudity not permitted). Parking lots are full at both beaches by late morning in summer; consider walking. There's a small entrance fee.

WHEN TO GO

There are a surprising number of P'town loyalists who won't set foot here during the frantic, crowded months of July and August, but those are the prime months: If you're looking for nightlife, tea-dance society, a good tan, and the height of gay and lesbian society, brave the crowds and higher prices (many guest houses have four-day, if not seven-day, minimum stays at this time) and jump into the fray. In general, the July crowd is more of the stand-and-model variety, the August bunch is a bit older and more refined. Couples often visit during the lovely, still-moderate months of May, June, September, and October. The ratio of women to men drops during the summer, when the buff beach boys seem to run amok. Don't discount winter, however. Though only a handful of guest houses and restaurants remain open, it's still an enchanting (in a gray, melancholy sort of way) time to stroll along the dunes and curl up before a roaring fire.

GETTING THERE

Provincetown is about a 2- or 2½-hour drive from either Boston or Providence. From New York City, it's about six hours. There are just two bridges onto the Cape, and both are unbelievably congested on weekends—give yourself plenty of time. Bus service is also available from these cities, and from Boston's Logan International Airport, but it's a long ride. From Boston, also consider taking the relaxing passenger ferry (☎ 508/487–9284; once daily; 3 hrs.) from Commonwealth Pier to P'town's MacMillan Wharf. If money isn't an issue, several flights are offered by **Cape Air** (☎ 508/771–6944 or 800/352–0714) daily between Provincetown Municipal Airport and Logan; it's a 20-minute trip that affords breathtaking views.

GETTING AROUND

Parking is a challenge. Some accommodations have ample parking, but just as many have either no designated parking or only enough for a few guests. Once in town, find a legal spot for your car (parking rules are enforced vigilantly), then leave it there. You can walk the entire length of Commercial Street in about an hour, and most points in town are within easy walking distance of one another. For the easiest access to points in town and the beaches, rent a bike at either **Gale Force Bicycle Rentals** (☎ 508/487–4849) or **Arnold's Bike Shop** (☎ 508/487–0844).

EATS

Provincetown's dining scene is typical of Cape Cod's—lots of lobster, clams, cod, bluefish, and other indigenous seafood, plus plenty of Italian and Portuguese recipes. Stop by the **Provincetown Portuguese Bakery** (299 Commercial St., ☎ 508/487–1803) to sample the delicious meat pies, pastries, rolls, and breads. Some of the more touristy restaurants close to MacMillan Wharf are slightly straighter, more family oriented, but gays are all over town. The few restaurants in the West End have the strongest followings among gay men and lesbians.

For price ranges, *see* Chart B at the front of this guide.

$$$–$$$$ **Front Street.** Chef Donna Aliperti is renowned for her innovative menus, which change weekly, usually offering dishes with a vaguely Continental spin, such as rack of lamb, grilled fish and softshell crab, or tea-smoked duck. This bistro, in the brick cellar of an old Victorian home, is an ideal spot for special occasions—one of the few places you might dress to dine. *230 Commercial St.,* ☎ *508/487–9715.*

$$$–$$$$ **Red Inn.** One of the most romantic settings on Cape Cod, the Red Inn is a Federal colonial in the West End, directly overlooking the bay. People occasionally complain about the high cost of the food, but the quality is stellar: Specialties include clam-and-corn chowder; chicken Véronique (with a reduction sauce made from grapes, white wine, and cream); and daily presentations of duck, swordfish, scallops, and lobster. The candlelit dining room looks as one imagines it might have a few hundred years ago. *15 Commercial St.,* ☎ *508/487–0050.*

$$$–$$$$ **Sal's.** For the best, though priciest, Italian fare in town, plan an evening at Sal's, which is in a quiet, residential span of the West End. This is not the trendy fare of sidewalk cafés but carbo-packed pasta dishes, broiled native fish, stuffed mushroom caps, and fresh mussels with white wine and herbs. There's outdoor seating on the water under a wind-sheltering awning. *99 Commercial St.,* ☎ *508/487–1279.*

$$–$$$$ **Mario's.** Popular for its diverse menu, deck seating, and bustling pace, Mario's Mediterranean restaurant has an informal pizza parlor up front (open late), and a full dining room in back, where there's always a daily selection of tapas, plus great vegetable kebabs, seafood *fra diablo* (a spicy tomato *coulis*), and clam chowder that's as good as you'll find. Bustling. *265–7 Commercial St.,* ☎ *508/487–0002.*

$$–$$$ **Boatslip Restaurant.** This is P'town's only serious gay restaurant, set in a contemporary, airy space overlooking the tea-dance deck and the harbor. With timber-and-glass walls, the views are grand. The American food here is decent, if predictable—a standout is the lobster niĉoise. *161 Commercial St.,* ☎ *508/487–2509.*

$$–$$$ **Bubala's.** Becoming more and more of a late-night fixture (all dishes are served until 11; the bar is open till 1), Bubala's setting, in a dull roadhouse on Commercial, lacks charm but has great bay views. The menu is quite sophisticated, however, with everything from tuna wasabi to native steamers to grilled tofu with Thai curry. Service is friendly but uneven, the decor bright and whimsical. Great breakfasts, too. *183 Commercial St.,* ☎ *508/487–0773.*

$$–$$$ **Gallerani's Café.** Gallerani's serves the kind of food you imagine the town's salty and sweaty Portuguese and Italian fishermen devoured after long days at sea: rich chowders, squid stew, shrimp scampi; the antifish types among you can savor the chicken sautéed with olive oil, capers, roasted red peppers, and sun-dried tomatoes. Extra points for the homey, untrendy interior: a large, open, storefront dining room with black-and-white wood tables. *133 Commercial St.,* ☎ *508/487–4433.*

$$–$$$ **Lobster Pot.** Don't leave P'town without having a meal at this tried-and-true, family-style tourist mecca overlooking the harbor and MacMillan Wharf. Come here to feast on the best lobster rolls in town, plus steamers, coquilles St. Jacques, and all the usual seaside suspects. Unusually polite service, considering the crowds. *321 Commercial St.,* ☎ *508/487–0842.*

$$–$$$ **Martin House.** A former captain's residence (circa 1750), the Martin House has several intimate dining rooms, many with fireplaces, original wide-plank floors, exposed brick, local paintings, pitched roofs, beamed ceilings and other charming touches—there's also a cheerful redbrick garden terrace in back. Here you'll find some of the fancier food in town: *crostini* with goat cheese, pecan-crusted chicken with bourbon molasses, veggie lasagna with a puree of wild mushroom, and, for dessert, an outstanding white chocolate flan. *157 Commercial St.,* ☎ *508/487–1327.*

$$–$$$ **Napi's.** Napi's has the most exotic menu in town, including such worldbeat fare as caponata, hummus, Brazilian steak, chicken teriyaki, Syrian falafel melts, and Thai noodles with shrimp. There's a long wine list, too. The atmosphere is festive, with old-fashioned laminated wooden tables

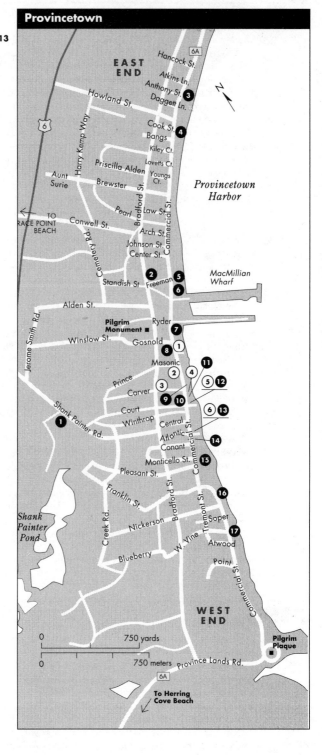

Provincetown

Eats ●

Bagel Factory, **1**
Boatslip Restaurant, **13**
Bubala's, **11**
Café Heaven, **9**
Front Street, **8**
Gallerani's Café, **15**
Lobster Pot, **6**
Mario's, **7**
Martin House, **14**
The Mews, **4**
Napi's, **2**
Pucci's, **3**
Red Inn, **17**
Sal's, **16**
Sebastian's, **12**
Snackattack, **5**
Spiritus, **10**

Scenes ○

Atlantic House, **2**
Backstreet, **3**
Boatslip, **6**
Crown & Anchor, **1**
Larry's Bar, **5**
Pied Piper Lounge, **4**

set closely together, amber lighting, and Tiffany-style lamps. Lots of lesbians hanging around the bar. *7 Freeman St.,* ☎ *508/487–1145.*

$–$$$ The Mews. Home of the best margarita in town and great live entertainment—from open-mike nights to drag shows. The pubby café upstairs has lighter fare (such as designer pizzas), a piano, and a popular bar. The downstairs dining room, with pickled-wood floors, mahogany wainscoting, and stylish sand-color, textured-plaster walls, is more formal. A favorite combination here is roasted whole garlic followed by roasted duck, which is accompanied each day by a different sauce, such as calvados. Both rooms have great harbor views. *429 Commercial St.,* ☎ *508/487–1500.*

$–$$ Pucci's. This informal spot is in an invitingly weathered cedar-shake house right on the water in the East End; the dining room, dressed down with paper napkins and austere wooden furniture, offers sweeping harbor views. Has the best burgers in town and is a major brunch spot. For breakfast, choose from hearty omelets or waffles; for dinner, try the scampi, baked chicken, or stuffed mushrooms. *539 Commercial St.,* ☎ *508/487–1964.*

$–$$ Sebastian's. Affording great bay views from its simple, fish-shanty interior, Sebastian's is a quick, cheap standby. The food is unexceptional—burgers, soups, lobster rolls—but it's a lively scene most afternoons. *177 Commercial St.,* ☎ *508/487–3286.*

$ Bagel Factory. Though it's up on Shank Painter Road, a good walk from Commercial Street, the bagels baked here every day are the best in town, and they come in all the usual varieties and with several types of spreads. Great sandwiches, too. A good spot for picking up picnic supplies before hitting the beaches. *100 Shank Painter Rd.,* ☎ *508/487–1610.*

$ Café Heaven. Noted for incredible, filling breakfasts (available all day), this small storefront hangout has long wooden benches, cream-color tables, and pale olive walls that contrast nicely with two huge bright murals of P'town's beach scene. Come for great omelets, sharp antipasti, or sandwiches like avocado, goat cheese, tomato, and lettuce on French bread. A full range of coffees. Long lines for brunch. *199 Commercial St.,* ☎ *508/487–9639.*

$ Snackattack. Just a great little snack stand with meat and veggie burgers, frozen yogurt, and many low-fat and nonfat choices. Perfect if you're on the go. Lesbian-operated. *331 Commercial St.,* ☎ *508/487–4749.*

$ Spiritus. If not the home of the town's best pizza, it's certainly where you'll find the best people-watching, especially late at night, especially in that golden hour between bar closing and Spiritus's closing (1 AM–2 AM). In addition to a variety of slices (the Greek has calamata olives, red onions, spinach, feta, and mozzarella), dozens of coffees and milk shakes are available. The service is usually rude and brusque. You can eat inside, but most people grab a slice and sit outside on the steps. *190 Commercial St.,* ☎ *508/487–2808.*

SLEEPS

P'town has an astounding number of B&Bs and inns. More than 60 of them are gay-owned, and a good many more have strong gay followings—especially in summer. Those that remain open in the off-season usually get a broader mix of straights and gays at that time. The West End is quieter and near the beach; Bradford Street is less scenic, but its higher elevations mean great views and soft breezes; and the East End is the straightest and a long walk from gay clubs and the beach. On Commercial Street, as you move toward the center of town from either end, you'll find most of the B&Bs, restaurants, and shops—it's more social here, but also more congested and noisy.

About two-thirds of P'town's gay-oriented lodgings are reviewed below. A few general notes: Very few lodgings could be considered even moderately luxurious. Most B&Bs here are glorified rooming houses. As many as a third of the rooms in town share baths; most establishments serve scant, bleak Continental breakfasts; few places have air-conditioning, private phones, extensive off-street parking, or substantial closet space; many are without TVs and radios. Only a smattering have swimming pools, though a good number have common hot tubs. If any of these amenities are important to you, be sure to ask when booking. You're not encouraged to spend much time in your room in Provincetown, and the houses, for the most part, lack the social—and sexual—buzz of the spreads in Palm Springs and Key West. Finally, tourism has been strong enough here over the past couple of years for many places to begin requiring four- to seven-night minimums in summer, especially around July 4 and Labor Day.

All of these factors might lead you to suspect that the lodging experience in Provincetown is an unpleasant one. On the contrary: Though accommodations are simple, they're also comparatively inexpensive (a shared bath in high season can be had for as little as $40, a private bath for $65), their atmosphere is casual, their pace is unhurried.

For price ranges, *see* Chart B at the front of this guide.

Hotels and Motels

🏠 Ground zero for P'town's frenetic party scene is the **Boatslip,** whose daily tea dances are not to be missed—there's also a lounge and restaurant here. Rooms are of the standard motel ilk: clean, bright, with functional baths. Street-side rooms lack water views but are much cheaper and cozier, with timber ceilings and sloped walls. You're paying for the location and atmosphere. *161 Commercial St., ☎ 508/487–1669. 45 rooms. Mixed gay/straight. $$$–$$$$*

🏠 Near Bradford's intersection with Shank Painter is the **Bradford House Motel,** which consists of a Victorian guest house, smartly furnished with period pieces, and a motel in back, with nondescript rooms that have knotty pine walls—a little pricey for what it is. *41 Bradford St., ☎ 508/ 487–0173. 19 rooms. Mostly mixed gay/lesbian. $$$*

🏠 Two creative women took over the previously uninspired **Dunes Motel** a couple years ago and have done wonders livening up the decor. The apartments are each themed differently: One has a Wild West motif, the Carnival Room is a colorful but tasteful tribute to gay Mardi Gras, and the Sunflower Room has sunflower-print spreads plus a spacious deck that's perfect for watching the sun set. The smaller motel rooms are adequate but not fancy. *125 Bradford St. Extension, ☎ 508/487–1956. 13 rooms, 6 apartments. Mostly mixed gay/lesbian. $$–$$$*

🏠 Decidedly youth- and male-oriented is the grand but tattered **Gifford House Inn,** the site of the Backstreet bar. This turn-of-the-century hotel is basically a gay boarding house. Rooms are simple but functional, many with bay or Monument views, but also with scarred wallpaper and dingy carpeting. The two-bedroom suites are great for four guys on a budget. Friendly staff. A likely place to make new friends. *9–11 Carver St., ☎ 508/487–0688. 25 rooms. Mostly gay male. $$–$$$*

🏠 The **Provincetown Inn** is a sprawling, weather-beaten, family-run and family-frequented motor lodge—but gay guests are welcome. It's beside the rotary in the extreme West End, minutes from Herring Cove Beach; the Pilgrims raved about this setting 375 years ago, and it's still impressive. *1 Commercial St., ☎ 508/487–9500. 102 rooms. Mostly straight. $$–$$$*

⌂ Built in the 1830s, the **Crown and Anchor** maintains a weather-worn, ragged veneer that suits Provincetown well. A party atmosphere pervades, largely because the ground floor hosts a complex of gay bars; upstairs are a couple floors of unfortunately tired and pockmarked rooms, although some have great views of the bay and Commercial Street. *247 Commercial St., ☎ 508/487–1430. 28 rooms. Mostly mixed gay/lesbian. $$*

Guest Houses

Central to West End

⌂ The closest any of Provincetown's gay guest houses come to being luxury inns, the **Brass Key**, which also has a successful outpost in Key West, has 10 rooms in the carefully preserved 1830 main house, plus two cottages—one with a pitched roof and a hot tub. The inn is done in a colonial folk theme, carried out with original antiques and hand-stenciling; other touches include pickled-wood tables and Hitchcock chairs. The pool and redbrick lanai are among the prettiest in town. Attracts a very professional crowd. *9 Court St., ☎ 508/487–9005 or 800/842–9858. 12 rooms. Mostly gay male. $$$–$$$$*

⌂ In the far West End, **Westwinds** comprises a small, yellow-and-white 1782 cape, a few cottages behind it, a pool and deck, and expansive grounds and gardens. Examples of the colonial folk decorating include braided rugs and rush-seated chairs; the main house has original wide-plank floors and wainscoting. The cottages are perfect for long-term stays; they have kitchens and allow plenty of privacy. *28 Commercial St., ☎ 508/487–1841. 2 cottages, 2 apartments. Mostly mixed gay male/lesbian. $$$–$$$$*

⌂ One of the more striking guest houses on Commercial Street, the Victorian **Anchor Inn** makes quite a statement with its dramatic white balcony, faux-Corinthian columns, and bay backdrop—there's usually a vintage auto parked outside, too. Rooms are less impressive—even a tad musty—with small baths, old fixtures, and plain furnishings. Many, however, have sliding glass doors that open onto decks and balconies; try to get a sea view. *175 Commercial St., ☎ 508/487–0432. 25 rooms. Mostly mixed gay male/lesbian. $$$*

⌂ Two outgoing London transplants have brought British elegance to the **Beaconlite,** thanks to the many antiques from their English home. The 1860 house is one of the most impressive in town: The grounds are lushly landscaped, a piano is often heard from in the living room, an octagonal roof deck affords panoramic views, and guest rooms are lavishly furnished and have private baths. Though the crowd is mostly male in season, lesbians are warmly received. A second house next door has four attractive guest rooms. *12–16 Winthrop St., ☎ 508/487–9603. 14 rooms. Mostly gay male. $$–$$$*

⌂ The **Fairbanks Inn** is one of the better values in Provincetown. The compound consists of a stately white clapboard colonial—a former captain's house that dates from 1776—a carriage house, and a Victorian next door. The rooms in the main house are cozy and thoughtfully appointed; the two that share a bath are a bargain. Many rooms have fireplaces, canopy beds, stenciled walls or period papering, and wide-plank floors. There's a homey common area with braided rugs and a TV and VCR, as well as a garden and a courtyard with a gas grill. *90 Bradford St., ☎ 508/487–0386. 14 rooms, 1 apartment. Mixed gay/straight. $$–$$$*

⌂ **Gabriel's** is the largest and most social women's guest house. Rooms are named and themed after famous women: The Georgia O'Keeffe room has Southwestern furnishings; the Diane Fosse room has a loft filled with stuffed gorillas. For general use are a large sundeck, two whirlpools, an extensive new gym and sauna, and a women's lending library. All in all, an excellent, professionally run guest house. *104 Bradford St., ☎ 508/487–3232. 20 rooms and apartments. Lesbian. $$–$$$*

☷ A former boarding house, the century-old **Sandpiper** strikes a successful balance between privacy and intimacy. Rooms in this gray, turreted Victorian are simply appointed, with plenty of hanging plants and large windows; the upper rooms have eaved ceilings and many look over the harbor. *165 Commercial St., ☎ 508/487–1928. 13 rooms. Mixed gay/straight. $$–$$$*

☷ At the **West End Inn,** rooms aren't memorable, but they're clean and eclectically decorated; they have peach, pink, and pale green walls, some papered and some painted. The top-floor suite sleeps four, has a private deck, and a half kitchen. *44 Commercial St., ☎ 508/487–9555. 7 rooms. Mostly mixed gay male/lesbian. $$–$$$*

☷ The **White Wind Inn,** a white Queen Anne near the Boatslip, has some of the only rooms in town with air-conditioning. Additionally, all have new berber carpeting, and many have four-poster or brass beds, Victorian settees and other period antiques, nautical paintings, and separate entrances. One room has a deck with terrific bay views. *174 Commercial St., ☎ 508/487–1526. 11 rooms. Mostly mixed gay male/lesbian. $$–$$$*

☷ One of a handful of accommodations clustered around the Pilgrim Monument, a couple blocks in from the bay, the **Chicago House** is one of Provincetown's original gay guest houses. This pretty white structure is actually two Federal capes joined together. Though it's set on a quiet side street away from the noise of Commercial Street, it's a very social, casual house—the kind of place where you can relax and kick back. A clean, simple interior. *6 Winslow St., ☎ 508/487–0537. 11 rooms, 3 apartments. Mostly mixed gay male/lesbian. $$*

☷ A dependable women's choice is the **Dusty Miller Inn,** a white colonial with black shutters, set near Town Hall on one of Provincetown's highest hills. It's a homey place, with lots of art, bric-a-brac, pillows, teddy bears, and personal touches. Dogs are allowed (call to arrange this), and men may rent any of the rooms with private baths. Adjacent are several nondescript motel units. Gets a young, friendly, social bunch. *82 Bradford St., ☎ 508/487–2213. 12 rooms, 1 apartment. Mostly lesbian. $$*

☷ Nearby, the stately **Four Bays** is painted pale green with intricate forest green and cream trim. Inside, rooms are decorated with seaside Victoriana; the largest has a screened-in porch. *166 Commercial St., ☎ 508/487–0859. 8 rooms. Mostly mixed gay male/lesbian. $$*

☷ One of the best values in the West End is **Lady Jane's,** a women's guest house, the cedar-shake guest wing of which overlooks a garden and contains 10 bright, immaculate rooms, each with baths with blue-tile floors, and a selection of walnut and mahogany antiques. Innkeeper Jane Antonil built several of the Adirondack chairs. A popular common room has a VCR and common fridge. *7 Central St., ☎ 508/487–3387. 10 rooms. Lesbian. $$*

☷ On a quiet lane behind the Fairbanks Inn is one of the town's best-kept secrets, **Six Webster Place.** The main 1750s house is one of the six oldest in town; it retains the original wide-plank pine floor and wavy-glass windows, and there are fireplaces and antiques everywhere. A second house has apartments, which can be rented by the week. This is a low-key, secluded spot, drawing mostly couples and professionals; Gary, the owner, is a great host. *6 Webster Pl., ☎ 508/487–2266 or 800/693–2773. 7 rooms, 3 apartments. Mostly mixed gay male/lesbian. $$*

☷ One of the more social guest houses in the neighborhood, the **Watership Inn** has a large pool and sundeck, is known to host informal parties and mixers from time to time, and has an affable staff. Built in the 1820s and the former home of a prominent sea captain, the house has original floors, beam ceilings, a smattering of antiques, and plenty of character. Rooms are neither memorable nor lacking comfort. *7 Winthrop St.,* ☎ *508/487–0094. 17 rooms. Mostly mixed gay male/lesbian. $$*

☷ The **1807 House** is a simple, weathered-shingle cape with several detached apartments in back. On broad, sweeping grounds with restful gardens and its own gym, this is a good place to chill out and meet fellow guests. Rooms have the ubiquitous blend of colonial-style furnishings and a few antiques, and four-poster or brass beds. *54 Commercial St.,* ☎ *508/487–2173. 3 rooms, 5 apartments. Mixed gay/straight. $–$$*

☷ The **Shire Max** is as much a social experience as it is a guest house. Community rooms are decked with hundreds of photos of the mostly repeat clientele, and the owners are very warm and outgoing. Rooms are quirkily decorated with bright colors and a mishmash of furniture—one has fox hunt prints, another a fluorescent orange and yellow radiator. There's a VCR in one common room; for use is the owners' collection of 900 movies. *5 Tremont St.,* ☎ *508/487–1233. 7 rooms, 2 apartments. Mostly gay male. $–$$*

☷ Of central budget accommodations, the **Revere Guest House** is a good bet. Newly furnished and clean, rooms are small but functional, with hardwood floors, paisley bedspreads, and a tasteful mix of reproduction furnishings. Some of the shared-bath rooms go for less than $50. *14 Court St.,* ☎ *508/487–2292. 8 rooms. Mostly gay male. $*

Central to East End

☷ Said to be a favorite hangout of such sapphic celebs as Melissa Etheridge, **Bradford Gardens,** deftly run by Susan Culligan, is the most luxurious gay-frequented inn on the island. Choose from rooms in the 1820s main house, four rose- and wisteria-wrapped cottages, or five two-bedroom town houses—all are set on a hilltop acre of exquisite gardens, noted for their plentitude of Oriental lilies. Even the smaller rooms here are large by Provincetown standards, with private baths, fine antiques, hardwood floors, braided rugs, and classy color schemes. There are also 15 fireplaces set among the several buildings. A delicious full breakfast is prepared daily. *178 Bradford St.,* ☎ *508/487–1616 or 800/432–2334. 8 rooms, 4 cottages, 5 town houses, 1 small penthouse. Mostly lesbian. $$$–$$$$*

☷ High on a hill on the eastern reaches of Bradford Street, the **Normandy House** is a clean, homey spot with VCRs in every room, a sundeck with great harbor views, a hot tub out back, and extremely friendly, straight owners. There are antiques in some rooms, but decor is mostly a loose mix of the old and the new—it's extremely comfortable here. The third-floor room of this 150-year-old house is highly sought after for its great views. *184 Bradford St.,* ☎ *508/487–1197. 8 rooms. Mostly mixed gay male/lesbian. $$–$$$*

☷ Run on a small scale but with great attention to detail and guest comforts, **Plums Bed and Breakfast** is a popular women's guest house in a white Victorian with distinctive lavender-and-plum trim and a fence out back hung with dozens of colorful buoys. Rooms are peaceful (no TVs) and have private baths, authentic Victorian furnishings, lace curtains, and flowered wallpaper. Great full breakfasts, too. *160 Bradford St.,* ☎ *508/487–2283. 5 rooms. Lesbian. $$–$$$*

☷ There are only a few gay-popular lodgings in the far East End, but the 1850 **Somerset House** is one of the nicest, filled with elegant reproduction and original antiques, pedestal sinks, brass beds, nautical prints, and presided over by Tootsie, a gregarious watchdog. *378 Commercial St.,* ☎ *508/487–0383. 13 rooms, 1 apartment. Mostly mixed gay male/lesbian. $$–$$$*

☑ Of guest houses with a somewhat frisky reputation, **The Tradewinds Inn** is the best of the bunch—attractive individually decorated rooms, outgoing guests, cute houseboys, and not a lot of attitude. Furnishings are generally contemporary; most rooms have large closets (rare in Provincetown), berber carpeting, and clean tile baths. A lot of care has been put into the inn's upkeep and appearance. *12 Johnson St., ☎ 508/487–0138. 16 rooms, 1 suite. Mostly gay male. $$–$$$*

☑ If the feel of yesteryear's Provincetown appeals to you, the **Admiral's Landing** is a wise choice. Nautically themed art, old tools, antiques, and collectibles fill the common areas and some rooms, which aren't fancy but are full of character. Most have pastel-painted furnishings and walls, and slightly worn but clean baths. *158 Bradford St., ☎ 508/487–9665. 6 rooms, 2 cottages. Gay male. $$*

☑ The late-Edwardian **Elephant Walk** was established in 1922, and artist Charles Hawthorne had his studio in back. The building has a popular screened-in porch in front and pretty gardens; rooms cultivate a farmhouse feel, with Oriental rugs, old captain's bureaus, and other antiques. *156 Bradford St., ☎ 508/487–2543 or 800/889–9255. 8 rooms. Mostly mixed gay male/lesbian. $$*

☑ The three women who operate the **Heritage House** strive to create the sort of friendly atmosphere in which both genders can mingle and have fun. There's lots of common space: The living room is large and bright, with a VCR, sofas, and antiques; and a second-floor veranda has Adirondack chairs and wicker. Unfortunately, though rooms are simply but smartly decorated, 13 of them share just four baths. *7 Center St., ☎ 508/ 487–3692. 13 rooms. Mostly mixed gay male/lesbian. $$*

☑ Ideal for long-term stays, the **Ravenwood,** which is well east on Commercial and overlooks the harbor, has several self-contained units with varying degrees of self-catering, lots of privacy, and an eye-pleasing selection of antiques. Rooms are oddly configured; one has a cozy sleeping loft, some have skylights, and all have private decks. The penthouse has great views. *462 Commercial St., ☎ 508/487–3203. 1 room, 4 apartments. Mostly lesbian. $$*

☑ One of only a few straight-operated inns that makes a point of attracting gay visitors, the **Sunset Inn** is a huge, memorable, white Victorian with a white-and-black-striped awning and a graceful second-floor veranda. It's a classic New England inn (an Edward Hopper depiction of it hangs at the Yale University Art Gallery). Rooms are bright and cheerful, with hardwood floors, floral bedspreads, and local paintings and prints. *142 Bradford St., ☎ 508/487–9810. 20 rooms. Mostly straight. $$*

☑ Exuding a definite social atmosphere, the **Swanberry Inn** has been recently refurbished with that ubiquitous Provincetown mix of reproduction antiques, brass beds, pedestal sinks, rattan and wicker furniture, and paisley bedspreads. Very clean and casual—some of the shared baths have two showers, which can lead to some unexpected, friendly greetings among the guests. *8 Johnson St., ☎ 508/487–4242 or 800/847–7926. 10 rooms. Mostly gay male. $$*

☑ One of the oldest gay inns in town, the **Coat of Arms** is run with plenty of tender loving care by an extremely charming owner. It's a social house, with a restored 1917 Chickering player piano, and vintage posters and playbills on many walls. Rooms, however, are a bit dated. *7 Johnson St., ☎ 508/487–0816. 11 rooms. Gay male. $*

SCENES

Of all gay summer resorts, Provincetown has the most varied nightlife scene (Fire Island runs a close second). But even with the diversity of options, several conventions seem to prevail: Most visitors—especially singles—head to the beach in the morning, drop by the Boatslip for the afternoon tea dance, rush home to shower and change, catch the end of the post–tea dance party at the Pied Piper, and then head off to dinner. After that, women generally congregate at the Pied Piper, men at the Atlantic House. Depending on the night, crowds swell at the Gifford House's Backstreet bar. Bars used to be very male or female; now the scene is quite mixed at most places on most nights, and just about every bar has a women's night once a week. In general, the crowd changes from night to night, as the bars here stage theme nights and throw parties.

At 1 AM, when the bars close, *everybody* heads to Spiritus Pizza for an hour of dishing, posing, and, ideally, discovering where the after-hours parties are. A little persistence is required if you're unfamiliar with the scene, but P'town's many houseboys/girls, waitrons, and retail workers are known to party until dawn. Ask around.

Atlantic House. Set inside one of the town's most historically significant buildings, the downstairs bar dates from 1798 and the hotel half was added in 1812. Tennessee Williams and Eugene O'Neill used to stay here. It's the main men's disco, and it has a small dance floor, a terrace out back that's good for talking, and a cozy lounge off the dance floor. The smaller upstairs bar, which has a separate entrance from the street, attracts a leather contingent. Of the many theme parties held all summer long, the Thursday-night full costume parties are undoubtedly the best. This is the only gay bar open year-round. *8 Masonic Pl.,* ☎ *508/487–3821. Crowd in main bar: 80/20 m/f, younger, very stand-and-model; upstairs: older, more leather and Levi's.*

Backstreet. The popularity of this bar in the Gifford House hotel seems to vary depending on the night of the week: It's jam-packed some nights, dead on others. Typically, one night is set aside for women, another for leather, another for townies. There's also a casual bar in the porch, which is open daily and caters mostly to the hotel guests. The main disco is open on weekends. Musical performers, such as the Dyketones, frequently perform here, too. *Gifford House, 9 Carver St.,* ☎ *508/487–6400. Crowd: generally gay, but otherwise totally varied.*

Boatslip. All summer long, the poseurs and party creatures—mostly men but plenty of women, too—mingle and cruise during the Boatslip's legendary tea dances, held daily 3:30 to 6:30. The party rocks on the long wooden deck, which has great harbor views, but there's also dancing in the enclosed disco. At night, the younger crowd heads elsewhere, but lots of locals gather in the lobby lounge for quiet chitchat; dance fans head to the downstairs disco for two-stepping (four nights weekly) and ballroom dancing (three nights weekly). *161 Commercial St.,* ☎ *508/487–1669. Tea-dance crowd: 70/30 m/f, mixed ages, fresh from the beach. Lobby-bar crowd: older, mixed m/f, more couples, regulars.*

Crown and Anchor. There are several distinct spaces on the ground floor of this shabby old seaside resort in the heart of town: There's a leather shop and a small lounge popular with boys in leather; a pool hall, which gets a good mix of men and women; and a cabaret, which showcases gay musical and comic talents. This definitely isn't the trendiest hangout in town, but the Crown and Anchor draws a devoted crowd. *247 Commercial St.,* ☎ *508/487–1430. Crowd: generally older, harder-edged, leather and Levi's; gender breakdown varies among the several bars.*

Larry's Bar. This tiny front bar at Sebastian's Restaurant, next door to the Boatslip, is famous for the ongoing, relentlessly bitchy, irreverent, obnoxious, and genuinely funny commentary and banter of Larry the bartender. Not the quietest spot in town, but always a trip. *At Sebastian's,*

177 Commercial St., ☎ 508/487–3286. Crowd: very mixed, big local following.

Pied Piper Lounge. This is the best women's disco of any gay resort town in the country. The dance floor is small but has a good sound system, and the intimacy makes it easy to get, well, intimate. Off the dance floor, however, is one of the loveliest decks in town, a great spot to savor the early evening during the Pied Piper's popular after-tea dance, or gaze at the moon later in the evening. *193A Commercial St., ☎ 508/487–1527. Crowd at after-tea dance: same as at Boatslip tea dance; crowd at other times: 80/20 f/m, very diverse.*

THE LITTLE BLACK BOOK

At Your Fingertips
Cape Cod Human Services AIDS/HIV Team: ☎ 508/483–4607. **Helping Our Women:** ☎ 508/487–4357. **Provincetown AIDS Support Group:** ☎ 508/487–9445. **Provincetown Business Guild (gay/lesbian business and tourism association):** 115 Bradford St., Box 421, 02657, ☎ 508/487–2313 or 800/637–8696. **Provincetown Chamber of Commerce:** MacMillan Wharf, 02657, ☎ 508/487–3424.

Gay Media
The Provincetown Business Guild, an alliance of businesses that cater to the gay community, puts out a useful directory detailing its members' services. The weekly, gay-friendly ***Provincetown Magazine*** (☎ 508/487–1000) has restaurant and nightlife listings and articles.

BOOKSTORES
Now, Voyager (357 Commercial St., ☎ 508/487–0848) is an excellent independent bookstore with a large selection of gay and lesbian books and periodicals.

Body and Fitness
The two principal workout spots are the **Provincetown Gym** (170 Commercial St., ☎ 508/487–2776), which moved to a better location in 1994 and gets a broad mix of lesbians and gay men, and **Mussel Beach** (56 Shank Painter Rd., ☎ 508/487–0001), which is a bit small, more male-oriented, and very cruisy.

21 *Out in Rehoboth Beach*

AFTER DRIVING THROUGH IT, you wouldn't expect Rehoboth Beach to be the lesbian and gay summer capital of the Mid-Atlantic states—the preferred resort for homos from Washington, D.C., Baltimore, Philadelphia, and, increasingly, New York City. Most East Coast gay enclaves grew up around small artists' colonies: Ogunquit, Provincetown, New Hope. Rehoboth's emergence was more of a historic accident.

The beach is fronted by a typically tacky boardwalk of saltwater taffy parlors, games booths and video arcades, and souvenir shops hawking everything from wood-grain toilet seats inscribed with inspirational epithets to porcelain toad candlesticks. We're bombarded constantly by signs that bemoan our collective inability to dress and behave appropriately: SHOES MUST BE WORN AT ALL TIMES, NO SHIRT, NO SERVICE, and PLEASE, NO SPITTING.

In June 1994, police arrested a man outside a gay bar for violating a recently passed noise ordinance. This was immediately taken as an affront to the gay community. Only one of the three candidates for two city council openings in 1994 courted the gay vote, and she ended up winning by the largest margin. The following year five candidates ran for the two other city council openings and this time they all courted the gay vote. There are plenty of shops and restaurants in town, especially along touristy Rehoboth Avenue, in which lesbian and gay couples are treated with anything from cool detachment to thinly veiled contempt.

There is considerable tension in Rehoboth between gay and straight people, between the pro- and antidevelopment camps, and, to a lesser extent, between the younger lesbians and gays who've been invading in greater numbers since the early '80s and the older lesbian and gay guard, who've been coming here since shortly after World War II.

Away from the hustle and bustle of the commercial areas is an attractive, middle-class slice of seaside suburbia—rows of ranch-style homes, most built between 1930 and 1960. It's a flat, salt-air village, as unhurried as it is unspectacular. Here, gays and straights seem far more integrated: Every fifth or sixth house shows evidence of gay occupancy, perhaps a rainbow flag hanging above the front door or a pink triangle decal on the rear window of a car in the driveway. For a gay resort town, the presence of gays seems limited. People often comment that Rehoboth looks only to be about 10% gay, which, according to the Kinsey Report, makes it a typical American town. The report may be a few percentage points high, or Rehoboth may just be a lot gayer than it looks—in any case, this is not your typical American town.

A couple of area bars began developing gay followings during the McCarthy years, probably owing to the fact that closeted Washington fags unable to risk braving the nightlife of D.C. found the summer beach region a relatively safe and anonymous place to test the waters. Lesbians and gays continued to settle here in dribs and drabs before Glenn Thompson decided to open a full-scale gay resort, the Renegade, in the western outskirts of town in 1980. Soon after, the Blue Moon restaurant and bar opened downtown. Both are still going strong, and just about every young dyke and queen within a three-hour drive makes it a point to party here at least once a summer. The formerly quiet, unobtrusive gay scene has blossomed quickly into something festive, at times political, and, perhaps most challenging of all, sexy—even if it is dwarfed by Rehoboth's straight contingent.

All this controversy and division has occurred in a town named, ironically enough, Rehoboth. This biblical name is borrowed from a passage in Genesis in which Isaac is forced from his home by a pesky brood of ignorant Philistines. He relocates, but is fought by quarrelsome herdsmen. He again relocates, but is again fought by quarrelsome herdsmen. Finally, he moves to a land where his presence comes under no fire—where he is at last made to feel welcome—and he names this land Rehoboth, saying ". . . for now the Lord has made room for us, and we shall be fruitful in the land." Unfortunately, it seems some pesky broods of ignorant philistines have found today's Rehoboth.

THE LAY OF THE LAND

The Beach

The beach is straight and family-oriented from the northern border of town down to about New Castle Street. Poodle Beach is officially from St. Lawrence Street down to Penn Street, but it can begin to get gay around New Castle Street. It's a fairly low-key scene that's popular with both genders. Going nude or topless is prohibited.

The boardwalk above the gay beach, a major cruise spot, is lit overhead by huge spotlights and police have been known to sweep through unexpectedly.

Downtown

Rehoboth Avenue, the main drag, runs perpendicular to the boardwalk and is not an especially gay-friendly strip—although there are a few gay-oriented shops. The main gay commercial strip is Baltimore Avenue, between 2nd Street and a couple hundred feet on the ocean side of 1st Street. Along here are dozens of terrific boutiques, antiques shops, and home-furnishing emporia. The two avenues north of and parallel to Baltimore, Maryland and Olive avenues also have a lot of gay shares and residents but are nevertheless mixed neighborhoods. The boardwalk and beach section that these avenues lead to are not gay. In fact, it's about a 15-minute walk from the corner of Baltimore and 1st to Poodle Beach. On the south side of Rehoboth, Wilmington Avenue has several gay-owned or -friendly restaurants and shops.

In town you can kill about an hour exploring either the **Anna Hazzard Museum** (17 Christian St., ☎ 302/227–7413), a small house museum with artifacts and memorabilia tracing Rehoboth's century of development, or the **Lewes Historical Society Complex** (3rd and Schipcarpenter, ☎ 302/645–8073), a group of historic buildings open for tours by appointment.

If you walk over to the dull, modern family resort, the **Boardwalk Plaza Hotel** (Olive Ave. at the Boardwalk), click your heels together and wish long enough, you may be able to channel visions of Rehoboth's first gay bar, the **Pink Pony,** which stood on this site through the 1950s. In the two decades prior to the 1980s, several bars opened and closed in this area before things began to boom.

Rehoboth Environs

Residentially, the area south of Rehoboth Avenue all the way down to Silver Lake is mixed straight and gay and is basically safe. The nicest homes are on the streets bordering or within a few blocks of Silver Lake. Several rather palatial homes have also gone up recently near Poodle Beach.

WHEN TO GO

The high season is from roughly late June through Labor Day. The shoulder season is usually from mid-April through mid-June and mid-September through mid-October—these are both wonderful, mild, and relatively uncrowded times to come, and everything is still open. From mid-October through mid-April, a number of businesses shut down, but just as many remain open. This period isn't much fun for singles on the make, but winter here can be very romantic for couples looking to escape from nearby cities.

GETTING THERE

The only practical way here is by car: Airports, train stations, and bus terminals are all too far away to justify their use. It's a straightforward three-hour drive from Washington, Baltimore, Philadelphia, or Norfolk, Virginia. From the northeast you can either take the Jersey Turnpike to Wilmington before heading south on U.S. 301. Or, for more scenery in the same amount of time, take the Garden State Parkway to Cape May, New Jersey. Then board the **Cape May–Lewes Ferry** (☎ 800/643–3779 or 609/886–9699; cars cost $18 one-way plus $4.50 for each additional passenger over 12) for Lewes, Delaware, which is 8 miles north of Rehoboth. There are no same-day reservations, and there's a $5 reservation fee. The ride takes 70 minutes. The first ferry heads south at 6:20 AM, the last at 7:40 PM.

GETTING AROUND

Everything is within walking distance. Only the Renegade resort and the shopping centers along Route 1 require a car. Taxis are unnecessary. Parking on residential streets is free and usually easy to find; at hotels and guest houses it's free and plentiful, and in commercial areas it's metered but somewhat hard to come by. Leave your car where you're staying.

EATS

Rehoboth has two distinct dining scenes. There are dozens of cheap, touristy seafood shanties, pizza parlors, taco joints, and other spots to grab a quick but often mediocre bite. Several of these places—mostly around Baltimore Avenue—are gay-owned or gay-oriented; a good many are not. There are also a bunch of sophisticated dining rooms with stellar cuisine, an extremely gay following, and very high prices. Unfortunately, only two or three places bridge the gap between these two extremes.

For price ranges, *see* Chart A at the front of this guide.

$$$$ **Back Porch Café.** Slightly out of place amid Rehoboth Avenue's jarring souvenir shops, the Back Porch has been a gay culinary institution for

Rehoboth Beach

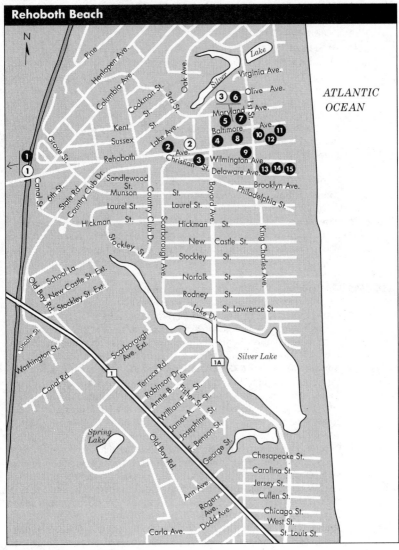

Eats ●

Adriatico Ristorante & Cafe, **10**
Back Porch Café, **12**
Bagel Bagel, **7**
Blue Moon, **6**
Chaf's Table, **1**
Dos Locos, **8**
Dream Café, **11**
Iguana Grill, **4**
La La Land, **14**
Mano's, **5**
Oscar's, **2**
Pierre's Pantry, **13**
Sidney's Side Street, **3**
Square One, **9**

Scenes ○

Blue Moon, **3**
Cloud 9, **2**
The Renegade, **1**

ages. The food is contemporary world-beat, with Asian, Caribbean, and Middle Eastern influences. The Sunday brunch is phenomenal. *59 Rehoboth Ave.,* ☎ *302/227–3674.*

$$$$ **La La Land.** This weathered, shingle house with a fanciful blue-and-purple color scheme and dappled chairs serves some of the best food in town. The inventive New American creations include smoked then pan-seared salmon with fennel-and-saffron mashed potatoes and roast loin of lamb with rosemary and a ratatouille tartlet topped with chèvre mousse. Very romantic. *22 Wilmington Ave.,* ☎ *302/227–3887.*

$$$$ **Square One.** California's architectural and culinary soul are captured in this chic, if slightly pretentious, Mediterranean-style stucco house, the interior of which is a sunny mix of high ceilings, hardwood floors, massive plate-glass windows, skylights, and contemporary art. The cutting-edge kitchen throws together a variety of veal, lamb, and seafood entrées accompanied by elaborate sauces and reductions. *37 Wilmington Ave.,* ☎ *302/227–1994.*

$$$–$$$$ **Blue Moon.** The classy Blue Moon is known equally as one of the area's best restaurants and as a lively gay bar. It has an airy, open dining room where you can feast eclectically on such dishes as Japanese griddle cakes filled with duck leg; shrimp and crawfish étouffée; and seafood burritos. A definite scene. *35 Baltimore Ave.,* ☎ *302/227–6515.*

$$$–$$$$ **Chef's Table.** Except for its unfortunate location in a drab shopping center a short drive from downtown, this prix-fixe dinner restaurant is charming. Its changing menu is stupendous: A four-course meal ($35) might consist of shellfish risotto with grilled asparagus, confit of duck with creamy polenta and wild mushrooms, and banana cheesecake dripping with mango coulis. *10 Henlopen Junction Mall, on Rehoboth Ave.,* ☎ *302/227–6339.*

$$–$$$ **Adriatico Ristorante & Cafe.** Your classic, no-frills Italian restaurant with traditional Southern Italy trappings. You can get pasta with any of eight traditional sauces, great mussels marinara, and the house specialty, steak *alla pizzaiola* (marinated in tomatoes and herbs). Huge portions. There's an awning-covered porch looking out over Baltimore Avenue. *N. 1st St. and Baltimore Ave.,* ☎ *302/227–9255.*

$$–$$$ **Oscar's.** There are two dining rooms in this seafood house. The one downstairs is a bit darker and much straighter; the one upstairs is brightened by a pitched roof and skylights, a small piano bar, and the presence of bubbly homosexuals—it can get very social up here. The sautéed softshell crabs are a specialty, but don't overlook any of the great seafood dishes. *247 Rehoboth Ave.,* ☎ *302/227–0789.*

$$–$$$ **Sydney's Side Street.** Sydney's oozes with character: Live jazz and blues bands perform nightly inside this peach-trimmed, brown-shingle cottage, and the high-ceilinged dining room is right out of the Garden District. The Creole and Cajun menu is designed for nibblers and sippers, offering both full and grazing portions as well as a wine list with several selections available by the glass. *25 Christian St.,* ☎ *302/227–1339.*

$$ **Iguana Grill.** This old beach cottage on the "gay strip" with a large and brightly painted wraparound porch and colorful laminated tables now has a Southwestern menu. The very popular brunch comes with $1 well drinks. Spotty service, decent food—nothing to write home about. *52 Baltimore Ave.,* ☎ *302/227–0948.*

$$ **Mano's.** Run by the people who operate Annie's Paramount Steak House, one of D.C.'s most popular gay restaurants, Mano's is informal, cheerful, and cavernous, with a vase of sunflowers brightening up each table. Good choices off the fairly priced menu are fried oysters, steak, and the crab imperial. It's hearty comfort food and it's issued in large portions that have been known to spoil many a girlish figure. *10 Wilmington Ave.,* ☎ *302/227–6707.*

$ Bagel Bagel. In a made-to-look-quaint mews-style minimall just two doors down from Lambda Rising. There's outdoor seating on green lawn furniture on a nicely landscaped brick patio. Very suburban looking. Hefty sandwiches, natural sodas, and other snacks. *33 Baltimore Ave.,* ☎ *302/227–7345.*

$ Dos Locos. The best of the few Mexican restaurants in town, Dos Locos clearly has the most exotic menu: Consider the Ole Mole—a chicken breast dunked in a spicy Oaxacan chili-and-fruit sauce—or the chicken topped with a smoky chipotle chili and peanut sauce. Has a great patio out back. *42½ Baltimore Ave.,* ☎ *302/227–5626.*

$ Dream Café. Gourmet coffees, rich Belgian waffles, and deli sandwiches (try the spicy Moroccan chicken) are served in this ugly post-modern building with a huge coffee cup sculpture perched above the front door—very L.A. looking and very gay. Closes at 3 PM daily. *26 Baltimore Ave.,* ☎ *302/226–2233.*

$ Pierre's Pantry. On your way to the beach, stop by this storefront eatery for any of the outstanding homemade soups (including red bell pepper with yellow squash and a spicy crab bisque) and sandwiches (including Cajun chicken breast with smoked Havarti and Italian sausage with marinara sauce). Their bagels are shipped regularly from New York City. *1st St. and Wilmington Ave.,* ☎ *302/227–7537.*

Coffeehouse Culture

Cuppa Jo'. Rehoboth's contribution to gay coffeehouse culture is right beside the Lambda Rising bookstore and open quite late (until midnight on weekdays, 12:30 AM on weekends). Tables outside are brightly colored; some have checkerboards painted on top. The shop, which has no indoor seating, has all the coffees, snacks, slushes, light sandwiches, and other goodies you'd expect. Equally popular with women and men. *39 Baltimore Ave.,* ☎ *302/226–9220.*

SLEEPS

Because Rehoboth lacks the grand architectural history of many other seaside resorts, its accommodations are disappointingly characterless and overpriced. Book well ahead, especially if you're trying for one of the relatively few gay-owned guest houses. You'll save 25% to 50% by visiting in spring or fall.

The entire waterfront is packed with interchangeable mid-rise motels that cater principally to families and straights, but if a sea view matters to you, you might consider one. The gay-oriented places are all a block or two from the water.

For price ranges, *see* Chart A at the front of this guide.

Hotels and Motels

⊞ The contemporary sand-color **Brighton Suites** has spacious rooms, each done in beachy pinks and teals. It's nothing fancy, but all rooms have a fridge, freezer, and wet bar—and though it caters mostly to families, it's very gay-friendly. *34 Wilmington Ave.,* ☎ *800/227–5788. 66 rooms. $$$–$$$$*

⊞ In the heart of the gay area, the three-story cement **Cape Suites** (think Berlin circa 1960) is impersonal, but rooms are mid-size, clean, and have private entrances and porches overlooking Baltimore Avenue. Mixed clientele. *47 Baltimore Ave.,* ☎ *302/226–3342 8 rooms. $$–$$$*

⊞ Run by the owners of Guest Rooms at Rehoboth, **Southside Suites** is just a block from the beach and gets a mostly gay clientele. Decor is tropical and contemporary, showing off dozens of original pieces by local artists. *44 Delaware Ave., ☎ 302/227–8355. 4 rooms, 2 apartments. $$–$$$*

The region's first and only fully gay resort is the **Renegade,** which is a 10-minute drive from the beach, near Route 1. Rooms are of the standard, nondescript motel variety. You stay here because you want to be where the action is—and the adjacent nightclub and disco are among the hottest on the eastern seaboard. *4274 Route 1, ☎ 302/227–1222. 20 rooms, 8 cabins. $–$$*

Guest Houses

The elder statesperson of area guest houses, the pale green **Beach House B&B** is the place to stay if proximity to the beach is your highest priority—it's but 10 houses from the boardwalk. The decor is simple and beach-tropical; rooms are bright, airy, and quite large. *15 Hickman St., ☎ 302/227–7074. 10 rooms. Mostly gay male/lesbian. $$–$$$*

Each of the five bedrooms at the charming **Guest Rooms at Rehoboth** has a different theme: Choose from Shaker, Victorian, Empire, art deco, or eclectic. The latter has a cozy sleigh bed that's perfect for snuggling away a rainy Sunday. This small cedar-shake house with peacock trim is in the heart of gay territory. *45 Baltimore Ave., ☎ 302/227–8355. 5 rooms. Mixed gay male/lesbian. $$–$$$*

The **Mallard House on Lake Street** is rather quiet and secluded—a traditional white-bread–looking '50s summer house that's been chopped up into clean, smartly furnished rooms. It's a 25-minute walk to the gay beach. *67 Lake Ave., ☎ 302/226–3448. 10 rooms. Mostly gay male. $$–$$$*

Silver Lake is the best of the bunch—new and clean, with friendly and professional innkeepers, and lovely views across Silver Lake and, from some rooms, of the ocean (Poodle Beach is a 10-minute walk). Rooms all have private baths and restful tropical themes, but this recently built brick home looks like any other suburban spread—it's a bit ordinary. *133 Silver Lake Dr., ☎ 302/226–2115 or 800/842–2115. 11 rooms. Mostly gay male. $$–$$$*

A homey, and at times very social, budget accommodation, the **Rehoboth Guest House** is in a white clapboard house with pale blue trim, a 15- to 20-minute walk from Poodle Beach but a block from the gay commercial strip. With somewhat dowdy furniture, simply furnished bedrooms, and a nice deck, the place has a summer rooming house feel. Most rooms share baths. *40 Maryland Ave., ☎ 302/227–4117. 12 rooms. Mixed gay male/lesbian. $–$$*

For those Gidgets who want a homey, beachy feel, there's **Sand In My Shoes.** This two-story former motel six blocks from the beach offers rooms with private baths and sundecks. Continental breakfast on weekdays, full breakfast on Saturdays, Belgian waffles on Sundays. Pets are welcome. *6th and Canal Sts., ☎ 302/226–2006. 12 rooms. Mostly lesbian. $–$$*

SCENES

The lounges at Oscar's and Square One restaurants compete with the Blue Moon and Cloud 9 for local action. None of the downtown spots are particularly wild; to cut loose, you have to get out to the Renegade. There are no women's bars, but dykes are abundant everywhere men are, though less so at the Blue Moon's bar. House parties are a significant social force here, though they tend to be cliquey and inaccessible to out-of-towners; if you're not bashful, hint around for an invitation at last call (12:45).

Blue Moon. One of the few gay-owned restaurants-cum-bars that could survive solely on the merit of either venue. The bar here is small but chatty and downright packed on weekends and during the daily late-afternoon tea dances. The tiny inside section is standing room only; the deck outside is semi-covered with tables and chairs. A zoo when it's crowded. *35 Baltimore Ave., 302/227–6515. Crowd: mostly male, mixed ages, very convivial and down-to-earth on weekdays.*

Cloud 9. The most recent addition to Rehoboth's gay nightlife scene, Cloud 9 is a bistro-style restaurant with a very popular stand-and-model bar, a small dance floor, and a sunny patio bar. *234 Rehoboth Ave.,* ☎ *302/226–1999. Crowd: similar to that at the Blue Moon.*

The Renegade. The classic gay resort, it's just off Route 1, a short way from town; if you don't drive (parking is plentiful but chaotic) you're in for a very long walk. Inside there's a main cruise bar with a pool table and some video games and beyond it a mid-size dance floor. The music, sound, and lighting are all stellar. One corner of the dance floor always seems to draw a lot of dykes; the rest of it packs in the shirtless pretty boys from D.C. The deck outside gets a much mellower—though still dense—crowd of lesbians and gay men. *4274 Route 1,* ☎ *302/227–4713. Crowd: 80/20 m/f, mostly under 35, varied, attitudy on the dance floor, friendlier out on the decks.*

THE LITTLE BLACK BOOK

At Your Fingertips
AIDS Hotline of Delaware: ☎ 800/422–0429. **Beebe Hospital:** ☎ 302/645–3300. **Camp Rehoboth** (lesbian/gay community service organization): 39 Baltimore Ave., Rehoboth Beach, 19971, ☎ 302/227–5620. **Delaware Lesbian & Gay Health Advocates:** ☎ 302/652–6776.

Gay Media
The nonprofit group **Camp Rehoboth** (*see above*), an outstanding community resource that has been instrumental in bridging the gap among opposing factions, publishes a helpful and informative newspaper, *Letters from Camp Rehoboth,* every two weeks from early March to late November. It's packed with articles, gossip, literary submissions, and a handy map of gay-friendly establishments in the area. Copies of the paper are free at many of the establishments it lists. The organization has also been a torchbearer here in AIDS fund-raising and lesbian and gay outreach.

BOOKSTORES
Stop by the small but extremely well-stocked outpost of the Washington and Baltimore lesbian/gay bookstore **Lambda Rising** (39 Baltimore Ave., ☎ 302/227–6969). The staff is friendly and knowledgeable. It's open daily 10 AM–midnight.

Body and Fitness
Body Shop Fitness Center (Virginia Ave. at the Boardwalk, ☎ 302/226–0920) is the local homo health club; it's open daily 8 to 7.

22 Out in St. Louis

FUR TRADERS FROM FRANCE founded this Mississippi River settlement in 1764, naming it for the canonized 13th-century king of France, Louis IX. When Thomas Jefferson orchestrated the Louisiana Purchase in 1803, explorers Meriwether Lewis and William Clark decided that St. Louis would make a logical base in their quest to find out what treasures lay west of the Mississippi. With that, an important gateway was born, and for the next century, just about every easterner with a yen to move west passed through this city. St. Louis boomed.

The railroad came through in 1857, helping to establish St. Louis as a major transportation and commercial center. The Mississippi, which joins the Missouri River a few miles north of town, had already turned the city into the country's premier inland port. In 1904 St. Louis hosted the United States's first Olympic Games and the magical World's Fair, which inspired the musical and Judy Garland film, *Meet Me in St. Louis.*

Had you suggested in 1904 that the St. Louis of the 1990s would rank lower than third or fourth on the list of America's most important metropolises, you'd have been met with considerable doubt. But since the turn of the century, St. Louis's population has dropped from about 890,000 to 390,000—it's no longer even the largest city on the Mississippi, trailing both Minneapolis/St. Paul and New Orleans.

Lewis and Clark saw the city as the gateway to the West, and people today still see it largely as a point of departure. It is significant that Charles Lindbergh's famous flight was aboard a plane dubbed the *Spirit of St. Louis.* St. Louis's fabled "spirit" seems very much to inspire its residents to chart new territories. The first spacecraft to orbit the earth was built here in St. Louis by McDonnell-Douglas—westward expansion indeed! Tennessee Williams grew up here but will always be identified with New Orleans—the same could be said about jazz music. T. S. Eliot hailed from St. Louis but made his name in Oxford. Tina Turner, Bobby McFerrin, Chuck Berry, Miles Davis, Josephine Baker, and Sheryl Crow left St. Louis and made it big musically elsewhere. St. Louis son Tom Dooley, who is believed to have been gay, earned distinction opening hospitals in Laos and Cambodia. Writers like Maya Angelou and Howard Nemerov are seldom associated with St. Louis, the city where they penned many of their best works. Native son Yogi Berra made it big playing baseball for the New York Yankees. And last year, composer Leonard Slatkin left the city to head Washington's National Symphony. The city instills in its children a pioneering spirit, and so while its sons and daughters bloom to profit otherwise, St. Louis trudges along largely unnoticed and unappreciated by the rest of the country.

St. Louis interests and entertains visitors without much fanfare. It's a big baseball city, a beer city, a working-class city. Families vacation here because St. Louis possesses the sort of attractions that would seem perfect for kids: dozens of museums and parks, a restored train station decked with shops and restaurants, and the magnificent St. Louis Arch, which reaches gracefully into the sky above the banks of the mighty Mississippi and its several gussied-up riverboats. Yet it's their *parents* who enjoy St. Louis.

Charmed by the city's embrace of the past, and by its nostalgic styles, tastes, and diversions, adults relate to St. Louis, which hasn't had the money or the interest over the past half century to mow down its old neighborhoods in favor of new high-rises. It's had little reason to fund fancy amusements and sightseeing venues. Most of the newer development has occurred west in St. Louis County, in places like Frontenac, Clayton, and West Port. St. Louis is just St. Louis—looking much as it has for three or four decades.

And now, as tourism has begun to improve again, as the city is beginning to pump some money into its appearance, preserving the past is *in*. And, just like Baltimore, another city whose renaissance occurred during the preservation-minded past decade, St. Louis is sprucing up some of its older neighborhoods and landmark buildings, rather than razing them and starting anew. Slowly but surely, the city is becoming a destination.

For all of their tradition and mainstream values, St. Louisians, those who remain inside the city limits anyway, are a fairly accommodating lot when it comes to gays and lesbians. The same can in no way be said for residents of St. Louis County, which grew as the majority of the city's well-to-do movers and shakers fled there following World War II. A huge controversy erupted recently in the suburbs when the county chapter of Parents and Friends of Lesbians and Gays (PFLAG) petitioned to adopt a span of highway, for the purposes of upkeep and litter removal. Hardly a radical cog in the gay political machine, PFLAG had to fight tooth-and-nail for their sponsorship in a state that has granted such aegis to the apparently more palatable Ku Klux Klan.

Those who have remained in the city, however, have weathered the horrible racial tensions of the 1960s. They've rolled with the punches and learned for the most part to leave well enough alone. And they've noticed that gays and lesbians have visibly transformed several neighborhoods, most notably the Central West End, from blighted victims of white flight into desirable blocks of restored homes.

Gay people are visible throughout the city. The community is large, spread out, and vibrant. St. Louis has an extensive antidiscrimination policy, and mayor Freeman Bosley has been decent to the gay community. Passage of civil rights laws protecting gays has been low-key and subtle, and there has been no movement to repeal these initiatives. The pride festival is said to be the fifth largest in the country, and a lesbian and gay picnic in Tower Grove Park on Memorial Day, 1994 drew 2,000 people.

St. Louis's lesbian and gay community is also a relatively mature one. Activism here has long been ardent and vocal, and it seems that many in the forefront of St. Louis's queer community have been so for many years. The "letters to the editor" pages of the three gay papers are usually jammed with lengthy, if soft-spoken, treatises regarding controversies within the community. The several area colleges infuse the city with younger voices, but most of them graduate and move elsewhere, in the St. Louis tradition. Remaining are the lifers, lesbians and gays who have been fighting for gay rights for so long they may not realize just how much they've accomplished, and how relatively well-adjusted St. Louis's gay community is.

THE LAY OF THE LAND

St. Louis's small downtown hugs the river, and distinctive neighborhoods surround it on all sides: Soulard and Benton Park are to the south, Lafayette Square and Tower Grove to the southwest; the Hill, Dogtown, and the Central West End to the west; and the Ville to the north. The character of downtown neighborhoods changes dramatically from street to street. Though the contrast can be fascinating, also bear in mind that it's easy to amble absent-mindedly into crime-ridden pockets of town.

Downtown/Riverfront/Laclede's Landing

An eclectic array of buildings representing the entire last century in architecture, the downtown proper is bounded roughly by the river to the east, Martin Luther King Drive to the north, 21st Street to the west, and I–64 to the south. Moored along the **Riverfront** are a few riverboats with restaurants and casinos. Above the river, however, is the **Jefferson National Expansion Memorial** (☎ 314/425–4465), a rolling green park that acts as a buffer between the city and the river, the centerpiece of which is the 630-foot **Gateway Arch.** The lines here can be a drag (try to go early in the morning), and the visitor center and museum are a bit hokey, but the tram ride to the top of this sleek tribute to westward expansion is memorable. On the west side of the park is St. Louis's oldest church, the **Old Cathedral** (the Basilica of St. Louis, the King, ☎ 314/231–3250), which dates from the 1840s. Two blocks west of here is the green-domed **Old Courthouse** (11 N. 4th St., ☎ 314/425–4468), site of the infamous case in which Dred Scott unsuccessfully sued for his freedom from slavery.

French furrier Pierre Laclède first debarked in St. Louis at a point just north of the Jefferson Memorial Park. **Laclede's Landing** later evolved into the city's warehouse district and is today a touristy nine-square-block network of gas lamps, cobblestone streets, bars, restaurants, shops, and a goofy wax museum. Though few gay couples roam these streets today, Pierre Laclède is said to have spent much of his time here in bed with his young footman.

About 20 blocks west of the riverfront, on Market Street, is the restored, century-old **St. Louis Union Station** (☎ 314/421–6655), formerly the world's largest and busiest rail terminal and now a collection of shops, restaurants, and the Hyatt Regency Hotel. Just north of the station is the **Drury Inn,** which was once the YMCA. During World War II, troops moving east to west were housed here midway through their journey— many a gay trick is said to have been turned during these stopovers. During the 1950s a gay bar, Martin's, was run out of the basement.

Just west of downtown is **Grand Center** (Grand Ave. and Lindell Blvd.), the city's theater and performing arts district. And bordering this area to the west is **St. Louis University;** a beguiling promenade spans much of the campus, starting where Vandeventer Avenue is met by West Pine Boulevard—this spot is close to several gay bars, so you never know what pretty thing might stroll by. Near here, at 4633 Westminster, is the otherwise ordinary brick apartment building in which Thomas "Tennessee" Williams grew up—the setting of *The Glass Menagerie.*

Central West End/U. City Loop

Following the World's Fair of 1904, which was held in Forest Park, the adjacent **Central West End** evolved into St. Louis's most fashionable neighborhoods. There are still enormous mansions along Hortense Place and Portman Place. In the middle of this century, however, as most of St. Louis's wealthier residents headed to the suburbs, the CWE fell into abandonment and disrepair. Hippies and counterculturists—many of them students and faculty at nearby Washington and St. Louis universities—moved in to many of these grossly undervalued, neglected homes. The CWE became something of a gay ghetto, and during the next couple of decades, the gay community thrived here. The Magic Wok, at the corner of Maryland and Euclid, was then Herbie's, one of the country's best gay discos. The CWE remains the city's urban anchor, but many of the gay men who brought it to prosperity died of AIDS during the '80s, and others hoping to settle here began finding the property values prohibitive. The shops and restaurants along Euclid Avenue have become increasingly costly, appealing to a broader, though still somewhat bohemian, mix of cosmopolitans.

Gracious **Washington University** is north of here, the hub of its campus at the northern border of 1,300-acre **Forest Park.** This sprawling rectangle has a skating rink, a golf course, a 7-mile jogging and cycling path and some of the Midwest's best museums, including the **St. Louis Art Museum** (1 Fine Arts Dr., ☎ 314/771–0072), the **St. Louis Science Center** (5050 Oakland Ave., ☎ 314/289–4444 or 800/456–7572), and the **History Museum** (Lindell Blvd. and Debaliviere Ave., ☎ 314/746–4599). Washington University also has an excellent collection of American and European painting at its **Gallery of Art** (1 Brookings Dr., Steinberg Hall, ☎ 314/935–5490).

A landmark study on cruising for sex, released as the book *Tearoom Trade,* was based allegedly on observations made at tearooms and cruising areas around Forest Park and in many of the buildings at Washington University, most notably the now-closed bathroom in the basement of Duncker Hall. It has been noted that Forest Park's cruising activity involved mostly married men and other closeted figures afraid of venturing into gay bars, whereas the transactions in the city's other major venue, Tower Grove Park, involved mostly hustling hoosiers (the local slang for white trash, not to be confused with natives of Indiana!).

East of Washington University, where Skinker runs into Delmar Boulevard, is the **U. City Loop,** a smaller, more alternative, and generally younger version of the restaurant-and-shopping row along the CWE's Euclid Avenue. So named because it's where the streetcar used to loop around before heading back downtown, the Loop's most famous establishment is **Blueberry Hill** (6504 Delmar Blvd., ☎ 314/727–0880), a lively nightclub tribute to American pop culture.

Soulard/Benton Park/Lafayette Square
Nowhere are St. Louis's richly hued red, orange, and brown bricks more evident than in **Soulard,** a residential row house neighborhood just south of downtown. The clay for these bricks came from nearby Alton, Illinois; the supply now depleted, many of St. Louis's buildings have been dismantled in recent years, their valuable bricks commanding high prices from builders in Chicago and Dallas.

Soulard, which is significantly gay-populated, is a walker's neighborhood. Just park your car and wander among the homes, Irish pubs, and bars—a couple of which are gay. At 7th Street and Lafayette is the **Soulard Market** (☎ 314/622–4180), a public food market for more than 200 years. Farther south is the **Anheuser-Busch Brewery** (12th and Lynch Sts., ☎ 314/577–2626; tours available), the only one of about 100 area breweries still remaining, and beyond that is the **DeMenil Mansion and Mu-**

seum (3352 DeMenil Pl., ☎ 314/771–5828), a Greek Revival mansion with period furnishings.

Just south and west of Soulard is **Benton Park,** home to the **Cherokee Street Antiques Row;** most of the shops are between Lemp and Jefferson streets. As families moved to St. Louis for short periods before continuing west, thousands of antiques were hawked and left behind, making St. Louis one of the antiques trade's better-kept secrets.

Northwest of Soulard, across I-55 and I-44, **Lafayette Square** is an increasingly gay neighborhood that has been improving slowly but surely since the 1970s. This was St. Louis's most desirable neighborhood until a tornado destroyed many of its most beautiful homes in 1896. Then the World's Fair was staged in Forest Park in 1904, drawing most of the city's wealth and prestige into the Central West End. Since that time, Lafayette Square has languished. The neighborhood's focal point, **Lafayette Park,** is the oldest park west of the Mississippi (the wrought-iron fence surrounding it is original). The roads fringing the square are lined with historic buildings, some of them restored painted ladies but just as many awaiting face-lifts. Park Avenue, between Mississippi and 18th streets, has a few good restaurants.

Just west of Benton Park, **Grand South Grand** is a short stretch of Grand Avenue between Utah and Arsenal streets, which has become increasingly known for its many ethnic restaurants and funky shops—several of them gay-owned. In the past several years, the residential neighborhood just west of here, **Tower Grove** (a.k.a. Dyke Heights), has become increasingly popular with lesbians. In the adjacent Tower Grove Park is the stellar **Missouri Botanical Garden** (4344 Shaw Ave., ☎ 314/577–5100), a 79-acre spread created by the allegedly gay Victorian horticulturist, Henry Shaw.

GETTING AROUND

You can cover St. Louis's downtown on foot, but the city's strengths are its colorful neighborhoods, which are most conveniently explored by car. Meter parking is easy to find outside downtown, and the streets are navigable with relative ease; you will need to garage your vehicle downtown (the fees are reasonable). St. Louis's recently introduced light-rail system, the **MetroLink** (☎ 314/231–2345), is good if you're hopping between some of the tourist sights like Laclede's Landing and Union Station, but it's not a viable means for seeing the whole city. Taxis are neither plentiful nor practical.

EATS

Thanks to its large number of German, Italian, and Irish immigrants, St. Louis is strong on food from those three cultures. Some places around town have spruced up their traditional meat-and-potatoes menus with contemporary touches. A neighborhood pub might serve the usual burgers but with toppings like sun-dried tomatoes or avocados; another locale might offer grilled fish with an interesting chutney or sauce. St. Louisians are a bit wary of radical foodies, however; overall, expect the emphasis to be on dependably good, well-prepared comfort food.

You'll find lots of sidewalk cafés and pubs along Euclid Avenue in the CWE and along Delmar Boulevard in the U. City loop. There aren't that many good restaurants downtown, though the converted Union Station has a few notable ones. Grand South Grand recently spawned a slew of Chinese, Thai, Indian, and other Asian eateries. Most of the gay bars serve food, with the Continental and American menu at **Clementine's** (*see below*) generally regarded as the best. St. Louis's most famous food neighborhood, however, is the Hill, a vibrant Little Italy of authentic pasta joints and food markets west of downtown. With its rows of 1950 clapboard and faux-brick homes, the Hill is not all that charming architecturally, but in the little quadrant defined by Shaw, Macklind, Bischoff, and Hereford avenues, every restaurant yields outstanding food. **Dominic's** (5101 Wilson Ave., ☎ 314/771–1632; $$$$) and **Giovanni's** (5201 Shaw Ave., ☎ 314/772–5958; $$$–$$$$) are considered the best and most formal; a bit more affordable are **Bruno's** (5901 Southwest Ave., ☎ 314/781–5988; $$), **Cunetto's** (5453 Magnolia Ave., ☎ 314/781–1135; $), and **Zia's** (5256 Wilson Ave., ☎ 314/776–0020; $–$$).

For price ranges, *see* Chart B at the front of this guide.

Central West End and Environs

$$–$$$ **Cafe Balaban's.** This may be the most popular of upper Euclid Avenue's infectiously spirited taverns. The best seating is on the glassed-in porch, but there's also a cozy pub inside with a variety of ales and wines. The extremely good American food here reflects plenty of foreign and contemporary influences. Beef Wellington in a golden raisin sauce is among the tasty dishes offered here. *405 N. Euclid Ave., ☎ 314/361–8085.*

$$–$$$ **Duff's.** Almost indistinguishable from nearby Cafe Balaban's, Duff's is another of CWE's sidewalk cafés, always abuzz with chatter and laughter. This is one of the few places with tables directly on the sidewalk as opposed to overlooking it through a glassed-in porch. Except for a smart new addition decked out with contemporary art, all of the interior rooms are pubby and traditional. A great Continental menu—try the bouillabaisse or chicken marsala. *392 N. Euclid Ave., ☎ 314/361–0522.*

$$–$$$ **Niner Diner.** Sandwiched between the gay bookstore and Magnolia's bar, the Niner Diner is a tiny place, and although the atmosphere is somewhat dinerish, the food is a cut above: gussied-up American dishes such as chicken magnolia (with artichoke hearts, tomatoes, black olives, and onions) as well as lots of inventive pastas and grills. *9 S. Vandeventer Ave., ☎ 314/652–6500.*

$$–$$$ **Redel's.** In a dull spot near Forest Park—away from the sidewalk bustle of Euclid Avenue and the U. City Loop but still in the northern reaches of the Central West End—Redel's is noted for its thin-crust pizzas, eclectic menu, and snazzy art deco dining room. Has an extremely gay following. *310 Debaliviere Ave., ☎ 314/367–7005.*

$–$$ **Blanche's.** This quiet neighborhood restaurant near St. Louis University and Magnolia's has a big lesbian and gay following, a popular tree-shaded patio, and a fairly standard menu of comfort foods. *33 N. Sarah St., ☎ 314/652–9960.*

$–$$ **Brandt's.** A fancy-food market and sidewalk café on the U. City Loop's main drag, where college students, self-styled intellectuals, and artistes of every background mingle. The food is wide-ranging, including pizzas, trendy sandwiches, and pastas, plus a vast selection of wines, beers, vodkas, and coffees. *6525 Delmar Blvd., ☎ 314/727–3663.*

$–$$ **Dressel's.** One of several yuppified hangouts on upper Euclid, Dressel's is notable for the warm downstairs tavern, where the walls are jammed with celeb photos, and for the authentic Welsh-style pub upstairs, where live jazz is performed on Wednesdays and a hearty pint of Felio-Edel ale always awaits you. Has burgers, some diverse veggie dishes, and St. Louis's best "chips." *419 N. Euclid Ave., ☎ 314/361–1060.*

$–$$ **Upper Crust Cafe.** Arguably the best breakfasts in the area are served at this tiny art-filled hole-in-the-wall near the corner of Euclid Avenue. In-

Eats ●
Blanche's, **11**
Brandt's, **2**
Cafe Balaban's, **5**
Cicero's, **1**
Dressel's, **4**
Duff's, **7**
Flaco's Tacos, **13**
Left Bank Coffee, **6**
Majestic, **9**
Niner Diner, **12**
Redel's, **3**
Sunshine Inn, **10**
Upper Crust Cafe, **8**

Scenes ○
Attitude's, **2**
Loading Zone, **1**
Magnolia's, **3**

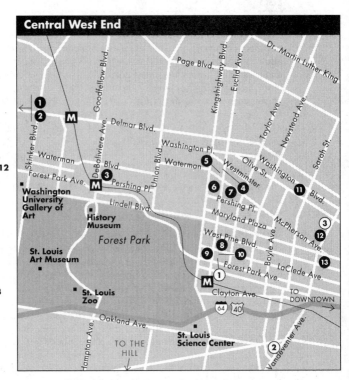

Central West End

Eats ●
Addisson's on the Square, **6**
Arcelia's, **4**
MoKaBe's, **1**
9th Street Abbey, **7**
Ricardo's, **5**
Sidney Street Cafe, **3**
South City Diner, **2**

Scenes ○
Clementine's, **4**
The Complex, **1**
Drake Bar, **2**
Fall Out, **3**

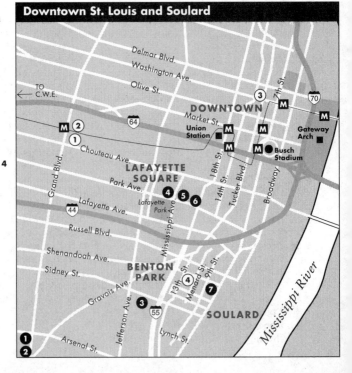

Downtown St. Louis and Soulard

timate, local, and often very gay, the Upper Crust has tasty Greek salads, stir-fries, and fluffy fruit pancakes. *4578 Laclede Ave.,* ☎ *314/367–3635.*

$ **Cicero's.** Right beside the inevitably packed Blueberry Hill bar and music club, Cicero's is another U. City Loop mainstay—loud, casual, and festive. Live music (often), standard pub food, good burgers, extraordinary desserts. *6510 Delmar Blvd.,* ☎ *314/862–0009.*

$ **Flaco's Tacos.** Slightly more formal than a fast-food restaurant, this bright red, green, and yellow taco house near St. Louis University has speedy service, healthful food, and a steady traffic of cute collegiate types. Specialties are fish tacos and burritos. *3852 Lindell Blvd.,* ☎ *314/534–8226.*

$ **Majestic.** Where all the boys take their dates the morning after—to parade them before the legions of hung-over revelers. The Majestic is a true gay diner, and the Greek fare here is above average—wonderful feta omelets, Greek salads, gyros, and flaky baklava. Has a bright patio overlooking Laclede and Euclid. *4900 Laclede Ave.,* ☎ *314/361–2011.*

$ **Sunshine Inn.** Another major brunch scene, this one is definitely less cruisy, less showy, and less gay-male than the Majestic's around the corner. The several smart, bright dining rooms have large plate-glass windows, and the veggie menu offers many juices, apple pancakes, guacamole omelets, and homemade soups. Smoke-free. *8½ S. Euclid Ave.,* ☎ *314/367–1413.*

Soulard and Environs

$$–$$$ **Sidney Street Cafe.** This lovely redbrick tavern in Benton Park, candlelit and with green plants hanging everywhere, attracts everybody from the antiquing tourists from Cherokee Street to workers from the nearby Anheuser-Busch Brewery. The ever-changing chalkboard menu ranges from fat, juicy burgers to crab cakes to chicken over spinach with prosciutto, artichoke hearts, and goat cheese. *2000 Sidney St.,* ☎ *314/771–5777.*

$$ **Adisson's on the Square.** This is first and foremost a wine bar, which is not to say the salads, gourmet sandwiches, and fresh cheese platters aren't great. More notable, however, are the more than 60 wines available by the glass and the restaurant's frequent tastings. The dining room is warmly lighted, with plenty of exposed brick. *1917 Park Ave.,* ☎ *314/621–8877.*

$–$$ **9th Street Abbey.** Eating in this dramatic 1850 abbey that's been converted into a restaurant may make you feel as if you're eating at a church potluck supper. The food is good—capellini in fresh tomato sauce, curried chicken salad, BLT sandwiches—though somewhat less memorable than the setting. Very gay following. *1808 S. 9th St.,* ☎ *314/621–9598.*

$–$$ **Ricardo's.** About 30 varieties of pasta are available at this smart Italian café just off Lafayette Park. Through the storefront windows is a classy but informal dining room. One of the more romantic settings in town. *1931 Park Ave.,* ☎ *314/421–4833.*

$–$$ **South City Diner.** Amid Grand South Grand's numerous Asian eateries is this traditional 24-hour greasy spoon. Trendily untrendy, the look is somewhat outdone by the menu, which includes, along with the usual breakfast-any-time and blue-plate specials, several upscale dishes, too. There are always a few fresh fish entrées, plus good homemade soups. *3141 S. Grand Blvd.,* ☎ *314/772–6100.*

$ **Arcelia's.** Once a Soulard standby, Arcelia's has moved to Lafayette Square and gotten a face-lift. The atmosphere is casual; the menu, unusual Mexican. Surrounded by cedar, stucco, exposed brick and, of course, the occasional sombrero, you can feast on *nopales* (stir-fried cactus) or the great chicken fajitas. There are two dining rooms (one is for smokers), and each has a bar. *2001 Park Ave.,* ☎ *314/231–9200.*

Coffeehouse Culture

Left Bank Coffee (395 N. Euclid Ave., ☎ 314/367–6703) is a bookstore café (*see* The Little Black Book, *below*) with light-hued wood furnishings, soft lighting, and large windows opening onto the street. It fosters a cosmopolitan but relaxed mood, and there's always plenty to read. **MoKaBe's** (3606 Arsenal St., ☎ 314/865–2009) feels half like a typical diner and half like a neighborhood bar—if only more coffeehouses had pool tables! Another plus is the live entertainment offered many weekends. Patrons have a choice of sitting at the long bar, or at several tables and booths. Just off Tower Grove Park.

SLEEPS

St. Louis was once a grand hotel city, but as the population and popularity of the city have waned, many of its finest properties—the Planters House, Chase, and Park Plaza hotels among them—have been razed or converted into luxury apartments. A few classics remain, but just as much of the region's hotel business has moved out to the rather dull suburb of Clayton.

In the city itself, most hotels are downtown, with only a few up near Forest Park and the Central West End. It's hard to find a place that's within walking distance of gay nightlife and restaurants. The accommodations around Union Station are ideally located because they're about equidistant from downtown attractions, Soulard, Lafayette Square, and the CWE.

For price ranges, *see* Chart B at the front of this guide.

Hotels

⌑ With many rooms looking out at the Arch and the Mississippi River, the 18-story **Adam's Mark** is the riverfront area's most popular hotel. It's contemporary and quite luxurious, though not especially memorable. *4th and Chestnut Sts., ☎ 314/241–7400 or 800/444–2326. 910 rooms. $$$–$$$$*

⌑ One of the more unusual properties is the **Hyatt Regency St. Louis,** which has been fashioned out of the city's former Union Station rail terminal. The lobby was the station's original grand concourse, and the gold-leaf plasterwork, stained glass, frescoes, and barrel-vaulted ceilings are still intact. *1 St. Louis Union Station, ☎ 314/231–1234 or 800/233–1234. 538 rooms. $$$–$$$$*

⌑ One of the most interesting of St. Louis's historic properties is the **Doubletree Suite Hotel,** formerly the Mayfair. Built in 1925, the downtown Mayfair hosted Harry Truman, Cary Grant, and many others during its heyday. The guest rooms are quite large, and the original, hand-operated elevator is still in use. *806 St. Charles St., ☎ 314/421–2500 or 800/222–8733 184 rooms. $$–$$$*

⌑ Around the corner from the Hyatt Regency is another historic hostelry, the **Drury Inn Union Station,** the city's former YMCA. *201 S. 20th St., ☎ 314/231–3900 or 800/325–8300. 176 rooms. $$*

⌑ Near the Adam's Mark in the riverfront area, but far more affordable, is the **Holiday Inn-Downtown Riverfront,** which gets mostly families and tourists but has hosted gay events in the past. *200 N. 4th St., ☎ 314/621–8200 or 800/925–1395. 456 rooms. $–$$*

⌑ Extremely close to CWE bars and restaurants is the clean but nondescript **Best Western Inn at the Park,** a good budget choice. *4630 Lindell Blvd., ☎ 314/367–7500 or 800/373–7501. 128 rooms. $*

Guest Houses

☐ New owners took over and ambitiously renovated **Napoleon's Retreat B&B** in 1994. This pale gray Victorian with shades of lavender, light blue, and charcoal and a mansard roof is just around the corner from Lafayette Park, about a mile from downtown. The rooms are huge, done with a smattering of antiques and period reproductions, and bright modern baths. Owners Jeff and Michael are friendly, helpful, and can tell you a great deal about the area. *1815 Lafayette Ave.,* ☎ *314/772–6979. 4 rooms. Mixed gay/straight. $–$$*

☐ In the Soulard/Benton Park area is the **Brewers House,** a restored mid-19th-century row house with a secluded garden hot tub, fireplaces in some rooms, and proximity to Soulard's bars and the antiques shops on Cherokee Street. *1829 Lami St.,* ☎ *314/771–1542. 2 rooms. Mostly gay/lesbian. $*

SCENES

St. Louis is not exactly abuzz with gay nightlife. Certainly nobody comes here expressly to party; there are, however, a few good clubs and bars, most of them easygoing and open to new faces. They tend to be either close to the Central West End (younger crowd) or Soulard (older crowd), but St. Louis doesn't have a specifically gay entertainment district. There are also several bars downtown, but they tend toward the seedy side.

Owing to St. Louis's location, you get a fairly good mix here of southern belles and corn-fed midwesterners—as though Chicago and New Orleans had merged. The decor and atmosphere of most bars reflects the city's straightforward, working-class mentality—lots of plain red-brick buildings, dark rooms with neon bar signs and sports pennants. The average St. Louis gay bar is largely indistinguishable from most of the mainstream Irish pubs and German beer halls around town. The crowd just happens to be gay.

There isn't much blending of gay men and lesbians in most bars—the Drake Bar is the most mixed. The average age of bar goers, even at the more popular discos, seems several years above the national average—most patrons are in their mid-30s. Consequently, you will do best to act like yourself and avoid trying to impress anybody. Where trendy club gear, gym-perfected bodies, and attitude might earn you points in Los Angeles, such affectations draw blank stares in St. Louis. It's extremely easy for a newcomer here to walk into a bar and strike up a conversation.

Club St. Louis (2625 Samuel Shepphard Dr., ☎ 314/533–3666) is the city's bathhouse and sauna, open 24 hours, with steamroom, tanning bed, sauna, gym, lockers, TV lounge, and all the usual fixtures.

Attitude's. The city's most popular dyke bar is in an old brick building in a somewhat seedy area—near where Manchester becomes Chouteau, at the intersection with Sarah Street. You won't see many professionals here; in fact, the crowd's a little rowdy. Darts, pool, a large central bar, and a small dance floor, which has country-western dancing some nights. *4100 Manchester Ave.,* ☎ *314/534–3858. Crowd: mostly female, loud, down-to-earth, mixed ages.*

Clementine's. A fixture of historic Soulard, Clementine's is the oldest gay bar in St. Louis, set in a charming redbrick town house with stained glass windows and original architectural details. The Oh My Darlin' Cafe is extremely popular and the best of the restaurants at gay bars, and although the crowd at the bar is almost exclusively male, the restaurant gets plenty of lesbians, too. There's a cute patio off the building. Used to be more of a leather bar, but has become more mainstream in recent years. This is a great place to go if you're new in town or here on business. Friendly staff. *2001 Menard St., ☏ 314/664–7869. Crowd: mostly male, some leather but more Levi's, mostly ages 40s and 50s, laid-back, friendly.*

The Complex. On weekend nights, guys go back and forth between here and Magnolia's, a five-minute drive away. The Complex is made up of several spaces, including a room with drag shows and musical performances, a dance floor, a renowned leather bar called "Mom's," a leather-and-lace boutique, and a patio. It's a bit less stuffy and stand-and-model than Magnolia's, but there are still plenty of cute guys. The festivities occur in a sprawling brick compound in the warehouse district west of downtown. *3511 Chouteau Ave., ☏ 314/772–2645. Crowd: mostly men but otherwise diverse—college students, leather men, drag queens, professionals, blue collars, good racial mix.*

Drake Bar. The Drake Bar is in an ancient redbrick house on a side street behind the Complex, sort of an unlikely location for a chatter bar. On one floor cappuccino is served, on another there's piano entertainment. It's all very civilized, and there's plenty of room to sit and talk. Not too cruisy—a good place to bring a date. *3502 Papin St., ☏ 314/865–1400. Crowd: good mix of men and women, mixed ages.*

Fall Out. The only true warehouse-style disco, Fall Out is downtown on the ground floor of an otherwise derelict turn-of-the-century office building. It's not especially large, and the dance floor can get crowded late on Saturdays, but it's jumping with energetic revelers. It's cruisier here than at similar clubs in many cities—some people come primarily to dance, others to date. Good mix of industrial, techno, and house music. Cover most nights. Thursday is students' night. *1324 Washington Ave., ☏ 314/421–0003. Crowd: mostly male on Saturday—more diverse Thursdays and Fridays; good racial mix; young, trendy, alternative.*

Loading Zone. This is a textbook video bar, with three floors of patrons staring each other down and making hollow conversation. It's as stand-and-model here as anywhere in St. Louis, but still largely free of snootiness. The decor is jet black and nondescript, but there are lots of video screens in every corner. Great happy hour bar. *16 S. Euclid Ave., ☏ 314/361–4119. Crowd: 75/25 m/f, young, cruisy, collegiate.*

Magnolia's. The crowded mishmash of rooms is similar to those at the Complex, though they're not as distinctly themed here. There's really no leather contingent to speak of here either, as most of those guys head to the Outpost down the block. Magnolia's is basically *the* main nightspot on weekends, and it even gets fairly crowded during the week. The decor and surroundings are a bit ordinary, and it can get a little cliquey. Within view of St. Louis University. *5 S. Vandeventer Ave., ☏ 314/652–6500. Crowd: 90/10 m/f, similar to crowd at Complex but somewhat more professional, neater, buttoned-down.*

If you're spending a lot of time in St. Louis, you might also want to check out one or more of the following downtown bars: **Ernie's Class Act** (3756 S. Broadway, ☏ 314/664–6221) is actually not all that classy, but it's a fairly popular, and rowdy, dyke bar; no men. The **Front Page** (2330 Menard St., ☏ 314/664–2939), in a 19th-century brick building in the heart of Soulard, is St. Louis's drag bar; has some good female impersonator acts—both on and off stage. **Gabriel's** (6901 S. Broadway, ☏ 314/832–0656), South St. Louis's main neighborhood pub, has its own dart shop and feels a bit like an Irish pub. The city's answer to *Cheers,* that quiet neighborhood bar where everybody knows your name (or at least asks) is the **Grey Fox Pub** (3503 S. Spring St., ☏ 314/772–2150). **Merlie's** (2917 S. Jefferson St., ☏ 314/664–1066), St. Louis's contribution to the country-western world, is unfortunately not all that exciting, but it does have a strong local following. Leather hands congregate at the otherwise characterless **Outpost** (17 S. Vandeventer Ave., ☎ 314/535–4100), a few doors down from Magnolia's.

THE LITTLE BLACK BOOK

At Your Fingertips

AIDS Hotline: ☎ 314/367–8400 or 800/337–2437. **Lesbian and Gay Community Center:** ☎ 314/725–3122 or 314/997–9897. **Lesbian and Gay Hotline:** ☎ 314/367–0084. **St. Louis Convention and Visitors Bureau:** 10 S. Broadway, Suite 1000, 63102, ☎ 314/421–1023 or 800/916–0040. **St. Louis Effort for AIDS:** ☎ 314/645–6451; information hot line, ☎ 314/647–1144.

Gay Media

TWISL (This Week in Greater St. Louis) (☎ 618/465–9370) is the gay bi-weekly covering news and entertainment. The monthly **LesTalk** (☎ 314/773–3220) is one of the most comprehensive lesbian newspapers in the country. Covering the entire state, but focusing chiefly on St. Louis and Kansas City, is the biweekly **News-Telegraph** (☎ 314/664–6411). The best mainstream resource is the **Riverfront Times** (☎ 314/231–6666), the alternative-scene arts-and-entertainment weekly.

BOOKSTORES

St. Louis has a terrific lesbian and gay bookstore, **Our World Too** (11 S. Vandeventer Ave., ☎ 314/533–5322), which is snug between a pair of gay bars, Magnolia's and the Outpost. The store has an extensive section of secondhand titles, plenty of out-of-state gay papers and magazines, and most of the common porn mags. **Left Bank Books** (399 N. Euclid Ave., ☎ 314/367–6731) is a terrific independent mainstream bookstore with a significant gay following and a great coffeehouse. Also on Euclid, **Pages Video & More** (10 N. Euclid Ave., ☎ 314/361–3420) has a mid-size selection of gay and lesbian titles, plus magazines and video rentals.

Body and Fitness

A gay-friendly gym is the **Maryland Fitness Center** (48 Maryland Plaza, ☎ 314/361–3603).

23 *Out in San Diego*

WESTERN U.S. CITIES ALWAYS SEEM to be stuck in a rut of being compared to one another: Phoenix to Las Vegas and L.A., L.A. to San Francisco, San Francisco to Seattle, Seattle to Vancouver and Portland. But you almost never hear anyone mention San Diego in the same breath with other cities (except, rarely, with L.A.). Perhaps a tad provincial, it stands almost entirely on its own. It's the second largest city in California and one of the largest in the country, and it motors along at a comfortable pace, pleasing all who visit, but never really knocking anybody's socks off. What gives?

For one thing, San Diego's very even keel keeps it out of the public eye; it has a steady, predictable personality, as seen in the resolute cheerfulness of its verdant neighborhoods and the consistently calm and sunny disposition of its weather. Of California's three children, San Diego is the proper middle child. L.A. is the oldest child—an arrogant, image-conscious, bossy dictator of America's styles and trends. San Francisco is the baby—always whining about injustice, always tattling on the politically incorrect, and often basking in its mandate to monitor America's conscience. Quiet, conservative, mild-mannered, and with a willingness to take orders, San Diego just marches along—speaking to America only when spoken to.

San Diego had hoped, during the latter half of the 19th century, to emerge as a much bigger player in America's expansion and commerce. After it won the bid to become the terminus of the Santa Fe railway, it blossomed in anticipation of its new status as Southern California's most important rail center. Alas, the railroad failed—the mountains east of the city proved to be inhospitable to the newly laid tracks, and year after year storms washed them away. The experiment soon died, and there is still no direct rail service to San Diego from the east.

In the early part of the 20th century, San Diego's safe harbor ensured it a different destiny: that of America's most significant naval—and eventually naval air force—base. For this entire century, naval operations have dominated the city's economic, political, and social landscape.

The effect of the navy's prominence on San Diego's gay community has been significant but also double-edged. Historically, wherever you have strong military operations, you have a strong gay presence—a phenomenon that has been well documented throughout this century. On the West Coast, rapid economic growth from mobilization for World War II occurred most dramatically in San Francisco, Long Beach, and San Diego. If you had to theorize, you might guess that putting tens of thousands of men together, without women, in close quarters, under tremendous pressure, for anywhere from several months to several years, would inspire—or at least allow—a number of men with same-sex leanings to test the waters. To a lesser extent, because there were fewer of them, the same theory can be applied to the many women who served here. After testing the waters, many of these men and women no doubt returned to their hometowns and went on to live straight lives. Others may have returned to live gay lives, but a significant chunk stuck around these cities where first they discovered their real sexual identities and preferences. And so, at the end of World War II, San Diego was teeming with gay men and a smaller number of lesbians—and their presence has never subsided.

On the other hand, because the military has always and continues to disallow and disapprove of same-sex relations, the impetus among enlistees to remain closeted is tremendous. And the impetus to quash liberal activism—whether in the form of gay rights or anti-war rallies—has also been strong among by-the-book military personnel, politicians, and industry leaders catering to military interests. San Diego's strong college presence and its significant population of "out" gays, hippie surfers, and California-style liberals have helped avoid a complete capitulation to right-wing homophobic policy making; but the city's conservative demeanor mitigates the sort of flamboyant gay presence you often see in other large cities. The military has made San Diego very gay, but it's made San Diego gays and lesbians something far short of militant.

As in any big city, there are exceptions to general rules. Though still a bastion of Republican politics, San Diego does have a gay councilwoman, and the police are well regarded for their handling of gay bashings and for their dealings in the community. And though not often associated with violent crime, the city has suffered through its share of gay hate crimes. But in general, life here moves along rather pleasantly for gays and lesbians.

One trait for which San Diego is known is its friendliness. There is not a city in America where the service people at restaurants go to more trouble to check on the well-being of their patrons, where shopkeepers utter more heartfelt gratitudes, and where strangers on the street are quicker to answer questions and help out visitors. With all the liberals and all the navy personnel living in each other's shadows, it's surprising everybody here remains so friendly, so willing to let their guard down. Perhaps the pervading civility is owing to the delightful climate and lush tropical surroundings. San Diegans truly seem to live under a blissful spell. This as much as anything might explain why visitors find San Diego so charming and relaxing, and at the same time why they so rarely leave with anything memorable to report about it.

THE LAY OF THE LAND

San Diego doesn't sprawl with quite the aggressive reach of L.A., but neither is it compact. The city's geographic center is the verdant, leafy, 1,400-acre Balboa Park. Downtown abuts the park on the south and west. Several older residential and mixed-use neighborhoods flank the park to the west and north—including the gay Hillcrest and Uptown districts. And several of the city's most Hispanic, and in some cases up-and-coming, neighborhoods are east and southeast of the park; of these, Azalea Park and Golden Hill—which is loaded with beautiful Victorian and Spanish architecture—are rapidly becoming gentrified by lesbians and gays. The beach communities of North Island, Coronado Beach, Point Loma, Ocean Beach, Mission Beach, Pacific Beach, La Jolla, and Del Mar are a short drive away. Automobile culture prevails here, but San Diego does have fairly walkable neighborhoods. Downtown, particularly around the Gaslamp Quarter, is particularly good for strolling.

Hillcrest, the Uptown District, and Environs

Hillcrest, the neighborhood at the northwest tip of Balboa Park, is a greatly toned-down version of San Francisco's Castro. Around its traditional crux, at the intersection of 5th and University avenues, you'll find many of the city's gay bars, restaurants, and shops. In recent years, however, the most concentrated commercial focus of San Diego's gay community has emerged in the eastern reaches of Hillcrest, just beyond Route 163, along the 1000 block of University Avenue.

The more gentrified blocks in this area are generally referred to as the **Uptown District,** but the name technically applies to a cluster of attractive pastel-hue, Spanish-style shopping centers that line the north side of University along this stretch. Several years ago, a massive, dumpy Sears store and its parking lot were plowed over in favor of this highly successful redevelopment project, which has lent warmth and color to what had been a flagging neighborhood. On the south side of the street are a strip of gay-oriented shops, eateries, and bars (sometimes called the Rainbow Block). As a whole, the Uptown District is one of the prettiest, liveliest, and newest gay enclaves in the country.

Hillcrest had for years been the primary settling spot for gays; it was a mostly residential neighborhood of older California bungalows and a relatively inexpensive source of desirable real estate. With its growing popularity, gays and lesbians are generally moving east and north of here, to the neighboring communities of **University Heights, North Park,** and **Normal Heights.** To a lesser degree, there's been similar gentrification west of here, in **Middletown.**

Downtown and the Gaslamp Quarter

San Diego's **Downtown** is a grid whose northeast corner touches I–5 and Balboa Park, and whose southwest corner touches San Diego Bay. It's bound roughly by Cedar Street to the north, 5th Avenue to the east, Market Street to the south, and Harbor Drive to the west.

If you take Harbor Drive along San Diego Harbor, you'll find the **Seaport Village** (☎ 619/235–4014), which anchors the **Embarcadero,** a touristy waterfront stretch of shops and restaurants that's more attractive but no more noteworthy than others you may have seen around the country. There's also the city's outstanding **Maritime Museum** (1492 Ash St., ☎ 619/234–9153). As you walk east from the water, you'll discover a fairly typical business district and, eventually, Downtown's main square: **Horton Plaza,** a six-block shopping, dining, and entertainment mall with a **Nordstrom,** a farmers' market, the excellent **San Diego Repertory Theater,** and a great variety of attractions. The mall was built in 1985, and was one of the first steps in reinventing a city center that had ceased to attract locals or visitors.

In fact, this Horton Plaza–centered renaissance was precipitated by the '70s restoration of the **Gaslamp Quarter,** a 16-block historic district that runs along 4th and 5th avenues from Broadway to Market Street. The city's commercial center during the late 19th century, the quarter turned into a nasty, red-light district in the early 20th century and remained crime-infested and undesirable until its overhaul and refurbishment began in 1974. Today it is one of the nation's most successful and aesthetically pleasing urban renovations. The original buildings have been remodeled and reopened as art galleries, coffeehouses, jewelry shops, restaurants, and antiques shops. There's even a gourmet cheese shop—a sure sign in the mid-'90s that yes, gentrification has arrived. On a typical weekend afternoon, you'll see mobs of both locals and tourists; all in all, the Quarter draws a more sophisticated, gay-friendly crowd than, say, Sea World. Several of the restaurants here are gay-owned and many have gay servers and fairly like-oriented followings. It's pretty easy and safe to park on the street, and when this is a problem, there are a few lots around, including a big one at Horton Plaza.

For a startling view, stand at the corner of Market and 5th and look north (away from the Harbor) up 5th Avenue. Every several minutes or so you'll witness an airplane executing its final descent into San Diego airport; the planes swoop down just behind the Downtown architectural horizon—appearing to just skim the tops of buildings.

Balboa Park

San Diego's major museums and sights are concentrated not Downtown but almost entirely within the rolling, emerald confines of **Balboa Park.** The most impressive of the structures, in an elaborate Spanish-Moorish tradition, were built during either the Panama–California International Exposition of 1915 or the California Pacific International Exposition of 1935–36. The highest concentration of attractions is in the center of the park, along El Prado (which you reach via 6th Avenue) to its junction with Park Boulevard. For general information on the attractions below, stop by or contact the **Balboa Park Visitors Center** (Plaza de Panama, in front of the San Diego Museum of Art, ☎ 619/239–0512).

Must-sees include the **Fleet Space Theater and Science Center** (☎ 619/238–1233); the **San Diego Natural History Museum** (☎ 619/232–3821); the **San Diego Museum of Art** (☎ 619/232–7931); the world-class, 100-acre **San Diego Zoo** (☎ 619/234–3153)—which can be explored either on foot (somewhat rigorous) or via an open-air tram—and the **Casa de Balboa** (☎ 619/232–6203), which houses four museums, the most notable of which is the **San Diego Historical Society Museum.**

Old Town

San Diego's 18th-century Spanish roots are preserved in **Old Town San Diego,** a small quadrant of historic blocks northwest of Downtown, just below where I–8 branches off from I–5. Within the few blocks are several of the city's oldest buildings, including a few museums. And a few blocks north is the hilly, green, 40-acre **Presidio Park,** where the city's Spanish presidio and mission once stood. For information on this extensive tribute to San Diego's early Colonial heritage, contact the Old Town **Visitor Center** (4002 Wallace St., ☎ 619/220–5422).

Coronado and the Beaches

At the top of **Coronado Island,** the mammoth **North Island Naval Air Station**—where Charles Lindbergh took off for his around-the-world flight—has been a fixture in the region since 1911. South of the base is the civilian-accessible part of the island; sights here include **Orange Avenue,** a popular stretch of boutiques and restaurants, and the grandiose **Hotel Del Coronado,** the century-old stunner in which electricity was first used to light a hotel and at which Jack Lemmon, Tony Curtis, and Marilyn Monroe frolicked during the filming of Billy Wilder's *Some Like it Hot.*

Hooking around San Diego Bay, and buffering Downtown and the North Island Naval Air Station from the Pacific Ocean, is dramatic **Point Loma,** a mix of military installations, well-heeled and modest residential blocks, and cluttered marinas. You can take a pretty excursion by following Catalina Drive to the tip of Point Loma, and by wandering along the cliffs and shores of **Cabrillo National Monument.** As the sun is setting, head back up Catalina Drive, turn left onto Hill Street, and right on Sunset

Cliffs Boulevard. Here you'll discover the awesome **Sunset Cliffs Park,** which provides panoramic views of the Pacific, and you'll see many more of the area's most impressive homes.

North of here are the beach suburbs of **Ocean Beach** and **Mission Bay,** the latter being famous as the home of **Sea World** (Sea World Dr., ☎ 619/226–3901), the vast marine-life amusement park. This is a fairly conservative area, and you might want to think twice in these parts about publicly pecking your partner on the cheek. That said, just north of the grand Bahia Resort Hotel, just off West Mission Bay Drive, is a small section of **gay beach and lawn** facing east toward the bay.

Also possessing a somewhat gay following is a funky stretch of **Pacific Beach,** north of Mission Beach, that begins just above the Crystal Pier and extends for a couple of hundred yards. Around the corner from here is a cute little gay beach bar called **The Matador** (*see* Scenes, *below*). You may or may not see gay couples along the beach, but you'll certainly see scads of buff surfer boys in tight wet suits and gorgeous women blading along the cliff sidewalk above the beach—so at least you can enjoy the scenery.

Continuing up the coast will lead you to **La Jolla,** San Diego's most prestigious resort and beach town—a bastion of seaside nobility. At the northern reaches of town, along the coast, is **Torrey Pines City Park Beach,** known locally as Black's Beach. This lovely stretch of sand, where nudity is officially not permitted but widely practiced, is the most openly gay of San Diego's beaches. To reach this somewhat secluded haven, follow Genesee Avenue west from I–5 to its intersection with Torrey Pines Road; here you'll find parking and several trails leading down the steep cliffs.

Tijuana

Being as close as you are to Mexico (San Diego is just 18 miles north of the border), consider a quick jaunt to **Tijuana,** which has a raucous—and distinctly young—gay nightlife, some terrific dining options, and hundreds of mediocre shops. You'll need a valid passport, or an original birth certificate plus a photo ID, to cross the border. The easiest way is to park at one of the lots on the U.S. side and walk over; Tijuana is not a big city, and you'll quickly find yourself in the heart of downtown. Most of the better, though still quite touristy, shopping and dining, lies along **Avenida Revolución,** which intersects Calle 2 near the town center. There's the city's major gay disco, **Mike's** (Av. Revolución 1220, ☎ 011/52/66/85–3534). Also, at the intersection of Calle 3 and Avenida Ninos Heroes, you'll find a coffeehouse called **Emilio's** (☎ 011/52/66/88–0267), which houses Tijuana's **Lesbian and Gay Information Center.** For general visitor information, contact **Tijuana/Baja Information** (7860 Mission Center Court, No. 202, San Diego, CA 92108, ☎ 619/299–8518 or 800/225–2786).

GETTING AROUND

It's possible to rely solely on the bus and trolley system to travel among major neighborhoods; to get from San Diego down to the U.S.–Mexican border, however, a car is best. Parking is relatively easy to find, on the streets and in lots, and streets are intelligently laid out and easy to navigate.

EATS

If there aren't more than a handful of extraordinary restaurants in town, there are hundreds of solid options, the most gay-frequented of which are around Hillcrest. None of the Gaslamp Quarter's restaurants have an especially gay following, but they all cater to a fairly trendy, artsy bunch—you'll never feel out of place there.

A disappointing note: Somehow, in California, the farther north you travel the better the Mexican food. Indeed, San Diego, just 18 miles north of Tijuana, has a fairly ordinary Mexican dining scene.

For price ranges, *see* Chart A at the front of this guide.

Downtown/Gaslamp Quarter

$$–$$$$ **Kansas City Steakhouse and Stingaree Saloon.** With ruby red walls, Victorian decor, and dim lighting, this steak house looks a bit like a brothel. It serves a wide array of fish, fowl, and juicy red meat—the 22-ounce porterhouse clearly separates the men from the boys, if you'll pardon the expression. Great ribs, too. *535 5th Ave.,* ☎ *619/557–0540.*

$$–$$$ **Café Sevilla.** For Spanish and Latin dining and entertainment, don't miss this place. Feast on such dishes as *cordero a la cordobesa* (slow-roasted leg of lamb in a mushroom and wine sauce); partake of sangria and tapas that are so authentic, you may have the urge to don a mantilla and a polka-dot gown and insist that everyone call you Carmen. Each evening five guitarists strum flamenco melodies on the intimate top floor. Indeed, there's music most nights: On Friday and Saturday, $19.50 buys a 3-course Spanish *comida* and admission to a flamenco *spectacolo;* on Sunday, there is Brazilian samba; Monday, Latin rock; Tuesday and Thursday, salsa and merengue. Wednesday brings Club 555, the longest continuously operated underground club in the city. *555 4th Ave.,* ☎ *619/233–5979.*

$$–$$$ **Croce's Restaurant & Jazz Bar.** In 1985, the wife of the late Jim Croce, Ingrid, boldy opened a restaurant that offered live music in a run-down part of town—an act that started the renaissance of a historic district and earned her the title of First Lady of the Gaslamp Quarter. As a tribute to her late husband, the exposed-brick walls are decorated with family photos, gold albums, guitars, and other memorabilia. Croce's offers culinary excellence at affordable prices, top-notch entertainment, and a nightclub ambience. Listen to live jazz while dining on such tantalizing dishes as Sante Fe Wellington (fillet of beef with a spicy sausage and raisin filling baked in a delicate pastry and served with jalapeño hollandaise sauce) or Pacific niçoise (charcoal-grilled swordfish served with new potatoes, niçoise olives, fresh tomatoes and french beans, dressed with a caper vinaigrette). You can also dine on Southwestern fare at the more casual **Ingrid Croce's Cantina & Sidewalk Cafe.** After your meal, retreat to the adjoining **Croce's Top Hat,** a nightclub that features live rhythm and blues nightly. The newest addition to the complex is **Upstairs at Croce's.** Situated in the atrium above the Top Hat and the Cantina, it has an ambience reminiscent of a '20s speakeasy. Its two parlors flank a grand bar/dining room that overlooks the Victorian architecture of 5th Avenue. There's also an upscale boutique. *802 5th Ave., 5th Ave. and F Sts., 619/232–4338.*

$$–$$$ **Dakota Grill & Spirits.** The Dakota Grill is a Californian version of a traditional Western eatery. The first floor was once home to a bank, so you'll find a curious, yet pleasant, mix of neoclassical architectural features and Western decor. A few of the high-quality, affordable dishes include penne with spice-charred shrimp served with scallions, cilantro, and fresh lime in a chile cream sauce or spit-roasted chicken with an orange chipotle glaze or Dakota's own BBQ sauce. After dinner, you may want to get your kicks at Club 66, located downstairs. *901 5th Ave., corner of 5th and E,* ☎ *619/234–5321.*

$$–$$$ **Ole Madrid.** A major hangout for the trendy set—straight and gay, Ole Madrid is one of the smartest eateries in the Gaslamp Quarter. It's set in

Eats ●

Scenes ○

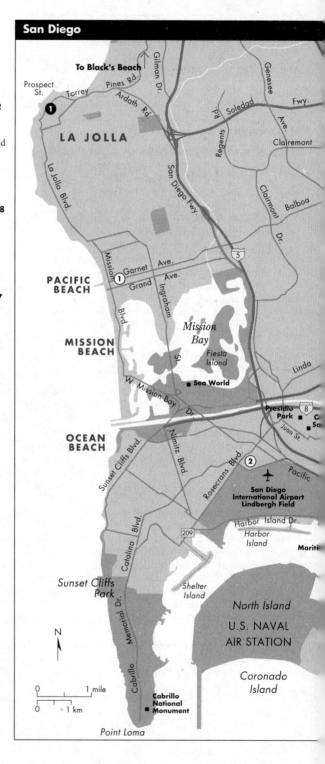

San Diego

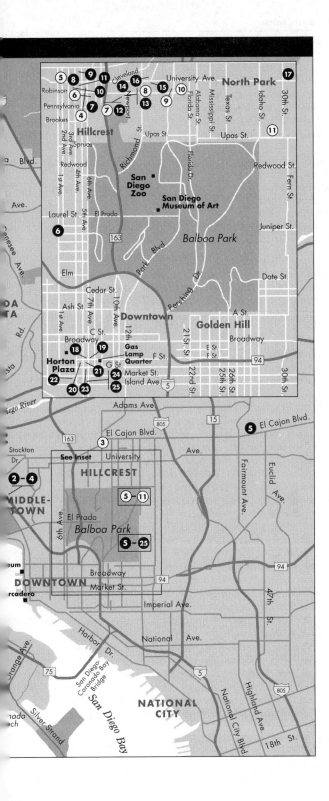

a two-tier dining room with a sweeping staircase, bright-red wooden chairs, and a slick, polished wood floor. A wide selection of tapas appears nightly, and the sangria is great, too. *755 5th Ave.,* ☎ *619/557–0146.*

$$ **Bayou Bar and Grill.** Of Gaslamp Quarter restaurants, this one is the campiest—note the tacky plaster fountain festooned with Mardi Gras beads that anchors the dining room. Some of the better dishes include an authentic Cajun version of red beans and rice, wonderful soft-shell crabs, oysters en brochette, and shrimp with Creole spices. *329 Market St.,* ☎ *619/696–8747.*

$–$$ **Beyond.** This is one of the best ethnic restaurants in the city—definitely a few cuts above your average, order-by-number, take-out joint. Contemporary Szechuan fare is served, including some tantalizing variations, such as *chinizzas* (Chinese wood-fired pizzas) and Kobi-style black-pepper steak. It's in a beguiling Victorian storefront restaurant with two large dining rooms. *618 5th Ave.,* ☎ *619/238–2328.*

Hillcrest

$$–$$$ **Banzai Cantina.** As the name suggests, Japanese and Mexican cuisines are united here in this airy, peach-and-teal restaurant just west of Hillcrest. Offerings range from a piquant Japanese bouillabaisse to several varieties of quesadillas to ahi with a teriyaki cream sauce. *3667 India St.,* ☎ *619/298–6388.*

$$–$$$ **California Cuisine.** Epitomizing California cooking, this restaurant utilizes minimalist decor and black-and-white photos so nothing distracts from the fabulous fare—such as grilled venison with wild mushrooms. Flashy patrons. On the Rainbow Block. *1027 University Ave.,* ☎ *619/543–0790.*

$$–$$$ **Canes.** It's hard to determine why a restaurant would dedicate itself to walking sticks (they hang all over the dining room), but overlooking the eccentricities of the decor, this is one of Hillcrest's finest restaurants. New American cuisine is featured—dishes like rainbow-trout cakes with peach-cilantro salsa and several designer pizzas—but you can get meat loaf, too. *1270 Cleveland St.,* ☎ *619/299–3551.*

$–$$ **Cafe Eleven.** Scenario: You can't spend a lot of money, but you do want that special someone out for a quiet, elegant, romantic dinner. The solution is to dine in this intimate country-French bistro, where local art on the walls brightens the atmosphere and veal sweetbreads, or pork chops with a black cherry sauce, can be had for a song. *1440 University Ave.,* ☎ *619/260–8023.*

$ **Corvette Diner.** This touristy, *Happy Days*–style diner goes a bit over-the-top with its decor, with Beatles memorabilia, framed photos of vintage roadsters, and even an early-model Corvette in the front room. It's a large, noisy place where the waitresses are trained to throw around a lot of attitude—not to mention straws and napkins and anything else they can think of. Expect big portions of better-than-usual diner fare. In the heart of Hillcrest. *3946 5th Ave.,* ☎ *619/542–1001.*

$ **El Indio.** For cheap, authentic Mexican food, you won't find a better option than El Indio. Nothing unusual—just inexpensive, filling, fresh tortillas and chips, enchiladas, chicken burritos, and several vegetarian dishes. Several locations, but the most popular is in Hillcrest. Great for takeout. *3695 India St.,* ☎ *619/299–0333; Downtown: 409 F St.,* ☎ *619/239–8151.*

$ **Hob Nob Hill.** San Diegans—including those gay navy men—have been coming here since 1944 for the kind of home-style fare you miss when you're on the road. Famous for great pecan rolls, coffee cakes, and other breads and sweets baked on the premises. There's always a fresh catch of the day, and breakfast is always available. Lots of regulars. *2271 1st Ave., ☎ 619/239–8176.*

$ **Saffron.** The top Thai eatery in town, it's well-known for Thai-roasted chicken (on a spit, over a fire) that comes with any of five hot sauces, including peanut and chili. Lots of salad rolls done with tofu and veggies. Some outdoor seating. *3731 India St., ☎ 619/574–0177.*

Coffeehouse Culture

Once a cheese shop (ergo, the name), **Pannikin** (523 University Ave., 619/295–1600) started percolating in 1978. This clean, laid-back café has two rooms: one quiet and sedate, the other colorful and very lesbian and gay. The clientele is over half homo, and, owing to its late closing time (2 AM), it's also popular with students. **The Study** (401A University Ave., ☎ 619/296-4847) has a meditative aura about it: walls are lined with books, jazz plays in the background, and lighting is subdued. You'll also find soup, sandwiches, scones, muffins, danishes, and—best of all—free refills.

Euphoria (1045 University Ave., 619/295–1769) is very laid-back. Leather chairs, changing artwork, and hot cider are some of the offerings at this java joint. Owing to its location between the bars Rich's and Flicks, Euphoria's crowd is trés gay. **The Living Room** has three locations (1417 University Ave., ☎ 619/295–7911; 1010 Prospect St., La Jolla, ☎ 619/459–1187; 5900 El Cajon Blvd., college area, ☎ 619/286–8434), all of which are furnished with authentic antiques (some of the pieces date from as far back as the 17th century). Sandwiches, pastries, and muffins are made fresh on the premises. The Hillcrest location is the gayest and grooviest. Popular with students is **North Park Coffee** (3028 University Ave., ☎ 619/298–1258). The decor, atmosphere, and menu are typical coffee bean.

Other popular coffeehouses in the area are **Espresso Roma Cafe** (406B University Ave., ☎ 619/295–0208) and **David's Place** (3766 5th Ave., ☎ 619/294–8908), the only nonprofit coffeehouse in San Diego—all its proceeds go to AIDS organizations.

SLEEPS

San Diego has an excellent variety of lodging options, and many of them cater specifically to the gay and lesbian community. Years ago, you'd have been bored out of your mind staying Downtown, but the revitalization of the area and several of its hotels has made it a perfectly pleasant base from which to explore the area. To be within walking distance of most nightlife, you'll need to stay in Hillcrest—but there your options are limited to a few smaller properties. For good access to both Hillcrest and the beach communities, consider staying in Mission Valley, where most of the national chain hotels have properties. This neighborhood is just off the San Diego Freeway, and you'll save money staying here.

For price ranges, *see* Chart A at the front of this guide.

Hotels

⊞ It's enormous, impersonal, and mobbed with conventioneers, but the twin-towered, 26-story **Marriott Hotel and Marina** has a choice location close to Downtown by the Seaport Village. *333 W. Harbor Dr., ☎ 619/234–1500 or 800/228–9290. 1,355 rooms. $$$$*

⊞ One of the more unusual properties on the West Coast, the **Horton Grand Hotel** is really two Victorian brick properties that were moved to the Gaslamp Quarter and rebuilt in 1986. Rooms have period furnishings and gas-burning fireplaces. High tea here is a much-celebrated event. *311 Island Ave., ☎ 619/544–1886 or 800/542–1886. 132 rooms. $$$–$$$$*

🏨 The **Doubletree–Horton Plaza Hotel** has a great location Downtown; it's connected to Horton Plaza and it fringes the Gaslamp Quarter. This is a property of understated class, with heavy use of marble, brass, and glass; some rooms have balconies. *910 Broadway Circle, ☎ 619/222–8733 or 800/222–8733. 450 rooms. $$–$$$*

🏨 The gay rodeo and other gay events are often hosted by the **Marriott Mission Valley;** set in the San Diego River Valley, it gets a fairly corporate clientele during the week. Rooms are clean and contemporary; the staff is efficient and friendly. *8757 Rio San Diego Dr., ☎ 619/842–5329 or 800/842–5329. 350 rooms. $$–$$$*

🏨 Run by the company that operates the Horton Grand Hotel, the similarly historic and elegant **U.S. Grant Hotel** across the street dates from 1910. It contains lovely Queen Anne–style reproductions in every room and handsomely restored public areas. *326 Broadway, ☎ 619/232–3121 or 800/237–5029. 280 rooms. $$–$$$*

🏨 Geared to budget travelers, the 11-story **Gaslamp Plaza Suites** was San Diego's first skyscraper and contained the city's first elevator. The atmosphere here is a cross between that of a European pension and that of a beach resort. The lobby and stairwells have Italian marble, and there are mosaic floors in several areas. Take in spectacular views of the city while relaxing in the Jacuzzi on the rooftop terrace. *520 E St., ☎ 619/232–8500 or 800/874–8770. 50 suites. $–$$*

Guest Houses and Small Hotels

🏨 It's pricier than other Hillcrest properties, but the classy, elegant **Balboa Park Inn** is still less expensive than Downtown lodgings. Rooms have individual themes and decors to match them; all have kitchenettes, and some have Jacuzzis. *3402 Park Blvd., ☎ 619/298–0823 or 800/938–8181. 26 rooms. Mixed gay/straight. $$–$$$$*

🏨 You'll feel as if you're visiting your groovy aunt Edna when you stay at the **Blom House.** Built in 1948, this cottage-style home offers impressive views of the Mission Valley from the 65-foot deck (equipped with a Jacuzzi) and the living room (equipped with a fireplace). The rooms have high ceilings, hardwood floors, and antiques; in-room amenities include VCRs, refrigerators, and irons. Roses, chocolates, wine, and cheese are never in short supply here. *1372 Minden Dr., ☎ 619/467–0890. 3 rooms. Mixed gay male/lesbian. $$*

🏨 For a good, inexpensive option in a residential North Park neighborhood, try **Carole's B&B,** a simple bungalow with a mostly straight clientele but a strong gay following. Furnishings are plain and homey. Rooms have refrigerators, and some baths are shared. *3227 Grim Ave., ☎ 619/280–5258. 8 rooms. Mostly straight. $–$$*

🏨 The **Keating House,** a peach-and-green confection a short walk west of Balboa Park and a 20-minute walk from Hillcrest, is one of the most attractive restored Victorians in San Diego. The rooms in both the house and cottage are furnished in period style. Good full breakfast. *2331 2nd Ave., ☎ 619/239–8585 or 800/995–8644. 8 rooms. Mixed gay/straight. $–$$*

🏨 One of the largest gay-oriented properties in Southern California, the **Park Manor Suites Hotel** is an older, all-suite property just west of Balboa Park—perhaps a 15- to 20-minute walk from most Hillcrest bars. Rooms are large and have rather dated furnishings, but ones on the upper floors have nice city views; the staff is knowledgeable about the gay scene. *525 Spruce St.,* ☎ *619/291–0999 or 800/874–2649. 80 rooms. Mixed gay/straight. $–$$*

☏ This is a cut above a youth hostel (and a very gay one at that), with simple, bare-bones rooms, but the **Hillcrest Inn** is perfectly located, within walking distance of the area's bars and restaurants. You get a refrigerator, bar sink, and microwave for an incredibly low rate. *3754 5th Ave.,* ☎ *619/293–7078 or 800/258–2280. 45 rooms. Mostly gay male. $*

SCENES

Few people would put San Diego's nightlife ahead of L.A.'s or San Francisco's. Certainly, there are fewer options here and fewer out-of-towners to play with—San Diego is nowhere near the gay mecca that its sister cities are. An argument can be made for San Diego, however, as the top club city in California. It's a city of remarkably tanned, toned, and extroverted souls—an easy place to meet people.

Bars are spread around town, but the highest concentration is in Hillcrest, along 5th and University avenues. Most of the others are either east or west of Hillcrest, but almost always north of Balboa Park. The one gay bar Downtown is a bit skanky.

An odd aspect of the zoning in San Diego is that adult bookstores have been permitted to open in virtually every neighborhood, and often at highly visible intersections (one suspects the strong navy presence is to thank for this). Sex shops and theaters aren't just relegated to slimy back alleys and red-light districts, as they are in most American cities. Many of the San Diego porn stores are gay, and most of these are well stocked and well utilized; they attract a fairly diverse and often well-heeled crowd. Most popular are the **F Street** bookstores, of which there are 10 branches in metropolitan San Diego—the most convenient are in North Park at the intersection of University Avenue and Florida Street, and in the Gaslamp Quarter at 4th and F streets.

Club San Diego (3955 4th Ave., tel 619/295–0850) is the biggest and most popular bathhouse in town. **Dave's Club** (4969 Santa Monica Ave., btw. Bacon and Cable, ☎ 619/224–9011), in Ocean Beach, has an outdoor pool and a Jacuzzi. **Mustang Spa** (4200 University Ave., ☎ 619/297–1661) attracts a diverse bunch. A little seedier than the others, **Vulcan Steam & Sauna** (805 W. Cedar St., ☎ , 619/238–1980) is downtown.

Bars and Nightclubs

Bourbon Street. You won't often see guys in suits in San Diego, but Bourbon Street usually draws a few of them. This is the city's most elegant piano bar, a good place to take a date and celebrate with a group of friends. In back is a patio that's meant to recall the jazzy courtyards of New Orleans's French Quarter. *4612 Park Blvd.,* ☎ *619/291–0173. Crowd: older, mostly male, smartly dressed, dignified.*

Brass Rail. The oldest gay bar in the city, the Brass Rail is the place devoted club-hoppers stop by midweek for a change of pace. It's also a bar popular with guys who want a night out on the town without all the posing. There's a decent drag show Monday and Tuesday, dancing other days of the week. Thursdays have a big Latin following. *3796 5th Ave.,* ☎ *619/298–2233. Crowd: mostly male, regular guys, 20s and 30s; cruisy.*

The Flame. This is the city's top lesbian bar, with a large dance floor and several bars scattered about. A mixed bunch comes on Friday night for the drag shows, and Tuesday is boys' night. Whenever you come, there's great music and a high-energy crowd. Check out country-western dancing on Thursday. *3780 Park Blvd., ☎ 619/295–4163. Crowd: 80/20 f/m most nights; a stylish, younger crowd.*

Flicks. Though it's *the* see-and-be-seen, video cruise bar in town, it's still incredibly friendly and down-to-earth. This neat, carpeted space is nicely done with framed posters of movie stars and flattering lighting; music is played at a level that allows conversation. It's on the yuppie side, but you'll meet nice guys you can take home to mom. Very friendly staff. Women are rare but welcome. Best on Friday nights. *1017 University Ave., ☎ 619/297–2056. Crowd: mostly male, young; clean-cut, guppie, stand-and-model, cruisy.*

The Hole. Close to the area's military installations but a short drive from Hillcrest, the Hole is a wild spot with pool tables, a patio, a stage (where there are drag shows from time to time), and lots of space for mingling. The place is famous for its unbelievable drink specials and unbelievably drunk guys. Sunday nights are best. It's such a big, festive place, you may feel tempted to dance in here, but beware—in California such activity is only allowed in bars with dancing permits; the Hole is not one of them. *2820 Lytton St., Point Loma, ☎ 619/226–9019. Crowd: mixed ages, mostly male; lots of navy guys and the men who prefer them.*

Kickers. As is often the case, the city's big, country-western dance hall is the friendliest bar in town—and this is in a city where bar patrons are already extremely outgoing. There's two-stepping and line-dancing in this large, nicely furnished place—and a Hamburger Mary's restaurant (casual American fare) in the same building. Has free lessons most weekday nights. *308 University Ave., ☎ 619/491–0400. Crowd: extremely mixed in age, about 60/40 m/f, racially diverse, friendly, country-western, great dancers.*

The Matador. This is one of SoCal's best beach bars—the kind of place where men and women hobble in for a beer after a long day sunning or surfing. Also, if you're out by La Jolla or Pacific Beach, it's your closest gay bar. Not a big or memorably decorated place: There's a long bar with a jukebox, a few places to sit down, and a patio out back. *4633 Mission Blvd., Pacific Beach, ☎ 619/483–6943. Crowd: 80/20 m/f; sun-bleached beach bums, Gidget-dykes; all ages, fairly local crowd.*

Number One Fifth Ave. Of the dozens of quiet neighborhood bars around town, this is one of the most popular. It's a casual saloon where you can kick your feet up and chat with the guys around you. There's piano entertainment some nights, and a patio out back. *3845 5th Ave., ☎ 619/299–1911. Crowd: 80/20 m/f, mostly thirtysomething and up; local, mellow, not so cruisy.*

Numbers. Across the from the Flame, the most distinctive aspect of this video, pool, and sports bar is the friendly, no-attitude crowd. A saloon-type atmosphere prevails with the nightly drink specials and the two bars. *3811 Park Blvd., ☎ 619/294–9005. Crowd: Fun T-shirt and Levi's boys in their 20s and 30s; casual, relaxed.*

Rich's. One of the hottest gay discos on the West Coast, though not as large or as glamorous as the warehouse discos of L.A. House music dominates the sound system. There's a smaller video bar up front, and the dance floor is in the back. There's a cover most nights. Thursdays and Saturdays, everybody stops in here. Since the West Coast Production Company closed late in 1995, Rich's has grown even more in popularity. *1051 University Ave., ☎ 619/497–4588. Crowd: young, mostly male; a fair racial mix; buffed, wired, lots of poseurs; serious dancers.*

Wolfs. Like its same-name cousins in Palm Springs and Long Beach, this is a leather-and-Levi's bar that's perfectly tolerant of preppy curiosity seekers. Good and popular because it's open late on weekends (till 4). Two large rooms, both very dark. A motorcycle hangs from one ceiling and the usual butch equipment hangs from the walls. A small leather and lube boutique on premises. *3404 30th St., ☎ 619/291–3730. Crowd: male, mixed ages; as hard-core as leather gets in San Diego.*

<u>DIVES</u>
The **Capri Lounge** (207 N. Tremont St., Oceanside, ☎ 619/722–7284) gets lots of military types. The **Caliph Lounge** (3100 5th Ave., ☎ 619/298–9495) is big with chickens and chickenhawks and has nice piano music. **Club Bombay** (3175 India St., ☎ 619/296–6789) is the mellower of the two lesbian clubs, drawing a diverse, local crowd to its small dance floor, great juke box, and Sunday barbecues. The **Loft** (3610 5th Ave., ☎ 619/296–6407) is a friendly neighborhood tavern. **Pecs** (2046 University Ave., ☎ 619/296–0889) gets a lot of guys stopping in on the way from or to the nearby F Street Adult Bookstore; lots of leather, facial hair, bears.

The owner of **The Eagle** (3040 N. Park Way, ☎ 619/295–8072) is from New York and enjoys the fact that his bar is similar to all the other Eagles in the country: dark, smoky, and cruisy with lots of leather and facial hair wherever you look. This bar has monthly events (such as Mr. Eagle in March) and throws beer busts every week.

As its name suggests, **Shooters** (3815 30th St., ☎ 619/574–0744), has many pool tables; it also has video games and attracts a local crowd of mixed ages. **Waterloo Station** (3968 5th Ave., ☎ 619/574–9329) draws a more sedate, mature local crowd. **Tidbits** (3838 5th Ave., ☎ 619/543–0300) is drag revue cabaret. The clientele is mixed in age but united in their love of singing and performing drag queens. **The Loft** (3610 5th Ave., ☎ 619/296–6407) attracts an older crowd that you could call inveterate regulars.

THE LITTLE BLACK BOOK

At Your Fingertips
AIDS Foundation San Diego Hotline: ☎ 619/686–5000; in Spanish: ☎ 619/686–5001. **Lesbian and Gay Community Center:** 3916 Normal St., ☎ 619/692–2077. **San Diego Convention & Visitors Bureau:** 401 B St., Suite 1400, 92101, no ☎. **San Diego Visitor Information Center:** 2688 E. Mission Bay Dr., 92109, ☎ 619/276–8200.

Gay Media
Based in San Diego but with coverage spanning Southern California, *Up-date* (☎ 619/299–0500) is the weekly, news-oriented community newspaper. The *Gay and Lesbian Times–Southern California's Weekly* (☎ 619/299–6397), a somewhat flashier magazine, is more entertainment-oriented and has better specific coverage on San Diego.

Serving Tijuana and the rest of Baja California is *Frontera Gay* (☎ 619/236–0984), a monthly paper written in Spanish that has one page of resources, tips, and club listings in English.

<u>BOOKSTORES</u>
The main lesbigay bookstore is **Obelisk** (1029 University Ave., ☎ 619/297–4171), a rather elegant fixture in the Uptown District's so-called Rainbow Block. More general-interest but also with a good selection of

feminist, lesbian, and gay titles is **Blue Door Books** (3823 5th Ave., ☎ 619/298–8610).

Body and Fitness

The major gay gyms are: **Bodybuilders Gym** (3647 India St., ☎ 619/299–2639) for true muscle sculptors; **Hillcrest Gym** (142 University Ave., ☎ 619/299–7867) for the see-and-be-seen set; and, for a mix of the two, **Bally's Holiday** (405 Camino del Río S, ☎ 619/297–6062).

24 *Out in San Francisco*

With the Russian River

PUNCTUATED BY HILLS, CONSUMED BY AN EERIE BLANKET of fog on summer mornings, and rarely marred by freezing temperatures, San Francisco is adored as much for its stunning natural setting as for its moderate climate. But a city is only as engaging as its inhabitants. In this regard, San Francisco's diverse ethnic makeup, its celebration of nonconformity, and its cerebral personality make it one of the world's most memorable metropolises.

Specifically, clichéd as it is, San Francisco is *the* gay mecca. Much of what makes the city popular with gays and lesbians—outstanding fine and performing arts, world-class restaurants, fascinating architecture, sophisticated shopping, and manageable layout—is what makes it popular with everybody. A case could be made that San Francisco's attractions are more adult-oriented than other hot tourist locations, such as Washington, Orlando, and Southern California. Relatively few gays and lesbians travel with families, after all. But there's definitely more to it than that.

Gay ghettos and entertainment districts have historically sprung up in the more licentious sections of cities. If you apply this reasoning on a larger scale, it makes sense that a vibrant gay community evolved in what was arguably the "loosest" city in America, at least during its first few decades. New England's settlers were puritan—San Francisco's settlers were anything but.

The city boomed in 1850, following the discovery of gold in the nearby Sierra foothills and later by a similar discovery of silver in Virginia City, Nevada. The population rose from 25,000 to about 350,000 during the 1850s, and a good many of these settlers were scrappy prospectors, rough-edged sailors, and other frontier spirits. For the remainder of the 19th century, San Francisco developed a reputation for drinking, brawling, gambling, and whoring. If you lived here at that time, you learned to tolerate the shady behavior of those around you. This was San Francisco's notorious Barbary Coast era—a time when brothels, saloons, and gaming houses boomed along Pacific Street, from Sansome Street to Grant Avenue. As the century drew to a close, the Barbary Coast district averaged one murder a week, and gangsters and cheats ran the city.

In 1906 the great earthquake and subsequent fire destroyed much of the Barbary Coast (the neighborhood has become the city's comparatively dull Financial District). Moral conservatives considered the disaster a judgment from the heavens: "San Francisco Punished!" was the headline of a Los Angeles newspaper days after the quake—a proclamation still bandied about today by certain right-wingers, in an entirely different, but no less nasty, context.

The few allegedly depraved operations that still thrived following the earthquake and fire were shut down by city leaders in 1917. But San Francisco continued to be popular with sailors and thugs, as well as actors and musicians (the social good-for-nothings of the era). In early-20th-century accounts, San Francisco is frequently referred to as one of the "gayest" places in America—though the word "gay" at that time had little to do with same-sex orientation. In fact, there aren't many recorded accounts of homosexual life in San Francisco prior to World War II, although one suspects it was always part of the landscape.

During World War II, San Francisco was the point from which many naval enlistees sailed for Pacific tours of duty. The city swelled with men, and the Polk Gulch neighborhood soon developed a reputation for male hustlers and covertly gay establishments. At about this time, discreet lesbian clubs also began to pop up around town.

The mid-'50s marked the beginning of two tumultuous decades of gay, and to a lesser degree, lesbian activism. In 1955 the nation's first major lesbian political organization, Daughters of Bilitis (DOB), was formed here under the leadership of Del Martin and Phyllis Lyon. Simultaneously, serveral mostly male-oriented homophile organizations, such as the Mattachine Society, sprung up around the city, and in 1959 the conservative *San Francisco Progress* ran a piece announcing that "sex deviates" had turned the city into the nation's "headquarters." Gay and lesbian bars became increasingly commonplace, though the owners had to pay off police to be allowed to remain in business.

By the mid-'60s the city's reputation as a haven for homosexuals had begun to gel. The San Francisco Police Department (SFPD), however, poured gasoline onto the fire that still smoldered from previous decades. At a 1965 fund-raiser sponsored by several gay political organizations, police attempted to harass the roughly 600 attendees. When two gay lawyers and two straight bystanders stepped up to prevent the officers from pushing through the ball, the four of them were abruptly handcuffed and thrown in jail. The American Civil Liberties Union (ACLU) agreed to defend those who were arrested, the mainstream press denounced the police officers' actions, and the defendants were found innocent. Chided for its strong-arm tactics, the police department struck back. To convince the public of what it saw as the tremendous threat posed by the city's homosexuals, the SFPD announced that as many as 70,000 gays and lesbians lived in San Francisco. (Even local homos had a hard time believing the number was that large.) The publicity spread rapidly, and the result was ironic: If you were a young "deviant" living elsewhere in America, you suddenly knew to pack your bags and move to San Francisco.

Up until this time, the Polk District had been the main gay neighborhood, although the countercultural Beat Generation had also forged a small, artsy, gay-friendly subculture in North Beach. Lesbians, despite the success of DOB, never really ghettoized in San Francisco—those who lived here lived all over, making their presence seem less pronounced. Greater concentrations of lesbians could be found in nearby Berkeley and Oakland, where the feminist movement was gaining momentum.

In the early '70s, the mostly Irish, working-class Castro neighborhood was transformed into one of the world's most recognizable gay ghettos. A smattering of gay men, led by the outspoken political activist Harvey Milk, who opened a camera shop on Castro Street, began to settle here. A tidal wave of gay male—mostly white and middle-class—immigration followed.

In Edmund White's *States of Desire,* David Goodstein, the controversial former publisher of the *Advocate,* had this to say about the Castro of the late '70s: "It's essentially a refugee culture made up of gay men, who, in a sense, are convalescing in the ghetto from all of those damaging years in Podunk."

Indeed, many Castro pilgrims of the '80s were born in Podunk—Podunk, Georgia; Podunk, Ohio; Podunk, Utah; and so on. The so-called "Castro Street clone" typically waited tables, worked behind sales counters, or collected unemployment benefits to support himself. He partied a great deal and had plenty of sex with many partners. Thousands of young, often disaffected, gay men bonded and felt, perhaps for the first time, that they were part of a much grander picture. Away from typically nonsupportive parents and siblings, they formed new, strong, family ties.

In 1978, a crisis further unified the Castro. A disgruntled, former city supervisor named Dan White assassinated San Francisco's gay-friendly mayor, George Moscone, and then supervisor Harvey Milk—who had risen to become the state's first, elected, openly gay, official. On May 21, 1979, White was sentenced to a prison term of just under eight years (with parole possible after five). That evening, thousands of angry gays protested the sentence on the steps of city hall. They left behind about a million dollars in damage, including 11 burned police cars and hundreds of smashed windows. The following night, the San Francisco police marched along Castro Street, yanking patrons from gay bars, and beating them up. One bar, the Elephant Walk, sued the city for damages and won.

In the 1980s, a much more severe emergency, the AIDS epidemic, struck the city—and most severely the Castro. Opinions vary as to effects that the disease has had on the character and personality of this once bacchanalian community. Though still bubbly in many ways, the Castro is certainly not what it once was—for better or for worse. The community appears older, more settled, and definitely more introspective. It still feels like a refugee culture of gays convalescing. Today's wounds, however, weren't inflicted in Podunk but rather right here, where, for 15 years, the community has learned to cope with thousands of losses.

The biggest difference between the gay San Francisco of today and that of two decades ago is that lesbians have stepped into many of the community's influential positions. The Castro is far more diverse today than it once was. People of all colors and classes now settle here, as do many lesbians. By the same token, more gays and lesbians live in other neighborhoods around the city. Perhaps most significant is the emergence of the nation's most visible and powerful dyke community, which has grown up right beside the Castro, in the lively Mission District.

The lesbian community, whose voice was for so many years denied a serious platform, is now highly organized and quite vocal. Great tension in the gay community has always existed between men and women, as the same "old boy" network that often prevented qualified women from advancement in mainstream society did the same in such gay political forums as the Mattachine Society. Tragically, AIDS took the lives of many of the men who had been at the forefront of San Francisco's gay movement. Lesbians not only picked up the slack, but also often grabbed the reigns and took charge. When you talk about San Francisco's homosexual community, you're including the legions of woman-owned businesses and woman-operated restaurants, and the many dyke performance spaces. The lesbian community has dedicated itself not only to the advancement of itself, but—through volunteer work, fund-raising, and political rallying—has also led the battle against a disease that struck down only a few of its own and many of those gay men who prior to 1980 held women in seemingly low regard.

San Franciscans have long shown an ability to confront disasters heroically—just consider how they have rebuilt the city following countless fires and two major earthquakes. The response to the AIDS crisis by both men and women, straight and gay, has been profoundly moving. The definition of the word may have changed, but San Francisco remains the "gayest" city in the country—if not the entire world.

THE LAY OF THE LAND

Ringed to the east and north by San Francisco Bay and to the west by the Pacific Ocean, San Francisco sits at the northern tip of a peninsula. Its terrain is hilly, and the land south of the city and also across from the bay is downright mountainous—wherever you go, you're almost never without spectacular views of both human and natural engineering. Within the city limits, you'll find dozens of small, and for the most part, lushly landscaped parks, as well as a few large ones, such as the Presidio and Golden Gate Park.

The most commercial and earliest developed section of the city lies at the northeastern tip of San Francisco, encompassing the Financial District, North Beach, Chinatown, Union Square, Nob Hill, Russian Hill, and the Waterfront. South of here are mostly industrial and working-class neighborhoods, the nearest of which, SoMa (as in "South of Market" Street), has become increasingly gentrified. West of downtown, from Pacific Heights clear out to Richmond and Sunset, the blocks become increasing residential but no less urban, and urbane. Due southwest of downtown, the old working-class immigrant neighborhoods, such as the Mission District, Noe Valley, and the Castro, have become anywhere from a quarter to three-quarters gay and lesbian over the years.

The Castro

The tiny **Castro,** the hub of the city's gay community, is bound by Market Street to the north, Noe Street to the east, 21st Street to the south, and Diamond Street to the west. The strongest commercial activity happens on **Market Street,** parallel-running **18th Street,** and **Castro Street,** which bisects the two of them.

Architecturally, the Castro is undistinguished in some areas, charmingly Victorian in others. It's a decent place to find cheap food, though it's generally put down for having the city's weakest dining scene. The neighborhood abounds with dozens of gay-oriented businesses, none of them especially high-end, including **A Different Light** (*see* Bookstores, *below*), the main lesbigay bookstore; **Under One Roof** (2362 Market St.), which sells gifts and T-shirts and whose profits benefit a slew of AIDS organizations; **All American Boy** (436 Castro St., ☎ 415/861–0444), an emporium of faggy fashion; **Jaguar** (4057 18th St.), which has a luscious array of sex toys, novelties, lube, and greeting cards; and **Louie's Barber Shop** (422 Castro St., ☎ 415/552–8472), a plain ole hair-cuttin' place frequented by plain ole dykes. In addition to being one of the top organic-food markets in the city, the **Harvest Ranch Market** (2285 Market St., ☎ 415/626–0805) doubles as a proven lesbian pickup spot.

The Castro has few cultural attractions. But you might check out **Harvey Milk Plaza** (above the Castro Muni Metro Station, at Market and Castro Sts.), which in 1985 was dedicated to the memory of the city's first, elected (and later assassinated) openly gay official. The plaque here has a moving inscription. Across the street stands the spectacular 1922 **Castro Theatre,** which hosts the city's esteemed Lesbian and Gay Film Festival each summer; at other times, it serves as an outstanding repertory movie house. The balcony at this marvelous, 1,500-seat, Spanish Baroque institution is, according to local lore, a great place to make out; so is the parking lot behind the theater. Up on Market Street, the **NAMES Project Foundation** (2362 A Market St., ☎ 415/863–1966) has a visitor center and panel-making workshop. The NAMES quilt, begun here in 1987, consists of more than 26,000 hand-sewn panels, each a tribute created by the loved ones of a person who has fallen to AIDS. You can come here to make your own panel (materials and encouragement are provided) and view the quilt's newest additions. People stop here from all over the world to visit the foundation. For many of them, it's part of a lengthy healing process; for anyone, it can be a deeply emotional experience.

The best way to see the Castro is to take the famed 3½-hour walking tour, **Cruisin' the Castro** (☎ 415/550–8110), given by Trevor Hailey, both a delightful speaker and a walking encyclopedia of local history. Ms. Hailey's tour includes brunch at the Elephant Walk.

The Mission

Due east of the Castro, the Mission District gets its name from the **Mission Dolores** (Dolores and 16th Sts., ☎ 415/621–8203), which has stood here since 1791. During the 19th century, this verdant area was San Francisco's resort community. It gradually changed into a working-class residential neighborhood; today it's largely inhabited by Latinos. Over the past couple of decades, the area has also emerged into a lesbian stronghold.

The major commercial thoroughfares are **16th Street,** from about Guerrero to Mission streets, and **Valencia Street,** from about 16th to 24th streets. Many of the blocks just off of these two thoroughfares are colorful as well. You'll find lots of cheap and tasty eateries, many left-leaning and lesbian-oriented shops and galleries, and most of the city's queer and women's performance spaces. Of course, this is still a major Latino community, with Spanish groceries and dry-goods stores alongside the artsy spots. The neighborhood, with its low, quirky skyline, is far more diverse—and less predictable—than the Castro.

If wandering the Mission, you'll discover great places to buy books on feminist issues, New Age themes, and Eastern religion (*see* Bookstores, *below*). The area is also home to **Community Thrift** (623 Valencia St.), where you'll find second-hand clothing, shoes, furniture, and household stuff; **Womencrafts West** (1007½ Valencia St.), a popular gallery; **Groger's Western Wear** (1445 Valencia St.), a good place to find the right gear for two-stepping; **Botanica Yoruba** (998 Valencia St.), which stocks incense, candles, and oils; and **Good Vibrations** (1009 Valencia St.), an attractive, well-lit, woman-owned emporium that may be the loveliest erotica boutique you'll ever encounter.

A striking mural illustrating the lives of prominent women over the centuries covers two sides of the **Women's Building** (3543 18th St., ☎ 415/431–1180). This community center holds events, readings, meetings, and workshops for women and many of the city's feminist and lesbian political and social organizations. It's a terrific resource. If you walk down Church Street to about 18th Street, you'll reach the expansive **Dolores Park,** a popular gay and lesbian "beach" during the day (the fog rarely affects this neighborhood); it is extremely dicey at night.

Southeast of the park, around the intersection of Army Street and Van Ness Avenue, is **Bernal Heights,** a modest residential neighborhood that has little of interest to the visitor. Supposedly, though, it has the highest number of lesbian-owned houses in the city.

Noe Valley

The lesbians who live in the Mission and Bernal Heights often aspire to live in the more fashionable Noe Valley, which has a mixed population of straight yuppies, gay couples, and lesbians with kids. This quiet, residential neighborhood lies due south of the Castro and southwest of the Mission. On any morning, you'll find both **Chloe's** (1399 Church St., ☎ 415/648–4116) and **Just For You** (see Eats, below), a couple of casual diners, packed with locals. Between Church and Diamond streets, **24th Street** has several restaurants, about a half-dozen coffeehouses, and some shops and galleries. It's a cruisy scene but in a cerebral way.

To the west and high above Noe Valley and the Castro is **Twin Peaks,** a double-hump mountain that affords perhaps the most spectacular view of the entire city. You can drive up here via Twin Peaks Boulevard, or, from Castro and Market streets, take Muni Bus 37.

Downtown

Downtown encompasses the dense triangle of urbanity that's east of Van Ness Avenue, north of Market Street, and fringed by the Embarcadero. This area serves as San Francisco's commercial center.

Most of the city's hotels and high-end department stores (Neiman-Marcus, Saks, Gump's, Nordstrom) are centered near or on **Union Square,** a neat, dull green rectangle. **Geary Street,** just west of the Square, constitutes the city's modest "Theater Row." And **Maiden Lane,** east of the square, is notable for having been San Francisco's red-light district until the 1906 earthquake and fire burned down all the brothels.

Northeast of Union Square, you'll reach the **Financial District,** whose spine, **Montgomery Street,** is often dubbed the "Wall Street of the West." Since the gold boom of 1849, San Francisco has been the western United States's financial capital. You'll find the city's tallest, and in some cases, most dramatic, skyscrapers on these blocks, most notably the 52-story, granite-and-marble **Bank of America** (Pine and Kearny Sts.), which has a lounge and restaurant (the Carnelian Room, ☎ 415/433–7500) on the top floor, and the 853-foot **Transamerica Pyramid** (600 Montgomery St.).

Immediately southeast of the Financial District, at the foot of Market Street, is the heart of the city's **Embarcadero,** a stretch of contemporary office blocks anchored by **Justin Herman Plaza**—a concrete park where corporate types spend recess chatting over sandwiches. On one side of the plaza stands the old **Ferry Building** with its distinctive 230-foot clock tower; on the other side is the mammoth **Embarcadero Center,** which houses offices, shops, a five-screen cinema, and the Hyatt Regency Hotel.

If you head west of the Financial District, you'll approach **Chinatown,** which, for full effect, you should enter via the ornate **Chinatown Gate** at Grant Avenue and Bush Street. This is one of the largest Chinese communities in North America. You're now on the eastern slope of **Nob Hill** (a.k.a. Snob Hill), where the city's old money has traditionally come to nest. At the peak of the hill, where California and Mason streets intersect, you'll find five of the city's most luxurious hotels and the stunning, extremely gay-friendly **Grace Cathedral** (1051 Taylor St.). California Street is one of the city's main, and quite dramatic, cable car routes—and in the Nob Hill area, you can visit the free **Cable Car Museum** (1201 Mason St., ☎ 415/474–1887). Just northwest of Nob Hill lies the similarly posh **Russian Hill,** with restored Victorians and fancy new high-rises lining the streets. The area is renowned for the oft-photographed, and steep, **Lombard Street** (a.k.a. the crookedest street in America), which switchbacks eight times from its apex at Hyde Street to its base at Leavenworth Street.

North of Nob Hill and Chinatown is the half-yuppie and half-Italian neighborhood of **North Beach,** whose lively **Columbus Avenue** and **Stockton Street** overflow with pastry shops and tony boutiques. In the '50s the area was home to the Beat Generation of Jack Kerouac and Lawrence Ferlinghetti. You can walk east of North Beach a few blocks along Filbert Street to reach **Telegraph Hill** and the steps to the distinctive **Coit Tower,** which has great views of San Francisco Bay and Alcatraz Island.

Polk Gulch and the Tenderloin

Here's a favorite San Francisco joke: "Whaddya do if you find a quarter lying on Polk Street? Kick it over to Van Ness and pick it up." **Polk Street** defines "rough trade" and the phrase, "Brother can you spare a dime?" Hustlers sit along the curb bumming smokes off passersby. Drunken old men stumble out of bars at two in the afternoon. The street is lined with the city's dreariest gay bars, plus some diners, dry-goods stores, and porn shops. Though Polk Street is actually rather fashionable up around Russian Hill, the section that runs through the heart of the **Polk Gulch** neighborhood, from about California to Market streets, is thoroughly seedy.

From the end of World War II, when San Francisco's gay community first began to emerge in strong numbers, until the early '70s, when the action shifted into the Castro, Polk Gulch was the city's most significant gay district. It actually looks better today than it did five years ago, as certain blocks are slowly being gentrified.

Just east of lower Polk Street, Eddy and Turk streets lead you into the city's infamous **Tenderloin,** where many of the city's gay and straight strip joints and seedy shops are found.

SoMa

The sprawling **SoMa** district has many of San Francisco's warehouses and resembles New York City's SoHo district in more ways than one. Here, the industrial businesses have been replaced with artists' lofts, factory-outlet shops, designers' studios, and nonprofit galleries. Literally south (well, southeast) of Market Street, SoMa is also bound by the Embarcadero to the northeast, Berry Street to the southeast, and the Central Skyway to the southwest.

The section of SoMa with the bulk of attractions lies between 4th and 2nd streets, including **Moscone Convention Center** and a couple of large hotels. A recent addition to this area is the **San Francisco Museum of Modern Art** (151 3rd St., ☎ 415/357–4000), which opened in 1995 to considerable acclaim. Head down 3rd Street, below the I–80 overpass, to reach **660 Center** (660 3rd St.), a mall containing 22 outlet shops. Nearby, running between 2nd and 3rd streets, is the somewhat incongruous **South Park,** a grassy square that recalls Victorian London far more than it does industrial San Francisco. A few up-and-coming eateries have opened around South Park.

At night SoMa comes alive as the city's major gay and straight club campus. For years the city's half dozen wildest gay leather bars have been here, mostly around 8th and 9th streets. They remain, even if their popularity has dwindled, and several big discos now glow with activity around Folsom and Harrison streets. The areas also has a couple of great leather shops: **Stormy Leather** (1158 Howard St.) is dyke-owned and has fetish wear, toys, harnesses, and other leather gear for women; the **Bear Shop** (367 9th St.) sells toys, videos, and magazines for "bears"; and **A**

Taste of Leather (317-A 10th St.) is one of the largest leather boutiques on the West Coast.

Fisherman's Wharf and the Marina District

San Francisco's northern shore, from the Golden Gate Bridge to North Beach, contains many of the city's most popular attractions. The most touristy and least-interesting span of waterfront is **Fisherman's Wharf** (foot of Taylor St.), the most well-known of several formerly industrial piers now refitted with amusements, schlocky shops, and overpriced restaurants. The action stretches from **Ghirardelli Square,** at the top of Polk Street, to **Pier 39,** home to the tackiest of souvenir stands and the brand-new **Underwater World** (415/544–9920). From several of the piers, you can book sightseeing cruises of the bay or excursions to **Alcatraz Island** (☎ 415/546–2628), the infamous island prison.

Just west of all of this action is the impressive **National Maritime Museum** (foot of Polk St., ☎ 415/556–8177), and beyond that lies **Fort Mason,** a former World War II supplies depot that now contains several fine cultural attractions, including the **Mexican Museum** (Bldg. D, ☎ 415/441–0404), the **Museo Italo-Americano** (Bldg. C, ☎ 415/673–2200), the **San Francisco African-American Historical and Cultural Society** (Bldg. C, ☎ 415/441–0640), and the **San Francisco Craft and Folk Art Museum** (Bldg. A, ☎ 415/775–0990).

Farther west is the **Marina District,** a monied neighborhood where yuppies nest in their large Art Deco homes. The only significant site here is the **Palace of Fine Arts** (corner of Baker and Beach Sts.), a massive study in rococo built for the 1915 Panama-Pacific International Exposition. Its interior houses the **Exploratorium** (☎ 415/561–0362), a science museum that resembles a dark, crowded airport hangar. Displays are hands-on. Touch this, listen to that, open these, put your finger under this, rest your chin about here—a bit like playing Twister with 700 strangers.

West of here is the 1,400-acre **Presidio,** now administered as part of the Golden Gate National Recreation Area. Since the time that Spanish settlers first claimed the area in 1776, the Presidio was a military post; most recently, the U.S. Army occupied it until 1994. At the northwest tip of the Presidio, the awesome **Golden Gate Bridge** stretches her arms 2 miles across the bay, connecting San Francisco with the Marin Headlands.

Southwest of the Presidio, you'll find the rugged 275-acre **Lincoln Park.** The park's sheer cliffs provide spectacular views of the Pacific Ocean, often accompanied by high winds, dense fog, and pounding surf. One of the most popular vantage points is **Land's End** (parking is at the end of El Camino del Mar). If you've read Armistead Maupin's *Tales of the City,* you'll remember this steep perch as being particularly fraught with danger—indeed, you'll want to be extremely careful around these trails. The beach down below is stunning—and a bit cruisy. Do not swim here or at any of the beaches off of Lincoln Park, however; there's a strong and violent undertow.

Lincoln Park's most visited attraction, the **Cliff House** (1066 Point Lobos Ave.), is worth seeing if only for the views. The food at its restaurant and trinkets sold at its gift shop are overpriced and mediocre.

Between the Presidio and Lincoln Park stretches popular **Baker Beach;** its southwesternmost end is pretty straight and easily accessible. As you hike along the rocky coastline in a northeasterly direction, toward the Golden Gate Bridge, you'll discover that much of the crowd is sunbathing in the nude (weather permitting), that many of these sunbathers are gay men, and that many of these men are a bit frisky. Always watch your footing along the steep trails and slippery rocks—and again, beware of the dangerous surf.

West of Van Ness Avenue

Between Van Ness Avenue and Golden Gate Park, below the Marina District and above Market Street, you have access to several highly explorable neighborhoods. To the north is ritzy **Pacific Heights,** a residential community known for its expensive homes, pretty gardens, and trendy shops and restaurants. This is a fairly straight area, populated by many of the yuppies who work in the Financial District; hence the neighborhood's nickname, "Specific Whites." On **Fillmore Street,** which runs north to south, you'll find dozens of cute shops and cafés. Just north of here is **Union Street,** another popular strip of boutiques and restaurants, running east to west from near Steiner to Gough (pronounced "Goff") Street.

South of Pacific Heights is **Japantown,** a contemporary though somewhat characterless neighborhood where the city's Japanese immigrants settled prior to World War II; during the war most of its population were placed in internment camps. Many Japanese still reside here, and much of the neighborhood's commercial activity takes place on **Geary Boulevard,** between about Laguna and Divisadero streets. The most popular attraction here is **Japan Center,** a mammoth complex of shops and restaurants.

Southeast of Japantown, near the intersection of Van Ness and Market, is the **Civic Center,** the city's central complex of governmental buildings and cultural attractions. Within these few blocks you'll find the dramatic, French Renaissance Revival **City Hall** (Polk and Grove Sts.); the brand-new **San Francisco Public Library** (Larkin and McCallister Sts., ☎ 415/557–4440), which contains one of the most extensive gay and lesbian archives in the world; the elaborate **War Memorial Opera House** (301 Van Ness Ave., ☎ 415/861–4008), home of the city's esteemed ballet and world-class opera companies; the **Louise M. Davies Symphony Hall** (201 Van Ness Ave., ☎ 415/552–8000); and the **San Francisco Performing Arts Library and Museum** (399 Grove St., ☎ 415/255–4800), which contains a large collection of memorabilia concerning the city's illustrious performing-arts history.

One constructive by-product of San Francisco's 1989 earthquake was the destruction of the Highway 101 Central Skyway, which used to pass directly over the **Western Addition,** the neighborhood just west of the Civic Center. This neighborhood, whose commercial heart runs along **Hayes Street,** from Van Ness to Alamo Square, is now referred to by most people as **Hayes Valley.** A largely gay and lesbian gentrification of this lovely neighborhood began as soon as Highway 101 tumbled. Galleries and funky restaurants now line Hayes Street and the blocks just off of it. **Alamo Square,** which you'll reach at the intersection of Hayes and Steiner, is a hilly green slope surrounded by many of the city's restored "painted ladies," those colorful Victorian row houses coated with as many as two dozen shades of paint.

Haight-Ashbury

Alamo Square lies perched at the northeast corner of perhaps the world's most recognizable bed of counterculturalism, the **Haight-Ashbury District.** Bound to the east by Divisadero Street, to the south by 17th Street, to the west by Stanyan Street, and to the north by Oak Street, the Haight's history is fairly typical of other hippie neighborhoods around the country. It has some of the city's biggest and most desirable—in this case Victorian wood-frame—homes. During the '50s and early '60s, when middle-class professionals began taking to the suburbs, young artists and radical thinkers began taking over the neighborhood, chopping up these oversize homes into affordable apartments. Progressive rockers, such as the Grateful Dead, Janis Joplin, and Jefferson Airplane lived here, as did their thousands of acid-infused followers.

This part of town remains a land of slackers and alternateens, an easy place to find crystal jewelry, incense, vintage duds, and illicit buds. It has changed some with the times, however: Deadheads are outnumbered by grungers, and rave-wear is more prevalent than tie-dyes. Most of the popular (if excessively commercial) shopping happens along Upper Haight Street, from about Divisadero Street to the park. Lower Haight Street, east of Divisadero, has more of an authentic, struggling-artist mood about it—a good spot to find genuinely cheap food and poor students nagging you for spare change.

Beautiful **Buena Vista Park** rises high above the center of the Haight District, allowing fabulous views in all directions. It is also the city's cruisiest park—no matter what time of day.

Golden Gate Park and Points West
The city's western neighborhoods are not particularly interesting for exploring. **Richmond,** which is north of Golden Gate Park, is an upper middle-class, residential enclave, and **Sunset,** below the park, is more middle-class. But don't miss **Golden Gate Park** itself, a wonderful spot for biking or blading—especially on Sundays when most of the park roads are closed to vehicles.

The park extends between Fulton Street and Lincoln Way, and stretches all the way from the Haight District to the Pacific Ocean. Across the Great Highway from the park, the beach is popular with both gays and straights. You may get wind of how cruisy the park is on the paths between the two windmills, which stand in the western quadrant of the park. While cruising is common here, especially near the working windmill to the north by the **Wilhelmina Tulip Garden,** the area is filled with tourists during the day, and it's rather unsafe at night. You should avoid cruising around here.

Meadows, groves of cypress trees, lakes, and trails meander through the park. The eastern half has several notable attractions, such as the **Strybing Arboretum** (☎ 415/661–1316); the **Asian Art Museum** (☎ 415/668–8921); and the **California Academy of Sciences** (☎ 415/750–7145), with a planetarium, an aquarium, an "earthquake floor" enabling visitors to experience a simulated quake, and several art and natural history exhibits.

The Russian River

On the edge of the Napa and Sonoma valley wine regions, the modest communities of **Guerneville** and **Monte Rio** comprise northern California's Russian River gay and lesbian resort community. Since the late '70s, when a couple of gays opened bed-and-breakfasts here, the region's popularity has soared. Unfortunately, the swift-flowing Russian River, which passes through the heart of both communities, floods frequently, and has completely wiped out the towns in both 1986 and 1994. Businesses rarely seem to fold, however, as most of those who settle here can't imagine a place they'd rather be.

Other than the wineries, there aren't many cultural attractions here. There is plenty to do, however. People come chiefly to escape urban pressures and to take advantage of the region's myriad outdoor offerings—from swimming to river rafting to hiking. Accommodations tend to be rustic, restaurants simple and inexpensive; although the nearby Marin Coast and Napa and Sonoma valleys offer quite a few luxury accommodations and sophisticated dining options. Towering redwoods and lush foliage grow densely through the valley—there are beaches along the river and sundecks at most resorts, but this is less a spot for sun bunnies than Palm Springs and Laguna Beach. Aging hippies and left-leaning thinkers make up a significant chunk of both the visiting and permanent population; about every sixth car is an old VW bus.

Guerneville is the region's commercial hub, where you'll find the only nightlife and most of the restaurants, shops, and accommodations. Although it doesn't have as intense a scene as Key West or Fire Island, the Russian River is consistently popular year-round, with high season in summer. The community is slightly more popular with gay men than it is with lesbians, but you'll always find a bit of a mix. And there are women's weekends each May and September. It takes from 90 minutes to two hours to drive here from San Francisco. Travel along U.S. 101 north through the small city of Santa Rosa, getting off at the River Road exit. Follow this west for about 20 minutes to reach Guerneville.

GETTING AROUND

Up until a few years ago, San Francisco was an easy driving city. It's still not too hard to find parking spaces west of Van Ness, but downtown as well as points north and south are tough—most parking requires a permit. Garages downtown are costly, too. Furthermore, this city has steep, hilly streets, which can prove tricky—especially if your car is a stick shift. The main reason to have a car here is to explore the outlying areas; in the city itself, unless you're dead set on being able to drive around at will, you should consider relying on mass transit and cabs.

Buses are a good way to travel among neighborhoods (from anywhere on Market Street, you can pick up Muni Bus 8 to reach the Castro). The fare is $1, exact change (bills or coins), and day passes are available. The cable cars are certainly fun and exciting, but they only hit a few major routes. Bay Area Rapid Transit (BART) is the region's rail system; while it's useful for getting out to Berkeley and Oakland, it's less practical for travel within San Francisco. Still, many people use it to commute between downtown and the Castro. Taxis are easy to use and not terribly expensive; it's a small city, so even a ride from downtown to the Castro shouldn't set you back more than $8. You can hail taxis, but this isn't done commonly; better to phone for one. In SoMa, plenty of taxis are usually available after the clubs close; in the Castro, you can often hail a cab around the intersection of 17th, Market, and Castro streets.

EATS

San Francisco may be America's best dining city—it is very difficult to stumble upon a bad meal. At worst, you'll pay too much in a few touristy areas, and the food will be decent but not great. Or in a few less expensive neighborhoods, you might sample a mediocre meal, but your financial loss will be minimal. In any case, disappointments are rare. All around town, you're apt to find good food at reasonable prices.

What follows are some broad guidelines to consider when exploring various neighborhoods:

Downtown and the Financial District: pricey, but usually pretty ambitious, well-prepared cuisine. **Chinatown:** maybe the best one in America; if you have to ask for chopsticks, move on. **North Beach:** delicious, moderately priced Italian food—all styles, including one that is purely North Beach. **Fisherman's Wharf:** Don't eat here. **Pacific Heights:** many darlings of regional Cal cuisine—healthy, light, but pricey; lots of interesting wine lists;

pretentious wine connoisseurs. **Japantown:** self-explanatory. **Hayes Valley and the Civic Center:** diverse, many up-and-coming bistros; becoming a place to nosh and be noticed. **The Haight District:** young, sullen misfits snarfing down cheap, comfort food. **Richmond and Sunset:** no glitter here, but some surprisingly good neighborhood spots—ask locals for favorites. **SoMa:** You just never know . . . some of San Francisco's hottest restaurants rub shoulders with some of its coldest cafeterias—any place within 200 yards of South Park is a guaranteed winner. **The Mission:** cheap, delicious, healthy fare—Formica tables, burritos, tofu. **Noe Valley:** Breakfast is serious business here—and there are plenty of greasy spoons to choose from; several upbeat coffeehouses, too. **The Castro:** lots of local color, but not a lot of good food—pick carefully.

For price ranges, *see* Chart A at the front of this guide.

The Castro, Noe Valley, and the Mission

$$–$$$ **Universal Café.** One of the area's rising stars, this café has a striking, postmodern dining room set inside a converted turn-of-the-century warehouse. Bountiful floral arrangements offset the spare look of the metal chairs and marble counters and tabletops. The menu concentrates on French and Italian Mediterranean fare. Try the roasted Muscovy duck on spaghetti squash with chanterelle and porcini mushrooms. The grilled flatbread, which comes with an array of toppings, is a popular starter. *2814 19th St.,* ☎ *415/821–4608.*

$$–$$$ **Val 21.** So named for its location at the corner of Valencia and 21st streets, Val 21 is a notable purveyor of healthful Cal cuisine. The menu changes every six weeks; it features several fish and free-range poultry dishes, vegetarian plates—such as grilled portobello mushrooms on a soft roasted-red-pepper polenta—and no red meat. Jazz music is pumped through the stylish, industrial-looking dining room. *995 Valencia St.,* ☎ *415/821–6622.*

$$ **Anchor Oyster Bar.** Meal for meal, this is the best restaurant in the Castro. You'll never be treated to less than a wonderful clam chowder or any of a number of fresh pastas and seafood grills. This remarkably clean restaurant has a cheerful staff. *579 Castro St.,* ☎ *415/431–3990.*

$$ **Eichelberger's.** Named after Ethyl Eichelberger, the renowned New York City performance artist, this informal supper club has a sassy bar downstairs, and a restaurant upstairs, whose American food is so-so but whose live entertainment is great. You come more for the atmosphere than for the grub. Wednesday nights the place turns into "Dykelberger's," an open-mike, lesbo salon. *2742 17th St.,* ☎ *415/863–4177.*

$–$$ **La Méditerranée.** This Middle Eastern and Greek eatery serves some of the best under-$10 dinners in the city. You'll find all the usual Greek dishes, plus healthy Lebanese kibbeh and tangy *baba ganoush.* The combo platters are hearty and inexpensive, and you can also get picnic meals to take to Buena Vista Park. Those resinous retsina wines are delicious. *288 Noe St.,* ☎ *415/431–7210.*

$–$$ **Pozole.** At this lively spot along Market Street, many admire the gorgeous wait staff (few of whom speak any English) known affectionately as the "boys of Pozole." The menu includes great Mexican and Latin food—the usual burritos, quesadillas, etc., which are not overly greasy. *2337 Market St.,* ☎ *415/626–2666.*

$–$$ **Radio Valencia Cafe.** Even for the Mission, this place is strange. It's a corner storefront that has old spool tables with fanciful scenes painted crudely on them. The linoleum floor is filthy, fabulous Latin music plays in the background, and the service is indifferent at best. The food—focaccia pizzas with pesto and veggies, a Texas tuna sandwich with apples, kidney beans, and onions—is good, not great. It's the kind of place that might inspire you to write a Raymond Carveresque short story. *1199 Valencia St., ☎ 415/826–1199.*

$–$$ Thai House. Several good Thai restaurants can be found in the Castro, yet no one seems to agree on which one is best. Here's a vote for Thai House, a snug, dependable restaurant with pungent green curries. Be sure to sample the sweet-and-smoky Thai iced coffee. *2200 Market St., ☎ 415/864–5006.*

$–$$ Ti-Couz. Lots of cute dykes work here, a delightful creperie where you can invent your own version or choose from a long list. These Gallic wonders are filling and reasonably priced. You might also pop in for one of the sweeter dessert creations. *3108 16th St., ☎ 415/252–7373.*

$ Bad Man José's. This *taqueria* has Aztec-influenced decor that's straight out of an archaeological dig—right down to the huge, earthen likenesses of Aztec gods lining the walls. Try the Tiburón Tacos: Two broiled, thresher shark tacos made with soft corn tortillas, cabbage, tartar sauce, and poblano hot sauce. The veggie tacos are great, too. *4077 18th St., ☎ 415/861–1706.*

$ Bagdad Café. Some people call it "the Fag Hag Café," but the crowd—and especially the staff—are actually rather lesbo-chic. The food at this 24-hour diner is better and healthier than Sparky's, the Castro's other post-disco nosh pit. *2295 Market St., ☎ 415/621–4434.*

$ Hot 'n' Hunky. Many people swear by the juicy burgers; though they're good and have amusing names (e.g., "I wanna hold your ham"), they're hardly the stuff of legend. Obviously, the name of the place suggests that you turn your eyes toward the waiters, and they do measure up nicely—not because they're all so beefy but rather because they're all so fun and dishy. Great jukebox. *4039 18th St., ☎ 415/621–6365.*

$ It's Tops. Though it bills itself as the original '50s diner, the look is more '70s—note the knotty-pine ceilings and walls, for instance. And how many '50s diners have espresso makers? There are, however, precious Seaburg Wall-O-Matic minijukes at every table. Typical diner food. *1801 Market St., ☎ 415/431–6395.*

$ Josie's Cabaret and Juice Joint. This crunchy, nonalcoholic café is an authentic Castro institution. During the day you can munch on inexpensive vegetarian food or sip yummy fruit smoothies; at night it becomes a cabaret with a diverse lineup of entertainment (*see* Scenes, *below*). *3583 16th St., ☎ 415/861–7933.*

$ Just For You. At this major breakfast spot for dykes with tykes, be sure to try the breakfast burritos. *1453 18th St., ☎ 415/647–3033.*

$ La Cumbre. Inside this stucco eatery, the walls are covered with colorful Mexican art. The menu includes huge, authentic burritos, rice-and-bean platters, and award-winning *carne asada* (grilled steak). This is one of the Mission's best taquerias, and there are many. *515 Valencia St., ☎ 415/863–8205.*

$ Marcello's. Across from the Castro Theatre and steps from several bars, Marcello's is a great option for a quick slice of pizza—even the ready-made slices have such creative toppings as ham-and-pineapple, or spinach, calamata olives, and feta. A whole pie can be pricey but will feed an army. *420 Castro St., ☎ 415/863–3900.*

$ Patio Café. Not surprisingly, a pretty garden patio (formerly a greenhouse) provides the setting. It has faux tropical birds and, again not surprisingly, is perhaps the queerest patio in America. The Sunday brunches are usually mobbed with hungover disco queens dishing about the prior night's tricks and treats. You'll enjoy the good food—especially the cheese blintzes. *531 Castro St., ☎ 415/621–4640.*

$ Sparky's. After the Castro bars close, a mostly young, vaguely trendy bunch of queens congregates here for filling tuna melts, burgers, fries, and other diner standbys. It's open all night. *242 Church St., ☎ 415/621–6001.*

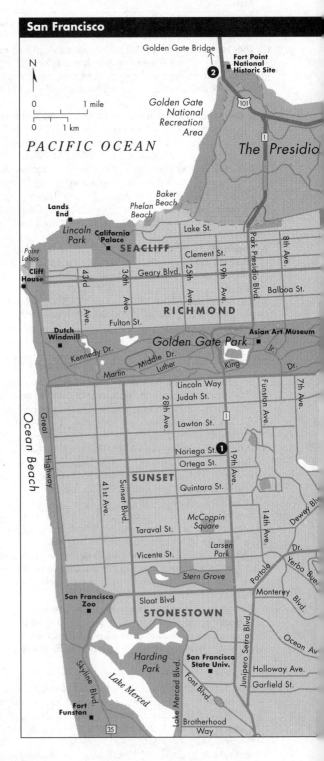

San Francisco Bay

TO ALCATRAZ ISLAND

3 Fort Mason

Marina Green

Pier 39

4 Fisherman's Wharf

Palace of Fine Arts

MARINA

Marina Bay St.

Aquatic Park

NORTH BEACH

Columbus Ave.

Coit Tower

Lombard St.

Hyde St.

RUSSIAN HILL

TELEGRAPH HILL

(tunnel)

Presidio Ave.

Divisadero St.

...tic Ave.

PACIFIC HEIGHTS

Broadway

Washington St.

CHINATOWN

FINANCIAL DISTRICT

San Francisco-Oakland

Sacramento St.

California St.

Grant Ave.

Powell St.

Bay Bridge

5

Geary

Masonic Ave.

...St.

Pine St.

Bush St.

Gough St.

Van Ness Ave.

NOB HILL

Post St.

Geary St.

UNION SQUARE

1st St.

2nd St.

3rd St.

Mission St.

4th St.

5th St.

80

Golden

Gate Ave.

Alamo Square

JAPAN-TOWN

Steiner St.

Laguna St.

Franklin St.

Turk St.

Fulton St.

Market St.

SOMA

6th St.

7th St.

Downtown

China Basin

Fell St.

Oak St.

10th St.

9th St.

Folsom

Harrison

Bryant St.

Brannan St.

Townsend St.

HAIGHT-ASHBURY

WESTERN ADDITION

Haight St.

Buena Vista Park

Duboce Ave.

Castro St.

101

Central Freeway

Potrero Ave.

7th St.

280

Central Basin

...anvan St.

Clayton St.

17th St.

Mariposa St.

Indiana St.

3rd St.

COLE VALLEY

Market St.

CASTRO

Mission Dolores Park

MISSION

20th St.

Harrison St.

South Van Ness Ave.

POTRERO

Pennsylvania Ave.

Dolores St.

Guerrero St.

Valencia St.

Mission St.

San Francisco General Hospital

Twin Peaks

25th St.

NOE VALLEY

César Chavez (Army) St.

Islais Cr. Channel

aight, Castro, and Mission

BERNAL HEIGHTS

280

Diamond St.

1

Oakdale Ave.

Quesada Ave.

Bosworth St.

Monterey Blvd.

Fwy.

Silver Ave.

GLEN PARK

Felton St.

South Basin

Southern

Balboa Park

Ave.

Excelsior Ave.

St.

Persia

Mission St.

Moscow St.

Ave.

John McLaren Park

Mansell St.

101

Gilman Ave.

Jamestown

St. 3rd

San Jose Ave.

Alemany Blvd.

France Ave.

Geneva Ave.

280

TO COW PALACE

TO SAN FRANCISCO INTERNATIONAL AIRPORT

Candlestick Park

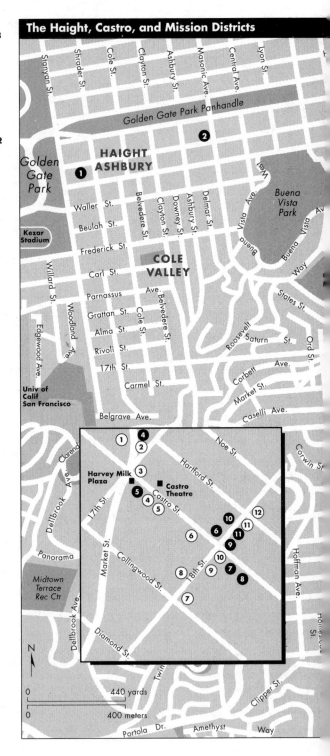

The Haight, Castro, and Mission Districts

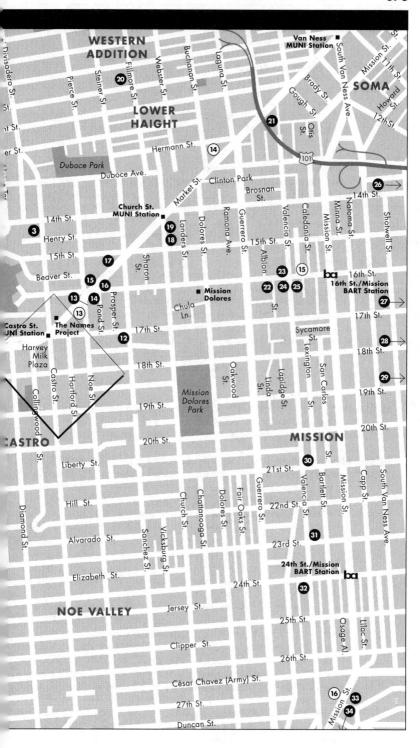

$ Take Sushi. Betty, the owner, is something of a neighborhood mother—she seems to know everyone who pops into her tiny Japanese restaurant. Best sushi in the Mission. *149 Noe St.,* ☎ *415/621–0290.*

West of Van Ness Avenue

$$$$ Stars. People take their friends here with the primary intention of impressing them, which can be a problem because Stars's holier-than-thou waitrons will probably blow you off once they realize you aren't famous. Nevertheless, this pioneer of California cuisine is justly famous for its inventive menu, which emphasizes healthful poultry and seafood grills. *150 Redwood Alley,* ☎ *415/861–7827.*

$$–$$$ Gaylord. Although many types of Asian cuisine are generously represented in San Francisco, there are only a handful of Indian restaurants. Gaylord helps make up for this lack, but don't expect a cheap tandoori parlor—it has an ambitious menu and a courtly dining room of Chippendale furnishings. You can't go wrong with any of the several lamb curries or the *navratan korma* (vegetables, farmers cheese, and nuts in a mild cream sauce). *Ghirardelli Square,* ☎ *415/771–8822.*

$$–$$$ Greens. It's a bit of a haul from any of the more interesting neighborhoods, but this innovative vegetarian restaurant has been turning heads for years. On weekends you can only order the five-course prix-fixe dinner; it's famous among food lovers nationwide and is a bargain when you consider the caliber of cooking. Be sure to sample the bakery's fresh bread and pastries. *Bldg. A, Fort Mason,* ☎ *415/771–6222.*

$$–$$$ Hayes Street Grill. Guppie central. This informal seafood bistro has a dapper dining room with varnished wood tables and soothing walls of cream and forest green. Some of the better entrées include the crispy, soft-shell crab meunière and the grilled fresh calamari. *320 Hayes St.,* ☎ *415/863–5545.*

$$–$$$ Ivy's. This upbeat gay spot serves typical New American dishes—grilled lamb chops with white bean, artichoke, and fennel gratin, or pan-fried mozzarella with tomatoes, basil, and smoked tomato cream. *398 Hayes St.,* ☎ *415/626–3930.*

$$–$$$ PlumpJack Café. One of the best of Pacific Heights's several slick neighborhood bistros, this café serves fine California cuisine. It's affiliated with the wine shop of the same name, which accounts for the more than 30 vintages of wine by the glass. *3127 Fillmore St.,* ☎ *415/563–4755.*

$$–$$$ Zuni Café. Synonymous in San Francisco with upscale gay dining, Zuni gets its share of celebs and movie moguls, too—definitely call well ahead for a table. Chic but rustic, the dining room is decorated as it ought to be in the wine country. A perfect meal: Start with Caesar salad (best on the planet), then sample a dozen oysters (best selection in the city), before moving on to the roast chicken for two (best bargain of the entrées). *1658 Market St.,* ☎ *415/552–2522.*

$$ Casa Aguila. You'll have to head way over to Sunset for the city's most amazing burritos, rich chicken mole, and spicy salsa. This little neighborhood joint has developed a big following, so you can expect long lines on weekend afternoons. You may want to finish your spicey meal with a dish of tropical ice cream. *1240 Noriega St.,* ☎ *415/661–5593.*

$$ Cha Cha Cha. Hungry in the Haight? Check out this noisy, festive eatery—one of the many excellent Caribbean and Latin American restaurants around town, this one has a Southwest twist. The tapas include plantains with black beans and sour cream or chili-spiked shrimp. Beware the long lines. *1801 Haight St.,* ☎ *415/386–5758 or 415/386–7670.*

$–$$ Isobune. If you can stand the touristy crowds at the Japan Center in Japantown, stop in for the inexpensive sushi at Isobune. Favorites such as octopus and salmon roe are unbelievably fresh; the food floats by you on little, wooden sushi boats along a countertop moat—you pluck whatever interests you. *1737 Post St., ☎ 415/563–1030.*

$–$$ Phnom Penh. A good, cheap spot near Polk Street, Phnom Penh brightens this dreary neighborhood with its inexpensive Cambodian fare. The lace curtains in the dining room are a major improvement upon the many scuzzy storefronts nearby. The top dishes are a refreshing, green papaya salad and the spicy curries (the best are with halibut). *631 Larkin St., ☎ 415/775–5979.*

$ Crescent City Cafe. Small and kind of greasy, this threadbare spot is blessed with outstanding Creole and Cajun fare, from oyster po'boys to andouille sausage hash. *1418 Haight St., ☎ 415/863–1374.*

$ Vicolo. This noisy, pink-and-peach dining room churns out the most inventive pizza in town. The place may be guilty of a little overkill on the toppings—the "olive" pizza has mozzarella, fontina, red onion, green and calamata olives, parmesan, garlic, and parsley—but everything tastes delicious. Slices are prepared and baked on the spot, so expect a 10-minute wait after placing your order. Gets plenty of beautiful people. *201 Ivy St., ☎ 415/863–2382.*

East of Van Ness Avenue

$$$$ Aqua. Most Americans live a lifetime without sampling the caliber of seafood served here. Supremely fresh, its preparation is also incredibly original, rooted in French and American traditions but always with an eye-opening twist: The rare *ahi* tuna comes with foie gras, and the delicious soufflées are made of mussels or lobster. *252 California St., ☎ 415/956–9662.*

$$$$ Fleur de Lys. Incredibly romantic. Hyperbolic fans rave that this may be the best French restaurant anywhere. Dishes such as the corn-pancake-wrapped salmon topped with golden caviar in a watercress sauce, may make you a believer. However, the chance to dine amid the zillions of yards of paisley that encase this intimate dining room is reason enough to visit. There's an innovative vegetarian tasting menu, too. *777 Sutter St., ☎ 415/673–7779.*

$$$$ Masa's. The service is refined, the dining room sumptuous, and the place remains unstuffy despite the hype. You can either opt for the menu *dégustation* or the menu du jour, which is slightly less costly. A sample dégustation might include foie-gras ravioli in a pheasant consommé with truffles, and a dessert of chocolate-pistachio terrine. *648 Bush St., ☎ 415/989–7154.*

$$$$ Ritz-Carlton Dining Room. This is a formal, elegant restaurant in a formal, elegant hotel. Gary Danko's exquisite cuisine suits the dapper setting perfectly; the service is positively doting. Danko is probably the highest profile gay chef in the country. *600 Stockton St., ☎ 415/296–7465.*

$$$–$$$$ One Market. With nice views of San Francisco Bay and Justin Hermann Plaza, this understated, elegant, split-level dining room has banquette seating, views into the open kitchen, and piano entertainment most nights. The dishes on the eclectic menu have one common denominator: creativity. Consider the fried-onion salad with maple-smoked salmon and creamy chervil dressing, or the steamed Thai snapper with preserved lemon-ginger vinaigrette and vegetable couscous. *1 Market St., ☎ 415/777–5577.*

$$$ Postrio. Although it's a tad overrated, this creation and part-time home of celebrity chef Wolfgang Puck still makes for a memorable dining experience. In the main dining room the crispy Chinese duck is a specialty. Consider saving a few bucks by eating in the bar, whose menu shows off Puck's signature designer pizzas. Wherever you sit, prepare to watch a lot of moving and shaking. You'll have to call at least a week ahead for a table in the main room. *545 Post St., ☎ 415/776–7825.*

Downtown San Francisco

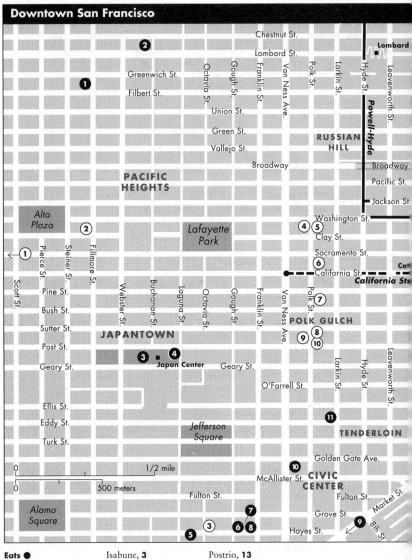

Eats ●

Aqua, **25**

Café Akimbo, **18**

Café Miramba, **2**

Cafe Tiramisu, **19**

Caffe Trieste, **21**

Caribbean Zone, **28**

City of Paris, **14**

Fleur de Lys, **12**

Fringale, **34**

Hamburger Mary's, **32**

Hayes Street Grill, **8**

House of Nanking, **20**

Isabune, **3**

Ivy's, **6**

Lori's, **15**

LuLu, **30**

MacArthur Park, **24**

Mad Magda's Russian Tea Room, **5**

Manora, **31**

Masa's, **16**

North Beach Pizza, **22**

One Market, **27**

Phnom Penh, **11**

Pizza Love, **33**

PlumpJack Café, **1**

Postrio, **13**

Ristorante Ecco, **29**

Ritz-Carlton Dining Room, **17**

Rubicon, **23**

Splendido, **26**

Stars, **10**

Vicolo, **7**

Yo-Yo, **4**

Zuni Café, **9**

Scenes ○

Alta Plaza, **2**

Cinch Saloon, **4**

Eagle, **11**

The Giraffe, **9**

Hole in the Wall
Saloon, **12**

Hunks/Reflections, **8**

Julie's Supper
Club, **13**

Lion's Pub, **1**

Marlena's, **3**

N'Touch, **6**

177 Townsend
Street, **16**

1015 Folsom
Street, **15**

Polk Gulch, **10**

QT II, **7**

Stud, **14**

The Swallow, **5**

$$$ Rubicon. Backed by such investors as Robin Williams and Robert de Niro, lesbian and award-winning chef Traci des Jardins is currently wowing locals with her stunning contemporary French fare. The setting is a stately stone building that dates from 1908. *558 Sacramento St.,* ☎ *415/434–4100.*

$$$ Yo-Yo. A princess of San Francisco's lesbian culinary elite, Elka Gilmore, oversees this chic Pan Asian seafood restaurant at the fabulous Hotel Miyako. The dining room's colorful murals provide an appropriate backdrop for such fare as salmon with soba noodles, bonita flakes, and shiitake consommé; and squab with balsamic figs and port sauce. *1611 Post St.,* ☎ *415/922–7788.*

$$–$$$$ Splendido. With views of San Francisco Bay, any of sunny Splendido's several rustic dining rooms provides the perfect place to enjoy a romantic dinner. The menu is largely southern French and Northern Italian; try the chicken saltimbocca with wild rice, designer pizzas, or oak-roasted clams with smoked bacon. *Embarcadero 4,* ☎ *415/986–3222.*

$$–$$$ Cafe Tiramisu. This charming sidewalk café takes the corporate edge off of all those Financial District stockbrokers—still, you'll witness a lot of intense power-lunch dates here. You can't go wrong with any of the light, leafy salads. Of course, save room for the splendid tiramisù. *28 Belden St.,* ☎ *415/421–7044.*

$$–$$$ MacArthur Park. No, this restaurant has nothing to do with the pop song later turned into a Donna Summer disco classic. But the converted redbrick warehouse, brightened with greenery and skylights, will get your juices flowing nonetheless. Just dig into these soul-meets-Seoul dishes, such as whole, fried, cornmeal-crusted catfish with Asian cole slaw, the Southern-style ribs, or the ahi sandwich with wasabi cream sauce. *607 Front St.,* ☎ *415/398–5700.*

$$ Café Akimbo. This may be the gayest of downtown options, an intimate, contemporary dining room with Mondrianesque walls done in muted jewel tones. Creative seafood dishes are standard fare. With many dishes around $10, it's a steal. *116 Maiden La.,* ☎ *415/433–2288.*

$$ Cafe Marimba. Here you'll sample the most authentic Oaxacan and Zihuatenejan cooking in the city; a pleasant contrast to sloppy, Sonoran Mexican food. Everything is prepared as it is in Mexico (note the dry-roasted tomatoes and peppers). Tamales with a savory mole *negro* sauce are a specialty of the house. *2317 Chestnut St.,* ☎ *415/776–1506.*

$$ City of Paris. Come to this Parisian-style bistro for the perfect place to catch a bite before seeing a show on theater row. Traditional French favorites include herb-roasted rotisserie chicken and skirt steak with frites. Many affordable wines are available. *101 Shannon Alley,* ☎ *415/441–4442.*

$–$$ House of Nanking. This no-frills restaurant has perfunctory service and suffers from long lines, but it's still one of the best eateries in Chinatown. A plate of heavenly shrimp cakes in peanut sauce will make you glad you came. *919 Kearny St.,* ☎ *415/421–1429.*

$–$$ North Beach Pizza. Not only touristy, this place is often populated by slightly horrifying mobs of straight kids from the suburbs. However, should dining on the city's best pizza be your mission, you must come here. The pies are huge—two slices is plenty for most people. *1499 Grant St.,* ☎ *415/ 433–2444.*

$ Lori's. You'll be thankful for this 24-hour diner near Union Square if you're clubbed-out, on your way back to your hotel, and still hungry. Decorated with '50s memorabilia, Marilyn Monroe photos, red-glitter vinyl seats, and Art Deco sconces, the setting will wake you up fast. Enjoy great burgers, vanilla malts, and unusually ungreasy fries. *336 Mason St.,* ☎ *415/ 392–8646.*

SoMa

$$–$$$ **Caribbean Zone.** This lively place is built around an actual airplane that appears to have "crashed" through the restaurant exterior and into the dining room. The authentic, stale-aired cabin serves as a cocktail lounge, giving patrons the chance to pretend they're Karen Black in *Airport '75*. Dining tables face the plane's exterior. The updated Caribbean fare (for example, swordfish with an avocado-coconut-mint coulis) is not particularly authentic but quite good. Only the sloppy service is a drawback. *55 Natoma St.,* ☎ *415/541–9465.*

$$–$$$ **Fringale.** This increasingly well-known French Basque-style restaurant is still a real find—a bright café with lemon-yellow walls that feels as if it should be out in the countryside, not on a nasty industrial street. People come from all over town for the reasonably priced fare that includes such delicacies as Roquefort ravioli. *570 4th St.,* ☎ *415/543–0573.*

$$–$$$ **Ristorante Ecco.** Part of the South Park culinary craze, Ecco will take you right to Tuscany, with its classical decor and verdant views. There's an extensive, deservedly renowned antipasto, plus a few unusual dishes, such as chickpea fritters with an eggplant vinaigrette. *101 South Park Ave.,* ☎ *415/495–3291.*

$$ **LuLu.** This hip, chic, family-style café is one of the hottest tickets in town. The setting is a fabulous renovation of a San Francisco warehouse with a lofty vaulted ceiling; pizzas and pastas with amazing combinations of ingredients keep company on the menu with the signature sizzling mussels roasted in an iron skillet. *816 Folsom St.,* ☎ *415/495–5775.*

$$ **Manora.** Of the two branches of San Francisco's best Thai restaurant, the one on Folsom is nicest. Fill up on the spicy fish cakes or the savory garlic quail. *1600 Folsom St.,* ☎ *415/861–6224; also in the Mission: 3226 Mission St.,* ☎ *415/550–0856.*

$ **Hamburger Mary's.** A major favorite of SoMa disco bunnies, Hamburger Mary's is a colorful, characterful burger restaurant (tofu patties are available) that's open till 1 in the morning (2 on weekends). *1582 Folsom St.,* ☎ *415/626–5767.*

$ **Pizza Love.** There's little to love about the mediocre pizza here except that it's available until 4 in the morning on weekends. *1245 Folsom St.,* ☎ *415/252–5683.*

Elsewhere

$$$–$$$$ **Chez Panisse Café.** This is the turf of Alice Waters, the legendary pioneer of New American cooking, and it's worth the trip over the Bay Bridge—if you've called ahead for a reservation. The Martha Stewart–looking dining room appears almost too perfect, but the food is wonderful, including such unusual creations as roast truffled breast of hen. You can also dine in the upstairs café on more familiar but no less creative fare, such as the garden salad with goat cheese. *1517 Shattuck Ave., Berkeley,* ☎ *510/548–5049.*

$–$$ **Old Sam's Anchor Café.** On the sunniest afternoon of your visit to San Francisco, consider driving over to Tiburon for a dockside meal overlooking the bay and the distant city skyline. The food should hardly matter at this point, but Sam's has good, affordable sandwiches, salads, and omelets (one is filled with oysters, bacon, and cheese). *27 Main St., Tiburon,* ☎ *415/435–4527.*

Coffeehouse Culture

THE CASTRO VICINITY

Often called Café Hairdo, **Café Flore** (2298 Market St., ☎ 415/621–8579) is San Francisco's gay ground zero. You can come for breakfast, stay through lunch, stick around for afternoon coffee, grab a beer before dinner, eat dinner, and finish things off with cordials and dessert. It's true, you never have to leave—some people never do. **Castro Country Club** (4058 18th St., ☎ 415/552–6102) originated in 1983 as a nonalcoholic alternative to the area's many bars. It remains a great pressure-free place for clean-and-sober meetings. The lavender-walled **Cup a Joe** (3801 17th St., ☎ 415/487–9773) is one of the newer java joints in the Castro, a good alternative if you simply want decently priced espresso. In addition to the usual coffees, you can get cookies and sweets. At the venerable purveyor of things fattening and delicious, **Just Desserts** (248 Church St., ☎ 415/626–5774), chomp on pastries and heavenly cheesecake. Though it's a chain, **Pasqua** (Castro and 18th Sts., ☎ 415/626–6263) is a highly queer—in a bronzed-and-buffed sort of way—coffeehouse.

THE MISSION VICINITY

In an attractive, three-story, teal-painted building, **Cafe Commons** (3161 Mission St., ☎ 415/282–2928) draws a retro thrift-shop crowd. It has a patio, an espresso bar, and a typical soup, quiche, and sandwich menu. In the Mission, latter-day Che Gueveras sit around the oak tables at **Café Macando** (3159 16th St., ☎ 415/863–6517) debating leftist politics over *lattes*. The omelets are delicious, as are the rich focaccia sandwiches. **Muddy's Coffee House** (24th and Valencia Sts., ☎ 415/647–7994; 16th and Valencia Sts., ☎ 415/863–8006) has a couple of outdoor tables and gets a good mix of locals, artists, and queers. The main room has very high ceilings and good sidewalk views. Nearby, you can get great bagels, veggie burritos, and other meatless fare at the divinely dyky **Red Dora's Bearded Lady** (485 14th St., ☎ 415/626–2805), an incredibly popular, smoke-free, PC, lesbian performance space. The votive candles are a nice touch.

ELSEWHERE

Gay Beat poet Allen Ginsberg and his pack regularly graced the old tables of **Caffe Trieste** (601 Vallejo St., ☎ 415/392–6739), a North Beach institution founded in 1956. If you're toddling around the Haight, you may want to pop your head inside the **Horseshoe** (566 Haight St., ☎ 415/626–8852); unless your head has been shaved, tattooed, pierced, or dyed an electric color, you may feel completely out of place—but that's part of the fun. The most eccentric spot you'll find in the newly gentrified Hayes Valley, **Mad Magda's Russian Tea Room** (579 Hayes St., ☎ 415/864–7654) is a nutty spot with an unaffected bohemian feel. You can have a tarot card reading while enjoying some of the best sandwiches (like the Fabergé eggplant with mozzarella and basil) in town. Live music many nights.

The Russian River

For price categories, *see* Chart B at the front of this guide.

$$$$ **John Ash & Co.** Named after chef John Ash, who is famous for his use of local game and organic products that complement the wines of Sonoma county, this critically acclaimed restaurant is surrounded by a 50-acre vineyard whose grapes are used in Ash's own Chardonnay. On cool evenings, dine by the fireplace; on warm ones, sit on the patio. The menu changes seasonally and has such offerings as sautéed Dungenesse crab cakes with serrano mayonnaise and grilled peppered beef fillet with a port sauce and Gorgonzola cheese. *4330 Barnes Rd., Santa Rosa, ☎ 707/527–7687.*

$$–$$$ **Village Inn.** The restaurant at this 1910 resort, where parts of Bing Crosby's *Holiday Inn* were filmed, is cozy and romantic, with warm lighting and the ambience of an old New England tavern. Favorites from the American and Continental menu are quiche Florentine, deep-fried prawns,

blackened red snapper, and pepper steak. *20822 River Blvd., Monte Rio,* ☎ *707/865–2304.*

$$ Sweet's Cafe. In the center of town, just a few blocks west of the bridge, Sweets is the closest Guerneville has to a see-and-be-seen restaurant. The prime people-watching is done from the many tables along the sidewalk. The cuisine is eclectic, with Southwestern, Continental, and Asian touches. Try the grilled *Niçoise* salad; any of the designer pizzas; or the Thai burrito with chicken, black beans, and Asian veggies in a Thai sauce. Nice beer and wine selection, too. *16251 Main St., Guerneville,* ☎ *707/869–3383.*

$–$$ Breeze Inn Bar-B-Q. Soon after you arrive in Guerneville, you'll notice a peculiar, three-wheel, motorized vehicle zipping around town delivering slow-cooked pork ribs, smoked salmon fillets, and barbecue chicken, all of which comes from the Breeze Inn Bar-B-Q. You can dine at this popular roadhouse, too. Vegetarians take heart: There are several options, including fettuccine or seasonal greens with cornbread. The sweet potato pie may topple you. *15640 River Rd., Guerneville,* ☎ *707/869–9208.*

$–$$ The Triple R. This dining room is the only place in the area that serves food after 10 PM (it's open till 4 AM). The traditional American food—pork chops, steak, eggs—is not especially memorable, but the staff and crowd are friendly and fun-loving. Attached are a motel, a pool, and a bar. *4th and Mill Sts., Guerneville,* ☎ *707/869–0691.*

$ Brew Moon. This is one of the few spots in the quaint Russian River are that captures the cosmopolitan air of San Francisco. Here you'll find an art gallery; jazz playing over the sound-system; and such fanciful decorating elements as abstract murals, delicate glass tables, and colorful directors chairs. There's a light menu of sandwiches and sweets, plus a vast array of coffees. *16248 Main St., Guerneville,* ☎ *707/869–0201.*

$ Lalita's Mexican Cantina. This is one of the wildest restaurants in the area; it's aglow with Mexican tapestries, piñatas, colorful flashing lights, and a mix of authentic and hokey collectibles. There's live music many nights, and loud, lively lesbians, gays, and straights often yuk it up at the bar or in the dining room. The food is ordinary at best—green enchiladas, quesadillas, chili—but come for the atmosphere. *16225 Main St., Guerneville,* ☎ *707/869–3238.*

SLEEPS

San Francisco

No matter what your price range, San Francisco is a marvelous metropolis for accommodations, with luxurious, Old World–inspired lodgings on a par with New York; charming, small hotels rivaled only by those in New Orleans; and the best selection of gay-friendly B&Bs of any city in the country. The Kimpton Group, which owns a handful of hotels in Seattle and Portland, has about a dozen intimate, smartly done accommodations in San Francisco. Several of them, especially the ones downtown, have a strong gay following, as does the Joie de Vivre chain, a diverse collection of inns and hotels presided over by the gay wunderkind of hotel hospitality, Chip Conley.

If you insist on being within a short walk of the Castro, you'll need to check into one of the area's guest houses. Most of the city's best gay-popular options are downtown, close to Nob Hill and Union Square. Here you're a 10-minute cab ride from the Castro and an even shorter ride (or a manageable walk) from the nightclubs in SoMa; you're also close to many of the city's top attractions. Keep in mind that hotel rooms in San Francisco fill up quickly in summer and during holidays—book at least a couple of months ahead whenever possible.

For price ranges, *see* Chart A at the front of this guide.

Hotels

DOWNTOWN VICINITY

☆ The **Mandarin Oriental,** situated on the top 11 floors (38–48) of the city's third-tallest building, has rooms with sensational views. Even from your tub, a massive plate window allows you to watch the fog lift above the Golden Gate Bridge. Rooms are decorated with understated Asian colors and furnishings; although they're luxurious, they're not as ornate as the sort of rooms you'll find on Nob Hill. *222 Sansome St., ☎ 415/885–0999 or 800/622–0404. 158 rooms. $$$$*

☆ Not just your ordinary **Ritz-Carlton,** the San Francisco property is one of the top two or three urban hotels in America. Inside a gorgeous, neo-classic building (1920), guests enjoy an immense fitness center, two outstanding restaurants, and the Ritz bar, which has the country's largest collection of single-malt whiskeys. *600 Stockton St., ☎ 415/296–7465 or 800/241–3333. 336 rooms. $$$$*

☆ Renowned for its personal service and small but classy rooms, the exclusive **Campton Place** lies a short walking distance from SoMa nightlife. The Campton Place restaurant, which serves New American cuisine, is excellent. *340 Stockton St., ☎ 415/781–5555 or 800/426–3135. 107 rooms. $$$–$$$$*

☆ The whimsical **Hotel Monaco** has a distinctly Parisian flair. Rooms have faux-bamboo writing desks, high-back chairs, four-poster beds, and wallpaper striped in bold colors. *501 Geary St., ☎ 415/292–0100 or 800/214–4220. 201 rooms. $$$–$$$$*

☆ Nob Hill's **Huntington Hotel** is less famous than its impressive neighbors, but it remains one of the top three or four places to stay in San Francisco. While the discreet staff aims to please, it also respects your privacy. The large, elegant rooms reflect a variety of decorating styles. A great hotel, from top to bottom. *1075 California St., ☎ 415/474–5400 or 800/227–4683. 140 rooms. $$$–$$$$*

☆ From the outside, the **Hyatt Regency** appears a bit stark, especially considering all the other enticing accommodations in nearby Union Square. Inside, however, you'll find stylish rooms and one of the Hyatt's spectacular trademark atriums. A groovy revolving restaurant and bar sit atop this reliable hotel, which has long been a friend to the city's gay community. *5 Embarcadero Center, ☎ 415/788–1234 or 800/233–1234. 803 rooms. $$$–$$$$*

☆ The first-rate staff at the **Prescott** contributes to making it a superior hotel. Guests staying on the concierge level are treated to a nightly evening reception of drinks and pizza from Wolfgang Puck's top-rated Postrio restaurant downstairs. Rooms are a bit small but luxurious. *545 Post St., ☎ 415/563–0303 or 800/283–7322. 165 rooms. $$$–$$$$*

☆ On the eastern slope of Nob Hill is the opulent **Stanford Court.** This former apartment building has spacious rooms with all sorts of novel creature comforts—doesn't every traveler yearn for a heated towel rack? The hotel claims one of the top Italian eateries in the city, Fournou's Ovens. *905 California St., ☎ 415/989–3500 or 800/227–4736. 400 rooms. $$$–$$$$*

☆ Built in 1928, the **Sir Francis Drake** lies just a block from Union Square's fancy shops. At this immensely popular boutique hotel the rooms—which are a bit froufrou—are quaintly decorated with California colonial-style furniture. The doormen look somewhat silly in their garish beefeater costumes—you'll be tempted to tease them. *450 Powell St., ☎ 415/392–7755 or 800/227–5480. 417 rooms. $$$*

☆ From the outside, the majestic **Fairmont,** which served as the basis for Arthur Hailey's novel *Hotel,* is still one of the most impressive hotels in

America. Rooms, especially in the newer wing, have lost some of their luster, but many boast beautiful views of the skyline and bay. *950 Mason St.,* ☎ *415/772–5000 or 800/527–4727. 597 rooms. $$–$$$$*

Popular with gays, Europeans, and corporate types (in some cases all three), the **York Hotel,** a rather imposing gray-stone property, has rooms decorated with Mediterranean-inspired colors and furnishings. There's a popular cabaret, the Plush Room, on the premises. *940 Sutter St.,* ☎ *415/885–6800 or 800/808–9675. 96 rooms. $$–$$$$*

Artists and designers favor the postindustrial **Hotel Diva** with its weathered chrome facade. In the heart of Theater Row, the lodging has rooms done up in black and silver, with stark furnishings. *440 Geary St.,* ☎ *415/885–0200 or 800/553–1900. 107 rooms. $$–$$$*

Among the Kimpton Group properties, the **Triton Hotel** is the one that might as well have a pink-triangle welcome mat outside its front door— it markets very openly to the gay and lesbian community. The stylish and rather avant-garde rooms recall the Manhattan's Royalton. The eight suites were each decorated by a different celeb designer, from Joe Boxer to Suzan Briganti. *342 Grant Ave.,* ☎ *415/394–0500 or 800/433–6611. 140 rooms. $$–$$$*

The romantic **Vintage Court** frequently runs ads courting the gay community. This reasonably priced, first-rate hotel has the atmosphere of a Wine Country inn, and it serves complimentary wine in the stately lobby each evening. Even if you don't stay here, you'll want to try Masa's—the city's best French restaurant. *650 Bush St.,* ☎ *415/392–4666 or 800/654–1100. 107 rooms. $$–$$$*

The 1913 **Victorian Hotel** remains one of the best bargains downtown, and it's extremely gay-friendly. The clean and cheerful rooms are furnished with Victorian reproductions. It's a short walk from all the Folsom bars. *54 4th St.,* ☎ *415/986–4400 or 800/227–3804. 166 rooms. $*

WEST OF DOWNTOWN

Hotel Majestic is one of the most glamorous properties west of Van Ness Avenue. A typical room inside this Edwardian palace has a fireplace, a four-poster bed, and French Empire and 19th-century English antiques. *1500 Sutter St.,* ☎ *415/441–1100 or 800/869–8966. 57 rooms. $$–$$$$*

A moderately priced choice near Hayes Valley and Polk Street, the **Atherton Hotel** has a Mediterranean-inspired lobby and small but comfortable rooms. *685 Ellis St.,* ☎ *415/474–5720 or 800/474–5720. 75 rooms. $–$$*

The functional, '60s **Becks Motor Lodge** is a dull but cheap budget option in the Castro. *2222 Market St.,* ☎ *415/621–8212. 57 rooms. $–$$*

From the outside, the Joie de Vivre–operated **Holiday Lodge** looks like any other motel, but rooms here are the model of cleanliness, plus they have kitchenettes and in-room laundry facilities. Beds are against mirrored walls, creating the curious illusion that there's a second couple in bed with you. *1901 Van Ness Ave.,* ☎ *415/776–4469 or 800/367–8504. 77 rooms. $–$$*

A cult favorite, the **Phoenix** bills itself as the city's "creative crossroads." It's also the gateway to the Tenderloin, but don't hold that against it. This fabulous hotel has hosted many trendy celebrities, including John Waters (alive, gay), River Phoenix (deceased, gay icon), Keith Haring (deceased, gay), Faye Dunaway (alive, gay icon), and Keanu Reeves (no comment). This '50s motor lodge had become seedy until hotelier Chip Conley converted it into a chic but still affordable lodging, famous for its pool parties and the more than 250 works of art hanging throughout the property. Be sure to check out the lively Caribbean restaurant, Miss Pearl's Jam House. *601 Eddy St.,* ☎ *415/776–1380 or 800/248–9466. 44 rooms. $–$$*

⊞ The **Abigail** may be the Joie de Vivre chain's most conventional establishment—it's a fairly gay, inexpensive, Victorian-style hotel with small rooms brightened by down comforters and turn-of-the-century lithographs and paintings. Midway between the Castro and downtown, it has a terrific vegetarian restaurant, the Millennium, on the ground floor. *246 McAllister St., ☎ 415/861–9728 or 800/243–6510. 60 rooms. $*

⊞ Along with the similar Atherton across the street, the **Essex Hotel** is one of the more gay-popular, European-style hotels in the city. The main difference between the two properties is that rooms here are cheaper; their rooms are comparable. *684 Ellis St., ☎ 415/474–4664 or 800/453–7739. 100 rooms. $*

⊞ Because of its location in the center of Polk Street's seedy bar district, the **Leland Hotel** has a somewhat sketchy reputation—it's a base for many of the neighborhood's young, eager self-starters. Nevertheless, if you're in a pinch, the rooms are clean and the staff polite. *315 Polk St., ☎ 415/441–5141 or 800/258–4458. 104 rooms. $*

⊞ This **Travelodge** is close to Polk Street and a short bus ride, or a long walk, from the Castro. *1707 Market St., ☎ 415/621–6775 or 800/578–7878. 84 rooms. $*

⊞ If you don't mind bare-bones, musty accommodations, the **Twin Peaks** offers great daily and weekly rates; it also has a good location, a block from Castro Street. *2160 Market St., ☎ 415/621–9467. 60 rooms. $*

Guest Houses and Small Hotels

THE CASTRO AND VICINITY

⊞ **Inn on Castro** is easily the nicest, though costliest, accommodation in the Castro. The light and airy rooms in this refurbished 1896 home have contemporary furnishings. *321 Castro St., ☎ 415/861–0321. 8 rooms. Mixed gay male/lesbian. $$–$$$*

⊞ The striking, pink **Inn San Francisco,** an Italianate Victorian in Mission Hill, has pleasant rooms with feather beds and 19th-century antiques. You'll find a sunny patio on the roof, and out back there's a verdant garden with a redwood hot tub. Midway between the Castro and SoMa bars, this inn provides the perfect setting for a gay vacation. *943 S. Van Ness Ave., ☎ 415/641–0188 or 800/359–0913. 22 rooms. Mixed gay/straight. $$–$$$*

⊞ Don't assume that because the **Black Stallion** is a leather-and-Levi's-theme guest house that all the rooms are painted black and have beer stains on the floors (as most leather bars do). Everything here is clean and bright, and if this type of place is your scene, you'll love the owners and patrons. *635 Castro St., ☎ 415/863–0131. 8 rooms. Mostly gay male. $$*

⊞ Not everybody adores the gritty feel of the Mission District, at least as a place to stay, but a visit to the **Dolores Park Inn** may change your outlook. Antiques fill this 1870s Italianate Victorian, and there's a delightful, lush garden in the back. Good breakfast, too. *3641 17th St., ☎ 415/621–0482. 4 rooms. Mixed gay/straight. $–$$*

⊞ You're bound to love the sprightly **House O'Chicks,** a homey, century-old Victorian whose rooms have VCRs (note the owners' hot collection of "chicks" porn) and CD players. This is a good place to celebrate your anniversary. *On 15th St. (call for details), ☎ 415/861–9849. 3 rooms. Lesbian. $–$$*

⊞ One of the Castro's more modest, but nevertheless homey options, the **Castillo Inn** has refrigerators and microwaves in its rooms. *48 Henry St., ☎ 415/864–5111 or 800/865–5112. 4 rooms. Mostly gay male. $*

EAST OF VAN NESS AVENUE

⊞ Female executives often choose the sumptuous **Lambourne,** a cross between an urban spa and a state-of-the-art business center. Guests have access to personal computers and laser printers and can also opt for an herbal wrap in the on-site spa. Rooms have contemporary furnishings and kitchenettes. *725 Pine St., ☎ 415/433–2287 or 800/274–8466. 20 rooms. Mixed gay/straight. $$–$$$*

☒ **Pensione International Hotel** is one of the most affordable options in the city, especially if you're willing to forego a private bath. It's surprisingly cheerful for a budget choice, and breakfast is included. *875 Post St., ☎ 415/775–3344. 46 rooms. Mixed gay/straight. $*

WEST OF VAN NESS AVENUE

☒ The sumptuous **Anna's Three Bears** has suites with full kitchens, Edwardian antiques, fireplaces, and private decks. It's quite a spot, and especially nice for a longer stay, with clear city views from its Buena Vista Heights location. If you factor in the self-catering option, the weekly rates of $1,000 to $1,400 can be bargains. *114 Divisadero St., ☎ 415/255–3167 or 800/428–8559. 10 rooms. Mixed gay/straight. $$$–$$$$*

☒ **Archbishops Mansion** is a popular backdrop for gay weddings, and one of the most romantic properties in California. The Second Empire–style edifice was built in 1904 for the city's archbishop. Rooms are enormous, many with separate sitting rooms and fireplaces. *1000 Fulton St., ☎ 415/563–7872 or 800/543–5820. 15 rooms. Mixed gay/straight. $$–$$$$*

☒ A pair of excessively ornate Queen Anne Victorians in Pacific Heights, the **Mansions** complex is as entertaining as it is functional. Curios and art objects abound, and each room features a striking mural of the famous person for which it is named. Every night the owner presents a live magic show; this tradition has become legend around town. A headless ghost supposedly haunts the premises. *2220 Sacramento St., ☎ 415/929–9444 or 800/826–9398. 21 rooms. Mixed gay/straight. $$–$$$$*

☒ Close to Hayes Valley's great restaurants (there's even one on the premises), the courtly, old **Albion House Inn** has vintage wallpaper and art, and many antiques and collectibles. *135 Gough St., ☎ 415/621–0896 or 800/625–2466. 8 rooms. Mixed gay/straight. $$–$$$*

☒ **Red Victorian** is one of the strangest properties in town, a true theme hotel: The Summer of Love room has a tie-dyed canopy bed; other rooms have similarly odd decorating schemes and quirky touches. The place may bring back memories of bad acid trips, but it's clean and run by a friendly bunch. *1665 Haight St., ☎ 415/864–1978. 18 rooms. Mostly straight. $–$$*

☒ If you don't mind staying in suburban-feeling Sunset, the lesbian-owned **Bock's B&B** is an inexpensive Edwardian home with period-style furnishings. (Non-smokers only; two-night minimum.) *1448 Willard St., ☎ 415/664–6842. 3 rooms. Mixed gay/straight. $*

☒ For a safe, friendly place for women, try the **Carl Street Unicorn House** near Buena Vista Park. The two rooms share one bath, but that's the only drawback. It's a beautiful 1895 house, filled with owner Miriam Weber's many collectibles. *156 Carl St., ☎ 415/753–5194. 2 rooms. Mostly women; mixed lesbian/straight. $*

☒ **Metro Hotel** is not too far from the Castro, about a 10-minute walk north into Haight-Ashbury. Distinctive for its huge neon sign, the lodging attracts a funky crowd, and rooms are quite large and pleasant. *319 Divisadero St., ☎ 415/861–5364. 23 rooms. Mixed gay/straight. $*

The Russian River

For price ranges, *see* Chart B at the front of this guide.

☒ There aren't many full-scale resorts in the region, but the **Doubletree Hotel** in Santa Rosa is a pleasant 30-minute drive from Guerneville, gives you the privacy and anonymity that smaller properties sometimes can't and is perfectly gay-friendly. There's a large pool and a fitness center; rooms are spacious and have decks or balconies. *3555 Round Barn Blvd., Santa Rosa, ☎ 707/523–7555 or 800/222–8733. 245 rooms. $$$*

⌘ Set on 56, hilltop, tree-studded acres above the Russian River, **Huckleberry Springs** is a resort with four cottages, each with a private bath, a skylight, and a wood-burning stove. This highly secluded retreat is just a 10-minute drive from the bars and restaurants of Guerneville. The folks here serve a terrific full breakfast, too. *Monte Rio, ☎ 707/865–2683 or 800/822–2683. 4 cottages. Mixed gay/straight. $$$*

⌘ The **Highland Dell Inn** is one of the most charming properties in all of Wine Country. Modeled after the chalets of Germany's Black Forest, this 1906 inn has stained- and leaded-glass windows and a mix of Victorian and early 20th-century antiques in both the guest rooms and public areas, and a magnificent wooden chandelier. The full breakfast is elaborate and filling, and on Saturday night talented hosts Glenn Dixon (who bakes) and Anthony Patchett (who cooks) concoct a locally renowned prix-fixe dinner that's open to guests and, by reservation only, to the public. *21050 River Blvd., Monte Rio, ☎ 707/865–1759 or 800/767–1759. 10 rooms. Mixed gay/straight. $$–$$$$*

⌘ The most luxurious accommodations in Guerneville are those at the **Fern Grove,** which consists of the main inn and several craftsman-style cottages, all dating from the mid-'20s. Rooms have TVs and VCRs (there's an on-site film library), fireplaces, knotty pine–paneled walls, a mix of antiques and contemporary pieces, and private baths. This is not as much a party place as some of the others; it's ideal for couples. *16650 River Rd., Guerneville, ☎ 707/869–9083 or 800/347–9083. 20 rooms and cottages. Mixed gay/straight. $$–$$$*

⌘ **Fifes** is the quintessential rustic resort; it's also the largest gay compound in the region, with a popular restaurant and a bar that has country-western dancing. Cabins and cottages are simple (there are also nearly 100 campsites), but many have wood-burning stoves, TVs, and wet bars. You can walk through the property's 15 acres of colorful rose gardens and wooded trails. There are also many on-site facilities and activities, including volleyball, a private beach, a sprawling pool and sundeck, a small gym, and canoeing. *16467 River Rd., Guerneville, ☎ 707/869–0656 or 800/734–3371. 50 cabins. Mixed gay male/lesbian. $–$$$*

⌘ **Highland's** is a modest, low-key gay resort on 4 acres, a short walk from downtown. There's a pool and a hot tub (nudity is permitted), and some of the rooms have kitchens. *14000 Woodland Dr., Guerneville, ☎ 707/869–0333. 16 rooms. Mixed gay male/lesbian. $–$$*

⌘ Comprising a sprawling old country lodge and a 60-site tent-and-RV campground, the **Willows** sits right on the Russian River, nestled amid groves of pine and willow trees. Guest rooms in the lodge have rich dark-wood paneling, TVs, and VCRs; there's also a homey common room with a fireplace and a grand piano. You're free to use the Willows's paddle-boats and canoes or to laze along the beach or on the sundeck. An excellent value. *15905 River Rd., Guerneville, ☎ 707/869–2824 or 800/953–2828. 13 rooms. Mixed gay male/lesbian. $–$$*

⌘ The **Russian River Resort** (a.k.a. the Triple R) has a devoted following of guys, many of whom have been coming here for years. The motel-style rooms are small, clean, and affordable; on-site facilities include a piano and video bar, a pool, a sundeck, and a restaurant. The resort is within walking distance of downtown. *4th and Mill Sts., Guerneville, ☎ 707/869–0691 or 800/417–3767. 23 rooms. Mostly gay male. $*

SCENES

San Francisco

The quality of San Francisco's nightlife is a somewhat touchy subject. On the one hand, you'll hear people describing it as an older and fairly tired scene. On the other, you'll be reminded that the city may have more gay bars per capita than any other city in the world. Of course, if you think about it, these two views are not mutually exclusive. San Francisco does in fact have about 80 gay bars and only about 750,000 residents. New York City has fewer gay bars and about 10 times the population. However, be warned that quantity does not guarantee variety.

This city had a wild and crazy '70s, and a rough '80s. In particular, if you check out the bars along lower Polk Street and in the Tenderloin, you're going to see a lot of walking wounded.

About 50 of the city's gay bars are small and sleepy, catering mostly to old drunks. This doesn't mean that these places aren't fun, or that you can't meet people in them. It's just that . . . well, there are times when you could swear that the guy across the room is staring at you because he has the hots for you. So maybe you smile back at him—you know, with one eyebrow arched. And he keeps staring. So you're feeling a little bold tonight; you walk over to him and introduce yourself. And, still, he just keeps staring. So, finally, you give him a quick tap on the shoulder, just to see if anybody is in there. And crash! He falls off his bar stool.

Better spots are described below. Within this grouping you'll find just about every flavor of gay watering hole known to humanity: leather, guppie, piano bar, sports bar, Latino, Asian, African-American, warehouse disco, drag, strip club—you name it. Only a couple of quasi-lesbian bars exist, however, which does seem strange for such a dyky city. Making up for their absence, however, are several, weekly, roving girl parties and a number of women's performance spaces.

All in all, for a city its size, San Francisco does have a fairly impressive nightlife. You have to sort through a good number of places to find your ideal crowd, but somewhere in this city there's a bar stool with your name on it. Now all you have to do is try not to fall off it.

Bars and Small Clubs

THE CASTRO AND VICINITY

Badlands. This is a terrific place for both its outstanding, eclectic selection of tunes, which range from oldies to rock to disco, and for its famed collection of oddly monogrammed license plates. It's a little larger than some nearby bars, but it fills up quickly, especially on Sundays, when there can be a long line outside. It has a vaguely Southwestern theme—cattle skulls, chaps—plus two pool tables and many pinball machines. Chatty, handsome bartenders. *4121 18th St.,* ☎ *415/626–9320. Crowd: mostly male; ages 20s and 30s; lots of flannel and denim; cruisy, cute but unpretentious.*

The Café. This is the Castro's most—some would say only—happening dance club. It originated as a lesbian bar, but pretty soon all of the boys realized it's a much nicer space than most of their own clubs, so now it's pretty mixed. You enter up a flight of stairs; there are festive bars on two sides and a small dance floor in the middle. The walls are lined with big windows, and on one side there's a great little balcony overlooking Market, Castro, and 17th streets. The only annoying things about this place (in addition, some might say, to the presence of men): There are often long lines to get in, and at about 10 minutes to closing they start kicking everybody out with great urgency—pulling drinks out of customers' hands and herding people down the stairs. Seeing as some people can barely walk at this point, it would be nice to be ushered out gently. *2367 Market St., ☎ 415/861–3846. Crowd: mixed m/f; fairly young, professional, collegiate; has a little more attitude than it should have.*

Castro Station. In addition to seeing many Tom of Finland–type works on the walls, you'll find several odd objets d'art meant to pay homage to the bar's train-station theme. These items include an ersatz-stained glass locomotive and, behind the bar, a speeding, neon, diesel engine. Neat. It's a very chatty place—a mellow cruise bar with a local following. *456 Castro St., ☎ 415/626–7220. Crowd: mostly male; all ages; all races; zero attitude.*

Daddy's. If you're lucky, you'll catch this place on a night when they're screening *Planet of the Apes* reruns. Other times they show campy old films or sporting events. The crowd is a bit bearish, but mostly in a warm, fuzzy, intoxicated sort of way. There's a long, narrow, front room with a bar, a pool table, and pinball; off the back there's a deck. A couple of cats always seems to be roaming around. *440 Castro St., ☎ 415/621–8732. Crowd: 75/25 m/f; mostly fortysomething; lots of facial hair, chest hair, back hair; fairly butch but down-to-earth.*

Detour. This is the Castro's tried-and-true pickup bar. It's decorated with chain-link fencing and strobe lights, giving the place the feel of a warehouse disco—in fact, it's a very small bar. And there's precious little open space, which, of course, forces guys to brush up against one another. The pool table up front is constantly in use, apparently even when the bar is closed—a couple of years ago Falcon Studios filmed a porn flick on top of it. The scant blue lighting casts a forbidding, somewhat sexy glow on everyone. *2348 Market St., ☎ 415/861–6053. Crowd: male; mostly under 35; a sea of denim and white T-shirts; professional oglers.*

The Edge. This casual bar has an "edge of the universe" motif, with a glow-in-the-dark model of our solar system laid out against the ceiling—much like your bedroom might have looked when you were a child. This, and the free peanuts, are the bar's only distinguishing features. Nevertheless, there's always a substantial crowd. *4149 18th St., ☎ 415/863–4027. Crowd: mostly male; thirtysomething; on their way to or from other Castro bars.*

Harvey's. This popular Castro piano bar changed recently from the Elephant Walk to Harvey's; people still come as much to chat as to eat the so-so pub fare and to people-watch (try to grab a table by the big windows looking over the corner of 18th and Castro streets). In addition to the many candlelit tables, there's lots of seating at the bar, too. It's rather cutesy, in an informal way, and has dark green walls and vintage wallpaper. It remains to be seen whether Harvey's will attain its predecessor's tremendous level of popularity. *500 Castro St., ☎ 415/431–4278. Crowd: mixed gay/lesbian; all ages; friendly, low-key; not at all cruisy.*

Metro. It's hard to know what to make of this bar. Were it not for its mysteriously mobbed, Tuesday karaoke nights and its lovely balcony overlooking the fascinating intersection of Noe, Market, and 16th streets, nobody might venture in here. The weeknight, early-evening happy hour is popular too. Other times it's just neon-infused and dated-looking bar. *3600 16th St., ☎ 415/703–9750. Crowd: 65/35 m/f; diverse in age; mixed bag of queens and dykes; in every other way middle-of-the-road.*

Midnight Sun. This cruisy video bar is probably the safest bet for tourists hoping to find boys just like the ones back home. The midsize room has lots of video screens, big crowds, and popular dance music. On the TV screens, the bar shows music videos, campy movie clips, and fag favorites, such as *Ab Fab. 4067 18th St., ☎ 415/861–4186. Crowd: mostly* *male; young, clean-shaven; professional, like the boys at Alta Plaza but without high-paying jobs.*

Moby Dick. Famous for its huge tropical fish tank and its literary name, which almost begs you to go up to the first cute guy you meet, tell him your name, smile, and declare: ". . . but you, my friend, you may call me Ishmael." (By all means, try this yourself.) Basically, Moby Dick is a video bar with a pool table, pinball, and all of the usual diversions. Sometimes people refer to it unkindly by exchanging the word "Moby" with "Moldy." *4049 18th St., no ☎. Crowd: mostly male; thirtysomething; a bit sleazier but otherwise similar to the guys at the Midnight Sun.*

Pendulum. This is San Francisco's only African-American bar, although you'll see men of color at many of the other spots (except maybe those two lily-white bars in Pacific Heights). Furthermore, you'll see a lot of white guys here. Inside, the bar looks like a party room in a frat house, packed with a pretty rowdy, outgoing bunch. Cruisy bathroom. It's been around for more than 25 years. *4146 18th St., ☎ 415/863–4441. Crowd: mostly male; mostly African-American; all ages, all types; very friendly.*

Phoenix. At the Castro's oldest dance bar, the space is relatively small, with a bar up front and a tiny dance floor in back. You'll get dizzy with the abundance of disco balls, strobe lights, and I-beams—the accompanying music and videos are fun, if a little dated. Gets a very young crowd, so young that the Phoenix has become about the only club in the Castro to card everybody. *482 Castro St., ☎ 415/552–6827. Crowd: 85/15 m/f; either very young men of color or older men of no color.*

Twin Peaks. This was the first bar in the nation to have clear street-level windows, thereby allowing curious straight people to observe us up close, in our native environment. It opened in 1972, and just because it attracts many of the Castro's old-timers, bitchy young people often call it a "wrinkle bar," which is mean—but true. It's also called a "fern bar," although there are no ferns. In any case, it's a cheerful haunt with Tiffany-style lamps and a crowd that seems to know one another on a first-name basis. Its best attribute is the intimate interior balcony, where lovers who are coping (fighting) often go to process (break up). *401 Castro St., ☎ 415/864–9470. Crowd: mostly male; mostly ages 35 to 75; cordial; white-collar, a bit cliquey.*

Even sleepier than some of the sleepy places listed above are the **Men's Room** (3988 18th St., ☎ 415/861–1310), which, behind its striking, red cedar-shake exterior, has a long bar that's short on customers; and **Uncle Bert's** (4086 18th St., ☎ 415/431–8616), a chummy, slow-pace spot where they've been known to show televised golf on Saturday nights. Horny tramps shouldn't overlook the **Jackhammer** (290 Sanchez St., ☎ 415/252–0290), a serious, leather-oriented cruise bar that makes the Detour look like Sunday school.

POLK STREET

Cinch Saloon. Except for the music, which is culled from a rather hip collection of CDs behind the bar, this is a Wild West–themed bar—sort of as if Disney had created it, but with the help of a few queens. Memorable touches include a cigar store Indian to greet you at the front door, swinging doors, fake cacti, Navajo rugs, wagon wheels, and a bas-relief Western mural on one wall showing cowboys under a lipstick sunset. Other walls have silly photos and signs with such endearing epithets as: "If you ain't a cowboy you ain't shit" and "Spitting on the floors and walls is prohibited." If all this doesn't get you excited, check out the incredible drink specials: This may be the easiest place in town to get tanked for under $5. *1723 Polk St., ☎ 415/776–4162. Crowd: mostly male; mostly thirtysomething; fun-loving, rowdy.*

The Giraffe. The most underrated bar in San Francisco, which means, unfortunately, that it can be pretty quiet some nights. Although it's on lower Polk Street, near all the sleaze, it's the one area bar that draws a nice (but still kind of cruisy) guy-next-door crowd. It doubled in size in 1993 by taking over the space next-door; now there's a small dance floor and an additional area up front for chatting. The original section still contains a pubby, nicely decorated bar. Bits of giraffe paraphernalia are strewn about, including the odd photo and statue. The cute and incredibly outgoing bartenders wear white Oxford shirts with snazzy ties. Give this place a shot—many come just to meet their James Deans. *1131 Polk St.,* ☎ *415/474–1702. Crowd: 80/20 m/f; mostly 20s and 30s; mix of working-class and white-collar; slightly rough but congenial.*

Hunks/Reflections. Popular among locals for its Keno games, old video games, and pool table, this run-down bar has dreary maroon industrial carpeting that adds a certain flavor—or odor—to the place. The name is not especially reflective of either the clientele or the decor. *1160 Polk St.,* ☎ *415/771–6262. Crowd: male; local; old.*

N' Touch. A sleek, contemporary disco just north of where Polk begins to get slimy. It's the city's most popular hangout among gay Asian men. The narrow bar up front can get somewhat claustrophobic on busy nights. In back, the compact dance floor has excellent music. On Thursdays strippers perform before a packed house. For such a small place, this is a very hot disco. Fun for everybody, but especially enjoyable if the words *Pacific Rim* excite you. *1548 Polk St.,* ☎ *415/441–8413. Crowd: mostly male; mostly Asian; young, lively; lots of disco bunnies.*

Polk Gulch. Whew! This place is scary. Rumor has it that not one but *two* men featured on *America's Most Wanted* have been discovered hanging out at the ole Gulch. Nevertheless, if you want to understand the heart and soul of Polk Street over the past two decades, you should stop by. It's a simple-looking place, with tubes of neon snaking across the wall, as well as several mirrors and a few TV screens. A good place to perfect your deadly glare. *1100 Polk St.,* ☎ *415/771–2022. Crowd: male; mostly 30s and 40s; rough trade; drunk; hustlers.*

QT II (a.k.a. Quick Tricks). Decorated presumably in about 1979, the QT looks like a cross between Studio 54 and a ski lodge. White, pink, and chrome cubes cling to the wall above the bar, creating an almost three-dimensional effect reminiscent of a Sylvester album cover. Vertical strips of mirror and white-stucco alternate on the other walls. In the back a small, elevated stage features a diverse range of entertainment, from experimental jazz combos to strippers (amateur contests on Tuesdays are great fun). Several TV screens show vintage, music videos, and when there isn't live music, Top 40 classics are piped in. Never a dull moment. *1312 Polk St.,* ☎ *415/885–1114. Crowd: 85/15 m/f; diverse in age; bad hair, hair pieces; tourists seeking respite from their dreary hotel rooms at the nearby Leland Hotel; sloppy drunks; many hustlers and dirty old men.*

The Swallow. The gold nameplate outside the front door is a bit much—you'd think you'd stumbled upon the Union Club or something. This is, however, the classiest bar on Polk Street, well north of the shadier places. Inside you'll discover a long bar and plenty of table seating. Every night but Tuesday you can hear some of the community's best piano performers—mostly playing popular show tunes. *1750 Polk St.,* ☎ *415/775–4152. Crowd: 85/15 m/f; mostly 40s and up; friendly; lots of ascots and velvet blazers.*

If you're still up for more Polk exploring, try **Kimo's** (1351 Polk St., ☎ 415/885–4535), which marks the beginning of the seedy span of Polk Street and has a show lounge with tired drag acts; the **P. S. Bar** (1121 Polk St., ☎ 415/885–1448), a dreary piano lounge that's all mirrors, neon, and black-tile floor, and whose patrons, strange as it might sound, all seem to be named "John"; and the **Polk Rendezvous** (1303 Polk St., ☎ 415/673–7934), a creepy cocktail lounge—a good place to rendezvous with your bookie or your pimp.

SOMA

Eagle. The Sunday beer blast here is phenomenally popular. At other times this is one of the city's best leather bars—the guys here take the theme very seriously. There's even a great leather shop on the premises, one of the best you'll find anywhere. Sometimes the place gets dark and a bit cramped; in good weather you can amble out onto the heated, outdoor patio. Hmmm. These guys may not be so tough after all. *398 12th St., ☎ 415/626–0880. Crowd: male; leather, brawny, butch; big, rough, he-man central.*

Hole in the Wall Saloon. The self-proclaimed "Nasty Little Biker Bar" is aptly named—it's a hellish sliver of a place where they play hard rock music and the guys throw each other deadly looks. If you're lucky, a fight will break out during your visit. If you want to increase the odds of this happening, wear a polo shirt and plenty of cologne. The doors open at 6 AM—gentlemen, start your engines. Because this is such a strangely wonderful place, it seems destined to get overrun with curiosity seekers; this will probably take away some of its edge. Hopefully, though, it will remain scary forever. *289 8th St., ☎ 415/431–4695. Crowd: male; leather; drunk by noon.*

Julie's Supper Club. Although it's not a gay place per se, it has a big queer following. It serves good food with a '50s version of refined atmosphere. You'll find lots of pre-clubbers sipping cocktails—the martinis have attained cult status. *1123 Folsom St., ☎ 415/861–0707. Crowd: mostly straight.*

Stud. Yet another of the popular roving-party venues in SoMa. It's a tight and compact place with a narrow, crowded bar for dancing and several other bars and areas for mingling. The Stud has been hot for many years. On Thursdays the two best queer DJs in the Bay Area, Junkyard and Zanne, host Junk. These two women play everything from tribal dance music to Neil Diamond. It's a wild party, about two-thirds lesbian. At the Wednesday Trash Disco parties, you'll hear an array of disco classics and New Wave favorites. Other nights different styles of music, from funk to acid jazz, are played. *399 9th St., ☎ 415/863–6623. Crowd: depends on the theme, but tends to be young; low attitude, mixed genders, and multiracial.*

The seedy **Lonestar** (1354 Harrison St., ☎ 415/863–9999) is called an "ego bar" by some, and that's not because everybody here has a big ego. **My Place** (1225 Folsom St., ☎ 415/863–2329) is one of the leather bars in SoMa that still has a reputation for back-room activity. The city's major country-western dance venue, the **Rawhide II** (280 7th St., ☎ 415/621–1197) gets a mixed gay male and lesbian crowd. It has lodgelike decor—deer heads, cowboy memorabilia—and Nashville sounds.

ELSEWHERE

Alta Plaza. Most evenings, a sea of lawyers and stockbrokers flock to this oft-teased bar, usually referred to as the "Ultra Plastic." In any other town this guppie bar wouldn't seem so out of place, but San Francisco's gay community is not usually thought to be status-conscious—the sight of guys in Armani suits swarming around a cream color, varnished-wood bar is a real anomaly. If you want to see the place in full swing, come after work for happy hour. Dinner here in the American grill is quite good; consider stopping by for a meal. *2301 Fillmore St., ☎ 415/922–1444. Crowd: mostly male; young, professional; lots of designer duds; sugar daddies, and even some sugar babies.*

El Rio. On Sunday afternoons at this dive in the Mission, there's live salsa music and great food—it's one of the liveliest parties in the city. The rest of the time this hangout combines the best attributes of a disco, a pool hall, and a restaurant, attracting a mix of both gay and straight, local Latinos and others from all around town. The back patio provides a great place to hang out on warm days. *3158 Mission St., ☎ 415/282–3325. Crowd: totally mixed—straight, gay; male, female; Hispanic, African American, white; old, young.*

Esta Noche. A fixture in the Mission since the '70s, the city's main, queer Latin disco still rages. Many white, self-proclaimed "taco queens" can be found lurking around at all hours, as though shopping for imported spices at a Hispanic market. This sort of behavior *may* not bother the regulars; but if you act like an outsider, you're apt to be treated like one (in other words, be ignored). The crowd is rather young and insular, so don't be shy. It's a great place to dance, to watch the campy drag shows on Wednesday nights, and to make a lot of noise. *3079 16th St., ☎ 415/861–5757. Crowd: mostly male; mostly Hispanic; young, loud, raucous.*

Lion's Pub. This guppie bar has been a fixture in Pacific Heights for more than 25 years. It's well-known for its incredibly hunky and friendly bartenders—the owner seems to handpick on the basis of their brawn. Also famous is the toasty fieldstone fireplace in back. Your parents would be at home amid the clubby decor—Tiffany-style lamps and windows, faux-Corinthian columns, and faux-marble tables. It's the Alta Plaza's major competitor, but both bars draw a lot of the same guys. As the night progresses, it gets livelier. A women's night on Tuesday. *2062 Divisadero St., ☎ 415/567–6565. Crowd: mostly male; young to middle-age professionals, guppies; more relaxed than Alta Plaza.*

Marlena's. The only bar in Hayes Valley, Marlena's is one of those friendly spots where everyone knows everyone else. After work there's often a good crowd, and outsiders are usually welcomed warmly. The decor is of the gay-tacky genre—lots of pink and a jukebox that spins old pop tunes. *488 Hayes St., ☎ 415/864–6672. Crowd: 60/40 m/f; mixed racially, mixed ages.*

Mint. At this terrific bar, it's easy to hear people talk. Regulars and tourists are friendly to one another, and it's also clean and well-lighted. And karaoke is on just about every night of the week—San Francisco appears to be obsessed with this phenomenon. The Mint has been up-and-running and gay since World War II. What did they do here all those years before karaoke? *1942 Market St., ☎ 415/626–4726. Crowd: 75/25 m/f; all ages; some suits; laid-back, friendly; some talented singers, some untalented singers.*

Company (1319 California St., ☎ 415/928–0677) is on the western slope of Nob Hill, making it a safe bet for gays staying at the Fairmont and too lazy to descend 400 feet to someplace decent. Another downtown option, the **Gate** (1093 Pine St., ☎ 415/885–2852) gets a pretty local, cliquey crowd. The **Motherlode** (1002 Post St., ☎ 415/928–6006), the city's main transgender club, lies in a rough part of the Tenderloin. In Haight-Ashbury, your only gay option is **Trax** (1437 Haight St., ☎ 415/864–4213), a casual neighborhood bar with a nice CD jukebox; it attracts a pleasant crowd.

Finocchio's (506 Broadway, ☎ 415/982–9388), in North Beach, has been celebrated since 1936 among straights and gays for its revue of female impersonators. The Mission's **Theater Rhinoceros** (2926 16th St., ☎ 415/861–5079) is the area's official queer performance space and always has plays and art pieces going on. North Beach's trendy celebrity hangout, **Tosca** (242 Columbus Ave., ☎ 415/391–1244), is a straight bar that's extremely gay-friendly—how could it not be with a jukebox that plays only opera selections?

Movable Fetes

On Saturday nights, the city's wildest, must-do parties are held at both **1015 Folsom Street** and nearby **177 Townsend Street.** The names and styles of parties change enough so that it's not worth mentioning them here, but you can always count on crowds that are huge, young, and wired— mostly male but some lesbians, and some straights. At 1015 Folsom there are three dance floors, a number of lounges, and a great rooftop patio. Set in an enormous, old warehouse, 177 Townsend has the larger dance space.

The Box (715 Harrison St., ☎ 415/647–8258), a multilevel disco in SoMa, packs them in for its Thursday night, funk-and-soul dance party. **Club Because** (9th and Howard, ☎ 415/765–7676) is a major Friday night party with '80s retro, funk, and industrial music; it's big with men and women.

Women's Bars and Hangouts

Wild Side West. The owners of this bar don't like to think of it as a lesbian bar, but come see for yourself: There are an awful lot of them in here. Whatever the makeup, it's way up in Bernal Heights, a 30-minute uphill walk from the Mission and not too convenient to anything. This small place has exposed brick, a pool table, chandeliers, and a long bar with a stained-glass window at the end. *424 Cortland St., ☎ 415/647– 3099. Crowd: 75/25 f/m; lots of straight local types.*

At **Osento Baths** (955 Valencia St., ☎ 415/282–6333), a soothing women's bathhouse in the Mission, sexual activity is forbidden—it's a relaxing spot to shake off a tense day. **Eros** (*see* Sleaze, *below*) is a sex club that holds lesbian nights.

Club Confidential (Embassy Lounge, 600 Polk St., ☎ 415/885–0842) is a monthly, dykes-dressed-as-guys party, which is usually packed and features a few cabaret performers. Very *Victor/Victoria.* **Faster Pussycat!** (Wed., ☎ 415/561–9771) has most recently been held at the otherwise straight **Covered Wagon Saloon** (911 Folsom St.). This lesbian party always features a live "grrrl" band, and the place usually rocks. Also at the Covered Wagon, **Muffdive** (Sun., ☎ 415/974–1585), one of the most popular dyke dance parties in town, is DJ'd by the famous women of Junk (*see* Stud, *above*).

The nonalcoholic **Josie's Juice Bar** (3583 16th St., ☎ 415/861–7933) actually gets a mix of men and women, but it showcases performances by some of the nation's best-known lesbian comics and music acts.

On the Wild Side

Sex clubs and private parties, as well as video arcades and porn shops, are popular and widely available in San Francisco. The most popular clubs are **Blow Buddies** (933 Harrison St., ☎ 415/863–4323), **Eros** (2051 Market St., ☎ 415/864–3767), and the **Night Gallery** (1365 Folsom St., ☎ 415/255–1852).

One of the most famous adult theaters in the country is the **Campus** (220 Jones St., ☎ 415/673–3384), in the heart of the Tenderloin. Tickets are a bit steep at $12, but they're good for the whole day (in-out privileges). Several other such theaters and video arcades are in the neighborhood. There are a couple of others in SoMa.

The Russian River

For a secluded community in the sticks, Guerneville offers a lively nightlife scene. Nonguests are perfectly welcome to party at some of the resorts, most notably **Fifes** (16467 River Rd., ☎ 707/869–0656), which has a country-western dance hall and piano and patio bars, and the **Triple R** (Russian River Resort, 4th and Mill Sts., ☎ 707/869–0691), which has a small video and piano bar with a pool table and a fireplace.

There are a couple of friendly local bars with mostly gay followings, including **Molly's Country Club** (14120 Old Cazadero Rd., ☎ 707/869–0511), which has country-western dancing and music, and the **Rainbow Cattle Company** (16220 Main St., ☎ 707/869–0206), which was once a straight gambling hall and is now a wild saloon that draws a pretty rowdy, butch gang of gay guys and some women.

The place to party, however, is the **Jungle** (16135 Main St., ☎ 707/869–1400), a movie theater that's almost as big and cosmopolitan as some of the warehouse discos in San Francisco's SoMa District. There are a few levels: The uppermost one has a pool table, the main level has a bar and lots of seating and standing room, and the lower one is a large dance floor spinning the latest house and hip hop. On Saturdays, especially in summer, big-name DJs from San Francisco guest host the Jungle's parties. The crowd here is a cross-section of all the kinds of people who visit the Russian River; just about everyone fits in.

Bars stop serving booze at 2, but many of them stay open later for dancing and hanging out. Both women and men are welcome at all of these places, although the Triple R and Rainbow Cattle Company are mostly male.

THE LITTLE BLACK BOOK

At Your Fingertips

AIDS Hotline: ☎ 415/863–2437. **AIDS Nightline:** ☎ 415/434–2437. **Community United Against Violence Hotline:** ☎ 415/333–4357. **Deaf Gay and Lesbian Center:** ☎ 415/255–0700, TTY: 415/255–9797. **Gay and Lesbian Helpline:** ☎ 415/772–4357. **Lyon-Martin Women's Health Services:** ☎ 415/565–7667. **Russian River Visitors Center:** Box 255, 14034 Armstrong Woods Rd., Guerneville, CA 95446, ☎ 707/869–9212. **San Francisco Convention and Visitors Bureau:** 201 3rd St., Suite 900, 94103, ☎ 415/974–6900. **"What's Up" Hotline for African American Lesbians:** ☎ 510/835–6126. **Women's Building** (a lesbian resource center): ☎ 415/431–1180.

Gay Media

The two most popular gay newspapers are the weekly *Bay Area Reporter* (☎ 415/861–5019) and the biweekly *San Francisco Bay Times* (☎ 415/227–0800). Of the two, the *Bay Times* has the most in-depth coverage, and speaks best to both lesbians and gay men, as well as to racial minorities. The monthly newspaper *Icon* (☎ 415/282–0942) serves as the best resource for lesbians.

The biweekly *Frontiers* San Francisco (☎ 415/487–6000) focuses mostly on entertainment and features stories. *Odyssey* (☎ 415/621–6514) is a terribly handy, biweekly fag rag with detailed boys' and girls' club information and lots of fun dish. *Q San Francisco* (☎ 800/999–9718) is a flashy bimonthly gay news and entertainment magazine, providing plenty of bar, restaurant, and arts coverage.

Both the *Bay Guardian* (☎ 415/255–3100) and the *San Francisco Weekly* (☎ , 415/541–0700) are valuable, free, alternative papers with fine performing-arts listings and interesting, left-of-center political commentary.

We The People (453 Stony Point Rd., Suite 166, Santa Rosa, 95491, no ☎) is the gay-and-lesbian monthly newspaper serving the Russian River and Wine Country.

BOOKSTORES

A Different Light Bookstore (489 Castro St., ☎ 415/431–0891) is the city's major lesbigay bookstore, and in many ways its unofficial welcoming center to gays. **Modern Times** (888 Valencia St., ☎ 415/282–9246) carries a strong selection of left-leaning texts, many of them relevant to lesbian and gay studies. If you're in Oakland, check out **Mama Bears** (6536 Telegraph Ave., ☎ 510/428–9684), the East Bay's best source of feminist and lesbian books.

Most mainstream bookstores in San Francisco have excellent lesbigay departments. A few of the more interesting spots include **City Lights** (261 Columbus Ave., ☎ 415/362–8193), which is owned by poet Lawrence Ferlinghetti and has long been associated with the Beat Generation; **Gaia Bookstore** (1400 Shattuck Ave., Berkeley, ☎ 510/548–4172), the region's foremost source of New Age titles; and **McDonald's Book Shop** (48 Turk St., ☎ 415/673–2235), one of the largest used bookstores in the country—a crazy, haphazard place with enough stacks of books and piles of magazines to keep you browsing for days.

Body and Fitness

Gay gyms are easy to find all around town. Some of the most popular include **The Muscle System** (364 Hayes St., ☎ 415/863–4701; also 2275 Market St., ☎ 415/863–4700), whose two locations draw scads of pretty buff boys; the coed **Market Street Gym** (2301 Market St., ☎ 415/626–4488), one of the most crowded and probably gayest gym in the city; the snazzy **Pacific Heights Health Club** (2356 Pine St., ☎ 415/563–6694), with separate facilities for both gay men and, regardless of their sexual orientation, women; and the **Women's Training Center** (2164 Market St., ☎ 415/864–6835), a smaller gym that's popular with both dykes and straight women, offering personal training and helpful service.

25 *Out in Santa Fe and Taos*

IF YOU WERE A LESBIAN HEADED to New Mexico about 15 years ago, you probably went to Taos; if you were a gay man, you went to Santa Fe. That these lines have blurred gradually over the years probably says more about the changing dynamic between gay men and lesbians more than the one between Taos and Santa Fe. If you're unfamiliar with New Mexico, you might be tempted to lump the two communities together: Both are set in the high desert, popular with New Agers and alternative thinkers, revered by artists and painters, notable for skiing and hiking, littered with great Southwestern restaurants, abundant with shops and galleries, and made up of a tricultural Hispanic, Native American, and Anglo population.

Taos has traditionally been strongest with New Agers, outdoors enthusiasts, hippies, and those without the funding to ensure a good time in Santa Fe, which is stronger in high-end shopping and gallery going, dining, and other cosmopolitan endeavors. Taos is perfect if you have an insatiable frontier spirit; Santa Fe is perfect if you have an insatiable frontier spirit *and* a weakness for espresso and European sports cars.

Earlier in this century, Santa Fe was a place where wealthy families sent their homosexual sons to dabble in the arts, to write, and, ideally, to stay as far from proper society as possible. Some of the moves here were self-imposed, others externally motivated, but for most gay men during this time, Santa Fe represented a cross between a gay summer camp and Devil's Island. Of course, being "banished" to Santa Fe hardly entailed making a heaven of hell; early residents discovered a splendid climate, magnificent natural scenery, miles of uninterrupted seclusion—in short, a natural artist's studio.

Today, few dilettantes settle in Santa Fe. Unless you've acquired a great deal of money pursuing some other endeavor, you'll need to excel at your craft to survive here. Real estate is expensive, and the arts community is fiercely competitive. Some of the world's premier photographers, painters, and sculptors live here.

"The City Different," as Santa Fe is sometimes called, means many things to many people, but it's not one of America's truly gay resorts. Because, for some people, sexual orientation has long been a matter of unconditional privacy, and Santa Fe has been a haven of privacy seekers, the idea that the city be called *gay*—the way that Palm Springs and Key West are—curdles the blood of some gay locals.

A desire for privacy and anonymity, plus the belief that you can be an innkeeper or a painter who happens to be gay as opposed to a gay innkeeper or gay painter, motivates many Santa Feans to distance themselves from their sexual orientation. People tend to move here to be themselves, to escape society's mores, to celebrate their identity not as part of a particular community but as an individual.

What one local lesbian described as the occasional flare-up in Santa Fe of internalized homophobia, another resident defended as a need to protect financial interests. Where Palm Springs has such a gay identity that many businesses can survive catering exclusively to gays and lesbians, Santa Fe's high cost of living and dependence upon mainstream tourism prevent most gay-specific businesses from surviving. The city's only gay disco, the Edge, went "straight" in April 1995 because the owners weren't making enough money. A restaurant could never survive by marketing itself primarily to gays and lesbians. And although a couple of gay guest houses have opened on the outskirts of town, no downtown B&Bs are, or wish to be thought of as, predominantly gay. In fact, one gay-owned B&B wished so strongly not to encourage patronage by the gay community that it refused to be reviewed in this book—even with the assurance that their clientele would be described as primarily straight (because it is) and the owners would not be mentioned.

As with any paradise, there is considerable debate in Santa Fe as to how to keep this city of 60,000 both a desirable home and a popular destination for years to come. The issue of gay tourism, which may be thought to affect the appeal of Santa Fe to straights, throws an especially controversial kink into the equation. That said, Santa Fe had its first lesbian, gay, and bisexual film festival in 1995. It's hard to imagine that the new gay disco, which opened in the fall of 1995, won't survive.

If Santa Fe is "The City Different," you might nickname Taos "The City Indifferent." Nobody seems as concerned here about social and political issues, whether they involve race, religion, or sexual orientation. A gay pride rally was staged on the Plaza here a few years ago. Several gay men and lesbians stood up and shared their stories. Nobody protested. Nobody objected. Nobody cared. Tolerance and diversity are cherished but rarely articulated; Taoseños promote individualism by leaving each other alone.

Life is slow in Taos. If you catch lunch at the Northtown Restaurant— an authentic local luncheonette—you'll see a town council member mingling with her daughter's kindergarten teacher who's lunching with the sculptor from Valdez whose booth is behind the realtor who sold him his studio. Everybody knows everybody. More important, in such a small community, everyone is linked by some matter of commerce or socializing. In many respects, Taos is just a small town with beautiful mountains.

It's less costly here than in Santa Fe, but economics rarely inform people's decisions to choose one city over the other. Those who chose Taos probably saw Santa Fe as a zoo: overcrowded, fraught with tension among the Native Americans, the Hispanics, and the Anglos and between the tourists and the locals; possessing a disconcerting level of politicking and bickering. They felt that homes were too close together, that overcrowding was imminent, that they were more likely to be hit up for change (which does happen, but far less often than in most American cities).

In reality, Taos is not free of any of these problems; it's simply several years behind Santa Fe in growth. Furthermore, the quality of life in both towns still compares favorably with that of many towns in America. Santa Feans are less critical of Taos; they can't understand what all the fuss is about. Taos is just fine, they offer, if you're into that whole hippie scene— stringing beads, doing drugs, baking bread—it's like a commune. Most

Santa Feans could never imagine living in Taos, and vice versa. These rival views are almost always offered tongue-in-cheek, but make no mistake, Taoseños and Santa Feans do perceive themselves differently.

In Taos there is a stronger awareness that artisans create in order to support themselves—often barely. Your B&B may share the street with other traditional pueblo homes as well as a few trailers and mobile homes, and many backyards contain chicken coops or bean fields. Attempts to introduce zoning have failed, mostly because the older generations of Hispanics and Native Americans see zoning as a controlling device employed by the Anglos. The intention of such proposals, in fact, has been to curb the development of strip malls, condo complexes, and fast-food restaurants—not to impinge upon Taos's tradition of using your home as a small farm or a crafts studio. In a land that has been continuously occupied for at least the past 1,000 years, change comes slowly.

Most tourists identify more with one city than the other, but if you're visiting for the first time, try to spend some time in each. Can Santa Fe find a way to balance its reliance on tourism with the interests of its residents? Can Taos remain unsullied by growth and technology? Hard to say. For now, both communities represent two slightly similar but stubbornly opposing visions of paradise.

THE LAY OF THE LAND

Santa Fe

Nearly 400 years ago, Santa Fe's small, glorious, tree-shaded **Plaza** was where settlers held their military and religious ceremonies; today it's a good spot to catch your breath between shopping and museum hopping. At the northern end of the Plaza is the **Palace of Governors,** the oldest public building in the country, which now houses the main branch of the **Museum of New Mexico,** a state system that includes four museums in Santa Fe: the **History Museum** (W. Palace Ave., ☎ 505/827–6474) is within the walls of the Palace; the adjacent **Museum of Fine Arts** (107 W. Palace Ave., ☎ 505/827–4455), which concentrates on Southwestern, Mexican, and Native American art by masters ranging from Georgia O'Keeffe to Diego Rivera; the **Museum of International Folk Art** (706 Camino Lejo, ☎ 505/827–6350), which is a couple miles south of the Plaza on the Old Santa Fe Trail and contains an exhaustive collection of handmade crafts and art spanning several centuries and regions of the world; and, next door to that, the **Museum of Indian Arts and Culture** (710 Camino Lejo, ☎ 505/827–6344), which documents the history and art of the area's Pueblo, Navajo, and Apache. Also in this neighborhood, behind the Museum of International Folk Art, is an art museum of Native American pieces, the **Wheelwright Museum of the American Indian** (704 Camino Lejo, ☎ 505/982–4636).

As you wander out from the Plaza, you'll pass through a maze of narrow streets, mostly lined with boutiques and upscale chain shops, restaurants, and hotels. It feels and looks a bit like a Southwestern village as envisioned by planners of Disney's Epcot Center. Buildings are not allowed to exceed five stories, and the architecture is always consistent with the pueblo style. Santa Fe's 125 galleries and many sophisticated specialty stores outshine those you'll find in Taos.

In addition to shops, you'll note several historic churches, including the French Romanesque **Cathedral of St. Francis** (131 Cathedral Pl., ☎ 505/982–5619), founded by the city's first archbishop, Jean Baptiste Lamy, who is the subject of Willa Cather's novel, *Death Comes for the Arch-*

bishop. Also try to catch a glimpse of the unusual, Zia Indian-inspired **State Capitol building** (Old Santa Fe Trail and Paseo de Peralta, ☏ 505/986–4589), a vast round structure designed to represent the Circle of Life.

The Western border of the downtown commercial area is **Guadalupe Street,** once the terminus of the 1,500-mile trade route, El Camino Real, which extended all the way from Mexico City. Just off this street is the historic **Old Railroad Depot,** the terminus of the famed Atchinson, Topeka, and Santa Fe Railroad. This neighborhood isn't quite the trade center it used to be, but the adjacent turn-of-the-century freight warehouse, the **Sanbusco Market Center,** has been converted into galleries, shops, and restaurants, and a popular farmers' market is held in the parking lot Monday through Saturday, from June through October. Stop by for fresh veggies, herbs, wreaths, and juicy watermelons.

About 7 miles north of town on U.S. 84/285 are two attractions that have nothing to do with each other but that nevertheless attract many of the same followers: **Trader Jack's Flea Market** (no ☏) and the **Santa Fe Opera** (☏ 505/986–5900). The market, which is open dawn to dusk from Friday to Sunday, March through November, has incredible bargains and stunning views of the desert beyond it. A favorite custom is to browse the 12 acres of wares, then stop by the nearby Tesuque Village Market afterward for lunch. The world-class opera, founded in 1957, is set inside a dramatic 1,200-seat, open-air amphitheater built on a hillside overlooking miles of mesas and mountains. Its season is only July and August, and good tickets can be tough to come by, so call as far ahead as possible.

Ten Thousand Waves (Hyde Park Rd., ☏ 505/982–9304) is a Japanese-style spa just 4 miles from town. Here you can take advantage of the private and communal hot tubs and get facials, salt glows, herbal wraps, and massages. This is an extremely gay-friendly facility, popular with everybody.

Taos

Taos is snuggled in at the base of the Sangre de Cristo range, the southernmost extension of the Continental Divide, which splits Colorado, to the north. Looming almost directly above town is 13,161-foot Wheeler Peak, the tallest in the state. To the west, a flat mesa, interrupted only by the sharp gorge of the Rio Grande River, extends for miles before giving way gradually to gentle mountains. To the north, east, and south, lush aspen- and piñon-coated slopes rise precipitously from the plain.

As in Santa Fe, activity in Taos centers around the **Plaza,** in this case a smaller, dustier, but more personable plot of grass surrounded by galleries and shops. Anywhere within a few hundred yards of the Plaza are lanes of more shops, galleries, and restaurants—most of them hawking Native American and Southwestern wares and fares. Though Taos has been rapidly commercialized, the shopping is generally of high caliber. It is no longer, however, much less expensive than Santa Fe. If there's any difference between the two, it's that these days you're apt to find many pieces in Santa Fe that aren't necessarily native to the region. Taos, on the other hand, is where generations of crafts makers still weave or whittle together in the same studio; here you're find less well known though no less promising artists with galleries of their own. The **Taos Art Association** (☏ 505/758–2052) has information on most of the galleries in town.

Also near the Plaza you'll find the town's two historic hotels: the handsome **Taos Inn,** whose lobby bar is the perfect place for afternoon refreshments, and the more ragged **La Fonda de Taos Hotel.** Inside La Fonda's manager's office is perhaps the most disappointing but fascinating "peep show" in America: A nominal entry fee allows you to survey D. H. Lawrence's erotic paintings, whose racy content (by Victorian standards) caused Britain to ban them. Lawrence clearly had a better grasp of the pen than the palette. Much is made of the great poet-novelist's association with Taos; in fact, he spent parts of only three years here in the mid '20s. This was toward the end of his life, when he was a frequent guest of noted arts patroness Mabel Dodge Luhan. He, his wife Frieda, and their friend, the literary doyenne Lady Dorothy Brett, lived just north of Taos at Kiowa Ranch. It's now called **D. H. Lawrence Ranch,** though he never owned it. Several years after Lawrence's death in France in 1930, Frieda had his ashes buried on the ranch's property, in front of a small memorial shrine. Though the buildings at the ranch are owned by the University of New Mexico and not open to the public, you can visit the shrine (Rte. 522, 15 mi north of the Plaza, ☎ 505/776–2245).

Near the Plaza is the **Kit Carson Home and Museum** (Kit Carson Rd., ☎ 505/758–0505), the 12-room home of the mountain man who defended Taos from Confederate sympathizers during the Civil War. Just north of the Plaza is one of the town's better-kept secrets, the **Firehouse Collection** (323 Placitas Rd., ☎ 505/758–3386), an exhibit inside the Volunteer Fire Department of more than 100 paintings by Taos masters. A couple blocks south of the Plaza are more collections of art from the early Taos colony: the **Blumenschein Home** (222 Ledoux St., ☎ 505/758–0505) and the **Harwood Foundation Museum** (238 Ledoux St., ☎ 505/758–9826).

The most engrossing museum in Taos is reached by taking a left at the Texaco gas station just before the blinking light at the intersection of highways 522, 64, and 150, as you drive north from the city. The **Millicent Rogers Museum** (☎ 505/758–2462) is the legacy of the eponymous Standard Oil heiress, an avid collector of Native American and Hispanic art. Within the walls of her striking pueblo home are more than 5,000 pieces—not just paintings but kachina dolls, rugs, jewelry, and local crafts as well.

The section of town south of the Plaza, centered at the intersection of Route 68 and Ranchitos Road, is called **Ranchos de Taos.** The town's Spanish roots can be traced through the area's homes and its dramatic **San Francisco de Asis Church.** A few miles west on Ranchitos Road (Rte. 240) is **La Hacienda de Don Antonio Severino Martinez** (☎ 505/758–1000), a massive 21-room adobe residence. The fortlike building on the banks of the Rio Pueblo served as the Martinez family's home and as a community refuge against raids by the original inhabitants of the region, the Comanche and Apache. The house has been fully restored and changing exhibits and demonstrations now chronicle the lifestyle of the Spanish Colonial era.

Three miles north of town is Taos's most famous attraction, the **Taos Pueblo** (☎ 505/758–9593), the center of a 95,000-acre complex that is now the full-time home of roughly 2,000 Native Americans. The largest multistory pueblo structure in the country, it is actually divided by a creek into two structures, each a seemingly haphazard arrangement of mud-and-straw adobe rectangles situated atop one another. It is believed that the pueblo has housed Taos-Tiwa Indians for as many as 1,000 years.

Just west of town on U.S. 64 is a spectacular photo op, the majestic **Rio Grande Gorge Bridge,** which, at 650 feet above the river, is the second-highest suspension bridge in the country. The views from the observation platforms along the bridge's length are breathtaking, though many visitors have reported feeling more queasy than elated.

The Outdoors

After gallery scouring and museum hopping, the leading activities in Taos and, to a lesser extent, Santa Fe, are pursued outdoors. The **Taos Outdoor Recreation Association** (☎ 505/758–3873 or 800/732–8267) and **Bureau of Land Management** (☎ 505/758–8851) have plenty of information on places to go and outfitters to contact. Hiking, cycling, horseback riding, llama trekking, snowmobiling, cross-country skiing, and white-water rafting are among the most popular options.

Taos has five downhill skiing facilities within a two-hour drive. Even if you're not a skier, try to make the picturesque 20-mile drive from town up to **Taos Ski Valley** (☎ 505/776–2291), one of the world's premier resorts; there are several restaurants and bars up here, and it's a good place to people-watch. Less spectacular but popular locally is the **Santa Fe Ski Area** (☎ 505/982–4429).

There's a soothing natural **hot springs resort** north of town along the Rio Grande. It's a perfect setting for relaxing muscles you've strained while skiing or hiking; it's not gay-oriented, per se, but neither is it an unlikely spot to meet other gays and lesbians. The springs are near the village of Honda Arroyo, along a dirt road off Route 522, but to get here you'll need directions, which almost any local can give you.

The High Road to Taos

Though the main road between Santa Fe and Taos, Route 68, is still scenic, the slightly slower excursion through the higher, easterly elevations and dusty Hispanic villages is an enchanting route if you have the time. Take U.S. 84/285 north 12 miles. Turn right onto Route 503 and head to the village of **Chimayo,** famed for its weaving—be sure to check out **Ortega's Weaving Shop** (junction of County Road 98 and NM 76, ☎ 505/351–4215). At this point, just a little more than 15 miles north of Santa Fe, you can stand along the roadside and see nothing but sagebrush-covered desert hills for miles. In Chimayo, turn left onto NM 76 and follow it toward the tiny village **Cordova,** which employs no fewer than two dozen wood carvers. Continue on NM 76 through the farming community of **Truchas,** which you may recognize as the town in which Robert Redford filmed *The Milagro Beanfield War*. Continue through the equally picturesque towns of **Trampas, Ojo Sarco,** and **Charmisal,** turn right onto Route 75 at **Peñasco,** continue to Route 518, onto which you turn left and drive through about 30 miles of Kit Carson National Forest on through Taos. The whole trip takes up to two hours without stops.

Day Trips from Santa Fe and Taos

The entire northern half of the state is within a three- to four-hour drive of the Santa Fe/Taos region. If you're here for a week, it's worth spending one day venturing to any of the places named below. The chamber of commerce in Taos and the convention and visitors bureau in Santa Fe can both give you detailed information.

One short trek is to **Ojo Caliente Mineral Springs,** about an hour from either Santa Fe or Taos (from Taos go north on U.S. 64 then south on U.S. 84/285; from Santa Fe go north on Route 68 to U.S. 84/285 until you reach Ojo Caliente; ☎ 505/583–2233). Here you can lounge in private or public springs, get a massage, and while away the better part of an afternoon. Just northwest of Taos, the **Wild Rivers Recreation Area** (take Rte. 522 past Questa; turn left onto Rte. 378) is set at the confluence of the Rio Grande and Red rivers; it's the deepest point of the Rio

Grande Gorge. There are several (fairly challenging) hiking trails down to the river, where you'll find hot springs and bunches of picnic tables along the rim of the gorge.

The drive up to Questa marks the beginning of a breathtaking 84-mile scenic drive, the **Enchanted Circle,** which passes through the villages of Red River, Eagle Nest, and Angel Fire. Off this loop are several other possible detours, including a drive along the **Valle Vidal Loop,** which leads through the Ski Rio resort and into Kit Carson National Forest's Valle Vidal sector, a 100,000-acre tract of wilderness in which elk, wild turkey, and black bear, thrive.

WHEN TO GO

Santa Fe and Taos are both at points where a flat desert mesa meets the Sangre de Cristo Mountains; the resultant climate is one that can be as severe in winter as that of the Colorado Rockies and as parched in summer as that of Mexico. Northern New Mexico has four distinct seasons. In summer, even on days when the temperature reaches 100°F, nights can be cool enough to require a light jacket—it's the most popular time to visit, and, especially in July and August in Santa Fe, hotel rates are among the highest in the nation. Winter is by no means a down time, however. It snows constantly in the mountains, and though it snows often in Taos and Santa Fe, the afternoon sun usually pushes temperatures into the upper 30s. Ski season runs from about Thanksgiving through early April. Fall and spring are beautiful, slightly less crowded and less expensive; there's never a significant shoulder season, but April and November are the quietest. January, after the holiday rush has died, offers the best lift-ticket prices at the slopes, lodgings in the ski areas are slashed in summer, and August is the monsoon season—a great time to photograph rainbows.

GETTING THERE

There are no commercial airports in Santa Fe or Taos. You must fly to Albuquerque, where you can rent a car and drive the hour to Santa Fe, and an additional hour to Taos. From the airport, frequent **Greyhound** shuttle service is available to Santa Fe and Taos, too.

GETTING AROUND

In either town, you can tour the areas around the Plaza on foot, but you'll need a car to reach many of the B&Bs and restaurants, not to mention the vast majority of the region's natural attractions. Roads twist and turn in these parts; get a detailed map.

EATS

No Southwestern-style restaurant in the rest of the country does this region's cooking justice. What you'll notice immediately is that the regional specialties here are lighter, fresher, and better for you than elsewhere. There are dozens of chili varieties here, and most dishes come with the option of either a green or red chili sauce (the former is the hotter). You'll also notice a number of dishes infused with the smoky chipotle variety of chili. Blue and red corn are as popular as yellow; black beans are as common as pintos. In short, there's considerable color, flavor, and variety coming out of the local kitchens.

If you don't swoon over Southwestern food—or you at least want to vary your diet while you're here—you'll find no shortage of other options: There are plenty of Italian trattorias, Western steak houses, Asian eateries, and even a few French restaurants. California's influence has made its way here, too, resulting in inventive dishes that combine ingredients and techniques from several cultures. All in all, this is one of the top destinations for America's food lovers, rivaled only by San Francisco and New Orleans.

Santa Fe

For price ranges, *see* Chart A at the front of this guide.

$$$–$$$$ **Santacafe.** One of the most romantic spots in town, the sparely decorated Santacafe also has some of the most outlandish cuisine—an exotic blend of Far Eastern and Southwestern cooking, with such specialties as duck with maple hoisin sauce and sesame bok choy, or filet mignon with roasted garlic and green chili mashed potatoes. *231 Washington Ave.,* ☏ *505/984–1788.*

$$$–$$$$ **Coyote Cafe.** The Cafe's celebrity chef, Mark Miller, is the man most strongly associated with Santa Fe's brand of New American-inspired Southwestern cuisine. This place is loud, expensive (there's a charge for salsa and chips), flashy, and prone to pretension; but the food—like buttermilk corn cakes with chipotle shrimp—is memorable. There is a prix-fixe menu for $50. If the dining room turns you off, turn on to the festive, open-air rooftop cantina, where the food is half the price and just as good. Locals like to knock this place, but when you're looking to shoot something down, you aim high. *132 W. Water St.,* ☏ *505/983–1615.*

$$$–$$$$ **Geronimo's.** One of the newer restaurants on Canyon Road, Geronimo's picked up a major gay following immediately after its opening in 1995. The cuisine is Continental-influenced Southwestern—lots of healthful seafood grills and composed salads. The two dimly lit dining rooms in this 200-year-old adobe building are very romantic, but if you and your date like the outdoors, you can try for a table in the courtyard. The tiny bar is always crowded. *724 Canyon Rd.,* ☏ *505/982–1500.*

$$$–$$$$ **Palace Restaurant.** The ruby velvet walls belie the Palace's colorful role in the history of the Wild West—indeed, the building has been a whorehouse, a saloon, and a gaming parlor. The Palace is a bit touristy these days, but it's nonetheless appealing. The hefty Caesar salads are prepared table-side, and an extensive—though unspectacular—list of steak, veal, and pasta dishes is offered. *142 W. Palace Ave.,* ☏ *505/982–9891.*

$$$–$$$$ **Pink Adobe.** For 50 years they've been talking about this sprawling downtown pink adobe—it's synonymous with Santa Fe dining, and you're sure to see some of the city's old guard holding court here. The emphasis is on old-fashioned, filling fare; steaks and shrimp reign supreme. Each of the several dining areas is hung with local art. *406 Old Santa Fe Trail,* ☏ *505/983–7712.*

$$$ **Paul's.** The fact that Paul's offers a discount to guests staying at local B&Bs is reason enough to come. But repeat visitors and locals know that, discounts aside, this quietly elegant storefront dining room is one of the best finds in Santa Fe. Among the favorites off the regionally inspired Continental menu are baked salmon with pecan herb crust and sorrel sauce, and the filling pumpkin bread (stuffed with pine nuts, corn, green chili, and squash) served with red chili sauce, queso blanco, and caramelized apples. *72 W. Marcy St.,* ☏ *505/982–8738.*

Santa Fe

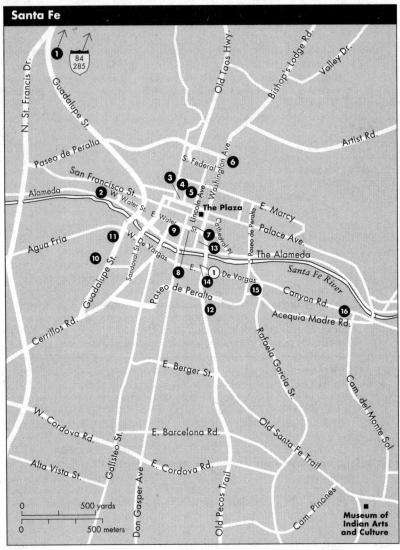

Eats ●

Babbo Ganzo
Trattoria, **5**

Blue Corn Cafe, **7**

Coyote Cafe, **8**

Downtown
Subscription, **15**

Galisteo, **9**

Geronimo's, **16**

Guadalupe Cafe, **11**

India Palace, **13**

Old Santa Fe Trail
Bookstore &
Coffeehouse, **12**

Palace Restaurant, **3**

Paul's, **4**

Pink Adobe, **14**

Pranzo, **10**

Santacafe, **6**

Tesuque Village
Market, **1**

Vanessie, **2**

Scenes ○

Club 414, **1**

\$\$-\$\$\$ **Babbo Ganzo Trattoria.** In an upscale shopping center a few blocks from the Plaza is this classy, Northern Italian bistro known for stellar service, a great wine list, fresh baked breads, and designer pizzas. Not especially Santa Fe, but who cares? It's great food. *130 Lincoln Ave., 2nd Floor,* ☏ *505/986-3835.*

\$\$-\$\$\$ **India Palace.** When you've overdosed on blue corn and chili sauce, it may be time to sample equally stimulating combinations of foods from another part of the world. There are, in fact, some similarities between the cuisines of India and the American Southwest—the heavy use of coriander, cumin, and other piquant spices, for example—but there are major differences, too. Come here for an intense refresher course: You'll be treated to some of the finest Indian food you've ever had, and, hey, there's belly dancing many nights. *227 Don Gaspar Ave.,* ☏ *505/986-5859.*

\$\$-\$\$\$ **Pranzo.** This sleek, contemporary restaurant is a popular power-lunch spot for local politicos. It serves first-rate cioppino, thin-crust pizzas, and rich desserts. *540 Montezuma, Sanbusco Center,* ☏ *505/984-2645.*

\$\$-\$\$\$ **Vanessie.** With the absence of gay bars in town, plenty of folks head to Vanessie, where live piano music warms the air and the smell of steak and ribs permeates it. The lodge ambience is created with high-beamed ceilings, massive oak tables, cow skulls on the walls, and roaring fireplaces. The food is simple and filling; the spicy onion loaf is famous. *434 W. San Francisco St.,* ☏ *505/982-9966.*

\$ **Blue Corn Cafe.** In the center of town, at the Mercado shopping center, this is an outstanding option for cheap, authentic Southwestern fare. It's always busy, has a young, outgoing staff, and is open late; dinners are served until 11, the bar closes at 2 AM. Best bets: the fiery chipotle and smoked-corn soup; the veggie tamales; and the margaritas, which may be the best in town. *133 Water St., Plaza Mercado,* ☏ *505/984-1800.*

\$ **Guadalupe Cafe.** Though many B&Bs in Santa Fe have great breakfasts, consider sneaking out one morning and eating where the locals do. The breakfast burritos here are famous, but such non-Southwestern standbys as raspberry pancakes are also tasty. The lunches and dinners are great, too, offering basic Mexican dishes. Finish things with the *sopaipillas* (fried bread with honey). Expect a long wait. *313 Guadalupe St.,* ☏ *505/982-9762.*

\$ **Tesuque Village Market.** This is the sort of trendy but local country-deli-cum-café where Porsches and BMWs are parked beside pickup trucks with muddy golden retrievers in the back. It's in sleepy Tesuque, 10 miles north of town, and perfect for people-watching (stop by on the weekend after visiting Trader Jack's flea market). The French owners are as proficient in croissant baking as they are in burrito stuffing. Be sure to try the red chili fries, too. *Rte. 591 off U.S. 285, Tesuque,* ☏ *505/988-8848.*

Taos

For price ranges, *see* Chart B at the front of this guide.

\$\$-\$\$\$ **Apple Tree.** Taos has only a few restaurants that match Santa Fe's in both price and ambience; the Apple Tree, set in an ancient territorial-style house near the Plaza, hits the mark. Each of the dining rooms abounds in straw chairs, beehive-shape *kiva* fireplaces, and other local touches. The food is Southwestern eclectic: smoked trout, veggie green curry, mango chicken enchiladas. Very fun and festive. *123 Bent St.,* ☏ *505/758-1900.*

\$\$\$ **Marciano's.** This intimate Italian bistro has a nice, ho-hum, small-town pace and views from some of the windows of the Sangre de Cristo Mountains. Pumpkin-orange walls, latilla ceilings, soft music, and mismatched chairs create a warm, slightly quirky atmosphere. The top-notch menu has a few colorful Southwestern touches (like the blue corn pasta, for example), plus there's a great wine list. Very romantic and gay-popular. *Junction of La Placita and Ledoux Sts.,* ☎ *505/751–0805.*

$$–$$$ **Doc Martin's.** Many locals as well as regular visitors—gay and straight—love to congregate at this remarkably comfy place. Though a bit pricey, the menu here is as good as any in town, offering such New American creations as black bean cakes, pecan-encrusted sea bass, and apple cider pork tenderloin. The elegant dining room has a *latilla* ceiling and thick adobe walls. *125 Paseo del Pueblo N,* ☎ *505/758–1977.*

$$–$$$ **Stakeout.** People come to this hilltop steak house as much for the outstanding views over the mesa west of town as for the thick pepper steaks flambéed in brandy, the rib-eye steaks, the baked trout with vegetables and herbs, the Alaskan king crab legs, or the fresh oysters (on the half-shell or broiled). *Stakeout Dr., off Rte. 68,* ☎ *505/758–2042.*

$$ **Bent Street Deli.** You can get New York-style Reubens here, and, at lunchtime anyway, it does feel like a deli. But then along comes dinner, and you can choose from an expanded menu that includes such options as chicken in East Indian spices with chipotle-peach chutney or creamy tortellini Alfredo. *120 Bent St.,* ☎ *505/758–5787.*

$ **Trading Post Cafe.** This sunny gallery-cum-café is on the approach into town, in the midst of a small complex of artisans. The California-style cuisine—mostly light composed salads, creative sandwiches, and grilled veggies—is very tasty and very reasonably priced. Long wine list with unusual choices. *Rte. 68 and Rte. 508,* ☎ *505/758–5089.*

$ **Amigos.** Taos's local food co-op is not only a great source of whole-food groceries but it also has a great little deli and a bulletin board for many of the New Age, holistic, outdoors-oriented, arts, and political groups in town. Order a creation from the juice bar to wash down your bean burrito or tofu salad. *326 Paseo del Pueblo S,* ☎ *505/758–8493.*

$ **The Burrito Wagon.** Behind the Central Taos Motorbank (which has a drive-through ATM) is a rusty tan camper known as the Burrito Wagon, from which you can get the finest, cheapest, and most authentic tacos, burritos, and tostadas in town. This place has even fewer frills than no-frills. You dine in your car. Closed weekends. *Jct. of Tewa La. and Paseo del Pueblo S,* ☎ *505/751–4091.*

$ **Casa Fresen.** Like the Tesuque Market outside Santa Fe, Casa Fresen is the perfect blend of upscale café and local gathering hole. It's officially just a bakery, but in addition to selling amazingly good fresh breads, rolls, and pastries, they also offer fancy coffees, salads, and cheeses; they'll even pack you a choice box lunch. Dogs lurk around the picnic benches in the dusty courtyard. *Arroyo Seco,* ☎ *505/776–2969.*

$ **Eske's Brew Pub.** Ski bums head down from the valley to check out the local scene and throw back a few at this funky, lackadaisical brew pub. The crunchy pub fare menu includes tabbouleh salad with feta, diced tomato, and pita; bangers and mash; green-chili stew (veggie or turkey); and a wide variety of teas. *106 Des Georges La.,* ☎ *505/758–1517.*

$ **Northtown Restaurant.** Just up the street from Wild and Natural (*see below*), this local institution has a simple, open cafeteria-style room that could be in any town in America but for its adobe facade and spectacular views of Wheeler Peak. A great place to mingle with locals and dine on hearty Southwestern fare. *908 Paseo del Pueblo N,* ☎ *505/758–2374.*

$ **Wild and Natural Cafe.** Owner Carole Wildman works hard to show that vegetarian food can both fill you up and please your taste buds: Specialties include classic green chili, hummus, tempeh burgers, Thai peanut pasta, and blue corn tostados piled with rice, beans, lettuce, guacamole, and salsa. There are also organic wines and fruit smoothies. *812B Paseo del Pueblo N,* ☎ *505/751–0480.*

Eats

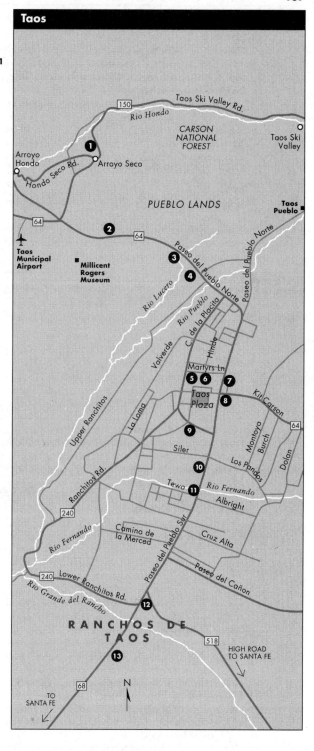

Coffeehouse Culture

Santa Fe

Galisteo (201 Galisteo St., ☎ 505/984–1316) is a gay-friendly newsstand that also serves coffees, sandwiches, good Texas chili stew, and other cheap eats; the patio seating is great for people-watching. At the **Old Santa Fe Trail Bookstore & Coffeehouse** (613 Old Santa Fe Trail, ☎ 505/988–8878), you can munch on a turkey, bacon, and avocado sandwich or a piece of raspberry rhubarb pie while listening in on a poetry reading. **Downtown Subscription** (376 Garcia St., ☎ 505/983–3085), is a good spot for cooling your heels after a long day of gallery visiting. The room is lined on three sides with newspaper and magazine racks (there are scads of titles); light food and coffees are available.

Taos

Magpies (Rte. 522 N, ☎ 505/758–0068), a cute coffeehouse in the Overland Sheepskin Company complex, is adjacent to several good galleries. If you choose to sit outside you'll enjoy great mountain views and the pleasant sound of sheep bleating in an adjacent field. Not especially gay, but fun. Light sandwiches.

SLEEPS

Santa Fe

The resorts and hotels in and around Santa Fe are expensive but usually correspondingly sumptuous. Most are built in the pueblo style and furnished in the Southwestern style. They are, with few exceptions, lovely. However, you might wish to consider a B&B accommodation in Santa Fe over one of the hotels. By and large, B&Bs are among the best in the country, and the rates are often half of what you'll pay at the hotels. The breakfasts are typically large enough so that you don't need lunch. Finally, the one concern that many travelers wary of guest houses seem to share—privacy—is not usually a concern here. At least half the guest house rooms in Santa Fe have private entrances, and rarely are they without private baths.

For price ranges, *see* Chart A at the front of this guide.

Resorts and Hotels

⊡ Perhaps the most celebrated resort in New Mexico, the **Bishop's Lodge** is a formal compound 3 miles north of town, in the shadows of the Sangre de Cristo Mountains. This resort offers guests a rundown of civilized activities, from horseback riding to lawn bowling to skeet shooting. Even if you don't stay here, consider stopping in for the Lodge's legendary Sunday brunch. *Bishop's Lodge Rd.,* ☎ *505/983–6377. 88 rooms. $$$$*

⊡ Highly recommended is the **Inn of the Anasazi,** another intimate adobe hotel close to the Plaza. Rooms here have kiva fireplaces, four-poster beds, and Southwestern furnishings; there's also an on-site library that has an outstanding selection of local literature and history books. *113 Washington Ave.,* ☎ *505/988–3030 or 800/688–8100. 59 rooms. $$$$*

⊡ Of the many exclusive, expensive inns downtown, the most memorable is the **Inn on the Alameda,** a small property on the Santa Fe River, a couple blocks from the Plaza and close to Canyon Road. Rooms are luxurious yet authentically Southwestern, with many handmade furnishings and local art. *303 E. Alameda,* ☎ *505/984–2121 or 800/289–2122. 66 rooms. $$$$*

⊡ The centrally located **Hotel St. Francis** dates from 1920, and though rooms are a bit small, they are filled with such classy touches as cherry wood antiques and brass-and-iron beds. *210 Don Gaspar Ave.,* ☎ *505/983–5700 or 800/529–5700. 83 rooms. $$$*

Guest Houses

⊡ A 20-minute walk from the Plaza, **Dos Casas Viejas** is luxurious and secluded. You enter the compound through a tall wooden gate; a long driveway then leads between two restored 1860s adobe buildings, whose rooms all have private entrances, kiva fireplaces, and such colorful pieces as mesquite-wood armoires, cowhide chairs, and hickory-wood tables. This is one of the few area B&Bs with a large pool. *610 Agua Fria St.,* ☎ *505/983–1636. 6 rooms. Mostly straight. $$$–$$$$*

⊡ With rooms as impressively decorated as any luxury hotel in town, **Adobe Abode,** a couple blocks off the Plaza, is a great bargain. Belying the modest exterior are six large rooms with large, modern baths, upscale amenities, an eclectic array of antiques and folk furniture, and a detailed notebook listing owner Pat Harbour's favorite sights and restaurants. *202 Chapelle,* ☎ *505/983–3133. 6 rooms. Mostly straight. $$–$$$*

⊡ The Adobe Abode's filling breakfasts are rivaled by those served at Louise Walter's nearby **Grant's Corner Inn.** Near the Plaza, this creaky turn-of-the-century home is a surprising presence downtown, where adobe construction is the norm. Rooms are done with classic Victorian pieces and a gentility and elegance that recalls Savannah or San Francisco. Walter's hotel background (her father owns the famous Camelback Inn in Scottsdale) is evident in the inn's many thoughtful touches, from the popular afternoon refreshment time in the parlor to a common room stocked with snacks, microwave popcorn, and soft drinks. *122 Grant Ave.,* ☎ *505/983–6678. 12 rooms. Mostly straight. $$–$$$*

⊡ California transplants Andrew Beckerman and John Daw built the cozy **Four Kachinas** in 1992, fulfilling a longtime dream to settle in Santa Fe. Rooms are clean, crisp, and uncluttered, with saltillo-tile floors and Southwestern furnishings; all have a private entrance to which a light breakfast is delivered each morning. There's also a small library with a wood-burning fireplace and sodas and brownies out for light snacks. It's just off Paseo de Peralta, a 10-minute walk from the Plaza. *512 Webber St.,* ☎ *505/982–2550 or 800/397–2564. 5 rooms. Mostly straight. $$*

⊡ A 10-minute walk from the Plaza is the **Preston House,** credited with beginning the Santa Fe B&B boom—it was the first guest house in New Mexico. The property offers both a Victorian and a Southwestern experience; the first can be had in the 1886 Queen Anne, which has several quirky, simple rooms, many with brass beds, ceiling fans, and stained glass windows. There are also two Queen Anne–style cottages in back, each with a fireplace—these are the best accommodations here. In a traditional adobe house across the street are several more rooms, done in traditional Southwestern style. *106 Faithway St.,* ☎ *505/982–3465. 15 rooms. Mostly straight. $–$$$*

⊡ For an affordable, central location, consider **El Paradero,** a modest property built in the early 19th century as a farmhouse and modified and expanded over the years. Rooms here are simple but accented with native materials and furnishings. *220 W. Manhattan Ave.,* ☎ *505/988–1177. 14 rooms. Mostly straight. $–$$*

⊡ Set alluringly in the sticks, 7 miles west of town, Cathy Bugliari's and Trish Pyke's **Hummingbird Ranch** is an extremely informal place, and the owners will rent out the rooms—and even their entire house—on a daily, weekly, or monthly basis. The house has two guest rooms; next door is a nice-size casita, and a few steps away is another small cottage with a VCR and stereo, but you must use the main house's bathroom. The location is incredible, with lovely sunset views off the back porch. Hummingbirds really do hover around the property, and you can board your horses here, too. This is the closest experience to staying with friends that you'll find in Santa Fe. *Rte. 10,* ☎ *505/471–2921. 4 rooms. Mixed gay/straight. $–$$*

⚅ A 25-minute drive south of downtown is Babette Miller's small guest house, the **Open Sky,** which is smack in the middle of nowhere, at the end of a long dirt road. Mountains views are had in every direction from this Santa Fe-style ranch, which is surrounded by Babette's many flower beds. Each guest room is done in a contemporary Southwestern theme; there's also a large main living room with a fireplace, and there's a hot tub in back. *134 Turquoise Trail,* ☎ *505/471–3475 or 800/244–3475. 3 rooms. Mostly gay male/lesbian. $–$$*

⚅ Just north of the village of Tesuque and the opera is the **Triangle Inn,** whose innkeepers are friendly Sarah Hryniewicz and Karen Ford (the latter hosts a local gay radio show, *Out Loud and Proud*). This rustic ranch has six individual adobe casitas, each tastefully decorated and with differing layouts; the largest, and nicest, has two bedrooms, a VCR, and a kitchenette, and is perfect for two couples. A low-key atmosphere prevails, there's a hot tub and sunning area in the courtyard, and Karen and Sarah are usually around to chat and offer sightseeing advice. *Rte. 11, Arroyo Cuyamungue,* ☎ *505/455–3375. 6 casitas. Mostly gay male/lesbian. $–$$*

Taos

Accommodations at both hotels and guest houses are consistently less expensive and simpler than in Santa Fe. They are still consistently stellar, and most of the places here, especially the guest houses, have quieter settings and better mountain views than in Santa Fe. If you're looking for accommodations at a hotel or condo near Taos Ski Valley, try calling **Taos Central Reservations** (☎ 505/758–9767 or 800/821–2437).

For price ranges, *see* Chart B at the front of this guide.

Resorts and Hotels

⚅ Though part of a chain, the **Best Western Kachina Lodge de Taos** retains an authentic Southwestern feel, with antique kachina dolls in many of the public areas and traditionally furnished guest rooms; it's just down the road from the Taos Pueblo. *413 N. Pueblo Rd.,* ☎ *505/758–2275 or 800/522–4462. 118 rooms. $$$*

⚅ The **Taos Inn** is the prize accommodation downtown, a charming, intimate, adobe structure, parts of which date from the 1600s. It's within a block of the Plaza, has one of the best restaurants and bars in town, and the rooms are furnished with antiques and bright, handmade Southwestern bedspreads and fabrics. Very warm and personable. *125 Paseo del Pueblo N,* ☎ *505/758–2233 or 800/826–7466. 38 rooms. $$–$$$*

⚅ The best no-frills motel in town—and it's always been very hospitable to gays and lesbians—is the **Sun God Lodge,** which is along the main drag a short drive from the Plaza, has a hot tub, allows pets, and has fairly large rooms. *919 Paseo del Pueblo S,* ☎ *505/758–3162. 55 rooms. $*

Guest Houses

⚅ Susan Vernon's stunning 1912 Spanish-style hacienda **Casa de Las Chimneas,** is one of the most luxurious spots in town—a 10-minute walk from the Plaza. Lush gardens and fountains fill the large yards; such antiques as restored writing desks and pewter chandeliers fill the lovely guest rooms, which have Southwestern influences but whose styles borrow from all over Europe and the United States. *405 Cordoba Rd.,* ☎ *505/758–4777. 4 rooms. Mostly straight. $$$*

⚅ **Casa Feliz** is as close to the Plaza as any guest house, but its setting around a quiet courtyard keeps you secure from what noise and traffic envelopes Taos on weekend afternoons. This historic adobe home has a variety of mid size, cozy, casual rooms with Southwestern furnishings; never overly cutesy. *137 Bent St.,* ☎ *505/758–9790 or 800/764–9790. 5 rooms. Mostly straight. $$–$$$*

🏠 A short drive north of downtown is the **Hacienda del Sol,** a home that once figured prominently in Taos's arts colony past. Once the home of Mabel Dodge Luhan, such luminaries as Willa Cather, Georgia O'Keeffe, and D. H. Lawrence have visited here. Parts of this complex of three buildings, which is marred only slightly by its proximity to the busy main highway, date from 1804; this is one of the most authentic examples of local adobe architecture in the region. The guest rooms are decorated in Southwestern and Native American style; all rooms have beehive ovens or gas fireplaces, most have lovely mountain views. *109 Maple Dodge La.,* ☎ *505/758–0287. 9 rooms. Mostly straight. $$–$$$*

🏠 If a secluded, dramatic setting is a priority, consider the **Little Tree,** one of the most inviting small guest houses in the Southwest. Built in 1991 by Kay and Charles Giddens, this pueblo-style house is set about midway between the ski valley and downtown. Rooms have latilla ceilings, native furnishings, and a few of Kay's handmade quilts. From every window and the courtyard are incredible mountain and mesa views—this makes for the best star-gazing in town. *Hondo-Seco Rd., El Prado,* ☎ *505/776–8467 or 800/334–8467. 4 rooms. Mostly straight. $$*

🏠 One of the better deals among centrally located guest houses is the cheerful **Ruby Slipper,** which is presided over by New York City transplants Beth Goldman and Diane Fichtelberg. All guest rooms have private entrances, warm tile floors, unpretentious and brightly painted handcrafted furnishings, and kiva fireplaces. Simple, restful living is emphasized here: Hammocks and a hot tub are available in a private backyard, the hearty breakfasts use all-natural ingredients, and there are no TVs! *416 La Lomita Rd.,* ☎ *505/758–0613. 7 rooms. Mixed gay/straight. $$*

🏠 A building contractor from California, Noel Stone, moved to the northern Taos County village of Valdez a few years back to build a dream house and rent out the rooms to visitors. His finished product, the **Taos Stone House,** makes for one of the most interesting and hospitable lodgings in the area (it's about 15 minutes north of town, toward the ski valley). Rooms of this adobe house are large, some with balconies offering vast views of the region; one has its own steam room. Guests can use the full kitchen and enjoy the run of the property. *Valdez,* ☎ *505/776–2146 or 800/771–2189. 3 rooms. Mostly gay male/lesbian. $$*

SCENES

If doing the nightclub circuit means a great deal to you, you'll have to drive down to Albuquerque, which can actually be a lot of fun on a weekend evening. Consider staying there overnight, however, as incidences of drunk driving are notoriously high in New Mexico; even if you remain sober, you can't count on other drivers. *Out! Magazine* has the scoop on the city's nightlife, which is heavily influenced by the presence of the University of New Mexico; a few of the better known clubs include the **Albuquerque Mining Co.** (7209 Central Ave. NE, ☎ 505/255–0925); the **Club on Central** (10030 Central Ave. SE, ☎ 505/291–1550); **Foxes Lounge** (8521 Central Ave. NE, ☎ 505/255–3060); and the **Ranch** (8900 Central Ave. SE, ☎ 505/275–1616). Otherwise, Santa Fe and Taos offer but a few gay-popular nightlife diversions.

Santa Fe

As the only gay/lesbian bar in Santa Fe, **Club 414** has had to rise to the challenge of offering something for everyone. The nightly happy hours (4 PM–7 PM) attract a more mature crowd; the dance music starts at 10

PM, and a younger crowd takes to the floor. Friday is country-western night, and Saturday there is a DJ. By far the most popular DJ night, however, is trash disco Wednesday: The crowd is so big that you can just barely shake your booty. In addition to the bar and dance floor, 414 also has pool tables and a courtyard. *414 Old Santa Fe Trail,* ☎ *505/986–9971. Crowd: mixed gay/lesbian of all ages and all stripes.*

In the absence of more specifically gay meeting places, several of Santa Fe's restaurant bars have fairly strong lesbian and gay followings, including **Vanessie** and **Geronimo's** (*see* Eats, *above*). Though less known as a gay hangout, the old-fashioned Victorian-style bar the **Staab House** (330 E. Palace Ave., ☎ 505/986–0000) at the La Posada Hotel is a great spot for after-dinner drinks.

Taos

In Taos there are even fewer options for gay and lesbian night owls than in Santa Fe. The top hangout for all Taoseños and visitors is the intimate **Adobe Bar** (125 Paseo del Pueblo N, ☎ 505/758–2233) at the Taos Inn. There's country dancing regularly at the **Sagebrush Inn** (S. Santa Fe Rd., Rte. 68, ☎ 505/758–2254), but few homos have been known to give it a twirl here; still, it's not likely you won't be welcome. Same goes for the several bars up at Taos Ski Valley, which draws a consistently crunchy, open-minded après-ski bunch.

THE LITTLE BLACK BOOK

At Your Fingertips
Common Bond Gay and Lesbian Info Line (Albuquerque): ☎ 505/266–8041. **Fire or Police:** ☎ 911. **New Mexico Association of People Living with AIDS:** ☎ 505/820–2437. **Santa Fe Convention and Visitors Bureau:** 201 W. Marcy St., Box 909, 87504, ☎ 505/984–6760 or 800/777–2489. **Taos County Chamber of Commerce:** Drawer 1, 87571, ☎ 505/758–3873 or 800/732–TAOS. **Taos County Health Office:** ☎ 505/758–2073.

Gay Media
Out! Magazine (☎ 505/243–2540) is New Mexico's lesbian/gay news monthly; coverage is skewed heavily toward Albuquerque. You can find *Out!* in Santa Fe at Downtown Subscription (376 Garcia St., ☎ 505/983–3085) and Galisteo News (201 Galisteo St., ☎ 505/984–1316); nobody carries it in Taos.

BOOKSTORES
There are no gay/lesbian stores in the region, but most of the general bookstores are strong in gay, lesbian, feminist, New Age, and religious titles. In Santa Fe, the best bookstore is **Old Santa Fe Trail Books** (613 Old Santa Fe Trail, ☎ 505/988–8878); **Galisteo News** (*see above*) has the best selection of gay periodicals; and **Downtown Subscription** (*see above*) has a comprehensive selection of newspapers and periodicals, including gay ones and a few porn titles. All three spots double as coffeehouses.

The two best sources of gay and lesbian titles in Taos are the **Taos Book Shop** (122D Kit Carson Rd., ☎ 505/758–3733) and **Moby Dickens** (124A Bent St., ☎ 505/758–3050). For gay periodicals you'll have to go to Santa Fe.

Albuquerque has the only true lesbigay bookstore in the Southwest (excluding Las Vegas), **Sisters' and Brothers' Bookstore** (4011 Silver Ave. SE, ☎ 505/266–7317).

Body and Fitness

In Santa Fe, the gym at the **Fort Marcy Pool** (490 Washington Ave., ☎ 505/984–6725.) is very nice and gay-friendly. In Taos, both **Northside Health and Fitness Club** (1307 Paseo del Pueblo N., ☎ 505/751–1242) and **Taos Spa and Court Club** (111 Doña Ana Dr., ☎ 505/758–1980) are excellent facilities.

26 Out in Seattle

AN EXAMINATION OF SEATTLE AND ITS PEOPLE reveals a city that's awfully difficult not to love. Of course, most locals want the city to be made fun of, derided, and scorned. Travel guides, it is hoped, will assure the world that Seattle is highly overrated and nobody need move here. In fact, Seattle is a wonderful city, frequently found on magazine surveys as one of the most livable places on earth. But it's also bursting at the seams, its narrow streets unable to handle any more traffic and its cost of living rising sharply. "If you want to visit, fine," seems to be the attitude of most Seattleites, "but for God's sake, don't move here!"

One common myth about the migration to Seattle is that most of it is by way of San Francisco. If you ask around, however, you'll find that newcomers hail from every corner of America. Why? It used to be that young, often disaffected men and women with a bent toward spirituality, environmentalism, and feminism moved to San Francisco. This is less true today, as San Francisco has developed a reputation, deserved or not, as a haven of aged hippies and outmoded feminists, and for being a city ravaged by AIDS. Seattle, on the other hand, seems young, vibrant, and moving forward. America's twentysomethings—in considering what to drink, what music to embrace, how to communicate, and how to preserve natural resources—take many of their cues from Seattle.

What do Seattleites drink? A funny thing about these fit, fair-skinned people is that they're obsessed with health. They walk, jog, rollerblade, and cycle everywhere they go. They eat healthily. They're early to bed and early to rise. And yet the entire urban population is addicted to coffee and microbrewed beer. Hmmm. . . .

What kind of music do Seattleites listen to? The heady, harsh alternative sounds emanating from the city's hottest clubs are generally called grunge, a term that not only describes that style of music but also the deliberately shaggy attire and sensitive, brooding attitude of its followers. Local bands such as Nirvana and Pearl Jam were grunge pioneers. Now Seattle has hundreds of budding, young, alternative rockers attempting to carry on the torch. Dozens of clubs around town have live music from three to seven nights weekly.

How do Seattleites communicate? The city's residents don't actually speak to one another, they hold referendums. There is always some landmark threatened with demolition or some group threatened by an unfair statute. The most recent controversy facing the city is typical. It's over the possible redevelopment of 400-plus commercial and residential acres stretching from Denny Way to Lake Union. About one-third of the $300 million needed to reinvent this mildly gloomy neighborhood will come out of the pockets of taxpayers, should the proposal to build Seattle Commons proceed as planned. Opponents see the project as a way for investors and developers to line their pockets while displacing the neighborhood's working-class residents; proponents see Seattle Commons as a beautification project that will ultimately pump money back into the local economy while eradicating a pocket of urban blight. The debate exposes the conflict within the community between an embrace of egalitarianism and a push for progress.

How else do Seattleites communicate? They surf the net. The nearby suburb of Redmond is headquarters to Microsoft, a major engineer of the world's information superhighway. The joke is that everybody in this city either works for Microsoft or is forming his or her own grunge band, if not attempting both. Everybody seems to possess a state-of-the-art computer—it's about as necessary here as owning a phone.

How are Seattleites preserving their natural resources? First, failing to recycle in Seattle is like robbing a bank elsewhere. A staggering 89% of the population recycles on a regular basis. Laws against pollution are strictly enforced—the vast waterways surrounding the city are among the cleanest in the United States. People carpool to work whenever possible. They blade and cycle instead of driving. Even the buses have bike racks on the fronts of them, and the buses are free within Downtown, to encourage people not to drive. Seattle is one of America's greenest cities.

On Capitol Hill, Seattle's Gen-X cultures of cutting-edge music, coffeehouses and microbreweries, liberal politics, computer technology, and environmentalism seem to bridge the gap between gays and straights; yet although Capitol Hill has the city's largest homosexual population, it is by no means a gay ghetto. Compared with neighborhoods that are defined by their predominant sexual orientation, Capitol Hill is usually described as having significant populations of students, yuppies, latter-day hippies, and young families.

In this sense, Seattle differs considerably from many U.S. cities, particularly those in the Northeast. And maybe Capitol Hill's demography says something about how urban neighborhoods, with regard to their identities as either gay- or straight-oriented, are changing. The neighborhood does not function as a gay zone to which people retreat to find strength and safety in numbers, but more as a desirable residential setting with great shops, clubs, and restaurants—and where people accept one another at face value. Were Seattle as a whole less tolerant, a more insular gay neighborhood might exist.

THE LAY OF THE LAND

Several bodies of water define the city's boundaries. To the west is Puget Sound, off which Elliott Bay is a snug harbor whose shores constitute the western edge of Downtown. To the east is Lake Washington. Snaking across the northern half of Seattle is a stretch of water that begins in the west as the Lake Washington Ship Canal, becomes Lake Union, continues on as Portage Bay, then Union Bay, before finally emptying into Lake Washington. From nearly every elevated point in Seattle—and this is a hilly city—water is visible.

A significant chunk of Seattle, the section west of I-5, above the West Seattle Freeway and below Mercer Street, actually looks urban—with industry and warehouses to the south and Downtown's glimmering, contemporary skyline to the north. The rest of Seattle, however, is unusually green, lush, and almost a bit suburban. Some of the tonier, older residential neighborhoods are between Downtown and Lake Washington, and in northern Seattle, above Lake Union, stretches a vast residential neighborhood of relatively young, middle-class residents.

Capitol Hill and Volunteer Park

The western border of gay-beloved **Capitol Hill** begins where I–5 cuts through the city. Its northern boundary is around Prospect Street and Volunteer Park, its eastern boundary 20th Avenue, and its southern boundary Union Street and Seattle University. Due south of Capitol Hill is **First Hill,** which is smaller and which contains many medical centers and lots of office buildings.

There aren't many attractions on Capitol Hill, but several commercial streets are excellent for shopping, club hopping, cheap dining, and people-watching. Up-and-coming **Pine** and **Pike** streets run east–west, side-by-side; even locals confuse them, so don't be alarmed if you do. These streets have the highest concentration of gay bars, plus several grungy, live-music halls, some coffeehouses, and a few great shops, such as **Toys in Babeland** (711 E. Pike St.), a women's erotica emporium; and **REI** (1525 11th Ave.), where outdoorsy dykes and fags arm themselves with tents, bikes, hiking boots, and Swiss Army knives. For better or for worse, Seattle has major plans to develop the Pike and Pine corridor; a Planet Hollywood, for instance, recently opened down on Pike just below I–5.

Broadway Avenue, from Pike about 10 blocks north to Roy Street, is a youthful mix of straight and gay-popular businesses. The common denominators are funkiness and thrift, although Broadway is gentrifying some as the hippest crowds migrate south toward Pine and Pike streets. Still, along Broadway you can find incredibly cheap food and lots of fun clothing and bric-a-brac. A must-visit is **Broadway Market** (300 Broadway Ave. E), the largest queer-themed, commercial space in America. This three-story atrium mall is new, attractive, and fun, loaded with gift shops and stalls, clothing stores, a few restaurants, a gay-and-lesbian gym, a parking garage, and a full cinema. Most notable is the **Pink Zone,** on the top floor, a much-talked-about, salon-cum-boutique that bills itself: "queer shears & visibly queer gear." Outside the Pink Zone there are a few seats and tables overlooking the shoppers down below—a great spot from which to gawk at the crowds.

The other major north–south thoroughfare is **15th Avenue,** from about Madison to Mercer streets. A tad more upscale and mature than Broadway, 15th Avenue has more substantial restaurants, some antiques stores, and **City Mercantile,** Seattle's dyke hardware store. One other small pocket of eateries and coffeehouses is at the intersection of **Olive** and **Denny ways.**

The rest of Capitol Hill is characterized by rolling, tree-lined streets and an amazingly eclectic selection of houses and apartment buildings, ranging from Victorian painted ladies to '50s Bauhaus cubes. Along 15th Avenue you're rewarded with dramatic views of Elliott Bay; along 23rd Avenue, you can see east across Lake Washington.

At the northern fringe of Capitol Hill is gorgeous **Volunteer Park** (14th Ave. and Highland Dr. are good streets from which to enter), home to an exotic-plant-filled **Conservatory** (☎ 206/684–4743) and a water tower from which you can enjoy panoramic views of Seattle. You'll find throngs of queens and lesbians lying about on the lawns, reading books and each other. At night, it's very cruisy (but heavily policed); Seattle, in fact, has an awful lot of cruisy outdoor parks.

Downtown

There are both more and less exciting commercial districts in America, but **Downtown Seattle** does have one major thing going for it: **Pike Place Market** (at the foot of Pike St., ☎ 206/682–7453). And to think that during the '60s urban planners were ready to tear it down, until Seattleites voted to protect it as a historic site. The sprawling 1907 structure is abuzz with fishmongers and food marketers of every ilk. It's on a steep hill; its lower floors have tons of genuinely interesting shops, and the ground floor leads you under the hideous, elevated Route 99 freeway to the waterfront, which encompasses 20 blocks of piers—many of them with restaurants, shops, boat tours, and other attractions. Just south, at Pier 59, is the **Seattle Aquarium** (☎ 206/386–4320), and just north, at Pier 66, is the new **Odyssey Contemporary Maritime Museum** (☎ 206/623–2120). Overall, the market and the waterfront are as touristy as Seattle gets, but the historic aspect and high quality of shopping and amusements makes this area worth braving even if you dislike crowds.

The rest of Downtown, which is bounded by Stewart Street to the north, I–5 to the east, and Pioneer Square to the south, is not particularly memorable. At night, the sidewalks are left largely to the homeless, and by day it's fairly corporate. The one site worth visiting is the striking, postmodern **Seattle Art Museum** (1320 2nd Ave., ☎ 206/625–8900), whose collection focuses on Asian, Native American, African, and pre-Columbian art.

Pioneer Square and the International District

Enigmatic **Pioneer Square** is one example of urban restoration that's had very mixed results. Technically part of Downtown, these blocks around the intersection of 1st and 2nd avenues and Yesler Way comprised the city's first business district. Many of the buildings date from just after 1889, the year a fire destroyed most of the city's wood-frame buildings. In the early years, industrialist Henry Yesler operated a saw mill and pier at the foot of what is now Yesler Way. The forests along the hillside provided timber; each tree was cut and rolled down the hill to the mill. The long, muddy, bare incline became known as Skid Road, which was later butchered into Skid Row, made famous by John Steinbeck. As the area eventually became overrun with brothels and saloons, and successful commerce moved north, Skid Row became forever synonymous with poverty and drunkenness.

After a long era of decline, from the Depression into the early '70s, the whole area of Pioneer Square was cleaned up and infused with lively shops and cafés, their buildings restored. Many of the original saloons and hangouts, including a couple of long-running but rather divy gay bars, are still here—as are many Skid Row panhandlers and drunks (try not to trip over the 40-ounce malt-liquor bottles strewn around the cobbled pedestrian malls). At night, the square is a mostly collegiate party area; by day it's a good place for wandering through art galleries and the **Downtown Antique Market** (2218 Western Ave.), which features 70 of the area's top dealers.

Because of an unpleasant waste-disposal problem (the rising tide constantly backed up the sewers), city leaders leveled the town in 1889 by shaving off several hills and elevating some valleys close to the waterfront. Pioneer Square was raised, its original ground-level sidewalks and stores converted into basements. Much of "Underground Seattle" still exists intact, albeit derelict, and can be seen on a colorful, though hokey, 90-minute tour given by the garrulous **Bill Spiedel** (☎ 206/682–1511), beginning at 610 1st Avenue. Note that just down the street, beside one of the entrances to the underground, is **South End Steam Baths** (115½ 1st Ave. S), one of the oldest gay bathhouses on the West Coast.

Just south of Pioneer Square and east of the massive Seattle Kingdome sports stadium is the century-old, 12-block **International District,** where many Chinese, Japanese, Laotian, Thai, Vietnamese, and Filipino immigrants live and work. Chinese workers hired to complete the transcontinental railroad first settled here, and despite anti-Chinese riots in the 1880s and the internment of Japanese-Americans during World War II, the neighborhood has continued to thrive. A highlight is **Uwajimaya** (519 6th Ave. S, ☎ 206/624–6248), an immense Japanese department store with an amazing food section.

Belltown
Just above Downtown and bounded by Stewart Street to the south, 6th Avenue to the east, Battery Street to the north, and the waterfront to the west, is **Belltown,** which has fast become a commercial and residential haven of artists, musicians, and bookish yuppies. You'll find great home-furnishing shops, galleries, restaurants, and some of the city's hottest music clubs—the highest concentrations are along 2nd and 1st avenues.

Seattle Center and Queen Anne Hill
Due north of Belltown, beginning above Denny Way, is a controversial, working-class neighborhood that might eventually be transformed into **Seattle Commons,** depending on the outcome of a major war between the city's anti- and pro-development camps.

Northwest of Belltown is the **Seattle Center,** the 74-acre tract on which the 1962 World's Fair was held. This is a kooky spot, highlighted by the **Space Needle** (☎ 206/443–2111), the retro-futurist 600-foot tower you can see from just about anywhere in the city. You can take an elevator to the top; the best thing about the view from the Space Needle is that you can't see the Space Needle. Nearby, you can also visit the **Pacific Science Center** (☎ 206/443–2880), which contains a bunch of touch-friendly exhibits. This all might have been pretty interesting 30 years ago, but today the Seattle Center provides a rather embarrassing look back at how earlier planners envisioned our world.

Just west of Seattle Center, you can head up steep Queen Avenue to **Queen Anne Hill,** a stately, historic neighborhood of restored houses and quaint businesses that sits 457 feet above Elliott Bay. Lots of yuppies—straight and gay—live here. North, across the Lake Washington Ship Canal, is far funkier **Fremont,** which was Seattle's hippie haven in the 1960s. A little less happening today, it's nonetheless a great place to visit on Sundays, when dealers at **Fremont Market** show crafts, antiques, and objets d'art on a two-block plot of land just off Fremont Avenue.

The Lake Washington Shoreline
Many visitors neglect the east side of Seattle, which encompasses the verdant, well-to-do neighborhoods of **Madison Valley** and **Madison Park.** It's well worth driving or cycling through these rolling neighborhoods overlooking scenic Lake Washington.

From Downtown, go east on Yesler Way all the way to **Lake Washington Boulevard,** which skirts the lake's shoreline. Head north a half mile or so until you reach **Denny-Blaine Park,** (a.k.a. Dyke-kiki, as in Waikiki), a neat but compact plot of lawn on the lake. This is the city's unofficial lesbian tanning salon. There are two levels; if you wish to go topless, head to the lower one, which has access to some great swimming. Note that from this park you can see the homes of two local icons: Behind you, on Lake Washington Boulevard, is the home of the late Kurt Cobain (his widow, Courtney Love and their daughter, Frances Bean, still reside here). Across the lake, on the sterling shores of fancy Bellevue, you can see the immense undertaking that someday (it's taken years to build) will be the palace of billionaire computer whiz Bill Gates, founder of Microsoft.

Continue north on Lake Washington Boulevard to Madison Street, at which a right turn will lead down the hill to **Madison Park,** a long, sandy beach overlooking the lake. Most of the space north of the lifeguard house is gay, and there's a float out in the water that looks like an ad for Speedo swimsuits on hot summer days. Madison Street and the blocks just off of it have a number of good shops and gay-popular restaurants, including **Cactus** (*see* Eats, *below*) and **Mangoes Thai Cuisine** (1841 42nd Ave. E, ☎ 206/324–6467).

Take Madison Street back up to Lake Washington Boulevard, hang a right, and follow it to the **University of Washington Park Arboretum,** a shady public park containing more than 5,000 varieties of plants and quite a few windy trails. If you continue to where Lake Washington Boulevard passes by the on-ramp to I–520, you can park at the nearby lot and follow the path to find the city's most popular cruise grounds. Plenty of people wander through here just to enjoy the scenery and nonhuman wildlife, as well.

Wallingford and the University District

Take I–5 over Lake Union to the Northeast 45th Street exit to reach two interesting northern Seattle communities, the University District and Wallingford. Heading east on 45th Street leads to the **University of Washington's** beautiful, hilly campus. This isn't an especially gay area, but it's full of quirky diversions, cheap eats, and vintage clothing stores—especially along the neighborhood's main drag, **University Way.**

From I–5, follow Northeast 45th Street west several blocks to its intersection with **Meridian Street,** and you'll find yourself in the heart of Seattle's most significant lesbian community, **Wallingford.** This is a low-key neighborhood with a few interesting shops. Stop by the **Wallingford Center** (4430 Wallingford Ave. N), a small, indoor shopping complex with a strong community following. If you need a bite to eat, or just want to meet a few local lezzies, check out **Julia's** (4401 Wallingford Ave. N, ☎ 206/633–1175), a bright little café and juice bar.

Continue north on Meridian Street to reach **Green Lake,** which is both a body of water shared by shells, rowboats, and swimmers and a grassy, green park that draws hordes of walkers, bladers, and cyclists. Very popular with dykes.

GETTING AROUND

You can definitely get by in Seattle without a car, especially Downtown and on Capitol Hill. But if you're here for more than a few days, consider renting a car to see some of the outer neighborhoods. Traffic is a drag: Seattle's dated network of streets is ill-equipped to handle the volume. Buses are fairly practical for getting around even the more remote neighborhoods, and they're free within Downtown. Taxis are quite easy to hail on the street and very reliable and reasonable.

EATS

Seattle is an easy place to eat well and eat cheaply. Washington, like Oregon and Northern California, has fertile soil and good farming just about year-round. This means chefs always have access to a terrific array of fresh produce. With all the water, you can count on plenty of fresh seafood. And then there are the many specialty food shops in the International District. The result is an abundance of Asian-influenced regional cooking (a.k.a.

Pacific Northwest cuisine). Obviously, authentic Chinese, Thai, and Japanese restaurants are easy to find, and Seattle is also strong on Italian food.

So that explains why it's easy to eat well; as for eating cheap, you have the huge population of students and twentysomethings to thank. The pricey restaurants are Downtown; everywhere else, especially on Capitol Hill and in the University District, cheap and filling burritos, sushi, veggie platters, pizzas, and *pad thais,* the popular pan-fried rice noodle dish, are omnipresent.

For price ranges, *see* Chart A at the front of this guide.

Downtown and Environs

$$$ Campagne. A very chichi but not overdone French restaurant by the Market. The country French specialties (often game) include a starter of seafood sausage and a cinnamon-roasted quail in carrot-and-orange sauce. This is a terrific place to celebrate your long-term romance or, perhaps, kick off a new one. There's outdoor dining overlooking Elliott Bay. *86 Pine St.,* ☎ *206/728–2800.*

$$$ Kaspar's. Many epicureans call the chef-owner here, Kaspar Donier, a genius. Sample his Alaskan king salmon in a potato crust, braised lamb shanks, and grilled free-range chicken with grapes and rosemary and decide for yourself. And check out the excellent wine list. One block west of Key Arena in Seattle Center. *19 W. Harrison St., 206/298–0123.*

$$$ Queen City Grill. This Belltown fixture has been converted from an old-fashioned saloon into an elegant wine bar and seafood bistro. The dining room glows with polished wood and black lacquer, and tables have simple white linen. It's a good spot to try out Seattle's exquisite raw oysters on the half shell—or start with clams sautéed with tomatoes, garlic, and vermouth. Lots of daily, fresh fish specials, too. *2201 1st Ave.,* ☎ *206/443–0975.*

$$–$$$ Al Boccolino. Not usually mentioned among the city's top eateries, Al Boccolino is nevertheless a stellar place for Italian food: rigatoni with gorgonzola, roasted quail wrapped in prosciutto. The romantic, triangular dining room has exposed brick, soft lighting, and high ceilings. *1 Yesler Way,* ☎ *206/622–7688.*

$$–$$$ Dahlia Lounge. Chef Tom Douglas, an early proponent of Pacific Northwest cuisine, oversees the kitchen at this trendy, colorful restaurant just north of Downtown. The place is richly decorated with an abundance of exotic-fish sculpture. The eclectic menu changes, but it might include rabbit grilled with roasted garlic or Asian-inspired lobster–and–shiitake mushroom pot stickers. *1904 4th Ave.,* ☎ *206/682–4142.*

$$–$$$ Flying Fish. The extensive menu of this contemporary fish house lists small plates, large plates, and platters for sharing. For instance, your party can order mussels with a chili-lime dipping sauce for $7.95 per pound. Or you can try a big dish of crab ravioli with a lemongrass cream sauce. The preparations are exotic, the seafood is always fresh, and the orange-and-yellow dining room is festive and chic. *2234 1st Ave.,* ☎ *206/728–8595.*

$$ Casa-U-Betcha. Yuppie breeders flood this Belltown favorite late most nights, turning it into a major straight pickup scene. But this is Seattle, after all, and same-sexers seem always to be warmly welcomed, particularly among Gen-Xers. Here you'll find mostly Mexican fare, but also some terrific Caribbean and Latin specialties, such as a delicious paella with mussels, clams, chicken, chorizo, and snapper. *2212 1st Ave.,* ☎ *206/441–1989.*

$$ Zasu. This offbeat option near Pioneer Square is a sleek, high-ceilinged haunt with dancing most nights. The kitchen serves up a diverse array of mostly European dishes, from traditional Welsh rarebit to a zesty Hungarian goulash. *608 1st Ave.,* ☎ *206/682–1200.*

$–$$ **Good Chow.** A departure from Belltown's more bohemian eats, Good Chow is a perky café with an airy, brick courtyard, and a staff that's variously perky and airy, too. Best bets from the regional menu are the crab sandwich, greens with crumbled gorgonzola, and grilled veggie sandwiches. *2331 2nd Ave.,* ☎ *206/443–5833.*

$ **The Crocodile.** Part of what is currently one of the hottest grunge clubs in the country, the Crocodile is often overlooked as a restaurant. True, it's nothing fancy—just a cavernous pseudo-diner with big, plate-glass windows and a high ceiling. But the pastas, sandwiches, and eggs are excellent. At lunchtime, it's actually very relaxed here. *2200 2nd St.,* ☎ *206/441–5611.*

$ **Trattoria Mitchelli.** This sprawling, pubby Italian restaurant off Pioneer Square has great sidewalk seating along Yesler Way, hearty pasta dishes (try the black-bean ravioli), and a huge list of microbeers. A bit touristy and noisy, but open most nights till 4 AM. *84 Yesler Way,* ☎ *206/623–3883.*

Capitol Hill

$$ **Coastal Kitchen.** If you're with a group of friends, consider the Coastal Kitchen's bright, white-tiled dining room—there always seems to be a bunch of chattering, laughing groups here. The cuisine is eclectic, from the rock shrimp–and–crab cakes to Caribbean seafood grill to pasta *puttanesca* (tomatoes, garlic, capers, black olives, and anchovies). *429 15th Ave. E,* ☎ *206/322–1145.*

$$ **Machiavelli.** Set in a large dining room with lots of windows and cheerful red chairs, this poor man's chic bistro serves decent, fair-priced Italian favorites. Try the penne with red-pepper pesto, the anchovy pizza, or the eggplant parmigiana. *1215 Pine St.,* ☎ *206/621–7941.*

$–$$ **The Easy.** Restaurants attached to gay bars are rarely as good as the dyky Easy, at which everybody is exceedingly welcome. The varied, affordable food includes a fine Caesar salad with roasted-garlic–and–anchovy dressing, a smoked chicken–and–brie baguette, and rigatoni Siciliano (with calamata olives, capers, fresh tomatoes, fresh herbs, and garlic with red wine). *916 E. Pike St.,* ☎ *206/323–8343.*

$–$$ **Hopvine Pub.** Though a pub, it has the ambience of a contemporary art gallery—muted lighting, royal-blue bar stools. Only the wooden booths impart a taverny feel. The young and trendy crowd comes here as much to hear good live music as to sample Seattle-style clam chowder, pesto pizza, thick grinders, and microbeers by the dozen. *507 15th Ave. E,* ☎ *206/328–3120.*

$–$$ **Jack's Bistro.** This peppy Tuscan-Provençal–inspired eatery has a sunny courtyard, some sidewalk seating, and a cozy, storefront dining room—whatever your mood, you'll find a good place to sit. The menu has good salads and pastas, and a variety of interesting starters, such as gorgonzola polenta. Friendly, low-key staff. *405 15th Ave. E,* ☎ *206/324–9625.*

$–$$ **Siam on Broadway.** There are a bunch of Thai restaurants on the Hill, of which this is easily the best—and that's considering some pretty strong company. The crowds that descend upon this place most nights attest to its great food and friendly service. The vegetables in a spicy curry are among the best dishes. *616 Broadway Ave. E,* ☎ *206/324–0892.*

$ **Dick's Drive-In Restaurant.** The garish orange sign of this renowned burger joint is probably visible from the space shuttle. The whole place is a tribute to '60s kitsch architecture, and it's usually packed late at night with hungry, drunk guys and grungers. The menu is simple: quarter-pound, all-beef patties, plus fries and old-fashioned ice cream. There's a cruisy

422

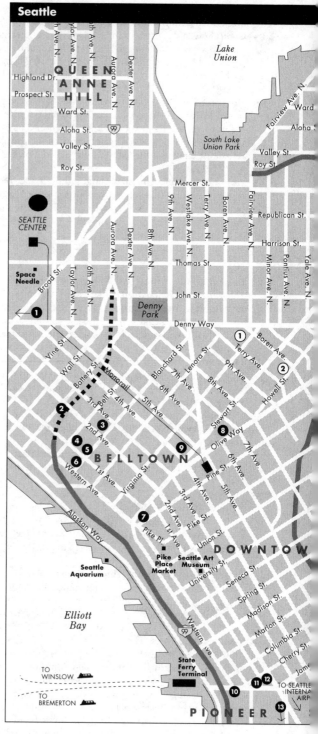

outdoor counter by the take-out window. *115 Broadway Ave. E, ☎ 206/ 323–1300.*

$ **Giorgina's.** Lesbian-owned and gay-frequented for many years, this is one of the classiest but most casual Italian restaurants on the Hill. The softly lighted, contemporary dining room is always aglow with smiling patrons, sampling from the list of designer pizzas (garlic clam is a favorite) and light pasta dishes. Many wines by the glass. *131 15th Ave. E, ☎ 206/329–8118.*

$ **Glo's.** As opposed to the city's zillion hip coffeehouses, Glo's is a real no-frills coffee shop, open from 7 AM to 3 PM and *the* breakfast choice among dykes and fags. Eggs Benedict, Belgian waffles, and bagels and lox should help you start your day. *1621 E. Olive Way, ☎ 206/324–2577.*

$ **Gravity Bar.** On the ground floor of the ultrafaggy Broadway Market, this postindustrial juice bar with massive chrome air ducts and pipes seems to be a magnet for cute lesbians. Many salads, open-face sandwiches, chapati-bread roll-ups, and rice-and-veggie platters are available. And yum . . . the wheatgrass juice is delicious . . . just like Mom's. *415 Broadway Ave. E, ☎ 206/325–7186; also in Belltown: 113 Virginia St., ☎ 206/ 448–8826.*

$ **Hamburger Mary's.** Looking like a giant fern bar is this cheerful version of the now ubiquitous, West Coast–restaurant chain. The tasty burgers and fries are the main offering, but you might also stop in for a late-night banana split. *1525 E. Olive Way, ☎ 206/324–8112.*

$ **Toshi's Teriyaki.** This is a tiny Japanese fast-food joint centrally located on 15th Avenue—inexpensive, quick, and convenient. Well-prepared take-out and eat-in (there are only a few seats) beef, chicken breast, pork, and stir-fried veggie options. *111 15th Ave. E, ☎ 206/329–5838.*

Elsewhere

$$ **Cafe Flora.** This handsome contemporary dining room is the most inventive vegetarian restaurant in the city. Menu highlights can include Oaxaca tacos with spicy mashed potatoes, diced peppers, cheddar and smoked-mozzarella cheeses, and a side of black-bean stew; an Indian chickpea stew; or an apple-jalapeño-chutney quesadilla appetizer. Probably the gayest scene off Capitol Hill: lots of power dykes and guppies. *2901 E. Madison St., ☎ 206/325–9100.*

$$ **Simpatico Bistro.** If you're looking to have a nice dinner near the University of Washington, this gay-popular Wallingford restaurant never fails. There are booths and tables inside, and also a shaded, arborlike patio. The food is Italian: Try lamb shank braised in Chianti with garlic and allspice, or the tangy goat-cheese polenta. *4430 Wallingford Ave. N., ☎ 206/632–1000.*

$–$$ **Cactus.** This funky (but not tacky) Mexican restaurant near the gay Madison Park Beach is a popular place after all that sunning, swimming, and scoping. The food is slightly contemporary, with dishes like papaya-and-avocado salad, and there's also a substantial tapas menu. *4220 E. Madison St., ☎ 206/324–4140.*

Coffeehouse Culture

This city is caffeine central. It's where the ever-expanding Starbucks chain originated in 1970, and there seems to be a coffeehouse on every corner. And, if you're still having trouble finding a cup of the jitters, simply look for one of the more than 200 licensed espresso carts roaming Seattle's streets.

B & O Espresso (204 Belmont Ave. E, ☎ 206/322–5028) is a Capitol Hill institution, drawing a fairly bookish and mellow gay crowd—lots of folks chipping away at dog-eared, dime novels hang here. On lower

Capitol Hill, **Bauhaus Books and Coffee** (301 E. Pine St., ☎ 206/625–1600) has stacks of art and architecture books and a stylish decor set off by lots of black, wrought-iron grillwork. **Book & Bean Espresso** (1635½ E. Olive Way, ☎ 206/325–1139) has all the usual beans, but also scads of used books regularly being pored over by cerebral sorts.

Perhaps the gayest coffeehouse in the city, **Cafe Paradiso** (1005 E. Pike St., ☎ 206/322–6960), is close to the city's two lesbian bars. There are two floors and big windows overlooking the action on Pike Street; more grunge than guppie, but plenty of both. Popular with alternateens, **Café Septième** (214 Broadway Ave. E, ☎ 206/860–8858) is a huge, dark, intentionally run-down-looking place with great sandwiches and a slightly affected ambience.

Cozy and crunchy, **Rosebud Espresso and Bistro** (719 E. Pike St., ☎ 206/323–6636) has real food—pastas, overstuffed sandwiches—good live jazz many nights, and whimsical decor of mismatched chairs and tables, sofas, and cushy wing chairs. There's a patio out back. The Pioneer Square location of **Torrefazione** (320 Occidental Ave. S, ☎ 206/624–5847) isn't nearly as gay as the Belltown one (622 Olive Way, ☎ 206/624–1429), but it has more character—with sidewalk seating along a cobblestone, pedestrian-only street of galleries.

SLEEPS

A drawback to visiting Seattle is that you can count on good weather only from about June through September: Since most everyone tries to come at this time, it's very hard to find a room then, even out by the airport. In-season rates have risen tremendously over the past five years, but there are still plenty of places to stay for less than $100 a night. Just book well ahead. The rest of the year, especially in winter, Seattle is a bargain. So, because it actually isn't much grayer here then than in places like New York City, Chicago, or Boston, don't reject an off-season vacation without considering the savings. And in Seattle, it may be raining, but it shouldn't be snowing. Guest houses, which were unheard of here 15 years ago, have boomed recently; you'll find plenty of gay-friendly options on Capitol Hill.

For price ranges, *see* Chart A at the front of this guide.

Hotels

⊞ Built in 1901, the luxurious **Alexis Hotel** is where stars and dignitaries often stay. Many suites have wood-burning fireplaces and Jacuzzis, and all rooms are done with a mix of antiques and period pieces. The only drawback to this four-story property is the lack of a view. *1007 1st Ave., ☎ 206/624–4844 or 800/426–7033. 54 rooms. $$$$*

⊞ The stylish **Hotel Vintage Park,** set in a striking 1922 building, is one of the city's most intimate, elegant properties. Rooms have cherry-wood furniture and rich, dark fabrics; some have fireplaces. *1100 5th Ave., ☎ 206/624–8000 or 800/624–4433. 129 rooms. $$$–$$$$*

⊞ The 35-story **Sheraton Hotel & Towers** is at the foot of Pike Street, a hilly but doable walk from most of the gay action. Though it has a bit of a convention feel, this is one of the brightest, most attractive Sheratons in the entire chain. Views from the top-floor health spa are incredible. *1400 6th Ave., ☎ 206/621–9000 or 800/325–3535. 864 rooms. $$$–$$$$*

⊞ Perched atop First Hill, a short way from Capitol Hill, the **Sorrento,** inspired by an Italian villa, has terrific views of the entire city. Rooms have a clubby feel, with plenty of antiques. The staff is well-trained and efficient. *900 Madison St., ☎ 206/622–6400. 76 rooms. $$$*

☉ Right across the street from Pike Place Market, the **Inn at the Market** is a relatively young property with the feel of an inn in the French countryside—dine downstairs at the hotel's Campagne (*see* Eats, *above*) restaurant if you're still not totally convinced. Rooms are spacious and contemporary; many have unobstructed views of Elliott Bay. *86 Pine St., ☎ 206/443–3600 or 800/446–4484. 65 rooms. $$–$$$*

☉ At the foot of Capitol Hill but still above I–5, **Plaza Park Suites** has a terrific location, spacious accommodations—many with a fireplace and kitchen—and provides complimentary Continental breakfasts. *1011 Pike St., ☎ 206/682–8282 or 800/426–0670. 194 rooms. $$–$$$*

☉ The **Camlin** is part of a chain of three, cheap restored early-20th-century hotels, all of them Downtown and all brimming with characters. The Camlin is the closest to Capitol Hill, but they're all convenient and relatively near one another; the others are the **Roosevelt** (1531 7th Ave., ☎ 206/621–1200 or 800/426–0670; 151 rooms; $) and the **Vance** (620 Stewart St., ☎ 206/441–4200 or 800/426–0670; 165 rooms; $). *1619 9th Ave., ☎ 206/682–0100 or 800/426–0670. 140 rooms. $*

☉ A cheap though somewhat sterile option up by the University of Washington and Wallingford is the **University Inn,** a small modern hotel. Its best attributes are a pleasant outdoor pool and its lively location. *4140 Roosevelt Way NE, ☎ 206/632–5055. 42 rooms. $*

Guest Houses and Small Hotels

☉ The **Capitol Inn** was built in 1903 and once served as a bordello. One room has a whirlpool and a fireplace. Eclectic decorating, yet very homey overall: Rooms have different themes, two have whirlpool tubs, and upstairs rooms are brighter but smaller. *1713 Belmont Ave., ☎ 206/323–1955. 6 rooms. Mixed gay/straight. $$–$$$*

☉ **Bacon Mansion,** a dramatic, Edwardian-style Tudor mansion with a separate cottage, is just east of all the action on Broadway. Rooms are fully modernized with TVs, phones, and modem lines; some have kitchenettes and refrigerators. *959 Broadway E, ☎ 206/329–1864 or 800/240–1864. 10 rooms. Mixed gay/straight. $–$$*

☉ Up in the University District, the **Chambered Nautilus** is a Georgian-style inn with great views of the Cascade Range and proximity to pretty Green Lake Park. There are four sundecks. Now, if only Seattle had sun. *5005 22nd Ave., ☎ 206/522–2536. 6 rooms. Mostly straight. $–$$*

☉ The **Gaslight Inn** is the best of the gay-oriented inns on the Hill. It's a lovely turn-of-the-century house with arts-and-crafts furnishings and an abundance of rich, oak paneling. There's a large, heated pool outside along with lots of space for sunning. Next door and owned by the same people is a more contemporary spot, **Howell Street Suites,** with kitchens and large sitting areas. A terrific value, both properties are extremely popular; book well ahead. *1727 15th Ave., ☎ 206/325–3654. 14 rooms. Mixed gay/straight. $–$$*

☉ **Hill House** is another of Capitol Hill's perfectly restored Victorians. Rooms are done up with antiques, lace curtains, and fluffy down comforters. The full breakfast is superb. *1113 E. John St., ☎ 206/720–7161 or 800/720–7161. 5 rooms. Mixed gay/straight. $–$$*

☉ The distinctive, craftsman-style **Landes House** is right off Volunteer Park. Several of the rooms have decks with views of Puget Sound and the city skyline. Great breakfasts. Named after the city's only female mayor. Down-to-earth, friendly hosts. Nice hot tub out back. *712 11th Ave. E, ☎ 206/329–8781. 11 rooms. Mostly mixed gay male/lesbian. $–$$*

SCENES

If Kate Moss is the sort of girl (or boy) you fancy, you'll love Seattle, whose population of gaunt, waiflike, morose-looking young people is perhaps the highest of any city in the world (or at least any city in a developed nation). On the other hand, with all the Californians creeping in here, a love of gyms and tanning salons has given the city more buffed-and-bronzed types in recent years. At a couple of clubs you'll see guys ripping off their shirts and vogueing, but for the most part, Seattleites dress down and behave modestly.

Visitors are often surprised by how mellow and polite bar goers tend to be. People at bars stand in a single file for drinks. It's a ritual that imparts an oddly formal air to such a countercultural community. Once you do finally get to the bar, you'll be titillated by a lengthy, exotic list of microbeers, plus a few of your usual standbys. This is one of the finest attributes of Seattle's nightlife—that so many varieties of beer are available, and usually at quite reasonable prices. If you're new to this racket, ask the bartender for a recommendation—or use your ignorance of local brews as a way to inflate the ego of the cute, hopefully knowledgeable, creature standing next to you.

Bathhouses here are generally quite clean and friendly. Most popular are **Basic Plumbing** (1104 Pike St., ☎ 206/682–8441), which is more of a cruisy sex club than a spa (you don't have to check your clothes), and **Club Seattle** (1520 Summit Ave., ☎ 206/329–2334), a traditional "spa." Though it's been around forever, don't overlook **South End Steam Baths** (115½ 1st Ave. S, ☎ 206/223–9091), a historic landmark.

A tip for lesbians: During the **University of Washington** (☎ for tickets 206/543–2200) women's basketball season, which runs from November through March, try to take in a game. These events are a big deal among Seattle dykes: Attendance averages more than 3,000—better than any lesbian bar in America!

Bars and Clubs

Brass Connection. This is a rather small disco with a big-city feel. It has a strange layout, with a bar up front, a tiny dance floor wedged into the back of the building, and then a little room with a pool table off to one side. Circulating is a challenge. The music and decor are a bit dated, and the entire club has a kind of seedy feel. But compared with Neighbours, up the street, the Brass Connection has considerably more character. *722 E. Pike St., ☎ 206/322–7777. Crowd: 80/20 m/f; mostly 20s and 30s; racially mixed; zero attitude; trampy and fun.*

C. C. Slaughter's. One section of C. C.'s is a '50s-style diner that isn't even especially gay. Next door (enter through the diner or by its separate entrance) is what looks like a small, hotel lounge with an '80s decorating sensibility. Lots of space to sit and mingle, plus tinted lights, glass brick, and a breathtaking, tropical fish tank. *1501 E. Madison Ave., ☎ 206/726–0565. Crowd: similar to Thumpers, but more casual.*

Changes. This is the only bar north of Lake Union, up in Wallingford and close to the University District. It mostly draws people too lazy to drive in to Capitol Hill—which can mean anyone. It's a fairly small, dark bar with pool, pinball, dart boards, and video games—not a lot of atmosphere, but some outgoing, good-looking folks. *2103 N. 45th St., ☎ 206/545–8363. Crowd: 75/25 m/f; diverse in age; lesbians from the neighborhood, some students, a nice mix.*

The Cuff. With the Eagle having gone grunge, the Cuff is the only place in Seattle that has a significant leather following, and even then only on weekends. The large room has a central bar, with Tom of Finland posters on the walls and chains dangling about. It's unusually well-lighted. The overflow bar in back is usually open only on weekends. Off the side of the main room stretches a narrow patio called the Dog Run. *1533 13th Ave., ☎ 206/323–1525. Crowd: male, mostly late-20s and early 30s; low-key, leather but also lots of Levi's; grunge, or any look with an edge.*

Eagle. Like most Eagles, this one began as a leather bar. But over the years, perhaps due to its location near Capitol Hill's many alternative music clubs and several colleges, it has begun to cultivate a fairly young, grungy crowd. There's a long, dark bar as you enter, a popular patio out back, an open balcony upstairs overlooking the action, and a smaller cruise bar with pool and pinball. The jukebox mostly plays alternative rock. This is where a lot of the guppies from R Place go when they're in the mood for a some good-natured sleazing. Friendliest bartenders in town. *314 E. Pike St., ☎ 206/621–7591. Crowd: mostly male; young; a fair racial mix; rough-looking, goatees, a touch of leather, cruisy.*

The Easy. Having recently opened a popular restaurant and expanded with a big dance floor, the Easy now gets a more diverse crowd than ever. To the left as you enter is the large restaurant and a long, spacious bar—a rustic spot with rough-hewn wooden floors where you can mingle and cruise, hang comfortably with a date, or grab a good meal. To the right is the big dance floor with hot lighting, high ceilings, and the beat of house music most of the time. Of the two lesbian bars, this one gets more men and more people of color. *916 E. Pike St., ☎ 206/323–8343. Crowd: 80/20 f/m; mostly under 35; varies from lipstick to diesel dykes; a lot of energy.*

Encore. This is a classy, almost upscale bar and restaurant—the sort of place you could take your mother. It has a long, wooden bar with over-head televisions; amber lighting and high ceilings are a plus, and half the space is an eating area with tables and chairs. A good spot to meet up with friends over microbeers or espresso. *1518 11th Ave. E, ☎ 206/ 324–6617. Crowd: 50/50 m/f; all ages; neighborhood types, laid-back; not very cruisy.*

Kid Mohair. Seattle's newest club opened in the fall of 1995 and has quickly cultivated a big after-work following early in the night and a more en-ergetic crowd later for dancing. It's an upscale place with a fireside lounge upstairs and an extensive wine list at all the bars. Sunday there's a tea dance. *1207 E. Pine St., ☎ 206/625–4444. Crowd: 80/20 m/f, mostly mid-20s to late 30s, a few suits, classy but laid-back.*

Neighbours. This is Seattle's big gay disco, and although it's neither bet-ter nor worse than similar clubs in other cities, it's disappointingly bland in a city that prides itself on alternative culture and music. The decor is industrial, with exposed piping, corrugated metal, and chain link fences. The music is house. Inside is a dance floor with lots of cruising and stand-ing space surrounding it, and upstairs is a cozy little balcony. On Fridays and Saturdays you can barely move in here, and the club stays open for dancing after the alcohol is cut off. *1509 Broadway, ☎ 206/324–5358. Crowd: mostly male but some straight females and even fewer dykes; young, white, guppies in disco duds; attitudy, clonish.*

R Place. This is Seattle's most popular cruise bar, a smartly furnished fern bar with three floors. On the first floor is a video bar with lots of space for mingling. The second floor has some seating and is partially open; you can see to downstairs. As you leave the seating area you can either head up an-other flight of stairs or into a space with two pool tables; there always ap-pears to be a line to use them. Upstairs is the most crowded: just a big video bar with loud dance music, another pool table, and lots of room to circu-late. For a guppie bar, there's not a lot of attitude. A great selection of mi-crobeers and ales. *619 E. Pine St., ☎ 206/322–8828. Crowd: mostly male; young, professional, button-down; stand-and-model, clean-cut.*

Re-bar. For some time, this has been one of Seattle's hottest discos—despite the fact that it's tiny. Every night sees a somewhat queer following, Saturdays get more dykes, but Thursday is officially Queer Disco night—with long, cruisy lines. Inside is a small dance floor with interesting props hanging about—the decor is thematic, usually postmodern, and it changes often. This miniature disco holds a determined crowd of dancers, some of whom climb atop the speakers for more elbow room—and a chance to vogue a little. Off the dance floor is a long corridor bar with some seating. Matt Dillon and k. d. Lang have been known to pop by (whether on queer or straight nights, no one could confirm). Music ranges from deep house to old New Wave to even older classic disco. Behave: The bouncer is an enormous drag queen named Isadora. *1114 Howell St., ☎ 206/233–9873. Crowd: mixed gay/straight, more gay male on Queer Disco nights, but some dykes and groovy straight people; other times young, alternative; Doc Martens and baggy jeans; strong dyke following on Saturday.*

Thumpers. This is the kind of bar that more settled professional guys head to, often to enjoy dinner at the terrace restaurant or to catch a cabaret—it's very congenial, and since it has been around for a long time, it also has an aura of comfortableness. With all these successful, mature men standing around, you can also expect to see a few younger, self-starters hoping to find somebody with deep pockets. *1500 E. Madison Ave., ☎ 206/328–3800. Crowd: mostly male; mostly over 40; casual but well-dressed with some suits, very clubby.*

Timberline Tavern. If you think good country music and line dancing are a Southern thing, you're mistaken. This bar is known throughout the West Coast. It's a beautiful space: A huge pitched ceiling and rustic, post-and-beam construction give it the feel of an old Western hunting lodge—well, one with a disco ball. The crowd is lively, loud, friendly, and energetic—very mixed, although the women seem to keep to the left and the guys to the right. There's a large dance floor, lots of viewing areas around it, and a festive bar in back. Even if you can't two-step or line-dance, you might just come to watch. The club publishes a handy, little newsletter with a dance-class schedule and line-dancing instructions: ". . . kick, step, heel, stomp, stamp, stump, bump. . . ." *2015 Boren Ave., ☎ 206/622–6220. Crowd: 50/50 m/f; all ages; some straights; fun-loving and friendly; lots of bolo ties, denim, and cowboy hats.*

Wildrose. More of a lesbian tavern than the Easy, the Wildrose is a mellow, chat spot with an attractive, pubby restaurant on one side and a bar with two, heavily trafficked pool tables on the other. Big plate-glass windows look onto Pike Street; you can walk by and check out who's inside (too bad more gay bars aren't set up this way). Not as boy-populated, but they're welcome if they recognize and respect where they are. Women often come here before going dancing at the Easy, across the street. *1021 E. Pike St., ☎ 206/324–9210. Crowd: mainly lesbian; mostly 20s and 30s; lots of Doc Martens and baseball caps.*

Neib Bars

Seattle has tons of neighborhood joints, and although they're small and draw basically local crowds, they're among the most interesting bars you'll find. Worth noting are the **Detour** (1501 E. Olive Way, ☎ 206/322–2802), a low-key, leathery cruise bar by Hamburger Mary's; **Double Header** (407 2nd Ave., ☎ 206/464–9918), which is supposedly the oldest gay bar on the West Coast; the **Elite** (622 Broadway Ave. E, ☎ 206/324–4470), a real old-timer's bar just down the street from the Broadway Market; in Pioneer Square, the **Six-Eleven Tavern** (611 2nd Ave., ☎ 206/345–9430), an old saloon; **Sonya's** (1532 7th Ave., ☎ 206/624–5377), a serious drinking bar that gets going early; **Spags** (1118 E. Pike St., ☎ 206/322–3232), which calls itself "Seattle's Den for Bears and Trappers"; and, popular with TVs and TSs, the **Tacky Tavern** (1706 Bellevue Ave., ☎ 206/322–9744).

An honorary mention goes to **Jimmy Wu's Jade Pagoda** (606 Broadway Ave. E, ☎ 206/322–5900), an otherwise unmemorable Chinese restaurant with a cozy, womblike bar in back that has a major gay following, the best Long Island iced teas in town, and a terrific jukebox.

Music Clubs

Seattle's youthful nightlife scene attracts a mixed crowd of gays and straights to many Capitol Hill and Belltown clubs. Below is a sampling of places that don't necessarily cultivate a gay following but are nonetheless bastions of alternative music, fashion, and culture. They tend to draw an open-minded crowd of Gen-Xers.

The **Comet Tavern** (922 E. Pike St., ☎ 206/323–9853) is one of the spots where grunge music began to explode—it's almost a bit touristy at this point. Belltown's version of the Comet Tavern, the **Crocodile** (2200 2nd St., ☎ 206/441–5611) is a major concert venue for cutting-edge bands. You can't beat **Linda's** (707 E. Pine St., ☎ 206/325–1220) ambience; filled with Courtney Love and Eddie Vedder wannabes, it's sort of a cross between *Twin Peaks* and Pearl Jam. Up-and-coming alternative bands perform here often. **Moe** (925 E. Pike St., ☎ 206/324–2406) gets the grunge bunch for coffee, food, and live music; it's queerest on Sunday nights. **Off-Ramp Music Cafe** (109 Eastlake Ave. E, ☎ 206/628–0232) has cabaret on Sunday nights and rock acts the rest of the week. **RKCNDY** (1812 Yale Ave., ☎ 206/623–6651) is not quite as popular a mosh mecca as it once was, but it's a regular on the thrash circuit and is queer on Sundays. A bit different from some of the other discos, the **Weathered Wall** (1921 5th Ave., ☎ 206/728–9398)—when not playing dance music—stages poetry readings and performance art; Wednesdays are gayest.

THE LITTLE BLACK BOOK

At Your Fingertips
Crisis Clinic Hotline: ☎ 206/461–3222 or 800/244–5767. **Lesbian Health Clinic:** ☎ 206/461–4503. **Lesbian Resource Center:** ☎ 206/322–3953. **Northwest AIDS Foundation:** ☎ 206/860–6241. **Police:** ☎ 911. **Seattle Convention and Visitors Bureau:** 520 Pike St., Suite 1300, 98101, ☎ 206/461–5800. **Seattle Gay Clinic:** ☎ 206/461–4540. **Seattle Visitor Center:** 800 Convention Pl., ☎ 206/461–5840.

Gay Media
Seattle's weekly gay newspaper, the **Seattle Gay News** (☎ 206/324–4297) is well written and extremely comprehensive. The monthly magazine **2002** (☎ 206/323–2332) takes a lively, Gen-X–rooted view of gay and lesbian issues. The monthly, pocket-size **Seattle's Alternative Guidebook** (☎ 206/726–9936) has a complete listing of bars and community resources, plus many restaurants.

Dykes can also consult the **Lesbian Resource Center Community News** (☎ 206/322–3953), a monthly newspaper with news features, community resources, and entertainment notes.

The **Stranger** (☎ 206/323–7101) is the more in-your-face of the city's left-leaning entertainment weeklies. More mainstream—and comprehensive—is **Seattle Weekly** (☎ 206/623–0500).

BOOKSTORES

Beyond the Closet (1501 Belmont Ave., ☎ 206/322–4609) has a handsome, lesbigay store with a helpful staff and an unusually good selection of both porn and mainstream gay and lesbian periodicals. The **Baily-Coy Bookstore** (414 Broadway Ave. E, ☎ 206/323–8842) is a great independent bookstore with a significant gay and lesbian following; it's across the street from the Broadway Market. The city's oldest independent bookstore, **Red & Black Books** (432 15th Ave. E, ☎ 206/322–7323), also has many gay titles.

Body and Fitness

BQ Workout (Broadway Market, 300 Broadway Ave. E, ☎ 206/860–3070) has long been popular with lesbians and gays. The *in* gym, however, is **World Gym** (at the Convention Center, 8th Ave. and Pike St., ☎ 206/583–0640), formerly known as Cascade.

27 *Out in South Beach*

With Miami and Fort Lauderdale

MIAMI BEACHERS ARE OBSESSED WITH preservation. Over the past decade, the median age here has dropped from 69 to 44. Perhaps more significant than the *actual* difference in age is the *apparent* one: 10 years ago, most of the enfeebled, destitute 69-year-olds looked about 89; today, most of the buffed and bronzed 44-year-olds look about 24. In 1513, Spanish explorer Ponce de Leon poked around South Florida in search of the "Fountain of Youth." It's taken about 500 years, but a posse of savvy, queer, New York City expatriates seems finally to have found it.

Indeed, the beauty factor is outrageously high. In South Beach (a.k.a. SoBe), the newly restored and buzzing southern tip of Miami Beach that's currently the trendiest gay and lesbian destination in America, people feel a need to look and be hot. Working out two hours daily is typical, as is sunning another hour or two. Bodies are tanned and toned, their sleek forms obscured by only the sheerest, skimpiest swimwear and club gear. Rollerblading is the unofficial mode of transportation, and posing is the most popular pastime.

The importance of personal preservation notwithstanding, *architectural* preservation has truly been the backbone of SoBe's complete and utter transformation from urban blight into beachfront splendor. In 1912, millionaire Carl Graham Fisher and the island's owner, a determined farmer named John Collins, teamed to develop what was an anemic spit of sand into America's greatest winter tourist destination. Miami Beach boomed through the early 1920s, was leveled by a 1926 hurricane, only to be reinvented in the 1930s by a small, innovative band of architects, led by Henry Hohauser, whose collective building aesthetic was defined by sleek, low-slung, modern structures with rounded edges and ornate Egyptian and Aztec influences.

By the mid-'50s, Miami Beach, which had been incorporated in 1915, was a formal place where music and film stars mingled and the wealthy lodged, and in some cases lived, at the magnificent Fontainebleau Hotel. Even in the heavy, humid heat of summer, you wore a shirt and tie or a light dress, you shopped along swank Lincoln Road—the Rodeo Drive of its time—and you entertained often and vigorously.

It's difficult to pinpoint exactly when and why the area's popularity began to flag, but slowly, wealthy snowbirds began migrating elsewhere, and SoBe's glamorous hotels became apartment houses for retirees. For thousands, the community was the last stop before death's door. By 1970, the best shops had moved to Palm Beach and Naples, and Lincoln Road and SoBe had become disaster areas.

If desertion and neglect weren't harsh enough, the city was besieged by boat lifts, during which waves of Castro-persecuted Cubans, brought here from that country's prisons, were settled into SoBe's prisonlike apartment buildings and hotels. At about this time, disenchanted northeasterners, many of them gay, began discovering the region. The rows of forgotten but potentially beautiful 1930s buildings stood amid the crack houses and tenements. Preservationists rallied to have South Beach protected by designating most of it the historic "Deco District."

Resistance was minimal from SoBe's existing population—most of it Hispanic or Jewish and quite sensitive to injustice and discrimination. Nobody else much wanted South Beach, despite its uninterrupted stretch of sand and its historic architecture. Gays and lesbians took this dreary, dilapidated neighborhood and reinvented it.

Hard work and a little luck have quickly turned South Beach into a glitzy playground—just as it was in the '50s, but without the formality. Film and fashion folk first fell in love with the renovated Art Deco beauties along Ocean Drive. Several gay discos opened. Top young hoteliers refurbished old properties, while top young chefs transformed empty storefronts into first-rate eateries. The first wave of development was the gentrification of Ocean Drive; the next came along a few blocks of commercial Washington Avenue. Collins Avenue, the rest of Washington Avenue, and the pedestrian mall, Lincoln Road, followed.

Miami Beach differs sharply from other gay resort destinations. Most notably, it is the only gay resort that is adjacent to a major international city. Proximity to Miami International Airport makes travel here from Latin America, Europe, and the rest of the nation relatively easy. Gay foreigners, especially South and Central Americans, vacation and settle here in droves. Rents have risen rapidly, but apartments still sell for less than those in Key West and a fraction of prices in Palm Springs, Fire Island, or Aspen.

The city's mix of body worship and urban toughness may leave you feeling a bit out of place, but this is a completely tolerant community. A human rights ordinance, not unlike the one that was rescinded in Gainesville in 1994, was passed here in 1992. Miami Beach has a gay-friendly mayor, gays on the city council, and gays on many city commissions. The local police force was the only one in the nation to take part in the March on Washington in 1993. South Beachers will proudly tell you that there are no "gay" restaurants or hotels, and that everyone is welcome everywhere. It's a community of unusual integration, harmony, and mutual respect for differing lifestyles, races, colors, and genders. And yet it wears not the clothing of some peacenik '60s commune but the cutting-edge duds of today's fashion industry.

THE LAY OF THE LAND

South Beach is the small, triangular tip of the larger island of Miami Beach (population 92,000). Only about a mile across at its widest point, South Beach proper extends about 2 miles from Dade Boulevard (which feeds into the Venetian Causeway) at its northern end down to South Pointe Park.

Ocean Drive

Ocean Drive resists labels of sexual orientation. It is touristy, it is local, it is gay, and it is straight. And it strives to be fabulous beyond words. This is where the most dramatic instances of Deco District revitalization have occurred; it's where celebrities, fashion designers, and models roam freely among stately hotels and landmarks, including the Mediterranean villa at 1114 Ocean Drive, formerly known as **Amsterdam Palace,** now the home of Italian fashion god Gianni Versace. For all the glamorous men and women strolling by, you acutely start to feel that everything has an unnatural aura—as though you're watching a carefully choreographed costume parade.

SoBe's **gay beach** is at 12th Street and Ocean. Things were beginning to stir at the beach up by the Shore Club (17th Street) until it closed in 1994; it remains to be seen whether the area will pick up once again. The Palace Bar and Grill at 1200 Ocean Drive marks the beginning of buff-boy territory. Although boyish poseurs make up the majority at this point, lesbians camp out here, too—not to mention a significant number of straight women hoping to ward off creeps. The beach can be cruisy at night, though the police patrol it heavily.

Washington Avenue

When only Cuban refugees and financially strapped retirees lived along Ocean Drive and Collins Avenue, they shopped for groceries, discount clothing, and cheap dry goods along **Washington Avenue.** This is still the island's chief commercial spine and offers a fascinating view of a city in transformation: Small discount stores and inexpensive restaurants are being replaced with fashion boutiques and home-furnishings stores. It's not as pricey as Ocean Drive or Lincoln Road, though: This is still where locals stock up on day-to-day goods, everything and anything from toilet paper to in-line skates, Cuban sandwiches to sushi. The pedestrian traffic, made up of poor and rich, gay and straight, young and old, white, black, Latino, and Orthodox Jew, is never dull.

At 10th and Washington is the world's most impressive collection of Art Deco and Art Nouveau, the **Wolfsonian Foundation Gallery** (1001 Washington Ave., ☎ 305/531–1001). A research center and museum, this 50,000-piece collection of decorative and fine arts, designs, and books provides one of the few good reasons in Miami Beach to stay inside for a few hours.

A few blocks over from Washington, along Meridian Avenue between 14th and 11th streets, is **Flamingo Park,** a popular cruising ground. As with the gay beach at Ocean and 12th, it's not especially safe, but that doesn't seem to stop plenty of boys from trying.

Lincoln Road Mall

In the '50s, **Lincoln Road** was a swank avenue dotted with America's top department stores. It died a decade later with the rest of South Beach; closed to traffic and turned into a pedestrian row, it never drew many pedestrians. With several million dollars pumped into it, however, Lincoln Road is now the hottest place to shop in the city. Major entertainment firms like Sony and MTV have offices here; dozens of galleries and home-furnishings stores have opened.

The most fashionable stretch is between Alton Road and Drexel Avenue; beyond Drexel, through Washington and Collins, it's basically a Fayva nightmare, though the KFC fast-food restaurant at Collins is, believe it or not, an impressive example of contemporary art deco.

By day Lincoln Road is more touristy: Bladers buzz by, families browse, business types gather for lunch. At night it's classy, though not particularly fancy, with chic homos eating out at the many sidewalk restaurants and smartly dressed couples walking arm in arm.

A few of the most notable sights along here include the four-story, Deco **Old Lincoln Theater** (541 Lincoln Rd., ☎ 305/673–3331), now home of

Michael Tilson Thomas's New World Symphony; the storefront practice space of the **Miami City Ballet** (905 Lincoln Rd., ☎ 305/532–7713 or 305/532–4880), where on many afternoons you can watch the dancers rehearse; and the **Colony Theater** (1040 Lincoln Rd., ☎ 305/674–1026), another of the great Deco theaters in the country, which hosts a variety of performing arts.

There are about a dozen art galleries along the mall, including the nonprofit **South Florida Arts Center** (924 Lincoln Rd., ☎ 305/674–8278), which houses 90 artists and is open to the public. Two popular weekend events held in the Lincoln Road pedestrian zone are the **antiques and collectibles market** (alternating Sun., 10–5), and the **Lincoln Road Farmers Market** (between Meridian and Euclid Aves., winter, Sun., 9–1). For information on these and other Lincoln Road events, call 305/531–3442.

Miami and Environs

Next to the United Nations, **Miami International Airport** (MIA) may be the world's most international gathering place. It is also your first hint that Miami is less a U.S. city than it is a Latin American one. Many signs are in Spanish; in fact, half the city identifies itself as Hispanic—much of the population is Cuban, but many others come from Central America, northern South America, and Creole French–speaking Haiti.

Since South Beach's emergence as a gay tourist mecca, few gay and lesbian leisure travelers stay in Miami proper or even spend an afternoon there. Recent isolated instances of violence directed at tourists are less of a reason to skip Miami than the fact that there simply isn't much to do. The city is difficult to navigate; it's densely trafficked, incoherently zoned and developed, and fairly unattractive. Miami's downtown is a busy, commercial, South Florida hub by day and an eerie wasteland at night. Slightly more interesting are **Little Havana,** the mostly Cuban neighborhood west of downtown across the Miami River, and the upscale **Coral Gables** and **Coconut Grove,** both worth exploring for their beautiful homes and for high-end shopping districts such as **CocoWalk** (3015 Grand Ave., Coconut Grove) and **The Shops at 550** (550 Biltmore Way, Coral Gables).

Fort Lauderdale and Environs

Fort Lauderdale, which drew zillions of poorly behaved college students on spring break from about 1965 through 1985, has grown up during the last decade. (You may find that it's grown too mature, with its goodly number of senior citizens.) The most notable difference between today's and yesterday's Fort Lauderdale has to do less with age than with mentality. Once slightly trashy and lowbrow, Fort Lauderdale now pulls in a fairly low-key, mellow, economically diverse group of visitors. You'll find more couples and a rapidly growing number of increasingly loyal gays and lesbians. Fort Lauderdale seems to be emerging as the perfect middle ground for comfort-seeking gay travelers who find South Beach too full of attitude, Miami menacing, Palm Beach snobby and straight, and Key West affable but sleazy.

A dull city to look at—a maze of six-lane roads and sullen shopping centers—there's little to do in Fort Lauderdale beyond sunning, swimming, fishing, and shopping (which is not to belittle any of these activities). **Ocean Boulevard's** beachfront, between Las Olas and Sunrise boulevards, is less a scene these days than when it provided the setting for the fluffy 1960 film *Where the Boys Are,* but the sands are still golden, and it's a nice place to plunk down your pale, paunchy, but no less personable body without worrying that a posse of SoBe clones is snickering at you (and so what if they are?). **Las Olas Boulevard** is the traditional avenue of high-end shopping; it leads east to the city's most expensive residential neighborhood, **The Isles.** Heading in the other direction, at the intersection of Andrews Avenue, is the **Museum of Art** (1 E. Las Olas Blvd., ☎ 305/525–5500), which houses a fine collection of Flemish and Dutch works, as well as Native American and pre-Columbian ethnographic art. Inland a couple of miles, where Southwest 2nd Street meets Southwest 7th Avenue, is **River-walk,** a pleasant if antiseptic promenade that runs along the banks of the New River. This thoroughfare takes you through the city's new **Arts and Science District,** a six-block stretch of new museums and attractions, including the **Museum of Discovery and Science** (401 S.W. 2nd St., ☎ 305/467–6637); the **Broward Center for Performing Arts** (201 S.W. 5th Ave., ☎ 305/462–0222); and the **Fort Lauderdale Historical Society Museum** (219 S.W. 2nd Ave., ☎ 305/463–4431).

GETTING THERE

The lower half of Miami Beach is connected to the city of Miami by three causeways. The **Venetian Causeway** is the middle one, which connects local streets. Travelers to and from mainland highways should take either the **Julia Tuttle Causeway** (I–195) from points north or the **MacArthur Causeway** (U.S. 41/Rte. A1A) from points south. Both Fort Lauderdale and Miami are easily reached by plane, train, and bus.

A taxi to Miami Beach or South Beach will cost upward of $20. The **Super Shuttle** (☎ 305/871–2000, or at the airport, look for a guy wearing a yellow Super Shuttle T-short) is the cheapest way to get from the airport to either area. The cost is $10 to a hotel, $13 to a residence. To get to the airport on the shuttle, call one day in advance.

WHEN TO GO

Generally, May through October is the down time, when hotel rates on South Beach are reduced as much as 50%. September and October are at the height of hurricane season, and although the most devastating storms come only once every 10 or 15 years, annoying two- to four-day low pressure systems can ruin a fall weekend getaway. January is probably the best time to come; prices are at their peak, but the Christmas crowds have returned north and families and spring breakers are still weeks away. Thanksgiving weekend kicks off a winter of absolutely dizzying SoBe party weekends, many of them anchored by crowded circuit parties.

GETTING AROUND

Miami Beach has grown at a pace that has strained its infrastructure. The island isn't really built for cars—traffic along Ocean Drive comes to a standstill on weekend evenings—and though plans are underway to add more parking by the late '90s, the city will never be able to handle cars in great numbers. It's best to park your car where you're staying and walk, blade, or bicycle.

EATS

Fashion and food have never been strangers, so it's not at all surprising that SoBe's culinary scene is thriving. Restaurants have been getting better and better, and many have cutting-edge chefs and managers from the Northeast. Miami proper had already developed a reputation for fine international cuisines—from Cuban and Spanish to Chinese and Thai—and SoBe now has options in all these categories.

SoBe's image-consciousness dictates that to be seen you must dine as often as possible along Ocean Drive, preferably near the sidewalk. The cafés along Lincoln Road rank second in image-boosting value. Washington Avenue's restaurants offer the most culinary bang for your buck (but no sidewalk seating).

For price ranges, *see* Chart A at the front of this guide.

South Beach

$$$–$$$$ Osteria Del Teatro. Osteria was one of the first of the new wave of stellar restaurants to open during SoBe's renaissance, and it's watched a lot of competitors come and go. The intimate dining room is always packed. The menu is pricey but exceptional. Salmon with fennel and orange sauce, and *pappardelle* with stone crab meat are among the stars. *1443 Washington Ave.,* ☏ *305/538–7850.*

$$$–$$$$ Pacific Time. Offering a pan-Pacific sampling of succulent and innovative dishes like chili-grilled shrimp with coriander and honey-roasted duck with fresh plum and plum wine sauce, Pacific Time is the best restaurant in SoBe. Great food and a nonchalant West Coast atmosphere. *915 Lincoln Rd.,* ☏ *305/534–5979.*

$$–$$$ Casablanca. On the ground floor of the Imperial Hotel, this Ocean Drive standby offers fairly traditional dishes like pasta, chops, sandwiches, and Caesar salads. Plenty of sidewalk seating at marble-top tables with black chairs. Pretty straight scene dominated by fashion plates, and a very good value. *650 Ocean Dr.,* ☏ *305/534–9463.*

$$–$$$ Chrysanthemum. A standout among the many strong Asian contenders in SoBe, Chrysanthemum is a classy spot that will tantalize your taste buds with sizzling Szechuan and Peking cooking. If you've never eaten frogs' legs, try them here; also great is the wonton ravioli with garlic and ginger. *1248 Washington Ave.,* ☏ *305/531–5656.*

$$–$$$ Farfalla. Why a shiny Harley-Davidson motorcycle anchors the dining room is anybody's guess; this otherwise elegant, high-ceilinged trattoria is one of the most sophisticated—and gay-popular—restaurants in town. Good nouvelle Northern Italian fare, from designer pizzas to grilled lamb with peppercorn and sage sauce. *701 Washington Ave.,* ☏ *305/673–2335.*

$$–$$$ Grillfish. As the name suggests, you come here to sample fresh grilled lobster, salmon, swordfish, tuna, marlin, grouper, snapper, trout, or monkfish. The dramatic decor recalls the classical ruins of Greece—although the brown vinyl table coverings could go. *1444 Collins Ave.,* ☏ *305/538–9908.*

$$–$$$ Jeffrey's. This gay-operated restaurant just off Lincoln Road keeps a low profile by South Beach standards, but it's always good and its slightly formal dining room with tall columns is a perfect venue for romantic dining. The mid-Atlantic bistro menu includes a crisp Cornish game hen and savory crab soup. *1629 Michigan Ave.,* ☏ *305/673–0690.*

$$ Joe's Stone Crab. Come prepared to wait (and wait and wait), to people-watch, and to chow delicious stone-crab claws—about a ton is served every-day—at this fourth-generation family restaurant. Fried green tomatoes, hash browns, and Key lime pie are other standouts. Not particularly gay, but a classic that no visitor should miss. *227 Biscayne St.,* ☏ *305/673–0365.*

$$ Lario's. Pop diva Gloria Estefan is part-owner of this chic, moderately priced, and consistently good Cuban restaurant. Try the tamale platter, chicken with yellow rice, and sweet plantains; finish it all off with the fresh gauva-and-cheese flan for dessert. The cutest Latino waiters alive. *820 Ocean Dr.,* ☏ *305/532–9577.*

$$ Van Dyke. Most of the seating at this smart Lincoln Road restaurant is outside, but much more pleasant is the elegant inner dining room with

438

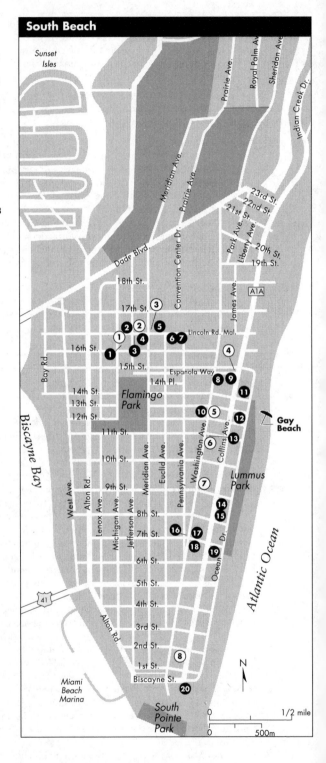

South Beach

its varnished wood, marble tables, and a classy little coffee bar. The traditional American food and service are uneven; the salads generally rise above the sandwiches. *846 Lincoln Rd.,* ☎ *305/534-3600.*

$$ World Resources Cafe. Despite a name that suggests food from many cultures, most of the dishes at this homey bistro are Thai—basil chicken, green curries, Thai teas. The eclectic furnishings, some of them Deco, are for sale. Impressive wine and beer list. *719 Lincoln Rd.,* ☎ *305/534-9095.*

$-$$ Beehive Diner. You can either dine inside amid the cartoonish colors or out in the courtyard on Lincoln Road Mall. The Beehive serves upscale diner favorites, including catfish marinara, a nice heavy meat loaf, pasta, and several kinds of pizza. *630 Lincoln Rd.,* ☎ *305/538-7484.*

$-$$ Lyon Frères et Compagnie. This tony market and self-service café is ideal if you need to stock your condo kitchen with salads, homemade soups, or focaccia sandwiches. The wine- and exotic-beer bar is a great place to make friends. *600 Lincoln Rd.,* ☎ *305/534-0600.*

$-$$ WPA. Best known for its Sunday gospel brunches at 1 and 2:30, WPA is one of the gayest spots in town—a cavernous dining room with murals of Works Progress Administration (WPA) scenes on the walls. The eclectic menu has a delicious Mediterranean antipasti plate, huge portions of turkey meat loaf, shrimp scampi, and rich ice cream desserts. *685 Washington Ave.,* ☎ *305/534-1684.*

$ 11th Street Diner. This stainless-steel deco diner was built in 1948 in Wilkes-Barre, Pennsylvania, and moved here in 1992. You get the usual diner food here, including a great Philly cheese steak and the most voluptuous vanilla malts in SoBe. In the spirit of traditional greasy spoons, the service is lousy, pissy to the point that waitpersons actually yell at their patrons. *11th St. and Washington Ave.,* ☎ *305/534-6373.*

$ Front Porch Café. On the upper stretch of Ocean Drive, the Front Porch fosters a truly lazy, devil-may-care atmosphere—a far cry from the stand-and-model spots down the block. It's known for its Thai noodles, pizzas, overstuffed sandwiches, muffins, breads, and hearty breakfasts. Strong gay following. *1420 Ocean Dr.,* ☎ *305/531-8300.*

$ Gertrude's. This café inspired by Gertrude Stein has a strong lesbian following. Ceiling fans whir overhead, the wall is a bright mural of 1920s flapper society, and the thick sandwiches are named after the likes of Fitzgerald and Hemingway. Has a festive coffee bar, too. *826 Lincoln Rd.,* ☎ *305/538-6929.*

$ News Café. Even though it's open 24 hours, serves decent food, and has an in-house newsstand, it's still difficult to understand why the News Café is the most popular spot on Ocean Drive. Among its negative attributes are the awful service, the brash and touristy crowd, and uncomfortable seating in a somewhat ugly building. Best bets are the gazpacho and anything from the little raw bar in back. *800 Ocean Dr.,* ☎ *305/538-6397.*

$ Palace Bar and Grill. This open-air hangout is where the girls and boys go between sun sessions at the gay beach across the street. It's a wonderful place for drinks, light food, and breakfast. Better meals of substance—and much better service—can be had elsewhere. *The* place to be a slacker on weekend afternoons. Great music. *1200 Ocean Dr.,* ☎ *305/531-9077.*

Coffeehouse Culture

Although several area restaurants have coffee bars, SoBe still lacks a proper java house. **Coccofresco** (710 Washington Ave., at 7th St., ☎ 305/531-5526) is a bright nook known for its rich gelato—white chocolate with hazelnut is the best flavor. But you can get all the usual coffees here, too.

Miami

$$$$ Mark's Place. Inside this adobe building in North Miami, chef Mark Militello creates regional Florida cuisine using an oak-burning oven imported from Genoa. Designer pizzas and pastas are available in the deco dining room—but it's hard to pass up eye-openers like red-tip crawfish flavored with ginger, lemongrass, chili, and garlic; or the pan-seared foie gras with huckleberry. *2286 N.E. 123rd St., ☎ 305/893–6888.*

$$–$$$$ East Coast Fisheries. An actual fish market on the Miami River, East Coast Fisheries gets its stock fresh daily from a fleet of nearly 40 fishing boats. From the dining area, you can watch the chefs below preparing your dinner to order. *360 W. Flagler St., ☎ 305/372–1300.*

$$ Tani Guchi's Place. It's up in North Miami, but if you're traveling between Fort Lauderdale and South Beach and you love Japanese food, stop here. Tuesdays they offer a two-for-one deal for gay couples. *2224 N.E. 123rd St., ☎ 305/892–6744.*

$ Islas Canarias. The food at this local institution is equal parts Canary Islands (the owners hail from there) and Cuba. Chips—both potato and plantain—or white rice and black beans come with the main dishes, which range from grilled chicken to ham hocks with boiled potatoes. Always abuzz with chatter. *285 N.W. 27th Ave., ☎ 305/649–0440.*

Fort Lauderdale

$$$ Mark's Las Olas. If food matters more than conversation, visit this hot spot whose metallic finishes make the place stylish but very noisy. Who cares though, when there's real West Indian callaloo, chayote, and plantain on the menu, exquisitely presented and imaginatively sauced. *1032 E. Las Olas Blvd., ☎ 305/463–1000.*

$$–$$$$ Café Arugula. This is one of the most gay-popular of the city's more elegant restaurants. Seafood dominates a menu that draws on the culinary traditions of warm climates from Mexico to the American Southwest to the Mediterranean. A good place for a special occasion. *3110 N. Federal Hwy., Lighthouse Point, ☎ 305/785–7732.*

$–$$$ Mangos. This airy spot on ritzy East Las Olas, just up the street from the guppie bar Cathode Ray's, is a good solid option for slightly nouvelle American food. One of the city's premier people-watching perches. *904 E. Las Olas Blvd., ☎ 305/523–5001.*

$ Lester's. After clubbing, queens from the nearby Copa and Stud pile into this 24-hour dive to recover over stacks of fluffy pancakes and fried eggs. *250 Rte. 84, ☎ 305/525–5641.*

SLEEPS

SoBe's hotel scene has improved. When the first few hotels along Ocean Drive and lower Collins Avenue were restored, the rates were relatively low for a resort area. Recently, however, they've come up to par with prices at hotels in similar destinations around the country. Most Deco hotels look stunning from the outside, and even the least expensive of the lot have worked hard on their lobbies. The guest rooms themselves, however, vary tremendously from property to property.

Most of these hotels were constructed on a smaller scale than the newer high-rises in mid- and North Miami Beach. Even in the fanciest South Beach hotels, bathrooms are sometimes tiny and functional, and in many of the less expensive properties, rooms are plain, small, and uninspired. In places like the Marlin, the Raleigh, and several other high-end properties, rooms have been given exotic, arty furnishings, and many have CD players and VCRs—but they still lack the sort of sumptuous trappings of the grand resorts of Coral Gables and Palm Beach.

Over the past few years, several gay guest houses have sprung up around town. Unfortunately, only a couple of them are worthy of recommendation. The rest are consistently worn, impersonal, and well beneath the standards of Key West's least desirable guest houses. No doubt, new properties will open as SoBe continues to boom.

South Florida is blessed with a top-notch gay reservation service, **South Beach Central** (☎ 305/538–3616 or 800/538–3616), which lists hotel and guest house accommodations, plus many short-term rentals throughout the area. Also popular is **Colours at the Mantell** (255 W. 24th St., ☎ 305/531–3601 or 800/277–4825), an on-site rental agent at a large studio condo complex.

For price ranges, *see* Chart A at the front of this guide.

South Beach

Hotels and Resorts

▦ Ian Schrager's lush new **Delano** is all about white: white draperies, white table linens, white slipcovers, even white TV sets. Designed by Philippe Starck, this playfully postmodern, hipper-than-thou hotel serves a clientele of trendsetters, Euro-chic, and stylish circuit boys. Among the main attractions are the David Barton Gym in the basement, the Madonna-owned Blue Door restaurant, and the staff of would-be models who are fully clad in—you guessed it—white. *1685 Collins Ave., ☎ 305/672–2000. 208 rooms. $$$$*

▦ The **Casa Grande** is not as conspicuously fabulous as the more renowned Raleigh (*see below*), but it's the top property in South Beach. Rooms have dhurrie rugs and other East Asian decorative touches, full kitchens, and huge baths, and guests are treated, as the old cliché goes, like royalty. *834 Ocean Dr., ☎ 305/672–7003 or 800/688–7678. 32 rooms. $$$–$$$$*

▦ The **Fontainebleau Hilton Resort and Spa** is actually north of South Beach, about at the middle of Miami Beach, a 10-minute drive from gay nightlife and beaches. This stunning dinosaur might remind you of a late-'50s Cadillac, with sleek, graceful lines and a gaudy, bigger-is-better sensibility. *4441 Collins Ave. ☎ 305/538–2000 or 800/548–8886. 1206 rooms. $$$–$$$$*

▦ Island Records mogul Chris Blackwell opened the quirky **Marlin Hotel** a few years back. Favored, appropriately, by music industry executives and recording artists, the Deco gem is also known for its Caribbean colors and furnishings, including exotic Jamaican bath amenities; some suites have kitchenettes and minibars. *1200 Collins Ave., ☎ 305/673–8770 or 800/688–7678. 12 rooms. $$$–$$$$*

▦ Of luxury properties, the **Raleigh** is tops with models, men and women who look like models, and admirers of all of the above. It's very gay, very retro, very '50s chic—rooms are done with an odd mix of angular and amoeba-shape furnishings in pasty pastels. The ground-floor restaurant is a SoBe society must-do. *1775 Collins Ave., ☎ 305/534–6300 or 800/848–1775. 107 rooms. $$$–$$$$*

▦ At the ultra-high-profile **Century Hotel,** the hipper-than-thou lounge about the memorable lobby, and wistful poseurs amble about hoping to be discovered by frequent guest Bruce Weber. It's the sort of place where guests spend three hours primping in their rooms before heading down to the lobby for coffee and a newspaper. *140 Ocean Dr., ☎ 305/674–8855. 47 rooms. $$–$$$$*

▦ Just across from the gay beach, the **Cavalier** has one of the most memorable facades on Ocean Drive and draws a strong list of fashion photography VIPs. Rooms are fitted with TVs, CD and cassette players, and VCRs. *1320 Ocean Dr., ☎ 305/534–2135 or 800/688–7678. 42 rooms. $$–$$$*

⌘ Very similar to the Cavalier, its sister, the **Leslie,** is a few steps from Gianni Versace's pad. *1244 Ocean Dr.,* ☎ *305/531–8800 or 800/688–7678. 50 rooms. $$–$$$*

⌘ The **Park Central Hotel** is as traditional a Deco hotel as you'll find, with period furnishings, vintage photos on the walls, mahogany ceiling fans, and a great little pool area off to the side. Gets a rather young, rather straight, rather dull crowd. *640 Ocean Dr.,* ☎ *305/538–1611 or 800/727–5236. 120 rooms. $$–$$$*

⌘ The **Essex** gets a fairly straight crowd and is worth touring even if you don't actually stay here. Ziggurat arches, hieroglyphic-inspired ironwork, a massive lobby mural, and rooms filled with oak antiques lend an exotic air. *1001 Collins Ave.,* ☎ *305/534–2700 or 800/553–7739. 60 rooms. $–$$$*

⌘ Yet-to-be-discovered models (i.e., those on a budget) love the **Avalon Hotel,** whose rooms and public areas are strictly Deco, and whose amusing restaurant, A Fish Called Avalon, makes for one of the better hotel dining options. *700 Ocean Dr.,* ☎ *305/538–0133 or 800/933–3306. 103 rooms. $–$$*

⌘ The vintage-1939 **Bayliss** is a modest, gay/lesbian property with studios with kitchens and two-bedroom units. It's nothing fancy, but it's just off Ocean Drive; rooms have private baths, and a little gay gift shop has video and VCR rentals. *504 14th St.,* ☎ *305/534–0010. 9 rooms. $–$$*

⌘ The peach and red **Penguin** strikes one of the more inspired poses on Ocean Drive. It has a major gay following, and though plain and simple, the rooms are clean and compact and outfitted with cable TV—all the essentials. In the afternoon, a local drag queen serves cocktails in the lobby bar. *1418 Ocean Dr.,* ☎ *305/534–9334 or 800/235–3296. 44 rooms. $–$$*

⌘ The predominantly gay **Kenmore** and **Park Washington** share a block and a pool and terrace, have basic motel-style rooms, and are conveniently situated across from the Twist gay bar. *Kenmore: 1050 Washington Ave.,* ☎ *305/674–1930. 60 rooms. $–$$. Park Washington: 1020 Washington Ave.,* ☎ *305/532–1930. 35 rooms. $*

⌘ The **Miami Beach International Youth Hostel** is one of the gayest in America—although plenty of bleary-eyed, straight European backpackers stay here, too. It's in a white Deco building that used to be the classy Clay Hotel, where Desi Arnaz and his band entertained way back when. It's a terrific location, two blocks from the beach and near bars. Private and group rooms. *1438 Washington Ave.,* ☎ *305/534–2988. 60 rooms. $*

Guest House

⌘ Though several blocks from the beach, the **Jefferson House** is without question the best of SoBe's gay guest houses. Units in a clean, if uninteresting, building behind this historic 1929 home near Flamingo Park are furnished with tropical resort furniture plus a few Art Deco pieces. The pool and deck added in 1995 vastly improved the place. *1018 Jefferson Ave.,* ☎ *305/534–5247. 7 rooms. Mostly gay/lesbian. $$*

Miami

None of the several outstanding, high-end hotels in Miami are especially popular with the gay community, and all of them cost a fortune. On the whole, however, though they lack trendy SoBe's buzz and chic clientele, they are the grandest properties south of Palm Beach. (If you're on a budget, stay in SoBe.)

⌘ Inland, in old-money Coral Gables, the 1926 **Biltmore** is Miami's grande dame, a completely modernized but no less classic monolith that rises above a golf course, tennis courts, and a waterway. Rooms are enormous and decorated with a Moorish flourish; the 15,000-square-foot spa and fitness center is among the best in the city. *1200 Anastasia Ave.,* ☎ *305/445– 1926 or 800/456–9126. 275 rooms. $$$$*

☎ The **Grand Bay Hotel** is a pyramid-shape high-rise on Biscayne Bay. It has an exceptional health club and pool area, and each of its rooms has a splendid view. *2669 S. Bayshore Dr.,* ☎ *305/858–9600 or 800/327– 2788. 181 rooms. $$$$*

☎ The best downtown hotel is the 34-story **Inter-Continental,** which has a five-story atrium; comfortable guest rooms decorated with a Latin flavor; and spectacular views of downtown. *100 Chopin Plaza,* ☎ *305/577– 1000 or 800/327–3005. 644 rooms. $$$$*

☎ Close to the Grand Bay and also near the sea is the **Mayfair House,** a discreet, European-style hostelry whose public rooms have Tiffany windows and lots of crystal, mahogany, and marble. Surrounding the hotel is a posh outdoor shopping plaza. About 50 suites have antique pianos, and all have whirlpool tubs. *3000 Florida Ave.,* ☎ *305/441–0000 or 800/433–4555. 182 rooms. $$$$*

Fort Lauderdale

Hotels and Resorts

☎ The 22-acre **Hyatt Regency Pier Sixty-Six** is a fancy high-rise with the ubiquitous—and touristy—revolving rooftop lounge and a great spa. *2301 S.E. 17th St.,* ☎ *305/525–6666 or 800/327–3796. 388 rooms. $$$$*

☎ The historic **Riverside Hotel** is a few blocks from the popular bar Cathode Ray's, along the leisurely shopping stretch of East Las Olas Boulevard. Rooms are decorated individually with antiques and prints. *620 E. Las Olas Blvd.,* ☎ *305/467–0671 or 800/325–3280. 109 rooms. $$–$$$*

Guest Houses

☎ The **Royal Palms Resort** is a small, expertly run, exclusively gay resort—probably the best in southern Florida. Lovely hosts and beautiful outdoor decks help to complete the experience. A better place for couples than for singles on the make. *2901 Terramar St.,* ☎ *305/564–6444 or 800/237–7256. 12 rooms. Gay male. $$$*

☎ The **Rainbow's Inn** was once a women's guest house but is now all guys. It is situated eight blocks from the beach, and it provides bikes for guests to get there. There are private gardens and a pool in back, upon which all the rooms overlook. The decor is tropical and art deco; rooms have kitchens and are painted in pastel. *1520 N.E. 26th Ave.,* ☎ *305/568– 5770 or 800/881–4814. 4 rooms. Gay male. $$*

☎ The **Blue Dolphin,** once for women, is now all guys. It's simple, cheap, and motel-style. *725 N. Birch Rd.,* ☎ *305/565–8437 or 800/893–2583. 18 rooms. Gay male. $*

SCENES

South Beach

Club society here is ritualized: Nobody would dare miss the Paragon on a Tuesday night or Amnesia's tea dance on a Sunday afternoon or dancing at Warsaw later that night. You'll find pretty much the same crowd at all major discos on their "designated" nights. As for the handful of smaller bars, they vary only in the degree to which they attract the stand-and-model set, with Twist leading the pack (though it's still far mellower than the discos).

The draw in South Beach is definitely its high-profile discos, which resemble New York's and L.A.'s massive warehouse scenes in terms of decor and clientele. SoBe is also a major stop on the circuit party rotation, with major events scheduled year-round. A few hints: A standard game at places like Kremlin and Warsaw is to arrive shortly after the bar opens to avoid the cover, get your hand stamped, and return much later, when the place is truly hopping. Also, although drinking is cut off at 2 AM, most major discos are open for dancing until dawn—brace yourselves, darlings.

Amnesia. At Amnesia's roaring Sunday afternoon tea dances—quite possibly the most exciting in the country—you will encounter all of the best and worst Miami Beach has to offer: the height of attitude, the smoothest abs, the deadliest sneers, the hottest dancing, the bitchiest comments, and the most stylish men and women in the world. This huge, whitewashed open-air compound looks like the lobby of a posh Caribbean resort. The dance floor is red marble, the walkways encircling the dance floor are red Spanish tile, the seats have plush tropical-print cushions, the music and lighting are stellar, and the stage is backed by a spectacular three-tier wedding-cake fountain. Other days of the week here are less clearly defined as gay; plenty of straights come on gay nights and gays on straight nights. *136 Collins Ave., ☎ 305/531–5535. Crowd: "I am soooo beautiful. Take my picture. Hurry!" Fairly balanced m/f mix.*

821. There's no sign over the door at 821 Lincoln Road, but inside you'll find a bright storefront space with a smart, long bar beside a sitting area with red and gold upholstered contemporary chairs and royal blue tables. Abstract paintings hang on the walls. Has cabarets and dancing many nights. *821 Lincoln Rd., ☎ 305/534–0887. Crowd: primarily women, most of them sassy and well-dressed.*

Hombre. For a while, this was SoBe's closest thing to a leather-and-Levi's bar. The current owners seem bent on encouraging a more diverse crowd. Has become a popular late-night hangout. *925 Washington Ave., ☎ 305/538–7883. Crowd: mostly male; ages 30s to 50s; low-key; Saturday is women's night.*

Icon 1235. The artist formerly known as Prince bought the old Paragon disco, renamed it the Glam Slam Club, and had been running it as a mostly straight club. But since 1995, Fridays here have been called Icon 1235 and cater to a mostly gay crowd—it's now one of SoBe's must-do homo events. The place is huge, packed with sweaty revelers, and has one of the hottest sound and video systems you'll ever find. There are lots of places to dance and mingle. *1235 Washington Ave., ☎ 305/531–1235. Crowd: see Amnesia, above.*

Kremlin. It's hard not to imagine the Kremlin's baroque interior—an all-out tribute to Old World Russia, with graceful columns, heavy gold drapes with swags, and three onion domes perched above the DJ booth— it's more kitsch than chic, though one wonders which was originally intended. Among the several rooms are one with two pool tables, a midsize dance floor, and a front bar meant to resemble a Russian salon. Not as popular as it once was, but booms on certain weeknights—especially Thursdays. Cover some nights. *727 Lincoln Rd., ☎ 305/673–3150. Crowd: compared with other SoBe discos, slightly older and more friendly, and better-than-average mix of dykes and fags.*

Twist. This is an all-around great little bar, with a tiny dance floor upstairs, a pool table, and an open-air porch off the back of the second floor. Downstairs is a long, traditional bar that's only open when it's crowded. Again, because it's so dark inside, making eye-contact is a challenge— although the porch is better lit. Basically the yuppiest of area bars. *1057 Washington Ave., ☎ 305/538–9478. Crowd: cute, mostly under 35,* *mixed locals and tourists, cruisy, mostly male, a bit more white-bread than the others.*

Warsaw. Though it's terribly popular on Sundays and Fridays, Warsaw still isn't quite as popular as Paragon on Saturdays. Once totally devoid of character—just a big, dark room with a midsize dance floor and a smaller second tier overlooking it—the place was revamped in 1995 and now has a number of classical Italian decorative touches that help to liven it up. The sound system is still too loud and bassy. A decent disco, but it could be so much better. *1450 Collins Ave.,* ☎ *305/531–4555. Crowd: young, attitudinal, New Yorkish, hot, 80/20 m/f, strong racial mix.*

West End. This pleasant corner bar and pool hall on Lincoln Road Mall chugs along nightly with its loyal following, ranging from older guys with tattoos and muscle shirts to lipstick lesbos to butch pool sharks to preppy college kids. The room is cast in red light, there are stools at the bar, and the decor is minimal. Slightly out of place but still inviting, a small bar in the back shows porn videos. *942 Lincoln Rd.,* ☎ *305/538–9378. Crowd: 60/40 m/f, totally diverse but low in attitude, mostly local.*

Miami

Most of the gay bars in Miami are local hangouts that are not especially popular with visitors.

O'Zone. For meeting cute Latino boys, the O'Zone is far better than any club in South Beach. This large, warehouse-style disco in an otherwise dull shopping center has a video bar, a cruisy industrial bar, an immense dance floor, and a lounge with cushy sofas. Good drag shows. Helps to be bilingual here, but a number of international gestures and expressions are understood. Sunday salsa nights give the clubs in SoBe a definite run for their money. *6620 Red Rd.,* ☎ *305/667–2888. Crowd: young, mixed genders, good racial mix, club kids.*

On the Waterfront. The city's—and maybe the country's—most popular Latino bar, On the Waterfront is famous for two things: incredible salsa music and dancing, and South Florida's most curvaceous drag queens. Has a lovely patio overlooking the Miami River. If you don't speak Spanish, go with somebody who's been here before. It's open very late on weekends. *3615 N.W. South River Dr.,* ☎ *305/635–5500. Crowd: 70/30 m/f, local Little Havana queens, less gay on Fridays.*

The **Club Body Center** (2991 Coral Way, ☎ 305/448–2214) is Miami's bathhouse.

Fort Lauderdale

Cathode Ray's. In terms of setting, ambience, attitude, and clientele, Cathode Ray's is one of the nicest video bars in the state. It overlooks a picturesque canal on Fort Lauderdale's ritzy Las Olas Boulevard; the patio along the canal is especially quiet and romantic. Inside is a homey, two-tiered tavern, long and narrow with trompe l'oeil murals on the walls. No sign of Miami Beach's grotesque steroid queens. *1105 E. Las Olas Blvd.,* ☎ *305/462–8611. Crowd: professional, guppie, nicely dressed, mostly male, mostly under 35.*

The Copa. This has long been the most famous club in Fort Lauderdale (it's also the closest one to Miami). Negative points include some awful, bitchy drag acts out on the patio, and a fair share of skanky kids with bad manners. On the plus side, the music is the best in town, and it's fun to watch balls of confetti explode every so often from the ceiling, dousing all the pretty boys and mussing up their hair. It's nicely decorated, with lots of glass brick, cool light shows, and fairly slick atmosphere. A smaller bar and pool room in back shows porn videos. *2800 S. Federal Hwy., ☎ 305/463–1507. Crowd: club kids, young, but shaggier than the SoBe bunch.*

Crescendo's. This elegant yet casual restaurant-lounge has a bright, pastel color scheme. There are two dance floors and a piano bar. Hot dance mixes are played after 11 PM, and there is Argentine tango every Thursday. More popular with lesbians than most Fort Lauderdale clubs. *3485 N. Federal Hwy., tel 305/568–0300. Crowd: 60/40 m/f; sophisticated and mature.*

Late Night. This disco is right beside several straight, alternative dance clubs. Great house and techno music blares over the large, loud, dance floor. There's a nice little bar off to the side. *120 S.W. 3rd Ave., ☎ 305/764–1111. Crowd: 80/20 m/f, as trendy as you'll find in Fort Lauderdale, young, energetic, cruisy, homogenous.*

The Stud. The Stud is your classic blockhead bar, big and brash and full of trash. The boys here have no rhythm, especially compared to the hot things in South Beach, but they give it their best shot. A motorcycle hangs over one bar, and chain-link fencing fringes many of the walls. Nice patio off the back, with a wooden deck and fence. Cover most nights. *1000 Rte. 84, ☎ 305/525–7883. Crowd: mixed ages, pumped up, roughedge, some leather and Levi's, industrial.*

The **Clubhouse II** (2650 E. Oakland Park Blvd., ☎ 305/566–6750) is Fort Lauderdale's gay bathhouse, steam room, and adult bookstore.

THE LITTLE BLACK BOOK

At Your Fingertips

AIDS Hotline: ☎ 800/352–2437. **Body Positive Resource Center:** 175 N.E. 36th St., Miami, ☎ 305/576–1111. **Center One** (resources for persons with AIDS/HIV): 3015 N. Ocean Blvd., Suite 111, Fort Lauderdale, ☎ 305/537–4111 or 800/339–2815. **Gay and Lesbian Center of Greater Fort Lauderdale:** ☎ 305/763–1530. **Gay and Lesbian Hotline (Miami and Miami Beach):** ☎ 305/759–3661. **Greater Fort Lauderdale Convention & Visitors Bureau:** 200 E. Las Olas Blvd., Suite 1500, Fort Lauderdale, 33301, ☎ 305/765–4466 or 800/227–8669. **Greater Miami Chamber of Commerce:** 701 Brickell Ave., Suite 2700, Miami, 33131, ☎ 305/539–3063 or 800/283–2707. **Lesbian, Gay, & Bisexual Community of Miami Beach:** 1335 Alton Rd., ☎ 305/531–3666. **Lincoln Road events:** ☎ 305/531–3442. **Miami Beach Chamber of Commerce:** 1920 Meridian Ave., Miami Beach, 33139, ☎ 305/672–1270. **Switchboard of Miami** (gay/lesbian referrals): ☎ 305/358–4357.

Gay Media

There are several gay papers in South Florida, most of them male-and nightlife-oriented. South Beach's weekly *Wire* (☎ 305/538–3111) does the best job of capturing the area's spirit and personality; not a gay paper per se, it aims to serve the whole community. If you're into the circuit party scene, which is as hot in Miami Beach as it is anywhere, consult the small but highly informative *Circuit Noize* (☎ 305/764–8210 or 800/325–2721), which comes out quarterly. *TWN* (☎ 305/757–6333) is a South Florida weekly. *Hotspots* (☎ 305/928–1862) is a mindless, flashy bar rag with lots of provocative bar ads and personals. It is a useful nightlife resource and has a bunch of fun, bitchy, gossip columns.

The monthly **Fountain,** "An Alternative Source for Women" (☎ 305/565–7479), is a cut above any of the male or mostly male South Florida periodicals in terms of both quality and depth.

Miami's **New Times** (☎ 305/372–0004) is the gay-friendly arts and entertainment weekly.

BOOKSTORES

The area's major gay and lesbian bookstore, **Lambda Passages Bookstore** (7545 Biscayne Blvd., Miami, ☎ 305/754–6900), is well stocked but it's out of the way for most tourists (it's well north of downtown on 76th Street). A smaller bookstore in South Beach, **GW** (720 Lincoln Rd. Mall, ☎ 305/534–4763) has a decent selection of gay titles, plus porn and other gay periodicals, novelties, cards, and gifts. In Fort Lauderdale, **Outbooks** (1239 E. Las Olas Blvd., ☎ 305/764–4333) has books, magazines, jewelry, clothing, and other gay goods; the bawdier **Fallen Angel** (3045 N. Federal Hwy., ☎ 305/563–5230) is a glorified adult bookstore selling lingerie, cards, leather gear, and other gay stuff.

Body and Fitness

Popular are **Club Body Tech** (1253 Washington Ave., ☎ 305/674–8222), which has a less cruisy diverse gay and straight clientele, and **Idol's Gym** (1000 Lincoln Rd., ☎ 305/532–0089), which has all the attitude and sweaty bodies of SoBe's best gay discos.

28 *Out in Tucson*

THIS IS A CITY WHERE LOCALS NEVER HESITATE to say "neat" and "right on"—and they're being completely genuine. In this sense and in many others, Tucson is unlike just about every other address in Arizona—especially its larger sister, Phoenix, 110 miles north. And yet, this is quintessential Arizona: immense stands of saguaro cacti; traditional adobe dwellings mingling alongside stately, contemporary Southwestern structures; a substantial Mexican immigrant population; a sunny, dry-as-death climate; and desert—to the nth power.

Of Southwestern cities, it's not at all like Las Vegas and Phoenix, but shares a number of similarities with Austin, Texas. Both share a population of well-educated, politically active, and liberal-leaning citizens, and both are in states where conservatism reigns supreme. Especially in Arizona, refuge of wealthy Republican retirees, it's startling to find such a gay-friendly, eco-sensitive community. But then who would have expected that the father of Arizona's conservative bent, Barry Goldwater, would emerge a latter-day champion of gay rights.

As in Austin, Tucson's enlightened mentality is derived principally from the presence of the state's major college, the University of Arizona, which has always fostered a more free-thinking, if bohemian, spirit than its rival institution, Phoenix's Arizona University. The U of A is central to downtown Tucson, making academics, artists, students, and other culturally hungry types the principal sidewalk strollers of the city center—much more so than nine-to-fivers.

This base of residents supports a lively arts scene. The city is one of 14 in America with a symphony, opera, theater, and ballet. Underground music, cutting-edge cuisine, and avant-garde arts scenes flourish here—just as they do in Austin. And in much of Tucson, gays, lesbians, and straights eat at the same cafés, walk the same streets, and frequent the same bars—again, as in Austin.

Setting Tucson apart from its peers is its natural environment. Consistently the color of terra cotta, the city is dry and bright (a blunt squint is the facial expression of choice), but surrounding it on all sides are precipitous mountain ridges affording some of the most incredible views in the Southwest from both the base and the foothills. In a matter of minutes, you can leave the somewhat unmemorable confines of metro Tucson, drive through a mountain pass, and find yourself in the middle of what appears to be a never-ending tract of desert. Few American cities have managed to keep wilderness so close at hand.

Awakening to the sun and the desert each morning engenders a feeling of breaking bread with nature. People here are good-natured, wide-eyed, and welcoming, yet, almost paradoxically, urbane, cultured, and mindful of sexual, racial, and religious diversity. America's largest cities represent the best and the worst of everything, and a huge fraction of Tucson's population hails from these busy metropolises. And that explains its charm: thousands of people who have fled urban settings with their mass transit, deadlines, rain, muggers, and pollution, yet who refuse to give up urban pleasures—Thai food, espresso, poetry, platform shoes, and the freedom to be themselves.

Traveling gays and lesbians blend right in here, at virtually every shop, restaurant, and hotel. Following the murder of a gay man here in 1976, a citywide ordinance was almost immediately to protect our rights. The mostly Democratic city council has stood behind the measure ever since.

For a variety of reasons, the lesbian and gay community is less centralized than in many cities. It's spread thinly geographically, as is the case throughout the Southwest. But it is huge and active, with more than 10,000 people attending its annual gay pride picnic. In a city of 500,000, that's quite impressive.

The lesbian community is especially powerful, and women-owned businesses abound. Tucson is small enough for one woman to start up a social group or develop a particular cause, yet large enough to back her idea and see it through. So there's a wealth of well-organized women's and lesbian social and political groups.

THE LAY OF THE LAND

Tucson is low, sprawling, and suburban in feel with a genuinely tiny downtown that's engaging but hardly bustling. Off this area are two more small, charming parts of town: the historic El Presidio district, to the north, and the 4th Avenue district, to the northeast. Farther east of the latter area are the campus and environs of the University of Arizona. Below downtown, South Tucson is where most of the city's Mexican population resides. These neighborhoods are the only well-defined ones in Tucson; beyond them, residential blocks—broken only by dull strip malls—stretch all the way to the mountains. Tucson is an astounding 500 square miles, and it can take a good 45 minutes without traffic to drive from corner to corner.

The University District

This is no gay ghetto as such, but it's a somewhat left-leaning rectangle in the vicinity of the university; it's bounded roughly by Grant Road to the north, Broadway Boulevard to the south, Main Avenue to the west, and Country Club Road to the east. Residentially, this region has the highest concentration of homos, though plenty of us are heading for the hills, as it were, taking advantage of outlying Tucson's stunning surroundings. A number of small roads have begun invading the mountainside where once there were none—thus fueling friction between developers and preservationists.

Museum lovers will be happiest on the 325-acre campus of the **University of Arizona** (☎ 520/621–5130). The **Center for Creative Photography** (1030 N. Olive Rd., ☎ 520/621–7968) has a vast cache of Ansel Adams's works; the **U of A Museum of Art** (Fine Arts Complex, Bldg. 2, ☎ 520/621–7567) has pieces from the Middle Ages to the present; the **Arizona Historical Society's Museum** (949 E. 2nd St., ☎ 520/628–5774) traces the state's growth from its Spanish heritage through its mining boom years to today; and the **Arizona State Museum** (University and Park Aves., ☎ 520/621–6302) focuses on archaeological and anthropological aspects of the state's pre-Westernized heritage.

4th Avenue

Fourth Avenue, from about 9th to 2nd streets, runs north–south through the western side of the semi-gay rectangle, acting as something of a bohemian Rodeo Drive—a busy stretch of Third World-inspired shops and eateries.

Downtown

Just off the southwest corner of the rectangle, Tucson's compact downtown is about as gay as any in America. Few people live in this amorphous pod of crooked thoroughfares, but lesbians and gays own many of the shops and galleries, work in the few office buildings, eat at the many trendy restaurants, and walk the streets. The best shopping is along Congress Street, from about Church Avenue east to 5th Avenue. There are also a few galleries and shops on Pennington Street and Broadway, which both run parallel to Congress, and along the roads that run perpendicular to the two. If not everyone around here is gay, they're at least living and dressing on the fringes of mainstream America. Downtown Tucson is certainly not bland.

El Presidio District

The westernmost section of the rectangle, the El Presidio district, brushes the top of downtown and contains Tucson's most aesthetically pleasing streets, speckled as they are with colorful vestiges of a rich, 135-year architectural history. El Presidio del Tucson originally stood within this district, an enormous, walled Spanish fortress (1776) whose duty it was to protect the territory of New Spain from "unruly" Native Americans; you can view a portion of the original fortress wall on the second floor of the Pima County Courthouse, on the east side of El Presidio Park. There are a few notable house museums in the El Presidio, including the **Tucson Museum of Art** (140 N. Main Ave., ☎ 520/624–2333); the 1868 **Edward Nye Fish House** (120 N. Main Ave., ☎ 520/624–2333); and **La Casa Cordova** (175 N. Meyer Ave., ☎ 520/624–2333), which houses the fascinating Mexican Heritage Museum. Good gallery-hopping is along Meyer and Court avenues, which run parallel to Main. Be sure to check out the Southwestern pieces in the **Old Town Artisans Complex** (186 N. Meyer Ave.).

Outer Tucson

Jagged peaks rim the city, but the sheerest, nearest, and most dramatic are the Santa Catalina Mountains to the north, which rise sharply from a mile or so beyond the Santa Cruz River. It's best to view them shortly before sunset, when the shadows accentuate their rugged features, and the sun paints them a fiery red.

Near here, gay sunbathers like to cruise, nap, and relax up at tranquil, rocky **Reddington Pass,** in the Sabino Canyon, where there's running water—in the way of waterfalls, streams, and swimming holes. From downtown, take Tanque Verde Road, turn left onto Sabino Canyon Road, and follow it into the Santa Catalina foothills to Sabino Canyon State Park; at the entrance, beyond which no cars are permitted, is a visitor center (☎ 520/749–8700) where you can get a detailed area map and directions to Reddington Pass.

West of Tucson are some of the most popular sights (take Speedway Boulevard west until it becomes Gates Pass Road; continue over the mountains and look for signs). You're in the desert, and if you've never been in one before you oughtn't leave without a visit to the world-renowned **Arizona-**

Sonora Desert Museum (2021 N. Kinney Rd., ☎ 520/883–2702), a true outdoor classroom that replicates the desert environment. Here you'll see every form of native wildlife in its natural habitat, plus exhibits on desert minerals, flora, and other environmental features. This is the best attraction in Tucson. Nearby is the western half of the **Saguaro National Park** (☎ 520/733–5100), formerly a national monument, where there's a great visitor center and many nature trails (the eastern sector is on the other side of Tucson). The park is dedicated to its forests of saguaro (pronounced suh-*wahr*-oh) cacti, which jut out of the ground like silly green forks. It takes as long as 15 years for them to grow a foot.

Very touristy and fraught with screaming toddlers is the **Old Tucson Studios** (201 S. Kinney Rd., inside Tucson Mountain Park, ☎ 520/883–0100), a theme park and still-operating film set that has seen the making of more than 250 films (including *Gunfight at the OK Corral* and *Rio Lobo*) and many television series (including *Little House on the Prairie* and *The Young Riders*). There are a lot of goofy amusements here—magic shows, souvenir shops, stagecoach rides—but the kitschier of your inner children will love them.

Day Trips

From Tucson, there are a number of enchanting places within a two-hour drive, including **Tubac** (45 mi south; chamber of commerce ☎ 520/398–2704), the state's oldest village (1752), which is today laced with ruins and historical artifacts; its Presidio museum commemorates the site of the region's major fort before it was moved to Tucson in 1787. Twenty-two miles south of Tubac and 67 miles south of Tucson is the Mexican border-town of **Nogales,** which, like Tijuana, is worth visiting for the variety of good restaurants and crafts shops, and for the sake of saying you've been to Mexico.

Increasingly touristy **Globe** (55 mi north of Tucson; chamber of commerce ☎ 800/425–4495), equidistant from Tucson and Phoenix, was built from fortunes made from cattle ranching and gold-, silver-, and copper-mining. Its boom years were from about 1870 to 1920, but more than 25 historic buildings still stand.

Southeast of Tucson and even more overrun with tourists is **Tombstone** (63 mi from Tucson; chamber of commerce ☎ 520/457–3911), famous in the late 1800s as a silver mine and the site of the battle at the OK Corral between the Clanton boys and the Earp family. Today you can witness stagings of the historic shoot-out, browse along Allen Street for souvenirs, and visit the tacky **Historama** museum, in which creepy Vincent Price narrates the story that put this town on the map.

The best, though longest, trip involves a journey to **Bisbee** (100 mi from Tucson; chamber of commerce ☎ 520/432–5421), a hippified and more recently yuppified haven of artists, dropouts, frayed urbanites, and a fair share of lesbians and gays. The town made a name for itself with copper mining and today has about 25 restaurants, a dozen historic bed-and-breakfasts (most of them gay-friendly), several excellent antiques stores, numerous galleries, concerts and poetry readings, and not a single traffic light. It even has a bar with a gay following, **St. Elmo's** (36 Brewery Gulch Ave., ☎ 520/432–5578).

GETTING AROUND

To get anywhere, you'll need a car. Many sights are a 10- to 40-minute drive from downtown. Even bars and restaurants within central Tucson are not typically within easy walking distance. In the very center of town, streets are numbered in a grid pattern: streets run east–west, avenues north–south. Outside the center but still within the city limits, where you'll find many bars, accommodations, and restaurants, the streets still run largely in a grid but have names. Outside Tucson, where the rivers and washes traverse the area and the hills and mountains begin to rise, you need a good map, as roads twist every which way.

Local buses and trolleys are impractical for tourists, as are, except in a bind, taxis, which are unregulated and costly.

EATS

Though there are no ostensibly self-styled gay eateries here, Tucson ranks among the country's best small cities for innovative and colorful dining— and virtually all the hot restaurants here are popular with the gay community. Yet despite its sophisticated, world-beat palate, there are few big-city pretensions. People are not likely to pose haughtily with a highball in one hand and an imported cigarette in the other, and when you eat out, you pretty much wear whatever you've been wearing all day and concentrate on pleasing your appetite, not on impressing your neighbor. Meals are rarely taken after 10 PM, so don't plan on much late-night noshing.

Mexican grub here is actually not much better than in other near-the-border locales. Tucson's best cooking is Southwestern, utilizing local ingredients and borrowing its techniques a bit from Mexico, a lot from California, and to varying degrees from New Orleans, France, Italy, and even Asia. Also, a few Tucson resorts have fine restaurants, most notably the New American-Continental **Ventana Room** at the Loews Ventana Canyon Resort (*see* Sleeps, *below*) and the traditional Continental **Gold Room** at the Westward Look Resort (☎ 520/297–1151). The jazz club **Café Sweetwater** (*see* Scenes, *below*) has excellent seafood, pasta, and Continental dishes.

For price ranges, *see* Chart B at the front of this guide.

Central Tucson

$$$–$$$$ Janos. One of the town's exemplary Southwestern restaurants, Janos is in a historic 1855 adobe building beside the Tucson Museum of Art. Regionally beloved chef Janos Wilder cooks under something of a French influence; a typical menu might show off chipotle-roasted rack of lamb or a grilled swordfish in a tomato coulis. Very trendy. *150 N. Main Ave.,* ☎ *520/884–9426.*

$$–$$$ Café Poca Cosa. Run by a former Mexico City model and attached to the mundane Park Inn, Poca Cosa defies just about every Tucson Mexican restaurant stereotype—that is, the food is contemporary, healthful, and stylish. The always-changing menu is presented daily on a chalkboard; consider something simmered in a delicious mole sauce. Entrées come with thick, leafy salads, too. May be the best meal in town for the money. *88 E. Broadway Blvd.,* ☎ *520/622–6400.*

$$–$$$ Kingfisher Bar and Grill. The Kingfisher is noted for many things: the raw bar that offers four kinds of oysters on the half shell plus mussels and house-smoked trout; a menu of about a dozen kinds of small-batch bourbons (the U.S. equivalent of single-malt whiskeys); and a grazing menu from 10 PM till midnight. Nice spot for a first date. *2564 E. Grant Rd.,* ☎ *520/323–7739.*

$$–$$$ Presidio Grill. Its occasional four-course cabaret show is always a hit in the gay community. But the urbane, contemporary look of high tin ceilings, black booths, and marble tables also helps to make this a popular homo haven. Follow an appetizer of whole garlic with brie and mixed peppers with the andouille sausage and shrimp sautéed with greens and roasted red pepper butter. *3352 E. Speedway Blvd.,* ☎ *520/327–4667.*

$$–$$$ **Vivace, Vivace.** This new northern Italian restaurant is presided over by the former owner of Daniel's, one of Tucson's finest Italian restaurants. It has quickly developed a strong lesbian and gay following, thanks to its upbeat, contemporary setting and warm staff. *4811 E. Grant Rd.,* ☎ *520/795–7221.*

$$ **Café Magritte.** Very gay, very "in," with decor and atmosphere that are a tribute to the surrealist painter René Magritte. The menu offers such creations as chicken tortilla soup, Caesar salad with the day's seafood, and a number of run-of-the-mill dishes made interesting with Southwestern ingredients. *254 E. Congress St.,* ☎ *520/884–8004.*

$$ **Maya Quetzal.** This gay-frequented storefront restaurant, across the street from Wingspan, is notable for a beautiful mural of El Salvador. Popular dishes include chili rellenos, *media lunas* (folded corn tortillas stuffed with spinach and walnuts), and, on Tuesdays, *carne gulsada* (stewed beef flavored with tomatillos, tomatoes, carrots, potatoes, and garlic). *429 N. 4th Ave.,* ☎ *520/622–8207.*

$–$$ **Cock Asian.** A play on many words; think for a while and you should come up with all of them (it's hard to know whether all were intended). This cheap and cheerful place is one of the best Vietnam-meets-China eateries around. *2226½ N. Stone Ave.,* ☎ *520/623–7765.*

$–$$ **Delectables.** As close to a classic New York deli as you're gonna find west of the Hudson River. The pubby dining room, formerly the city's Harley-Davidson showroom, has curried turkey salad, several types of deli sandwiches, a variety of deli "boards"—including chilled smoked rainbow trout fillets with cream cheese—and plenty of veggie options. *533 N. 4th Ave.,* ☎ *520/884–9289.*

$–$$ **El Charro.** Claims to be oldest family-run Mexican restaurant in the United States (1922) and to have originated the greasy but irresistible chimichanga—supposedly the result of someone having accidentally dropped a burrito into a vat of sizzling oil (culinary derring-do at its least eloquent). This is a truly cheesy (pardon the pun) restaurant, with its own gift shop and a touristy, rather gay, following. *311 N. Court Ave.,* ☎ *520/622–1922.*

$ **Egg Garden.** It's actually more of an omelet hall. Some 30 varieties of the folded, fluffy delicacies are available here, from those stuffed with avocado, bacon, and Swiss to several Southwestern creations. Lots of sandwiches and burgers, too. Cheap and friendly, it has a loyal gay following. *509 N. 4th Ave.,* ☎ *520/622–0918.*

$ **Marelene's Hungry Fox.** A diner you hang out in when you're feeling homesick and long for your mom's cooking. The food, especially at breakfast, exceeds typical diner fares—try the homemade breads and golden hash browns. The lovable, frumpy waitresses call everyone "honey." *4637 E. Broadway Blvd.,* ☎ *520/326–2835.*

$ **Sprouts.** Just a terrific vegetarian restaurant, this place offers better fare than its name suggests (does anyone really *eat* sprouts?). Sample a basmati rice stir-fry or the hefty plate of pinto beans, or maybe just have a drink from the extensive juice bar. Across from Antigone Bookstore. *621 N. 4th Ave.,* ☎ *520/620–1938.*

Outer Tucson

$$$–$$$$ **Tack Room.** Here's the scenario: You and your lover want to savor a special dinner, only his/her parents are also in town (though at least they're paying); said would-be father-in-law, however, has notorious indigestion and an aversion to offbeat cooking. Solution: the Tack Room. It's gar-

454

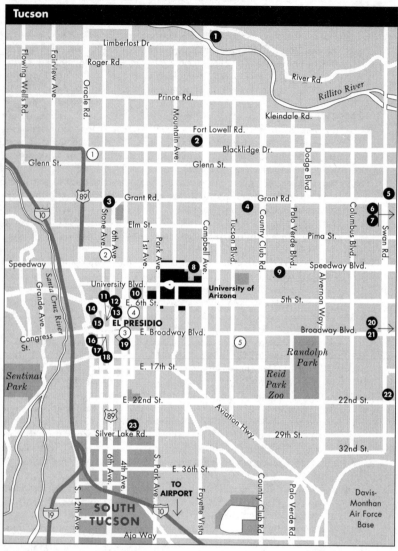

Eats ●

Bailey & Bailey, **17**
Bentley's House of
Coffee and Tea, **8**
Café Magritte, **16**
Café Poca Rosa, **18**
Café Terra Cotta, **1**
Cock Asian, **3**
Cup Café, **19**

Egg Garden, **11**
El Charro, **14**
Good Earth
Restaurant and
Bakery, **21**
Janos, **15**
Jerome's, **7**
Kingfisher Bar and
Grill, **4**
Marlene's Hungry
Fox, **20**

Maya Quetzal, **13**
Milagro, **2**
Mi Nidito, **23**
Presidio Grill, **9**
Sprouts, **10**
Tack Room, **6**
Vivace, Vivace, **5**
Womyn's Third
Friday Coffeehouse, **22**

Scenes ○

Ain't Nobody's
Bizness, **5**
Club Congress and
the Tap Room, at
Hotel Congress, **3**
Club 2520, **1**
IBT's (It's 'Bout
Time), **4**
Venture-N, **2**

nered major awards, it's in a classy, family-owned hacienda, and the Southwestern food is middle of the road. You'll need to dress a bit for this one. *2800 N. Sabino Canyon Rd.,* ☎ *520/722–2800.*

$$$ Café Terra Cotta. The embodiment of the trendy Southwestern dining experience. With its light woods and bright, regional hues, the dining room, in an upscale shopping center is chic, the food is daring, and the service somewhat uppity. But the restaurant is one of the best in Arizona, offering designer pizzas cooked in a wood-burning oven and such succulent dishes as salmon cakes on wilted spinach with tomatillo salsa. *4310 N. Campbell Ave.,* ☎ *520/577–8100.*

$$–$$$ Jerome's. Surprise: an outstanding Cajun-and-Creole restaurant in the middle of the desert. Not only is the food great and slightly Southwesternized (note the generous use of mesquite), but the atmosphere is spirited and sophisticated. The Sunday brunch buffet makes for a near-perfect act of immediate gratification (you can taste everything in sight and it's all delicious), and the raw bar throws out a divine calamari ceviche. *6958 E. Tanque Verde Rd.,* ☎ *520/721–0311.*

$–$$ Good Earth Restaurant and Bakery. More than 150 items are prepared daily at this locally famed health food restaurant that's been hot for more than 15 years. Only high-quality, whole-food ingredients are used; woks and broilers are favored over deep fryers and boilers. *El Mercado, 6366 E. Broadway Blvd.,* ☎ *520/745–6600.*

$–$$ Mi Nidito. You have to split hairs to determine the best of the South 4th Avenue Mexican restaurants. This one is certainly in the running. You'll find all the traditional Sonoran dishes, along with a few attempts at healthful cooking, including a taco jammed with cheese, avocado, tomatoes, onions, and sprouts. The spicy salsa will freak out most gringos. *1813 S. 4th Ave.,* ☎ *520/622–5081.*

Coffeehouse Culture

The U of A, which has more than its share of left-leaning intellectuals, avant-garde artists, and crunchy environmentalists, fuels and is fueled by the city's high concentration of coffeehouses; the city is wild about java—there's even a coffeehouse column in the biweekly *Metro* arts and entertainment newspaper.

A short walk from many of the city's galleries, **Bailey & Bailey** (135 S. 6th Ave., ☎ 520/792–2623) has cultivated a distinctly artsy clientele—lots of black-turtleneck types. The setting is charming, with high ceilings and bold black-and-white tiles. A nice selection of sandwiches, salads, and pâtés. The crowd at **Bentley's House of Coffee and Tea** (1730 E. Speedway Boulevard, ☎ 520/795–0338) is more academic than funky. It has a wide selection of potables and edibles and an excellent bulletin board, and it occasionally hosts live music. Off the lobby of the fabulous, deliriously nonconformist Hotel Congress is **Cup Café** (311 E. Congress St., ☎ 520/798–1618), a two-room, high-ceilinged, coffee-and-sandwiches hangout, typically crawling with waifish Meat Puppets groupies and boys in black mascara. There's also some seating out along the sidewalk. It's a fun place from which to watch the world go by, and the desserts are killers. **Milagro** (3073 N. Campbell Ave., ☎ 520/795–1700) is a chic, upscale coffeehouse where you can also get a full meal. The emphasis is on pastas and California-inspired Italian dishes. There's a selection of books for sale and a newsstand, too. Up near the Café Terra Cotta restaurant, Milagro gets a more professional, well-heeled crowd than the spots closer to the university. **Womyn's Third Friday Coffeehouse** (Unitarian Universalist Church, 4831 E. 22nd St., no ☎) is a monthly lesbian-only event that's highly popular. If you happen to be in town on the third Friday of the month, come on over. Sometimes live music is presented, and there's always discussion—from "best and worst coming-out stories" to any number of social and political issues affecting lesbians. The group meets at 7:30; bring a brown-bag dinner.

SLEEPS

Tucson, because it is both a leisure and business destination, has a terrific variety of accommodations, a few gay-operated and most of them gay-friendly. You'll find bed-and-breakfasts, both downtown and in the desert outskirts, plus luxury resorts and the usual city hotels and motor lodges.

Unless you're here on business or yearn to see Tucson's urban side, you should spend at least part of your stay out in the desert—nowhere are you more than a half-hour's drive from good restaurants and bars, and the scenery is simply spectacular. Phoenix and neighboring Scottsdale are Arizona's best-known first-class resort areas, but only the spreads in Tucson give visitors a true taste of the region's wilderness.

For price ranges, *see* Chart B at the front of this guide.

Downtown Hotels

⛬ The **Arizona Inn** is the most luxurious property in Tucson proper, a historic 14-acre resort just east of the U of A. *2200 E. Elm St.,* ☎ *520/ 325–1541. 80 rooms. $$$–$$$$*

⛬ The slick, contemporary **Doubletree** is east of downtown but still central to everything. It's across the road from the Randolph Park municipal golf course, which hosts an LPGA tournament every year—always drawing a good lesbian following. *445 S. Alvernon Way,* ☎ *520/881– 4200 or 800/528–0444. 295 rooms. $$$*

⛬ A short walk from the U of A, the **Plaza Hotel and Conference Center** is booked during school-related events but has a somewhat gay following, owing partly to its welcoming staff. *1900 E. Speedway Blvd.,* ☎ *520/327–7341 or 800/843–8052. 150 rooms. $$*

⛬ The gayest game in town is the **Ramada Downtown Tucson,** a clean and cheerful hotel that always hosts the gay rodeo and actively markets itself to the community. It's just off the interstate, near 4th Avenue's and Congress Street's nightlife and restaurants. *475 N. Granada,* ☎ *520/622– 3000 or 800/228–2828. 300 rooms. $$*

⛬ The delightfully peculiar and historic **Hotel Congress** has a heavily gay-frequented coffeehouse, dance club, and tap room, and ultra cheap, no-frills, somewhat crummy rooms. *311 E. Congress St.,* ☎ *520/622–8848 or 800/722–8848. 40 rooms. $*

⛬ The **Park Inn/Santa Rita** is an older hotel that has been smartly renovated. *88 E. Broadway Blvd.,* ☎ *520/622–4000 or 800/622–1120. 165 rooms. $*

Outlying Resorts

⛬ The **Loews Ventana Canyon Resort** is the best money can buy, but gets a lot of stuffed shirts and dishes out too much attitude. Still, it's undeniably sumptuous and sensitively designed to blend in with the Coronado National Forest rising up behind it. *7000 N. Resort Dr.,* ☎ *520/ 299–2020 or 800/234–5117. 398 rooms. $$$$*

⛬ Sports enthusiasts will be happier at the **Sheraton El Conquistador,** which is snug below Pusch Ridge's 2,000-foot granite cliffs and has 45 holes of golf, 31 lighted tennis courts, 11 indoor racquetball courts, stables, pools, and a pair of fitness centers. *10000 N. Oracle Rd.,* ☎ *520/742–7000 or 800/325–7832. 438 rooms. $$$$*

Downtown Bed-and-Breakfasts

☒ The **Catalina Park Inn** was opened in 1994 and has a San Francisco-meets-Santa Fe look, with a variety of antiques and arts and crafts, Art Deco, and Art Nouveau details; the woodwork of this 1927 Neoclassical Revival house is Mexican mahogany. *309 E. 1st St.,* ☎ *520/792–4541 or 800/792–4885. 2 rooms, 1 suite, and 1 cottage, all with bath. Mixed gay/straight. $$–$$$*

☒ Just down the street from the Catalina Park (*see above*), Phyllis Florek's gay-friendly **Casa Alegre** is set in an unfancy yet warm 1915 stucco house filled with Craftsman-inspired built-in cabinets, turn-of-the-century furnishings, and hand-stenciling; each room has a different theme—the Hacienda Room has hand-carved Mexican pieces, another has Southwestern decor. *316 E. Speedway Blvd.,* ☎ *520/628–1800 or 800/628–5654. 4 rooms. Mostly straight. $$*

Outlying Bed-and-Breakfasts

☒ For about half of what you might pay at a fancy resort, you can surround yourself with luxury at the posh **Suncatcher,** set on 5 acres of desert in the farthest eastern reaches of town, by the Saguaro National Park East. Rooms, which are plush beyond imagination, are fashioned after those in famous hostelries around the world. *105 N. Avenida Javalina,* ☎ *520/ 885–0883 or 800/835–8012. 4 rooms. Mixed gay/straight. $$$*

☒ In case you'd forgotten the definition of remote, the wonderful **Casa Tierra** is smack in the middle of the desert, just over the mountains west of Tucson. Rooms surround a lushly landscaped, shady, terraced courtyard, which is steps from an outdoor Jacuzzi. Especially popular with lesbians. *11155 W. Calle Pima,* ☎ *520/578–3058. 3 rooms. Mixed gay/straight. $–$$*

☒ The only predominantly gay establishment here is **Tortuga Roja,** a 1950s adobe-brick home on the usually dry Santa Cruz River, just north of town. Rooms, which are quite large, have tile floors, beam ceilings, and TVs and VCRs. There's a Jacuzzi and pool out by the pretty red-brick patio, and opposite that is the cottage, which has its own kitchen and fireplace—a great value. *2800 E. River Rd.,* ☎ *520/577–6822 or 800/467–6822. 2 rooms and 1 cottage. Gay male/lesbian. $–$$*

SCENES

The gay nightlife in Tucson is unflashy but gregarious, small but diverse. No two bars are alike, both women and men are welcome at every gay establishment, and a number of predominantly straight clubs and bars—especially around 4th Avenue and the university—have gay followings.

Tucson is unusual in that its lesbian and gay alliance actually went to the city's gay-bar owners and demanded that they encourage a coed clientele, although you're unlikely to find lesbians at the Venture-N, the Stonewall/Eagle, or the Graduate.

No section of town has a high concentration of gay bars; in fact, nowhere is it practical to walk from one watering hole to another—they're all at least a five-minute drive apart. The only exception is 4th Avenue, where the only officially gay bar is IBT's, but several gay-friendly bars and music clubs are along the same stretch.

Like Seattle and Austin, Tucson fosters a strong underground music and arts scene. The under-30 set spends a lot of time, money, and energy trying to look dirty and dated, and, as with most countercultural scenes, this one is suspiciously uniform in its shagginess. Nose rings, tattoos, ripped baggy jeans, and Day-Glo dyed hair are far more fashionable here than any of the club gear popular elsewhere. At most gay bars, expect to see either full cowboy regalia or extremely casual duds—jeans and T-shirts, flannel, some leather. You might see a collared Oxford shirt at Club 2520, but preppy attire is rare, and business attire even rarer. Tucson's small-town flavor keeps the typical bar atmosphere open and chatty, and distinctly uncruisy.

There is one "sex plex" in town, the outrageous and entirely gay-friendly **Tropicana Hotel and Adult Bookstore** (617 W. Miracle Mile, ☎ 520/622–2289), a ready source of cheap dates, cheap rooms (at hourly rates), and plenty of porn. On the premises are a rather extensive magazine, video, and sex-toy boutique, a peep-show arcade, and an adult theater. Shady, to be sure, but fun.

Bars and Nightclubs

Ain't Nobody's Bizness. This is the snazziest gay bar in the city, with soft lighting, plenty of seating, good music, pool tables, a great dance floor, and go-go dancers on weekends. Most intriguing is a small, soundproof, no-smoking parlor off the main room, done with colonial reproductions, and strongly resembling the lobby of a fancy hotel—it even has a house phone. The staff is amiable and outgoing. Same owners as the club of the same name in Phoenix. *2900 E. Broadway Blvd.,* ☎ *520/318–4838. Crowd: 70% to 90% women but men welcome; stylish, yuppie, lots of lipstick and good hair, mostly under 35.*

Club Congress and the Tap Room at Hotel Congress. The gay-friendly Hotel Congress has a small beer tavern, a coffeehouse, and a club with terrific live acts. The crowd is diverse, drawing lots of grungers, alternateens, students, and artists. Most bands are cutting-edge, and plenty of big names come here. The Tap Room has a small bar with stools and some booths, and it gets a loud, chatty, heavy-smoking crowd of all different types—gays, straights, Deadheads, punks. Very groovy—kind of like Seattle in the desert. *311 Congress St.,* ☎ *520/622–8848. Crowd: mostly straight but totally gay-friendly; young, wild, and grungy in club; all ages and types but mellower in Tap Room.*

Club 2520. This was *the* dance club in Tucson, drawing whatever stand-and-model crowd exists here, up until Paragon's opening in 1995. (Whether Paragon diminishes Club 2520's cachet remains to be seen.) Its success to date has to do with its schizophrenic layout: One dance floor is devoted to country music, another to club, house, and disco; club kids and cowhands mingle (to a certain extent, anyway) in a small, somewhat quiet bar between them. After Paragon, this is the city's largest gay nightclub. Cover some nights. *2520 N. Oracle Rd.,* ☎ *520/882–5799. Crowd: 70/30 m/f, very mixed racially, both the disco and two-stepping crowd, generally mid-30s and under, quite cruisy, good mix of club kids and preppy types.*

IBT's (It's 'Bout Time). This is a nice bar to mix with locals; it's just up the street from the Antigone feminist bookstore, the gay community center, and all of 4th Avenue's artsy buzz. Has a small dance floor and plenty of seating. It's pleasantly ragged and unpretentious inside—the kind of place where the bartenders learn your name. *616 N. 4th Ave.,* ☎ *520/882–3053. Crowd: 90% gay, 70/30 m/f, somewhat country-western, extremely welcoming, artists, diverse in age but lots of students.*

Venture-N. This is Tucson's only rough-and-tough leather bar, but the staff and patrons are very approachable and don't seem to mind people who aren't leather aficionados. Nevertheless, there is a small leather boutique on the premises that offers all the usual pain-inducing trinkets and tools. The atmosphere is dark and shady; construction signs line the otherwise dark walls. Has a decent-size patio, too. *1239 N. 6th Ave.,* ☎ *520/882–8224. Crowd: mostly male, leather with a cowboy slant, mostly 30s and up, very butch.*

DIVES
The small, dark, smoky, seedy, but fun-filled **Graduate** (23 W. University Ave., ☎ 520/622–9233) hosts a colorful assortment of guys—many of whom have graduated to social security. **Hours** (3455 E. Grant Rd., ☎ 520/327–3390) is a mixed-gay/lesbian, "no bullshit, no attitude" bar, low on ambience. The **Stonewall/Eagle** (2921 N. 1st Ave., ☎ 520/624–8805), once a leather bar, is now divided in two, being more of a neighborhood place on one side and a dance hall on the other.

STRAIGHT BUT NOT NARROW
Café Sweetwater (340 E. 6th St., ☎ 520/622–6464) has consistently great jazz acts. The **Fourth Avenue Social Club** (424 N. 4th Ave., ☎ 520/622–0376) books a good mix of rock, acoustic, and blues acts. The **Shanty Café** (401 E. 9th St., ☎ 520/623–2664) is a popular tavern with a great selection of imported beers.

THE LITTLE BLACK BOOK

At Your Fingertips
Arizona/Sonora Proyecto SIDA: ☎ 520/882–3933. **Gay and Lesbian Information Hotline:** ☎ 520/624–1799. **Metropolitan Tucson Convention and Visitors Bureau:** 130 S. Scott Ave., Tucson, 85701, ☎ 520/624–1817 or 800/638–8350. **Rape Crisis Line:** ☎ 520/327–7273. **Shanti Foundation (AIDS resource):** ☎ 520/622–7107. **Tucson AIDS Project Hotline:** ☎ 520/326–2437. **Wingspan Gay and Lesbian Community Center:** 422 N. 4th Ave., ☎ 520/624–1779. **Women's Information and Referral Service** ☎ 520/881–1794.

Gay Media
The weekly **Observer** (☎ 520/622–7176) has served the gay and lesbian community for 20 years. Phoenix-based rags with limited information on Tucson and the general Southwest include **Echo** (☎ 602/266–0550) magazine, the **Western Express** (☎ 602/254–1324) newspaper, **"Transformer"** (☎ 602/973–5682), a small bar and resources pamphlet, and **X-Factor** (☎ 602/266–0550), a gay-male adult entertainment biweekly. All the above are free and found at many bars.

A couple of grass-roots homo rags are published in Tucson, including, for lesbians, the well-written monthly **Ruby Fruit Journal** (☎ 520/888–5371, $1.50), and the provocative, male-oriented **"Going Homo"** (Box 3403, Tucson, AZ 85722, no ☎), a sporadically published, low-budget pamphlet containing deliciously scandalous poetry, essays, and odd stories.

The two local arts and entertainment papers, which are both quite gay-friendly, are the **Tucson Weekly** (☎ 520/792–3630) and biweekly **Metro** (no ☎).

BOOKSTORES
Given the magnitude of the city's lesbian and gay population, it's surprising that the community is without a bookstore. **Antigone Books** (600 N. 4th Ave., ☎ 520/792–3715) is a stellar feminist bookstore, with a wealth of material for lesbians but nothing specifically for gay men. Women should definitely stop in and leaf through the community resources notebook; there's plenty of information inside. The *Ruby Fruit Journal* is also sold here.

More general stores that carry lesbian and gay titles include **The Bookmark** (5001 E. Speedway Blvd., ☎ 520/881–6350), which is the largest mainstream bookstore in town, and **Bookstop** (2504 N. Campbell Rd., ☎ 520/326–6661), which specializes in used titles.

Body and Fitness

This is not a big stand-and-model city, so people who work out generally do so to keep in shape, not to bulk up for the discos. There isn't a gay gym, per se, but any fitness center in the area will be more than accommodating. The downtown **YMCA** (60 W. Alameda Ave., ☎ 520/623–5200) charges $7 for a day pass. **World Gym** (1240 N. Stone Ave., ☎ 520/882–8788) offers day passes for $7 and week passes for $20.

29 Out in Washington, DC

IN TERMS OF THE SIZE AND VISIBILITY of its gay population, Washington is one of America's great gay cities. In both political and social terms, Washington compares with New York, Los Angeles, San Francisco, and Chicago. More gay and lesbian organizations have their headquarters here than in any other American city: the AIDS Action Council, Dignity, the Human Rights Campaign Fund, the Log Cabin Republicans, the National Coalition of People with AIDS, the National Center for Lesbian Rights, the National Coalition of Black Gays and Lesbians, the National Federation of Parents and Friends of Lesbians and Gays (PFLAG), the National Gay and Lesbian Task Force, the National Leadership Coalition on AIDS, the National Lesbian and Gay Health Foundation, the Network of Gay and Lesbian Alumni Association, and the World Congress of Gay and Lesbian Jewish Organizations—and that's just a partial list.

Some people outside the Beltway think of Washington's gays as fairly loud, shaggy throwbacks to '60s grass-roots activists—constantly demonstrating, petitioning, and getting their hands dirty fighting the good fight. The fact is that Washington is hardly a city of guerilla warfare. If you want to fight for gay rights by working within the system, you come to DC; activists here are among America's most conservative (as far as the means by which they mobilize). In many other cities, activists are more strident and more radical in their approaches.

A good many of DC's gay residents keep a lid on their sexual orientation—their careers often depend on remaining closeted. But just as many others have carved their livelihood out of their sexual identity. Plenty of gays work for think tanks, lobbies, or organizations that either exist for gay activism or at least relate to it in a positive way. Or, they might work for the government, in which case being either openly gay or remaining closeted has a significant bearing on their political identity. Even if they don't work for the government, they live in a city whose personality is dominated by politics—the significance of their sexual orientation is lost on few people.

More so here than in many large cities, relatively few residents were born and raised in the city. Many saw Washington as a town where they could come out of the closet. But many others moved here to build political careers. It's a city where your orientation can play an integral part in who you are and what role you're expected to play both at work and at cocktail parties. At times, the tendency of Washingtonians to pigeonhole you according to your sexual orientation—or for that matter according to any characteristic that might neatly define your political outlook—can be annoying. You're never merely the congressional aide who happens to be gay, you're the gay congressional aide. You're the gay bookstore owner, tour operator, dentist, realtor. Your party lines, religion, gender, ethnicity, education, socioeconomic background, sexual orientation—all of these labels precede you, your thoughts, and your personality.

There was a time not so long ago when the only way you could make progress on behalf of gay rights was to work from outside the system. Doors have opened slowly in Washington, but they have opened. There's now incentive to dress the part of an insider, learn the ropes, and work the system. Conforming and assimilating are the keys to success for many. The effects of this "respectable" gay sensibility are fairly obvious in the District. In gay bars, you see more collared shirts than leather, drag, or short shorts. And although being openly and proudly gay is fashionable, being "queer" (as in politically militant) or "faggy" (as in effeminate and campy) are widely frowned upon. Ditto for a pierced septum, suggestive disco garb, leather chaps, a backwards baseball cap, or pink-triangle earrings, all of which may get you ignored.

This may explain why visiting gays and lesbians return from the nation's capital with sharply diverging assessments of the city's hospitality. There is no question that Washington's gay community is more conservatively dressed and discreet than that of all cities except, perhaps, Boston and Dallas. Depending on your own styles and attitudes, you may encounter either a warm handshake or a cold shoulder. In bars, locals are apt to determine your desirability according to how well your image jibes with theirs.

THE LAY OF THE LAND

Locals are constantly defending DC's bizarre street grid as logical and simple to navigate; were this even remotely true, they wouldn't need to defend it so often. The District is divided into four quadrants: northwest, northeast, southwest, and southeast, with the Capitol Building at the center. Downtown streets run at right angles and come in two flavors: Those that run north–south are numbered; most of those that run east–west are lettered A through W (note that J does not exist and that I is often spelled "Eye"). Avenues, which are named after states, emanate diagonally from various traffic circles and run in every which direction. It's important to know the quadrant of any address you're trying to find. The same intersection, 4th and D for instance, may appear in all four quadrants; the NE, NW, SE, or SW at the end of the address tells you which quadrant it's in. The street address itself is determined by which streets the building falls between. An address in the 1400s on R street falls between 14th and 15th streets; an address in the 700s on 15th Street falls between G and H streets (the seventh and eighth letters of the alphabet).

Safety is a legitimate concern in Washington, which has one of the nation's highest crime rates. It's best not to stray off the beaten path, particularly in the NE and SE quadrants. At night, especially, avoid walking alone. Lesbians and gays will find the city extremely tolerant on the whole. In almost any of the neighborhoods described below, same-sex couples can walk together without much fear of harassment. In Dupont Circle, and to some extent in Adams-Morgan and Foggy Bottom, the lesbian and gay population is quite conspicuous.

Dupont Circle

This district just a few blocks northwest of the White House is one of the gayest neighborhoods in the country. Especially fabulous is the area along P Street west of the circle, Connecticut Avenue north of the circle, and most of the streets in between. In the past few years, the formerly down-and-out stretch of 17th Street between P and S streets has become a major hangout, too.

Washington is a city of open spaces, parks, statuary, and lovely 19th-century architecture, and nowhere is this more evident than around Dupont Circle. Development was begun here shortly after the Civil War and it was then that many of the capital's most beautiful mansions were built. During the years following World War II, upper-class professionals left Dupont Circle and northwest Washington for the Maryland and Virginia suburbs, abandoning the area to hippies, lesbians and gays, activists, and other counterculturalists. Although yuppies have rediscovered the neighborhood over the past two decades, a tolerant, liberal mood remains. A couple of the area's best museums are the **Textile Museum** (2320 S St. NW, ☎ 202/667–0441), which houses thousands of textiles and carpets from around the world; and the stunning **Phillips Collection** (1600–1612 21st St. NW, ☎ 202/387–2151), the first permanent museum of modern art in the nation; strongly represented are Georges Braque, Pierre Bonnard, Mark Rothko, Paul Klee, and Henri Matisse.

Many of the city's chic and trendy shops are on or near Dupont Circle; start out by exploring along Connecticut Avenue north of the circle, and on P Street to the east. **Rock Creek Clothiers** (2029 P St. NW, ☎ 202/429–6940) is one of the gayest (men's) clothiers in town; they have an attractive, friendly staff and reasonably priced casual clothing and sportswear. **Universal Gear** (1601 17th St. NW, ☎ 202/319–1157) is where your typical club kid buys his duds before heading downstairs to Trumpets (*see* Scenes, *below*) to stand and pose with a Rolling Rock in hand.

Follow P Street from Dupont Circle a couple blocks to Rock Creek, and you'll discover a large plot of grassy slope and dense shrubbery dubbed, affectionately, the **P Street Beach.** At night, this area is somewhat cruisy; by day, in warm weather, it's nature's gay tanning salon.

North and West

Adams-Morgan, bounded by Connecticut Avenue and 16th Street NW, begins at around Florida Avenue, several blocks north of Dupont Circle. An artsy but gentrified set began moving here in the early '80s, weaving a pattern of offbeat shops and hip eateries in with the existing rows of West African, Asian, and Latino restaurants and residential enclaves. Plenty of lesbians and gay men live, shop, and eat here, but the population is principally straight, a mix of immigrants and young professionals trying to elude the tight grip of conformity present in Washington's other yuppie neighborhoods.

This enclave is a popular hunting ground for Art Deco, Art Nouveau, and other 20th-century furnishings (pieces you might recall from the living rooms of Samantha Stevens and Carol Brady). Most of these spots are along 18th Street between Florida Avenue and Columbia Road. A must-see is the **Brass Knob** (2311 18th St. NW, ☎ 202/332–3370), but all of them are great. For Ghanian carvings, clothing, jewelry, and crafts, check out **Kobos** (2444 18th St. NW, ☎ 202/332–9580).

West of here is **Cleveland Park,** a tony neighborhood that many of DC's bigwigs call home—this is where you'll find the 160-acre **National Zoological Park** (3001 Connecticut Ave. NW, ☎ 202/673–4800 or 202/673–4717).

The formerly nightmarish **U Street Corridor** (around the intersection of 14th St. NW) has become a mid-'90s version of Adams-Morgan. Along here are several new restaurants and nightclubs, a couple of them drawing a mixed gay and straight crowd. Check out both the **Bent** (1344 U St. NW, ☎ 202/986–6364), a hip disco, and the **Grand Poohbah** (2001 14th St. NW, ☎ 202/588–5709), a popular video bar—both are big with men and women.

Georgetown and Foggy Bottom

Straddling the shores of Rock Creek are these two upscale neighborhoods. Both are within walking distance of Dupont Circle and both are home to a good number of lesbian and gay couples. Georgetown has the bulk of Washington's oldest homes, including DC's only pre-Revolutionary building, the **Old Stone House** (3051 M St. NW, ☎ 202/426–6851), which is now a museum. Here you can walk along the historic **Chesapeake & Ohio Canal,** or, if nature isn't your thing, you can shop till you drop along **M Street** and **Wisconsin Avenue.** Not much here is specifically gay-oriented, but you could easily spend an afternoon digging around in the tony boutiques and upscale chain stores. **Georgetown Park** (3222 M St. NW, ☎ 202/298–5577), a multilevel extravaganza with a number of high-ticket stores (Polo/Ralph Lauren, Godiva Chocolates, F.A.O. Schwarz) is one of the more successful and attractive urban malls in the country.

The nightlife here, however, is not as good as the shopping. In part because of the proximity of Georgetown University, the club and bar scene can be oppressively straight and fairly obnoxious.

The Mall and Capitol Hill

The area around the Mall, Capitol Hill, and Metro Center is where most government and commercial activity occurs, and with the exception of blocks east and north of the Capitol, it's mostly nonresidential. There are a smattering of gay bars around here, and the area is relatively safe—although at night, when businesses and museums have closed, it can be a little too quiet for comfort. Old Downtown and Chinatown, north of the Mall between Pennsylvania and Massachusetts avenues and 14th and 6th streets, are largely commercial neighborhoods that have been plagued for years by neglect; they're currently staging a comeback under the guidance of urban renewal.

To see even the must-sees among Washington's many monuments, galleries, museums, and famous sights, you'd need a good week. The best of the best are listed below.

Like many visitors to DC, you can begin your day at the Mall, where you'll find the many **Smithsonian museums** (☎ 202/357–2700)—including the National Air and Space Museum, the National Museum of American History, and the National Galleries of Art; the moving **U.S. Holocaust Memorial Museum** (100 Raoul Wallenberg Pl. SW, ☎ 202/488–0400); the **Washington Monument** (☎ 202/426–6840); the **Jefferson Memorial** (☎ 202/426–6821); the **Lincoln Memorial** (☎ 202/426–6895); and the **Vietnam Veterans Memorial** (☎ 202/634–1568). Virtually all the sights in this area are free. The monuments, though magnificent by day, are particularly striking at night when illuminated by spotlight. The **White House** (1600 Pennsylvania Ave., ☎ 202/755–7798), due north of the Washington Monument, is, despite long lines to see it, definitely worth touring.

There are two outstanding galleries nearby: The Second Empire **Renwick Gallery** (Pennsylvania Ave. and 17th St. NW, ☎ 202/357–2700) houses one of the nation's best collections of crafts and furnishings, and the Beaux-Arts **Corcoran Gallery of Art** (17th St. and New York Ave. NW, ☎ 202/638–1439) contains more than 11,000 works of art. Its emphasis is on late-19th- and early 20th-century European painting, American painting and portraiture, and photography. At the eastern end of the Mall is the **U.S. Capitol** (☎ 202/224–3121), much of which is open to the public; its 68 acres were landscaped by Frederick Law Olmsted. Near here also are the **U.S. Botanic Gardens** (1st St. and Maryland Ave. SW, ☎ 202/225–8333), a massive indoor plant conservatory; the **Library of Congress** (Independence Ave. between 1st and 2nd Sts. NE, ☎ 202/707–6400), which contains more than 100 million items of which 30 million are books; and the **Supreme Court Building** (1st and E. Capitol Sts. NE, ☎ 202/479–3000), designed by Cass Gilbert.

Several blocks north of the Mall, in Old Downtown, is the outstanding **National Museum of Women in the Arts** (1250 New York Ave. NW, ☎ 202/783–5000). The permanent collection includes works by the likes of Georgia O'Keeffe, Mary Cassatt, Frida Kahlo, and Judy Chicago. Also near here are two other Smithsonian museums, the **National Portrait Gallery** and the **National Museum of American Art,** both housed in the Old Patent Office Building (8th and G Sts. NW, ☎ 202/357–2700). Walk south down 8th Street a few blocks to the **Federal Triangle,** a complex of federal offices built in the '20s and '30s, which is bounded by Pennsylvania and Constitution avenues and 15th Street. Buildings here include the **Department of Commerce,** the **National Archives,** and the hideous **J. Edgar Hoover F.B.I. Building**—named, of course, for quite possibly the most homophobic homosexual in recent history.

Arlington

Until 1845 part of the District of Columbia but now a northern Virginia suburb, **Arlington** has a few of the area's top attractions and a sizable lesbian and gay community—one that is generally more settled than DC's. The **Pentagon** (off I–395, ☎ 703/695–1776) is here but makes for a fairly dull tour. Better to see the **Arlington National Cemetery** (☎ 703/607–8052), which has more than 200,000 graves, including those of John F. Kennedy and Jackie Onassis, Robert Kennedy, and many distinguished war veterans, as well as the Tomb of the Unknowns. Just north of the park, on the southern border of the neighborhood of Rosslyn, is the 78-foot-tall **U.S. Marine Corps War Memorial** (a.k.a. the Iwo Jima Memorial), a memorial to marines who have given their lives. Today, however, it's gained notoriety as one of the cruisiest spots in DC.

The Maryland Burbs

The Maryland bedroom communities north of DC are settled heavily by lesbians and an increasing number of gay men. There aren't many attractions here, but something of a lesbian hangout and a wonderful place to shop is the **Takoma Park Silver Spring Co-op** (623 Sligo Ave., Silver Spring, MD, ☎ 301/588–6093), which sells organic foods, earth-friendly paper products and cleaners, homeopathic items, and books and magazines. Similar is the **Bethesda Co-op Nature Food Market** (6500 7 Locks Rd., Bethesda, MD, ☎ 301/320–2530).

GETTING AROUND

Washington is a confusing city to drive in—particularly downtown's maze of traffic circles and diagonal cross streets—and it's generally hard to find parking. Conditions are a little better around Dupont Circle and Adams-Morgan, where you can usually find a parking spot on the street, but you're still better off parking in a hotel or private lot, most of which charge about $12–$15 a day. Don't play around with tow-away zones; you'll often be snagged within minutes.

Opened in 1976, DC's Metro is one of the cleanest and safest systems in the country. Though it doesn't reach all of the neighborhoods you might want to play in (Georgetown or the southeast, for example), it does run a good ways into the Maryland and Virginia burbs. Taking a taxi in the District is a crapshoot. Sometimes they'll stop for you, sometimes they won't. Most know the locations of gay bars, but many drivers are surly and will take advantage of DC's meterless zone system by whisking unsuspecting tourists circuitously to their destination, hitting as many zones as possible and working up the fare. Drivers can pick up additional passengers along the way—this is only supposed to be done with your permission, but they'll often do it anyway. On the whole, they will get you where you're going, and the fare will be less than it is in most major cities, but no two drivers will take you somewhere the same two ways and charge the same fare.

EATS

Washington is a great dining town for several reasons. For one thing, politicking involves a lot of hobnobbing, backscratching, and other types of schmoozing that work best over a bottle of wine and a good meal. Add to the hungry politicians a constant stream of hungry tourists, and you can see why the city has so many eateries. But more impressive than the quantity of restaurants is the culinary diversity; from Latin American to Central African to East Asian to Central European, every conceivable cuisine is well-represented.

The gay dining scene is concentrated primarily in the Dupont Circle area, especially along P Street out to 23rd Street, up Connecticut Avenue, and a few blocks over on 17th Street between Q and S streets. Many of the District's best ethnic eateries are around 18th and Columbia streets in gay-friendly Adams-Morgan. The scene around Capitol Hill is fairly straight—but there are plenty of great restaurants. Georgetown is another fairly straight bastion of good eating. Nowhere in Washington, however, will two lesbians gazing at each other over a candlelit dinner be met with much surprise.

For price ranges, *see* Chart A at the front of this guide.

$$$$ **Jean-Louis.** Jean-Louis Palladin, one of DC's top chefs, cleverly combines contemporary French fare with regional American ingredients. Dining is prix-fixe; choose from four-, five-, or six-course menus. Dress is formal, and waiters are French (dishing out attitude as only the French can); but don't let that stop you—this is a must-eat on any food lover's visit to the capital. *2650 Virginia Ave. NW, the Watergate Hotel,* ☎ *202/ 298–4488.*

$$$–$$$$ **Red Sage.** Now it can be told. George Bush and Bill Clinton have one thing in common: They've both dined amid the barbed wire and lizards in this extravagantly decorated, faux adobe warren of dining rooms, the second home of Santa Fe chef Mark Miller. Check out the chili bar upstairs, or go for the artfully arranged fare downstairs (duck breast with *habanero* peppers and fig sausage, red chili risotto, etc.). *605 14th St. NW,* ☎ *202/638–4444.*

$$$–$$$$ **Vidalia.** Dutch cabinets display antique plates, and dried arrangements of fruits and vegetables serve as wall hangings at this take on a country manor. Indigenous American foods star: Maine oysters, Shenandoah trout, Virginia veal, and the eponymous onions from Georgia—which appear in more than half of the dishes. *1990 M St. NW,* ☎ *202/659–1990.*

$$$ **Two Quail.** This Capitol Hill standout has long been regarded as one of the city's top eateries, owing to its fantastic country French cuisine—the juicy apricot-stuffed pork chops are a typical offering. It's quite big with lesbians: This is where you take somebody you're already fairly sure about (save the first dates for 17th Street). Avoid eating here if you're in a hurry—

the service is deliberate and dignified. *320 Massachusetts Ave. NE,* ☎ *202/543–8030.*

$$$ Vincenzo. This spiffy, contemporary spot is perhaps the best Italian seafood restaurant in DC. Swordfish, red snapper, and grilled tuna are always delicious; the methods of preparation for all change regularly. The many fancy appetizers and desserts are presented on carts, and it's quite difficult to keep from choosing more than you can possibly finish. *1606 20th St. NW,* ☎ *202/667–0047.*

$$–$$$ Café Atlántico. This Downtown hangout for hotshot politicos is notable for its dramatically presented, inventive Latino-Caribbean fare: soy-marinated quail with beet sauce and coconut risotto, chicken sausage with pepper *coulis* and shiitake-coconut polenta. Loud and stylish. *405 8th St. NW,* ☎ *202/393–0812.*

$$–$$$ Café Berlin. If you're in a Christopher Isherwood kind of mood, stop by the Café and fill up on hearty German dishes and the smiles of cute men. It's below Two Quail (*see above*) and has outdoor seating in summer. *322-B Massachusetts Ave. NE,* ☎ *202/543–7656.*

$$–$$$ Il Radicchio. Local restaurateur Roberto Donna is responsible for several of the city's top Italian restaurants. Il Radicchio is the most popular among gays, and although some deride the food for being overpriced and foofy, it's still one of the best eateries on 17th Street. If you're on a budget, stick to the terrific wood-fired pizzas. It's flashier than its neighbors, but jeans and T-shirts are still perfectly suitable. *1509 17th St. NW,* ☎ *202/986–2627.*

$$–$$$ La Tomate. You can stare at the pretty passersby from Tomate's triangular, arbored patio, which is at the queeny intersection of 20th and R streets and Connecticut Avenue. The chichi Northern Italian food is dependable, the service less so. *1701 Connecticut Ave. NW,* ☎ *202/667–5505.*

$$–$$$ Perry's. A popular Japanese restaurant with one of the city's better sushi bars, Perry's is most famous for its Sunday drag brunch—a delightful experience if you don't mind a towering drag queen plopping down on your lap and scrambling your eggs to the disco remix of "Don't Cry for Me, Argentina." The non-Japanese, all-you-can-eat brunch buffet is excellent—raw oysters and mussels, broiled fish, and chicken, all served with a variety of spicy, Latin-inspired sauces. The decor is best summed up as Gumby meets Dali—a florid blend of cartoonism and surrealism. On warm days, you can dine on the roof deck. *1811 Columbia Rd. NW,* ☎ *202/234–6218.*

$$–$$$ Sala Thai. One of the best Thai restaurants in town, this eatery is right along P Street's row of gay bars. The dining room is classy and subdued, with soft lighting and mirrors. Try the shrimp in curry-peanut sauce. *2016 P St. NW,* ☎ *202/872–1144.*

$$–$$$ Trumpets. It's rare to find serious food at a restaurant that is known primarily as a gay bar, but Trumpets manages to churn out excellent, if contrived, California-inspired grub. The presentation of the food is so artful that even the most demanding queen will be pleased. *17th and Q Sts.,* ☎ *202/232–4141.*

$$ Annie's Paramount Steakhouse. For years the city's gayest restaurant, Annie's is smack in the middle of 17th Street's long row of gay-friendly, mediocre eateries. The menu emphasizes steak and eggs, burgers, and other meat-and-potatoes dishes. A pretty butch crowd (the men and the women) tends to hang out at the fairly cruisy bar. The popular midnight brunch offers a pleasant break if you find yourself hopping between nearby J. R.'s and Trumpets (*see* Scenes, *below*). *1609 17th St. NW,* ☎ *202/232–0395.*

$$ Carmella Kitty's. Tucked away in a charming old 19th-century brownstone, Carmella Kitty's is one of the most popular restaurants on 17th Street. The roster of authentic, well-seasoned, New Orleans–style grub—

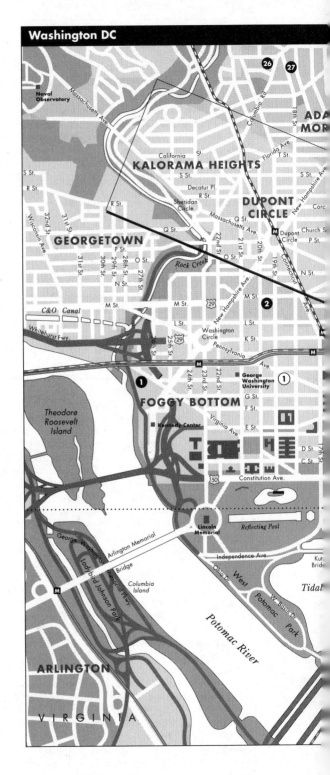

Washington DC

470

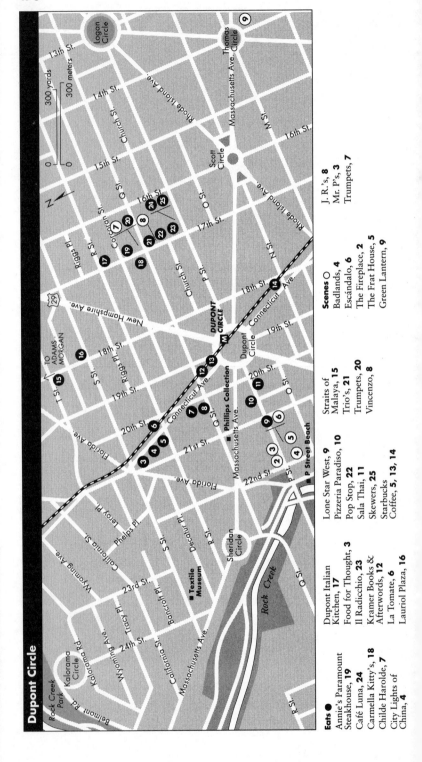

Dupont Circle

Eats ●

Annie's Paramount Steakhouse, **19**
Café Luna, **24**
Carmella Kitty's, **18**
Childe Harolde, **7**
City Lights of China, **4**

Dupont Italian Kitchen, **17**
Food for Thought, **3**
Il Radicchio, **23**
Kramer Books & Afterwords, **12**
La Tomate, **6**
Lauriol Plaza, **16**

Lone Star West, **9**
Pizzeria Paradiso, **10**
Pop Stop, **22**
Sala Thai, **11**
Skewers, **25**
Starbucks Coffee, **5, 13, 14**

Straits of Malaya, **15**
Trio's, **21**
Trumpets, **20**
Vincenzo, **8**

Scenes ○

Badlands, **4**
Escándalo, **6**
The Fireplace, **2**
The Frat House, **5**
Green Lantern, **9**

J. R.'s, **8**
Mr. P's, **3**
Trumpets, **7**

including po'boys, gumbo, crawfish, and jambalaya—is hard to beat. Could it be that this strip is beginning to demand good food? *1601 17th St. NW,* ☎ *202/667–5937.*

$$ Childe Harolde. Upstairs there's a rather elegant dining room with dark wood furniture and white napery; downstairs there's a darkly lit pub with exposed brick and old wooden benches. The latter is a nice place to while away one of DC's cool, damp, winter Sundays. Sandwiches, burgers, omelets, veal, steaks, and pasta are served in both rooms. There are a few sidewalk seats in summer. *1610 20th St. NW,* ☎ *202/483–6702.*

$$ Lauriol Plaza. The menu is a mix of Spanish, Mexican, Tex-Mex, Peruvian, and Cuban, and it's all very good, especially the fajitas and the *pollo asado* (roasted chicken) topped with Spanish onions. It's very noisy inside, but almost all the seats have good sidewalk views of this cruisy neighborhood. In good weather, you can sit under umbrellas on the patio. The excellent, affordable house wines are a steal. *1801 18th St. NW,* ☎ *202/387–0035.*

$–$$ Café Luna. Very queer Luna serves a straightforward array of pastas and pizzas. The food is a good value and usually pretty good, but the main point here is to see and be seen. The decor—broken mirror shards tacked to the walls—is unique, if a bit jarring. Has video showings and poetry readings many nights. *1633 P St. NW,* ☎ *202/387–4005.*

$–$$ City Lights of China. DC's top Chinese restaurant is very close to Dupont Circle. Best bets: the fried dumplings as a starter, the orange chicken as an entrée. *1731 Connecticut Ave. NW,* ☎ *202/265–6688.*

$–$$ Lone Star West. The entrance to this Tex-Mex restaurant is immediately off the dance floor of the gay bar Escándalo (*see* Scenes, *below*)—hence the decidedly queer crowd. The long, narrow dining room packs everyone tightly together at little tables the color of Fiestaware. The waiters are spicier than the food, which is still quite good, except for the clumpy, bland refried beans. *2122 P St. NW,* ☎ *202/822–8909.*

$–$$ Mr. Henry's. This Capitol Hill spot has long been a friend to Washington's lesbian and gay community. Mr. Henry's has a pubby feel to it and one of the best (antique) jukeboxes in town. The burgers are great and come with all sorts of odd toppings. Upstairs is Mr. Henry's Smoke Free restaurant, which has live folk music many nights and a major lesbian following. *601 Pennsylvania Ave. SE,* ☎ *202/546–8412.*

$–$$ Skewers. Above Café Luna (*see above*), the name of the game here is— as you might guess—kebabs. You'll find plenty of good veggie dishes, too (try hummus with warm baked beans). Skewers has jazz on weekends and displays the works of local artists on its walls. Gets very crowded Thursday through Sunday. *1633 P St. NW,* ☎ *202/387–7400.*

$–$$ Straits of Malaya. This somewhat formal Malaysian restaurant has huge windows looking out onto the street and a lively little side bar—many gay folks stop in for drinks before heading elsewhere. A favorite on the menu is the fiery Malaysian beef curry. *1836 18th St. NW,* ☎ *202/483–1483.*

$ Dupont Italian Kitchen. Another renowned but unimpressive member of 17th Street's gay-eats row, the Kitchen has a convivial, festive atmosphere with outdoor seats that are perfect for ogling the parade of boys off the Hill. The food is hearty, heavy, and Italian, and offers no surprises. *17th and R Sts. NW,* ☎ *202/328–3222.*

$ Fasika's. It's almost de rigueur among Washingtonians to take out-of-town guests to Adams-Morgan for Ethiopian food. Though Meskerem, across the street, is also quite good, Fasika's has a slightly warmer ambience. Meals center around a spicy stew called *watt,* which may contain chicken, lamb, beef, or shrimp. You use no silverware·but instead scoop up your food with the aid of *injera,* a spongy flat bread. *2447 18th St. NW,* ☎ *202/797–7673.*

$ **Food for Thought.** A brigade of Birkenstockers descends regularly on this earthy storefront eatery, which is known for its terrific folk music (most nights) and its community bulletin board (one of the best in town). Among the meatless good-for-you adventures are a Reuben of Russian dressing, sauerkraut, and vegetables on rye and the legendary black bean dip. *1738 Connecticut Ave. NW, ☎ 202/797–1095.*

$ **Kramer Books & Afterwords.** This popular bookstore and café is notable for its cozy atmosphere, book selection, and outside dining. *1517 Connecticut Ave. NW, ☎ 202/387–1400.*

$ **Pizzeria Paradisio.** The brick-oven wood-fired pizzas here have earned Paradisio many kudos and extremely long lines (come early, around 5 PM, to avoid the crowds). The small dining room looks right into the open-air kitchen full of cute young men and women preparing these thin-crust wonders. The trompe l'oeil columns and blue sky ceiling are clever, but the acoustics leave something to be desired. *2029 P St. NW, ☎ 202/ 223–1245.*

$ **Trio's.** This standard pizza-and-subs joint with cheap food and pitchers of beer has an extremely gay following—owing partly to its fabulous cast of diva-ish waitrons. It's open late and is popular for takeout and delivery. *1537 17th St. NW, ☎ 202/232–6305.*

Coffeehouse Culture

The 17th Street headquarters of Washington's alternafags, **Pop Stop** (1513 17th St. NW, ☎ 202/328–0881; open all night on weekends) is sometimes cruisier than J. R.'s, a few doors over (*see* Scenes, *below*); unfortunately, it can also bristle with attitude. The second floor looks like the lounge of a college dorm—people read in here for hours.

There are dozens of branches of **Starbucks Coffee** all around town. The gayest of the bunch are along Connecticut Avenue, one right on Dupont Circle across from the Dupont Plaza Hotel (younger, hipper, friendlier), another a few blocks up (older, snobbier, embassy types), and another just below the Circle. The one on the Circle has an odd triangular sipping area that's all windows—you'll feel like you're in a fishbowl, but the tight space does encourage mingling. *Dupont Cir. N, 1501 Connecticut Ave. NW, ☎ 202/588–1280; Dupont Cir. S, 1301 Connecticut Ave. NW, ☎ 202/785–4728; Connecticut and R NW, ☎ 202/232–6765.*

SLEEPS

Perhaps it's because the International Gay Travel Association has convened in Washington on several occasions; maybe it's because of the room demand generated by 1993's March on Washington; or it could simply be because hoteliers here are unusually savvy: Whatever the reason, DC's hotels—even the major chains—show a visible interest in our business.

If the relatively high cost of hotel rooms bothers you, consider one of the excellent smaller guest houses in DC, or try one of the properties in Arlington, Virginia. It's only a few Metro stops from most Washington attractions and has some of the best hotel bargains in the region, especially on weekends.

For price ranges, *see* Chart A at the front of this guide.

Hotels

DC

🖼 Impressive on a much more intimate scale, the **Hay-Adams Hotel** was built in 1927 on the site of John Hay's and Henry Adams's former homes. The much-talked-about guest rooms are decked in 23 colors; those facing south have White House views. If nothing else, come for the memorable afternoon tea. *1 Lafayette Sq. NW,* ☎ *202/638–6600 or 800/424–5054. 143 rooms. $$$$*

☎ Just off Dupont Circle, the **Ritz-Carlton Washington** is a dignified, handsome old property—formerly a luxury apartment building, where Vice President Al Gore spent his childhood. Rooms are small by luxury hotel standards, but still furnished with the traditional hunt-club look for which Ritz-Carltons are known. *2100 Massachusetts Ave. NW,* ☎ *202/293–2100 or 800/241–3333. 206 rooms. $$$$*

☎ Of downtown luxury hotels, the **Stouffer Renaissance Mayflower** is the most impressive—and it's only about a 15-minute walk from Dupont Circle. Opened in 1925 for President Coolidge's inauguration, many of the original touches remain—notably, the lavish gilt-trimmed lobby and the nonworking fireplaces in 76 suites. *1127 Connecticut Ave. NW,* ☎ *202/347–3000 or 800/468–3571. 659 rooms. $$$$*

☎ Across Rock Creek from Dupont Circle, on a tony Georgetown block full of shops, the intimate **Georgetown Inn** blends the ambience of a small hotel with the amenities of a much larger property. The guest rooms are outfitted with writing desks, black-lacquered cabinets, French armoires, gilt-frame mirrors, and lavish baths. *1310 Wisconsin Ave. NW,* ☎ *202/333–8900 or 800/424–2979. 95 rooms. $$$–$$$$*

☎ Though its facade recalls a large city hospital, the **Omni Shoreham Hotel** has a supreme location overlooking Rock Creek Park. Rooms of this 1930s Art Deco palace retain a grand, albeit fading, charm—many have fireplaces and half overlook the park. *2500 Calvert St. NW,* ☎ *202/234–0700 or 800/333–3333. 770 rooms. $$$–$$$$*

☎ Extremely gay-friendly and relatively inexpensive, the **Dupont Plaza Hotel** is an eight-story Bauhaus dinosaur. It's always a dependable choice, despite its worn veneer. About half the rooms have new and attractive furnishings; the rest have shag carpeting and are a bit dingy. The first-floor Collector's Restaurant is popular with local lesbians and gays. Equidistant from 17th Street's and P Street's bar scenes. *1500 New Hampshire Ave. NW,* ☎ *202/483–6000 or 800/841–0003. 314 rooms. $$–$$$*

☎ Very near Union Station but a short cab ride from Dupont Circle, the **Quality Hotel Capitol Hill** is a smart budget choice (some rooms are as low as $59). The rooms are very basic and have minibars and tiny baths. *415 New Jersey Ave. NW,* ☎ *202/638–1616 or 800/456–4329. 346 rooms. $$–$$$*

☎ Once an apartment house and then the Omni Georgetown, the **Radisson Barceló Hotel** has a gloomy exterior and rooms furnished in a fairly perfunctory manner, but you can't beat the location—smack in the middle of P Street's bar scene. Other strengths include a great restaurant, a chic marble lobby, and a lovely outdoor pool. *2121 P St. NW,* ☎ *202/293–3100 or 800/333–3333. 300 rooms. $$–$$$*

☎ The all-suite **St. James** in Foggy Bottom is one of the city's best-kept secrets. The enormous suites have separate living rooms and full kitchens and are decorated with matching floral-print bedspreads and curtains; there are also 10 full studios. Has an excellent fitness center. *950 24th St. NW,* ☎ *202/457–0500. 196 suites. $$–$$$*

☎ The **Carlyle Suites** is a terrific, affordable option near Dupont Circle with funky art deco touches and a fabulous restaurant. There's nothing at all special about the rooms, but you can't beat the price—especially when you consider that each room has a fully equipped kitchen and sitting area. *1731 New Hampshire Ave. NW,* ☎ *202/234–3200 or 800/964–5377. 170 rooms. $$*

☎ Just around the corner from the St. James, the **River Inn** is a boutique hotel frequented mostly by parents of students at nearby George Washington University. The suites are quirkily decorated with leather furniture, mirrored walls, and glass-top tables; some have full kitchens. *924 25th St. NW, ☎ 202/337–7600 or 800/424–2741. 127 rooms. $$*

⊡ The **Best Western Skyline** is recommended with considerable reservations, mostly owing to its seedy southeast DC location. On the plus side, it's clean inside, inexpensive, and gay-friendly; it's also the only hotel close to Tracks (*see Scenes, below*) and the bulk of DC's sex clubs. Still, at night, you'll want to cab it even short distances. Highlights are the lobby lounge, which has leatherette chairs the color of caterpillar guts and the pool and patio out back. *10 I St. SW, ☎ 202/488–7500 or 800/458–7500. 203 rooms. $–$$*

Arlington

⊡ The **Ritz-Carlton, Pentagon City** towers above the spiffiest shopping mall in greater Washington and has great views of the Capitol from many rooms. This is a classic Ritz with Chippendale-style furniture, silk bed coverings, and a museum's worth of fine art. Has a spectacular fitness center, too. *1250 S. Hayes St., ☎ 703/415–5000 or 800/241–3333. 345 rooms. $$$$*

⊡ For a fraction of what you'd pay for comparable accommodations in DC, the **Doubletree Hotel–Pentagon City** offers large, bright, pleasant guest rooms, an indoor pool with great city views, and easy Metro access to the Mall and Dupont Circle. The deluxe suites, with balconies and Jacuzzis, are ideal for a splurge. *300 Army/Navy Dr., ☎ 703/416–4100 or 800/222–8733. 632 rooms. $$–$$$*

⊡ Despite the monolithic concrete exterior, the **Stouffer Renaissance Concourse Hotel** is all class inside, from the upbeat and efficient staff to a couple of great restaurants to rooms dressed elegantly in Colonial antiques. Because it's primarily a business hotel, the Stouffer offers some eye-popping weekend specials. *2399 Jefferson Davis Hwy., ☎ 703/418–6800 or 800/468–3571. 386 rooms. $$–$$$*

⊡ Arlington's leading budget choice is the HoJo-esque **Americana Hotel,** which is a couple blocks from the Crystal City Metro stop. Rooms are clean and have vanities and original baths (circa 1963 but still working just fine). Parking is free and ample, the staff is personable (it's family owned), and Continental breakfast is included. *1400 Jefferson Davis Hwy., ☎ 703/979–3772 or 800/548–6261. 102 rooms. $*

Guest Houses and Small Hotels

⊡ Actually a grouping of four turn-of-the-century town houses (three of them close together on a secluded lane in Adams-Morgan, one in snazzy Woodley Park), the **Kalorama Guest House** is one of the top values in the city. Furnishings—from the antique oak tables and chairs to the brass or wooden beds—have a somewhat faded charm. Though none of the rooms has a phone or TV and a few are quite small, it's hard not to feel at home here. *1854 Mintwood Pl. NW, ☎ 202/667–6369; or 2700 Cathedral Ave. NW, ☎ 202/328–0860. 50 rooms. $–$$*

⊡ The popular **Brenton** is a three-story Victorian town house, with a brownstone and redbrick facade, just around the corner from 17th Street's bar and restaurant scene. Rooms are beautifully decorated with elaborate Victorian antiques and Oriental rugs; beds have feather pillows and bright linens. *1708 16th St. NW, ☎ 202/332–5550 or 800/673–9042. 8 rooms. $*

⊡ Its location across the Anacostia River in southeast Washington may seem a bit out of the way and seedy, but the **Little White House Bed & Breakfast** is just a short bus ride from Capitol Hill. The 1910 Colonial Revival, with is distinct columned front portico, is not unlike its namesake, and rooms are warmly furnished. On weekends, the already generous Continental breakfast is expanded into a full one. *2909 Pennsylvania Ave. SE,* ☎ *202/583–4074. 4 rooms. $*

SCENES

Because there's some disagreement as to whether Washington's nightlife is friendly—some say it's unbelievably so, others insist it's chilly—let's just say that your results may vary. When most visitors speak of DC's bar scene, they're really talking about 10 bars in the vicinity of Dupont Circle, most of which have a reputation for being white, male, young, and preppy. If your idea of sexy is an amalgam of subjects culled from Norman Rockwell paintings, you'll love it. If you're a lesbian, or a guy into diversity of age, dress, and background, you may be disappointed. And you may feel out of place. You can pass in a business suit at almost any Dupont Circle club; country-club garb prevails.

Washington has a substantial African American population and a few predominantly black gay bars; Tracks and a few of the P Street bars are diverse, but 17th Street's bars and restaurants have never cultivated much of a black following. Lesbians are even more invisible at night, with only one bar of their own and perhaps three others with small lesbian followings.

Most of the raunchier gay bars and sex clubs are in a rough southeastern Washington neighborhood down near the Navy Yard. You should never walk around here at night—even by day it's a little dicey.

Badlands. The only disco near Dupont Circle is in an old brick building that comprises two floors, several rooms, and at least a half-dozen bars. It's best on Fridays (on Saturdays you're better off at Tracks), though the large dance floor is still not big enough to handle peak crowds. This is where you'll find the sort of innocuous pretty boy who sincerely believes that removing his Polo shirt and tying it around his 28-inch waist will earn him an appearance in Madonna's next video. In back is a dark video bar with blue lights. Upstairs is a rec room with pool tables and, behind it, the Wild West-themed Last Chance Saloon; this room is smoke-free, but to enjoy it you must endure a tedious drag act. *1415 22nd St. NW,* ☎ *202/296–0505. Crowd: 80/20 m/f, twentysomethings who look even younger, clean-shaven, clonish, stand-and-model.*

DC Eagle. Washington has one of the nation's lamest leather scenes (perhaps a sign of a city that takes itself too seriously). But what scene there is congregates at the Eagle, a large, two-floor bar—they play rock on the lower floor, country-and-western upstairs. *639 New York Ave. NW,* ☎ *202/347–6025. Crowd: male, mostly age 35 and up, a fair amount of leather but more Levi's, gritty, lots of facial hair.*

Escándalo. Long and narrow, with brightly colored peppers painted on the walls in Keith Haringesque strokes, this delightfully brash little place is supposed to be a dance spot, though everyone seems happiest crowded around the small bar up front. The Lone Star West (*see* Eats, *above*) restaurant is attached. Used to be Friends, a piano bar. *2122 P St. NW,* ☎ *202/822–8909. Crowd: mostly male, lots of Latinos, mixed ages, a fair share of club kids.*

The Fireplace. Guys go to J. R.'s (*see below*) to pose and sneer, they come here when they're really ready to meet somebody (and it's late, and their standards have dropped a couple notches . . .). Like a pair of old, comfortable shoes, the Fireplace keeps bringing them back. It actually looks more like a fern bar than most fern bars (the plant is ubiquitous here); and oddly, it has no fireplace. Downstairs, guys gather around a central bar; upstairs, serious looking young men stare blankly at music videos and each other. Crowded every night, especially Sunday. Formerly known as P Street Station. *2161 P St. NW, ☎ 202/293–1293. Crowd: mostly male, trashy-preppy, collegiate, fairly strong racial mix, local.*

The Frat House. The grandpa of Dupont Circle bars is in a converted carriage house one alley away from Escándalo and one away from Badlands. Downstairs a small disco has a strong African American following (cover most nights). Upstairs there's a noisy video bar (lots of suggestive staring); a dark room with one tiny TV showing porn (lots of groping); and a roadhouse-style room—the Arcade—with pinball machines and a pool table, a few tables with chairs, and soul and soft rock playing softly (lots of phone-number exchanging). *2123 Twining Ct. (off P St. NW), ☎ 202/223–4917. Crowd: mostly male, high testosterone levels, but otherwise varies a great deal depending on the room you're in: generally more African American downstairs, same crowd as the Fireplace upstairs.*

Green Lantern. This refreshingly unpretentious bar in an old carriage house is a 20-minute walk from Dupont Circle, just off Thomas Circle and down an alley behind a Holiday Inn. There's a big, fairly safe parking lot outside with *lots* of VA and MD license plates. The split-level first floor has a bar below and a pool table up top. Upstairs patrons intermittently cast their gaze on the screens mounted above the huge bar (some show porn, others music videos). There's an itsy-bitsy groping area (a.k.a. the Bermuda Triangle) in one corner, which fits only about three people (not that this discourages anyone). *1335 Green Ct. NW, ☎ 202/638–5133. Crowd: mostly male, flannel and Levi's, butch and beefy, late-20s to mid-30s, friendly, casual, unpretentious.*

Hung Jury. Given that Washington has more women than men and that it has a highly active lesbian community, it's kind of surprising that there aren't more nightspots for women. Virtually every gay bar in Dupont Circle is at least 90% male. This is not to take anything away from the Hung Jury, however, which is a great bar, in the safe residential neighborhood of Foggy Bottom. Inside is a mid-size dance bar, lots of seating, video games and a pool table, and it's all well-lit. *1819 H St. NW, ☎ 202/785–8181. Crowd: mostly lesbian, mix of lipstick meets soft butch, lots of guppies, wide age range.*

J. R.'s. Welcome to the bar that everybody loves to hate. A work of hunter green, brass, and mirrors, J. R.'s is maligned because it epitomizes the city's standoffish, glaring manner—but the ones who dump on it the loudest can't seem to get enough of the place. It's always packed. The bar itself is long and narrow; upstairs is an even smaller area for chatting, from which you can gawk at the crowd below. *1519 17th St. NW, ☎ 202/328–0090. Crowd: male, boys from the Hill, starched collars and stuffed shirts.*

Mr. P's. Mr. P's best attributes are that it's a decent place for blacks and whites to mingle and that it's the quietest of the P Street hangouts. There's a nice deck off the back, but it closes early. Porn videos. *2147 P St. NW, ☎ 202/293–1064. Crowd: mostly male, racially mixed, 30s and 40s, a slightly tragic bunch—lots of broken heels and runny mascara.*

Remington's. It's taken some time to catch on, and it's odd that more women don't come here, but Remington's, the District's only country-western bar, is one of the up-and-coming night spots. The crowd is often bigger after work than late at night. Has some pool tables, lots of video screens showing Travis Tritt, and a slightly cramped dance floor. Gets a lot of Capitol Hill staffers and boys from Virginia. *639 Pennsylvania Ave. SE, ☎ 202/543–3113. Crowd: mostly male, thirtysomething, some cowboy garb, low on attitude.*

Tracks. The largest dance club in Washington is officially gay on Saturday but welcomes gays at all times. Women's night (once a month, usually on a Tuesday or Thursday), is known as one of the most happening dyke parties on the East Coast. This extraordinary place has dozens of bars, a couple of dance floors, counters hawking hot dogs and popcorn, and an outdoor volleyball court. Music is standard house and techno, with the odd disco classic. There are plenty of places to stand around, make new friends, discard old ones. To get in you have to pass through a metal detector and by dozens of doormen—some of them obnoxious. Valet parking available. Tracks is in a nasty neighborhood; Navy Yard Metro station is on the corner, but consider a cab. *1111 1st St. SE,* ☎ *202/488–3320. Crowd: spans genders and races, generally young, serious about dancing, wired; breakdown depends on the night; Saturdays are mostly gay and 80% male, Fridays mostly straight, Sundays more African American, weekdays vary.*

Trumpets. Despite a silly name more suitable for the dreary lounge of a Holiday Inn in suburban Maryland, this is one of the area's liveliest spots. It can be very fun if you're here with friends, but daunting if you're alone. Though the boys here are theoretically the same bunch you see at nearby J. R.'s, they seem a little more stuck up. The entrance is down a flight of stairs off 17th Street (it feels as if you're headed into a Metro station). Even midweek the long room, which has a fair number of red vinyl seats and booths, is packed. A full restaurant (*see* Eats, *above*) in back serves excellent Cal-cuisine. *1603 17th St. NW,* ☎ *202/232–4141. Crowd: mostly male, guppie, a bit narcissistic.*

Strip Clubs

La Cage Aux Follies. The best club on DC's infamous, and impressive, sex block, La Cage is a must for many visitors. Washington is among the few U.S. cities where strippers shed *all* of their clothes. La Cage has a stable of guys who shake and gyrate out of their scant attire (it's against the law to touch them, but . . . it's amazing what goes on here, and for that matter, what a couple of bucks can get you). Hanging around gay strip clubs is surprisingly acceptable among most circles in DC; you're apt to see all kinds of guys here. *18 O St. SE,* ☎ *202/554–3615. Crowd: male, horny, all ages but tending to the older side, lots of suits on weekdays.*

Near La Cage are several similar clubs, including the **Edge/Wet** (56 L St. SE, ☎ 202/488–1200), which also has strippers; **Club Washington** (20 O St. SE, ☎ 202/488–7317), a gay bathhouse; and **Ziegfeld's** (1345 Half St. SE, ☎ 202/554–5141), which has strippers but is better known for drag acts. All are in the extremely seedy Navy Yard neighborhood, southeast of the Capitol—about a 10-minute walk from Tracks. Watch your back, your front, and your wallet.

THE LITTLE BLACK BOOK

At Your Fingertips

AIDS Hotline: ☎ 800/342–2437; in Spanish, ☎ 800/344–7432. **Arlington Convention and Visitors Service:** 1400 N. Uhle St., Suite 102, Arlington, VA 22201 (mailing address), ☎ 703/358–3988 or 800/296–7996; 735 S. 18th St., Arlington, VA 22202 (visitor center), ☎ 703/358–5720 or 800/677–6267. **DC Crisis Hotline:** ☎ 202/223–2255. **Lesbian and Gay Switchboard:** ☎ 202/628–4667. **Police:** ☎ 202/727–4326. **Washington DC Convention and Visitors Association:** 1212 New York Ave. NW, Suite 610, 20005, ☎ 202/789–7000. **Whitman-Walker Medical Clinic:** ☎ 202/ 797–3500.

A terrific social resource is the **Coffee House for HIV+ Friends, Family, and Lovers** (2111 Florida Ave. NW, ☎ 202/483–3310), a very casual and friendly hangout open Saturdays from 7:30 PM on.

Gay Media

The city's free bar rag is *Metro Arts & Entertainment Weekly (MW)* (☎ 202/344–7640); in addition to the latest on drink specials, it usually has a few fluffy—and usually silly—features on lesbian and gay goings on. The *Washington Blade* (☎ 202/797–7000) is one of the most respected lesbian and gay newsweeklies in the nation. The focus is political and the writing no-nonsense—serious almost to a fault. Coverage of gay issues spans the globe and the paper is packed with local resources, detailed arts coverage, a reliable real estate section, and a sizable personals listing. *Off Our Backs* (☎ 202/234–8072) is a feminist news journal.

Of the city's two mainstream newspapers, the *Washington Post* is the gay-friendlier; the *Washington Times* is not well thought of among lesbians and gays. The free entertainment weekly, *City Paper,* gives detailed coverage of arts events and social happenings; it's extremely gay-friendly and always lists lesbian/gay-related concert series, art exhibitions, and film festivals.

BOOKSTORES

The city's largest gay bookstore, **Lambda Rising** (1625 Connecticut Ave. NW, Washington, 20009, ☎ 202/462–6969; send $2 for a mail-order catalogue), is just north of Dupont Circle and stocks virtually every lesbian and gay title in print. It's a browser-friendly place with a laid-back staff who'll help you through the maze of books, videos, music, periodicals, and greeting cards. (There are branches in Rehoboth Beach and Baltimore, too.)

Lammas–Women's Books & More (1426 21st St. NW, ☎ 202/775–8218) has a mostly lesbian (and virtually all-female) clientele, a popular community bulletin board, Sunday readings, and lesbian-oriented books, cards, and music. If you want to find the pulse of the lesbian community, stop here.

Not specifically gay-oriented but definitely gay-frequented, **Vertigo Books** (1337 Connecticut Ave. NW, ☎ 202/429–9272) specializes in international studies, African American titles, and world literature. **Kultura Books and LPs** (1741 Connecticut Ave. NW, ☎ 202/462–2541) has used books—many of them rare—and old records and **Kramer Books and Afterwords–A Café and Grill** (1517 Connecticut Ave. NW, ☎ 202/387–1400) is a comfy independent store with a café just off Dupont Circle.

Body and Fitness

Muscle Beach (2007 18th St. NW, ☎ 202/328–5201), in Adams-Morgan, is big with the free-weights crowd, sometimes referred to locally as "the dumb and the buffed." The **Washington Sports Club** has three branches in the city and another out in Bethesda, MD; the gayest of the bunch is north of Dupont Circle (1835 Connecticut Ave. NW, ☎ 202/332–0100). **Bally's Total Fitness** (2000 L St. NW, ☎ 202/331–7898) gets a stronger racial mix than the others.

INDEX

NOTES

NOTES

NOTES

NOTES

NOTES

NOTES

NOTES

Fodor's Travel Publications

Available at bookstores everywhere, or call 1–800–533–6478, 24 hours a day.

Gold Guides
U.S.

Alaska	Florida	New Orleans	Santa Fe, Taos, Albuquerque
Arizona	Hawaii	New York City	
Boston	Las Vegas, Reno, Tahoe	Pacific North Coast	Seattle & Vancouver
California		Philadelphia & the Pennsylvania Dutch Country	The South
Cape Cod, Martha's Vineyard, Nantucket	Los Angeles		U.S. & British Virgin Islands
The Carolinas & the Georgia Coast	Maine, Vermont, New Hampshire	The Rockies	USA
Chicago	Maui	San Diego	Virginia & Maryland
Colorado	Miami & the Keys	San Francisco	Waikiki
	New England		Washington, D.C.

Foreign

Australia & New Zealand	Egypt	Madrid & Barcelona	Provence & the Riviera
Austria	Europe	Mexico	Scandinavia
The Bahamas	Florence, Tuscany & Umbria	Montréal & Québec City	Scotland
Bermuda	France	Moscow, St. Petersburg, Kiev	Singapore
Budapest	Germany	The Netherlands, Belgium & Luxembourg	South Africa
Canada	Great Britain		South America
Cancún, Cozumel, Yucatán Peninsula	Greece	New Zealand	Southeast Asia
Caribbean	Hong Kong	Norway	Spain
China	India	Nova Scotia, New Brunswick, Prince Edward Island	Sweden
Costa Rica, Belize, Guatemala	Ireland		Switzerland
	Israel	Paris	Thailand
Cuba	Italy	Portugal	Tokyo
The Czech Republic & Slovakia	Japan		Toronto
Eastern Europe	Kenya & Tanzania		Turkey
	Korea		Vienna & the Danube
	London		

Fodor's Special-Interest Guides

Branson	Fodor's London Companion	Shadow Traffic's New York Shortcuts and Traffic Tips	Where Should We Take the Kids? California
Caribbean Ports of Call	France by Train		
The Complete Guide to America's National Parks	Halliday's New England Food Explorer	Sunday in New York	Where Should We Take the Kids? Family Adventures
		Sunday in San Francisco	
Condé Nast Traveler Caribbean Resort and Cruise Ship Finder	Healthy Escapes	Walt Disney World, Universal Studios and Orlando	Where Should We Take the Kids? Northeast
	Italy by Train		
Cruises and Ports of Call	Kodak Guide to Shooting Great Travel Pictures	Walt Disney World for Adults	

Special Series

Affordables
Caribbean
Europe
Florida
France
Germany
Great Britain
Italy
London
Paris

Fodor's Bed & Breakfasts and Country Inns
America's Best B&Bs
California's Best B&Bs
Canada's Great Country Inns
Cottages, B&Bs and Country Inns of England and Wales
The Mid-Atlantic's Best B&Bs
New England's Best B&Bs
The Pacific Northwest's Best B&Bs
The South's Best B&Bs
The Southwest's Best B&Bs
The Upper Great Lakes' Best B&Bs

The Berkeley Guides
California
Central America
Eastern Europe
Europe
France
Germany & Austria
Great Britain & Ireland
Italy
London
Mexico
Pacific Northwest & Alaska
Paris
San Francisco

Compass American Guides
Arizona
Chicago
Colorado
Hawaii
Idaho
Hollywood
Las Vegas
Maine
Manhattan
Montana
New Mexico
New Orleans
Oregon
San Francisco
Santa Fe
South Carolina
South Dakota
Southwest
Texas
Utah
Virginia
Washington
Wine Country
Wisconsin
Wyoming

Fodor's Citypacks
Atlanta
Hong Kong
London
New York City
Paris
Rome
San Francisco
Washington, D.C.

Fodor's Español
California
Caribe Occidental
Caribe Oriental
Gran Bretaña
Londres
Mexico

Nueva York
Paris

Fodor's Exploring Guides
Australia
Boston & New England
Britain
California
Caribbean
China
Egypt
Florence & Tuscany
Florida
France
Germany
Ireland
Israel
Italy
Japan
London
Mexico
Moscow & St. Petersburg
New York City
Paris
Prague
Provence
Rome
San Francisco
Scotland
Singapore & Malaysia
Spain
Thailand
Turkey
Venice

Fodor's Flashmaps
Boston
New York
San Francisco
Washington, D.C.

Fodor's Pocket Guides
Acapulco
Atlanta
Barbados

Jamaica
London
New York City
Paris
Prague
Puerto Rico
Rome
San Francisco
Washington, D.C.

Rivages Guides
Bed and Breakfasts of Character and Charm in France
Hotels and Country Inns of Character and Charm in France
Hotels and Country Inns of Character and Charm in Italy

Short Escapes
Country Getaways in Britain
Country Getaways in France
Country Getaways in New England
Country Getaways Near New York City

Fodor's Sports
Golf Digest's Best Places to Play
Skiing USA
USA Today The Complete Four Sport Stadium Guide

Fodor's Vacation Planners
Great American Learning Vacations
Great American Sports & Adventure Vacations
Great American Vacations
National Parks and Seashores of the East
National Parks of the West